PEARSON CUSTOM BUSINESS RESOURCES

Compiled by

The Legal and Ethical
Environment of Business

Pearson Custom Publishing

New York   Boston   San Francisco
London   Toronto   Sydney   Tokyo   Singapore   Madrid
Mexico City   Munich   Paris   Cape Town   Hong Kong   Montreal

Senior Vice President, Editorial and Marketing: Patrick F. Boles
Senior Sponsoring Editor: Robin J. Lazrus
Development Editor: Abbey Lee Briggs
Marketing Manager: Jack Cooney
Associate Editor: Ana Díaz-Caneja
Operations Manager: Eric M. Kenney
Database Product Manager: Jennifer Berry
Art Director: Renée Sartell
Cover Designer: Renée Sartell

Cover Art: Courtesy of EyeWire/Getty Images and PhotoDisc/Getty Images. Photodisc, "Globe surrounded by business people on computer monitors," courtesy of Photodisc/Getty Images. Dave Cutler (Artist), "Man Dropping Coins Into Glass Jar," courtesy of David Cutler/Images.com. Dave Cutler (Artist), "Three Coins in Glass Jar," courtesy of David Cutler/Images.com.

This special edition published in cooperation with Pearson Custom Publishing.

Printed in the United States of America.

Please visit our web site at *www.pearsoncustom.com.*

Attention bookstores: For permission to return any unsold stock, contact us at *pe-uscustomreturns@pearson.com.*

**Pearson
Custom Publishing**
is a division of

www.pearsonhighered.com

ISBN 10: 0558265618
ISBN 13: 9780558265618

Editorial Advisory Board

Contents

Critical Thinking and Legal Reasoning
Nancy K. Kubasek, Bartley A. Brennan, M. Neil Browne 1

Introduction to Law and the Legal Environment of Business
Nancy K. Kubasek, Bartley A. Brennan, M. Neil Browne 19

The American Legal System
Nancy K. Kubasek, Bartley A. Brennan, M. Neil Browne 39

The International Legal Environment of Business
Nancy K. Kubasek, Bartley A. Brennan, M. Neil Browne 79

Ethics in Business
Gerald F. Cavanaugh 117

Business Ethics and Social Responsibility
Ronald J. Ebert, Ricky W. Griffin 157

Ethics, Social Responsibility, and the Business Manager
Nancy K. Kubasek, Bartley A. Brennan, M. Neil Browne 175

Social Responsibility and Managerial Ethics
Stephen P. Robbins, Mary Coulter 203

Ethics of Managers and Social Responsibility of Business
Henry R. Cheeseman 237

Ethics, Social, and Political Issues in E-Commerce
Kenneth C. Laudon, Carol Guercio Traver 261

The Foundation of Ethical Thought
Peter A. Stanwick, Sarah D. Stanwick 333

Establishing a Code of Ethics and Ethical Guidelines
Peter A. Stanwick, Sarah D. Stanwick 345

Index 363

Critical Thinking and Legal Reasoning

From Chapter 1 of *The Legal Environment of Business: A Critical Thinking Approach*, 5/e. Nancy K. Kubasek. Bartley A. Brennan. M. Neil Browne. Copyright © 2009 by Pearson Prentice Hall. All rights reserved.

Critical Thinking and Legal Reasoning

- THE IMPORTANCE OF CRITICAL THINKING
- A CRITICAL THINKING MODEL
- THE CRITICAL THINKING STEPS
- USING CRITICAL THINKING TO MAKE LEGAL REASONING COME ALIVE
- APPLYING THE CRITICAL THINKING APPROACH

The Importance of Critical Thinking

critical thinking skills
The ability to understand the structure of an argument and apply a set of evaluative criteria to assess its merits.

Success in the modern business firm requires the development of **critical thinking skills**: the ability to understand what someone is saying and then to apply evaluative criteria to assess the quality of the reasoning offered to support the conclusion. Because they are under increasing competitive pressure, business and industry need managers with advanced thinking skills.[1] Highlighting this need, a report by the secretary of education states that because "one of the major goals of business education is preparing students for the workforce, students and their professors must respond to this need for enhancing critical thinking skills."[2]

Calls for improvements in critical thinking skills also come from persons concerned about business ethics: "Managers stand in need of sharp critical thinking skills that will serve them well [in tackling] ethical issues," according to an editorial in *Management Accounting Quarterly*.[3] As a future business manager, you will experience many ethical dilemmas: Where should our facilities be located? Whom should we hire? What are the boundaries of fair competition? What responsibilities do firms owe various stakeholders? All such questions require legal analysis and ethical understanding, guided by critical thinking.

The message is clear: Success in business today requires critical thinking skills, and there is no better context in which to develop them than in the study of the

---

[1] C. Sormunen and M. Chalupa, "Critical Thinking Skills Research: Developing Evaluation Techniques," *Journal of Education for Business* 69: 172 (1994).

[2] *Id.*

[3] P. Madsen, "Moral Mazes in Management," *Management Accounting Quarterly* 56 (July 1990).

laws that affect business. Critical thinking skills learned in the legal environment of business course will be easily transferred to your eventual role as a manager, entrepreneur, or other business professional. The law develops through argument among various parties. Critical thinking about these arguments gives direction to the development of more effective law.

Legal reasoning is like other reasoning in some ways and different in others. When people, including lawyers and judges, reason, they do so for a purpose. Some problem or dilemma bothers them. The stimulus that gets them thinking is the issue. It is stated as a question because it is a call for action. It requires them to do something, to think about answers.

For instance, in our legal environment of business course, we are interested in such issues as the following:

1. When are union organizers permitted under the National Labor Relations Act to enter an employer's property?
2. Do tobacco manufacturers have liability for the deaths of smokers?
3. Must a business fulfill a contract when the contract is made with an unlicensed contractor in a state requiring that all contractors be licensed?

These questions have several possible answers. Which one should you choose? Critical thinking moves us toward better choices. Some of your answers could get you into trouble; others could advance your purpose. Each answer is called a conclusion. The **conclusion** is a position or stance on an issue.

Business firms encounter legal conclusions in the form of laws or court decisions. Business managers, therefore, are both consumers of and contributors to legal conclusions. As businesses learn about and react to decisions or conclusions made by courts, they have two primary methods of response:

conclusion A position or stance on an issue; the goal toward which reasoning pushes us.

1. Memorize the conclusions or rules of law as a guide for future business decisions.
2. Make judgments about the quality of the conclusions.

This book encourages you to do both. What is unique about this text is its practical approach to evaluating legal reasoning. This approach is based on using critical thinking skills to understand and evaluate the law as it affects business.

There are many forms of critical thinking, but they all share one characteristic: They focus on the quality of someone's reasoning. Critical thinking is active; it challenges each of us to form judgments about the quality of the link between someone's reasons and conclusions. In particular, we will be focusing on the link between a court's reasons and conclusions.

A Critical Thinking Model

You will learn critical thinking by practicing it. The text will tutor you. Your efforts, however, are the key to your skill as a critical thinker. Because people often learn best by example, we will introduce you to critical thinking by demonstrating it in a model that you can easily follow.

We now turn to a sample of critical thinking in practice. The eight critical thinking questions listed in Exhibit 1 and applied in the sample case that

EXHIBIT 1

THE EIGHT STEPS TO LEGAL REASONING

> **8.** Is there relevant missing information?
> **7.** How appropriate are the legal analogies?
> **6.** What ethical norms are fundamental to the court's reasoning?
> **5.** Does the legal argument contain significant ambiguity?
> **4.** What are the relevant rules of law?
> **3.** What are the reasons and conclusion?
> **2.** What is the issue?
> **1.** What are the facts?

follows illustrate the approach you should use when reading cases to develop your critical thinking abilities.

As a citizen, entrepreneur, or manager, you will encounter cases like the one that follows. How would you respond? What do you think about the quality of Judge Cedarbaum's reasoning?

CASE 1

United States of America v. Martha Stewart and Peter Bacanovic
United States District Court for the Southern District of New York
2004 U.S. Dist. LEXIS 12538

Defendants Martha Stewart and Peter Bacanovic were both convicted of conspiracy, making false statements, and obstruction of an agency proceeding, following Stewart's sale of 3,928 shares of ImClone stock on December 27, 2001. Stewart sold all of her ImClone stock after Bacanovic, Stewart's stockbroker at Merrill Lynch, informed Stewart that the CEO of ImClone, Samuel Waksal, was trying to sell his company stock. On December 28, 2001, ImClone announced that the Food and Drug Administration (FDA) did not approve the company's cancer-fighting drug Erbitux, after which the Securities and Exchange Commission and the United States Attorney's Office for the Southern District of New York began investigations into the trading of ImClone stock, including investigations of Stewart and Bacanovic. Following Stewart and Bacanovic's criminal convictions, the defendants filed a motion for a new trial, alleging that expert witness Lawrence F. Stewart, director of the Forensic Services Division of the United States Secret Service, had committed perjury in his testimony on behalf of the prosecution. As the "national expert for ink analysis," Lawrence Stewart testified about the reliability of Defendant Bacanovic's personal documents that contained information about Martha Stewart's investments in ImClone.

Judge Cedarbaum

Rule 33 provides: "Upon the defendant's motion, the court may vacate any judgment and grant a new trial if the interest of justice so requires." However, "in the interest of according finality to a jury's verdict, a motion for a new trial based on previously-undiscovered evidence is ordinarily 'not favored and should be granted only with great caution.'" In most situations, therefore, "relief is justified under Rule 33 only if the newly-discovered evidence could not have been discovered, exercising due diligence, before or during trial, and that evidence 'is so material and non-cumulative that its admission would probably lead to an acquittal.'"

But the mere fact that a witness committed perjury is insufficient, standing alone, to warrant relief under Rule 33. "Whether the introduction of perjured testimony requires a new trial initially depends on the extent to which the prosecution was aware of the alleged perjury. To prevent prosecutorial misconduct, a conviction obtained when the prosecution's case includes testimony that was known or should have been known to be perjured must be reversed if there is any reasonable likelihood that the perjured testimony influenced the jury." When the Government is unaware of the perjury at the time of trial, "a new trial is warranted only if the testimony was material and 'the court [is left] with a firm belief that but for the perjured testimony, the defendant would most likely not have been convicted.'"

Since *[United States v.] Wallach,* the Second Circuit has noted that even when the prosecution knew a witness was committing perjury, "where independent evidence supports a defendant's conviction, the subsequent discovery that a witness's testimony at trial was perjured will not warrant a new trial."

Defendants have failed to demonstrate that the prosecution knew or should have known of Lawrence's perjury. However, even under the stricter prejudice standard applicable when the Government is aware of a witness's perjury, defendants' motions fail. There is no reasonable likelihood that knowledge by the jury that Lawrence lied about his participation in the ink tests and whether he was aware of a book proposal could have affected the verdict.

The verdict, the nature of Lawrence's perjury, and the corroboration that Lawrence's substantive testimony received from the defense's expert demonstrate that Lawrence's misrepresentations could have had no effect on defendants' convictions.

First, the jury found that the Government did not satisfy its burden of proof on the charges to which Lawrence's testimony was relevant. Defendants do not dispute that Bacanovic was acquitted of the charge of making and using a false document, and that none of the false statement and perjury specifications concerning the existence of the $60 agreement were found by the jury to have been proved *beyond a reasonable doubt*. . . . In other words, the jury convicted defendants of lies that had nothing to do with the $60 agreement. The outcome would have been no different had Lawrence's entire testimony been rejected by the jury, or had Lawrence not testified at all.

Defendants argue that acquittal on some charges does not establish that the jury completely disregarded Lawrence's testimony. They contend that the $60 agreement constituted Stewart and Bacanovic's core defense and that the "@60" notation was evidence which supported that defense; thus, to the extent that awareness of Lawrence's perjury could have caused the jury to discredit his testimony and have greater confidence in the existence of the agreement and the validity of the notation, the jury would have been more willing to believe defendants' version of the events.

This argument is wholly speculative and logically flawed. The existence of the $60 agreement would not have exonerated defendants. It would not have been inconsistent for the jury to find that defendants did make the $60 agreement, but that the agreement was not the reason for the sale. Defendants do not persuasively explain

how knowledge of Lawrence's lies could have made the jury more likely to believe that the agreement was the reason for the sale.

Second, Lawrence's false statements were entirely collateral to the substance of his testimony and to defendants' culpability for the crimes charged. Courts have consistently held that no new trial is warranted under Rule 33 when the allegedly perjured testimony comes from a witness who is not key to the prosecution's case or when the perjury touches on matters collateral to the facts in dispute or to the defendants' guilt or innocence.

As an initial matter, defendants overstate the importance of the $60 agreement to this prosecution. That a $60 agreement was the reason for Stewart's sale was only one of many lies defendants were charged with telling investigators to conceal that Stewart sold her stock because of Bacanovic's tip.

Third, in the words of Bacanovic's lawyer, the prosecution and defense experts "really agreed on almost everything about the main important points." Lyter agreed that the "@60" notation was made with ink which was different from the rest of the ink the Government had tested and that it was not possible to tell whether the "@60" notation was made at the same time as the other notations. Accordingly, even putting aside indications that the jury did not give credence to Lawrence's testimony, it is clear that the impeachment value of Lawrence's perjury would be severely limited since the most critical aspects of his scientific analysis were corroborated by the defense.

In addition to the substantial basis for concluding that the jury's decision could not have been affected by the revelation of Lawrence's misrepresentations, ample evidence unrelated to the $60 agreement or to Lawrence's testimony supports defendants' convictions.

The testimony of Faneuil, Perret, and Pasternak supports the jury's determinations that Stewart lied when she told investigators that she did not recall being informed of Waksal's trading on December 27. . . .

Finally, Faneuil's testimony supports the jury's determination that Stewart lied when she claimed not to have spoken with Bacanovic about the Government investigation into ImClone trading or Stewart's ImClone trade (Specifications Six and Seven of Count Three). Faneuil stated that Bacanovic repeatedly told him in January 2002 and afterward that Bacanovic had spoken to Stewart and that everyone was "on the same page."

But defendants fail to explain how the revelation of this perjury—if in fact it is perjury—could have affected the verdict. Defendants cannot escape the fact that the jury acquitted Bacanovic of Count Five and both defendants of making false statements relating to the existence of the $60 agreement, and the fact that ample evidence supports the charges of which the jury convicted defendants.

Motion for a new trial *denied.*

First, review the eight steps of a critical thinking approach to legal reasoning in Exhibit 1. We will call these the critical thinking questions throughout the book. Notice the primary importance of the first four steps; their purpose is to discover the vital elements in the case and the reasoning behind the decision. Failure to consider these four foundational steps might result in our reacting too quickly to what a court or legislature has said.

The answers to these four questions enable us to understand how the court's argument fits together and to make intelligent use of legal decisions. These answers are the necessary first step in a critical thinking approach to legal analysis. The final four questions are the critical thinking component of legal reasoning. They are questions that permit us to evaluate the reasoning, to form our reaction to what the court decided.

Our reactions to legal arguments shape our efforts to either support the status quo in the legal environment of business or support the institution of particular changes. Without the last four questions, legal reasoning would be sterile. Why are we even curious about the legal environment? The answer is we want it to be the best we can create.

You will develop your own workable strategies for legal reasoning, but we urge you to start by following our structure. Every time you read a case, ask yourself these eight questions. Then improve upon this set of questions as you become comfortable with the questions.

The remainder of this section will demonstrate the use of each of the eight steps in order. Notice that the order makes sense. The first four follow the path that best allows you to discover the basis of a particular legal decision; the next four assist you in deciding what you think about the worth of that decision.

The Critical Thinking Steps

FACTS

First we look for the most basic building blocks in a legal decision or argument. These building blocks, or facts, provide the context in which the legal issue is to be resolved. Certain events occurred; certain actions were or were not taken; particular persons behaved or failed to behave in specific ways. We always wonder, What happened in this case? Let's now turn our attention to the Stewart case:

1. Martha Stewart sold 3,928 shares of her ImClone stock on December 27, 2001.
2. On December 28, 2001, ImClone announced the FDA's rejection of its new cancer-fighting drug, causing the company's stock to lose value.
3. Stewart and Bacanovic were convicted of conspiracy, making false statements, and obstruction of an agency proceeding.
4. Expert witness Lawrence Stewart was accused of perjuring himself in the testimony he gave prior to the defendants' conviction.
5. According to a federal rule and case law, perjury of a witness could constitute grounds for a new trial.

ISSUE

In almost any legal conflict, finding and expressing the issue is an important step in forming our reaction. The issue is the question that caused the lawyers and their clients to enter the legal system. Usually, there are several reasonable perspectives concerning the correct way to word the issue in dispute.

1. In what instances may a court grant a new trial?
2. Does perjury of a witness mean that defendants should have a new trial?
3. Do the regulations associated with Rule 33 and relevant case law permit the defendants to have a new trial?

Do not let the possibility of multiple useful ways to word the issue cause you any confusion. The issue is certainly not just anything that we say it is. If we claim something is an issue, our suggestion must fulfill the definition of an issue in this particular factual situation.

REASONS AND CONCLUSION

Judge Cedarbaum held that the defendants should not have a new trial. This finding by Judge Cedarbaum is her conclusion; it serves as her answer to the legal issue. Why did she answer this way? Here we are calling for the **reasons,** explanations or justifications provided as support for a conclusion.

reason An explanation or justification provided as support for a conclusion.

1. Under Rule 33 and relevant case law, perjury is not sufficient to warrant a new trial, unless (a) the government knew about the perjury or (b) the perjured testimony was so material that the verdict would probably result in acquittal of the defendants.
2. The defendants did not demonstrate that the government knew or should have known about the perjured testimony.
3. The jury would have still convicted the defendants apart from Lawrence's testimony.
4. Defense experts agreed with Lawrence on the "most critical aspects of his scientific analysis."

Let's not pass too quickly over this very important critical thinking step. When we ask *why* of any opinion, we are showing our respect for reasons as the proper basis for any assertion. We want a world rich with opinions so we can have a broad field of choice. We should, however, agree with only those legal opinions that have convincing reasons supporting the conclusion. So to ask *why* is our way of saying, "I want to believe you, but you have an obligation to help me by sharing the reasons for your conclusion."

RULES OF LAW

Judges cannot offer just any reasoning that they please. They must always look back over their shoulders at the laws and previous court decisions that together provide an anchor for current and future decisions.

This particular case is an attempt to match the words of the Federal Rules of Criminal Procedure, specifically Rule 33, and its regulations with the facts in this instance. The court also references case law, specifically the Second Circuit's ruling in *United States v. Wallach*. What makes legal reasoning so complex is that statutes and findings are never crystal clear. They may be clear, but judges and businesspeople have room for interpretive flexibility in their reasoning.

AMBIGUITY

ambiguous Susceptible to two or more possible interpretations.

The court's reasoning leans on its implied assumptions about the meaning of several ambiguous words or phrases. (An **ambiguous** word is one capable of having more than one meaning in the context of these facts.) For instance, Judge Cedarbaum stated that Rule 33 permits the court's granting a new trial if the "interest of justice so requires." But what is the "interest of justice"?

Does the interest of justice entail strict conformity to legal precedents? Or could the court's reliance on certain precedents result in some form of injustice in the Stewart case? To assume the former definition, we would be more inclined to conclude that the judge's denying the defendants' motion for a new trial was consistent with the "interest of justice." However, if the legislators who created Rule 33 intended a definition of justice that placed a stronger emphasis on judicial fairness, for example, in that defendants should be entitled to a fair trial in which perjury does not taint the verdict, perhaps we would be less supportive of Judge Cedarbaum's decision. The kind of justice that we assume is relevant to the amount of support we have for the judge's decision.

Another illustration of important ambiguity in the decision is the court's use of the term *reasonable likelihood,* referring to the probability that Lawrence's alleged perjury could not have affected the jury's verdict; but what degree of probability is a "reasonable likelihood"? Does this level of probability suggest that knowledge of Lawrence's testimony could have affected the jury's verdict? If we interpret "reasonable likelihood" as still including the possibility that knowledge of Lawrence's perjury could have affected the jury, we might reach a conclusion that differs from the court's decision. If we assume a definition of "reasonable likelihood" similar to the "beyond a reasonable doubt," however, we would be more inclined to agree with the judge's decision. Hence, until we know what "reasonable likelihood" means, we cannot fairly decide whether the judge made the appropriate decision.

ETHICAL NORMS

The primary ethical norms that influence judges' decisions are justice, stability, freedom, and efficiency. Judge Cedarbaum expresses herself as a defender of efficiency. (Here is a good place to turn to Exhibit 2 to check alternative definitions of efficiency.) She is unwilling to grant a new trial simply on the grounds that one of the witnesses allegedly committed perjury. Instead of granting the defendants' motion, Judge Cedarbaum elevates the "interest of according finality to a jury's verdict," even if the prosecution knew or should have known about the alleged perjury. Citing previous case law, she holds to those precedents that grant new trials only in rare instances.

Although the court does not explicitly address its feelings about stability, that ethical norm is assigned low priority by the reasoning. The court rejects the possibility of deviating from certain restrictions of previous case law in its argument, acting more consistently with a judge's belief in judicial restraint than judicial activism.

A judge's claiming or implying allegiance to a particular ethical norm focuses our attention on a specific category of desired conduct. We have, or think we have, an understanding of what is meant by freedom and other ethical norms.

But do we? Ethical norms are, without exception, complex and subject to multiple interpretations. Consequently, to identify the importance of one of the ethical norms in a piece of legal reasoning, we must look at the context to figure out which form of the ethical norm is being used. The types of conduct called for by the term *freedom* not only differ depending on the form of freedom being assumed, but at times they can contradict each other.

As a future business manager, your task is to be aware that there are alternative forms of each ethical norm. Then a natural next step is to search for the form used by the legal reasoning so you can understand and later evaluate that reasoning.

The following alternative forms of the four primary ethical norms can aid you in that search.

ETHICAL NORMS	*FORMS*
1. Freedom	To act without restriction from rules imposed by others
	To possess the capacity or resources to act as one wishes
2. Security	To possess a large enough supply of goods and services that basic needs are met
	To be safe from those wishing to interfere with your property rights
	To achieve the psychological condition of self-confidence such that risks are welcomed
3. Justice	To receive the product of your labor
	To provide resources in proportion to need
	To treat all humans identically, regardless of class, race, gender, age, and so on
	To possess anything that someone else was willing to grant you
4. Efficiency	To maximize the amount of wealth in our society
	To get the most from a particular input
	To minimize costs

EXHIBIT 2

CLARIFYING THE PRIMARY ETHICAL NORMS

We certainly cannot say as a result that Judge Cedarbaum does not value stability. Surely she does! But for this fact pattern, stability has a lower ethical pull on the reasoning than is provided by the ethical norm of efficiency.

ANALOGIES

Ordinarily, our examination of legal analogies will require us to compare legal precedents cited by the parties with the facts of the case we are examining. Those precedents are the analogies on which legal decision making depends. In this case, Judge Cedarbaum relies on several legal precedents as analogies for her ruling, including *United States v. Wallach*.

In this particular precedent, the Second Circuit held that even if the prosecution knew of a witness's perjury, the court should not grant a new trial when independent evidence is sufficient to convict a defendant. The worth of this analogy depends on a greater understanding of independent evidence. In other words, what constitutes independent evidence? And is the strength of independent evidence in the Stewart case comparable to the independent evidence in Wallach? Or are there significant differences between the two cases such that the court's reliance on Wallach is unwarranted in this case?

To feel comfortable with the analogy, we would need to be persuaded that, like *United States v. Wallach,* the independent evidence in the Stewart case is similar to the independent evidence in the precedent.

MISSING INFORMATION

In the search for relevant missing information, it is important not to say just anything that comes to mind. For example, where did the defendants last eat Thanksgiving dinner? Anyone hearing that question would understandably wonder why it was asked. Ask only questions that would be helpful in understanding the reasoning in this particular case.

To focus on only relevant missing information, we should include with a request for additional information an explanation for why we want it. We have listed a few examples here for the Stewart case. You can probably identify others.

1. How well informed is Judge Cedarbaum with respect to the deliberations of the jury? If her understanding of the jurors' preverdict discussions is very limited, the defendants' request for a new trial might be more convincing because Judge Cedarbaum repeatedly contends that jurors' knowledge of Lawrence's alleged perjury would not have affected the jurors' decision.

2. Congress, as it does with any legislation, discussed the Rules of Criminal Procedure before passing them. Does that discussion contain any clues as to Congress's intent with respect to the various conditions required for a defendant to receive a new trial? The answer would conceivably clarify the manner in which the court should apply Rule 33.

3. Are there examples of cases in which courts have examined similar fact patterns as the Stewart case but reached different conclusions about a new trial? The answer to this question would provide greater clarity about the appropriateness of using certain case precedents, thereby corroborating or undermining Judge Cedarbaum's decision.

Many other critical thinking skills could be applied to this and other cases. In this book, we are focusing on the ones especially valuable for legal reasoning. Consistently applying this critical thinking approach will enable you to understand the reasoning in the cases and to increase your awareness of alternative approaches our laws could take to many problems you will encounter in the legal environment of business. The remaining portion of this chapter examines each of the critical thinking questions in greater depth to help you better understand the function of each.

You will have plenty of practice opportunities in this text to apply this set of critical thinking questions to the cases you read. You should also answer the questions contained in the "Critical Thinking About the Law" boxes that follow many of the cases.

Using Critical Thinking to Make Legal Reasoning Come Alive

Our response to an issue is a conclusion. It is what we want others to believe about the issue. For example, a court might conclude that an employee, allegedly fired for her political views, was actually a victim of employment discrimination and is entitled to a damage award. Conclusions are reached by following a path that is produced by reasoning. Hence, examining reasoning is especially important when we are trying to understand and evaluate a conclusion.

There are many paths by which we may reach conclusions. For instance, I might settle all issues in my life by listening to voices in the night, asking my uncle, studying astrological signs, or just playing hunches. Each method could produce conclusions. Each could yield results.

But our intellectual and legal tradition demands a different type of support for conclusions. In this tradition, the basis for our conclusions is supposed to consist of reasons. When someone has no apparent reasons, or the reasons don't match the conclusion, we feel entitled to say, "But that makes no sense." We aren't impressed by claims that we should accept someone's conclusion "just because."

This requirement that we all provide reasons for conclusions is what we mean in large part when we say we are going to think. We will ponder what the reasons and conclusion are and whether they mesh. This intense study of how a

certain conclusion follows from a particular set of reasons occupies much of the time involved in careful decision making.

Persons trained to reason about court cases have a great appreciation for the unique facts that provoked a legal action. Those facts, and no others, provide the context for our reasoning. If an issue arises because environmentalists want to prevent an interstate highway from extending through a wilderness area, we want to know right away—What are the facts?

Doesn't everyone want to know about the context for an event? Unfortunately, the answer is no. Many people rush to judgment once they know the issue. One valuable lesson you can take with you as you practice legal analysis is the fundamental importance of the unique set of facts that provides the setting for the legal dispute.

Legal reasoning encourages unusual and necessary respect for the particular factual situation that stimulated disagreement between parties. These fact patterns, as we call them, bring the issue to our attention and limit the extent to which the court's conclusion can be applied to other situations. Small wonder that the first step in legal reasoning is to ask and answer the question: What are the facts?

LEGAL REASONING

Step 1: What Are the Facts? The call for the facts is not a request for all facts but only those that have a bearing on the dispute at hand. That dispute tells us whether a certain fact is pertinent. In some cases, the plaintiff's age may be a key point; in another, it may be irrelevant.

Only after we have familiarized ourselves with the relevant legal facts do we begin the familiar pattern of reasoning that thoughtful people use. We then ask and answer the following question: What is the issue?

Step 2: What Is the Issue? The issue is the question that the court is being asked to answer. For example, courts face groups of facts relevant to issues such as the following:

1. Does Title VII apply to sexual harassment situations when the accused and the alleged victim are members of the same sex?
2. Does a particular merger between two companies violate the Sherman Act?
3. When does a governmental regulation require compensation to the property owner affected by the regulation?

As we pointed out earlier, the way we express the issue guides the legal reasoning in the case. Hence, forming an issue in a very broad or a highly narrow manner has implications for the scope of the effect stemming from the eventual decision. You can appreciate now why parties to a dispute work very hard to get the court to see the issue in a particular way.

You will read many legal decisions in this book. No element of your analysis of those cases is more important than careful consideration of the issue at hand. The key to issue spotting is asking yourself, What question do the parties want to be answered by the court? The next logical step in legal analysis is to ask, What are the reasons and conclusion?

Step 3: What Are the Reasons and Conclusion? The issue is the stimulus for thought. The facts and the issue in a particular case get us to start thinking critically about legal reasoning; but the conclusion and the reasons for that conclusion provide flesh to the court's reaction to the legal issue. They tell us how the court has responded to the issue.

To find the conclusion, use the issue as a helper. Ask yourself: How did the court react to the issue? The answer is the conclusion. The reasons for that conclusion provide the answer to the question: Why did the court prefer this response to the issue rather than any alternative? One part of the answer to that question is the answer to another question: What are the relevant rules of law?

Step 4: What Are the Relevant Rules of Law? The fourth step in legal reasoning reveals another difference from general nonlegal reasoning. The issue arises in a context of existing legal rules. We do not treat each legal dispute as if it were the first such dispute in human history. On the contrary, society has already addressed similar disputes in its laws and court findings. It has already responded to situations much like the ones now before the court. The historical record of pertinent judicial decisions provides a rich source of reasons on which to base the conclusion of courts. These prior decisions, or legal precedents, provide legal rules to which those in a legal dispute must defer. Thus, the fourth step in legal reasoning requires a focus on those rules. These legal rules are what the parties to a dispute must use as the framework for their legal claims. How those rules and the reasoning and conclusions built on them are expressed, however, is not always crystal clear. So another question—one that starts the critical thinking evaluation of the conclusion—is, Does the legal argument contain significant ambiguity?

Step 5: Does the Legal Argument Contain Significant Ambiguity? Legal arguments are expressed in words, and words rarely have the clarity we presume. Whenever we are tempted to think that our words speak for themselves, we should remind ourselves of Emerson's observation that "to be understood is a rare luxury." Hence, legal reasoning possesses elasticity. It can be stretched and reduced to fit the purpose of the attorney or judge.

As an illustration, a rule of law may contain the phrase *public safety*. At first glance, as with any term, some interpretation arises in our mind; however, as we continue to consider the extent and limits of public safety, we realize it is not so clear. To be more certain about the meaning, we must study the intent of the person making the legal argument. Just how safe must the public be before an action provides sufficient threat to public safety to justify public intervention?

As a strategy for critical thinking, the request for clarification is a form of evaluation. The point of the question is that we cannot make the reasoning our own until we have determined what we are being asked to embrace.

What we are being asked to embrace and the reasoning behind it usually involve an ethical component. So an important question to ask is, What ethical norms are fundamental to the court's reasoning?

Step 6: What Ethical Norms Are Fundamental to the Court's Reasoning? The legal environment of business is established and modified according to ethical norms. A **norm** is a standard of conduct, a set of expectations that we bring to social encounters. For example, one norm we collectively understand and obey is that our departures are ordinarily punctuated by "good-bye." We may presume rudeness or preoccupation on the part of someone who leaves our presence without bidding us some form of farewell.

norm A standard of conduct.

ethical norms Standards of conduct that we consider good or virtuous.

Ethical norms are special because they are steps toward achieving what we consider good or virtuous. Goodness and virtue are universally preferred to their opposites, but the preference has little meaning until we look more deeply into the meaning of these noble aims. As you are well aware, there are dozens of alternative visions about what it means to be good or to have a good society.

Conversations about ethics explore these alternative visions. They do so by comparing the relative merit of human behavior that is guided by one ethical norm or another. Ethical norms represent the abstractions we hold out to others as the most fundamental standards defining our self-worth and value to others.

For example, any of us would be proud to know that others see us as meeting the ethical norms we know as honesty, dependability, and compassion. Ethical norms are the standards of conduct we most want to see observed by our children and our neighbors.

The legal environment of business has received ethical guidance from many norms. Certain norms, however, play a particularly large role in legal reasoning. Consequently, we highlight what we will refer to as the four **primary ethical norms**: freedom, stability, justice, and efficiency. (See Exhibit 2 for clarification of these norms.) The interplay among these four provides the major ethical direction for the laws governing business behavior. As you examine the cases in this text, you may identify other ethical norms that influence judicial opinions.

primary ethical norms The four norms that provide the major ethical direction for the laws governing business behavior: freedom, stability, justice, and efficiency.

As critical thinkers, we will want to always search for the relevant ethical norms. To do so requires us to infer their identity from the court's reasoning. Courts often do not announce their preferred pattern of ethical norms, but the norms are there anyway, having their way with the legal reasoning. As critical thinkers, we want to use the ethical norms, once we find them, as a basis for evaluating the reasoning. Another element used in arriving at legal conclusions is the device of reasoning by analogy. Part of the critical thinking process in the evaluation of a legal conclusion is another question: How appropriate are the legal analogies?

Step 7: How Appropriate Are the Legal Analogies? A major difference between legal reasoning and other forms of analysis is the heavy reliance on analogies. Our legal system places great emphasis on the law, as it has evolved from previous decisions. This evolutionary process is our heritage, the collective judgments of our historical mothers and fathers. We give them and their intellects our respect by using legal precedents as the major support structure for judicial decisions. By doing so, we do not have to approach each fact pattern with new eyes; instead, we are guided by similar experiences that our predecessors have already studied.

analogy A comparison based on the assumption that if two things are alike in some respect, they must be alike in other respects.

The use of precedent to reach legal conclusions is so common that legal reasoning can be characterized as little but analogical reasoning. An **analogy** is a verbal device for transferring meaning from something we understand quite well to something we have just discovered and have, as yet, not understood satisfactorily. What we already understand in the case of legal reasoning is the precedent; what we hope to understand better is the current legal dispute. We call on precedent for enlightenment.

To visualize the choice of legal analogy, imagine that we are trying to decide whether a waitress or waiter can be required to smile for hours as a condition of employment. (What is artificial about such an illustration, as we hope you already recognize, is the absence of a more-complete factual picture to provide context.) The employer in question asks the legal staff to find appropriate legal precedents. They discover the following list of prior decisions:

1. Professional cheerleaders can be required to smile within reason, if that activity is clearly specified at the time of employment.

2. Employees who interact regularly with customers can be required as a condition of employment to wear clothing consistent with practice in the trade.

3. Employers may not require employees to lift boxes over 120 pounds without the aid of a mechanical device under the guidelines of the Employee Health Act.

Notice that each precedent has similarities to, but each has major differences from, the situation of the waiter or waitress. To mention only a few:

- Is a smile more natural to what we can expect from a cheerleader than from a waiter or waitress?

- Were the restaurant employees told in advance that smiling is an integral part of the job?

- Is a smile more personal than clothing? Are smiles private, as opposed to clothing, which is more external to who we are?

- Is a plastered-on smile, held in place for hours, a serious risk to mental health?

- Is a potential risk from smiling as real a danger as the one resulting from physically hoisting huge objects?

The actual selection of precedent and, consequently, the search for appropriate analogies are channeled by the theory of logic that we find most revealing in this case. For example, if you see the requirement to smile as an invasion of privacy, you will likely see the second precedent as especially appropriate. Both the precedent and the case in question have employment situations with close customer contact.

The differences, however, could be significant enough to reject that analogy. Do you see your clothing as part of your essence in the same fashion as you surely see the facial form you decide to show us at any given moment? Furthermore, the second precedent contains the phrase *consistent with practice in the trade*. Would not a simple field trip to restaurants demonstrate that a broad smile is a pleasant exception?

As you practice looking for similarities and differences in legal precedents and the legal problem you are studying, you will experience some of the fun and frustration of legal reasoning within a business context. The excitement comes when you stumble on just the perfect, matching fact pattern; then, after taking a closer look, you are brought back to earth by those annoying analogical differences that your experience warns you are always present.

Ambiguity, ethical norms, and legal analogies are all areas in which legal arguments may be deficient; but even if you are satisfied that all those considerations meet your standards, there is a final question that must not be overlooked in your critical analysis of a conclusion: Is there relevant missing information?

Step 8: Is There Relevant Missing Information? When we ask about the facts of a case, we mean the information presented in the legal proceedings. We are, however, all quite aware that the stated facts are just a subset of the complete factual picture responsible for the dispute. How could any of us expect to ever have all the facts about a situation? We know we could use more facts than we have, but at some point we have to stop gathering information and settle the dispute.

You might not be convinced that the facts we know about a situation are inevitably incomplete; however, consider how we acquire facts. If we gather them ourselves, we know the limits on our own experience and perceptions. We often see what we want to see, and we consequently select certain facts to file in our consciousness. Other facts may be highly relevant, but we ignore them. We can neither see nor process all the facts.

Our other major source of information is other people. We implicitly trust their intentions, abilities, and perspective when we take the facts they give us and make them our own. No one, however, gives us a complete version of the facts. For several reasons, we can be sure that the facts shared with us are only partial.

Armed with your awareness of the incompleteness of facts, what can you do as a future businessperson or employee to effectively resolve disagreements and apply legal precedents?

You can seek a more complete portrayal of the facts. Keep asking for detail and context to aid your thinking. For example, once you learn that a statute requires a firm to use the standard of conduct in the industry, you should not be satisfied with the following fact:

On 14 occasions, our firm attempted to contact other firms to determine the industry standards. We have bent over backwards to comply with the ethical norms of our direct competitors.

Instead, you will persist in asking probing questions designed to generate a more-revealing pattern of facts. Among the missing information you might ask for would be the extent and content of actual conversations about industry standards, as well as some convincing evidence that "direct" competitors are an adequate voice, representing "the industry."

Applying the Critical Thinking Approach

Now that you have an understanding of the critical thinking approach, you are ready to begin your study of the legal environment of business. Remember to apply each of the questions to the cases as you read them.

After you become proficient at asking these questions of every case you read, you may find that you start asking these evaluative questions in other contexts. For example, you might find that, when you read an editorial in the *Wall Street Journal,* you start asking whether the writer has used ambiguous terms that affect the quality of the reasoning, or you start noticing when important relevant information is missing. Once you reach this point, you are well on your way to becoming a critical thinker whose thinking skills will be extremely helpful for functioning in the legal environment of business.

ASSIGNMENT ON THE INTERNET

You have now been introduced to the critical thinking steps that create a working strategy to evaluate legal reasoning. In the same manner that you evaluated *United States of America v. Martha Stewart and Peter Bacanovic,* practice evaluating the legal reasoning on a case of your choosing.

Go to **www.law.cornell.edu** for current legal issues and cases. Find a case of interest to you, and evaluate the reasoning using the critical thinking steps outlined in this chapter. The following Web sites on critical thinking may assist you in evaluating legal reasoning.

ON THE INTERNET

commhum.mccneb.edu/argument/summary.htm Use this site for practice, identifying reasons and conclusions in arguments.

www.austhink.org/critical

pegasus.cc.ucf.edu/~janzb/reasoning Both sites contain numerous links for those wishing additional reading and practice with the critical thinking skills learned in this chapter.

FOR FUTURE READING

Browne, M. Neil, and Stuart Keeley. *Asking the Right Questions: A Guide to Critical Thinking.* 8th ed. Upper Saddle River, NJ: Prentice Hall, 2007.

Damer, T. Edward. *Attacking Faulty Reasoning: Practical Guide to Fallacy-Free Arguments.* 5th ed. Belmont, CA: Wadsworth, 2004.

LeGault, Michael R. *Think: Why Crucial Decisions Can't Be Made in the Blink of an Eye.* New York: Threshhold Editions, 2006.

Introduction to Law and the Legal Environment of Business

From Chapter 2 of *The Legal Environment of Business: A Critical Thinking Approach*, 5/e. Nancy K. Kubasek. Bartley A. Brennan. M. Neil Browne. Copyright © 2009 by Pearson Prentice Hall. All rights reserved.

Introduction to Law and the Legal Environment of Business

- DEFINITION OF THE LEGAL ENVIRONMENT OF BUSINESS
- DEFINITION OF LAW AND JURISPRUDENCE
- SOURCES OF LAW
- CLASSIFICATIONS OF LAW
- GLOBAL DIMENSIONS OF THE LEGAL ENVIRONMENT OF BUSINESS

This book is about the legal environment in which the business community operates today. Although we concentrate on law and the legal variables that help shape business decisions, we have not overlooked the ethical, political, and economic questions that often arise in business decision making. In this chapter, we are especially concerned with legal variables in the context of critical thinking. In addition, we examine the international dimensions of several areas of law. In an age of sophisticated telecommunication systems and computer networking, it would be naive for readers to believe that, as citizens of a prosperous, powerful nation situated between two oceans, they can afford to ignore the rest of the world. Just as foreign multinational companies must interact with U.S. companies and government agencies, so must U.S. entities interact with regional and international trade groups.

The United States, Canada, and Mexico created the North American Free Trade Agreement (NAFTA) to lower trade barriers among themselves. In the Asian-Pacific Economic Cooperation (APEC) forum, the United States and 17 Pacific Rim nations are discussing easing barriers to trade and investments among themselves and creating a Pacific free trade zone extending from Chile to China. In 2004, the European Union added 10 new member nations, bringing its total to 25. The World Trade Organization continues to lower trade barriers among the 144 nations that have joined it. No nation is an island unto itself today, and economic globalization is sure to accelerate in the twenty-first century.

CRITICAL THINKING ABOUT THE LAW

This chapter serves as an introduction to the legal and ethical components in the environment of business. You will learn about different schools of jurisprudence and about sources and classifications of law. In addition, this chapter offers the opportunity to practice the critical thinking skills you just learned. The following critical thinking questions will help you better understand the introductory topics discussed in this chapter.

1. Why should we be concerned with the ethical components of the legal environment of business? Why should not we just learn the relevant laws regarding businesses?

   Clue: Which critical thinking questions address the ethical components of the legal environment of business?

2. As you will soon discover, judges and lawyers often subscribe to a particular school of legal thought. Judges and lawyers, however, will probably not explicitly tell us which school of thought they prefer. Why do you think this knowledge might be beneficial when critically evaluating a judge's reasoning?

   Clue: Think about why we look for missing information. Furthermore, why do we want to identify the ethical norms fundamental to a court's reasoning?

3. You tell your landlord that your front door lock is broken, but he does not repair the lock. A week later, you are robbed. You decide to sue the landlord, and you begin to search for an attorney. As a legal studies student, you ask the potential lawyers what school of jurisprudence they prefer. Although you find a lawyer who prefers the same school of jurisprudence you prefer, your decision is not complete. What else might you want to ask the lawyer?

   Clue: Think about the other factors that might affect a lawyer's performance.

Definition of the Legal Environment of Business

Scholars define the "legal environment of business" in various ways, according to the purposes of their studies. For our purposes, the study of the legal environment of business shall include the following:

- The study of legal reasoning, critical thinking skills, ethical norms, and schools of ethical thought that interact with the law.
- The study of the legal process and our present legal system, as well as alternative dispute resolution systems, such as private courts, mediation, arbitration, and negotiations.
- The study of the administrative law process and the role of businesspeople in that process.
- The study of selected areas of public and private law, such as securities regulation, antitrust, labor, product liability, contracts, and consumer and environmental law. In each of these areas, we emphasize the processes by which business managers relate to individuals and government regulators.
- The examination of the international dimensions of the legal environment of law.

Our study of the legal environment of business is characterized by five features:

1. *Critical thinking skills.*

2. *Legal literacy.* A survey by the Hearst Corporation found that 50 percent of Americans believe that it is up to the criminally accused to prove their innocence, despite our common-law heritage that a person is presumed innocent until proven guilty. Only 41 percent were able to identify the then chief justice (Warren Burger) and the first woman Supreme Court justice (Sandra Day O'Connor). Of those responding to the survey, 49.9 percent had served on a jury, and 31 percent were college graduates.

3. *An understanding that the law is dynamic, not static.* The chapters on discrimination law, securities regulation, antitrust law, and labor law, especially, have had to be constantly updated during the writing of this book because federal regulatory agencies issue new regulations, rules, and guidelines almost daily.

4. *Real-world problems.* You will be confronted with real, not theoretical, legal and ethical problems. As the great American jurist Oliver Wendell Holmes once pointed out, the law is grounded in "experience." In reading the cases excerpted in this book, you will see how business leaders and others either were ignorant of the legal and ethical variables they faced or failed to consider them in making important decisions.

5. *Interdisciplinary nature.* Into our discussions of the legal environment of business we interweave materials from other disciplines that you either are studying now or have studied in the past, especially economics, management, finance, marketing, and ethics. You may be surprised to learn how often officers of the court (judges and attorneys) are obliged to consider material from several disciplines in making decisions. Your own knowledge of these other disciplines will be extremely helpful in understanding the court decisions set out in this book.

The connections to other areas of business are so significant that we have chosen to highlight many of them in subsequent chapters of the book. As you are reading, you will encounter boxes entitled "Linking Law and Business." These boxes contain material from other business disciplines that is related to the business law material you are studying. By highlighting these connections, we hope to provide greater cohesiveness to your education as a future business manager.

As listed in Exhibit 1, there are a number of benefits to be gained by studying the legal environment of business.

EXHIBIT 1

TOP 10 REASONS FOR STUDYING THE LEGAL ENVIRONMENT OF BUSINESS

1. Becoming aware of the rules of doing business.
2. Familiarizing yourself with the legal limits on business freedom.
3. Forming an alertness to potential misconduct of competitors.
4. Appreciating the limits of entrepreneurship.
5. Being able to communicate with your lawyer.
6. Making you a more fully informed citizen.
7. Developing an employment-related skill.
8. Exploring the fascinating complexity of business decisions.
9. Providing a heightened awareness of business ethics.
10. Opening your eyes to the excitement of the law and business.

Definition of Law and Jurisprudence

Jurisprudence is the science or philosophy of law, or law in its most generalized form. Law has been defined in different ways by scholarly thinkers. Some idea of the range of definitions can be gained from the following quote from a distinguished legal philosopher:

> We have been told by Plato that law is a form of social control; by Aristotle that it is a rule of conduct, a contract, an ideal of reason; by Cicero that it is the agreement of reason and nature, the distinction between the just and the unjust; by Aquinas that it is an ordinance of reason for the common good; by Bacon that certainty is the prime necessity of law; by Hobbes that law is the command of the sovereign; by Hegel that it is an unfolding or realizing of the idea of right.[1]

jurisprudence The science or philosophy of law; law in its most generalized form.

The various ideas of law expressed in this passage represent different schools of jurisprudence. To give you some sense of the diversity of meaning the term *law* has, we will examine seven accepted schools of legal thought: (1) natural law, (2) positivist, (3) sociological, (4) American realist, (5) critical legal theory, (6) feminist, and (7) law and economics. Exhibit 2 summarizes the outstanding characteristics of each of these schools of jurisprudence.

NATURAL LAW SCHOOL

For adherents of the natural law school, which has existed since 300 B.C., law consists of the following concepts: (1) There exist certain legal values or value judgments (e.g., a presumption of innocence until guilt is proved); (2) these values or value judgments are unchanging because their source is absolute (e.g., nature, God, or reason); (3) these values or value judgments can be determined by human reason; and (4) once determined, they supersede any form of human law. Perhaps the most memorable statement of the natural law school of thought in this century was made by Martin Luther King, Jr., in his famous letter from a Birmingham, Alabama, city jail. Here is how he explained to a group of ministers why he had violated human laws that discriminated against his people:

SCHOOL	CHARACTERISTICS
Natural Law School	Source of law is absolute (nature, God, or reason)
Positivist School	Source of law is the sovereign
Sociological School	Source of law is contemporary community opinion and customs
American Realist School	Source of law is actors in the legal system and scientific analysis of their actions
Critical Legal Theory School	Source of law is a cluster of legal and nonlegal beliefs that must be critiqued to bring about social and political change
Feminist School	Jurisprudence reflects a male-dominated executive, legislative, and judicial system in which women's perspectives are ignored and women are victimized
Law and Economics School	Classical economic theory and empirical methods are applied to all areas of law in order to arrive at decisions

EXHIBIT 2

SCHOOLS OF JURISPRUDENCE

---

[1] See H. Cairns, *Legal Philosophy from Plato to Hegel* (Baltimore: John Hopkins University Press, 1949).

There are just laws and there are unjust laws. I would be the first to advocate obeying just laws. One has not only a legal but moral responsibility to obey just laws. Conversely, one has a moral responsibility to disobey unjust laws. I would agree with Saint Augustine that "an unjust law is no law at all."

Now what is the difference between the two? How does one determine when a law is just or unjust? A just law is a man-made code that squares with the moral law or the law of God. An unjust law is a code that is out of harmony with the moral law. To put it in the terms of Saint Thomas Aquinas, an unjust law is a human law that is not rooted in eternal and natural law. Any law that uplifts human personality is just. Any law that degrades human personality is unjust. All segregation statutes are unjust because segregation distorts the soul and damages the personality.

Let us turn to a more concrete example of just and unjust law. An unjust law is a code that a majority inflicts on a minority that is not binding on itself. This is difference made legal. On the other hand, a just law is a code that a majority compels a minority to follow that it is willing to follow itself. This is sameness made legal.

Let me give another explanation. An unjust law is a code inflicted upon a minority which that minority had no part in enacting or creating because they did not have the unhampered right to vote.[2]

Adherents of other schools of legal thought view King's general definition of law as overly subjective. For example, they ask, "Who is to determine whether a man-made law is unjust because it is 'out of harmony with the moral law'?" Or: "Whose moral precepts or values are to be included in the 'moral law'?" The United States is a country of differing cultures, races, ethnic groups, and religions, each of which may reflect unique moral values.

POSITIVIST SCHOOL

Early in the 1800s, followers of positivism developed a school of thought in opposition to the natural law school. Its chief tenets are (1) law is the expression of the will of the legislator or sovereign, which must be followed; (2) morals are separate from law and should not be considered in making legal decisions (thus, judges should not take into consideration extralegal factors such as contemporary community values in determining what constitutes a violation of law); and (3) law is a "closed logical system" in which correct legal decisions are reached solely by logic and the use of precedents (previous cases decided by the courts).

Disciples of the positivist school would argue that when the Congress of the United States has not acted on a matter, the U.S. Supreme Court has no power to act on that matter. They would argue, for example, that morality has no part in determining whether discrimination exists when a business pays workers differently on the basis of their sex, race, religion, or ethnic origin. Only civil rights legislation passed by Congress, and previous cases interpreting that legislation, should be considered.

Positivism has been criticized by adherents of other schools of thought as too narrow and literal minded. Critics argue that the refusal to consider social, ethical, and other factors makes for a static jurisprudence that ill serves society.

---

[2] See M. L. King, Jr., *Letters from a Birmingham Jail* (April 16, 1963), reprinted in M. McGuaigan, Jurisprudence (Free Press 1979), p. 63.

SOCIOLOGICAL SCHOOL

Followers of the sociological school propose three steps in determining law:

1. A legislator or a judge should make an inventory of community interests.
2. Judges and legislators should use this inventory to familiarize themselves with the community's standards and mores.
3. They should rule or legislate in conformity with those standards and mores.

For those associated with this school of legal thought, human behavior or contemporary community values are the most important factors in determining the direction the law should take. This philosophy is in sharp contrast to that of the positivist school, which relies on case precedents and statutory law. Adherents of the sociological school seek to change the law by surveying human behavior and determining present community standards. For example, after a famous U.S. Supreme Court decision stating that material could be judged "obscene" on the basis of "contemporary community standards,"[3] a mayor of a large city immediately went out and polled his community on what books and movies they thought were obscene. (He failed to get a consensus.)

Critics of the sociological school argue that this school would make the law too unpredictable for both individuals and businesses. They note that contemporary community standards change over time and, thus, the law itself would be changing all the time and the effects could harm the community. For example, if a state or a local legislature offered a corporation certain tax breaks as an incentive to move to a community and then revoked those tax breaks a few years later because community opinion on such matters had changed, other corporations would be reluctant to locate in that community.

AMERICAN REALIST SCHOOL

The American realist school, though close to the sociological school in its emphasis on people, focuses on the actors in the judicial system instead of on the larger community to determine the meaning of law. This school sees law as a part of society and a means of enforcing political and social values. In a book entitled *The Bramble Bush,* Karl Llewellyn wrote: "This doing of something about disputes, this doing it reasonably, is the business of the law. And the people who have the doing of it are in charge, whether they be judges, or clerks, or jailers, or lawyers, they are officials of the law. What these officials do about disputes is, to my mind, the law itself."[4] For Llewellyn and other American realists, anyone who wants to know about law should study the judicial process and the actors in that process. This means regular attendance at courthouses and jails, as well as scientific study of the problems associated with the legal process (e.g., plea bargaining in the courtroom).

Positivists argue that if the American realist definition of law were accepted, there would be a dangerous unpredictability to the law.

---

[3] *Roth v. United States,* 354 U.S. 476, 479 (1957).

[4] K. Llewellyn, *The Bramble Bush* (Oceana Publications 1950), p. 12.

CRITICAL LEGAL STUDIES SCHOOL

As a contemporary extension of American legal realism, critical legal studies seeks to connect what happens in the legal system to the political–economic context within which it operates. Adherents of critical legal jurisprudence believe that law reflects a cluster of beliefs that convinces human beings that the hierarchical relations that they live and work under are natural and must be accommodated. According to this school, this cluster of beliefs has been constructed by elitists to rationalize their dominant power. Using economics, mass communications, religion, and, most of all, law, members of society's elite have constructed an interlocking system of beliefs that reinforces established wealth and privilege. Only by critiquing these belief structures, critical legal theorists believe, will people be able to break out of a hierarchical system and bring about democratic social and political change.

Traditional critics argue that the critical legal theorists have not developed concrete strategies to bring about the social and political changes they desire but have constructed an essentially negative position.

FEMINIST SCHOOL

There is a range of views as to what constitutes feminist jurisprudence. Most adherents of this school, believing that significant rights have been denied to women, advocate lobbying legislatures and litigating in courts for changes in laws to accommodate women's views. They argue that our traditional common law reflects a male emphasis on individual rights, which at times is at odds with women's views that the law should be more reflective of a "culture of caring." To other adherents of this school of jurisprudence, the law is a means of male oppression. For example, some feminists have argued that the First Amendment, forbidding Congress from making any laws abridging the freedom of speech, was authored by men and is presently interpreted by male-dominated U.S. courts to allow pornographers to make large profits by exploiting and degrading women.

Traditional critics of feminist jurisprudence argue that it is too narrow in scope and that it fails to account for changes taking place in U.S. society such as the increasing number of women students in professional and graduate schools and their movement into higher-ranking positions in both the public and the private sectors.

LAW AND ECONOMICS SCHOOL

The law and economics school of jurisprudence started to evolve in the 1950s, but it has been applied with some rigor for the last 20 years. It advocates using classical economic theory and empirical methods of economics to explain and predict judges' decisions in such areas as torts, contracts, property, criminal administrative law, and law enforcement. The proponents of the law and economics school argue that most court decisions, and the legal doctrines they depend on, are best understood as efforts to promote an efficient allocation of resources in society.

Critics of the school of law and economics argue that there are many schools of economic thoughts, and thus, no single body of principles governs economics. For example, neo-Keynesians and classical market theorists have very different views of the proper role of the state in the allocation of resources. A related criticism is that this school takes a politically conservative approach to the legal solution of economic or political problems. Liberals and others argue that it is a captive of conservative thinkers.

Sources of Law

The founders of this country created in the U.S. Constitution three direct sources of law and one indirect source (see Appendix: The Constitution of the United States). The legislative branch (Article I) is the maker or creator of laws; the executive branch (Article II), the enforcer of laws; and the judicial branch (Article III), the interpreter of laws. Each branch represents a separate source of law while performing its functions (Table 1). The fourth (indirect) source of law is administrative agencies, which will be briefly discussed in this chapter.

THE LEGISLATURE AS A SOURCE OF STATUTORY LAW

Article I, Section 1, of the U.S. Constitution states, "All legislative Powers herein granted shall be vested in a Congress of the United States which shall consist of a House and Senate." It is important to understand the process by which a law (called a statute) is made by the Congress, because this process and its results

TABLE 1 WHERE TO FIND THE LAW

Leave of Government	Legislative Law	Executive Orders	Common Law/Judicial Interpretations	Administrative Regulations
Federal	• United States Code (U.S.C.) • United States Code Annotated (U.S.C.A.) • United States Statutes at Large (Stat.)	• Title 3 of the Code of Federal Regulations • Codification of Presidential Proclamations and Executive Orders	• United States Reports (U.S.) • Supreme Court Reporter (S. Ct.) • Federal Reporter (F., F.2d) • Federal Supplement (F. Supp.) • Federal agency reports (titled by agency; e.g., F.C.C. Reports) • Regional reporters • State reporters	• Code of Federal Regulations (C.F.R.) • Federal Register (Fed. Red.)
State	• State code or state statutes (e.g., Ohio Revised Code Annotated, Baldwin's)	• Executive Orders of Governors and Proclamations		• State administrative code or state administrative regulations
Local	• Municipal ordinances		• Varies; often difficult to find. Many municipalities do not publish case decisions but do preserve them on microfilm. Interested parties usually must contact the clerk's office at the local courthouse.	• Municipality administrative regulations

EXHIBIT 3

HOW A BILL BECOMES A LAW

This graphic sets out steps in the legislative process outlined in the text. Although this route is simpler, it should be noted that there are other more complex ways for a bill to become a law. These bills are subject to amendments and changes as part of the process shown here.

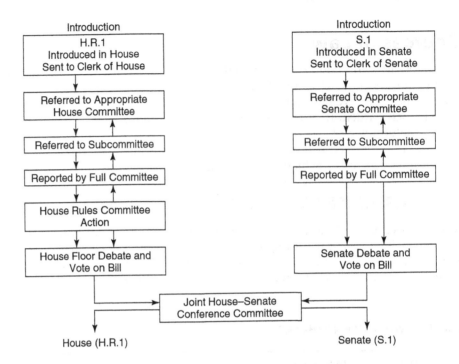

A compromise version of the original bills is sent back to both the House and Senate for a vote. If a compromise bill is approved, the compromised version is sent to the president of the United States for his signature or to become law in 10 days without his signature. The president may veto the bill, which may then become law only if two-thirds of the House and Senate approve.

have an impact on such diverse groups as consumers, businesspeople, taxpayers, and unions. It should be emphasized that at every stage of the process, each of the groups potentially affected seeks to influence the proposed piece of legislation through lobbying. The federal legislative process described here (Exhibit 3) is similar in most respects to the processes used by state legislatures, though state constitutions may prescribe some differences.

Steps in the Legislative Process

STEP 1 A bill is introduced into the U.S. House of Representatives or Senate by a single member or by several members. It is generally referred to the committee of the House or Senate that has jurisdiction over the subject matter of the bill. (In most cases, a bill is simultaneously introduced into the Senate and House. Within each body, committees may vie with each other for jurisdictional priority.)

STEP 2 Let's briefly follow through the House of Representatives a bill proposing to deregulate the trucking industry by doing away with the rate-making power of the Interstate Commerce Commission (ICC). This bill would be referred to the House Committee on

Energy and Commerce, which, in turn, would refer it to the appropriate subcommittee.

STEP 3 The House subcommittee holds hearings on the bill, listening to testimony from all concerned parties and establishing a hearing record.

STEP 4 After hearings, the bill is "marked up" (drafted in precise form) and then referred to the subcommittee for a vote.

STEP 5 If the vote is affirmative, the subcommittee forwards the bill to the full House Energy and Commerce committee, which either accepts the subcommittee's recommendation, puts a hold on the bill, or rejects it. If the House committee votes to accept the bill, it reports it to the full House of Representatives for a vote by all members.

STEP 6 If the bill is passed by the House of Representatives and a similar bill is passed by the Senate, the bills go to a Senate–House Conference Committee to reconcile any differences in content. After compromise and reconciliation of the two bills, a single bill is reported to the full House and Senate for a vote.

STEP 7 If there is a final affirmative vote by both houses of Congress, the bill is forwarded to the president, who may sign it into law or veto it. When the president signs the bill into law, it becomes known as a statute, meaning it is written down and codified in the United States Code Annotated. In the event of a presidential veto, a two-thirds vote of the Senate and House membership is required to override the veto. If the president takes no action within 10 days of receiving the bill from Congress, it automatically becomes law without the president's signature.

The single exception to this procedure occurs when Congress adjourns before the 10-day period has elapsed: In that case, the bill would not become law. It is said to have been "pocket-vetoed" by the president: The president "stuck the bill in a pocket" and vetoed it by doing nothing. With either type of veto, the bill is dead and can be revived only by being reintroduced in the next session of Congress, in which case the procedure begins all over again.

THE JUDICIAL BRANCH AS A SOURCE OF CASE LAW

The federal courts and most state courts make up the judicial branch of government. They are charged by their respective constitutions with interpreting the constitution and statutory law on a case-by-case basis. Most case interpretations are reported in large volumes called reporters. These constitute a compilation of our federal and state case law.

When two parties disagree about the meaning of a statute, they bring their case to court for the court to interpret. For example, when the bill to deregulate the trucking industry and take away the rate-making function of the ICC was signed by the president and became law, two parties could have disagreed about its meaning and asked the federal courts to interpret it. If the law had been challenged, the court would have first looked at the law's legislative history in order to determine the intent of the legislature. This history can be found in the hearings held by the subcommittees and committees previously referred to, as well as any debates on the Senate and House floors. Hearings are published in the U.S. Code Congressional News and Administrative Reports, which may be ordered from the Government Printing Office or found in most university libraries in the government documents section. Debates on a bill are published in the daily *Congressional Record,* which may also be found in most university libraries.

The U.S. Supreme Court and most state supreme courts have the power of judicial review—that is, the power to determine whether a statute is constitutional. Although this power was not expressly provided for in the U.S. Constitution, the Supreme Court established it for the judiciary in the landmark case *Marbury v. Madison*[5]. The right of judicial review gives the U.S. Supreme Court the ultimate power to check the excesses of either the legislative or the executive branch.

Furthermore, this decision establishes case law precedents, which are followed by all federal and state courts. Thus, through its case-by-case interpretation of the Constitution and statutes, the U.S. Supreme Court establishes a line of authoritative cases on a particular subject that has to be followed by the lower courts, both federal and state. Similarly, state supreme courts establish precedents that must be followed by lower courts in their particular state systems.

Restatements of the Law. Scholars writing in areas of the law inclusive of torts, contracts, agency, property, security, and conflicts of laws have published summaries of the case law generally followed by the 50 states. The American Law Institute published these scholarly compilations. The Restatements are secondary sources, which in and of themselves may not have the force of law, but are often still relied upon by judges in making decisions. Throughout this text, you may see references to the Restatements, for example, the Restatement (Second) of Contracts. Over a number of years, the areas referred to here have been updated to the second or third edition as the case law has evolved.

THE EXECUTIVE BRANCH AS A SOURCE OF LAW

The executive branch is composed of the president, the president's staff, and the cabinet, which is made up of the heads of each of the executive departments (e.g., the secretary of state, the secretary of labor, the secretary of defense, and the secretary of the treasury) and the counselor to the president. The Executive Office is composed of various offices, such as the Office of Management and Budget (OMB) and the Office of Personnel Management (OPM). The executive branch is a source of law in two ways.

Treaty Making. The president has the power, subject to the advice and consent of the Senate, to make treaties. These treaties become the law of the land, on the basis of the Supremacy Clause of the U.S. Constitution (Article VI), and supersede any state law. When President Carter entered into a treaty returning the Panama Canal Zone to the nation of Panama under certain conditions, it became the law of the land, and the treaty provisions superseded any federal or state laws inconsistent with the treaty.

---

[5] 5 U.S. (1 Branch) 137 (1803).

Executive Orders. Throughout history, the president has made laws by issuing executive orders. For example, President Reagan, by virtue of an executive order, ruled that all executive federal agencies must do a cost–benefit analysis before setting forth a proposed regulation for comment by interested parties. President Truman, by executive order, directed the secretary of commerce to seize all the nation's steel mills to prevent a strike in this essential industry during the Korean War. President Johnson issued Executive Order No. 11246 requiring government contractors to set out an affirmative action plan for hiring and promoting minorities and women.

The executive order as a source of law is also used by state governors to deal with emergencies and with budget functions. Often, a governor will call out the national guard or, in some states, implement particular aspects of the budget by executive order. For example, a governor may order a freeze on the hiring of employees in the state university system or order an across-the-board cut in budgets in all state departments.

ADMINISTRATIVE AGENCIES AS A SOURCE OF LAW

Less well known as a source of law are the federal regulatory agencies, among which are the Securities and Exchange Commission (SEC), the Federal Trade Commission (FTC), the Equal Employment Opportunity Commission (EEOC), and the Occupational Safety and Health Administration (OSHA). Congress has delegated to these agencies the authority to make rules governing the conduct of business and labor in certain areas. This authority was delegated because it was thought to be in the public interest, convenience, and necessity. Because each of the agencies must notify the public of proposed rule making and set out a cost–benefit analysis, all proposed and final rules can be found in the Federal Register. Administrative agencies constitute what many have called a fourth branch of government. They exist at the state and local levels as well.

Classifications of Law

Besides **statutory law** made by the legislative branch and **case law** resulting from judicial interpretation of constitutions and statutes, there are several other classifications of law that are necessary to know about in order to understand the legal environment of business.

statutory law Law made by the legislative branch of government.

case law Law resulting from judicial interpretations of constitutions and statutes.

CRIMINAL LAW AND CIVIL LAW

Criminal law comprises those federal and state statutes that prohibit wrongful conduct such as arson, rape, murder, extortion, forgery, and fraud. The purpose of criminal law is to punish offenders by imprisonment or fines as well as rehabilitation. The plaintiff in a criminal case is the United States, State X, County X, or City X, representing society and the victim against the defendant, who is most likely to be an individual but may also be a corporation, partnership, or a single proprietorship. The plaintiff must prove beyond a reasonable doubt that the defendant committed a crime.

Crimes are generally divided into felonies and misdemeanors. In most states, felonies are serious crimes (e.g., rape, arson, and criminal fraud) that are punishable by incarceration in a state penitentiary. Misdemeanors are less serious

criminal law Composed of federal and state statutes prohibiting wrongful conduct ranging from murder to fraud.

crimes (e.g., driving while intoxicated) that are usually punishable by shorter periods of imprisonment in a county or city jail or by fines. An act that is a misdemeanor in one state could be a felony in another state.

civil law Law governing litigation between two private parties.

Civil law comprises federal and state statutes governing litigation between two private parties. Neither the state nor the federal government is represented in most civil cases (exceptions will be pointed out in future chapters). Rather than prosecutors, there are plaintiffs, who are usually individuals or businesses suing other individuals or businesses (the defendants) to obtain compensation for an alleged breach of a private duty. For example, A, a retailer, enters into a contract with B, a manufacturer, who agrees to supply A with all the bicycles of a certain brand that the retailer can sell. A advertises and sales exceed all expectations. B refuses to ship any more bicycles, and A's customers sue him for reneging on the rain check he gave them. In turn, A sues B for breach of contract. A must show by a preponderance of evidence (a lower standard of proof than the "beyond a reasonable doubt" standard that prevails in criminal cases) that B is liable (legally obligated) to fulfill the contract. Note that A is not seeking to put B in prison or to fine B. A is seeking only to be compensated for his advertising costs, his lost sales, and what it may cost him in lawyers' fees, court costs, and damage to settle with his customers (Table 2).

PUBLIC AND PRIVATE LAW

public law Law dealing with the relationship of government to individual citizens.

Public law deals with the relationship of government to individual citizens. Constitutional law, criminal law, and administrative law fit this classification. Constitutional law comprises the basic principles and laws of the nation as set forth in the U.S. Constitution. It determines the powers and obligations of the government and guarantees certain rights to citizens. Examples of questions that fall under constitutional law: Does an individual citizen have a Sixth Amendment right to counsel when stopped by a police officer, taken into custody, and interrogated? Is it cruel and unusual punishment under the Eighth Amendment to electrocute a person when that person has been found guilty of certain crimes, such as first-degree murder or killing a police officer in the line of duty? We have already touched on criminal law. Administrative law covers the process by which individuals or businesses can redress grievances against regulatory agencies such as the FTC and the SEC. It prevents the agencies from acting in an arbitrary or

TABLE 2 COMPARISON OF CIVIL AND CRIMINAL LAW

	Civil Law	*Criminal Law*
Parties	Individual or Corporate Plaintiff (in most cases) versus Individual or Corporate Defendant (in most cases)	County, City, State, or Federal Prosecutor versus Individual or Corporate Defendant (in most cases)
Purpose	Compensation Deference-deterrence	Punishment Deference-deterrence Rehabilitation
Burden of proof and sanctions	Preponderance of Evidence Monetary Damages Equitable Terms	Beyond a Reasonable Doubt Imprisonment Fines

capricious manner and from extending their power beyond the scope that Congress has given them. For example, when the Federal Communications Commission (FCC) ruled that cable television corporations had to set aside so many channels for access by any public group that requested time, the courts reversed this FCC rule, deciding that it was beyond the agency's authority and in violation of a provision of the Federal Communications Act. Administrative law also covers the process whereby government agencies represent individuals or classes of individuals against business entities—for example, when the EEOC represents individuals alleging discrimination in pay under the provisions of the Civil Rights Act of 1964.

Private law is generally concerned with the enforcement of private duties between individuals, between an individual and a business, and between two businesses. Contracts, torts, and property law fall under this classification. Note that the government is not a concerned party in most private law cases.

private law Law dealing with the enforcement of private duties.

SUBSTANTIVE AND PROCEDURAL LAW

Substantive Law. Substantive law creates and regulates legal rights. For example, the rules of contract law determine whether an agreement between two parties is binding and, thus, an enforceable contract.

Procedural Law. Procedural law sets forth the rules of enforcing substantive rights in a court of law. In effect, procedural law defines the manner by which to obtain a remedy in a court of law. When there is a possible breach of contract, the plaintiff will have to file a complaint indicating the basis for the suit, and the defendant will set forth an answer responding to the complaint, indicating why the defendant should not have to compensate the plaintiff.

CYBERLAW

Over the last 15 years, the use of the Internet to carry out commercial transactions has brought about a body of law that is largely traditional in the above categories, but often unique to cyberspace communication. Cyberlaw is not really a new type of law but traditional categories (e.g., private law—contracts and torts) based on a relatively new form of communication (online). Those prepared to enter business today need to know traditional laws and their application dealing with cyberlaw issues.

Global Dimensions of the Legal Environment of Business

At the beginning of this chapter, we stated that managers need to be aware of the impact of international variables on their business. As of the year 2004, approximately 30 percent of all jobs in the United States depended on exports, and in the view of many experts, that percentage will soon rise to 50 percent. Additionally, many jobs are being outsourced to other countries by American corporations for cost purposes. Trade treaties will make the international dimensions of the legal environment of business increasingly important to U.S. firms. Throughout this book, therefore, we discuss the international dimensions of product liability, tort, contracts, labor, securities and antitrust law, as well as ethics whenever appropriate. For example, current U.S. securities laws include the Foreign Corrupt Practices Act of 1977 (FCPA), as amended in 1988. If the laws of Country X do not forbid bribery in order to obtain a $10 million contract to build an oil pipeline, should U.S. companies be constrained by the FCPA prohibitions against such bribery? Ethical and cultural relativists would say no: "When in Rome do as the Romans do." Normative ethical theorists, such as rule utilitarians, would say yes, arguing that rules agreed upon by the world community, or a preponderance of it, cannot be compromised by a particular situation. They would point out that both the United Nations' Multinational Code and the laws of most of the UN member states prohibit bribery.

SUMMARY

The study of the legal environment of business includes the study of legal reasoning, critical thinking skills, and ethical norms; the legal and administrative law processes; selected areas of public and private law; and relevant international law. Jurisprudence is the science or philosophy of law, or law in its most generalized form. The major schools of jurisprudence are natural law, positivism, sociological, American realism, critical legal theory, feminism, and law and economics.

The three direct sources of law are the legislative (statutory), judicial (case law), and executive (executive orders) branches of government. Administrative agencies, which promulgate regulations and rules, constitute the fourth (indirect) source of law. The international dimensions of law include legal, financial, economic, and ethical variables that have an impact on business decision making.

REVIEW QUESTIONS

1 Contrast the natural law school's definition of law with that of the positivist school.

2 Explain how the critical legal theory and the feminist school of jurisprudence are similar.

3 Describe how the executive branch of government is a source of law.

4 What is the difference between statutory law and case law? Explain.

5 If the president vetoes a bill passed by Congress, is there any way that the bill can become law? Explain.

6 Distinguish between the pairs of terms in each of these three classifications of law:

   a. public law, private law

   b. civil law, criminal law

   c. felonies, misdemeanors

REVIEW PROBLEMS

7 Three men are trapped in a cave with no hope of rescue and no food. They roll dice to determine who will be killed and eaten by the others in order to survive. The two survivors are rescued 10 days later and tried for murder. Judge A finds them guilty, saying that the unjustifiable killing of another is against the

homicide laws of State X. He bases his decision solely on statutory law and case precedents interpreting the law. To which school of legal thought does Judge A belong? Explain.

8 Basing his decision on the same set of facts as given in Problem 7, Judge B rules that the survivors are not guilty because they were cut off from all civilized life, and in such a situation, the laws of nature apply, not man-made laws. To which school of legal thought does Judge B belong? Explain.

9 Basing her decision on the same set of facts as given in Problem 7, Judge C rules that the two survivors are not guilty because, according to a scientific survey of the community by a professional polling organization, the public believes that the survivors' actions were defensible. To which school of legal thought does Judge C belong? Explain.

10 Imagine that you were a judge in the case set forth in Problem 7. How would you decide the case? On the basis of the reasons for your decision, explain which legal philosophy you think you hold.

11 Madison and his adult son lived in a house owned by Madison. At the request of the son, Marshall painted the house. Madison did not authorize the work, but he knew that it was being done and raised no objection. Madison refused to pay Marshall, arguing that he had not contracted to have the house painted.

Marshall asked his attorney if Madison was legally liable to pay him. The attorney told Marshall that, in their state, several appellate court opinions had established that when a homeowner allows work to be done on his home by a person who would ordinarily expect to be paid, a duty to pay exists. The attorney stated that, on the basis of these precedents, it was advisable for Marshall to bring a suit to collect the reasonable value of the work he had done. Explain what the attorney meant by precedent and why the fact that precedent existed was significant.

12 Smith was involved in litigation in California. She lost her case in the trial court. She appealed to the California appellate court, arguing that the trial court judge had incorrectly excluded certain evidence. To support her argument, she cited rulings by the supreme court of North Dakota and the supreme court of Ohio. Both the North Dakota and Ohio cases involved facts that were similar to those in Smith's case. Does the California court have to follow the decisions from North Dakota and Ohio? Support your answer.

CASE PROBLEMS

13 Walt Disney Company entered into a contract with Irving Berlin, Inc., assigning musical copyrights in exchange for a share of Berlin revenues. The agreement exempted from copyright protection Disney's use of the assigned music in motion pictures. The music was used in several Disney feature-length cartoons that were later made available for sale on videocassette. Berlin's heirs brought suit, alleging infringement. Was this new technology an infringement? How would a judge's legal philosophy affect how he or she would rule in this case? *Bourne v. Walt Disney Co.,* 68 F.3d 621 (2d Cir. 1995).

14 Three same-sex couples who are residents of Vermont have lived together in committed relationships for a period. Two of the couples have raised children together. All three couples applied for marriage licenses and were refused a license on the grounds that they were ineligible under the state marriage laws. Plaintiffs sought a declaratory judgment that the refusal to issue them a license violated the marriage statutes and the Vermont constitution. They argued that it violated the Common Benefits Clause of the Vermont constitution, which provides "[t]hat government is, or ought to be instituted for the common benefit, protection, and security of the people, nation, or community, and not for the particular emolument or advantage of a single person, family, or set of persons, who are part of that community. . . ." They argued that in not having access to a civil marriage license, they are denied many legal benefits and protections, including coverage under a spouse's medical, life, and disability insurance, hospital visitation and other medical decision-making privileges, and spousal support. Argue whether Vermont's marriage license law violates the same-sex couples' rights under the Vermont constitution. Which school of jurisprudence would you apply in your reasoning?

15 Beattie was seriously injured in an automobile accident in Delaware and was a quadriplegic following the accident. She filed suit against her husband for damages, alleging that his negligence was the cause of her injuries. Because the Beatties had substantial liability insurance, Margaret Beattie would have received a large sum in damages if she were able to establish her case. Unfortunately for her, Delaware follows the precedent of not allowing one spouse to sue the other spouse in tort. Should this precedent prevent Margaret from being allowed to sue her husband for damages in this case? *Beattie v. Beattie,* 630 A.2d 1096 (Del. 1993).

16 The federal Equal Employment Opportunity Commission (EEOC) brought suit against the Commonwealth of Massachusetts, challenging a statute mandating that state police must retire at 50 as a violation of the Age Discrimination Act. In an earlier suit brought by a state policeman named Mahoney, who held a desk job, the federal courts upheld the Massachusetts law on the grounds that being under 50 was a bona fide occupational requirement. The district court rejected the EEOC's challenge to the law on the basis of the ruling in Mahoney's case. The EEOC appealed, arguing that Mahoney's case should not be considered binding precedent for all members of the state police force. How did the EEOC appeal this case? Did it represent the agency or individuals or both? Who won? *EEOC v. Trabucco,* 791 F.2d 283 (1986).

17 A&M Records, plaintiffs, are in the business of the commercial recording, distribution, and sale of copyrighted musical compositions and sound recordings. It filed suit against Napster Inc. (Napster) as a contributory and vicarious copyright infringer. Napster operates an online service for "peer-to-peer file sharing" (www.Napster.com) so that users can, free of charge, download recordings via the Internet through a process known as "ripping," which is the downloading of digital MP3 files. *MP3* is the abbreviated term for audio recordings in a digital format known as MPEG-3. Napster's online service provides a search vehicle for files stored on others' computers and permits the downloading of the recordings from the hard drives of other Napster users. Napster provides technical support as well as a chat room for users to exchange information. The result is that users, who register and have a password through Napster, could download single songs and complete CDs or albums via the peer-to-peer file sharing. The district court granted a preliminary injunction to the plaintiffs enjoining Napster from "engaging in, or facilitating others in copying,

downloading, uploading, transmitting, or distributing plaintiffs' copyrighted musical compositions and sound recordings, protected by either federal or state law, without express permission of the rights owner." Who won? *A&M Records v. Napster,* 239 F.3d 1004 (9th Cir. 2001).

18 A short time after the bombing of the federal building in Oklahoma City in April 1995, a message was posted anonymously on an America Online (AOL) bulletin board advertising "Naughty Oklahoma T-Shirts." The posting advertised the sale of shirts featuring offensive and tasteless slogans celebrating the tragic bomb blast, which killed 168 people. The advertisement stated that interested buyers should call "Ken" at a phone number in Seattle. The telephone number given was the actual number of Mr. Kenneth Zeran, who had nothing to do with the posting and most definitely had no such T-shirts for sale.

During the following few weeks, Mr. Zeran received hundreds of telephone calls and voice mail messages. These calls caused him a great deal of distress. He notified AOL by telephone, letters, and e-mail about the bogus posting and harassment and asked AOL to immediately remove it and issue a public retraction. Although AOL did remove the original posting (the parties dispute how quickly this occurred), soon thereafter the unknown prankster posted another message advertising new T-shirts with more offensive slogans related to the Oklahoma City bombing, again giving Mr. Zeran's telephone number and also stating, "Please call back if busy."

For the next few days, Mr. Zeran's telephone rang almost every 2 minutes with irate messages. Meanwhile, the perpetrator of the hoax continued to post new messages on AOL, advertising several new distasteful items (fictitious) such as bumper stickers and key chains celebrating the Oklahoma City massacre and again giving Mr. Zeran's telephone number. An Oklahoma City radio station read the messages on the air and encouraged listeners to express their outrage. Mr. Zeran sued AOL for its slowness in removing the posting. The federal district court dismissed the suit, holding the Communications Decency Act prevented the suit. The Fourth Circuit Court of Appeals affirmed. Explain how the legal philosophy one adheres to would make one more or less supportive of the court's ruling in favor of AOL. *Zeran v. AOL,* 129 F.3d 327 (4th Cir. 1997).

THINKING CRITICALLY ABOUT RELEVANT LEGAL ISSUES

Although there is debate over the various schools of jurisprudence, not all options are of equal merit. In that the law is meant to offer protection and to guide society, not all philosophies can best achieve this desired outcome. In order to have a just legal system, laws need to be based on absolute principles that provide clarity in the prescribed rules to follow, as well as justice in the result of following the laws. Therefore, the natural law school best provides for the maintenance of law, order, and justice in society.

One advantage of the natural law school is the acknowledgment of the black and white nature of legal issues. When someone commits a crime and harms another, one party is wrong and the other is harmed because of the wrong. Certain actions, such as murder, are simply wrong acts that are never permissible. The natural law school of jurisprudence readily recognizes moral absolutes and seeks to create a legal system around these absolutes, ultimately strengthening the resulting laws. Good and evil exist, and natural law sides with the good against the evil.

The basis in moral absolutes grounds natural law in the pursuit of the right and the good. These moral absolutes exist and are available to those who study and think about what is right and just. People, by considering these moral absolutes, can come upon the naturally right code of conduct, and make laws that will ensure people live up to this naturally right code of conduct. No other school of jurisprudence adequately tells people the proper way to conduct their lives. After all, the role of the law is to maintain peace and justice in society by creating the laws that best channel people toward following right actions

and avoiding wrong actions. Only an application of natural law jurisprudence can guide society for the good of all.

In addition to prescribing proper conduct for citizens, law grounded in moral absolutes can avoid subjective approaches to laws. A quick review of almost any legal issue will demonstrate that judges and lawyers do not always agree upon what a law means. When laws are firmly grounded in moral absolutes, however, the subjective element of the law is removed. No longer would judges need to ponder over what a law means and when it applies. Instead, judges would have to look at the law and determine the relevant moral truth the law upholds. By enforcing the moral absolutes underlying the law, judges would no longer apply their subjective beliefs to laws, and instead would create a more consistent and predictable legal system.

- How would you frame the issue and conclusion of this essay?

- What is the primary ethical norm underlying the author's argument?

- Does the argument contain significant ambiguity in the reasoning?

  Clue: Which word or phrases could have multiple meanings, where changing the meaning used either strengthens or weakens the argument?

- Write an essay that someone who holds an opposition opinion to the author might write.

  Clue: How might reasonable people disagree with the author's conclusion?

ASSIGNMENT ON THE INTERNET

This chapter introduces you to seven different schools of jurisprudence, each with distinct elements. Yet, the various schools also share a number of similarities that often blur the lines separating one from the other. Using the Internet, research at least two of the schools of jurisprudence discussed here to go beyond the information provided in this chapter. Then apply critical thinking skills to compare the two schools you researched. How are they similar? How are they different?

For example, if you wanted to compare critical legal theory to the feminist school, you could begin by visiting this page on critical legal theory: **www.law.cornell.edu/topics/critical_theory. html**. Then visit a site exploring the feminist school. One such site can be found at **www.law.cornell. edu/topics/feminist_jurisprudence.html**. The following sites may also be of use in better understanding theories of jurisprudence.

ON THE INTERNET

www.seanet.com/~rod/marbury.html Learn about the jurisprudence of access to justice from this page.
www.iep.utm.edu/j/jurisfem.htm The various components of feminist jurisprudence, discussed in greater detail, can be found at this site along with reading recommendations for further study.
www.fact-index.com/v/vi/virtue_jurisprudence.html Seven schools of legal thought or jurisprudence are discussed in this chapter, yet other theories of jurisprudence exist. This site provides an overview to virtue jurisprudence.
www.archives.gov/federal_register/executive_orders/executive_orders.html This is the Web site of the Federal Register, which allows you to search and read executive orders.
thomas.loc.gov Search, read, and follow the legislative progress of bills through both houses of Congress by using this research site.

FOR FUTURE READING

Elias, Stephen, and Susan Levinkind. *Legal Research: How to Find & Understand the Law.* Berkeley, CA: Nolo Press, 2007.

Fuller, Lon. "The Case of the Speluncean Explorers." *Harvard Law Review* 62, no. 4 (1949): 616-45.

Murphy, Jeffrie, and Jules Coleman. *Philosophy of Law: An Introduction to Jurisprudence.* Boulder, CO: Westview Press, 1990.

Suber, Peter. *The Case of the Speluncean Explorers: Nine New Opinions.* 1998. Reprint, New York: Routledge, 2002.

The American Legal System

- JURISDICTION

- VENUE

- THE STRUCTURE OF THE COURT SYSTEM

- THE ACTORS IN THE LEGAL SYSTEM AND THEIR RELATIONSHIP TO THE BUSINESS COMMUNITY

- THE ADVERSARY PROCESS

- STEPS IN CIVIL LITIGATION AND THE ROLE OF BUSINESSPERSONS

- GLOBAL DIMENSIONS OF THE AMERICAN LEGAL SYSTEM

We are all subject to both state and federal laws. Under our dual court system, all lawsuits must be brought in either the federal or the state court system. In some cases, an action may be brought in either. Thus, it is important that those in the business community understand how the decisions are made as to which court system can resolve their grievances. This chapter first considers the principles that determine which court system has the power to hear various types of cases and then examines in greater detail the structure of the two basic divisions of our dual court system. Next, it focuses on the primary actors who play major roles in our litigation process. Finally, it examines the philosophy behind our American legal system and traces the procedures that must be followed when using one of our courts.

Jurisdiction

The concept of jurisdiction is exceedingly simple, yet at the same time, exceedingly complex. At its most simple level, **jurisdiction** is the power of the courts to hear a case and render a decision that is binding on the parties. Jurisdiction is complex, however, because there are several types of jurisdiction that a court must have in order to hear a case.

jurisdiction The power of a court to hear a case and render a binding decision.

ORIGINAL VERSUS APPELLATE JURISDICTION

Perhaps the simplest type of jurisdiction to understand is the distinction between original and appellate jurisdiction, which refers to the role the court plays in the

CRITICAL THINKING ABOUT THE LAW

Our American legal system can seem confusing at first. Using your critical thinking skills to answer the following questions as you read this chapter will help you understand how our legal system operates.

1. Critical thinkers recognize that ambiguous words—words that have multiple possible meanings—can cause confusion. Sam boldly asserts that the court of common pleas has **jurisdiction** over *Jones v. Smith*, while Clara asserts equally strongly that the court of common pleas does not have jurisdiction over the case. Explain the ambiguity that allows these two apparently contradictory statements to both be true.

   Clue: Is it possible for a court to have one type of jurisdiction and not another?

2. Our legal system contains numerous procedural requirements. Which of the primary values is furthered by these requirements?

3. Many say that the adversary system is consistent with the American culture. What value that is furthered by our adversary system is important to our culture?

---

original jurisdiction The power to initially hear and decide (try) a case.

appellate jurisdiction The power to review a previously made decision by the trial court.

in personam jurisdiction (jurisdiction over the person) The power of a court to render a decision that affects the legal rights of a specific person.

plaintiff Party on whose behalf the complaint is filed.

defendant Party against whom an action is being brought.

complaint The initial pleading in a case that states the names of the parties to the action, the basis for the court's subject matter jurisdiction, the facts on which the party's claim is based, and the relief that the party is seeking.

judicial hierarchy. A court of **original jurisdiction,** usually referred to as a trial court, has the power to initially hear and decide a case. It is in the court of original jurisdiction that a case originates; hence, its name.

A court with **appellate jurisdiction** has the power to review a previously made decision to determine whether the trial court erred in making its initial decision.

JURISDICTION OVER PERSONS AND PROPERTY

Before the court can render a decision affecting a person, the court must have **in personam jurisdiction** or jurisdiction over the person. In personam jurisdiction is the power to render a decision affecting the specific persons before the court. When a person files a lawsuit, that person, called the **plaintiff,** gives the court in personam jurisdiction over him or her. By filing a case, the plaintiff is asking the court to make a ruling affecting his or her rights. The court must acquire jurisdiction over the party being sued, the **defendant,** by serving him or her with a copy of the plaintiff's complaint and a summons. The **complaint,** discussed in more detail later in this chapter, is a detailed statement of the basis for the plaintiff's lawsuit and the relief being sought. The **summons** is an order of the court notifying the defendant of the pending case and telling him or her how and when to respond to the complaint.

Personal **service,** whereby a sheriff or other person appointed by the court hands the summons and complaint to the defendant, has been the traditional method of service. Today, other types of service are more common. Residential service may be used, whereby the summons and complaint are left by the representative of the court with a responsible adult at the home of the defendant. Certified mail or, in some cases, ordinary mail is also used to serve defendants. Once the defendant has been properly served, the court has in personam jurisdiction over him or her and may render a decision affecting his or her legal rights, regardless of whether the defendant responds to the complaint.

When one thinks about how the rules of service would apply to a suit against a corporation, the question arises: How do you serve a corporation? The legal system has solved this question. Most states require that corporations appoint an agent for service when they are incorporated. This agent is a person who has been given the legal authority to receive service for the corporation. Once the agent has been served, the corporation is served. In most states, service on the president of the corporation also constitutes service on the corporation.

A court's power is generally limited to the borders of the state in which it is located. So, traditionally, a defendant had to be served within the state in which the court was located in order for the court to acquire jurisdiction over the person of the defendant. This restriction imposed severe hardships when a defendant who lived in one state entered another state and injured the plaintiff. If the defendant never again entered the plaintiff's state, the plaintiff could bring an action against the defendant only in the state in which the defendant lived. Obviously, this restriction would prevent many legitimate actions from being filed.

To alleviate this problem, most states enacted **long-arm statutes.** These statutes enable the court to serve the defendant outside the state as long as the defendant has engaged in certain acts within the state. Those acts vary from state to state, but most statutes include such acts as committing a tort within the state or doing business within the state. The following case demonstrates the application of such a statute.

> **summons** Order by a court to appear before it at a certain time and place.
>
> **service** Providing the defendant with a summons and a copy of the complaint.
>
> **long-arm statute** A statute authorizing a court to obtain jurisdiction over an out-of-state defendant when that party has sufficient minimum contacts with a state.

CASE 1

World-Wide Volkswagen Corporation v. Woodson
District Judge of Cook County
Supreme Court of the United States
444 U.S. 286 (1980)

Mr. and Mrs. Robinson, the plaintiffs in the original case, filed a product liability action against defendant World-Wide Volkswagen in a state court in Oklahoma to collect compensation for damages they incurred as a result of an accident involving an automobile they had purchased in New York. The defendants in that case, the retailer and the wholesaler of the car, were both New York corporations.

Defendants claimed that the Oklahoma court could not exercise jurisdiction over them because they were nonresidents and they lacked sufficient "minimum contacts" with the state to be subject to its in personam jurisdiction.

The trial court rejected defendant petitioner's claims. The Oklahoma Supreme Court likewise rejected their claims, and so they petitioned the U.S. Supreme Court. Note that the case that went to the Supreme Court is against the trial court, because the issue on appeal is whether the trial court acted properly in asserting jurisdiction.

Justice White

The issue before us is whether, consistently with the Due Process Clause of the Fourteenth Amendment, an Oklahoma court may exercise in personam jurisdiction over a nonresident automobile retailer and its wholesale distributor in a products liability action, when the defendants' only connection with Oklahoma is the fact that an automobile sold in New York to New York residents became involved in an accident in Oklahoma.

As has long been settled, and as we reaffirm today, a state court may exercise personal jurisdiction over a nonresident defendant only so long as there exist "minimum contacts" between the defendant and the forum State. The concept of minimum contacts, in turn, can be seen to perform two related, but distinguishable, functions. It protects the defendant against the burdens of litigating in a distant or inconvenient forum. And it acts to ensure that the States, through their courts, do not reach out beyond the limits imposed on them by their status as coequal sovereigns in a federal system.

The protection against inconvenient litigation is typically described in terms of "reasonableness" or "fairness." We have said that the defendant's contacts with the forum State must be such that maintenance of the suit "does not offend 'traditional notions of fair play and substantial justice.'"

The limits imposed on state jurisdiction by the Due Process Clause, in its role as a guarantor against inconvenient litigation, have been substantially relaxed over the years. This trend is largely attributable to a fundamental transformation in the American economy.

Today many commercial transactions touch two or more States and may involve parties separated by the full continent. With this increasing nationalization of commerce has come a great increase in the amount of business conducted by mail across state lines. At the same time modern transportation and communication have made it much less burdensome for a party sued to defend himself in a State where he engages in economic activity.

Nevertheless, we have never accepted the proposition that state lines are irrelevant for jurisdictional purposes, nor could we, and remain faithful to the principles of interstate federalism embodied in the Constitution.

Applying these principles to the case at hand, we find in the record before us a total absence of those affiliating circumstances that are a necessary predicate to any exercise of state court jurisdiction. Petitioners carry on no activity whatsoever in Oklahoma. They close no sales and perform no services there. They avail themselves of none of the privileges and benefits of Oklahoma law. They solicit no business there either through salespersons or through advertising reasonably calculated to reach the State; nor does the record show that they regularly sell cars at wholesale or retail to Oklahoma customers or residents or that they indirectly, through others, serve or seek to serve the Oklahoma market. In short, respondents seek to base jurisdiction on one isolated occurrence and whatever inferences can be drawn therefrom: The fortuitous circumstance that a single Audi automobile sold in New York to New York residents happened to suffer an accident while passing through Oklahoma.

It is argued, however, that because an automobile is mobile by its very design and purpose it was "foreseeable"

that the Robinsons' Audi would cause injury in Oklahoma. Yet "foreseeability" alone has never been a sufficient benchmark for personal jurisdiction under the Due Process Clause.

If foreseeability were the criterion, a local California tire retailer could be forced to defend in Pennsylvania when a blowout occurs there, a Wisconsin seller of a defective automobile jack could be hauled before a distant court for damage caused in New Jersey, or a Florida soft-drink concessionaire could be summoned to Alaska to account for injuries happening there.

This is not to say, of course, that foreseeability is wholly irrelevant. But the foreseeability that is critical to due process analysis is not the mere likelihood that a product will find its way into the forum State. Rather, it is that the defendant's conduct and connection with the forum State are such that he should reasonably anticipate being hauled into court there. When a corporation "purposefully avails itself of the privilege of conducting activities within the forum State," it has clear notice that it is subject to suit there and can act to alleviate the risk of burdensome litigation by procuring insurance, passing the expected costs on to customers, or, if the risks are too great, severing its connection with the State. Hence, if the sale of a product of a manufacturer or distributor such as Audi or Volkswagen is not simply an isolated occurrence but arises from the efforts of the manufacturer or distributor to serve directly or indirectly the market for its product in other States, it is not unreasonable to subject it to suit in one of those States if its allegedly defective merchandise has there been the source of injury to its owner or to others.

But there is no such or similar basis for Oklahoma jurisdiction over World-Wide or Seaway in this case. Seaway's sales are made in Massena, New York. World-Wide's market, although substantially larger, is limited to dealers in New York, New Jersey, and Connecticut. There is no evidence of record that any automobiles distributed by World-Wide are sold to retail customers outside this tristate area. It is foreseeable that the purchasers of automobiles sold by World-Wide and Seaway may take them to Oklahoma. But the mere "unilateral activity of those who claim some relationship with a nonresident defendant cannot satisfy the requirement of contact with the forum State."

Reversed in favor of World-Wide Volkswagen Corporation.

Contrast the facts in the foregoing case with those in the 2004 case of *Snowney v. Harrah's Entertainment, Inc.*,[1] in which the court came to a contrary decision. In *Snowney,* the defendant, a California resident, filed a class action suit against Harrah's and other Nevada casino operators, in a California state court, alleging unfair competition, breach of contract, and false advertising. The trial court

---

[1] 11 Cal.Rptr. 3d 35 (Ct. App., Calif., 2004).

dismissed the suit for lack of personal jurisdiction. The California Court of Appeals overturned the dismissal, explaining that when the court was deciding whether it could exercise its jurisdiction over a nonresident, it must consider (1) the burden on the defendant of defending an action in the forum; (2) the forum state's interest in adjudicating the dispute; (3) the plaintiff's interest in obtaining relief; (4) judicial economy; and (5) the states' shared interest in furthering fundamental substantive social policies. In finding that there were sufficient minimum contacts with the state to justify exercising jurisdiction, the court cited the facts that the hotels and casinos (1) purposefully directed advertising at California residents, (2) conducted business with some residents by an interactive Web site, and (3) solicited and received the patronage of California residents.

In Rem Jurisdiction. If a defendant has property within a state, the plaintiff may seek to bring the action directly against the property rather than against the owner. For example, if a Michigan defendant owned land in Idaho on which taxes had not been paid for 10 years, the state could bring an action to recover those taxes. The Idaho court would have **in rem jurisdiction** over the property and, in an in rem proceeding, could order the property sold to pay the taxes. Such proceedings are often used when the owner of the property cannot be located for personal service.

> **in rem jurisdiction** The power of a court to render a decision that affects property directly rather than the owner of the property.

SUBJECT MATTER JURISDICTION

One of the most important types of jurisdiction is **subject matter jurisdiction,** the power of the court to hear certain kinds of cases. Subject matter jurisdiction is extremely important because if a judge renders a decision in a case over which the court does not have subject matter jurisdiction, the decision is void or meaningless. The parties cannot give the court subject matter jurisdiction. It is granted by law, as described in the subsequent sections.

> **subject matter jurisdiction** The power of a court to render a decision in a particular type of case.

At the beginning of this chapter, you learned that we have a dual court system, comprised of both a state and a federal system. The choice of the system in which to file a case is not purely a matter of deciding which forum is most convenient or which judge would be most sympathetic. Subject matter jurisdiction determines which court may hear the case. When you think about the concept of subject matter jurisdiction, it is easiest to think of it in two steps. First, which court system does the case fall within? Once you know which court system has jurisdiction over the case, you then need to ask whether there is a special court within that system that hears that specific type of case. When asking which court system has subject matter jurisdiction, there are three possible answers: state jurisdiction, exclusive federal jurisdiction, or concurrent federal jurisdiction (Exhibit 1).

State Jurisdiction. The **state court** system has subject matter jurisdiction over all cases not within the exclusive jurisdiction of the federal court system. Only a very limited number of cases fall within the exclusive jurisdiction of the federal courts. Consequently, almost all cases fall within the state court's jurisdiction. Suits for breach of contract, products liability actions, and divorces are just a few of the types of cases falling within the state court system's jurisdiction.

> **state court jurisdiction** Applies to cases that may be heard only in the state court system.

Exclusive Federal Jurisdiction. A few types of cases may be heard only in the federal courts. Such cases are within the exclusive jurisdiction of the federal

43

EXHIBIT 1

SUBJECT MATTER JURISDICTION

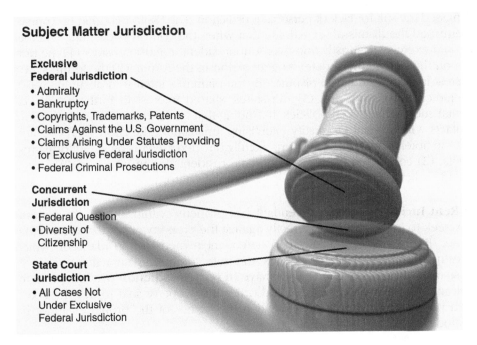

Subject Matter Jurisdiction

Exclusive Federal Jurisdiction
- Admiralty
- Bankruptcy
- Copyrights, Trademarks, Patents
- Claims Against the U.S. Government
- Claims Arising Under Statutes Providing for Exclusive Federal Jurisdiction
- Federal Criminal Prosecutions

Concurrent Jurisdiction
- Federal Question
- Diversity of Citizenship

State Court Jurisdiction
- All Cases Not Under Exclusive Federal Jurisdiction

exclusive federal jurisdiction Applies to cases that may be heard only in the federal court system.

concurrent jurisdiction Applies to cases that may be heard in either the federal or the state court system.

court system. If these cases were tried in a state court, any decision rendered by the judge would be void. Cases that fall within the exclusive jurisdiction of the federal courts include such matters as admiralty, bankruptcy, federal criminal prosecutions, claims against the United States, and claims arising under those federal statutes that include a provision for **exclusive federal jurisdiction.** Many of these last cases are of particular concern to those in business. For example, one statute that gives exclusive jurisdiction to the federal court system is the National Environmental Policy Act. Cases brought under this act must be filed in a federal district court.

Concurrent Federal Jurisdiction. Many cases may be heard in either the federal or the state court. These cases are said to fall within the federal court's **concurrent jurisdiction,** meaning that both court systems have jurisdiction, so the plaintiff may file in the trial court of either system. There are two types of such cases. The first are federal question cases. If a case requires an interpretation of the U.S. Constitution, a federal statute, or a federal treaty, it is said to involve a federal question and may be heard in either state or federal court. Many people make the mistake of thinking that when a person believes his or her rights under the federal Constitution have been violated, the case must go to the federal courts. They are wrong. Such a case involves a federal question and is, therefore, within the concurrent jurisdiction of both court systems.

The second means by which a case may fall within the federal court's concurrent jurisdiction is through diversity of citizenship. If the opponents in a case are from different states, there is said to be diversity of citizenship. The diversity must be complete. If any two parties on opposing sides reside in the same state, diversity is lost. For example, if the plaintiff is an Ohio resident and one of the defendants lives in Michigan and the other in Indiana, diversity exists. If an Ohio plaintiff is bringing an action against a Michigan defendant and an Ohio defendant, however, there is not complete diversity and, therefore, no concurrent federal jurisdiction. When the basis for federal jurisdiction is diversity of citizenship, there must be an amount in excess of $75,000 in controversy.

When a case falls within the federal court's concurrent jurisdiction because of either a federal question or diversity of citizenship, the suit may be filed in either state or federal court. If the case is filed in state court, the defendant has a right of removal, which means that he or she may have the case transferred to federal court. All the defendant has to do is file a motion with the court asking to exercise his or her right of removal and the case must be transferred to federal court; the judge has no discretion but must comply with the request.

The right of removal arises only when the case is filed in state court; there is no right of removal to state court. As a result, whenever there is a case under concurrent jurisdiction, if either party wants the case heard in federal court, that is where it will be heard.

Why should both parties have the right to have such a case heard in federal court? In certain cases, a party may fear local prejudice in a state court. Juries for a state court are generally drawn from the county in which the court is located. The juries for federal district courts are drawn from the entire district, which encompasses many counties. Juries in state court are, therefore, usually more homogeneous than those of a district court. One problem that this homogeneity may present to the out-of-state corporate defendant occurs when the county in which the court is located is predominantly rural. If the case involves an injury to a member of this rural community, the defendant may feel that the rural jurors would be more sympathetic to the local injured party, whereas jurors drawn from a broader area, including cities, may be more likely to view the victim less sympathetically. City residents are also more likely to work for a corporation and, thus, may not regard corporations as unfavorably as might rural residents.

When a case involves a federal question, some people believe federal judges are better qualified to hear such cases because they have more experience in resolving questions that require an interpretation of federal statutes. Finally, if a party anticipates that it may be necessary to appeal the case to the U.S. Supreme Court, bringing the case first in a federal district court may save one step in the appeals process.

When one party wishes to have the case tried in federal court and the other prefers state court, the issue of whether the case is within the concurrent jurisdiction of the federal courts sometimes arises. The following case provides an illustration of such a situation.

CASE 2

Ambrosia Coal & Construction Company v. Hector Carlos Morales, et al.
United States Court of Appeals for the Eleventh Circuit
482 F.3d 1309 (2007)

Ambrosia, a Pennsylvania-based corporation, entered into a real estate transaction with Garita Hotel Limited Partnership, an Ohio-based partnership. Ambrosia provided Garita L.P. with four million dollars in order for Garita L.P. to purchase a 99-year-leasehold interest in beachfront property in Puerto Rico. In exchange for supplying the financing, Ambrosia received a 100 percent ownership interest in Garita Hotel Corporation, a Puerto

Rican corporation. The corporate structure of Ambrosia and the Garita entities is that of parent and subsidiaries, respectively. After Ambrosia won a case regarding an unlawful sale of the leasehold, Ambrosia reached a settlement deal with Isla Verde in 1994. According to the agreement, Ambrosia agreed to relinquish its rights to the leasehold in exchange for enumerated considerations.

Ambrosia, feeling that post-settlement changes made by Isla Verde violated the settlement agreement, believed their ability to collect payment on the settlement was jeopardized. Subsequently, Ambrosia's subsidiaries, Garita L.P. and Garita Hotel Corp., assigned their claims under the 1994 settlement agreement to Ambrosia. Thus, Ambrosia's Puerto Rico and Ohio subsidiaries were not parties to the action when Ambrosia, as the sole plaintiff, commenced litigation against Isla Verde and related parties. The district court dismissed the complaint for lack of subject matter jurisdiction, holding that there was a lack of complete diversity between Ambrosia (and its subsidiaries) and Appellees, and there were no viable federal claims that would allow the court to exercise federal question jurisdiction over the matter. Ambrosia appeals the motion to dismiss and asks this Court to find that the district court has subject matter jurisdiction over both the state and federal law claims.

Judge Nangle

Ambrosia alleged the existence of federal jurisdiction over its state law claims through diversity of citizenship. Although on its face the action appears to have complete diversity amongst the parties, the district court found that Ambrosia improperly manufactured diversity jurisdiction in violation of 28 U.S.C. § 1359 when the Garita entities assigned their causes of action to Ambrosia. Section 1359 states that "[a] district court shall not have jurisdiction of a civil action in which any party, by assignment or otherwise, has been improperly or collusively made or joined to invoke the jurisdiction of the court." The district court arrived at this conclusion by first applying a presumption of collusion against Ambrosia, which shifted the burden to Ambrosia to demonstrate that it had a legitimate business reason for the assignment. The court then found that Ambrosia failed to rebut the presumption and held that Ambrosia achieved diversity of citizenship in violation of the anticollusion statute. Accordingly, the court dismissed the claims for lack of subject matter jurisdiction.

This Court reviews de novo the district court's conclusion that it lacked proper subject matter jurisdiction to decide the case.

Appellees contend that the district court correctly applied a presumption of collusion against Ambrosia, as other Circuits have done in evaluating assignments made between related entities. Contrary to Appellees' position, we hold that the district court erred in applying a presumption of collusion to the case at bar.

While other Circuits have reasoned that a presumption of collusion is appropriate when certain closely related entities assign claims amongst themselves, there is no such binding precedent in this Circuit. Neither the Supreme Court nor the Eleventh Circuit has held that in cases where diversity jurisdiction is premised on the assignment of claims from a subsidiary to a parent corporation, a presumption of collusion is triggered. However, both the Supreme Court and the Eleventh Circuit have opined on the general topic of parties collusively obtaining federal diversity jurisdiction. . . . [W]e decline to follow the law of other Circuits that apply the presumption of collusion to cases such as the one before us, and evaluate the assignment from the Garita entities to Ambrosia under existing precedent.

In *Kramer v. Caribbean Mills,* 394 U.S. 823 (1969), the Supreme Court held that when the assignor retains an interest in the assigned claims, the assignee has no previous connection in the matter, and the assignment is made for the sole purpose of accessing the federal courts, the assignment is collusive in violation of 28 U.S.C. § 1359. Likewise, we focus on the nature of the transfer, namely, whether the assignor has retained an interest in the assigned claim.

However, in Kramer, the Court explicitly stated that it was not disturbing prior decisions in cases where a claimant makes a bona fide, absolute transfer of its claims to a diverse citizen for the purpose of invoking federal jurisdiction. In such cases, the Court has held that federal jurisdiction is proper, and the motives of the transfer are irrelevant. For instance, in *Black & White Taxicab & Transfer Co. v. Brown & Yellow Taxicab & Transfer Co.*, 276 U.S. 518 (1928), the Court held that it was not collusive for a nondiverse corporation to dissolve and transfer its property into a new corporation for the purpose of creating diversity of citizenship. The Court stated, "[s]o long as [t]he succession and transfer were actual, not feigned or merely colorable . . . courts will not inquire into the motives when deciding jurisdiction."

In evaluating the nature and validity of absolute transfers, the Supreme Court has also examined the consideration exchanged for the assigned claim.

We conclude that subject matter jurisdiction over Ambrosia's state law claims is proper and does not violate the anticollusion statute. Ambrosia is the real party in interest in this litigation, and the Garita entities retained no interest in the assigned claims at issue. Since 1985, Ambrosia has been involved in the dispute relating to the title over the lease; it is Ambrosia that provided the four million dollars to purchase the lease in Puerto Rico; and, Ambrosia, on behalf of itself and its subsidiaries, spearheaded the litigation efforts ever since the Pennsylvania litigation. Furthermore according to the sworn statement by the president of Ambrosia, Carmen Schick, the assignment of claims between the Garita entities and Ambrosia were absolute transfers made in exchange for valuable consideration—in exchange for the claims, which Garita held pursuant to the

1994 settlement agreement, Ambrosia reduced its judgment against the Garita entities by $100,000. Ambrosia has placed and kept this judgment on its financial and accounting books, and as a result of the reduction in the judgment, Ambrosia was able to reduce its tax liability. Therefore, the district court erred in dismissing the state law claims for lack of subject matter jurisdiction.

Reversed and remanded in favor of Ambrosia Coal & Construction Company.

CRITICAL THINKING ABOUT THE LAW

Understandably, courts must have rules about when they will hear a case and when they will not. Parties to a legal action often search for avenues whereby they can acquire access to particular courts. The courts are watchful that jurisdiction has not been "created" by methods that are contrived. In this case, the court had to acknowledge that it did not make the same presumption of collusion when closely related entities assign claims among themselves.

1. What would be the reasoning that would lead a court to presume that collusion is responsible for assignments between closely related parties?

   Clue: What would be gained by such a transfer?

2. To what extent is the rule of law here different from the presumption of collusion in other circuits? In other words, are the rules dramatically different or only slightly different?

   Clue: Once the presumption of collusion is dropped, will demonstrated collusion lead to a different result in the Eleventh Circuit?

Venue

Subject matter jurisdiction should not be confused with venue. Once it is determined which court system has the power to hear the case, **venue** determines which of the many trial courts in that system is appropriate. Venue, clearly prescribed by statute in each state, is a matter of geographic location. It is usually based on the residence of the defendant, the location of the property in dispute, or the location in which the incident out of which the dispute arose occurred. When there are multiple defendants who reside in various geographic locations, the party filing the lawsuit may usually choose from among the various locales. If the location of the court in which the case is filed presents a hardship or inconvenience to one of the parties, that person may request that the case be moved under the doctrine of forum *non conveniens,* which simply means that the location of the trial court is inconvenient. The judge in the case will consider the party's request and decide whether to grant the party's request. Unlike the right of removal, the request for change of venue is granted at the judge's discretion. There will usually be a hearing on the issue of whether the judge should grant the motion, because the plaintiff generally filed the case in a particular court for a reason and will, therefore, be opposed to the defendant's motion.

One example of a case where a party sought to have the trial location changed due to *forum non conveniens* is Ex Parte Kia Motors America, Inc.[2] In this case, four people were riding in Florida in a 1998 Kia Sephia that was involved in a high-speed car accident; the car was forced from the road, caught

venue County of the trial court; prescribed by state statute.

---

[2] 881 So. 2d 396 (2003).

TECHNOLOGY AND THE LEGAL ENVIRONMENT

The Internet and In Personam Jurisdiction

Is the sponsor of a Web site that can be visited from every state subject to in personam jurisdiction in every state? As long as the sponsor is not conducting any business or trying to reach customers in a state, many courts have held that mere access to the Web site is not sufficient to grant in personam jurisdiction.

One case that illustrates this point involved two organizations that both used the name Carefirst. Carefirst of Maryland, a nonprofit insurance company, accused Carefirst Pregnancy Center (CPC), a Chicago-based nonprofit organization, of trademark infringement.[a] Carefirst of Maryland operated a Web site from which the company promoted its products to consumers who are located primarily in the Mid-Atlantic region, with the majority of its consumers living in Maryland. CPC also operated a Web site, which was accessible anywhere in the world, for the purpose of promoting its services for women with pregnancy-related crisis and to generate donations for the organization. CPC's operations were confined almost entirely to the state of Illinois.

Since CPC began using the name Carefirst, the Chicago-based organization has received only one donation from a Maryland resident via the company's Web site. From 1991 to 2001, CPC claimed that only 0.0174 percent of its donations came from Maryland residents. The only means through which CPC has contact with Maryland residents is CPC's Web site. Therefore, a district court in Maryland and the appellate court both dismissed the case for lack of personal jurisdiction, concluding that even though CPC's Web site could be contacted from anywhere, its purpose was to provide information about the organization and solicit donations primarily from Illinois residents. While the court noted that the donations received from Maryland residents were negligible, the court

also held that CPC made no effort to target Maryland donors. Furthermore, the court observed that CPC had no agents, employees, or offices located in Maryland. Hence, there was not sufficient contact with Maryland to support personal jurisdiction.

If the potential defendant, however, is actively trying to do business in other states via a Web site, the outcome of a case may be different. For example, in *Gator.com Corp v. L.L.Bean, Inc.*[b] the Ninth Circuit Court of Appeals held that L.L.Bean was subject to in personam jurisdiction in California. Gator.com, a company that develops software for consumers who make online purchases, also created pop-up coupons that would appear on L.L.Bean's Web site for L.L.Bean's competitors, like Eddie Bauer. In response to its receiving a cease-and-desist letter from L.L.Bean, Gator.com sought a declaratory judgment that its actions were not illegal according to state and federal laws. L.L.Bean filed a motion to dismiss, after which a district court in California ruled that the court did not have in personam jurisdiction. The Ninth Circuit reversed on appeal, noting that 6 percent of L.L.Bean's $1 billion in annual sales is attributable to California customers. The court also observed that L.L.Bean "targets" California consumers with its direct e-mail solicitations, although maintaining a highly interactive Web site, from which numerous California customers make online purchases and interact with L.L.Bean sales representatives. Hence, the Ninth Circuit found these e-mail solicitations and Web site services to California consumers to be sufficient minimum contacts for in personam jurisdiction.

---

[a]*Carefirst of Maryland, Inc. v. Carefirst Pregnancy Centers, Inc.*, 334 F.3d 390 (2003).

[b]*Gator.com, Inc. v. L.L.Bean*, 341 F.3d 1072 (2002).

---

fire, and burned. Three of the four passengers did not survive. The families of the deceased sued Kia for product liability and negligence, among other claims, in Alabama courts. Kia filed a motion for *forum non conveniens* to have the case moved to Florida stating that the car was purchased in Florida, the deceased were residents of Florida, the claims were to be tried according to Florida law, and 25 of the witnesses were also Florida residents. The Supreme Court of Alabama ruled that the motion for *forum non conveniens* was appropriate and the case should be moved to Florida.

The Structure of the Court System

As noted previously, our system has two parallel court structures, one federal and one state system. Because of subject matter jurisdiction limitations, one often does not have a choice as to the system in which to file the case. Once a case is filed in a system, it will stay within that system, except for appeals to the U.S. Supreme Court. The following sections set forth the structure of the two systems. As you will see, they are indeed very similar. Their relationship is illustrated in Exhibit 2.

THE FEDERAL COURT SYSTEM

Federal Trial Courts. As you already know, trial courts are the courts of original jurisdiction. In the federal court system, the trial courts are the U.S. district courts. The United States is divided into 96 districts, and each district has at least one trial court of general jurisdiction. General jurisdiction means that the court has the power to hear cases involving a wide variety of subject matter and that it is not limited in the types of remedies that it can grant. All cases to be heard in the federal system are filed in these courts, except those cases for which Congress has established special trial courts of limited jurisdiction.

Trial courts of limited jurisdiction in the federal system are limited in the type of cases they have the power to hear. Special federal trial courts of limited jurisdiction have been established for bankruptcy cases; claims against the U.S. government; and copyright, patent, and trademark cases. In an extremely limited number of cases, the U.S. Supreme Court also functions as a trial court of limited jurisdiction. Such cases include controversies between two or more states and suits against foreign ambassadors.

Intermediate Courts of Appeal. The second level of courts in the federal system is made up of the U.S. circuit courts of appeal. The United States is divided into 12 geographic areas, including the District of Columbia, each of which has a circuit court of appeals. Exhibit 2 illustrates this division. There is also a federal circuit court of appeals and a recently established United States Veterans' Court of Appeals. Each circuit court of appeals hears appeals from all of the district courts located within its geographic area. These courts also hear appeals from administrative agencies located within their respective circuits. In some cases, appeals from administrative agencies are heard by the Federal Circuit Court of Appeals. The Veterans' Court of Appeals hears appeals of benefits decisions made by the Veterans Administration.

Court of Last Resort. The U.S. Supreme Court is the final appellate court in the federal system. In a limited number of instances, discussed in the last section of this chapter, the U.S. Supreme Court also hears cases from the court of last resort in a state system. As previously noted, the U.S. Supreme Court also functions as a trial court in a limited number of cases. The federal court system is illustrated in Exhibit 3.

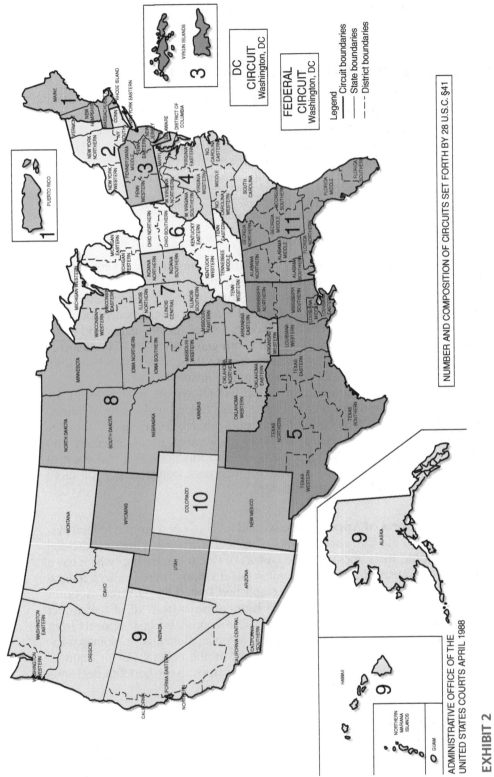

NUMBER AND COMPOSITION OF CIRCUITS SET FORTH BY 28 U.S.C. §41

Legend
—— Circuit boundaries
—— State boundaries
– – – District boundaries

DC
CIRCUIT
Washington, DC

FEDERAL
CIRCUIT
Washington, DC

ADMINISTRATIVE OFFICE OF THE
UNITED STATES COURTS APRIL 1988

EXHIBIT 2

GEOGRAPHIC BOUNDARIES OF UNITED STATES COURTS OF APPEALS AND UNITED STATES DISTRICT COURTS

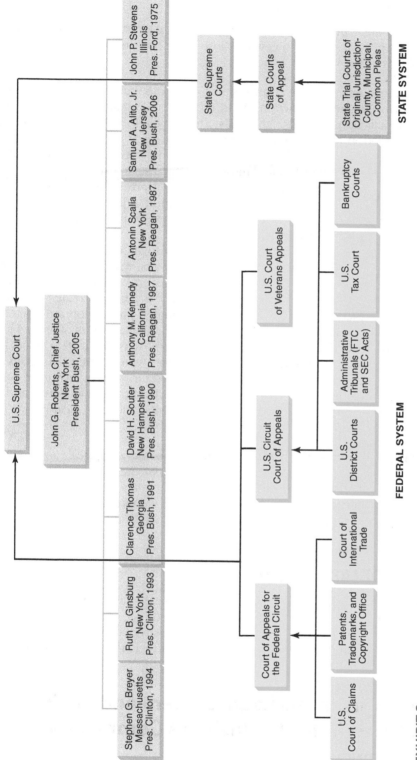

U.S. Supreme Court

John G. Roberts, Chief Justice
New York
President Bush, 2005

Stephen G. Breyer
Massachusetts
Pres. Clinton, 1994

Ruth B. Ginsburg
New York
Pres. Clinton, 1993

Clarence Thomas
Georgia
Pres. Bush, 1991

David H. Souter
New Hampshire
Pres. Bush, 1990

Anthony M. Kennedy
California
Pres. Reagan, 1987

Antonin Scalia
New York
Pres. Reagan, 1987

Samuel A. Alito, Jr.
New Jersey
Pres. Bush, 2006

John P. Stevens
Illinois
Pres. Ford, 1975

STATE SYSTEM

State Supreme Courts

State Courts of Appeal

State Trial Courts of Original Jurisdiction-County, Municipal, Common Pleas

FEDERAL SYSTEM

Court of Appeals for the Federal Circuit

U.S. Circuit Court of Appeals

U.S. Court of Veterans Appeals

U.S. Court of Claims

Patents, Trademarks, and Copyright Office

Court of International Trade

U.S. District Courts

Administrative Tribunals (FTC and SEC Acts)

U.S. Tax Court

Bankruptcy Courts

EXHIBIT 3

THE STRUCTURE OF THE COURT SYSTEM

STATE COURT SYSTEMS

There is no uniform state court structure because each state has devised its own court system. Most states, however, follow a general structure similar to that of the federal court system.

State Trial Courts. In state court systems, most cases are originally filed in the trial court of general jurisdiction. As in the federal system, state trial courts of general jurisdiction are those that have the power to hear all the cases that would be tried in the state court system, except those cases for which special trial courts of limited jurisdiction have been established. These trial courts of general jurisdiction are distributed throughout each state, usually by county. The names of these courts vary from state to state but are usually called courts of common pleas or county courts. New York uniquely calls its trial courts of general jurisdiction supreme courts. In some states, these courts may have specialized divisions, such as domestic relations or probate.

Most states also have trial courts of limited jurisdiction. These courts are usually limited in the remedies that they may grant. Some may not issue injunctions or orders for specific performance. A common court of limited jurisdiction in most states is the small claims court, which may not grant damage awards in excess of specified amounts. Some courts of limited jurisdiction are limited to certain types of cases, such as traffic cases. Some criminal courts of limited jurisdiction may be limited to hearing misdemeanors. It is difficult to generalize about these courts because they vary so much from state to state. The main distinction between trial courts of general and limited jurisdiction, however, is that the former hear almost all types of cases that are filed in the state system and are unlimited in the remedies they can provide, whereas the latter hear only a particular type of case or may award only limited remedies.

Intermediate Courts of Appeal. Intermediate courts of appeal, analogous to the federal circuit courts of appeal, exist in approximately half the states. These courts usually have broad jurisdiction, hearing appeals from courts of general and limited jurisdictions, as well as from state administrative agencies. The names of these courts also vary by state. They may be called courts of appeal or superior courts.

COURTS OF LAST RESORT

In almost all cases filed in the state court system, the last appeal is to the state court of last resort. This court is frequently called the supreme court. In some states, it is known as the court of appeals. In approximately half of the states, it is the second court to which an appeal can be made; in the remaining states, it is the only appellate court.

The Actors in the Legal System and Their Relationship to the Business Community

THE ATTORNEY

An understanding of the structure of the legal system would be incomplete without an awareness of the primary actors within the system. The party with whom businesspersons usually have the most frequent contact is the attorney. Although the exact qualifications for being an attorney vary from state to state, most require that an attorney have a law degree, have passed the state's bar examination, and be of high moral character. Attorneys are the legal representatives of the parties before the court. Some corporations have full-time attorneys, referred to as in-house counsel. Other corporations send all their legal work to an outside law firm. Many larger businesses have in-house counsel and also use outside counsel when a problem arises that requires a specialist.

Attorney–Client Privilege. The attorney can provide effective representation only when he or she knows all the pertinent facts of the case. The businessperson who withholds information from his or her attorney may cause irreparable harm if the hidden facts are revealed by the opposing side in court. To encourage client honesty, the **attorney–client privilege** was established. This privilege provides that information furnished in confidence to an attorney, in conjunction with a legal matter, may not be revealed by that attorney without permission from the client. There is, however, an important exception to this rule. If the lawyer knows that the client is about to commit a crime, the lawyer may reveal confidential information in order to prevent the commission of that crime. Revealing such information, however, is not required of the attorney; it is simply allowed. This protection also extends to the attorney's work product under what is known as the **work-product doctrine.** The work product includes those formal and informal documents prepared by the attorney in conjunction with a client's case.

One of the problems arising out of the use of the attorney–client privilege in the corporate setting is the definition of the client. The client is the corporation, but the communication sought to be protected is that between the attorney and upper-, middle-, or lower-level employees of the corporation. In such cases, the corporate attorney usually tries to rely on the work-product doctrine to protect the information that he or she has gathered from employees, especially when such information is in the form of written communications. Such an approach has generally been successful, but the courts have not yet precisely defined the parameters of the attorney–client privilege and the work-product doctrine as they apply to the corporate setting.

Additional Functions of the Attorney. Attorneys are probably best known for representing clients in litigation, but they also provide other services for business clients. Attorneys represent their clients not only in courtroom litigation but also before administrative boards. Attorneys may be called on to represent their corporate clients in negotiations with labor unions or with other firms.

Corporate attorneys also serve as advisors or counselors, reviewing proposed corporate activities and advising management of legal problems that may arise as a result of such activities. In-house counsel familiar with the various activities of the firm are often in the best position to fulfill this role. Thus, businesspersons should attempt to establish a good working relationship with in-house counsel, using them as a resource whenever legal issues arise. Managers should not assume that they know all the legal ramifications of all the business activities in which they engage. Most in-house counsel would prefer to be consulted before an activity is undertaken rather than after it results in a legal problem.

Finally, the attorney may serve as a draftsperson, drawing up contracts, deeds, the corporate charter, securities registration statements, and all other

attorney–client privilege
Provides that information furnished by a client to an attorney in confidence, in conjunction with a legal matter, may not be revealed by the attorney without the client's permission.

work-product doctrine
Provides that formal and informal documents prepared by an attorney in conjunction with a client's case are privileged and may not be revealed by the attorney without the client's permission.

legal documents needed by the corporation. Thus, it is clear that the attorney is one actor in the American legal system who is of special importance to the business manager.

THE JUDGE

The role of the judge is especially important in our legal system. The judge's function changes, depending on whether he or she is a trial or appellate court judge. A trial court judge presides over the trial, making sure the case is heard with reasonable speed; rules on all motions made in the case; and decides all questions of the law. One of the most crucial functions of the trial court judge is ruling on whether or not certain pieces of evidence are admissible. Failure of the judge to admit certain items into evidence may be determinative of the outcome of a case, and a judge's ruling on any piece of evidence may subsequently become the basis for the appeal of an unfavorable decision. If the parties waive their rights to a jury trial, or if they are not entitled to a jury, the judge also decides the facts in the case and renders a decision accordingly. A single judge presides over each case.

Appellate judges serve on panels. They review lower-court cases to determine whether errors of law were committed by the lower courts. Their review consists primarily of reading the transcript of the trial, reading written arguments by counsel for both parties, and sometimes hearing oral arguments from both parties' attorneys.

State court judges are usually elected, although some are appointed, whereas federal court judges are appointed by the president with the advice and consent of the Senate. This appointment process is a good example of how the legislative and executive branches serve as checks on each other. The president has the greatest role because he makes the nomination, but he cannot choose just anyone. The president will usually select a list of potential nominees that will then be rated by a committee of the American Bar Association. The bar association will look at the nominees' legal experience and read their written opinions and published articles in an attempt to ensure that only the most qualified candidates will be named to the federal bench. The Senate will also scrutinize the list and give the president an idea in advance of whether or not the various potential nominees will have a high likelihood of being confirmed. Once the president makes a nomination, the Senate judiciary subcommittee will hold formal hearings on the nominees' fitness for office. After the hearings, the full Senate will vote on the nomination. Although the president will generally try to nominate someone with a similar ideological background, if the Senate is dominated by the opposite political party, a nominee who has too strong an ideology is not likely to be confirmed. In recent years, the appointment process has become familiar to most Americans as the hearings on Supreme Court nominees have been televised. Federal court judges serve for life, whereas state court judges generally serve definite terms, the length of which varies from state to state.

There is a lot of debate over whether judges should be appointed for life or elected for specific terms. The rationale behind appointment for life is that it takes the politics out of the judicial process. A judge will be selected based on his or her credentials as opposed to the quality of his or her campaign skills. Once in office, the judge is free to make honest decisions without having to worry about the impact of any decision on reelection.

Of course, this independence is just what makes some people prefer elected judges. They argue that the members of every other branch of government are elected and are, therefore, forced to represent the will of the people, and judges should represent the people no less than members of the other branches.

The Power of Judicial Review. One very important power that the judges have is the power of judicial review, that is, the power to determine whether a law passed by the legislature violates the Constitution. Any law that violates the Constitution must be struck down as null and void. The justices of the Supreme Court are the final arbiters of the constitutionality of our statutory laws.

This power of judicial review was not explicitly stated in the Constitution. This power was established in the classic 1803 case of *Marbury v. Madison*,[3] wherein the Supreme Court stated, "It is emphatically the province and duty of the judicial department to say what the law is. Those who apply the rule to particular cases must of necessity expound and interpret that rule. If two laws conflict with each other, the courts must decide which of these conflicting rules governs the case. This is of the very essence of judicial duty."

When individual justices exercise this power of judicial review, they do so with different philosophies and attitudes. Their philosophies can have a powerful effect on how they make decisions.

One distinction that is frequently made with respect to judicial philosophies is the difference between a judge who believes in **judicial activism** and one who believes in judicial restraint.

A judge who believes in **judicial restraint** believes that the three branches are coequal, and the judiciary should refrain from determining the constitutionality of an act of Congress unless absolutely necessary to keep from interfering in the congressional sphere of power. These justices tend to believe that social, economic, and political change should result from the political process, not from judicial action. They consequently give great deference to actions of the state and federal legislatures.

Those who believe in judicial restraint will be much less likely to overturn an existing precedent. They tend to focus much more on the facts than on questioning whether the law needs to be changed. They tend to uphold lower-court decisions unless these decisions are clearly wrong on the facts.

Judicial activists tend to see a need for the court to take an active role in encouraging political, economic, and social change because the political process is often too slow to bring about necessary changes. They believe that constitutional issues must be decided within the context of today's society and that the framers meant for the Constitution to be an evolving document.

Judicial activists are much less wedded to precedent and are result oriented. They are much more likely to listen to arguments about what result is good for society. Activist judges are responsible for many social changes, especially in the civil rights area.

judicial activism A judicial philosophy that says the courts need to take an active role in encouraging political, economic, and social change.

judicial restraint A judicial philosophy that says courts should refrain from determining the constitutionality of a legislative act unless absolutely necessary and that social, political, and economic change should come out of the political process.

THE JURY

The jury is the means by which citizens participate in our judicial system. It had its roots in ancient Greek civilization, and it is often seen as the hallmark of democracy. A jury is a group of individuals, selected randomly from the

---

[3] 5 U.S. 137 (1803).

geographic area in which the court is located, who will determine questions of fact. There are two types of juries: petit and grand.

petit jury A jury of 12 citizens impaneled to decide on the facts at issue in a criminal case and to pronounce the defendant guilty or not guilty.

Petit Juries. Businesspersons are primarily concerned with **petit juries.** These juries serve as the finders of fact for trial courts. Originally composed of 12 members, most juries in civil cases are allowed to have fewer members in many jurisdictions. Traditionally, jury decisions had to be unanimous. Today, however, more than half the jurisdictions no longer require unanimity in civil cases. This change in the jury system has been made primarily to speed up trial procedures.

An important decision to be made by any corporate client and his or her attorney is whether to have a jury. In any civil action in which the plaintiff is seeking a remedy at law (money damages), a jury may hear the case. If both parties to the case agree, however, the jury may be waived, and a judge decides the facts of the case. There is no rule about when a jury should be chosen, but a few factors should frequently be considered. One is the technical nature of the case. If it is a case that is highly technical, it may be a case that can be more fairly decided by a judge, especially one with expertise in the area in dispute. Another factor is the emotional appeal of the case. If the case is one for which the opponent's arguments may have strong emotional appeal, a judge may render a fairer decision.

indictment A formal written accusation in a felony case.

grand jury A group of 12 to 23 citizens convened in private to decide whether enough evidence exists to try the defendant for a felony.

Grand Juries. Grand juries are used only in criminal matters. The Fifth Amendment requires that all federal prosecutions for infamous crimes (including all federal offenses that carry a term of imprisonment in excess of 1 year) be commenced with an **indictment** (a formal accusation of the commission of a crime, which must be made before a defendant can be tried for the crime) by a **grand jury.** This jury hears evidence presented by the prosecutor and determines whether there is enough evidence to justify charging a defendant. The prudent business manager who carefully heeds the advice of an attorney should not be faced with a potential indictment by a grand jury. Increasingly, however, corporate managers are facing criminal charges for actions taken to benefit their corporate employers.

The Adversary Process

adversarial system System of litigation in which the judge hears evidence and arguments presented by both sides in a case and then makes an objective decision based on the facts and the law as presented by each side.

Our system of litigation is accurately described as an adversary system. In an **adversarial system,** a neutral fact finder, a judge, hears evidence and arguments presented by both sides and then makes an objective decision based on the facts and the law as presented by the proponents of each side. Strict rules govern the types of evidence that the fact finder may consider.

Theoretically, the adversary system is the best way to bring out the truth because each side will aggressively seek all the evidence that supports its position. Each side will attempt to make the strongest possible argument for its position.

CRITICISMS OF THE ADVERSARY SYSTEM

Many people criticize this system. They argue that because each side is searching for only that evidence that supports its position, a proponent who discovers evidence helpful to the other side will not bring such evidence to the attention of the court. This tendency to ignore contrary evidence prevents a fair decision, one based on all the available evidence, from being rendered.

Another argument of the critics is that the adversary process is extremely time-consuming and costly. Two groups of "investigators" are seeking the same evidence. Thus, there is a duplication of effort that lengthens the process and increases the cost unnecessarily.

Others argue that the adversary system, as it functions in this country, is unfair. Each party in the adversarial process is represented by an attorney. Having the most skillful attorney is a tremendous advantage. As the wealthier a party is, the better the attorney she or he can afford to hire; the system unjustifiably favors the wealthy.

Law professor Marc Galanter has written an interesting critique of our adversary system that has generated a lot of discussion.[4] He argues that given the structure of our system, certain parties tend to have a distinct advantage in our system.

Galanter divides litigants into two groups: the repeat players (RPs), those who are engaged in similar litigations over time, and the one-shotters (OSs), those who have only occasional recourse to the courts. RPs would typically be large corporations, financial institutions, landlords, developers, government agencies, and prosecutors. Typical OSs would be debtors, employees with grievances against their employers, tenants, and victims of accidents.

According to Galanter, the RPs have a distinct advantage over the OSs in litigation. Because of their experience, RPs are better prepared for trial; they know what kinds of records to keep and how to structure transactions so that they will have an advantage in court. RPs will have developed expertise in the area and will have access to specialists. They will have low "start-up costs" for a case because they have been through it before. RPs will have developed helpful informal relationships with those at the courthouse. The RP knows the odds of success better because of his or her experience and can use that knowledge to calculate whether to settle. Finally, RPs can litigate for rules or for an immediate outcome.

Thus, in a typical case involving an RP and an OS, the RP has a distinct advantage. Some people believe this advantage is significant enough to prevent our current system from dispensing justice in these cases.

Steps in Civil Litigation and the Role of Businesspersons

THE PRETRIAL STAGE

Every lawsuit is the result of a dispute. Business disputes may result from a breach of contract, the protested firing of an employee, or the injury of a consumer who uses the corporation's product. This section focuses on dispute resolution in this country under the adversary system. It examines the procedure used in a civil case, the stages of which are outlined in Exhibit 4. The rules that govern such proceedings are called the **rules of civil procedure.** There are federal rules of civil procedure, which apply in all federal courts, as well as state rules, which apply in the state courts. Most of the state rules are based on the federal rules.

rules of civil procedure The rules governing proceedings in a civil case; federal rules of procedure apply in all federal courts, and state rules apply in state courts.

---

[4] Marc Galanter, "Why the Haves Come Out Ahead: Speculation on the Limits of Legal Change," *J. L. & Soc. Rev.* 9: 96 (1974).

EXHIBIT 4

ANATOMY OF A CIVIL LAWSUIT

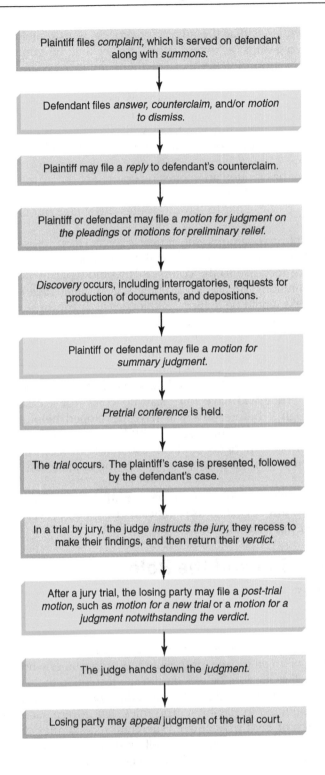

Plaintiff files *complaint*, which is served on defendant along with *summons*.

Defendant files *answer, counterclaim,* and/or *motion to dismiss*.

Plaintiff may file a *reply* to defendant's counterclaim.

Plaintiff or defendant may file a *motion for judgment on the pleadings* or *motions for preliminary relief.*

Discovery occurs, including interrogatories, requests for production of documents, and depositions.

Plaintiff or defendant may file a *motion for summary judgment.*

Pretrial conference is held.

The *trial* occurs. The plaintiff's case is presented, followed by the defendant's case.

In a trial by jury, the judge *instructs the jury,* they recess to make their findings, and then return their *verdict.*

After a jury trial, the losing party may file a *post-trial motion,* such as *motion for a new trial* or a *motion for a judgment notwithstanding the verdict.*

The judge hands down the *judgment.*

Losing party may *appeal* judgment of the trial court.

Informal Negotiations. For the businessperson involved in a dispute, the first step is probably going to be to discuss the dispute directly with the other disputing party. When it appears that the parties are not going to be able to resolve the problem themselves, the businessperson will then discuss the dispute with an attorney. It is important that the attorney be given all relevant information, even if it does not make the businessperson look good. The more relevant facts the attorney has, the better the attorney's advice will be. Together, the attorney and the client may be able to resolve the dispute informally with the other party.

Initiation of a Legal Action. Once a party decides that an informal resolution is not possible, the parties enter what is often called the pleading stage of the lawsuit. **Pleadings** are papers filed by a party in court and then served on the opponent. The basic pleadings are the complaint, the answer, the counterclaim, and the motion to dismiss. Exhibit 5 provides an illustration of a typical complaint. The attorney of the businessperson who feels he or she has been wronged

pleadings Papers filed by a party in court and then served on the opponent in a civil lawsuit.

EXHIBIT 5

COMPLAINT

THE COURT OF COMMON PLEAS
OF LUCAS COUNTY, OHIO

Pam Streets, Plaintiff v. Daniel Lane, Defendant
COMPLAINT FOR NEGLIGENCE
Case No. _____

Now comes the plaintiff, Pam Streets, and, for her complaint, alleges as follows:

1. Plaintiff, Pam Streets, is a citizen of Lucas County, in the state of Ohio, and Defendant, Daniel Lane, is a citizen of Lucas County in the state of Ohio.
2. On December 1, 1987, the Plaintiff was lawfully driving her automobile south on Main Street in Toledo, Ohio.
3. At approximately 4:00 p.m., on December 1, 1987, the Defendant negligently ran a red light on Starr Avenue, and as a result crashed into Plaintiff's car.
4. As a result of the collision, the Plaintiff suffered lacerations to the face and a broken leg, incurring $10,000 in medical expenses.
5. As a result of the above described collision, her car was damaged in the amount of $12,000.
6. As a result of the foregoing injuries, the Plaintiff was required to miss eight weeks of work, resulting in a loss of wages of $2,400.

WHEREFORE, Plaintiff demands judgment in the amount of $24,400, plus costs of this action.

Sam Snead
Attorney for Plaintiff
124 East Broadway
Toledo, OH 43605

JURY DEMAND
Plaintiff demands a trial by jury in this matter.

Sam Snead
Attorney for Plaintiff

initiates a lawsuit by filing a complaint in the appropriate court. A complaint is a document that states the names of the parties to the action, the basis for the court's subject matter jurisdiction, the facts on which the party's claim is based, and the relief that the party is seeking. Remember that the party on whose behalf the complaint is filed is the plaintiff, and the defendant is the party against whom the action is being brought.

In determining the appropriate court in which to file the complaint, the attorney must determine which court has subject matter jurisdiction over the case. Once that determination has been made, the attorney must ascertain the proper venue for the case. The means used by the attorney to determine the subject matter jurisdiction and venue were discussed earlier in this chapter.

Service of Process. Once the complaint is filed, the court serves a copy of the complaint and a summons on the defendant. The reader should remember that service is the procedure used by the court to ensure that the defendant actually receives a copy of the summons and the complaint. Service of process gives the court in personam jurisdiction over the defendant and provides his or her due process right of notice of the charges filed against him or her.

Defendant's Response. Once the defendant has been properly served, he or she files an answer and possibly a counterclaim. The answer is a response to the allegations in the plaintiff's complaint. The answer must admit, deny, or state that the defendant has no knowledge about the truth of each of the plaintiff's allegations. The answer may also contain affirmative defenses, which consist of facts that were not stated in the complaint that would provide justification for the defendant's actions and a legally sound reason to deny relief to the plaintiff. These defenses must be stated in the answer. If they are not raised in the answer, the court may not allow these defenses to be raised later. The defendant is required to plead his or her affirmative defenses in the answer in order to give the plaintiff notice of all the issues that will be raised at the trial.

As an illustration, two affirmative defenses to a breach-of-contract action might be that the plaintiff procured the defendant's signature on the contract through fraud and that the contract was illegal because its enforcement would result in a violation of the antitrust laws. Another example would be, if a manufacturer were being sued because the plaintiff was injured by the manufacturer's negligently produced defective product, the defendant might raise the affirmative defense of contributory negligence, arguing that the plaintiff's injury would not have occurred if the plaintiff had not also been negligent. Notice the use of an affirmative defense in the sample answer in Exhibit 6. It is important that the businessperson who is being sued try immediately to think of any potential affirmative defenses that might excuse his or her actions.

When a defendant, upon receiving the complaint, believes that even if all of the plaintiff's factual allegations were true and the plaintiff would not be entitled to a favorable judgment, the defendant may file a **motion to dismiss.** There are no factual issues being debated, so the judge accepts the facts as stated by the plaintiff and makes a ruling on the legal questions in the case. Judges are generally not receptive to such motions, granting them only when it appears beyond doubt that the plaintiff can prove no set of facts in support of his claim, which would entitle him to relief.

If the defendant believes that he or she has a cause of action against the plaintiff, this will be included as a **counterclaim.** The form of a counterclaim is

motion to dismiss Defendant's application to the court to put the case out of judicial consideration because even if the plaintiff's factual allegations are true, the plaintiff is not entitled to relief.

counterclaim Defendant's statement of facts showing cause for action against the plaintiff and a request for appropriate relief.

EXHIBIT 6

**AFFIRMATIVE DEFENSES
AND COUNTERCLAIM**

THE COURT OF COMMON PLEAS
OF LUCAS COUNTY, OHIO

Pam Streets, Plaintiff v. Daniel Lane, Defendant
ANSWER AND COUNTERCLAIM
Case No. _____

Now comes the Defendant, Daniel Lane, and answers the complaint of Plaintiff herein as follows:

FIRST DEFENSE

1. Admits the allegations in paragraphs 1 and 2.

2. Denies the allegation in paragraph 3.

3. Is without knowledge as to the truth or falsity of the allegations contained in paragraphs 4, 5, and 6.

SECOND DEFENSE

4. If the court believes the allegations contained in paragraph 3, which the Defendant expressly denies, Plaintiff should still be denied recovery because she was negligently driving in excess of the speed limit and without her glasses, both of which contributed to the cause of the accident.

COUNTERCLAIM

5. Defendant lawfully drove his automobile in an eastbound direction on Starr Avenue on December 1, 1987.

6. At approximately 4:00 p.m., on December 1, 1987, Plaintiff negligently drove her automobile at an excessive speed through a red light on Main Street where Said Street crosses Starr Avenue, colliding into Defendant's automobile.

7. As a result of the collision, Defendant suffered bruises and a concussion, resulting in $5,000 in medical bills.

8. Defendant further suffered $6,000 in property damage to his automobile.

WHEREFORE, Defendant prays for a judgment dismissing the Plaintiff's complaint, granting the Defendant a judgment against Plaintiff in the amount of $11,000 plus costs of this action.

Shelly Shaker
Attorney for Defendant
216 Nevada
Toledo, OH 43605

just like that of a complaint. The defendant states the facts supporting his or her claim and asks for the relief to which he or she feels entitled. Exhibit 6 also contains a counterclaim.

If the defendant files a counterclaim, the plaintiff generally files a reply. A reply is simply an answer to a counterclaim. In the reply, the plaintiff admits, denies, or states that he or she is without knowledge of the truth of the facts asserted by the defendant in the counterclaim. Any affirmative defenses that are appropriate must be raised in the reply.

Pretrial Motions. The early pleadings just described serve to establish the legal and factual issues of the case. Once these issues have been established, either the plaintiff or the defendant may file a motion designed to bring the case to an early conclusion or to gain some advantage for the party filing the motion. A motion is simply a request by a party for the court to do something. A party may request, or move, that the court do almost anything pertaining to the case, such as a motion for some form of temporary relief until a decision has been rendered. For example, if a suit is brought over the right to a piece of property, the court may grant a motion prohibiting the current possessor of that property from selling it; or a party may file a motion to proceed in forma pauperis, a motion to proceed without payment of fees if the party feels they have good reasons for why the court should allow the case to proceed even if they do not have the money to pay the fees up front, with the assumption being that after successful suit they will be able to pay the fees. Sometimes, a defendant may believe that even if everything the plaintiffs plead in complaint were true, there would still be no legitimate basis for a lawsuit. In such a situation, the defendant may file a motion to dismiss.

Many of the really frivolous lawsuits that are filed are dismissed in response to pretrial motion. For example, in 2007, Jehovah J. God, Jesus J. Christ, the Jehovah Witness Foundation Inc., and William E. Moore filed a $9 million lawsuit against the University of Arizona, arguing that the university was using God's autobiography, the Bible, without paying him royalties. In dismissing the case on hearing the motion to proceed in forma pauperis, the court said that the allegations were "both fanciful and factually frivolous," a finding that is made when the facts alleged rise to the level of the irrational or wholly incredible, whether or not there are judicially recognized facts available to contradict them.[5]

When a party files any motion with the court, a copy is always sent to the opposing attorney. That attorney may respond to the motion, usually requesting that the judge deny the motion. In many cases, the judge will simply rule on the motion, either granting or denying it. In some cases, the judge may hold a hearing at which the two sides orally present their arguments.

Discovery. Once the initial pleadings and motions have been filed, the parties gather information from each other through **discovery.** At this stage, the businessperson is frequently asked by his or her attorney to respond to the opponent's discovery requests. There are a number of tools of discovery. One of the most common is interrogatories, which are a series of written questions that are sent to the opposing party, who must truthfully answer them under oath. The interrogatories are frequently accompanied by a request to admit certain facts. The attorney and the client work together to answer these interrogatories and requests for admission of facts.

A request to produce documents or other items is another tool of discovery. Unless the information requested is privileged or is irrelevant to the case, it must be produced. Photographs, contracts, written estimates, and forms that must be filed with governmental agencies are among the items that may be requested. One party may also request that the other party submit to a mental or physical examination. This motion will be approved only when the party's mental or physical health is at issue in the case.

discovery The pretrial gathering of information from each other by the parties.

---

[5] *God, et al. v. Arizona State University,* U.S. Dist. LEXIS 38679 (2007).

Finally, testimony before trial may be obtained by the takings of a **deposition.** At a deposition, a witness is examined under oath by attorneys. A court reporter (stenographer) records every word spoken by the attorneys and witnesses. The testimony is usually transcribed so that both parties have a written copy. If a businessperson is to be deposed in a case, it is very important that he or she and the attorney talk extensively about what kinds of questions may come up at the deposition and how such questions are to be answered. The party who requested the deposition not only is seeking information but also is laying the groundwork for identifying any inconsistencies that may arise between a person's testimony at the deposition and in court. If such inconsistencies exist, they will be brought to the attention of the fact finder and may result in a loss of credibility for the courtroom testimony.

> **deposition** Pretrial testimony by witnesses who are examined under oath.

Depositions may also be used when a potential witness is old or ill and may die before the trial. They are useful if witnesses may be moving or for some other reason may not be available at the time of the trial.

As a result of discovery, each party should have knowledge of most of the facts surrounding the case. This process is supposed to prevent surprises from occurring in the courtroom.

Parties must comply with requests for discovery, or the court may order that the facts sought to be discovered be deemed to be admitted. Thus, it is important that the businessperson involved in litigation produce for the attorney all requested discovery material. An attorney who feels that certain material should not be discovered makes arguments about its lack of relevance to the case, but if the court disagrees, the information must be supplied.

Pretrial Conference. If the judge finds that questions of fact do exist, he or she usually holds a pretrial conference. This is an informal meeting of the judge with the lawyers representing the parties. At this meeting, they try to narrow the legal and factual issues and work out a settlement if possible. When the lawsuit begins, there are many conflicting assertions as to what events actually led up to the lawsuit. Questions about what actually happened are referred to as questions of fact. Many times, as a result of discovery, parties come to agree on most of the facts. Remaining factual disputes may often be resolved at the conference. Then the only questions left are how to apply the law to the facts and what damages, if any, to award.

By the time of the pretrial conference, the businessperson should have determined the limits on any settlement to which he or she is willing to agree and should have communicated those limits to his or her attorney, who may be able to reach a settlement at the conference. Judges frequently try very hard to help the parties reach agreement before trial. If no settlement can be reached, the attorneys and the judge discuss the administrative details of the trial, its length, the witnesses, and any pretrial stipulations of fact or law to which the parties can agree.

THE TRIAL

Once the pretrial stage has concluded, the next step is the trial. As stated previously, if the plaintiff is seeking a legal remedy (money damages), he or she is usually entitled to a jury trial. The judge is the fact finder when an equitable remedy (an injunction or other court order) is being sought or the parties have waived their right to a jury. For example, when a plaintiff in a product liability action requests a judgment for $10,000 in medical expenses, he or she would be seeking a legal remedy and would be entitled to a jury trial. A plaintiff seeking an injunction, however, under the antitrust laws, to prohibit two defendant corporations from merging would be requesting an equitable remedy and would not be entitled to a jury. It is important for the business manager to determine at the outset whether a jury is desirable, because a jury must be demanded in the complaint.

The stages of the trial are (1) jury selection, (2) the opening statements, (3) the plaintiff's case, (4) the defendant's case, (5) the conference on jury instructions, (6) closing arguments, and (7) post-trial motions.

Jury Selection. An important part of a jury trial is the selection of the jury. A panel of potential jurors is selected randomly from a list of citizens. In the federal court system, voter lists are used. In a process known as **voir dire,** the judge or the attorneys, or both, question potential jurors to determine whether they could render an unbiased opinion in the case.

voir dire Process whereby the judge and/or the attorneys question potential jurors to determine whether they will be able to render an unbiased opinion in the case.

When a juror's response to a question causes an attorney to believe that this potential juror cannot be unbiased, the attorney will ask that the potential juror be removed "for cause." For example, in an accident case, a potential juror might reveal that he had been in a similar accident, or the potential juror may have filed a similar lawsuit against one of the defendant's competitors 5 years ago. Attorneys are given an unlimited number of challenges for cause. In most states, each attorney is allowed to reject a minimal number of potential jurors without giving a reason. These rejections are called peremptory challenges.

While the legitimate rationale for peremptories is that they recognize a lawyer's "gut reaction" to a potential juror who does not say anything that technically reveals a bias, there has been some abuse of peremptories in the past. One potential source of abuse was to use peremptories to discriminate against certain classes, such as race or gender.

In 1986, in the case of *Batson v. Kentucky,*[6] the U.S. Supreme Court ruled that prosecutors could not use race-based peremptory challenges in criminal cases. Subsequently, the Supreme Court extended the ban to the use of race-based challenges by either party in civil cases. Several unsuccessful attempts were made to extend the prohibition to challenges based on gender. Finally, in 1994, the Court in the following case extended the equal protection guarantee to cover gender.

CASE 3

J.E.B. v. Alabama, EX REL. T.B.
Supreme Court of the United States
511 U.S. 127 (1994)

On behalf of T.B., the unwed mother of a minor child, the State of Alabama filed a complaint for paternity and child support against J.E.B. A panel of 12 males and 24 females was called by the court as potential jurors. After the court removed three individuals for cause, only 10 males remained. The state used its peremptory challenges to remove nine male jurors and J.E.B. removed the tenth, resulting in an all-female jury. The court rejected J.E.B.'s objection to the gender-based challenges, and the jury found J.E.B. to be the father.

J.E.B. appealed to the court of appeals, who affirmed the trial court's decision that the Equal Protection Clause

---

[6] 476 U.S. 79 (1986).

does not prohibit gender-based challenges. The Alabama Supreme Court denied certiorari, and J.E.B. then appealed to the U.S. Supreme Court.

Justice Blackmun

Today we reaffirm what should be axiomatic: Intentional discrimination on the basis of gender by state actors violates the Equal Protection Clause, particularly where, as here, the discrimination serves to ratify and perpetuate invidious, archaic, and overbroad stereotypes about the relative abilities of men and women.

Discrimination on the basis of gender in the exercise of peremptory challenges is a relatively recent phenomenon. Gender-based peremptory strikes were hardly practicable for most of our country's existence, since, until the 20th century, women were completely excluded from jury service.

Many States continued to exclude women from jury service well into the present century, despite the fact that women attained suffrage upon ratification of the Nineteenth Amendment in 1920.

Despite the heightened scrutiny-afforded distinctions based on gender, respondent argues that gender discrimination in the selection of the petit jury should be permitted, though discrimination on the basis of race is not. Respondent suggests that "gender discrimination in this country . . . has never reached the level of discrimination" against African-Americans, and therefore gender discrimination, unlike racial discrimination, is tolerable in the courtroom.

While the prejudicial attitudes toward women in this country have not been identical to those held toward racial minorities, the similarities between the experiences of racial minorities and women, in some contexts, "overpower those differences." Certainly, with respect to jury service, African-Americans and women share a history of total exclusion.

Discrimination in jury selection, whether based on race or on gender, causes harm to the litigants, the community, and the individual jurors who are wrongfully excluded from participation in the judicial process. The litigants are harmed by the risk that the prejudice which motivated the discriminatory selection of the jury will infect the entire proceedings. The community is harmed by the State's participation in the perpetuation of invidious group stereotypes and the inevitable loss of confidence in our judicial system that state-sanctioned discrimination in the courtroom engenders.

When state actors exercise peremptory challenges in reliance on gender stereotypes, they ratify and reinforce prejudicial views of the relative abilities of men and women. Because these stereotypes have wreaked injustice in so many other spheres of our country's public life, active discrimination by litigants on the basis of gender during jury selection "invites cynicism respecting the jury's neutrality and its obligation to adhere to the law."

In recent cases we have emphasized that individual jurors themselves have a right to nondiscriminatory jury selection procedures.

As with race-based Batson claims, a party alleging gender discrimination must make a prima facie showing of intentional discrimination before the party exercising the challenge is required to explain the basis for the strike. When an explanation is required, it need not rise to the level of a "for cause" challenge; rather, it merely must be based on a juror characteristic other than gender, and the proffered explanation may not be pretextual.

Equal opportunity to participate in the fair administration of justice is fundamental to our democratic system. It reaffirms the promise of equality under the law—that all citizens, regardless of race, ethnicity, or gender, have the chance to take part directly in our democracy. When persons are excluded from participation in our democratic processes solely because of race or gender, this promise of equality dims, and the integrity of our judicial system is jeopardized.

In view of these concerns, the Equal Protection Clause prohibits discrimination in jury selection on the basis of gender, or on the assumption that an individual will be biased in a particular case for no reason other than the fact that the person happens to be a woman or happens to be a man. As with race, the "core guarantee of equal protection, ensuring citizens that their State will not discriminate . . ., would be meaningless were we to approve the exclusion of jurors on the basis of such assumptions, which arise solely from the jurors' [gender]."

Reversed and remanded in favor
of Defendant, J.E.B.

Justice Scalia, Dissenting

Today's opinion is an inspiring demonstration of how thoroughly up-to-date and right-thinking we Justices are in matters pertaining to the sexes, and how sternly we disapprove the male chauvinist attitudes of our predecessors. The price to be paid for this display—a modest price, surely—is that most of the opinion is quite irrelevant to the case at hand. The hasty reader will be surprised to learn, for example, that this lawsuit involves a complaint about the use of peremptory challenges to exclude men from a petit jury. To be sure, petitioner, a man, used all but one of his peremptory strikes to remove women from the jury (he used his last challenge to strike the sole remaining male from the pool), but the validity of his strikes is not before us. Nonetheless, the Court treats itself to an extended discussion of the historic exclusion of women not only from jury service, but also from service at the bar (which is rather like jury service, in that it involves going to the courthouse a lot). All this, as I say, is irrelevant since the case involves state action that allegedly discriminates against men.

The Court also spends time establishing that the use of sex as a proxy for particular views or sympathies is unwise and perhaps irrational. The opinion stresses the lack of statistical evidence to support the widely held belief that, at least in certain types of cases, a juror's sex has some statistically significant predictive value as to how the juror will behave. This assertion seems to place the Court in opposition to its earlier Sixth Amendment "fair cross-section" cases. ("Controlled studies . . . have concluded that women bring to juries their own perspectives and values that influence both jury deliberation and result.")

Of course the relationship of sex to partiality would have been relevant if the Court had demanded in this case what it ordinarily demands: that the complaining party have suffered some injury. Leaving aside for the moment the reality that the defendant himself had the opportunity to strike women from the jury, the defendant would have some cause to complain about the prosecutor's striking male jurors if male jurors tend to be more favorable towards defendants in paternity suits. But if men and women jurors are (as the Court thinks) fungible, then the only arguable injury from the prosecutor's "impermissible" use of male sex as the basis for his peremptories is injury to the stricken juror, not to the defendant. Indeed, far from having suffered harm, petitioner, a state actor under precedents, has himself actually inflicted harm on female jurors. The Court today presumably supplies petitioner with a cause of action by applying the uniquely expansive third-party standing analysis of according petitioner a remedy because of the wrong done to male jurors. Insofar as petitioner is concerned, this is a case of harmless error if there ever was one; a retrial will do nothing but divert the State's judicial and prosecutorial resources, allowing either petitioner or some other malefactor to go free.

The core of the Court's reasoning is that peremptory challenges on the basis of any group characteristic subject to heightened scrutiny are inconsistent with the guarantee of the Equal Protection Clause. That conclusion can be reached only by focusing unrealistically upon individual exercises of the peremptory challenge, and ignoring the totality of the practice. Since all groups are subject to the peremptory challenge (and will be made the object of it, depending upon the nature of the particular case) it is hard to see how any group is denied equal protection.

Even if the line of our later cases guaranteed by today's decision limits the theoretically boundless Batson principle to race, sex, and perhaps other classifications subject to heightened scrutiny, much damage has been done. It has been done, first and foremost, to the peremptory challenge system, which loses its whole character when (in order to defend against "impermissible stereotyping" claims) "reasons" for strikes must be given. The right of peremptory challenge "is," as Blackstone says, "an arbitrary and capricious right; and it must be exercised with full freedom, or it fails of its full purpose."

And damage has been done, secondarily, to the entire justice system, which will bear the burden of the expanded quest for "reasoned peremptories" that the Court demands. The extension of Batson to sex, and almost certainly beyond, will provide the basis for extensive collateral litigation. . . . Another consequence, as I have mentioned, is a lengthening of the voir dire process that already burdens trial courts.

The irrationality of today's strike-by-strike approach to equal protection is evident from the consequences of extending it to its logical conclusion. If a fair and impartial trial is a prosecutor's only legitimate goal; if adversarial trial stratagems must be tested against that goal in abstraction from their role within the system as a whole; and if, so tested, sex-based stratagems do not survive heightened scrutiny—then the prosecutor presumably violates the Constitution when he selects a male or female police officer to testify because he believes one or the other sex might be more convincing in the context of the particular case, or because he believes one or the other might be more appealing to a predominantly male or female jury. A decision to stress one line of argument or present certain witnesses before a mostly female jury—for example, to stress that the defendant victimized women—becomes, under the Court's reasoning, intentional discrimination by a state actor on the basis of gender.

I dissent.

CRITICAL THINKING ABOUT THE LAW

The reasoning in Case 3 is played out with *Batson v. Kentucky* standing tall and visible in the background. The legal system reinforces our ethical preference for order. The resulting dependability of our legal rules serves as a guide for business decisions, facilitating the many transactions required by modern business.

Yet the courts recognize that rules must evolve as our social needs and understandings change. Hence, the courts must struggle with achieving a balance between order and flexibility. J.E.B. provides an opportunity to use our critical thinking to see this tension in action.

1. What facts in our society have become more visible such that Justice Blackmun feels it appropriate to expand the application of Batson?

   Clue: What about our history that makes Blackmun's reasoning less likely to have been the basis for a Supreme Court decision in 1950?

2. **Justice Blackmun disagrees with the respondent concerning the comparative "level of discrimination" experienced by nonwhites and women. Our reasoning frequently contains phrases like *level of discrimination* that require some numerical determination. Recognize that clear numbers measuring such a level are hard to come by. As critical thinkers, you can often see soft spots in reasoning by asking: Now how are they measuring that concept? Could you help Justice Blackmun measure "level of discrimination" by suggesting what data might be useful for this determination?**

   Clue: **Start with the number of people affected, the probability they would be affected, and the extent of the harm.**

3. **Justice Scalia does not categorically disagree with extension of Batson. What facts would have had to be different for Scalia to have concurred with the majority?**

   Clue: **Find the section in his dissent in which he explains the inadequacies in the majority's reasoning.**

The voir dire process has changed significantly over the years, and to many lawyers, a successful voir dire is the essential element in winning a case. Jury selection today has become a "science," and in most cases involving large potential judgments, at least one side, and often both, use a professional jury selection service. An example of one such service is Litigation Sciences, a firm established in 1979. By 1989, 10 years later, the firm claimed to have handled over 900 cases, with a win figure of 90 to 95 percent. It employed a full-time staff of over 100, and the average cost of its services was approximately $200,000, although some cases ran into the millions.[7] Its clients include both major law firms and corporations.

Some of the services include identifying demographic data to help lawyers build a profile of the ideal juror, helping design questions for the lawyers to ask during voir dire, and providing such post–voir dire services as mock juries and shadow juries.

A **mock jury** is a body of individuals whose demographic makeup matches that of the actual jury. The lawyers practice their case before the mock jury to find out how receptive the "jurors" are to the arguments and how the mock jurors relate to the witnesses. Lawyers can gain valuable information about what they need to change before presenting the case. Depending on how much money a client has, lawyers may go through multiple "trials" before a mock jury.

A **shadow jury** again matches the demographics of the real jury, but the shadow jury actually sits in the courtroom during the trial. They "deliberate" at the end of each day, so the lawyer has an ongoing idea of how the case is going. The shadow jury's deliberations may let a lawyer know when damage has been done to the case that needs to be repaired. After the trial is finished, the shadow jury deliberates for a predetermined, brief period of time. Their "verdict" then helps the lawyer decide whether to try to settle the case before the jury comes back with a verdict. (Remember, the parties can agree to settle at any time until the judge hands down the final decision in the case.)

You can see from this brief discussion how valuable a jury selection service can be. You can also see why many argue that such services should not be

mock jury Group of individuals, demographically matched to the actual jurors in a case, in front of whom lawyers practice their arguments before presenting their case to the actual jury.

shadow jury Group of individuals, demographically matched to the actual jurors in a case, that sits in the courtroom during a trial and then "deliberates" at the end of each day so that lawyers have continuous feedback of how their case is going.

---

[7] Maureen E. Lane, "Twelve Carefully Selected Not So Angry Men: Are Jury Consultants Destroying the American Legal System?" *Suffolk U. L. Rev.* 32: 463 (1999).

allowed. After all, they give a tremendous advantage to the client with more money to spend on the trial.

Opening Statements. Once a jury has been impaneled, or selected, the case begins with the opening statements. Each party's attorney explains to the judge and the jury what facts he or she intends to prove, the legal conclusions to which these facts will lead, and how the case should be decided.

Plaintiff's Case. The plaintiff then presents his or her case, which consists of examining witnesses and presenting evidence. The procedure for each witness is the same. First, the plaintiff's attorney questions the witness in what is called direct examination. The plaintiff's lawyer asks questions designed to elicit from the witnesses facts that support the plaintiff's case. Then the opposing counsel may cross-examine the witness; only questions pertaining to the witness's direct examination may be asked. The purpose of cross-examination is often to "poke holes" in the witness's testimony or to reduce the credibility of the witness. The plaintiff's attorney then has the opportunity for **redirect examination** to repair any damage done by the cross-examination. The opposing counsel then has a last opportunity to cross-examine the witness to address facts brought out in redirect examination. This procedure is followed for each of the plaintiff's witnesses.

Immediately following the plaintiff's case, the defendant may make a motion for a directed verdict. In making such a motion, the defendant is stating to the court that even if all the plaintiff's factual allegations are true, the plaintiff has not proved his or her case. For example, to prove a case of negligence, the plaintiff must prove that the defendant breached his or her duty to the plaintiff, causing compensable injury. If the plaintiff offers no evidence of any compensable injury, then there can be no judgment for the plaintiff. In such a case, a motion for a directed verdict would be granted, and the case would be dismissed. Such motions are rarely granted, because the plaintiff will usually introduce some evidence of every element necessary to establish the existence of his or her case.

A motion for a directed verdict also may be made by either party after the presentation of the defendant's case. The party filing the motion (the moving party) is saying that even if the judge looks at all the evidence in the light most favorable to the other party, it is overwhelmingly clear that the only decision the jury could come to is that the moving party is entitled to judgment in his or her favor.

Defendant's Case. If the defendant's motion for a directed verdict is denied, the trial proceeds with the defendant's case in chief. The defendant's witnesses are questioned in the same manner as were the plaintiff's, except that it is the defendant's attorney who does the direct and redirect examination, and the plaintiff's attorney is entitled to cross-examine the witnesses.

Conference on Jury Instructions. If the case is being heard by a jury, the attorneys and the judge then retire for a conference on jury instructions. Jury instructions are the court's explanation to the jury of what legal decision they must make if they find certain facts to be true. Each attorney presents to the judge the set of jury instructions he or she feels will enable the jury to accurately apply the law to the facts. Obviously, each attorney tries to state the law in the manner most favorable to his or her client. The judge confers with the attorneys regarding their proposed instructions and then draws up the instructions for the jury.

redirect examination
Questioning by the directing attorney following cross-examination. The scope of the questions is limited to questions asked on the cross-examination.

Closing Arguments. The attorneys' last contact with the jury then follows. The attorneys present their closing arguments. The party who has the burden of proof, the plaintiff, presents the first closing argument; the defendant's closing argument follows. Finally, the plaintiff is entitled to a **rebuttal.** The judge then reads the instructions to the jury, and the jurors retire to the jury room to deliberate. When they reach a decision, the jurors return to the courtroom, where their verdict is read.

rebuttal A brief additional argument by the plaintiff to address any important matters brought out in the defendant's closing argument.

Post-trial Motions. The party who loses has a number of options. A motion for a judgment notwithstanding the verdict may be made. This motion is a request for the judge to enter a judgment contrary to that handed down by the jury on the grounds that as a matter of law the decision could only have been different from that reached by the jury. For example, if a plaintiff requests damages of $500 but introduces evidence of only $100 in damages, the jury cannot award the plaintiff the $400 for unsubstantiated damages. If they do so, the defendant would file a motion for a judgment notwithstanding the verdict. Alternatively, the dissatisfied party may file a motion for a new trial on the grounds that the verdict is clearly against the weight of the evidence. If neither of these motions is granted and the judge enters a judgment in accordance with the verdict, the losing party may appeal the decision.

APPELLATE PROCEDURE

As explained earlier, the court to which the case is appealed depends on the court in which the case was originally heard. If a case was heard in a federal district court, it is appealed to the U.S. Circuit Court of Appeals for the geographic region in which the district court is located. If heard in a state trial court, the case is appealed to that state's intermediate appellate court or, if none exists, to the state's final appellate court.

To appeal a case, the losing party must allege that a prejudicial error of law occurred during the trial. A prejudicial error is one that is so substantial that it could have affected the outcome of the case. For example, the judge may have ruled as admissible in court certain evidence that had a major impact on the decision, when that evidence was legally inadmissible. Or the party may argue that the instructions that the judge read to the jury were inaccurate and resulted in a misapplication of the law to the facts.

When a case is appealed, there is not a new trial. The attorney for the appealing party (the appellant) and the attorney for the party who won in the lower court (the appellee) file briefs, or written arguments, with the court of appeals. They also generally present oral arguments before the appeals court. The court considers these arguments, reviews the record of the case, and renders a decision. The decisions of the appellate court can take a number of forms. The court may accept the decision of the lower court and **affirm** that decision. Alternatively, the appellate court may conclude that the lower court was correct in its decision, except for granting an inappropriate remedy, and so it will **modify** the remedy. If the appellate court decides that the lower court was incorrect in its decision, that decision will be **reversed.** Finally, the appeals court may feel that an error was committed, but it does not know how that error would have affected the outcome of the case, so it will **remand** the case to the lower court for a new trial.

affirm Term used for an appellate court's decision to uphold the decision of a lower court in a case that has been appealed.

modify Term used for an appellate court's decision that, although the lower court's decision was correct, it granted an inappropriate remedy that needs to be changed.

reverse Term used for an appellate court's decision that the lower court's decision was incorrect and cannot be allowed to stand.

remand Term used for an appellate court's decision that an error was committed that may have affected the outcome of the case and that therefore the case must be returned to the lower court.

Although the appeals procedure may sound relatively simple compared with the initial trial procedure, appeals require a great deal of work on the part of the attorneys. They are consequently expensive. Thus, when deciding whether to appeal, the businessperson must consider how much money he or she wishes to spend. If a judgment is rendered against a businessperson, it may be less expensive to pay the judgment than to appeal.

Another factor to consider when one is deciding whether to appeal is the precedential value of the case. The case may involve an important issue of law that a party hopes may be decided in her or his favor by an appeals court. If she or he anticipates similar suits arising in the future, it may be important to get a favorable ruling, and if the case appears to be strong, an appeal may be desirable.

Appellate courts, unlike trial courts, are usually composed of a bench of at least three judges. There are no juries. The decision of the court is determined by the majority of the judges. One of the judges who votes with the majority records the court's decision and their reasons in what is called the majority opinion. These have precedential value and are used by judges to make future decisions and by attorneys in advising their clients as to the appropriate course of behavior in similar situations. If any of the judges in a case agrees with the ultimate decision of the majority but for different reasons, he or she may write a concurring opinion, stating how this conclusion was reached. Finally, the judge or judges disagreeing with the majority may write their dissenting opinion, giving their reasons for reaching a contrary conclusion. Dissenting opinions may be cited in briefs by attorneys arguing that the law should be changed. Dissents may also be cited by an appellate judge who decides to change the law.

For most cases, only one appeal is possible. In some states, where there is both an intermediate and a superior court of appeals, a losing party may appeal from the intermediate appellate court to the state supreme court. In a limited number of cases, a losing party may be able to appeal from a state supreme court or a federal circuit court of appeals to the U.S. Supreme Court.

Appeal to the U.S. Supreme Court. Every year, thousands of individuals attempt to have their appeals heard by the U.S. Supreme Court. The Court hears, on average, however, only about 80 cases every year. When a party wishes to have his or her case heard by the highest court in the nation, he or she files a petition with the Court, asking it to issue a writ of certiorari, which is an order to the lower court to send to the Supreme Court the record of the case.

As you may guess from the number of cases heard by the Supreme Court, very few writs are issued. The justices review the petitions they receive and will issue a writ only when at least four justices vote to hear the case. The Court is most likely to issue a writ when (1) the case presents a substantial federal question that has not yet been addressed by the Supreme Court; (2) the case involves a matter that has produced conflicting decisions from the various circuit courts of appeal and is, therefore, in need of resolution; (3) a state court of last resort holds that a federal law is invalid or upholds a state law that has been challenged as violating federal law; or (4) a federal court has ruled that an act of Congress is unconstitutional.

It is often difficult to project whether the Court will hear a case. In the first instance described above, for example, a federal question is simply an issue arising under the federal Constitution, treaties, or statutes. Substantiality is a more difficult issue to define. If the decision would affect a large number of people or is likely to arise again if not decided, it may be considered substantial. Sometimes, however, a case may in fact involve a very important federal question of statutory interpretation, yet the Supreme Court may believe that the problem was unclear drafting by Congress, and so it may choose to not hear the case in anticipation of an amendment of the federal statute whose interpretation is at issue. If the Supreme Court refuses to hear a case, this refusal has no precedential effect.

CLASS ACTIONS

In discussing the stages of civil litigation, we have been talking as if there is only one plaintiff and one defendant, but remember, there can be multiple parties joined as plaintiffs and multiple parties joined as defendants. For example, if a person gets injured using a defective product, he or she would probably sue both the manufacturer and the retailer.

There is a special kind of case, however, in which the plaintiff is not a single party, or even a few parties, but rather a large group of individuals who may not even know each other but who all share a common complaint against the defendant. This kind of case is referred to as a class action. For example, all of the shareholders of a corporation may want to sue a member of the board of directors. One of the most common class actions involves product liability cases, situations in which numerous people injured by the same product join together to sue that product's manufacturer. Other kinds of cases that may give rise to class action suits include discrimination claims and antitrust claims. Sometimes, people will come together to bring a class action because their individual claims may be so small that separate litigation really is not feasible, but when all the claims are combined, the amount is large enough that it will be profitable for a lawyer to take the case.

Class actions are seen by some as efficient because instead of all the individuals filing and trying individual cases based on the same issue, all of the claims can be brought in one action. This efficiency seems even more significant when there are complex issues involved and high costs of trial preparation. When a class action is brought, the case is usually filed in the name of one or two of the parties and all others who are similarly situated. The named plaintiffs in the case have to pay all of the court costs, including the costs of finding the names and addresses of everyone in the class and notifying them.

The first step in a class action suit, which differentiates it from other suits, is certification of the class. The court will review the claims to ensure that all the named plaintiffs indeed share a common interest that can be adequately raised by the named plaintiffs. Defendants will often challenge the certification of the class, knowing that if the class does not get certified, the named plaintiffs may not have the resources to bring the case as an individual action.

Once the class has been certified, the parties will often enter into settlement negotiations. The court will approve the classwide settlement only if it is fair and equitable and benefits the entire class, not just the named plaintiffs and their lawyers. Once a settlement has been approved by the court, it legally satisfies the claims of all the class members.

In an effort to reform class action lawsuits, Congress passed, and President Bush signed, the Class Action Fairness Act of 2005. The Class Action Fairness Act had several intended goals. First, the Act sought to limit the enormous legal fees attorneys representing plaintiff classes frequently received as part of their service. Second, the Act was written to allow the defendants in class action lawsuits to have greater access to federal courts. Finally, the Act was intended to protect the interests of the individual class members to guarantee them equitable compensation.

As part of the new regulations on attorney fees, attorneys now receive compensation based on the actual amount class members claim as compensation and not based on the gross sum awarded to the plaintiff class. In addition, the court must first approve the award the plaintiff class members are to receive to ensure that the award does not violate the defendants' due process rights. If the attorney's fees are not to be determined by the amount of the award, the attorney's compensation is to be limited to actual time spent working on the case.

Moving beyond attorneys' fees, the Class Action Fairness Act changes the requirements for diversity of citizenship in class actions, as well as the general requirements for federal jurisdiction. The Act provides federal courts with jurisdiction over any class action where there is partial diversity of citizenship; that is, if any of the class members is a citizen of a different state than any of the defendants, the federal courts have jurisdiction. The federal courts also have jurisdiction whenever any plaintiff or defendant is a foreign state or the citizen of a foreign state. These new requirements under the act allow more class actions to fall within federal jurisdiction and make it much harder for plaintiffs to pursue their actions in state courts. Business defendants are typically happy with this last change, as they tend to face smaller awards in federal courts than in state courts.

Despite the greater access to federal courts, the act also allows some discretion for federal courts in accepting jurisdiction. A district court can choose to not accept jurisdiction over a class action if between one-third and two-thirds of the plaintiff class members and the primary defendants are citizens of the same state. There are also two situations where the federal court has no choice regarding jurisdiction. When fewer than one-third of the plaintiff class members are residents of the same state as the primary defendants, then the class action will be subjected to federal jurisdiction. If over two-thirds of the plaintiff class members are residents of the same state as the primary defendants, however, there will be no federal jurisdiction in the case.

As mentioned previously, the act contains a number of provisions that are intended to protect the interest of the individual plaintiff class members. For example, the act forbids any settlement that would result in a net loss to the class members. That is, class members cannot accept a settlement where the award does not cover their damages, unless the court decides that other, non-monetary, benefits are valuable enough to outweigh the net monetary loss. In addition, class members cannot be awarded different monetary amounts based upon their geographical location. All class members, barring differences in their actual damages, are awarded the same monetary amount.

Global Dimensions of the American Legal System

This chapter has focused on the American legal system. With the growth of multinationals and increasing trade among nations, Americans may increasingly become involved in disputes in foreign nations, and foreigners will increasingly become involved in disputes with Americans and American corporations.

When parties make international agreements, they can incorporate as a term of the agreement their choice of which nation's court will hear any disputes arising under the agreement. Because of differences between our litigation system and

LINKING LAW AND BUSINESS

Management

In your management class, you may have learned about a concept known as cost-benefit analysis. This idea is defined as the process by which managers weigh the benefits or revenues of a particular activity in comparison to the costs of performing the action. Usually, managers will decide to pursue an action if the benefits outweigh the costs.

Managers or other decision makers can effectively come to a conclusion as to which alternative to pursue after the options have been evaluated. There are three basic steps in this evaluation that decision makers should follow: (1) Estimate, as accurately as possible, the potential effects of each of the possible actions; (2) Assign probabilities to each of the expected effects of each decision if the idea was implemented; and (3) Compare the possible effects of each alternative decision and the probabilities of each. Meanwhile, consideration should be given to organizational objectives. After these three steps have been followed, managers will have a better understanding about the benefits of alternative decisions. Therefore, a choice can be made that will hopefully be most advantageous to the organization.

This concept of cost-benefit analysis can also be applied when a businessperson is faced with the decision of whether to appeal a court decision. The businessperson should examine the costs of the appellate procedures, the probability of the outcome in the appeals court, and the time involved with the appeals process. Thereafter, a decision can be made by the businessperson that will potentially be most beneficial.

Source: S. Certo, *Modern Management* (Upper Saddle River, NJ: Prentice Hall, 2000), 152, 432. Reproduced by permission.

COMPARATIVE LAW CORNER

The Judicial System in Germany

The United States and Germany are major trading partners and have many similarities, but the German judicial system is very different from the American judicial system. German law is based on a civil law tradition rather than a common law tradition. The United States has a common law system, which relies on precedents set by previous cases to rule on current cases. German judges make decisions based on the extensive civil codes, rather than previous decisions. German judges are not elected as many American judges are; instead, most are appointed for life, after a probationary period.

The judicial system is a federal system, as in the United States, but German courts are separated by field. The ordinary courts hear most criminal and civil cases, the specialty courts (for labor, patents, social, administrative, and fiscal issues) hear cases related to their individual area, and constitutional courts hear cases involving constitutional issues. The courts all have local, land (state), and federal levels. The highest court in Germany is the Bundesverfassungsgericht, the Federal Constitutional Court, which deals only with constitutional issues, unlike the United States' Supreme Court. Each specialty court has its own highest court of appeals, such as the Federal Court of Germany for the ordinary courts.

Germany does not have any jury trials; all cases are heard by a judge or a panel of judges. Also, the judges are the primary questioners of witnesses. Lawyers can question witnesses after the judges have finished. This legal fact-finding method differs from the American method of examination and cross-examination.

73

others, it is important to compare the procedures in each country before choosing a forum. For example, in Japan, there is no procedure comparable with discovery, and so, parties go to trial not knowing what evidence the other side has.

With the increase in trade, many foreigners now purchase American goods. Because of some differences between court systems, many citizens of foreign countries injured by U.S. corporations will prefer to sue in the United States. In Japan, for example, there are no contingency fees, and an injured plaintiff must pay his or her lawyer's fees up front, at a cost of 8 percent of the proposed recovery plus nonrefundable court costs. Also, in Japan, there are no class actions.

SUMMARY

Our American legal system is really composed of two systems: a federal system and a state system. When one has a legal dispute, subject matter jurisdiction determines which court system will hear the case. Almost all cases fall within the state court's jurisdiction. Only the limited number of cases within the exclusive jurisdiction of the federal courts do not. A case may be heard in either court when there is concurrent jurisdiction. Concurrent jurisdiction exists when (1) the case involves a federal question, or (2) there is diversity of citizenship between the plaintiff and the defendant. Besides having subject matter jurisdiction, a court must also have in personam jurisdiction and proper venue to hear a case.

Cases are filed in courts of original jurisdiction. In the state system, these courts are usually called the courts of common pleas or county courts. In the federal system, the courts of original jurisdiction are called the district courts. In the state system, state courts of appeals and state supreme courts have appellate jurisdiction. Depending on the state, there may be either one or two levels of appeal. In the federal system, cases are appealed to the circuit court of appeals and then to the U.S. Supreme Court.

Cases are guided through the courts by attorneys. Juries act as finders of fact in trials. Judges resolve questions of law and, in bench trials, also serve as finders of fact.

There are four basic stages in a lawsuit. In the pretrial stage, there are (1) informal negotiations, (2) pleadings, (3) pretrial motions, (4) discovery, and (5) a pretrial conference. Next comes the trial, with (1) jury selection, (2) opening statements, (3) the plaintiff's case, (4) the defendant's case, (5) jury instructions, and (6) closing arguments. Third are the post-trial motions, which may include a motion for a judgment notwithstanding the verdict and a motion for a new trial. The final stage is the appellate stage, during which the party who lost at the trial appeals his or her case.

REVIEW QUESTIONS

1 Identify the different types of jurisdiction and explain why each is important.

2 Explain the two situations that cause the state and federal courts to have concurrent jurisdiction.

3 What is venue?

4 What is the relationship between federal district courts and courts of common pleas?

5 What is the attorney-client privilege and what is the rationale for its existence?

6 Explain the importance of the work-product doctrine.

REVIEW PROBLEMS

7 Jacobson, a Michigan resident, sued Hasbro Corporation for negligence after one of Hasbro's truck drivers fell asleep and ran his semi off the road and into Jacobson's house, causing structural damage of approximately $80,000. Hasbro has small plants in Michigan, Ohio, and Indiana. The company is incorporated in Illinois and has its central offices there. Jacobson files his case in the state court in Michigan. Hasbro files a motion for removal, which Jacobson contests, arguing that the case does not fall within the concurrent jurisdiction of the federal courts. Should the case be transferred? Why or why not?

8 Bill, a white male, is charged with spousal abuse. His attorney uses his peremptory challenges to remove all white females from the jury. The prosecution objects. Was there any impropriety in the jury selection process?

9 Marx Corporation is incorporated in the state of Delaware, but all of the firm's business is conducted within the state of New York. Sanders, a Delaware resident, is injured by one of Marx Corporation's products and subsequently files suit against Marx Corporation in Delaware State Court. Marx files a motion to dismiss the case on grounds that Delaware cannot assert jurisdiction over the corporation because it does not conduct business in Delaware but is only incorporated there because it gained certain legal advantages from incorporating in that state. Explain why the Delaware state court system does or does not have jurisdiction over this case.

10 Carson is a resident of Clark County, Nevada. He sued Stevens, a resident of Washoe County, Nevada, for injuries he received in an accident that took place in Washoe County. Carson filed the case in Clark County. Can Stevens get the case moved to Washoe County? How would he try to do so?

11 Attorney Fox represented Davis in a number of drunk driving cases. Davis shows up at Fox's office to discuss having the attorney draw up a will for him. The attorney recognizes that Davis is clearly intoxicated. The attorney offers to pay for a cab to take Davis home, but he refuses the offer. Fox's secretary suggests that he call the state highway patrol. If Fox calls the highway patrol, is he violating the attorney–client privilege? Why or why not?

12 Watson brought a negligence case against the Hasbro Drug Store to recover damages for injuries he received from falling on the wet floor of the store. He believed that the store was negligent for marking the floor with only a small sign that said "Slippery When Wet." The trial court refused to let Watson introduce evidence that after his fall the store started marking wet floors with cones and a large sign saying, "Caution—Floor Is Wet and Slippery." Watson lost in the trial court and lost his appeals to the state appeals court and state supreme court. Will he be able to appeal to the U.S. Supreme Court? Why or why not?

CASE PROBLEMS

13 Frank Snowney, a California resident, reserved a hotel room in Las Vegas by phone from his California residence. Snowney was told that the room would cost $50 a night plus tax; however, he was not informed about a $3 energy surcharge he would receive at check out. Snowney sued the hotel owners for himself and all others who were not informed about the energy surcharge and thus were charged more than the advertised price. The hotel owners filed a motion to quash the summons on the grounds of a lack of personal jurisdiction. The hotel owners argued that they are incorporated in Nevada or Delaware and conduct their main business in Nevada. In addition, the owners do not conduct business in California, nor do they have bank accounts in California. The owners, however, did admit that they own a subsidiary that conducts business in California.

Snowney argues that the owners advertised extensively via billboard and publication media in California, maintained a Web site and toll free number that catered to out-of-state guests that included guests from California, accepted reservations from California residents through the hotel's Web site and toll free number, obtained a significant number of their guests from California residents, and sent mailings to California residents that participated in the hotel's "Total Rewards" program. The state trial court granted the hotel's motion to quash the summons finding

California did not have proper jurisdiction. The state court of appeals reversed, and the hotel owners appealed to the Supreme Court of California. If you were a justice with the Supreme Court of California, how would you have ruled and why? *Snowney v. Harrah's Entertainment, Inc.,* 112 P.3d 28 (2005).

14 Wallace R. Brown hired Jeffrey Thaler, an attorney with Berman & Simmons, to represent him in an effort to recover damages for three of his commercial fishing vessels that suffered from an oil spill. During the time of representation, Thaler moved from Berman & Simmons to Bernstein, Shur, Sawyer & Nelson (BSSN). Unhappy with Thaler's work, Brown filed a complaint with the Superior court against Thaler, Berman & Simmons, and BSSN, seeking damages. Brown used certified mail to send the summons and complaint to the defendants. According to Maine law, to complete service by mail (1) the summons and complaint must be mailed to the person to be served; (2) the served documents must be accompanied by a notice and acknowledgement form and a prepaid envelope to be returned to the sender with the signed acknowledgement form; and (3) the signed acknowledgement form must be filed with the court. None of the defendants acknowledged service, and filed suit to dismiss Brown's claims for lack of proper notification. The court dismissed Brown's claim. If you were Brown, what could you have done to have ensure proper service was given? *Brown v. Thaler,* 880 A.2d 1113 (2005).

15 Atlas Global Group, a Texas-based partnership, filed a state lawsuit against Grupo Dataflux, a Mexican corporation, in federal court on the grounds that there was diversity jurisdiction. The federal district court ruled in favor of Atlas, but before judgment was entered, the Mexican corporation moved to dismiss, claiming that even though two Mexican members of the partnership left the Texas partnership, they were still partners when Atlas filed suit. Hence, the Mexican corporation claimed that the court did not have subject matter jurisdiction because the parties were not diverse when the suit was filed. The magistrate judge agreed with the Mexican corporation and dismissed the case because diversity did not exist when the case was filed, even though the Mexican partners left Atlas before the trial. The appellate court reversed, claiming that because the jurisdictional error was not initially identified, the change of partnership after the filing cured the jurisdictional error. Explain how you think the United States Supreme Court ruled on appeal. *The Grupo Dataflux v. Atlas Global Group,* 124 S. Ct. 1920 (2004).

16 Joseph Hazel, a tractor-trailer operator for R & D Transport, was involved in a car accident while working. Hazel's tractor-trailer struck a vehicle in which A.H., a minor, was a passenger. The accident occurred in Dearborn County, and Hazel's residence and R & D Transport's principal place of business are in Hendricks County. Sarah Richardson, suing for herself and as the guardian of A.H., filed suit in Porter County where they reside. Richardson sued, in part, for damages to "orthotic devices [and] clothing" for A.H. that were normally kept in Porter County. Hazel and R & D filed a motion to have the case transferred to either Hendricks County or Dearborn County. What is the proper venue for the trial? *R & D Transport, Inc. v. A.H.,* 859 N.E.2d 332 (2006).

17 Prior to his becoming governor of California, Arnold Schwarzenegger resided as a citizen of California. Schwarzenegger brought suit against Fred Martin Motors, an Ohio-based car dealer, in a California district court. Schwarzenegger claimed that Fred Martin advertised his used cars in the *Akron Beacon Journal,* a locally owned Ohio newspaper, while inappropriately using Schwarzenegger's photograph as the "Terminator," thereby constituting an alleged violation of Schwarzenegger's right to publicity. Fred Martin regularly purchased imported automobiles from California, but he dealt only with their representatives in Illinois and New Jersey. In addition, Fred Martin relied on the services of a California-based marketing company to implement direct-mail advertisements. Explain why the state court in California can or cannot exercise personal jurisdiction over the defendant. *Arnold Schwarzenegger v. Fred Martin Motors,* 374 F.3d 797 (2004).

18 Plaintiff, a Virginia resident, sued the defendants, residents of Texas and New Mexico, in the Eastern District Court of Virginia for defamation and intentional infliction of emotional distress from comments they posted on AOL's Usenet groups. The defendants have never been to Virginia, and they posted their comments using a service provider from California. The defendants sought to dismiss the case on the grounds that Virginia lacked jurisdiction. The plaintiff argued that there was jurisdiction under the state long-arm statute that provides jurisdiction over a defendant who commits a tort in the state. The plaintiff alleged that the defamatory action occurred in Virginia because the defendants posted their statements using their AOL account, and AOL's server is located in Virginia. Thus, the defamatory messages would have been temporarily stored in Virginia and then would have been transmitted worldwide from Virginia. With which party do you believe the court sided? Why? *Bochan v. LaFontaine,* 68 F. Supp. 2d 692 (1999).

19   Jim Barber, a paralegal with the Bennett Law Offices, used one of Bennett's order forms to request a credit report from National Data Research (NDR), an investigative information service provider. Barber requested the credit report on Automated Recovery Systems (ARS) pursuant to a personal case he had against ARS but not through his employer, Bennett. Barber also orally requested a credit report on Timothy and Samuel Myers, who own and operate ARS. The Myers sued Bennett for the improper request on the Myers' credit. The Myers live and work in Nevada and filed suit in Nevada against Bennett, whose offices are in Utah, where it conducts the vast majority of its business.

Bennett filed a motion to dismiss for lack of personal jurisdiction and improper venue. Was Bennett successful in its motion? What would the Myers have to prove to be successful in defeating Bennett's motion? *Myers v. The Bennett Law Offices,* 238 F.3d 1068 (9th Cir., 2000).

20   Arnold Holloway was convicted of first-degree murder and sentenced to death. During the voir dire for the case, the prosecutor used 12 peremptory strikes, 11 of which were used to remove African Americans. Holloway, an African American, challenged the prosecutor's use of the peremptory challenges as being purposeful discrimination on the basis of race. Did the court of appeals overturn Holloway's conviction? Why or why not? *Arnold Holloway v. Martin Horn,* 355 F.3d 707 (2004).

THINKING CRITICALLY ABOUT RELEVANT LEGAL ISSUES

The Election of Judges

Despite a lack of consensus among legal commentators, there is a clear answer to the debate about whether judges should be elected or appointed. America is a democracy; it is only right that the American people would get to elect all judges. Like the legislative and executive branches of government, the judicial branch functions to provide services to the American people. Those very people deserve to elect their judges just as they elect members of Congress and the president. One of the keys to democracy is having a responsible and responsive government. Judges will be neither responsible nor responsive unless they must face the American people periodically and ask for their votes.

Part of holding judges accountable for their legal decisions is not only choosing to elect or reelect them but also having the ability to remove a judge who is not performing his duty adequately. The American people should have the option of removing a judge when he fails to uphold the standards and morals of the community. Accordingly, allowing voters to have recall elections would further prevent a judge from engaging in undue judicial activism. Judges who are appointed for life terms are beholden to no one; that life tenure challenges the very essence of democracy.

Sometimes a judge's ideology or judicial philosophy will change over time; this change affects the decisions the judge will make. When a judge changes her decision-making process, she is no longer staying true to why she was elected in the first place.

One way to fix unexpected changes is to have periodic elections for judges. These elections will help to keep judges consistent in their rulings and interpretations, while also preventing surprises for the American people who elected the judges in the first place.

By having elections, out-of-touch judges who do not reflect the current social climate can be removed in favor of a judge who is in touch with the American people. This last point has the added benefit of possibly bringing younger people to the bench, thus opening up the possibility for a wider group of Americans to shape the law.

1. How would you frame the issue and conclusion of this essay?

2. What ethical norms does the author most use in arguing for why judges should be elected?

3. Part of being a critical thinker is avoiding this temptation to dichotomize (look at everything as an either-or situation) and to look for other reasonable alternatives. Does the author engage in any dichotomous thinking? If so, what are other reasonable alternatives?

   Clue: What either-or situations does the author create, and are there third and fourth possibilities?

4. Write an essay that someone who holds an opposition opinion to the author might write.

   Clue: What other ethical norms could influence an opinion on this issue.

ASSIGNMENT ON THE INTERNET

As you learned in this chapter, the question of jurisdiction determines whether a court has the power to render a meaningful decision. The growth of Internet commerce, however, brings additional jurisdictional questions and concerns that have yet to be resolved. Use the Web site **library.findlaw.com/ 1999/Jan/1/241482.html** to familiarize yourself with the interactive and passive-use distinctions made in cases of Internet jurisdiction.

Next, apply this distinction to the case of *Barton Southern Company, Inc. v. Manhole Barrier Systems, Inc. and JFC Company*, 318 F. Supp. 2d 1174 (2004). which can be found using findlaw.com or through the Lexis-Nexis database. Does the interactive/passive distinction help resolve the issue of jurisdiction in this case? Why or why not?

 ## ON THE INTERNET

www.allbusiness.com/legal/961805-1.html This Web site contains an article discussing the difficulties and possible ways in which businesses can seek to obtain in personam jurisdiction over foreign "cybersquatters," who are people in other countries who have bought up popular domain names and are using them to their own personal gain and to the detriment of the owner of the products with the purchased domain names.
writ.news.findlaw.com/amar/20040220.html In his column, Vikram David Amar discusses some problems with juries as well as possible changes to the jury selection process that might improve juries.
www.litigationresources.com/HomePage/tabid/681/Default.aspx Litigation Resources is a company that offers business and legal professionals many tools and services they might need to ease the litigation process.
www.martindale.com This is the site of the Martindale-Hubble Law Directory, which provides information about lawyers and law firms. Typical entries include area of special expertise, address, and telephone number.
www.lexisone.com/legalresearch/legalguide/codes_statutes/federal_rules_of_civil_procedure.htm This site will lead you to a number of sites that contain the federal rules of civil procedure in a variety of formats.
www.lawresearch.com/v2/statute/statstat.htm Go to this page to find a link to your state's constitution, statutes, and rules of civil procedure.
www.supremecourtus.gov/about/about.html This site provides a wealth of information about the U.S. Supreme Court.

FOR FUTURE READING

Anenson, T. Leigh. "Creating Conflict of Interest: Litigation as Interference with the Attorney-Client Relationship." *American Business Law Journal* 43 (2006): 173.

Bonfield, Lloyd. *American Law And the American Legal System in a Nutshell*. St. Paul, MN: West Publishing, 2006.

Lande, John. "How Much Justice Can You Afford?: Defining the Courts' Roles and Deciding the Appropriate Number of Trials, Settlement Signals, and Other Elements Needed to Administer Justice." *Journal of Dispute Resolution* (2006): 213.

Magier, David S. "Tick, Tock, Time Is Running Out to Nab Cybersquatters: The Dwindling Utility of

the Anticybersquatting Consumer Protection Act." *IDEA: The Intellectual Property Law Review* 46 (2006): 415.

Stoltz, Brian W. "Rethinking the Peremptory Challenge: Letting Lawyers Enforce the Principles of Batson." *Texas Law Review* 85 (2007): 1031.

Walkowiak, Vincent S, ed. *Attorney-Client Privilege in Civil Litigation: Protecting and Defending Confidentiality*. 3rd ed. New York: American Bar Association, 2005.

Wishman, Seymour. *Anatomy of a Jury*. New York: Penguin Books, 1987.

The International Legal Environment of Business

From Chapter 9 of *The Legal Environment of Business: A Critical Thinking Approach*, 5/e. Nancy K. Kubasek. Bartley A. Brennan. M. Neil Browne. Copyright © 2009 by Pearson Prentice Hall. All rights reserved.

The International Legal Environment of Business

- DIMENSIONS OF THE INTERNATIONAL ENVIRONMENT OF BUSINESS

- METHODS OF ENGAGING IN INTERNATIONAL BUSINESS

- RISKS OF ENGAGING IN INTERNATIONAL BUSINESS

- LEGAL AND ECONOMIC INTEGRATION AS A MEANS OF ENCOURAGING INTERNATIONAL BUSINESS ACTIVITY

- GLOBAL DISPUTE RESOLUTION

U.S. managers can no longer afford to view their firms as doing business on a huge island between the Pacific and the Atlantic oceans. Existing and pending multilateral trade agreements open vast opportunities to do business in Europe and Asia, throughout the Americas, and indeed throughout the world. If present and future U.S. managers do not become aware of these opportunities, as well as the attendant risks, they and their firms will be at a competitive disadvantage vis-à-vis foreign competitors from all over the world.

CRITICAL THINKING ABOUT THE LAW

This chapter (1) introduces the international environment of business; (2) sets forth the methods by which companies may engage in international business; (3) indicates the risks involved in such engagement; (4) describes organizations that work to bring down tariff barriers and, thus, encourage companies of all nations to engage in international business; and (5) indicates the means by which disputes between companies doing business in the international arena are settled. Please note carefully that when we use the word companies in an international context, we are referring not only to private sector firms but also to nation-state subsidized entities and government agencies that act like private sector companies.

Because of the widespread international opportunities and advances in communication, business managers must be aware of the global legal environment of business. As you will soon learn, the political, economic, cultural, and legal dimensions are all important international business considerations. The following questions will help sharpen your critical thinking about the international legal environment of business.

1. Consider the number of countries that might participate in an international business agreement. Why might ambiguity be a particularly important concern in international business?

   Clue: Consider the variety of cultures as well as the differences in languages. How might these factors affect business agreements?

2. Why might the critical thinking questions about ethical norms and missing information be important for international businesses?

   Clue: Again, consider the variety of cultures involved in international business. Why might identifying the primary ethical norms of a culture be helpful?

3. What ethical norm might influence the willingness to enter into agreements with foreign companies?

   Clue: How might international agreements differ from agreements between two U.S. companies?

Dimensions of the International Environment of Business

Doing international business has political, economic, cultural, and legal dimensions. Although this chapter emphasizes the legal dimensions of international business transactions, business managers need to be aware of those other important dimensions as well.

POLITICAL DIMENSIONS

Managers of firms doing international business must deal with different types of governments, ranging from democracies to totalitarian states. They are concerned with the stability of these governments and with whether economic decisions are centralized or decentralized. In the Marxist form of government, such as that which existed in the former Soviet Union and in Eastern Europe until recent years, economic decisions were centralized, and there was political stability. This would seem to be an ideal environment in which to do business from a multi-national business manager's perspective. But it was not ideal, because a centralized economy limits the supply of goods coming from outside a country, the price that can be charged for goods inside the country, and the amount of currency that can be taken out of the country by multinational businesses.

In 1998, 88 of the world's 191 countries were categorized as "free" in the sense that they were perceived as having high political and civil liberties (e.g., Australia, Belgium, Luxembourg, Finland, and the United States, to name a few). Fifty-three countries were classified as "partly free" because they enjoyed limited political rights and civil liberties (e.g., Egypt, China, Ethiopia, and North Korea).[1] A trend toward democratization seems to be under way. The percentages of the total population living in free, partly free, and not free conditions in recent years are as follows:[2]

	1990	*1998*	*2003*
Free	38.9	21.7	41.4
Partly free	21.8	39.1	23.2
Not free	19.0	39.2	35.4

[1] Adrian Karatnycky, *Freedom Gains,* San Diego Union Tribune 61 (Dec. 27, 1998).

[2] Adrian Karatnycky, *Freedom in the World* 6 (Freedom House, 2002).

Despite the collapse of communism and the development of new political systems professing support of free enterprise in Eastern Europe and throughout the former Soviet Union, companies in the industrialized nations have delayed investing in most of these areas because they are uncertain of their political stability and willingness to adhere to economic agreements. In China, an early rush to invest had been slowed by foreign companies' experiences with a seemingly capricious government. For example, McDonald's leased a prime location in Beijing from the centralized government but found itself ousted a few years later when the government revoked the lease in order to allow a department store to be built on that site. Moreover, doubts about the Chinese government's intention to honor its agreement with the British government that Hong Kong would retain its separate political and economic status for 50 years after the 99-year British lease expired in 1997 led one longtime Hong Kong trading company, Jardine, to move its headquarters to the Bahamas. Despite these early political problems in the late 1990s, China's growth rate in 2007 proceeded at an annual GDP of 10–12 percent. Further, China has brought investment capital to other Asian and African nations, along with political influence.

ECONOMIC DIMENSIONS

Every business manager should do a country analysis before doing business in another nation-state. Such an analysis not only examines political variables but also dissects a nation's economic performance as demonstrated in its rate of economic growth, inflation, budget, and trade balance. There are four economic factors that especially affect business investment:

1. Differences in size and economic growth rate of various nation-states. For example, when McDonald's decided to engage in international business, the company initially located its restaurants only in countries that already had high growth rates. As more and more developing nations moved toward a market economy, McDonald's expanded into Russia, China, Brazil, Mexico, and other countries deemed to have potentially high growth rates.

2. The impact of central planning versus a market economy on the availability of supplies. When McDonald's went into Russia, it had to build its own food-processing center to be certain it would get the quality of beef it needed. Furthermore, because of distribution problems, it used its own trucks to move supplies.

3. The availability of disposable income. This is a tricky issue. Despite the fact that the price of a Big Mac, french fries, and a soft drink equals the average Russian worker's pay for 4 hours of work, McDonald's is serving thousands of customers a day at its Moscow restaurant.

4. The existence of an appropriate transportation infrastructure. Decent roads, railroads, and ports are needed to bring in supplies and then to transport them within the host country. McDonald's experience in Russia is commonplace. Multinational businesses face transportation problems in many developing countries.

The World Bank classifies economies into one of the following categories according to per capita GNP:[3]

---

[3] *The World Bank Atlas, 2003,* (The World Bank, 2002).

Low income	755 or less
Middle income	756–9,265
High income	9,266 or more

CULTURAL DIMENSIONS

Culture may be defined as learned norms of a society that are based on values, beliefs, and attitudes. For example, if people of the same area speak the same language (e.g., Spanish in most of Latin America, with the exception of Brazil and a few small nations), the area is often said to be culturally homogeneous. Religion is a strong builder of common values. In 1995, the Iranian government outlawed the selling and use of satellite communications in Iran on the grounds that they presented "decadent" Western values that were undermining Muslim religious values.

A failure to understand that some cultures are based on ascribed group membership (gender, family, age, or ethnic affiliation) rather than on acquired group membership (religious, political, professional, or other associations), as in the West, can lead to business mistakes. For example, gender- and family-based affiliations are very important in Saudi Arabia, where a strict interpretation of Islam prevents women from playing a major role in business. Most Saudi women who work hold jobs that demand little or no contact with men, such as teaching or acting as doctors only for women.

Another important cultural factor is the attitude toward work. Mediterranean and Latin American cultures base their group affiliation on family and place more emphasis on leisure than on work. We often say that the Protestant ethic, stressing the virtues of hard work and thrift, is prevalent in Western and other industrialized nations. Yet the Germans refuse to work more than 35 hours a week and take 28 days of paid vacation every year. The average hourly wage is higher in Germany than in the United States, and German workers' benefits far outpace those of U.S. workers.

Business managers must carefully consider language, religion, attitudes toward work and leisure, family versus individual reliance, and numerous other cultural values when planning to do business in another nation-state. They also need to find a method of reconciling cultural differences between people and companies from their own nation-state and those from the country in which they intend to do business.

culture The learned norms of a society that are based on values, beliefs, and attitudes.

CORRUPTION AND TRADE

The nature of trade between nations, between multinationals, and between multinationals, and nation-states has led to global competition, and sometimes bribery, and thus corruption. Attempts through bilateral and multilateral agreements to lessen such bribery has been led by the United States Foreign Corrupt Practice Act of 1977 (FCPA) and the Convention on Combating Bribery of Foreign Officials in International Business Transactions (CCBFOIBT) drafted by the Organization for Economic Cooperation and Development (OECD) and signed by 34 countires in 1998. The Convention adopts the standards of the FCPA. Facilitating payments made to obtain permits, licenses or other official documents associated with contract performance, or movement of goods across a country are considered lawful. The Justice Department, as well as other agencies and individuals, may enforce the FCPA. Activities that constitute a bribe are often the basis for legal action. The case excerpted here deals with this problem.

CASE 1

U.S. v. Kay
359 F. 3d 738 (5th Cir. 2004)

David Kay (defendant) was an American citizen and a vice president for marketing of American Rice, Inc. (ARI), who was responsible for supervising sales and marketing in the Republic of Haiti. Douglas Murphy (defendant) was an American citizen and president of ARI.

Beginning in 1995 and continuing to about August 1999, Kay, Murphy, and other employees and officers of ARI paid bribes and authorized the payment of bribes to induce customs officials in Haiti to accept bills of lading and other documents that intentionally understated the true amount of rice that ARI shipped to Haiti for import, thus reducing the customs duties owed by ARI and RCH to the Haitian government.

In addition, beginning in 1998 and continuing to about August 1999, Kay and other employees and officers of ARI paid and authorized additional bribes to officials of other Haitian agencies to accept the false import documents and other documents that understated the true amount of rice being imported into and sold in Haiti, thereby reducing the amount of sales taxes paid by RCH to the Haitian government.

Kay directed employees of ARI to prepare two sets of shipping documents for each shipment of rice to Haiti, one that accurately reflected and another that falsely represented the weight and value of the rice being exported to Haiti.

Kay and Murphy agreed to pay and authorized the payment of bribes, calculated as a percentage of the value of the rice not reported on the false documents or in the form of a monthly retainer, to customs and tax officials of the Haitian government to induce these officials to accept the false documentation and to assess significantly lower customs duties and sales taxes than ARI would otherwise have been required to pay.

ARI, using official Haitian customs documents reflecting the amounts reported on the false shipping documents, reported only approximately 66 percent of the rice it sold in Haiti and thereby significantly reduced the amount of sales taxes it was required to pay to the Haitian government.

In 2001, a grand jury charged Kay with violating the FCPA and subsequently returned the indictment, which charges both Kay and Murphy with 12 counts of FCPA violations. Both Kay and Murphy moved to dismiss the indictment for the failure to state an offense, arguing that obtaining favorable tax treatment did not fall within the FCPA definition of payments made to government officials in order to obtain business. The district court dismissed the indictment, and the United States of America appealed.

Justice Wiener

The principal dispute in this case is whether, if proved beyond a reasonable doubt, the conduct that the indictment ascribed to defendants in connection with the alleged bribery of Haitian officials to understate customs duties and sales taxes on rice shipped to Haiti to assist American Rice, Inc. in obtaining or retaining business was sufficient to constitute an offense under the FCPA. Underlying this question of sufficiency of the contents of the indictment is the preliminary task of ascertaining the scope of the FCPA, which in turn requires us to construe the statute.

Because an offense under the FCPA requires that the alleged bribery be committed for the purpose of inducing foreign officials to commit unlawful acts, the results of which will assist in obtaining or retaining business in their country, the questions before us in this appeal are (1) whether bribes to obtain illegal but favorable tax and customs treatment can ever come within the scope of the statute, and (2) if so, whether, in combination, there are minimally sufficient facts alleged in the indictment to inform the defendants regarding the nexus between, on the one hand, Haitian taxes avoided through bribery, and, on the other hand, assistance in getting or keeping some business or business opportunity in Haiti.

No one contends that the FCPA criminalizes every payment to a foreign official: It criminalizes only those payments that are intended to (1) influence a foreign official to act or make a decision in his official capacity, or (2) induce such an official to perform or refrain from performing some act in violation of his duty, or (3) secure some wrongful advantage to the payor. And even then, the FCPA criminalizes these kinds of payments only if the result they are intended to produce—their *quid pro quo*—will assist (or is intended to assist) the payor in efforts to get or keep some business for or with "any person."

Stated differently, how attenuated can the linkage be between the effects of that which is sought from the foreign official in consideration of a bribe (here, tax minimization) and the briber's goal of finding assistance or obtaining or retaining foreign business with or for some person, and still satisfy the business nexus element of the FCPA?

Invoking basic economic principles, the SEC reasoned in its amicus brief that securing reduced taxes and duties on imports through bribery enables ARI to reduce its cost of doing business, thereby giving it an "improper advantage" over actual or potential competitors, and enabling it to do more business, or remain in a market it might otherwise leave.

Section 78dd-1(b) excepts from the statutory scope "any facilitating or expediting payment to a foreign official . . . the purpose of which is to expedite or to service the performance of a routine governmental action by a foreign official . . ." 15 U.S.C. §78dd-1(b).

For purposes of deciding the instant appeal, the question nevertheless remains whether the Senate, and concomitantly Congress, intended this broader statutory scope to encompass the administration of tax, customs, and other laws and regulations affecting the revenue of foreign states. To reach this conclusion, we must ask whether Congress's remaining expressed desire to prohibit bribery aimed at getting assistance in retaining business or maintaining business opportunities was sufficiently broad to include bribes meant to affect the administration of revenue laws. When we do so, we conclude that the legislative intent was so broad.

Obviously, a commercial concern that bribes a foreign government official to award a construction, supply, or services contract violates the statute. Yet, there is little difference between this example and that of a corporation's lawfully obtaining a contract from an honest official or agency by submitting the lowest bid, and—either before or after doing so—bribing a different government official to reduce taxes and thereby ensure that the under-bid venture is nevertheless profitable. Avoiding or lowering taxes reduces operating costs and thus increases profit margins, thereby freeing up funds that the business is otherwise legally obligated to expend. And this, in turn, enables it to take any number of actions to the disadvantage of competitors. Bribing foreign officials to lower taxes and customs duties certainly can provide an unfair advantage over competitors and thereby be of assistance to the payor in obtaining or retaining business. This demonstrates that the question whether the defendants' alleged payments constitute a violation of the FCPA truly turns on whether these bribes were intended to lower ARI's cost of doing business in Haiti enough to have a sufficient nexus to garnering business there or to maintaining or increasing business operations that ARI already had there, so as to come within the scope of the business nexus element as Congress used it in the FCPA. Answering this fact question, then, implicates a matter of proof and thus evidence.

Given the foregoing analysis of the statute's legislative history, we cannot hold as a matter of law that Congress meant to limit the FCPA's applicability to cover only bribes that lead directly to the award or renewal of contracts. Instead, we hold that Congress intended for the FCPA to apply broadly to payments intended to assist the payor, either directly or indirectly, in obtaining or retaining business for some person, and that bribes paid to foreign tax officials to secure illegally reduced customs and tax liability constitute a type of payment that can fall within this broad coverage. In 1977, Congress was motivated to prohibit rampant foreign bribery by domestic business entities, but nevertheless understood the pragmatic need to exclude innocuous grease payments from the scope of its proposals. The FCPA's legislative history instructs that Congress was concerned about both the kind of bribery that leads to discrete contractual arrangements and the kind that more generally helps a domestic payor obtain or retain business for some person in a foreign country; and that Congress was aware that this type includes illicit payments made to officials to obtain favorable but unlawful tax treatment.

Reversed and *remanded* in favor of the United States.

CRITICAL THINKING ABOUT THE LAW

Congressional intent is a guiding principle of judicial interpretation. Here the court is asked to make a judgment about the scope of legislation. They answer that question by examining the purpose of the law and the applicability of that purpose to the facts of this case.

1. What is the difference between bribery and "innocuous grease payments"?

   Clue: For a payment to be innocuous, what effects would it have had to avoid?

2. What ethical norm is advanced by enforcing the statute in this case?

   Clue: How is fairness affected by permitting a firm to escape some of its tax liability?

COMPARATIVE LAW CORNER

Corruption generally discourages foreign investment according to data published by Transparency International in its annual Corruption Perception Index (CPI). The CPI is determined by an annual survey of business people, academicians, and analysts in each of 91 countries. The CPI in its latest published data see Nigeria, Uganda, Indonesia, Bolivia, Kenya, Cameroon, and Russia as countries most prone to corruption. Finland, Denmark, New Zealand, Iceland, Singapore, Sweden, and Canada are shown as having the least corruption. The United States ranks 17th.[a]

When doing business with countries where corruption is rampant (e.g., U.S. company trading oil equipment with Nigeria), it would be careful to learn what "facilitating payments" are lawful under U.S. law (FCPA), and what payments are legal, if there exists such statutes, under host-country laws (e.g., Nigeria). In countries that have similar statutes, it is also significant to check with counsel to determine exceptions to host-countries' laws (e.g., when a U.S. company is trading oil equipment with Canada), even when laws seem very similar. In both cases, one should not presume that either Nigeria or Canada's laws are similar with regard to "facilitating payments" (grease payment) as set out in the FCPA.

---

[a]Corruption Perception Index, 2002, from **www.transparency.org**. © 2002 Transparency International e.V.

LEGAL DIMENSIONS

Business managers have to be guided both by the national legal system of their own country and the host country and by international law when they venture into foreign territory.

National Legal Systems. When deciding whether to do business in a certain country, business managers are advised to learn about the legal system of that country and its potential impact in such areas as contracts, investment, and corporate law. The five major families of law are (1) common law, (2) Romano-Germanic civil law, (3) Islamic law, (4) socialist law, and (5) Hindu law (Table 1).

TABLE 1 FAMILIES OF NATIONAL LAW AND HOW THEY AFFECT INTERNATIONAL BUSINESS

Family	Characteristics
Common law	Primary reliance is on case law and precedent instead of statutory law. Courts can declare statutory law unconstitutional.
Romano-Germanic Civil law	Primary reliance is on codes and statutory law rather than case law. In general, the high court cannot declare laws of parliament unconstitutional (an exception is the German Constitutional Court).
Islamic law	Derived from the Shari'a, a code of rules designed to govern the daily lives of all Muslims.
Socialist law	Based on the teachings of Karl Marx. No private property is recognized. Law encourages the collectivization of property and the means of production and seeks to guarantee national security. According to classical Marxist theory, both the law and the state will fade away as people are better educated to socialism and advance toward the ultimate stage of pure communism.
Hindu law	Derived from the Sastras. Hindu law governs the behavior of people in each caste (hereditary categories that restrict members' occupations and social associations). Primarily concerned with family matters and succession. Has been codified into India's national legal system.

86

The common-law family is most familiar to companies doing business in the United States, England, and 26 former British colonies. The source of law is primarily case law, and decisions rely heavily on case precedents. As statutory law has become more prominent in common-law countries, the courts' interpretation of laws made by legislative bodies and of regulations set forth by administrative agencies has substantially increased the body of common law.

Countries that follow the Romano-Germanic civil law (e.g., France, Germany, and Sweden) organize their legal systems around legal codes rather than around cases, regulations, and precedents, as do common-law countries. Thus, judges in civil-law countries of Europe, Latin America, and Asia resolve disputes primarily by reference to general provisions of codes and secondarily by reference to statutes passed by legislative bodies. As the body of written opinions in civil-law countries grows, and as they adopt computer-based case and statutory systems such as Westlaw and Lexis, however, the highest courts in these countries are taking greater note of case law in their decisions. Civil-law systems tend to put great emphasis on private law, that is, law that governs relationships between individuals and corporations or between individuals. Examples are the law of obligations, which includes common-law contracts, torts, and creditor–debtor relationships. In contrast to common-law systems, civil-law systems have an inferior public law: This is a law that governs the relationships between individuals and the state. In fact, their jurists are not extensively trained in such areas as criminal, administrative, and labor law.[4]

More than 600 million Muslims in approximately 30 countries that are predominantly Muslim, as well as many more Muslims living in countries where Islam is a minority religion, are governed by Islamic law.[5] In many countries, Islamic law, as encoded in the Shari'a, exists alongside the secular law. In nations that have adopted Islamic law as their dominant legal system (e.g., Saudi Arabia), citizens must obey the Shari'a, and anyone who transgresses its rules is punished by a court. International business transactions are affected in many ways by Islamic law. For example, earning interest on money is forbidden, though a way around this stricture can be found by setting up Islamic banks that, in lieu of paying interest on accounts, pay each depositor a share of the profits made by the bank.

Socialist-law systems are based on the teachings of Karl Marx and Vladimir Lenin (who was, incidentally, a lawyer). Right after the Bolshevik Revolution of 1917 in Russia, the Czarist legal system, which was based on the Romano-Germanic civil law, was replaced by a legal system consisting of People's Courts staffed by members of the Communist Party and peasant workers. By the early 1930s, this system had been replaced by a formal legal system with civil and criminal codes that has lasted to this day. The major goals of the Soviet legal system were to (1) encourage collectivization of the economy; (2) educate the masses as to the wisdom of socialist law; and (3) maintain national security.[6] Most property belonged to the state, particularly industrial and agricultural property. Personal (not private) property existed, but it could be used only for the satisfaction and needs of the individual, not for profit—which was referred to as "speculation" and was in violation of socialist law. Personal ownership ended either with the death of the individual or with revocation of the legal use and

---

[4] See R. Davids and J. Brierly, *Major Legal Systems in the World Today* (Free Press, 1988).

[5] *Id.* at 437–38.

[6] *Id.* at 437–38.

enjoyment of the property. Socialist law is designed to preserve the authority of the state over agricultural land and all means of production. It is still enforced in North Korea, Cuba, and to some degree, Libya, but the countries that made up the old Soviet Union and the East European bloc have been moving toward Romano-Germanic civil-law systems and private-market economies in the last decade.

Hindu law, called Dharmasastra, is linked to the revelations of the Vedas, a collection of Indian religious songs and prayers believed to have been written between 100 B.C. and A.D. 300 or 400.[7] It is both personal and religious. Hindus are divided into social categories called castes, and the rules governing their behavior are set out in texts known as Sastras. The primary concerns of Hindu law are family matters and property succession. Four-fifths of all Hindus live in India; most of the remaining Hindus are spread throughout Southeast Asia and Africa, with smaller numbers living in Europe and the Americas. After gaining independence from England in 1950, India codified Hindu law. Today it plays a prominent role in Indian law alongside secular statutory law, which, especially in the areas of business and trade, uses legal terminology and concepts derived from common law. Both the Indian criminal and civil codes strongly reflect the British common-law tradition.[8] The civil code is particularly important today when issues involving outsourcing to and from India are discussed by multinationals and governments involved.

public international law Law that governs the relationships between nation-states.

private international law Law that governs the relationships between private parties involved in international transactions. Includes international business law.

International Law. The law that governs the relationships between nation-states is known as **public international law. Private international law** governs the relationships between private parties involved in transactions across national borders. In most cases, the parties negotiate between themselves and set out their agreements in a written document. In some cases, however, nation-states subsidize the private parties or are signatories to the agreements negotiated by those parties. In such instances, the distinction between private and public international law is blurred.

The sources of international law can be found in (1) custom; (2) treaties between nations, particularly treaties of friendship and commerce; (3) judicial decisions of international courts such as the International Court of Justice; (4) decision of national and regional courts such as the U.S. Supreme Court, the London Commercial Court, and the European Court of Justice; (5) scholarly writings; and (6) international organizations. These sources will be discussed throughout this text.

International business law includes laws governing (1) exit visas and work permits; (2) tax and antitrust matters and contracts; (3) patents, trademarks, and copyrights; (4) bilateral treaties of commerce and friendship between nations and multilateral treaties of commerce such as the North American Free Trade Agreement (NAFTA), the European Union (EU), and the World Trade Organization (WTO). All will be explored later in this chapter.

The U.S. Constitution grants the president the power to enter into treaties with the advice and consent of the U.S. Senate (two-thirds must concur). The Constitution prohibits the state from entering into "any Treaty, Alliance or Conferedation."[9] The U.S. Supreme Court, however, has allowed the states to enter

---

[7] *Id.* at 176–79.

[8] *Id.* at 468–71.

[9] U.S. Const. art 1, §10.

into treaties that "do not encrouch upon or impair the supremacy of the United States."[10] The states' power to enter into treaties is very limited as indicated by the case below. This issue has become of some significance in today's world as states are presently seeking to enter trade and other agreements independent of the federal government.

CASE 2

Crosby v. National Foreign Trade Council
Supreme Court of the United States
530 U.S. 363 (2000)

In 1996, the Commonwealth of Massachusetts passed a law barring governmental entities in Massachusetts from buying goods or services from companies doing business with Burma (Myanmar). Subsequently, the U.S. Congress enacted federal legislation imposing mandatory and conditional sanctions on Burma. The Massachusetts law was inconsistent with the new federal legislation. The National Foreign Trade Council sued on behalf of its several members, claiming that the Massachusetts law unconstitutionally infringed on federal foreign affairs power, violated the Foreign Commerce Clause of the U.S. Constitution, and was preempted by the subsequent federal legislation. The district and appeals courts ruled in favor of the council, and the Common wealth appealed.

Justice Souter

The Massachusetts law is preempted, and its application is unconstitutional under the Supremacy Clause of the U.S. Constitution. State law must yield to a congressional act if Congress intends to occupy the field, or to the extent of any conflict with a federal statute. This is the case even where the relevant congressional act lacks an express preemption provision. This Court will find preemption where it is impossible for a private party to comply with both state and federal law and where the state law is an obstacle to the accomplishment and execution of Congress's full purposes and objectives. In this case, the state act is an obstacle to the federal act's delegation of discretion to the president of the United States to control economic sanctions against Burma. Within the sphere defined by Congress, the statute has given the President as much discretion to exercise economic leverage against Burma, with an eye toward national security, as law permits. It is implausible to think that Congress would have gone to such lengths to empower the President had it been willing to compromise his effectiveness by allowing state or local ordinances to blunt the consequences of his actions—exactly the effect of the state act.

In addition, the Massachusetts law interferes with Congress's intention to limit economic pressure against the Burmese Government to a specific range . . . Finally, the Massachusetts law conflicts with the President's authority to speak for the United States among the world's nations to develop a comprehensive, multilateral Burma strategy. In this respect, the state act undermines the President's capacity for effective diplomacy.

The Court affirmed the lower courts in favor of the defendant, National Foreign Trade Council.

Methods of Engaging in International Business

For purposes of this chapter, methods of engaging in international business are classified as (1) trade, (2) international licensing and franchising, and (3) foreign direct investment.

TRADE

We define **international trade** generally as exporting goods and services from a country and importing the same into a country. There are two traditional theories

international trade The export of goods and services from a country and the import of goods and services into a country.

---

[10] *Virginia v. Tennessee* 148 U.S. 503, 518 (1893).

LINKING LAW AND BUSINESS

Global Business

Your management class may have discussed the growing trend of globalization. One level of an organization's involvement in the international arena is the multinational corporation. There are three basic types of employees in multinational corporations: (1) expatriates—employees living and working in a country where they are not citizens; (2) host-country nationals—employees who live and work in a country where the international organization is headquartered; (3) third-country nationals—employees who are expatriates in a country (working in one country and having citizenship in another), while the international organization is located in another country. Typically, organizations with a global focus employ workers from all three categories. The use of host-country nationals, however, is increasing, considering the cost of training and relocating expatriates and third-country nationals. By hiring more host-country nationals, managers may spend less time and money training employees to adapt to new cultures, languages, and laws in foreign countries. In addition, managers may avoid potential problems related to sending employees to work in countries where they do not have citizenship or understand the culture; thus, managers may still obtain organizational objectives through cheaper and respectable means by hiring a greater number of host-country nationals.

Source: S. Certo, *Modern Management* (Upper Saddle River, NJ: Prentice Hall, 2000), pp. 78, 84–85.

of trade relationships. The theory of absolute advantage, which is the older theory, states that an individual nation should concentrate on exporting the goods that it can produce most efficiently. For example, Sri Lanka (formerly Ceylon) produces tea more efficiently than most countries can and, thus, any surplus in Sri Lanka's tea production should be exported to countries that produce tea less efficiently. The theory of comparative advantage arose out of the realization that a country did not have to have an absolute advantage in producing a good in order to export it efficiently; rather, it would contribute to global efficiency if it produced specialized products simply more efficiently than others did. To illustrate this concept, let's assume that the best attorney in a small town is also the best legal secretary. Because this person can make more money as an attorney, it would be more efficient for her to devote her energy to working as a lawyer and to hire a legal secretary. Similarly, let's assume that the United States can produce both wheat and tea more efficiently than Sri Lanka can. Thus, the United States has an absolute advantage in its trade with Sri Lanka. Let us further assume that U.S. wheat production is comparatively greater than U.S. tea production vis-á-vis Sri Lanka. That is, by using the same amount of resources, the United States can produce two and a half times as much wheat but only twice as much tea as Sri Lanka. The United States then has a comparative advantage in wheat over tea.[11]

In this simplified example, we made several assumptions: that there were only two countries and two commodities involved; that transport costs in the two countries were about the same; that efficiency was the sole objective; and that political factors were not significant. In international trade, things are far more complex. There are many nations and innumerable products involved, and political factors are often more potent than economic considerations.

---

[11] J. Daniels, L. Radebaugh, and D. Sullivan, *International Business: Environments and Operations* 148, 149, 10th ed. (Upper Saddle River, NJ: Pearson Prentice Hall, 2004).

Trade is generally considered to be the least risky means of doing international business, because it demands little involvement with a foreign buyer or seller. For small and middle-sized firms, the first step toward involvement in international business is generally to hire an export management company, which is a company licensed to operate as the representative of many manufacturers with exportable products. These management companies are privately owned by citizens of various nation-states and have long-standing links to importers in many countries. They provide exporting firms with market research, identify potential buyers, and assist the firms in negotiating contracts.

Export trading companies, which are governed by the Export Trading Act in the United States, comprise those manufacturers and banks that either buy the products of a small business and resell them in another country or sell products of several companies on a commission basis. Small and medium-sized exporting companies may also choose to retain foreign distributors, which purchase imported goods at a discount and resell them in the foreign or host country. Once a company has had some experience selling in other countries, it may decide to retain a foreign sales representative. Sales representatives differ from foreign distributors in that they do not take title to the goods being exported. Rather, they usually maintain a principal–agency relationship with the exporter.

INTERNATIONAL LICENSING AND FRANCHISING

International licensing is a contractual agreement by which a company (licensor) makes its trade secrets, trademarks, patents, or copyrights (intellectual property) available to a foreign individual or company (licensee) in return either for royalties or for other compensation based on the volume of goods sold or a lump sum. All licensing agreements are subject to restrictions of the host country, which may include demands that its nationals be trained for management positions in the licensee company, that the host government receive a percentage of the gross profits, and that licensor technology be made available to all host-country nationals. Licensing agreements can differ vastly from country to country.

International franchising permits a licensee of a trademark to market the licensor's goods or services in a particular nation (e.g., Kentucky Fried Chicken franchises in China). Often companies franchise their trademark to avoid a nation-state's restrictions on foreign direct investment. Also, political instability is less likely to be a threat to investment when a local franchisee is running the business. Companies considering entering into an international franchise agreement should investigate bilateral treaties of friendship and commerce between the franchisor's nation and the franchisee's nation, as well as the business laws of the franchisee country.

In some instances, licensing and franchising negotiations are tense and drawn out because businesses in many industrialized nations are intent on protecting their intellectual property against "piracy" or are adamant about getting assurances that franchising agreements will be honored. These are major legitimate concerns. For example, between 1994 and 1999, the United States threatened to impose sanctions against China because of that nation's sale of pirated U.S. goods as well as its failure to comply with international franchising requirements. a series of last-minute agreements encouraged by Chinese and U.S. businesses averted the sanctions, which would have proved expensive for private and public parties in both countries. By the year 2000, the Congress and the president of the United States granted normal trade relations with China and left

international licensing
A contractual agreement by which a company (licensor) makes its intellectual property available to a foreign individual or company (licensee) for payment.

international franchising
A contractual agreement whereby a company (licensor) permits another company (licensee) to market its trademarked goods or services in a particular nation.

open the opportunity for the latter to join the WTO.[12] In June 2001, with a China–U.S. agreement on agriculture, a major barrier to entrance was overcome.

In November 2001, China and Taiwan entered the WTO after considerable negotiations between the western nations over many issues. For example, at China's insistence, all membership documents refer to China as the People's Republic of China, while Taiwan will be referred to as the Separate Customs Territory of Taiwan, Penghu, Kinmen, and Matsu. The latter three islands are under the control of Taiwan. Taiwan is not recognized as an independent nation but as a territory belonging to the mainland.

FOREIGN DIRECT INVESTMENT

foreign subsidiary A company that is wholly or partially owned and controlled by a company based in another country.

Direct investment in foreign nations is usually undertaken only by established multinational corporations. Foreign direct investment may take one of two forms: The multinational either creates a wholly or partially owned and controlled **foreign subsidiary** in the host country or enters into a joint venture with an individual, corporation, or government agency of the host country. In both cases, the risk for the investing company is greater than is the risk in international trade and international franchising and licensing because serious amounts of capital are flowing to the host country that are subject to its government's restrictions and its domestic law.

Large multinationals choose to create foreign subsidiaries for several reasons: (1) to expand their foreign markets, (2) to acquire foreign resources, including raw materials, (3) to improve their production efficiency, (4) to acquire knowledge, and (5) to be closer to their customers and competitors. Rarely do all these reasons pertain in a single instance. For example, U.S. companies have set up foreign subsidiaries in Mexico, Western Europe, Brazil, and India for quite different reasons. Mexico provided cheap labor and a location close to customers and suppliers for U.S. automobile manufacturers. In the case of Western Europe, the impetus was both a threat and an opportunity. The member nations of the EU have been moving to eliminate all trade barriers among themselves, although at the same time imposing stiffer tariffs on goods and services imported from non-EU countries. U.S. companies have been rushing to establish foreign subsidiaries in EU countries, not only to avoid being shut out of this huge lucrative market but also to expand sales among its approximately 380 million people. Brazil is not only the largest potential market in Latin America, but it also offers low labor and transportation costs, making it ideal for U.S. automakers desiring to export to neighboring Latin American countries. Union Carbide, Inc., a producer of chemicals and plastics, decided to establish a subsidiary in India, where cheap labor (including highly skilled chemists and engineers) and low-cost transportation enabled the parent company to produce various materials cheaply and, thus, boost its bottom line. The Indian subsidiary turned out to be a very expensive investment for Union Carbide after the Bhopal disaster. The civil suit that resulted illustrates an issue that is often overlooked by managers of multinationals when setting up subsidiaries in foreign nation-states: Should a parent corporation be held liable for the activities of its foreign subsidiary? Although the case presented here is framed in a jurisdictional context (whether a U.S. court or an Indian court should hear the suit), you should bear in mind the issue of corporate parent liability as you read it.

---

[12] See *Backers Hope China Pact Will Promote Reform*, USA Today 10 (Sept. 20, 2000).

CASE 3

In Re Union Carbide Corporation Gas Plant Disaster at Bhopal, India, in December, 1984 v. Union Carbide Corporation
United States Court of Appeals 809 F.2d 195 (2d Cir. 1987)

The Government of India (GOI) and several private class action plaintiffs (Indian citizens) sued Union Carbide India Limited (UCIL) and the parent corporation, Union Carbide Corporation (UCC), for over $1 billion after a disaster at a chemical plant operated by UCIL in 1984. There was a leak of the lethal gas methylisocyanate from the plant on the night of December 2, 1984. The deadly chemicals were blown by wind over the adjacent city of Bhopal, resulting in the deaths of more than 2,000 persons and the injury of more than another 200,000 persons. UCIL is incorporated under the laws of India; 50.9 percent of the stock is owned by UCC, 22 percent is owned or controlled by the government of India, and the balance is owned by 23,500 Indian citizens. The federal district court (Judge Keenan) granted UCC's motion to dismiss the plaintiffs' action on the grounds that Indian courts, not U.S. courts, were the appropriate forum for the suit. The plaintiffs appealed this decision.

Judge Mansfield

As the district court found, the record shows that the private interests of the respective parties weigh heavily in favor of dismissal on grounds of *forum non conveniens*. The many witnesses and sources of proof are almost entirely located in India, where the accident occurred, and could not be compelled to appear for trial in the United States. The Bhopal plant at the time of the accident was operated by some 193 Indian nationals, including the managers of seven operating units employed by the Agricultural Products Division of UCIL, who reported to Indian Works Managers in Bhopal. The plant was maintained by seven functional departments employing over 200 more Indian nationals. UCIL kept daily, weekly, and monthly records of plant operations and records of maintenance, as well as records of the plant's Quality Control, Purchasing, and Stores branches, all operated by Indian employees. The great majority of documents bearing on the design, safety, start-up, and operation of the plant, as well as the safety training of the plant's employees, is located in India. Proof to be offered at trial would be derived from interviews of these witnesses in India and study of the records located there to determine whether the accident was caused by negligence on the part of the management or employees in the operation of the plant, by fault in its design, or by sabotage. In short, India has greater ease of access to the proof than does the United States.

The plaintiffs seek to prove that the accident was caused by negligence on the part of UCC in originally contributing to the design of the plant and its provision for storage of excessive amounts of the gas at the plant. As Judge Keenan found, however, UCC's participation was limited and its involvement in plant operations terminated long before the accident. Under 1973 agreements negotiated at arm's length with UCIL, UCC did provide a summary "process design package" for construction of the plant and the services of some of its technicians to monitor the progress of UCIL in detailing the design and erecting the plant. However, the UOI controlled the terms of the agreements and precluded UCC from exercising any authority to "detail design, erect and commission the plant," which was done independently over the period from 1972 to 1980 by UCIL process design engineers who supervised, among many others, some 55 to 60 Indian engineers employed by the Bombay engineering firm of Humphreys and Glasgow. The preliminary process design information furnished by UCC could not have been used to construct the plant. Construction required the detailed process design and engineering data prepared by hundreds of Indian engineers, process designers, and subcontractors. During the ten years spent constructing the plant, the design and configuration underwent many changes.

In short, the plant has been constructed and managed by Indians in India. No Americans were employed at the plant at the time of the accident. In the five years from 1980 to 1984, although more than 1,000 Indians were employed at the plant, only one American was employed there and he left in 1982. No Americans visited the plant for more than one year prior to the accident, and during the five-year period before the accident the communications between the plant and the United States were almost nonexistent.

The vast majority of material witnesses and documentary proof bearing on causation of and liability for the accident is located in India, not the United States, and would be more accessible to an Indian court than to a United States court. The records are almost entirely in Hindi or other Indian languages, understandable to an Indian court without translation. The witnesses for the most part do not speak English but Indian languages understood by an Indian court but not by an American court. These witnesses could be required to appear in an Indian court but not in a court of the United States. India's interest is increased by the fact that it has for years treated UCIL as an

Indian national, subjecting it to intensive regulations and governmental supervision of the construction, development, and operation of the Bhopal plant, its emissions, water and air pollution, and safety precautions. Numerous Indian government officials have regularly conducted on-site inspections of the plant and approved its machinery and equipment, including its facilities for storage of the lethal methylisocyanate gas that escaped and caused the disaster giving rise to the claims. Thus India has considered the plant to be an Indian one and the disaster to be an Indian problem. It therefore has a deep interest in ensuring compliance with its safety standards.

Affirmed in favor of Defendant, Union Carbide.

COMMENT: The Bhopal victims filed their claims in U.S. courts against UCC because the parent company had more money than the subsidiary (UCIL). Also, suing the parent made it more likely that the case would be heard in U.S. courts, which are considered to be far better forums for winning damages in personal injury actions than Indian courts are. After the lawsuits were removed to an Indian court, UCC agreed to pay $470 million to the Bhopal disaster victims. Union Carbide's stock substantially decreased in value, and UCC was threatened by a takeover (the attempt was thwarted in 1985). More than half of UCC was subsequently sold or spun off, including the Indian subsidiary (UCIL). In 1989, the Indian Supreme Court ordered UCC to pay $470 million to compensate Bhopal victims. Criminal charges against the company and its officials were dropped. About 12,000 people worked for UCC in 1995, in contrast to the 110,000 employed by the company a decade earlier. In 1998, Dow Chemical acquired Union Carbide. By 2007 there had been no cleanup to the area where the explosion took place 23 years earlier.

CRITICAL THINKING ABOUT THE LAW

Please refer to Case 3 and consider the following questions:

1. Highlight the importance of facts in shaping a judicial opinion by writing an imaginary letter that, had it been introduced as evidence, would have greatly distressed Union Carbide Corporation (UCC).

   Clue: Review the first part of the decision, in which Judge Mansfield discussed the extent of UCC's involvement in the plant where the accident occurred. What facts would counter his statement that the parent company had only "limited" involvement?

2. Suppose a U.S. plant exploded, resulting in extensive deaths in the United States. Further, suppose that all the engineers who built the plant wrote and spoke German only. Could Judge Mansfield's decision be used as an analogy to seek dismissal of a negligence suit against the owners of the plant?

3. What additional information, were it to surface, would strengthen Union Carbide's request for a dismissal of the case described?

   Clue: Notice the wide assortment of facts that Judge Mansfield organized to support his decision.

Joint ventures, which involve a relationship between two or more corporations or between a foreign multinational and an agency of a host-country government or a host-country national, are usually set up for a specific undertaking over a limited period of time. Many developing countries (such as China) allow foreign investment only in the form of a joint venture between host-country nationals and the multinationals. Recently, there have been three-way joint ventures among United States–based multinationals (e.g., automobile companies such as Chrysler and General Motors), Japanese multinationals (e.g., Mitsubishi and Honda), and Chinese government agencies and Chinese nationals. Joint ventures are also used in host countries with fewer restrictions on foreign investment, often to spread the risk or to amass required investment sums that are too large for one corporation to raise by itself. Some of these joint ventures are private associations, with no host-government involvement.

joint venture Relationship between two or more persons or corporations, or an association between a foreign multinational and an agency of the host government or a host-country national, set up for a specific business undertaking or a limited time period.

Risks of Engaging in International Business

Unlike doing business in one's own country, the "rules of the game" are not always clear when engaging in business in a foreign country, particularly in what we have classified as middle- and low-income economies. Here we set out the four primary risks that managers engaged in international business may face: (1) expropriation of private property by the host foreign nation, (2) the application of the sovereign immunity doctrine and the act-of-state doctrine to disputes between foreign states and U.S. firms, (3) export and import controls, and (4) currency controls and fluctuations in currency values.

EXPROPRIATION OF PRIVATE PROPERTY

Expropriation—the taking of private property by a host-country government either for political or for economic reasons—is one of the greatest risks companies take when they engage in international business. Thus, it is essential for business managers to investigate the recent behavior of host-country government officials, particularly in countries that are moving from a centrally planned economy toward one that is market oriented (e.g., Russia and Eastern European nations). One method of limiting risk in politically unstable countries is to concentrate on exports and imports (trade) and licensing and franchising. Another method is to take advantage of the low-cost insurance against expropriation offered by the Overseas Private Investment Corporation (OPIC). If a U.S. plant or other project is insured by OPIC and is expropriated, the U.S. firm receives compensation in return for assigning to OPIC the firm's claim against the host-country government.

expropriation The taking of private property by a host-country government for political or economic reasons.

Bilateral investment treaties (BITs), which are negotiated between two governments, obligate the host government to show fair and nondiscriminatory treatment to investors from the other country. The BIT also includes a promise of prompt, adequate, and effective compensation in the event of expropriation or nationalization.

bilateral investment treaty Treaty between two parties to outline conditions for investment in either country.

SOVEREIGN IMMUNITY DOCTRINE

Another risk for companies engaged in international business is the **sovereign immunity doctrine,** which allows a government expropriating foreign-owned private property to claim that it is immune from the jurisdiction of courts in the owner's country because it is a government rather than a private sector entity.

sovereign immunity doctrine States that a government expropriating foreign-owned private property is immune from the jurisdiction of courts in the owner's country.

In these cases, the company whose property was expropriated often receives nothing because it cannot press its claims in its own country's courts, and courts in the host country are seldom amenable to such claims.

The sovereign immunity doctrine has been a highly controversial issue between the United States and certain foreign governments in developing nations. To give some protection to foreign businesses without impinging on the legitimate rights of other governments, the U.S. Congress in 1976 enacted the Foreign Sovereign Immunities Act (FSIA), which shields foreign governments from U.S. judicial review of their public, but not their private, acts. The FSIA grants foreign nations immunity from judicial review by U.S. courts unless they meet one of the FSIA's private exceptions. One such exception is the foreign government's involvement in commercial activity. Case 4 clarifies the U.S. Supreme Court's definition of commercial activity under the FSIA. Note how the Court emphasizes the nature of the Nigerian government's action by asking whether it is the type of action a private party would engage in.

CASE 4

Keller v. Central Bank of Nigeria
United States Court of Appeals
277 F. 3d. 811 (6th Cir. 2002)

Prince Arthur Ossai, a government official in Nigeria, entered into a contract with Henry Keller (plaintiff), a sales representative for H.K. Enterprises, Inc., a Michigan-based manufacturer of medical equipment. They agreed that among other things, Ossai would have exclusive distribution right to sell H.K. products in Nigeria, which would buy $4.1 million of H.K. equipment for $6.63 million, plus a $7.65 million "licensing fee." Ossai said that, first, $25.5 million on deposit in the Central Bank of Nigeria (CBN) had to be transferred into an account set up by Keller. CBN employees charged Keller $28,950 in fees for the transaction, but the funds were never transferred. Keller and H.K. filed a suit in a federal district court against the CBN and others, asserting in part a claim under the Racketeer Influenced and Corrupt Organizations Act (RICO). The defendants filed a motion to dismiss under the Foreign Sovereign Immunities Act (FSIA). The court denied the motion, concluding that the claim fell within the FSIA's "commercial activity" exception. The defendants appealed to the U.S. Court of Appeals for the Sixth Circuit.

Justice Norris

[The defendants] claim that the illegality of the deal alleged precludes a finding that it is a commercial activity. The FSIA defines "commercial activity" as "either a regular course of commercial conduct or a particular commercial transaction or act." The commercial character of an activity shall be determined by reference to the nature of the course of conduct or particular transaction or act, rather than by reference to its purpose. [W]hen a foreign government acts, not as regulator of a market, but in the manner of a private player within it, the foreign sovereign's actions are commercial within the meaning of the FSIA.

In the instant case, the conduct was a deal to license and sell medical equipment, a type of activity done by private parties and not a "market regulator" function. The district court correctly concluded that this was a commercial activity, and that any fraud and bribery involved did not render the plan non-commercial.

Defendants claim that plaintiffs cannot establish another element of the commercial activity exception, namely, that there was a direct effect in the United States. [A]n effect is "direct" if it follows as an immediate consequence of the defendant's activity.

In this case, defendants agreed to pay but failed to transmit the promised funds to an account in a Cleveland bank. Other courts have found a direct effect when a defendant agrees to pay funds to an account in the United States and then fails to do so. The district court in the instant case correctly concluded, in accord with the other [courts], that defendant's failure to pay promised funds to a Cleveland account constituted a direct effect in the United States.

Affirmed for Plaintiff.

CRITICAL THINKING ABOUT THE LAW

Context plays a vital role in any legal decision. The existence or nonexistence of certain events directly affects the court's verdict. In Case 4, the court applies the regulations of FSIA to the specific facts of the case. If certain facts exist, the federal statute protects the plaintiff, and the court should appropriately reject the defendant's motion to dismiss. Otherwise, the CBN is immune, and the statute does not protect the plaintiff.

Understanding the facts is the starting point for legal analysis. The following questions encourage you to consider the significance of the facts in Case 4.

1. What are the facts that are critical in the court's ruling in favor of the plaintiff?

   Clue: Reread the introductory paragraph.

2. Look at the facts you found. To illustrate the importance of context, which fact, if it had not been included in the case, might have resulted in the court's granting the defendant's motion to dismiss?

   Clue: Find the elements of the federal statute that the judge discusses and use these elements as a guide to highlight the most significant facts.

ACT-OF-STATE DOCTRINE

The **act-of-state doctrine** holds that each sovereign nation is bound to respect the independence of every other sovereign state and that the courts of one nation will not sit in judgment on the acts of the courts of another nation done within that nation's own sovereign territory. This doctrine, together with the sovereign immunity doctrine, substantially increases the risk of doing business in a foreign country. Like the sovereign immunity doctrine, the act-of-state doctrine includes some court-ordered exceptions, such as when the foreign government is acting in a commercial capacity or when it seeks to repudiate a commercial obligation.

Congress made it clear in 1964 that the act-of-state doctrine shall not be applied in cases in which property is confiscated in violation of international law, unless the president of the United States decides that the federal courts should apply it. As Case 5 demonstrates, the plaintiff has the burden of proving that the doctrine should not apply—that is, the courts should sit in judgment of public acts of a foreign government, in this case, a former government.

act-of-state doctrine States that each sovereign nation is bound to respect the independence of every other sovereign national and that the courts of one nation will not sit in judgment on the acts of the courts of another nation.

CASE 5

Republic of the Philippines v. Ferdinand E. Marcos
United States Circuit Court of Appeals
862 F.2d 1355 (9th Cir. 1988)

The Republic of the Philippines (plaintiff) brought a civil suit against its former president, Ferdinand Marcos, and his wife, Imelda (defendants), asserting claims under the Racketeer Influenced Corrupt Organizations Act (RICO) and other applicable U.S. law. The Republic alleges that the Marcoses (and other defendants) arranged for investments in real estate in Beverly Hills, California, of $4 million fraudulently

obtained by the Marcoses; that the Marcoses arranged for the creation of two bank accounts in the name of Imelda Marcos at Lloyds Bank of California totaling over $800,000, also fraudulently obtained by the Marcoses; and that the Marcoses transported into Hawaii money, jewels, and other property worth over $7 million, also fraudulently obtained by them. The key to the Republic's entire case is the allegation that the

Marcoses stole public money. The federal district court entered a preliminary injunction enjoining the Marcoses from disposing of any of their assets except to pay attorneys and their living expenses. The Marcoses appealed.

Justice Noonan

Before determining whether issuance of an injunction was appropriate we must consider two defenses which, if accepted, would block trial of the case the Marcoses maintain. First, that their acts are insulated because they were acts of state not reviewable by our courts, and second, that any adjudication of these acts would involve the investigation of political questions beyond our court's competence. The classification of certain acts as "acts of state," with the consequence that their validity will be treated as beyond judicial review, is a pragmatic device, not required by the nature of sovereign authority and inconsistently applied in international law. The purpose of the device is to keep the judiciary from embroiling the courts and the country in the affairs of the foreign nation whose acts are challenged. Minimally viewed, the classification keeps a court from making pronouncements on matters over which it has no power, maxmally interpreted, the classification prevents the embarrassment of a court defending a foreign government that is "extant at the time of suit." The "continuing vitality" of the doctrine depends on its capacity to reflect the proper distribution of functions between the judicial and political branches of the government on matters bearing upon foreign relations.

As a practical tool for keeping the judicial branch out of the conduct of foreign affairs, the classification of "act of state" is not a promise to the ruler of any foreign country that his conduct, if challenged by his own country after his fall, may not become the subject of scrutiny in our courts. No estoppel exists insulating a deposed dictator from accounting. No guarantee has been granted that immunity may be acquired by an ex-chief magistrate invoking the magic words "act of state" to cover his or her past performance.

In the instant case the Marcoses offered no evidence whatsoever to support the classification of their acts as acts of state. The burden of proving acts of state rested upon them. They did not undertake the proof.

Bribetaking, theft, embezzlement, extortion, fraud, and conspiracy to do these things are all acts susceptible of concrete proof that need not involve political questions. The court, it is true, may have to determine questions of Philippine law in determining whether a given act was legal or illegal. But questions of foreign law are not beyond the capacity of our courts. The court will be examining the acts of the president of a country whose immediate political heritage is from our own. Although sometimes criticized as a ruler and at times invested with extraordinary power, Ferdinand Marcos does not appear to have had the authority of an absolute autocrat. He was not the state, but the head of the state, bound by the laws that applied to him. Our courts have had no difficulty in distinguishing the legal acts of a deposed ruler from his acts for personal profit that lack a basis in law.

Affirmed for Plaintiff, Republic of the Philippines.

CRITICAL THINKING ABOUT THE LAW

1. At the outset of Case 5, Justice Noonan acknowledges a key ambiguity in this case that will require clarification before announcing his decision. How does that ambiguity affect the reasoning?

   Clue: Notice the key concept in the first of the two defenses used by the Marcoses.

2. What behavior of the Marcoses made it highly unlikely that the first defense would be effective?

   Clue: Review Justice Noonan's rationale for not honoring the defense.

3. What ethical norm is implicit in the Marcoses' struggle against the preliminary injunction?

   Clue: Look back at the discussion of the ethical norms and eliminate those that seem inconsistent with the Marcoses' behavior and interests.

EXPORT AND IMPORT CONTROLS

Export Controls. Export controls are usually applied by governments to militarily sensitive goods (e.g., computer hardware and software) to prevent unfriendly nations from obtaining these goods. In the United States, the Department of State, the Department of Commerce, and the Defense Department bear responsibility, under the Export Administration Act and the Arms Export Control Act, for authorizing the export of sensitive technology. Both criminal and administrative sanctions may be imposed on corporations and individuals who violate these laws.

Export controls often prevent U.S. companies from living up to negotiated contracts. Thus, they can damage the ability of U.S. firms to do business abroad.

Import Controls. Nations often set up import barriers to prevent foreign companies from destroying home industries. Two such controls are tariffs and quotas. For example, the United States has sought historically to protect its domestic automobile and textile industries, agriculture, and intellectual property (copyrights, patents, trademarks, and trade secrets). Intellectual property has become an extremely important U.S. export in recent years, and Washington has grown more determined than ever to prevent its being pirated. After several years of frustrating negotiations with the People's Republic of China, the U.S. government decided to threaten imposition of 100 percent tariffs on approximately $1 billion of Chinese imports in 1995, and again in 1996 and 1997. In retaliation, the Chinese government has threatened several times to impose import controls on many U.S. goods. Washington took action only after documenting that hundreds of millions of dollars' worth of "pirated" computerized software (including videodiscs, law books, and movies) was being produced for sale within China and for export to Southeast Asian nations in violation of the intellectual property laws of both China and the United States, as well as international law. The documentation showed that 29 factories owned by the state of Communist Party officials were producing pirated goods. A last-minute settlement in which the Chinese government pledged to honor intellectual property rights prevented a trade war that would have had bad implications for workers in import–export industries in both countries. American consumers also would have suffered because Chinese imports would have been twice as expensive had the 100 percent tariff taken effect—though the effect on consumers would have been offset by an increase in imports of the affected goods from other foreign countries (e.g., English and Japanese bikes would have replaced Chinese bikes in demand).

Another form of import control is the imposition of antidumping duties by two U.S. agencies, the International Trade Commission (ITC) and the International Trade Administration (ITA). The duties are levied against foreign entities that sell the same goods at lower prices in U.S. markets than in their own to obtain a larger share of the U.S. market (i.e., entities that practice "dumping"). An illustration of this conflict is set out in Case 6.

CURRENCY CONTROLS AND FLUCTUATIONS IN CURRENCY VALUES

Currency Controls. Currency controls are usually found in lower-income and lower-middle-income countries where regulations may restrict the conversion of domestic currency into foreign currency (e.g., the U.S. dollar) and the repatriation of foreign currency (e.g., taking U.S. dollars out of India). The latter type of restriction limits foreign multinationals from repatriating more than a certain percentage of the funds they have invested in the host country. Some countries impose an income (withholding) tax on repatriated earnings. Businesspeople need to be aware that currency controls are common both in developing and developed nations and that doing business in countries that impose them requires investment for the long term.

Currency Fluctuations. Doing international business involves the exchange of foreign currencies in the buying and selling of goods and services. Significant fluctuations in currency values, especially if they are unanticipated and, therefore, unprepared for, can present painful problems for businesses. For example, in July through September 1997, the world saw currencies of some Asian countries, vis-à-vis the U.S. dollar, fall dramatically. For many years, these countries had linked their currencies to the dollar. When their currencies were delinked, high growth rates, inflation, and easy bank loans led to financial crises. Some Asian political leaders blamed the crises on monetary speculators, who in turn placed the blame on more-fundamental economic indicators. With the resulting devaluation of currencies, such countries as Malaysia, Thailand, Indonesia, the Philippines, and South Korea saw their exports to developed nations plunge and investors flee. If it took many more ringgits (Malaysia), bahts (Thai), rupiahs (Indonesia), pesos (Philippines), and wons (Korea) per U.S. dollar to recover their return on investments, investors moved their money to other locations (e.g., the United States, Europe, Latin America). In economies that were highly dependent on foreign investment, this strategy led to cutbacks on major projects that would have provided local growth and employment. Most important, in October and November 1997, stock markets fell worldwide for several days, showing the interdependency of national and international institutions. The International Monetary Fund, the U.S. government, and private U.S. commercial banks "pumped" more than $100 million into the five nations mentioned here in January 1998. The opposite effect took place during 2002 to 2004 when the U.S. dollar fell vis-à-vis other currencies. Japan sought to temporarily hold the dollar value stable (Exhibit 1).

EXHIBIT 1

MANIPULATING EXCHANGE RATES

Source: Bloomberg Financial Markets, Ministry of Finance. Market manipulation by Japan, NYT Graphics. Reprinted with permission from the New York Times.

Japan has spent nearly 15 trillion yen, or $142 billion, so far this year to prop up the dollar and protect the value of its exports. Japan's intervention has also had an effect on other currencies, including the euro.

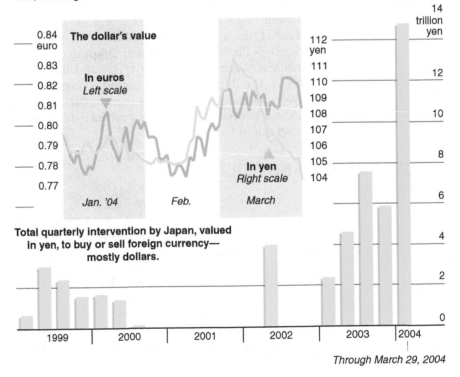

INTERNATIONAL COMMERCE AND CURRENCY MARKETS

As shown in Exhibit 1, exchange rates and currency fluctuations manipulated by the Japanese government cost it nearly ¥15 trillion ($142 billion) in order to prop up the U.S. dollar during the period from January to March 29, 2004. Without the Japanese action, the dollar would have slid lower and Japanese exporters would have had difficulty in selling abroad. Note in the exhibit that near the end of March, Japan decided not to prop up the currency as it had in previous months and the dollar dropped 1.2 percent to a 4-year-low of $104.35 and 0.9 percent against the euro, the latter rising to $1.23. Japan's withdrawal has important implications: (1) Its huge intervention up until the end of March translated into losses for big U.S. banks and hedge funds and lessened performance for Americans' overseas investments; and (2) the market manipulation by Japan ran counter to the traditional supply-and-demand mechanism that Japan and the United States had long agreed to when dealing with the foreign exchange market. By intervening in the market, Japan created an artificial volatility in these markets.

In such a financial crisis, United States and other exporters hedge against exchange risks by contracting with a bank. In return for a fee (based on risk), the bank assumes the risk of currency fluctuation by guaranteeing the exporter a fixed number of dollars in exchange for the foreign currency it receives. **Hedging** is a practice managers involved in international business should be thoroughly knowledgeable about, especially if they are dealing with developing nations where currency fluctuations can be quite erratic.

hedging Exporting companies contract with a bank that guarantees the exporter a fixed number of U.S. dollars in exchange for payment of the goods it receives in a foreign currency. The exporting company pays a fee to the bank. The fee is based on the risk the bank is taking that the foreign currency will fluctuate.

CASE 6

United States v. Haggar Apparel Company
United States Supreme Court
526 U.S. 380 (1999)

Haggar Apparel Company (Haggar) ships a fabric to Mexico with threads and zippers to make pants. A subsidiary has the trousers sewn and permapressed and then shipped back to the United States. Under federal agency regulations, this process of shipping out goods and reshipping back to the United States is exempt from a duty that is charged against other imports. The U.S. Custom Service, however, levied a duty on Haggar pants, under a regulation that makes all permapressing operations to be an additional step in manufacturing, not incidental to the assembly process. Haggar filed a suit against the United States in the U.S. Court of International Trade, seeking a refund of the duty. The court ruled in Haggar's favor, and the U.S. Court of Appeals for the Federal Circuit affirmed. The federal government appealed.

Justice Kennedy

The [Haggar Company] claims the regulation binds the Custom Service when they classify imported merchandise but does not bind the importers. The statutory scheme does not support this limited view of the force and effect of regulation.

Respondent [Haggar] relies on the specific direction to the Secretary to make rules of classification for "the various ports of entry" to argue that the statute authorizes promulgation of regulations that do nothing more than ensure that customs officers in field offices around the country classify goods according to a similar and consistent scheme. The regulations issued under the statute have no bearing, says respondent, on the right of the importer. We disagree. The phrase in question is explained by the simple fact that classification decisions must be made at the port where goods enter. We shall not assume Congress was concerned only to ensure that customs officials at the various ports of entry make uniform decisions but that it had no concern for uniformity once the goods entered the country and judicial proceedings commenced. The tariffs do not mean one thing for customs officers and another for importers. [Emphasis added.] Particularly in light of the fact that the

101

agency utilized the notice-and-comment rulemaking process before issuing the regulations, the argument that they were not intended to be entitled to judicial deference implies a sufficient departure from conventional contemporary administrative practice that we ought not to adopt it absent a different statutory structure and more express language to this effect in the regulations themselves.

Reversed the lower court's decisions in favor of the United States.

Legal and Economic Integration as a Means of Encouraging International Business Activity

Table 2 summarizes a number of groups that have been formed to assist businesspeople in carrying out international transactions. These groups range from the WTO (formerly the General Agreement on Tariffs and Trade), which is attempting to reduce tariff barriers worldwide, to the proposed South American Common Market, which would form a duty-free zone for all the nations of South America. The most ambitious organization is the EU, which is in the process of forming a Western European political and economic community with a single currency and a common external tariff barrier toward nonmembers.

Multinational corporations are learning that doing international business is much easier when they are aware of the worldwide and regional groups listed in the table. We will describe three of these groups: the WTO, the EU, and NAFTA. We chose to examine these three because they represent three different philosophies and structures of legal and economic integration, not because we do not appreciate the major effects of other integrative groups outlined in Table 2.

THE WORLD TRADE ORGANIZATION

Purpose and Terms. On January 1, 1995, the 47-year-old General Agreement on Tariffs and Trade (GATT) organization was replaced by a new umbrella group, the WTO. The WTO has the power to enforce the new trade accord that evolved out of seven rounds of GATT negotiations, with more than 140 nations participating. All 144 signatories to this accord have agreed to reduce their tariffs and subsidies by an average of one-third on most goods over the next decade, agricultural tariffs and subsidies included. Economists estimate that this trade pact will result in tariff reductions totaling $744 billion over the next 10 years.

Moreover, the accord, which the WTO will supervise, prohibits member countries from placing limits on the quantity of imports (quotas). For example, Japan will have to end its ban on rice imports, and the United States will have to end its import quotas on peanuts, dairy products, and textiles. Furthermore, the agreement bans the practice of requiring high local content of materials for manufactured products such as cars. It also requires all signatory countries to protect patents, trademarks, copyrights, and trade secrets.

General Impact. The accord created the WTO, which consists of all nations whose governments approved and met the GATT–Uruguay Round Accord.[13]

---

[13] Uruguay Round Amendments Act, P. L. 103–465, was approved by Congress on December 8, 1994. One hundred eight states signed the final act embodying the results of the Uruguay round of multilateral trade negotiations. *Bureau of National Affairs,* International Reporter 11 (Apr. 20, 1994). Sixteen more states have joined since 1994.

TABLE 2 LEGALLY AND ECONOMICALLY INTEGRATED INSTITUTIONS

Name	Members and Purpose
World Trade Organization (WTO)	Replaced General Agreement on Tariffs and Trade (GATT) in 1995 and the most favored nation clause with the normal trade relations principle. Composed of 144 member nations. Goal is to get the nations of the world to commit to the trade principles of nondiscrimination and reciprocity so that, when a trade treaty is negotiated between two members, the provisions of that bilateral treaty will be extended to all WTO members. All members are obligated to harmonize their trade laws or face sanctions. The WTO, through its arbitration tribunals, is to mediate disputes and recommend sanctions.
European Union (EU)	Composed of 25 European member states. Established as the European Economic Community (later called the European Community) by the Treaty of Rome in 1957. Goal is to establish an economic "common market" by eliminating custom duties and other quantitative restrictions on the import and export of goods and services between member states. In 1986, the treaty was amended by the SEA, providing for the abolition of all customs and technical barriers between nations by December 31, 1992. In 1991, the Maastricht Summit Treaty proposed monetary union, political union, and a "social dimension" (harmonizing labor and Social Security regulations) among EU members. All aspects have not been approved by all members.
North American Free Trade Agreement (NAFTA)	The United States, Canada, and Mexico are members at present; Chile has been invited to join. NAFTA seeks to eliminate barriers to the flow of goods, services, and investments among member nations over a 15-year period, starting in 1994, the year of its ratification. Unlike the EU, NAFTA is not intended to create a common market. Whereas EU states have a common tariff barrier against non-EU states, members of NAFTA maintain their own individual tariff rates for goods and services coming from non-NAFTA countries.
Organization for Economic Cooperation and Development (OECD)	Established in 1951. Western European nations with Australia, New Zealand, United States, Canada, Japan, Russia, and some Eastern European nations as associate members. The OECD's original purpose was to promote economic growth after World War II. Today it recommends and evaluates options on environmental issues for its members and establishes guidelines for multinational corporations when operating in developed and developing countries.
European Free Trade Association (EFTA)	Founded in 1960 and originally composed of Finland, Sweden, Norway, Iceland, Lichtenstein, Switzerland, and Austria. EFTA has an intergovernmental council that negotiates treaties with the EU. Finland, Sweden, and Austria left the EFTA in 1995 and joined the EU. EFTA in the future will have only minor significance.
Andean Common Market (ANCOM)	Composed of Bolivia, Venezuela, Colombia, Ecuador, and Peru. ANCOM seeks to integrate these nations politically and economically through a commission, the Juanta Andean Development Bank, and a Reserve Fund and a Court of Justice. Founded in 1969, its goals have been set back by national interests.
Mercado Commun del Ser Mercosul (Mercosul)	Composed of Argentina, Brazil, Paraguay, and Uruguay. Mercosul's purposes are to reduce tariffs and eliminate nontariff barriers among members and to establish a common external tariff. The organization was founded in 1991, and these goals were to be met by December 31, 1994. For political reasons, they have not been fully met.
South American Common Market	A duty-free common market comprised of countries in the ANCOM and Mercosul groups came about on January 1, 1995. On that date, tariffs were ended on 95 percent of goods traded among Brazil, Argentina, Paraguay, and Uruguay. All three nations adopted common external tariffs.
Asia-Pacific Economic Corporations (APEC)	Formed in 1989. A loosely organized group of 15 developed and developing Pacific Group (APEC) nations, including Japan, China, United States, Canada, and New Zealand. APEC is not a trading bloc and has no structure except for a secretariat.
Association of Southeast Asian Nations (ASEAN)	Formed in 1967. Composed of Indonesia, Malaysia, Vietnam, Philippines, Singapore, Thailand, and Brunei. ASEAN's purpose is to encourage economic growth of member nations by promoting trade and industry. There have been tariff reductions between members, and ASEAN's secretariat has represented nations vis-à-vis other regional groups such as the EU.
Gulf Cooperation Council (GCC)	Founded in 1982. Composed of Saudi Arabia, Kuwait, Bahrain, Qatar, the United Arab Emirates, and Oman. The GCC's purposes are to standardize industrial subsidies, eliminate trade barriers among members, and negotiate with other regional groups to obtain favorable treatment for GCC goods, services, and investments.

Each member state has one vote in the Ministerial Conference, with no single nation having a veto. The conference meets at least biannually, and a general council meets as needed. The conference may amend the charter created by the pact—in some cases, by a two-thirds vote; in others, by a three-fourths vote. Changes will apply to all members, even those that voted *no*.

The WTO has been given the power to set up a powerful dispute-resolution system with three-person arbitration panels. Each panel follows a strict schedule for dispute-resolution decisions, and WTO members may veto its findings. This is a matter of great concern to the United States, and it figured prominently in the House and the Senate debates preceding approval of the WTO. U.S. farmers (and other groups), who had previously won decisions before GATT panels, saw these decisions vetoed by the EU countries that subsidize the production of soybeans and other agricultural products; they enthusiastically supported the new WTO process. Environmentalists and consumer groups, on the other hand, feared that the WTO would overrule U.S. environmental laws and in other ways infringe on the sovereignty of the nation. To assuage these fears, the framers of the accord added a provision that allows any nation to withdraw upon 6 months' notice. Congress also attached a condition to its approval that calls for the setting up of a panel of U.S. federal judges to review the WTO panels' decisions.

Impact on Corporate Investment Decision Making. The WTO pact makes it less risky for multinationals to source parts—that is, to have them built in cheap-labor countries and then brought back to the multinational's home country for use in making a product (e.g., brakes for automobiles). Industries that are expected to shift quickly to buying parts from all over the world for their products include computers, telecommunications, and other high-tech manufacturing. It is anticipated that with a freer flow of goods across borders, businesses will gain increased economies of scale by building parts-manufacturing plants at a location that serves a wide market area.

Because the tariff cuts are to be introduced gradually over a 6-year period and are to be finalized only after 10 years, the impact on trade will not be immediate. Once the major nations ratify the WTO pact, however, companies will begin to make investment and employment decisions predicated on dramatic reductions in tariffs, subsidies, and other government-established deterrents to free trade.

THE EUROPEAN UNION

Purpose. Today's 25-member EU grew out of the European Economic Community (later called the European Community), established by six Western European nations through the Rome Treaty of 1957. Its goals are to create a "customs union" that would do away with internal tariffs among the member states and to create a uniform external tariff to be applied to all nonmembers. The EU is thoroughly committed to achieving the free movement of goods, services, capital, and people across borders (Exhibit 2).

The EU's ambitious plan to create an immense "common market" of 380 million people and $4 trillion worth of goods was greatly strengthened by the 1986 signing of the Single European Act (SEA), which set a deadline for economic integration of December 31, 1992, and instituted new voting requirements to make passage of EU legislation easier. A treaty that was proposed at the Maastricht Summit in 1991 was ratified in 1993. It provided for (1) monetary union

104

EXHIBIT 2

FROM 15 TO 25: THE EU SPREADS TO THE EAST

Source: "The Legal Environment of Business and On Line Commerce," 5E, by Henry Cheeseman (© 2007) p. 77, Ex. 5-2. Reproduced by permission of Pearson Education, Inc., Upper Saddle River, New Jersey.

through the creation of a single currency for the entire EU, (2) political union, and (3) a "social dimension" through the establishment of uniform labor and Social Security regulations. The leaders of the 12 nations at the time agreed to the creation of a European Monetary Institute by 1994, a European Central Bank by 1998, and a uniform European currency unit (ECU) by 1999 (Table 3). Three new members (Finland, Austria, and Sweden) joined the EU in 1994, bringing the total to 15 nations.

In May 2004, 10 nations joined the EU: Cyprus, Czech Republic, Estonia, Hungary, Latvia, Lithuania, Malta, Poland, Slovakia, and Slovenia. Bulgaria and Romania were accepted into the EU in 2007, and Turkey's applications may be accepted later.

Structure. The EU consists of (1) a Council of Ministers, (2) a Commission, (3) a Parliament (Assembly), (4) the European Court of Justice (with the addition of the Court of First Instance) and (5) the European Central Bank (ECB) and the European Monetary Union (EMU).

1. *Council of Ministers.* The Council of Ministers is composed of one representative from each of the member nations. Its purposes are to coordinate the economic policies of member states and, more recently, to negotiate with nonmember states. In the past, the council generally rubber-stamped legislation proposed by the Commission, but this docility is less assured as the council begins to flex some of the authority granted it by the SEA and the Maastricht Treaty.

2. *Commission.* The Commission consists of 20 members who represent the EU, not national concerns. It is responsible for the EU's relations with international

TABLE 3 KEY ELEMENTS OF THE TREATY OF MAASTRICHT

Agreement	Goals and Stumbling Blocks
Monetary Union	European Monetary Institute was created on January 1, 1994, and started operating on January 1, 1999. A single currency issued any day after January 1, 1999, is the goal of 25 nations who meet three standards: (1) Annual budget deficit cannot exceed the ceiling of 3 percent of gross domestic product; (2) the public debt limit for each country must not exceed 60 percent of gross domestic product; and (3) a country's inflation rate must be lower than 2.9 percent, based on a complex formula set out in 1997. Great Britain was allowed to opt out of the EC currency union until an unspecified date. It opposes monetary union for ideological reasons. Denmark was also allowed to opt out pending a referendum on the issue, a constitutional requirement. The Danish government backs monetary union.
Political Union	EC jurisdiction in areas including industrial affairs, health, education, trade, environment, energy, culture, tourism, and consumer and civil protection. Member states vote to implement decisions. Increased political cooperation under a new name—European Union. Permanent diplomatic network of senior political officials created in the EC capitals. Great Britain rejected EC-imposed labor legislation, forcing the removal of the so-called social chapter from the treaty. It will be implemented separately by the other 14 members, officials said.
Federalism	EC leaders dropped reference to an EC "with a federal goal." Instead, the political Union accord describes the community as "an ever-closer union in which political decisions have to be taken as near to the people as possible." Great Britain rejected the "federalism" as the embodiment of what it feels would be an encroaching EC superstate.
Foreign Affairs	EC states move toward a joint foreign policy, with most decisions requiring unanimity. Great Britain wanted the ability to opt out of any joint decision. How this provision will be interpreted by the various sides is yet to be seen.
Defense	The Western EU, a long-dormant group of nine EC states, will be revived to act as the EC's defense body but linked to the NATO alliance. Although France and Germany supported a greater military role for the Union, Great Britain, Italy, and others did not want to see NATO's influence diluted.
European Parliament	The 518-member EC assembly gets a modest say in shaping some EC legislation. Its new powers fall short of what the assembly had sought (i.e., an equitable sharing of the right to make EC laws with the EC governments). Great Britain and Denmark refused to grant the assembly broader powers.

organizations such as the United Nations and the WTO. Member states are apportioned voting power in the Commission on the basis of their population and economic power. The Commission elects a president from among its members. Each Commission member supervises a functional area (e.g., agriculture or competition) that may be affected by several directorates. There are 22 directorates (Exhibit 3), that are actually run by "supranational" civil servants called director generals. In theory, the directorates serve the Commission, but, in fact, the director generals often heavily influence legislation as it moves through the Commission.

3. *Parliament.* The Parliament (Assembly) is made up of representatives elected from each nation-state for a term set by the nation-state. The representatives come from most of the major European political factions (Socialists, Christian Democrats, Communists, Liberals, etc.), and each of the parties in the Parliament also exists in the member states. The Parliament elects a president to preside over its deliberations. The Parliament's general powers are to (1) serve as a consultative body to the council, (2) refer matters affecting EU interests to the Commission or Council, (3) censure the Commission when necessary, (4) assent to trade agreements with countries

EXHIBIT 3

DIRECTORATES OF THE EUROPEAN UNION

- External Relations
- Economic and Financial Affairs
- Internal Market and Industrial Affairs
- Competition
- Employment, Social Affairs, and Education
- Agriculture
- Transportation
- Development
- Personnel and Administration
- Information, Communication, and Culture
- Environment, Nuclear Safety, and Civil Protection; Science; Research and Development
- Telecommunication, Information Industry, and Innovation
- Fisheries
- Financial Institutions and Company Law
- Regional Policy
- Energy
- Credit and Investment
- Budgets
- Financial Control
- Customs Union and Indirect Taxation
- Coordination of Structural Instruments
- Enterprise Policy, Distributive Trades, Tourism, and Cooperatives

outside the EU, (5) amend the EU budget, and (6) participate with the Commission in the legislative procedure.

4. *European Court of Justice.* The European Court of Justice performs the functions of arbiter and final decision maker in conflicts between EU law and individual member states. The national courts of member states are obligated to follow EU law and Court of Justice decisions. The Court of First Instance was established in 1989 to reduce the workload of the Court of Justice. It has jurisdiction over appeals of the Commission's decisions on mergers and acquisitions. It also sets the penalties for price fixing when non-EU companies are involved.

Impact. *Unity of Law.* Agricultural, environmental, and labor legislation is being made uniform throughout the 25 member nations, with allowances and subsidies for the poorer members. The national courts of member states are now following decisions of the European Court of Justice.

Economic Integration. The SEA and the Maastricht Treaty have pushed the EU members to eliminate tariff and nontariff barriers among themselves. British and French differences over the creation of a single currency have forced the suspension of this goal.

Political Union. The political union envisioned by the Maastricht Treaty has been an elusive goal for the EU, because member states (and their citizens) have proved more reluctant to make the necessary compromises on national sovereignty than the treaty's architects anticipated. Nonetheless, the EU is the only regional organization that has in place the sophisticated structure required to make political union a realistic possibility. A draft of the new charter for the EU was under consideration in 2004.

The European Central Bank and the European Monetary Union. The Maastricht Treaty required all member states of the EU to converge their economic and monetary policies with the good of creating a single currency, the euro. The criteria set forth required the harmonization of budget deficits, inflation levels and long-term interest rates, and specific levels of currency inflations to achieve exchange rate stability. The European Monetary Union (EMU) was created on January, 1999. By giving up their national currencies, members of the EMU have relinquished control of their exchange rates and monetary policy to an independent European Central Bank (ECB) based in Frankfurt. The primary duty of the ECB is to maintain price stability, by lowering or raising interest rates. With the exception of Denmark and Great Britain, most members of the EMU have adopted the euro.

NORTH AMERICAN FREE TRADE AGREEMENT

Purpose. The NAFTA, ratified in 1994, seeks to eliminate barriers to the flow of goods, services, and investments among Canada, the United States, and Mexico over a 15-year period. NAFTA envisions a gradual phasing out of these barriers, with the length of the phaseout varying from industry to industry. The ultimate goal is a totally free trade zone among the three member states, with eventual inclusion of Central and Latin American countries. So far, the only country invited to join the founding members is Chile.

Structure. NAFTA is administered by a three-member Trade Commission, which oversees a Secretariat and arbitral panels.

Trade Commission. Staffed by trade ministers from each of the three nations, the Trade Commission meets once a year and makes its decisions by consensus. It supervises the implementation of the treaty and resolves disputes over interpretation. The daily operations of NAFTA are conducted by ad hoc working groups appointed by the three governments.

Secretariat. The permanent Secretariat is composed of national sections (departments) representing each member country. Its purposes are to provide technical support for the Trade Commission and to put together arbitral panels to resolve disputes between members.

Arbitral Panels. The treaty has detailed arbitration provisions for settling disputes, particularly those involving dumping of goods (selling a good in a member country at a lower price than at home) and interpretations of the treaty. Although the arbitration proceedings are designed especially to resolve disputes between member nations, the treaty encourages private parties to use them as well. If they do, they must agree to abide by the arbitral panel's decision.

Each arbitral panel has five members, chosen from a roster of 30 legal experts from NAFTA and non-NAFTA countries. Within 90 days, the panel will give the disputant countries a confidential report. Over the next 14 days, the disputants may present their comments on the report to the panel. Within 30 days of the issuance of the initial report, the arbitral panel must present its final report to the parties and to the Trade Commission, which publishes it. The countries then have 30 days to resolve their dispute, or if the panel has found one party wrong, the other may legally retaliate.

Impact. NAFTA has not only brought together three North American neighbors of different historical and cultural background but it has also provided a model of economic integration for other countries in Central and Latin America.

It has had an impact on each country's exports and imports. It has served as an institution to arbitrate disputes. For example, the U.S. government has filed a complaint on behalf of United Parcel Service (UPS), and one of the first arbitral panels was set up. UPS believed that it was being hampered by NAFTA government regulations in Mexico, which limit the size of delivery trucks to be used in delivering packages. The arbitral panel ruled in favor of UPS.

TECHNOLOGY AND THE LEGAL ENVIRONMENT

WTO Says U.S. Ban on Online Gambling Violates International Law

The island nation of Antigua and Barbuda (plaintiff) brought a case against the United States to a WTO panel. The nation licenses companies (19) that offer (sports) betting and casino games (e.g., blackjack) over the Internet. It argued that the United States is in violation of international law by prohibiting cross-border gambling operations via the Internet. The plaintiff argues that the U.S. trade policy does not prohibit cross-border gambling operations.

The WTO panel ruled in favor of Antigua and Barbuda. In its decision in 2004, the panel stated that U.S. policy prohibiting online gambling operations emanating from the plaintiff nation violates international law. WTO panels do not have to give reasons for their decisions. The United States has a right to appeal the decision to a separate court of appeals and is expected to do so.

Some important legal, political, and cultural considerations:

1. WTO panel decisions only apply to the set of facts and case before it. Internet gambling using credit cards takes place in the Caribbean, Costa Rica, Great Britain, and Canada. Although this case is not a precedent, the United States should expect more legal action as several million customers are at stake, and revenues from offshore casinos are important to nation-states that operate Internet casinos.

2. Present federal law in the United States makes it illegal to bet over the Internet if not allowed by individual states. Although untested as legal theory, the Justice Department is seeking to crack down on broadcasters and print media that accept advertising from offshore Internet casinos claiming that they are aiding and abetting an illegal enterprise. The airwaves are controlled by the Federal Communications Commission. Some questions are being raised: (a) Is the lobbying of American gambling companies against Internet betting (emanating from abroad) the real reason for the U.S. government stand? American companies have a lock on U.S. gambling and do not want to lose it to worldwide Internet casino interests; (b) On the basis of international trade law, countries allowing online casino gambling may seek to raise tariffs on services or goods of U.S. companies doing business (e.g., AT&T) within their jurisdiction as a way of retaliating against U.S. Policy. Will this bring an expression of concern from U.S. companies to members of Congress? Does AT&T contribute to the reelection of members of Congress? Do gambling interests provide funds for reelection bids? Will there be a clash of interests?

Global Dispute Resolution

Many times, when private or public parties enter into an international business agreement, they incorporate means for resolving future disputes (e.g., arbitration clauses) into the agreement. Another form of protection for firms doing business internationally is the insurance some nation-states offer domestic companies to encourage them to export (e.g., United States Overseas Private Investment Corporation). Still, the two methods used most frequently to resolve irreconcilable differences between parties involved in international transactions are arbitration and litigation.

ARBITRATION

arbitration A dispute-resolution method whereby the disputant parties submit their disagreement to a mutually agreed upon neutral decision maker or one provided for by statute.

Arbitration is a dispute-resolution process whereby parties submit their disagreements to a private individual decision maker they agree on or to a panel of decision makers whose selection has been provided for in the contract the parties signed. Arbitration clauses in contracts involving international business transactions should meticulously stipulate what law will govern the arbitration, where and when the arbitration will take place, what language will be used, and how the expenses of arbitration will be shared. They also stipulate a waiver of judicial (court) review by both parties to the dispute. All these matters should be carefully negotiated when the contract is being drafted. Arbitration of disputes may also come about through treaties. For instance, the United Nations Convention on the Recognition of Foreign Arbitral Awards encourages use of arbitration agreements and awards. The World Bank's International Center for the Settlement of Investment Disputes (ICSID), created in 1965 by treaty (the Washington Convention), provides to disputants arbitration rules as well as experienced arbitrators, and the International Chamber of Commerce offers a permanent arbitration tribunal. Finally, individual countries have arbitration associations that provide experienced arbitrators to parties desiring assistance in settling their disputes.

Here we provide a case that demonstrates how important it is for businesses to understand the nature of international arbitration and the meaning of any documents they sign.

CASE 7

Republic of Nicaragua v. Standard Fruit Company and Steamship Company
United States Court of Appeals 937 F.2d 469 (9th Cir. 1991)

Plaintiff-appellant Nicaragua sued Standard Fruit and its parent companies, the defendants. Standard Fruit, a wholly owned subsidiary of Standard Fruit Company (SFC) and Steamship Company (Steamship), was involved in the production and purchase of bananas in Nicaragua.

Steamship purchased the bananas from SFC. In 1979, a Nicaraguan rebel group known as the Sandinistas overthrew the government of Nicaragua and attempted to negotiate with Standard Fruit for more control over the banana industry in their country. When the negotiations proved unsuccessful, the Sandinistas took over the industry by decree and nullified all leases of plantations and purchase contracts. Standard Fruit stopped doing business in Nicaragua. After three days of negotiations, Steamship signed a memorandum, termed "an agreement in principal," that provided for the renegotiation of existing contracts and included an arbitration clause that stated, "Any and all disputes arising under the arrangements contemplated hereunder . . . will be referred to mutually agreed mechanisms or procedures of international arbitration, such as the rules of the London Arbitration Association."

The implementing contracts provided for in the memorandum were never renegotiated, but Standard Fruit resumed business in Nicaragua for two years and then left the country for good in 1982. Nicaragua then sued in a United States District Court, requesting the court to compel Steamship to arbitrate Nicaragua's breach-of-contract suit. Steamship argued that the arbitration clause in the memorandum was too vague and broad to be enforceable and that it merely referred to the creation of a formal clause that would be included in the renegotiated contracts. The district court agreed and ruled in favor of the defendants, granting their request for a summary judgment. Nicaragua appealed.

Judge Ferguson

We hold that although it was the court's responsibility to determine the threshold question of arbitrability, the district court improperly looked to the validity of the contract as a whole and erroneously determined that the parties had not agreed to arbitrate this dispute. Instead, it should have considered only the validity and scope of the arbitration clause itself. In addition, the district court ignored strong evidence in the record that both parties intended to be bound by the arbitration clause. As all doubts over the scope of an arbitration clause must be resolved in favor of arbitration, and in light of the strong federal policy favoring arbitration in international commercial disputes, Nicaragua's motion to compel arbitration should have been granted. Whether the Memorandum was binding, whether it covered banana purchases, and whether Standard Fruit Company was bound by it are all questions properly left to the arbitrators. Finally, genuine disputes of fact exist as to the intent of the parties and the validity and scope of the Memorandum.

Reversed in favor of Plaintiff-Appellant, Nicaragua.

LITIGATION

When contracts do not contain arbitration clauses and there is no other alternative (such as mediation or conciliation) available, **litigation** may be the only way to resolve a dispute between parties. In some private international business contracts, a choice-of-forum clause is included so that the parties know which family of law is to be applied in case of a dispute and what nation's courts will be used. When negotiating contracts in the international arena, managers should make sure that choice-of-forum clauses are specific as to these questions. Either or both can make a major difference in the outcome. Because there is no single international court or legal system capable of resolving all commercial disputes between private parties, a choice-of-forum clause should be negotiated in all agreements involving major transactions. London's Commercial Court, established in 1895, is the most popular neutral forum for resolving commercial litigation, owing to its 100 years of experience.

litigation A dispute-resolution process that involves going through the judicial system; a lawsuit.

Most of the international and regional organizations discussed in this chapter emphatically encourage the arbitration of private contractual disputes because the arbitration process is a quicker and less public means of resolving disputes than litigation. In certain areas of the world (particularly the Far East), companies and governments seek to avoid litigation.

GLOBALIZATION OR NOT?

In the following table you will find a debate that is taking place all over the world. We invite you to participate in this sometimes vigorous discussion of whether globalization of business helps or hurts societies all over the world. It is skillfully summarized by Professor Murray Wiedenbaum in his text *Business and Government in the Global Marketplace*.

Pros	*Cons*
"Accelerates economic growth, increasing living standards"	"Generates widespread poverty in the pursuance of corporate greed"
"Offers consumers greater variety of products and at lower prices"	"Results in greater income inequality"
"Increases jobs and wages and improves working conditions"	"Moves jobs to low-wage factories that abuse workers' rights"
"Encourages a greater exchange of information and use of technology"	"Provides opportunity for criminal and terrorist groups to operate on a global scale"
"Provides wealth for environmental cleanup"	"Pollutes local environments that lack ecological standards"
"Helps developing nations and lifts millions out of poverty"	"Traps developing countries in high debt loads"
"Extends economic and political freedoms"	"Threatens national sovereignty"
"Raises life expectancy, health standards, and literacy rates"	"Worsens public health and harms social fabrics of agricultural-based societies"

Source: M. Wiedenbaum, *Business and Government in the Global Marketplace,* 7th ed. (Upper Saddle River, N.J.: Prentice Hall, 2004), p. 190.

SUMMARY

The political, economic, cultural, and legal dimensions of the international environment of business need to be considered by managers undertaking international business ventures, although the emphasis in this book is on legal and ethical issues. The major families of law are common law, which relies primarily on case law and precedent; civil law, which relies primarily on codes and statutory law; Islamic law, which relies on the Shari'a, a religious code of rules; socialist law, which is based on Marxism–Leninism and does not recognize private property; and Hindu law, which relies primarily on the Sastras, a religious code.

International law is divided into public international law, governing the relationships between nation-states, and private international law, governing the relationships between private parties involved in international transactions.

The major methods of engaging in international business are trade, international licensing and franchising, and foreign direct investment. The principal risk of engaging in international business are expropriation, the sovereign immunity doctrine and the act-of-state doctrine, export and import controls, and currency controls and fluctuations (particularly in developing nations).

World and regional integrative organizations, especially the WTO, the EU, and NAFTA, are making a strong impact on international business. Arbitration and litigation are the major methods of international dispute resolution.

REVIEW QUESTIONS

1 Contrast the common-law family with the socialist-law family.

2 Which of the methods of engaging in international business discussed in this chapter is least risky for a foreign multinational company? Explain.

3 Define the following:
   a. expropriation
   b. doctrine of sovereign immunity
   c. act-of-state doctrine
   d. arbitration clause
   e. choice-of-forum clause

4 Explain how currency fluctuations affect companies doing international business.

5 Why was the GATT Pact, creating the World Trade Organization, so important to doing international business? Explain.

6 Why is arbitration preferred to litigation as a means of resolving international business disputes? Explain.

REVIEW PROBLEMS

7 Royal Bed and Spring Company, a U.S. distributor of furniture products, entered into an exclusive distributorship agreement with a Brazilian manufacturer of furniture products. Under the terms of the contract, Royal Bed was to distribute in Puerto Rico the furniture products manufactured by Famossul in Brazil. The contract contained forum-selection and choice-of-law clauses, which designated the juridical district of Curitiba, State of Parana, Brazil, as the judicial forum and the Brazilian Civil Code as the law to be applied in the event of any dispute. Famossul terminated the exclusive distributorship and suspended the shipment of goods without just cause. Puerto Rican law refuses to enforce forum-selection clauses providing for foreign venues as a matter of public policy. In what jurisdiction should Royal Bed bring suit? Explain.

8 A, a U.S. company, entered into a contract with C, a Swiss subsidiary of General Motors, to sell Chevrolet automobiles in Aruba. An arbitration clause in the parties' agreement provided that all disputes would be settled by arbitration in accordance with Aruban law. Aruba follows Dutch civil law. A argues that only U.S. law can apply because the contract was made in the United States. Is A correct? Explain.

9 Zapata entered into a contract with a German corporation to use one of Zapata's oil-drilling rigs off the coast of Italy. The contract stated, "Any dispute arising must be treated before the London Court of Justice." A severe storm damaged the oil rig as it was being towed through the Gulf of Mexico. Zapata filed suit in federal district court. Does the U.S. court have jurisdiction to decide the dispute? What is the purpose

behind a choice-of-forum clause, and should the clause be enforced?

10 The members of the International Association of Machinists (IAM) were disturbed by the high price of oil and petroleum-derived products in the United States. They believed that the actions of the Organization of Petroleum Exporting Countries (OPEC) were the cause of the high prices. Therefore, the IAM sued OPEC's member countries in a federal district court, alleging that these countries' price-setting activities violated U.S. antitrust law. OPEC argued the act-of-state doctrine as a defense. Who do you think won? Explain why.

11 Dr. Will Pirkey, a U.S. otolaryngologist, signed an employment contract in which he agreed to work for 2 years at the King Faisal Hospital in Saudi Arabia. Before his departure, Pirkey received his employment contract, which contained a clause providing that his agreement with the hospital would be construed in accordance with Saudi Arabian law. Because of the assassination of King Faisal and for other reasons, Pirkey did not go to Saudi Arabia as agreed and is now contesting the choice-of-law provision of his employment contract as unconscionable. He asks that his home state's laws (New York) should apply. Who will win this case? Explain why.

12 U.S. Company owned a subsidiary in France that had a contract to deliver compressors for use in the Soviet natural gas pipeline then under construction. The U.S. government banned the export of goods to the Soviet Union by U.S. companies or U.S.-controlled foreign companies, and U.S. company complied with

the ban by ordering its French subsidiary to stop delivery of the compressors. The French government, however, ordered delivery. U.S. Company delivered the compressors. The U.S. government thereupon instituted a criminal action against U.S. Company. What is U.S. Company's defense? Explain.

CASE PROBLEMS

13   Tonoga, Ltd., (Taconic) is a manufacturer incorporated in Ireland with its principal place of business in New York. In 1997, Taconic entered into a contract with a German construction company to supply special material for a tent project designed to shelter religious pilgrims visiting holy sites in Saudi Arabia. Most of the material was made in and shipped from New York. The company did not pay Taconic and eventually filed for bankruptcy. Another German firm, Werner Voss Architects and Engineers, acting as an agent for the government of Saudi Arabia, guaranteed the payments due Taconic to induce it to complete the project. When Taconic received all but the final payment, the firm filed a suit in a federal district court against the government of Saudi Arabia, claiming breach of the guaranty and seeking to collect, in part, about $3 million. The defendant filed a motion to dismiss based, in part, on the doctrine of sovereign immunity. Under what circumstances does this doctrine apply? Should this suit be dismissed under the "commercial activity" exception? Explain. *Tonoga, Ltd. v. Ministry of Public Works and Housing of Kingdom of Saudi Arabia,* 135 F. Supp. 2d 350 (N.D.N.Y. 2001).

14   DaimlerChrysler Corp. makes and markets motor vehicles. DaimlerChrysler assembled the 1993 and 1994 model years of its trucks at plants in Mexico. Assembly involved sheet metal components sent from the United States. DaimlerChrysler subjected some of the parts to a complicated treatment process, which included the application of coats of paint to prevent corrosion, to impart color, and to protect the finish. Under federal law, goods or U.S.-made parts that are assembled abroad can be imported tariff free. A federal statute provides that painting is "incidental" to assembly and does not affect the status of the goods. A federal regulation states that "painting primarily intended to enhance the appearance of an article or to impart distinctive features of characteristics" is not incidental. The U.S. Customs Service levied a tariff on the trucks. DaimlerChrysler filed a suit in the U.S. Court of International Trade, challenging the levy. Should the court rule in DaimlerChrysler's favor? Explain. *DaimlerChrysler Corp. v. United States,* 361 F.3d 1378 (Fed. Cir. 2004).

15   In 1996, the International Trade Administration (ITA) of the U.S. Department of Commerce assessed antidumping duties against Koyo Seiko Co., NTN Corp., on certain tapered roller bearings and their components imported from Japan. In assessing these duties, the ITA requested information from the makers about their home market sales. NTN responded in part that its figures should not include many sample and small-quantity sales, which were made to enable customers to decide whether to buy the products. NTN provided no evidence to support this assertion, however. In calculating the fair market value of the bearings in Japan, the ITA determined, among other things, that sample and small-quantity sales were within the makers' ordinary course of trade. Koyo and others appealed these assessments to the U.S. Court of International Trade. NTN objected in part to the ITA's inclusion of sample and small-quantity sales. Should the court order the ITA to recalculate its assessment on the basis of NTN's objection? Explain. *Koyo Seiko Co. v. United States,* 186 F. Supp.2d 1332 (Court of International Trade [CIT] 2002).

THINKING CRITICALLY ABOUT RELEVANT LEGAL ISSUES

Margaux de Chien, a naturalized U.S. citizen, was born in France. She went to work for Vin Enterprises, a wholly owned subisdiary of a Delaware corporation licensed to do business in Colorado. The parent company, Spanish Wines Are Us, has its principal place of business in Spain. Margaux worked in the United States for 2 years and then was transferred, at her request, to the company headquarters in Spain. Unfortunately, Margaux did not get along well in Spain. It seems that she was always being harassed because of her strong feelings about the superiority of French versus Spanish wine and culture. After 3 years at Vin Enterprises in Spain, Margaux was terminated. Margaux filed a charge of discrimination with the Equal Employment Opportunity Commission seeking relief under both Colorado law and Title VII of the Civil Rights Act of 1964 on the grounds that Vin Enterprises discriminated against her and ultimately fired her because of her national origin. Vin Enterprises claims that Title VII does not apply to the employment practices of U.S. employers who are subsidiaries of foreign-owned companies doing business in their home countries. What is the result? Discuss the legal and ethical aspects of this case using a critical thinking approach.

ASSIGNMENT ON THE INTERNET

As this chapter demonstrates, there are many important issues to consider before engaging in international business. Pick a country that you know little about, and using the Web site **www.lib.uchicago.edu/~llou/forintlaw.html**, research the issues you think most important to consider before doing business in that country. What are its cultural, economic, political, and legal dimensions? What are its trade laws? Does it belong to any international treaties or organizations?

If you cannot find all the information you need, make a list of detailed questions you would want answered. Finally, for each of the questions you researched, explain why that question was significant in your thinking.

 ## ON THE INTERNET

www.asil.org/resource/ergintr1.htm#Researching Use this site, maintained by the American Society of International Law, to guide you in researching international law issues on the Internet.

www.washlaw.edu/forint/forintmain.html This page provides links to primary foreign and international legal resources, research aids, and sites useful for international business.

www.loc.gov/law/guide/nations.html This link to the Law Library of Congress's Nations of the World contains legal information for each country around the world.

www.icj-cij.org This page contains information about and ruling of the International Court of Justice.

www.un.org/law This Web site of the United Nations International Law provides useful information, including treaties governing business transactions and trade law.

www.nafta-sec-alena.org/DefaultSite/index.html The homepage of the North American Free Trade Agreement (NAFTA) contains many legal texts as well as methods for dispute settlement.

FOR FUTURE READING

Mayer, Don. "Community, Business Ethics, and Global Capitalism." *American Business Law Journal* 38 (2001): 215.

Stoltenberg, Clyde D. "Law, Regulation, and International Business." *American Business Law Journal* 40 (2003): 445.

Ethics in Business

*When looking for managers, I basically look for three things—
integrity, intelligence and energy. The truth is that if you don't have
the first, the other two will kill you because if you have someone who
doesn't have integrity, you really want them to be dumb and lazy. It is
only if they have the first that the second two count.*

WARREN BUFFET (1930–), CEO, BERKSHIRE HATHWAY

A billion dollars doesn't go as far as it used to.

J. PAUL GETTY (1892–1976), FOUNDER, GETTY OIL COMPANY

*No one was ever honored for what he received. Honor has
been the reward for what he gives.*

CALVIN COOLIDGE (1872–1933), PRESIDENT OF THE
UNITED STATES, 1923–1929

It is better to love than be loved.

ST. FRANCIS ASSISI (1181–1226)

The ethical failures of managers at Enron, Arthur Andersen, WorldCom, and Tyco
underscore the need for ethics. An ethical adult needs moral maturity, the ability to
make ethical judgments, and a developed habit of doing so. We examined moral
development in the last chapter. In this chapter, we will (1) provide the tools for

From Chapter 3 of *American Business Values: A Global Perspective*, 6/e.
Gerald F. Cavanaugh. Copyright © 2010 by Pearson Prentice Hall. All rights reserved.

making ethical judgments and (2) describe how the individual person develops good moral habits, virtue, and character. In the first portion of the chapter we will ask: How does one make a judgment about what is morally right and wrong? What norms, models, and techniques are available for helping us to make ethical decisions?

Ethics can be defined as the principles of conduct governing an individual or a group, and the methods for applying them. Ethics provides the tools to make moral judgments. Let us provide a few examples of situations that call for ethical judgments:

> Jason Stacy, a California graduate student, downloads copyrighted music from the Internet for his own use. He gives some of that music to friends, and also sells it to fellow students.

> A Canadian woman visiting San Francisco mistakenly left her purse with jewelry and cash worth about a million dollars in a park. John Suhrhoff found the purse and returned it, saying "Every person I know would have done the same thing." But a San Francisco police sergeant said that Suhrhoff is unusual, and most people would have kept the find.

> Andrew S. Fastow, MBA from Northwestern and former Chief Financial Officer of Enron, pled guilty to fraud and is in jail. He admitted setting up false accounts to hide losing transactions of billions of dollars from investors and employees and enriching himself.[1]

> In a study of managers' ethics, 47% of top executives, 41% of controllers and 76% of graduate business students were willing to commit fraud by understating write-offs that cut into their company's profits. In addition, 29% of teenagers say that one has to "bend the rules to succeed" in business.[2]

> More than 4/5 (82%) of young people admitted that they lied to their parents about something significant at least once in the past year; 60% admitted that they cheated on an exam at least once in the past year; 28% acknowledged stealing something from a store during this same period. Yet, in contrast, 98% said that it was important for them to be a person of good character, and 74% rated their character higher than their peers.[3]

> A Pennsylvania man advertised "Blank receipts, 100 restaurant receipts, 50 styles, $5.98. Satisfaction guaranteed." The blank receipts are attractively designed to look like the receipts of restaurants anywhere in America: Captain's Table, Trophy Room, Village Green, P.J.'s, and so on. The purchaser, after filling in the dates, number of diners, and total bill, can use them in reporting expenses. An IRS spokesperson says that selling blank receipts is not illegal.

What are the ethical issues in each of the above cases? How would you go about judging the ethics of each case? Almost all important business decisions

---

[1] Jack Hitt, "American Kabucki: The Ritual of Scandal," *The New York Times,* July 18, 2004, Sec. 4, pp. 1, 3.
[2] "For Many Executives, Ethics Appear to Be a Write-Off," *The Wall Street Journal,* March 26, 1996, pp. C1, C13; for teenagers, *BusinessWeek,* September 20, 2004, p. 16.
[3] "2006 Josephson Institute Report Card on the Ethics of American Youth," Polling done by and reported by the Josephson Institute of Ethics, at http://www.josephsoninstitute.org/reportcard/, accessed July 19, 2007.

contain an ethical component. One purpose of this chapter is to better equip us to make effective ethical judgments.

FACTS, VALUES, AND ACTS

Ethics provides the tools for making **ethical judgments**, and helps develop the habits that result in morally good behavior. Good behavior requires the ability to make moral decisions. So in this chapter we offer a model to help a person make ethically good decisions. Making ethical judgments involves three steps: (1) gathering relevant factual information, (2) selecting the moral norm(s) that most help to make the decision, and (3) making the ethical judgment on the rightness or wrongness of the act or policy (see Figure 1).

Ethical judgments are not always easy to make. The facts of the case are often not clear, and the ethical norms to be used are not always agreed on, even by the experts. Hence, to many people, ethics seems ill-defined, subjective, and so not very useful. Just as is true with politics and religion, there is often more heat than light generated by ethical discussions. This lack of knowledge of ethics is unfortunate, because without ethical behavior, it is everyone for him or herself. In such a situation, trust, which is essential to any business transaction, is lost.[4]

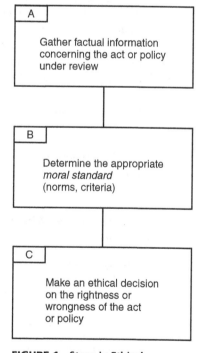

FIGURE 1 Steps in Ethical Decision Making

---

[4] For an overview of the importance of trust in organizations, see LaRue Tone Hosmer, "Trust: The Connecting Link Between Organizational Theory and Philosophical Ethics," *Academy of Management Review*, 20 (April 1995): 379–403; see also Roger C. Mayer, James H. Davis, and F. David Schoorman, "An Integrative Model of Organizational Trust," *Academy of Management Review*, 20 (July 1995): 709–734.

Dilemmas to Decisions

Let us begin our examination of ethical decision making by assessing a case that was first judged by 1,700 business executive readers of the *Harvard Business Review*. This case was part of an early large-scale study of business ethics by Raymond C. Baumhart, S.J.[5]

> An executive earning $150,000 a year has been padding her expense account by about $7,500 a year.

Is it ethical to pad one's expense account? On numerous occasions over the decades, hundreds of other managers have been asked to judge this case, and the results have been substantially the same. Replying to an anonymous questionnaire, 85 percent of executives both in the United States and in Japan think that this sort of behavior is simply unacceptable. Perhaps more important, almost two-thirds of them think their business colleagues would also see such behavior as unacceptable under any circumstances.

Why would padding an expense account be considered wrong by these executives? An expense account is not a simple addition to one's salary. It is intended to pay for expenses incurred in doing one's work.

Pocketing a pencil or making a personal long-distance phone call from the office may seem relatively trivial. Perhaps, but fabricating expenses up to 5 percent of one's salary is not trivial; it is substantial, and thus a violation of justice. The executive in the case is stealing money not owed to her. Presumably the executive's salary is fair compensation for her work; the extra $7,500 is not legitimate salary, nor is it recognized by law as such.

Circumstances are cited that might mitigate the injustice. Some may say, "Many others are also doing it" or "My superior knows about it and says nothing." In the cited study, only about a quarter of the executives thought that their peers would justify such actions for these reasons. Few (about 10%) said that they themselves thought that it would be acceptable in such circumstances. Let us further examine these circumstances.

Others Are Doing It; My Superior Knows About It and Says Nothing

The fact that many people are performing certain actions never in itself makes those actions ethically acceptable. For example, the fact that superiors ordered actions was not accepted as a defense for the unethical managers at Enron. It is not a defense for

---

[5] Raymond C. Baumhart, S.J., *Ethics in Business* (New York: Holt, Rinehart & Winston, 1968), p. 21. For later assessments using the same instrument, see Steven Brenner and Earl Molander, "Is the Ethics of Business Changing?" *Harvard Business Review*, 55 (January–February 1977): 57–71; the dollar figures have been adjusted for inflation. Also, S. T. Vitell and T. A. Festervand, "Business Ethics: Conflicts, Practices, and Beliefs of Industrial Executives," *Journal of Business Ethics*, 5 (1987): 111–122; and Chiake Nakano, "A Survey Study on Japanese Managers' Views of Business Ethics," Society for Business Ethics, Vancouver, B.C., 1995. An expense account is available for expenses that are incurred in the course of one's work. It is not fair to ask an employee to use personal funds, without reimbursement, for legitimate business expenses.

the military guards who tortured Iraqi prisoners at Abu Ghraib prison outside Baghdad. Nor was it a defense for concentration camp officers at the post–World War II Nuremberg war crime trials. Although ethics is influenced by conditions, a moral principle is not established by majority vote.

Let us go back to the case of the expense account. It would benefit the executive if she could increase her salary by $7,500; it would be in her self-interest. Focusing primarily on her own benefit could lead her to be less objective in her search for the right action and would make her more prone to look for excuses to take the money.

Justice calls for a fair distribution of the benefits and burdens of society. In this case, we are concerned with benefits. Is it ever ethical to claim funds from an expense account that were not true expenses? The executive's family is not starving because she has an abnormally low salary, so justice tells us that the expense account should not be used as a salary supplement. Ignorance and coercion can lessen responsibility. However, in this case, the executive can hardly claim that she did not know what an expense account was or that she was forced into taking the money.

But if it is not likely that she would be caught, why shouldn't she pad her expense account? Practically all businesspeople agree that a businessperson should be ethical. That is, individuals should try to do good and avoid evil, not only on the job but in all aspects of life. An essential foundation for business transactions is confidence that most businesspeople are trustworthy and truthful. If one could not trust businesspeople, it would be difficult to purchase goods, sell property or securities, or do most of the exchange that we are accustomed to in modern society.

Admittedly there can be a short-term financial benefit for an embezzler or a supplier who charges $10 million and delivers defective goods. It is because of individuals like this that we have laws, courts, and jails. Yet not all activities can be regulated, nor can all unethical acts be fully punished (in this life, anyway). However, if most businesspeople did not pay their bills and cheated their partners, the market system would collapse.[6]

ETHICAL PRINCIPLES FOR BUSINESS ACTIONS

How to make better ethical decisions has been deliberated for centuries. The norm of **rights and duties** is based on the human dignity of each individual person and results in personal entitlements. Immanuel Kant[7] (personal rights) and John Locke[8] (property rights) developed the theory of rights and duties. The norm of **justice** is also based on the dignity of each person and has a longer tradition, going back to Plato and Aristotle in the fourth century BC.[9]

---

[6] See Nobel prize winning economist Amartya Sen, "Economics, Business Principles and Moral Sentiments," *Business Ethics Quarterly,* 7 (July 1997): 5–15; also James H. Davis and John A. Ruhe, "Perceptions of Corruption: Antecedents and Outcomes," *Journal of Business Ethics,* 43 (April 2003): 275–288.

[7] Immanuel Kant, *The Metaphysical Elements of Justice,* trans. J. Ladd (New York: Library of Liberal Arts, 1965).

[8] John Locke, *The Second Treatise of Government* (New York: Liberal Arts Press, 1952).

[9] Aristotle, *Ethics,* trans. J. A. K. Thomson (London: Penguin, 1953); for influence of firm's culture, see Thomas M. Jones, Will Felps, and Gregory A. Bigley, "Ethical Theory and Stakeholder-Related Decisions: The Role of Stakeholder Culture," *Academy of Management Review,* 32, no. 1 (2007): 137–155.

Businesspeople are most familiar using the ethical norm of **utilitarianism**. This is because the norm examines consequences of actions, and traces its origins to Adam Smith, the father of modern economics. The main proponents of utilitarianism are Jeremy Bentham[10] and John Stuart Mill[11], who both helped to formulate the theory. Utilitarianism evaluates actions on the basis of their outcomes. In any given situation, the action that would result in the greatest net gain for all concerned parties is considered to be the right, or morally obligatory, action.

The ethical norm of caring was developed more recently from feminist ethics.[12] Work on each of these ethical norms continues to the present.[13] For an overview of these four ethical norms—their history, strengths, weaknesses, and areas of application—see Table 1.

Individual Rights and Duties

A moral right is an important, justifiable claim or entitlement to something. Moral rights and duties flow from each person's human dignity and ultimately from the Creator, and are often supported by law; our rights of freedom of conscience and freedom of speech are written into the U.S. Constitution. Moral rights enable individuals to pursue their own interests, and they also impose duties or correlative requirements or prohibitions on others.[14]

Legal rights are stated in laws, rules, or a constitutional system. The U.S. Bill of Rights and the United Nations Universal Declaration of Human Rights spell out individual rights in detail. Most legal rights stem from moral rights; but not all moral rights are enacted into law, and some bad law even attempts to deny human rights (e.g., rights of women in Saudi Arabia, blacks in pre-1960s in the United States, and Jews in Nazi Germany.)

Every right has a corresponding obligation or duty. Your right to freedom of speech places an obligation on others to respect that right; moreover, your right to freedom of conscience demands that you may not unnecessarily limit that freedom for others. In business my right to be paid for my work corresponds to the duty of my employer to provide that compensation. In the latter case, both the right and duty stem from the right to private property, which is a traditional pillar of American life and law. However, the right to private property is not absolute. A factory owner may be forced by morality and by law to install pollution control or safety equipment, even though it is expensive. For a listing of selected rights and other ethical norms, see Figure 2.

---

[10] Jeremy Bentham, *An Introduction to the Principles of Morals and Legislation* (New York: Hafner, 1948).

[11] John Stuart Mill, *Utilitarianism* (Indianapolis: Bobbs-Merrill, 1957).

[12] See Carol Gilligan, *In a Different Voice* (Cambridge: Harvard University Press, 1982); and Nel Noddings, *Caring* (Berkeley: University of California Press, 1984).

[13] For example, see Thomas Donaldson, Patricia Werhane, Patricia Hogue; Joseph Van Zandt, *Ethical Issues in Business: A Philosophical Approach*, 8th ed. (Upper Saddle River, NJ: Prentice-Hall, 2007); and John Rawls, *A Theory of Justice* (Cambridge, MA: Harvard University Press, 1971).

[14] Velasquez Manuel, *Business Ethics: Concepts and Cases*, 6th ed. (Upper Saddle River, NJ: Prentice Hall, 2006), pp. 71–84; also Richard T. De George, *Business Ethics*, 6th ed. (Upper Saddle River, NJ: Prentice Hall, 2006), pp. 77–84. For a comprehensive European view, see Andrew Crane and Dirk Matten, *Business Ethics*, 2nd ed. (Oxford: Oxford University Press, 2007).

TABLE 1 Models for Business Decisions

Definition and Origin	Strengths	Weaknesses	Example	When Used	
				Summary	
1. Norm of Rights and Duties Individual's freedom is not to be violated: Locke (1635–1701)—property Kant (1724–1804)—personal rights	1. Ensures respect for individual's personal freedom and property 2. Parallels political Bill of Rights	1. Emphasis on rights can encourage individualistic, selfish behavior	1. Unsafe workplace 2. Flammable children's toys 3. Lying to superior or subordinate	1. Where individual's personal rights or property are in question 2. Use with, for example, employee privacy, job tenure, work dangerous to person's health	
2. Norm of Justice Equitable distribution of society's benefits and burdens: Aristotle (384–322 BC) Rawls (1921–2002)	1. The "democratic" principle 2. Does not allow a society to become status- or class-dominated 3. Ensures that minorities, poor, handicapped receive opportunities and a fair share of the output	1. Can result in less risk, incentive, and innovation 2. Encourages sense of entitlement	1. Bribes, kickbacks, fraud 2. Delivery of shoddy goods 3. Low wages to Hispanic, African, American, or women workers 4. Sweatshops	1. Fairness, equal opportunity for poor and unemployed 2. Setting salaries for workers vs. executives 3. Public policy decisions: to maintain a floor of living standards for all 4. Use with, for example, performance appraisal, due process, distribution of rewards and punishment	

(continued)

TABLE 1 *(continued)*

Definition and Origin	Strengths	Weaknesses	When Used Example	When Used Summary
3. *Utilitarianism* "The greatest good for the greatest number": Bentham (1748–1832) Adam Smith (1723–1790) David Ricardo (1772–1823)	1. Concepts, terminology, methods are easiest for business people to use 2. Promotes view of entire system of exchange beyond "this firm" 3. Encourages entrepreneurship, innovation, productivity	1. Impossible to measure or quantify all important elements 2. "Greatest good" can degenerate into self-interest 3. Can result in abridging another's rights 4. Can result in neglecting less powerful segments of society	1. Plant closing 2. Pollution 3. Condemnation of land or buildings for "development"	1. Use in all business decisions, and will be dominant criteria in most 2. Version of model is implicitly used already, although scope is generally limited to "this firm"
4. *Caring* Responsibility to a person because of relationship: Gilligan (1936–) Noddings (1929–)	1. Emphasizes care and responsibility for people 2. Builds trust, healthy communications, and teamwork 3. Supports community and good for group	1. Poor at discriminating various responsibilities and equities 2. Without personal relationship there are no obligations	1. Mentoring colleagues and subordinates 2. Flexible hours and flexible leave policy or sake of family duties 3. At time of delivery of poor performance report or layoffs	1. Emphasizes interpersonal relationships 2. Care for employees and members of work group 3. Concern for those with personal or family needs

124

Rights and Duties

1. *Life and Safety:* Each person has the right not to have her or his life or safety unknowingly and unnecessarily endangered.

2. *Truthfulness:* The individual has the right not to be intentionally deceived by another, especially on matters about which the individual has the right to know.

3. *Privacy:* The individual has the right to do whatever he or she chooses to do outside working hours and to control information about his or her private life.

4. *Freedom of conscience:* The individual has the right to refrain from carrying out any order that violates those commonly accepted moral or religious norms to which the person adheres.

5. *Free speech:* The individual has the right to criticize conscientiously and truthfully the ethics or legality of corporate actions so long as the criticism does not violate the rights of other individuals within the organization.

6. *Private property:* The individual has the right to hold private property, especially far as this right enables the individual and his or her family to be sheltered have the basic necessities of life.insoand to

Justice

1. *Fair treatment:* People who are similar to each other in the relevant respects should be treated similarly; people who differ in some respect relevant to the job they perform should be treated differently in proportion to the difference between them.

2. *Fair administration of rules:* Rules should be administered consistently,fairly, and impartially.

3. *Fair compensation:* A person should be compensated for the cost of their injuries by the party that is responsible for those injuries.

4. *Fair blame:* Individuals should not be held responsible for matters over which they have no control.

5. *Due process:* A person has a right to a fair and impartial hearing when he or she believes that personal rights are being violated.

Utilitarianism

1. *Organizational Goals* should aim at *maximizing the satisfactions* of the organizations constituencies.

2. The members of an organization should attempt to attain its goals as *efficiently* as possible by consuming as few inputs as possible and minimizing external costs which organizational activities impose on others.

3. The employee should use *every effective means* to achieve the goals of the organization and should neither jeopardize those goals nor enter situations in which personal interests conflict significantly with the goals.

Caring

1. Each person has responsibility for the well-being of those people with whom one has a relation.

2. The responsibility to care increases as the dependency of the other person increases.

3. One cannot be obligated to provide care that one is incapable of providing.

FIGURE 2 Selected Ethical Norms

People also have the right not to be lied to or deceived, especially on matters about which they have a right to know. Hence, a supervisor has a duty to give helpful feedback on work performance even if it is time consuming and difficult for the supervisor to do so. Each of us has the right not to be lied to by salespeople or advertisements, even though this right is often violated. Perjury under oath is a serious crime; lying on matters where another has a right to accurate information is seriously unethical. Truthfulness is a basic ethical norm, and it is essential for business.

Rights and duties are moral requirements that protect the individual person, including protection from the encroachment and demands of society or the state. Utilitarian standards promote the group's interests and are relatively insensitive regarding a single individual except insofar as the individual's welfare affects the good of the group.

A business contract establishes rights and duties that did not exist before: the right of the purchaser to receive what was agreed and the right of the seller to be paid what was agreed. Formal written contracts and informal verbal agreements establish new rights and duties and are essential to business transactions.

Americans are more individualistic than any other culture,[15] and so emphasize personal rights more than others. German Philosopher **Immanuel Kant** (1724–1804) recognized that such an emphasis on rights can lead people to focus excessively on what is due them. Kant sought to broaden this perspective, so he emphasized what he called the "categorical imperative." The first formulation is: *I ought never to act except in such a way that I can also will that my principle should become a universal law.* An equivalent statement is: *An action is morally right for a person in a certain situation if and only if the person's reason for carrying out the action is a reason that he or she would be willing to have every person act on, in any similar situation.*[16]

Kant's second formulation of the categorical imperative cautions us against using other people as a means to our own ends: Never treat another person simply as a means, but always also as an end. An action is morally right for a person if and only if in performing the action the person does not use others merely as a means for advancing his or her own interests, but also both respects and develops their capacity to choose for themselves. The **Golden Rule,** "Do unto others as you would have them do unto you," mirrors Leviticus (19:18) and Jesus, "Love your neighbor as yourself'" (Matthew 22:19).

Capital, networks, and business firms are means, and are to be used to serve the purposes of people. On the other hand, a person is not to be used merely as a means to achieve my goals. Thus, respect for human dignity places a duty on me that I not deceive, manipulate, or exploit other people.

Norm of Justice

Justice requires that all persons be guided by fairness, equity, and impartiality. Justice calls for evenhanded treatment of groups and individuals (1) in the distribution of

---

[15] Hofstede Geert, *Culture's Consequences: Comparing Values, Behaviors, Institutions, and Organizations Across Nations,* 2nd ed. (Thousand Oaks: Sage, 2001), p. 215.
[16] Immanuel Kant, *Groundwork of the Metaphysics of Morals,* trans. H. J. Paton (New York: Harper & Row, 1964), pp. 62–90.

the benefits and burdens of society, (2) in the administration of laws and regulations, and (3) in the imposition of sanctions and the awarding of compensation for wrongs suffered.

Standards of justice are generally considered to be more important than the utilitarian consideration of consequences. If a society is unjust to a group (e.g., segregation, job discrimination), we consider that society to be unjust and we condemn it, even if the injustices bring about greater productivity. On the other hand, we are willing to trade off some equality if the results will bring about greater benefits for all. For example, differences in income and wealth are justified when they bring greater prosperity *for all*.

Standards of justice are not as often in conflict with individual rights as are utilitarian norms. Both justice and moral rights are based on the recognition of the **dignity of human beings**. The moral right to be treated as a free and equal person, for example, undergirds the notion that benefits and burdens should be distributed equitably. Personal moral rights (e.g., right to life, freedom of conscience, the right to free consent) are so basic that generally they may not be taken away to bring about a better distribution of benefits within a society. On the other hand, property rights may be sacrificed for the sake of a fairer distribution of benefits and burdens (e.g., graduated income tax, limits on pollution).

Distributive justice becomes important when a society has sufficient goods but everyone's basic needs are not satisfied. The question then becomes, what is a just distribution? The fundamental principle is that equals should be treated equally and that unequals should be treated according to their inequality. For example, few would argue that a new person hired for a job should receive the same pay as a senior worker who has 20 years of experience. People who perform work of greater responsibility or who work longer hours should also receive greater pay. Hence, pay differentials should be based on the work itself, not on some arbitrary bias of the employer. Even knowing all of the above, we still wouldn't be able to determine a fair distribution of society's benefits and burdens. In fact, quite different notions of equity are proposed. For example, the capitalist model (benefits based on contribution) is radically different from the socialist (from each according to abilities, to each according to needs).

John Rawls (1921–2003) contributed important ideas to the theory of justice.[17] Rawls would have us construct a system of rules and laws for society as if we did not know what roles we were to play in that society. We do not know if we would be rich or poor, female or male, African or European, manager or slave, physically and mentally fit or handicapped. Rawls calls this the "**veil of ignorance**." Constructing a system of rules under the veil of ignorance allows us to rid ourselves of the biases we have as a result of our own status. Rawls proposes that in such circumstances, each of us would try to construct a system that would be to the greatest benefit to all and that would not undermine the position of any group. According to Rawls, people under the veil of ignorance would agree to two principles:

1. Each person would have an equal right to the most extensive liberty compatible with similar liberty for others.

---

[17] Rawls, *op. cit.*

2. Social and economic inequalities would be arranged so that they are reasonably expected to be to everyone's advantage and attached to positions and offices open to all.

The first principle is parallel to the American sense of liberty and thus is not controversial in the United States. The second principle is more egalitarian and also more controversial. However, Rawls maintains that if people honestly choose as if they were under the veil of ignorance, they would opt for a system of justice that is most fair to all members of society.[18] We now turn to a norm that observes the *consequences* of actions on the entire group.

Norm of Utilitarianism

Utilitarianism examines the **consequences** of an act. It judges that an action is right if it produces the greatest utility, "the greatest good for the greatest number." The calculation is similar to a cost–benefit analysis applied to all parties who would be affected by the decision. That action is ethical which produces the **greatest net benefit** when all benefits to all the affected parties are added and the costs to parties are subtracted. Although it would be convenient if these costs and benefits could be measured in some comparable unit, this is rarely possible. Many important values (e.g., human life and liberty) cannot be quantified. Thus, the best we can do is to list the effects and estimate the magnitude of their costs and benefits as accurately as possible.

The utilitarian norm says that the ethical action is that which produces the greatest net benefit over any other possible action. This does not mean that the right action produces the greatest good for the person performing the action. Rather, it is the action that produces the greatest net good for all those who are affected by the action. The utilitarian norm is most useful for complex cases that affect many parties. Although the methodology is clear in theory, carrying out the calculations is often difficult. Taking into account so many affected parties, and the extent to which the action affects them, can be a tallying nightmare.

Hence several shortcuts have been proposed that can reduce the complexity of utilitarian calculations. Each shortcut involves a sacrifice of accuracy for ease of decision. Among these shortcuts are (1) calculation of costs and benefits in dollar terms for ease of comparison; (2) restriction of consideration to those directly affected by the action, putting aside indirect effects. In using these shortcuts, an individual should be aware that they result in simplification and that some interests may not be sufficiently taken into consideration.

In the popular mind, the term *utilitarianism* sometimes suggests exploitation. We do not intend this meaning. However, a noteworthy weakness of the ethical norm of utilitarianism is that it can advocate, for example, abridging an individual's right to a job or even life for the sake of the greater good of a large number of people. This

---

[18] An organization that treats its employees justly reaps many rewards, see Blair H. Shepard, Roy J. Lewicki, and John W. Minton, *Organizational Justice: The Search for Fairness in the Workplace* (New York: Lexington, 1992).

and other difficulties are discussed elsewhere.[19] There is an additional rule in using utilitarianism: It is considered unethical to choose narrower benefits (e.g., personal goals of career or money) at the expense of the good of a larger number, such as a firm, neighborhood, or a nation. Utilitarian norms emphasize the **good of the** *group*. However, as a result an individual and what is due to that individual may be overlooked. Hence the norm of utilitarianism must be balanced by the use of the norms of justice, rights and duties, and, the norm we will discuss next, caring.

Norm of Caring

Over the centuries ethicists, who were almost all male, developed the norms of rights and duties, justice, and utilitarianism. These norms highlight impartiality and abstract principles. A norm of *caring* has been recognized in the last few decades.[20] Caring is built upon relations between people and is an extension of family life. Rather than autonomous individuals making objective, impartial ethical judgments, we instead experience numerous **relationships**, and these relationships influence our ethical obligations. We care for each other, and we have responsibilities to each other.

Ethicists who advocate caring as a norm demonstrate how women's moral experience has been neglected. When facing moral dilemmas, women tend to focus on the relationships of people rather than on impartial, theoretical principles. Gilligan amended the levels of moral development in the light of the experience of women. The male matures by developing autonomy and sees himself in opposition to the other. Thus he insists on personal rights. However, if a businessperson is unduly influenced by rights and competition, it can result in paranoid tendencies that can cause difficulty relating to others or relating to others only by contract.

The female matures by developing relationship-based morality. Although feminist ethicists are reluctant to analyze caring too exactly, we can note some qualifications of the norm of caring. First, the obligation to care is proportional to one's relationship. In extended relationships, caring does not require action if that action is very costly. Second, one's roles and obligations influence the responsibility to care. Caring for one's child has greater priority than caring for someone in one's work group. Third, one cannot be obligated to provide care that one is incapable of providing. For the manager, caring is a relevant norm for many current business challenges. Trust, teamwork, good personal relationships, and communications build upon caring, and must be achieved, if the firm is to be successful.[21]

---

[19] Robert Audi, "Can Utilitarianism Be Distributive? Maximization and Distribution as Criteria in Managerial Decisions," *Business Ethics Quarterly*, 17 (October 2007): 593–611; Gerald F. Cavanagh, Dennis J. Moberg, and Manuel Velasquez, "The Ethics of Organizational Politics," *Academy of Management Review*, 6 (July 1981): 363–374; Manuel Velasquez, *Business Ethics: Concepts and Cases*, 6th ed. (Upper Saddle River, NJ: Prentice-Hall, 2006), pp. 60–71.

[20] See Rosemarie Tong, *Feminine and Feminist Ethics* (Belmont, CA: Wadsworth, 1993), esp. chapters 3 and 4; Gilligan, *op. cit.*

[21] Jeanne M. Liedtka, "Feminist Morality and Competitive Reality: A Role for the Ethic of Care?" *Business Ethics Quarterly*, 6 (April 1996): 179–200; Gerald F. Cavanagh, Dennis J. Moberg, and Manuel Velasquez, "Making Business Ethics Practical," *Business Ethics Quarterly*, 5 (July 1995): 399–418.

Caring engages our emotions, but in order to do *any* ethical reasoning, our emotions must be involved. While ethics is not feeling, it is a sterile intellectual exercise if one's feelings are not engaged in ethical decision making. In making ethical judgments it is essential to consider the interests of others. In order to incorporate the interests of others into one's decision-making processes, one must be able to feel and to empathize with those that are affected by one's decisions. In Kohlberg's terms, one must at least have achieved Level 2 moral development. In order to be an ethical decision maker, one must learn how to habitually put oneself in the position of other persons. One must learn how others perceive a situation and sense what others feel and suffer. Without this ability to care for others on a sensible level, it is impossible to examine the moral dimensions of life in any significant way.

Ethical Norms for Global Business

Some claim that the varying business customs and practices in countries around the world demand new norms for international business ethics. They propose a variety of different models, based upon rights, social contract, and negative and modified utilitarianism.[22] Other scholars, however, have found common basic ethical values in business in different cultures. While global business norms do not yet exist, the various attempts to achieve norms and the codes of ethics that we will examine in Chapter 9 are developing an international policy regime.[23] This is gradually providing a consensus of moral expectations for the global firm.

Manuel Velasquez applied the new proposed models to several cases in global business ethics.[24] He demonstrates the limitations of each of those new proposals. On the other hand, he found that the comprehensive model containing the norms of rights and duties, justice, utilitarianism, and caring as presented in this chapter is more flexible and effective for the global business manager. Let us now use these norms to solve some ethical problems.

SOLVING ETHICAL PROBLEMS

A good judgment is preceded by four steps: gather the facts, articulate accurately the issue, select the appropriate norm to use, and make an ethical judgment (see Figure 3). Before any ethical dilemma can be assessed, it is essential that all the **relevant facts** be considered. Omissions can result in a faulty judgment: failure to

---

[22] Thomas Donaldson and Thomas W. Dunfee, *Ties That Bind: A Social Contracts Approach to Business Ethics* (Boston: Harvard Business School Press, 1999); also Andrew Spicer, Thomas Dunfee, and Wendy J. Bailey, "Does National Context Matter in Ethical Decision Making? An Empirical Test of Integrative Social Contracts Theory," *Academy of Management Journal,* 47 (August 2004): 610–620.

[23] Duane Windsor, "The Development of International Business Norms," *Business Ethics Quarterly,* 14 (October 2004): 729–754; see the business ethics text in both Chinese and English, Stephan Rothlin, *Eighteen Rules of International Business Ethics* (Beijing, 2004); Japanese business managers have roughly the same values as do American, according to Chaiki Nakano, "A Survey on Japanese Managers' Views of Business Ethics," *op. cit.*

[24] Manuel Velasquez, "International Business Ethics: The Aluminum Companies in Jamaica," *Business Ethics Quarterly,* 5 (October 1995): 865–882; Hans Kung, "A Global Ethic in an Age of Globalization," *Business Ethics Quarterly,* 7 (July 1997): 17–31.

gather all the data, an inadequate understanding of ethical norms, and making an important decision too quickly.[25] To help select the most **appropriate ethical norm**, we have described rights and duties, justice, utility, and caring. Figure 3 is a schematic diagram of how ethical decision making can best proceed. Although it contains greater detail than Figure 1, it includes the same three steps, data gathering, analysis, and judgment. Even Figure 3 is simplified, but nevertheless it can aid in solving ethical dilemmas.

Note that each of the four ethical norms is listed in Figure 3. In order to make an ethical decision, we decide which norm is best able to assess the particular case. Basic moral rights, such as the right to life, may not be negated by others, even if doing so would effect greater benefits. The norm of caring may outweigh impartiality when the situation involves close relationships and privately held resources.

To summarize, one can come to an ethical decision when one follows the steps:

1. Gather the **relevant facts** of the case;
2. What is the principal **ethical issue**? [i.e., "Is it ethical to . . . "];
3. Choose the most appropriate **ethical norm**(s);
4. Apply the norm(s) and make an ethical **judgment**.

Let us apply this process and our norms to the case presented earlier of the executive who padded her expense account. We will accept the limited data provided in the case. The ethical issue: Is it ethical for an executive to obtain an additional $7,500 per year by padding her expense account? The rights norm is not so useful here: The executive has no right to the extra money, although we might argue that the shareholders' and customers' right to goods due them is being violated. Using the justice norm, we note that salary and commissions constitute ordinary compensation for individuals. Expense accounts have a different purpose. Most managers responding to the case held that it was unethical for the executive to pad her expense account. John Rawls would maintain that all of us would set the rules to prohibit such padding of expenses if we did not know what roles we ourselves would have in society. Using the utility criterion, we judge that padding her expense account benefits the executive but not others. Her actions hurt shareholders, customers, and honest executives; padding one's expense account adds to the cost of business and in this way also violates utility. Claiming nonexistent expenses does not indicate care for others in the firm. Hence, we conclude that padding one's expense account is unethical on all four ethical norms, and is therefore morally wrong. Note that 73 percent of the executives who were asked came to the same judgment.

Let us consider a case from the beginning of the chapter. Are our ethical norms violated when a student cheats on an exam? If a student looks at another student's paper or takes a "cheat sheet" into an exam, that student's finished exam does not represent what she actually knows. She has "stolen" answers that are not hers, and thus violates justice; she seeks to obtain credit for material that she does not know. Other students, who are playing by the rules, do not have access to

---

[25] Paul C. Nutt, *Why Decisions Fail: Avoiding the Blunders and Traps That Lead to Debacles* (San Francisco: Berrett-Koehler, 2002).

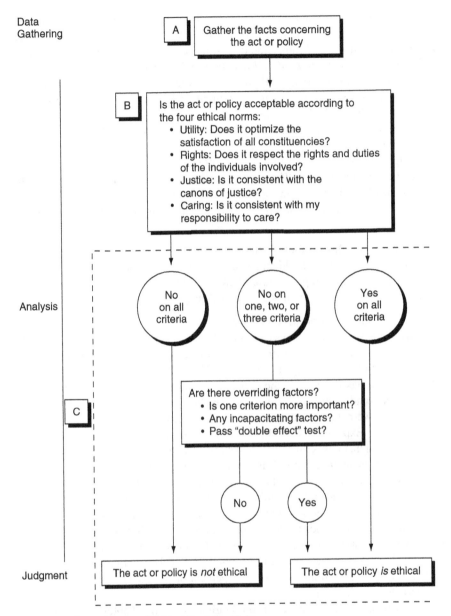

Data
Gathering

Analysis

Judgment

A — Gather the facts concerning the act or policy

B — Is the act or policy acceptable according to the four ethical norms:
- Utility: Does it optimize the satisfaction of all constituencies?
- Rights: Does it respect the rights and duties of the individuals involved?
- Justice: Is it consistent with the canons of justice?
- Caring: Is it consistent with my responsibility to care?

No on all criteria

No on one, two, or three criteria

Yes on all criteria

C

Are there overriding factors?
- Is one criterion more important?
- Any incapacitating factors?
- Pass "double effect" test?

No

Yes

The act or policy is *not* ethical

The act or policy *is* ethical

FIGURE 3 Flow Diagram of Ethical Decision Making

Source: Adapted from Gerald F. Cavanagh, Dennis J. Moberg, and Manuel Velasquez, "Making Business Ethics Practical," Business Ethics Quarterly *(July 1995); Manuel Velasquez, Gerald F. Cavanagh, and Dennis Moberg, "Organizational Statesmenship and Dirty Politics,"* Organizational Dynamics *(Fall 1983).*

answers. So the cheating student is taking unfair advantage of her fellow students. From the utilitarian perspective, the only person who benefits is the cheater. The other students all suffer because their performance is considered to be relatively poorer than the one who cheated. Cheating may hurt even the cheater, because she will not have the knowledge that a future employer may expect her to have. Moreover, cheating can easily become a habit, and that could cause one to be fired for cheating on the job. So, while cheating may benefit one in the short term, in the long term it is not a benefit even to the cheater.

What about the entrepreneur who advertised official-looking blank receipts of fictitious restaurants? Salespeople and managers could fill out the receipts and submit them for reimbursement. The receipts would document meals that never were purchased. Using our norms, how do we judge the ethics of the person selling such receipts? Or of the person buying them and using them? Respond to this case using the flow chart in Figure 3. Examine Andrew Fastow's case using the same norms.

When deciding on what is ethical behavior, two short-cut tests may help. First, could my conduct bear the scrutiny of a probing reporter? Would I do it if I knew that my actions were going to be featured in tomorrow's news? Second, could I acknowledge what I did to my mother or another for whom I have respect?

Decision Making Using the Model

Let us examine another case:

> Brian Curry, financial vice president of Digital Robotics Corporation, is about to retire and has been asked to recommend one of his two associates for promotion to vice president. Curry knows that his recommendation will be acted on. He also realizes that since both associates are about the same age, the one not chosen will have difficulty getting future promotions. Debra Butler is bright, outgoing and has better leadership skills. She is the most qualified for the position. Moreover, her father is president of the largest customer of Digital, and Curry reasons that Digital will more likely keep this business if his daughter is made an officer. On the other hand, John McNichols has been with the company longer, has worked seventy-hour weeks, and has pulled the company through some very difficult situations. He has continued putting in extra effort because he was told some time ago that he was in line for the vice presidency. Nevertheless, Curry recommends Butler for the job.

Let us again use our norms and Figure 3 to decide this case. Neither Butler nor McNichols has a right to the position. Is it ethical to promote Butler? As for justice, we conclude that because the promotional decision was made on the basis of relevant abilities, it did constitute fair treatment. On the other hand, McNichols worked extra hours because of the promised promotion. Much of his extra work was based on a false promise. McNichols had a right to know the truth and to be treated fairly. Utility tells us that the selection of Debra Butler optimally benefits shareholders, customers, management, and most of the workers, because she is a better leader.[26] Caring is not a primary norm to use in such a case.

Thus, according to the norms of justice and utility, the appointment of Butler is morally acceptable. However, because of the promise earlier made to McNichols, which resulted in extended work weeks, he is being treated wrongly. We can then ask if there are any "overriding factors" that ought to be taken into consideration.

Overriding Factors

Overriding factors are factors that may, in a given case, justify overriding one or perhaps two of the four ethical norms: rights and duties, justice, utility, or caring (see Figure 3). Overriding factors can be examined when there is a conflict in the conclusions drawn from the ethical norms. For example, there might be **incapacitating factors**, such as a *lack of information* or *coercion*. If there are any elements that *coerce* an individual into doing a certain action, then that individual is not fully responsible. Let us take the example of Bausch and Lomb. CEO Daniel Gill expected division managers to show double-digit earnings each quarter. Under this unrelenting pressure, the managers faked sales of sunglasses and forced distributors to accept unneeded products. This eventually resulted in a collapse of revenues and an SEC investigation. What the managers did was unethical, but to the extent that they were coerced their guilt is less because they were pressured by their CEO.[27] Also, a *lack of information* may be an incapacitating factor that might prevent someone might from utilizing a norm. A manager might suspect that another manager is embezzling from the firm. However, to report him to superiors could ruin his reputation. Therefore, even though stealing is a violation of justice, in this instance there is not yet sufficient information to act. In addition, a manager may be sincerely uncertain of the norm or its applicability in a particular case.[28]

Consider again our case of appointing a financial vice president. Utility calls for recommending Debra Butler for the position. The right to full information and perhaps justice support McNichols' claim. McNichols has worked more hours and harder because of a promised reward. Because the position was promised to him, fair treatment requires giving him special consideration. On the basis of the importance of a verbal promise and of justice, we might conclude that McNichols should get the position.

There is now a conflict between these two norms. Is one norm more important? The effective operation of the firm is an important ethical goal, because many jobs and family incomes depend upon it. How much better a manager is Butler and how would her selection affect the firm's performance and the jobs of others at Digital?

In examining incapacitating factors, coercion does not seem to be involved. That Debra Butler's father is president of Digital's largest customer might constitute psychological pressure. However, Curry seems to have made his decision freely.

---

[26] A manager can score him- or herself as being predominantly a user of the utility, justice, or rights norm by using a set of questions developed by Marshall Sashkin. See his *Managerial Values Profile* (Bryn Mawr, PA: Organizational Design and Development, 1986).

[27] "Blind Ambition: How Pursuit of Results Got Out of Hand at Bausch and Lomb," *Business Week,* October 23, 1995, pp. 78–92, 146.

[28] For how incapacitating factors lessen a moral agent's responsibility, see Oswald A. J. Mascarenhas, "Exonerating Unethical Marketing Executive Behaviors: A Diagnostic Framework," *Journal of Marketing,* 59 (April 1995): 43–57.

Another factor to consider is exactly what promise was made to McNichols? Was it clear and unequivocal? If the "promise" was in fact a mere statement that McNichols had a good chance at the promotion and if Butler's performance in the VP job is expected to be significantly better than McNichols', then Curry could ethically recommend Butler. However, some compensation should then be made to McNichols.

Selling Cigarettes Globally

Let us assess the ethics of the following case:

U.S. based Altria spun off Philip Morris International (PMI) and moved its headquarters to Switzerland in 2008. This made the tobacco firm's international operations beyond the reach of U.S. regulations, and the legal and public relations headaches that have stood in the way of its growth. With sales of $22 billion PMI is the third most profitable consumer goods firm in the world after Procter & Gamble (P&G) and Nestle. Smoking rates in developed countries have declined, but have increased dramatically in developing countries (for example, since 2001, up 42% in Pakistan; 36% in Ukraine and 18% in Argentina). China's 350 million smokers annually generate about $30 billion in tax revenue for the country.[29]

Roughly 430,000 Americans and globally almost 5,000,000 people die prematurely each year of tobacco related illness. Medical scientists estimate that 30 to 40 percent of all who smoke will die of cancer, cardio-vascular disease, or chronic obstructive lung disease caused by their smoking. Including medical costs and lost productivity, smoking costs the U.S. $167 million per year, according to the American Cancer Society.

Tobacco executives have initiated strategies to market cigarettes to teenagers, minorities, women and people in developing countries. They employ advertising and widespread distribution of free samples. Advertising shows members of the dominant social or racial group smoking cigarettes in attractive surroundings. The market share for U.S. firms in four Asian countries rose 600%, and cigarette smoking was found to be about 10% higher than it would be if it were not for the U.S. cigarettes and advertising. Experts predict the death rate due to tobacco world-wide will reach 10,000,000 annually by the year 2020.[30]

Is it ethical to sell cigarettes? Let us apply our ethical norms to the case. Cigarette executives claim that they are not violating anyone's right to life by selling cigarettes, because information is available on the health hazards. However, some people, especially youth and the poor, may not be aware of the likelihood of serious

---

[29] Vanessa O'Connell, "Philip Morris Readies Aggressive Global Push: Division Spinoff Enables Blitz of New Products; High-Tar Smokes in Asia," *The Wall Street Journal*, January 29, 2008, p. AI.

[30] David Kessler, *A Question of Intent: A Great American Battle with a Deadly Industry* (New York: Public Affairs, 2001); see also Philip Hilts, *Smokescreen: The Truth Behind the Tobacco Industry Cover-up* (Reading, MA: Addison Wesley, 1996); and Richard Kluber, *Ashes to Ashes: America's Hundred-Year Cigarette War, the Public Health, and the Unabashed Triumph of Philip Morris* (New York: Knopf, 1996).

disease and death that follow the use of tobacco. Both justice and rights demand that cigarette sellers be truthful in advertising products with such deadly consequences.

Utilitarians calculate that those who benefit are the cigarette companies, their employees, and the user who is able to feed his nicotine addiction. On the other hand, the user's health is often seriously impaired. This can result in large health and dollar costs to the smoker, their dependents, and employers. Society as a whole pays, because income is lost and insurance costs rise because of the many serious tobacco-related illnesses. Justice calls for tobacco firms, which reap large profits from cigarette sales, to share the burden of paying the additional health costs.

Health concerns and caring might lead tobacco executives to stop attracting new smokers and possibly even to withdraw tobacco products from the market altogether. There do not seem to be any overriding factors in this case, or any incapacitating factors such as coercion. Have we been too harsh on the executives of cigarette firms? How would you analyze the case?

The ethical model and principles described in this chapter are widely used. The model enables the manager to use ethical analysis in business decisions, and to thus balance financial and marketing analyses. Yet problems of conscience can still sometimes face a member of an organization.

Loyalty and Whistle-Blowing

In addition to making ethical decisions, a member of an organization sometimes faces a situation where superiors seem to ignore or be blind to unethical acts. Sherron Watkins of Enron, Cynthia Cooper of WorldCom, and Coleen Rowley of the FBI were named *Time Magazine*'s "persons of the year" for blowing the whistle internally at their organizations.[31] At Enron, WorldCom, and the FBI, they found that information was being falsified, thus misleading important stakeholders of their organization. Whether to blow the whistle is a difficult dilemma and ultimately demands courage. Let us examine the following case, where the stakes are high:

An engineer in the design section of an airplane manufacturing firm is convinced that the latch mechanism on a plane's cargo door does not provide sufficient security. She is convinced that the door could blow out, causing decompression and a crash; the door should be redesigned to make it more secure. She goes to her supervisor and presents the information, and is told that the U.S. Federal Aviation Administration (FAA) has given the required approval and that she should not "rock the boat." She goes to the president of the firm and gets the same answer.

Would that engineer be justified in making this information public, and perhaps taking it to the news media? The answer to this question is extremely important. The danger to the lives of hundreds of passengers might argue for going public.[32] On the other hand, the reputation and perhaps the financial viability of the aircraft

---

[31] Richard Lacayo and Amanda Ripley, "Persons of the Year," *Time*, January 6, 2003, pp. 30–60.

[32] Janet P. Near, Michael Rehg, James Van Scotter, and Marcia Miceli, "Does the Type of Wrongdoing Affect the Whistle-Blowing Process?" *Business Ethics Quarterly*, 14, no. 2 (2004): 219–242.

manufacturing firm are also to be weighed. A mistake on either side could cause disaster. So it is important to do the ethical analysis very carefully.

The right to life and safety is at issue. If the engineer is correct that the faulty latch mechanism puts the plane in danger of a crash, then the lives of the passengers would be of primary importance in the calculations. While the engineer owes loyalty to her employer, nevertheless justice requires that future passengers should not unknowingly be in danger of their lives due to the faulty design.

Utilitarians would total up the costs and benefits to all parties affected. Redesigning the aircraft and recalling planes already in service would cost the firm hundreds of millions of dollars. More immediately, taking the issue to the scandal-oriented media people would undermine the reputation of the firm. On the other hand, assuming that 300 people are aboard a plane that might crash, how much are 300 lives worth? Utilitarians, too, would conclude that the designer would be justified in taking the issue outside the firm. Caring would cause the engineer to opt for the safety of the passengers also. Even 69 percent of the corporate executives who examined the case thought that the designer was justified in breaching loyalty and taking the issue to the media.[33]

When to Blow the Whistle

Because opportunities for whistle-blowing are more common and the stakes are high, it is important to examine the conditions that would allow and sometimes require whistle-blowing. Whistle-blowing has been defined as "the disclosure by organization members (former or current) of illegal, immoral, or illegitimate practices under the control of their employers, to persons or organizations that may be able to effect action."[34] This definition covers both blowing the whistle internally to upper management (as the three *Time* Women-of-the-Year did) and also to external parties (e.g., government agencies or the media). To be ethical, one should meet several criteria for whistle-blowing:[35]

1. The purpose should be moral: to benefit the public interest.
2. What is protested should be of major importance and should be specific.
3. The facts of the case must be certain; they should be checked and rechecked.
4. In the case of external whistle-blowing, all other avenues for change within the organization must already be exhausted.

Let us examine these criteria. The first demands that the purpose of whistle-blowing should not be to attract attention, to seek revenge, or to achieve some personal goal. Whistle-blowers sometimes are seeking vengeance on a supervisor or a company that they believe has been unfair to them. Perceptions regarding one's grievances can be biased and do not provide a solid basis for whistle-blowing. Instead, the revelation of wrongdoing should be for the **common good**.

---

[33] "Business Executives and Moral Dilemmas," *Business and Society Review,* Spring, 1975, p. 52.

[34] Marcia P. Miceli and Janet P. Near, "Understanding Whistle- Blowing Effectiveness: How Can One Person Make a Difference," in *The Accountable Corporation,* ed. Marc J. Epstein and Kirk O. Hanson, vol. 4 (Westport, CT: Praeger, 2006), p. 203.

[35] Sissela Bok, "Whistleblowing and Professional Responsibilities," in *Ethics Teaching in Higher Education,* ed. Daniel Callahan and Sissela Bok (New York: Plenum Press, 1980).

Second, whistle-blowing requires that the wrongdoing be a serious breach of ethics. Much is at stake, and the action should not be taken lightly. The unethical act protested should be a specific act, not a vague attitude that is hard to document.

Third, the facts of the case must be ascertained, and the **evidence** must be double-checked. The fourth criterion demands that higher officials in the organization who could rectify the situation have been **informed** and that they still refuse to do anything. This requires going to the president and the board before going to an outside party. If a federal regulatory agency could be involved, then, assuming all internal avenues have been tried, the agency is to be preferred to the news media.

U.S. law provides financial rewards to whistle-blowers who find fraud with regard to federal contracts. These rewards have been successful in reducing such fraud, and thus rewards seem to be justified.[36] However, to compensate for possible personal bias, one should seek competent objective advice so as not to blow the whistle on the basis of partial or misleading information. Ideally, the whistle-blower should be willing to accept responsibility for providing the information. This takes courage, since the person's job may be on the line. It is also a test of one's motives. Moreover, anonymous informers are not as trusted.

Let us apply the criteria to the case of the aircraft designer. Her purpose in blowing the whistle is to serve the public interest by preventing an airplane crash and saving hundreds of lives. The facts of the situation should be checked. In this case, let us presume that the engineer is mentally stable, has checked her data with competent peers, and has nothing to gain from the revelations. The whistle-blower has already gone to her supervisor and to the president. The FAA does not seem to recognize the design problem. However, before going to the media, the designer should check to see if the FAA is aware of it. If not, telling the FAA of the design flaw could achieve the safety goal without a public splash, and thus prevent severe loss to the manufacturer and to the airlines that use the plane. Because the whistle-blower has not yet acted, we do not know whether she will identify herself. We also know nothing of her character, but let us presume that no personal advantage will be gained by the whistle-blowing.

In conclusion, the whistle-blower, assuming she has the correct facts, would be justified in going to an external agency. This case is not fictitious. Had someone recognized and protested the cargo door latch problem on the DC-10, a Turkish airliner taking off from Paris would not have crashed and taken more than 300 lives.[37]

Wrongdoing within the firm can damage a company's profitability, hurt its reputation, demoralize its employees, and result in costly fines or lawsuits. Hence, in order for management to obtain information on such potentially damaging actions or products, it should provide a vehicle for an employee to report wrongdoing internally.[38]

---

[36] Thomas L. Carson, Mary Ellen Verdu, and Richard E. Wokutch, "Whistle-Blowing for Profit: An Ethical Analysis of the Federal False Claims Act," *Journal of Business Ethics*, 77 (2008): 361–376.

[37] Paul Eddy, Elaine Potter, and Bruce Page, *Destination Disaster* (New York: New York Times Book Co., 1976), esp. pp. 33–63.

[38] Roberta Ann Johnson, *Whistleblowing: When It Works and Why* (Boulder, CO: Lynne Rienner, 2002); and Michael Gundlach, Scott Douglas, and Mark Martinko, "The Decision to Blow the Whistle: A Social Information Processing Framework," *Academy of Management Review*, 28 (January 2003): 107–123; Marcia P. Miceli and Janet P. Near, "Whistleblowing: Reaping the Benefits," *Academy of Management Executive*, 8 (August 1994): 65–72.

A serious deterrent to whistle-blowing is the fact that many whistle-blowers are penalized by being demoted, frozen out, or fired. They are labeled as "stool pigeons" and "squealers." Legislation has provided some protection for whistle-blowers. People cannot be fired for whistle-blowing, at least under restricted circumstances.

Only when a firm has bad management, poor communications, and managers who do not want to hear bad news, does whistle-blowing occur. Ethical problems do not arise when a firm has, for example, accurate and honest financial reporting, good design of the product, and open communications. Whistle-blowing occurs when supervisors do not listen to subordinates and their concerns. Sometimes these concerns are not well founded, but it is essential that they be heard. An ambitious manager can encourage cheaper, substandard practices and pretend he does not see them as he tries to show higher quarterly profits. In short, blowing the whistle is more likely to occur when an organization has poor management, is not performing well, or both.

GOOD HABITS BUILD VIRTUE AND CHARACTER

Given recent and too common business scandals, executives ask how good character can be developed within the organization. Character development includes the good habits of trust, loyalty, and integrity.[39] Recall CEO Warren Buffet's words in his annual letter to shareholders, "When looking for managers, I basically look for three things—integrity, intelligence and energy. The truth is that if you don't have the first, the other two will kill you; because if you have someone who doesn't have integrity, you really want them to be dumb and lazy. It is only if they have the first that the second two count." Without integrity and good character, intelligence and energy destroy value rather than increase it. The global marketplace makes the need for integrity and character even more important; far-flung operations demand greater cooperation and honesty. Executives cannot build trust, commitment, and effort among the stakeholders of the firm without giving attention to integrity and character development. Moreover, an organization that is virtuous has been shown to be more effective and more profitable.[40] With fewer middle managers today, greater personal responsibility is demanded of members of organizations in order to perform their ordinary tasks. This has been described and measured, and is called "organizational citizenship."[41]

---

[39] See Edwin M. Hartman, "Can We Teach Character: An Aristotelian Answer," *Academy of Management Learning and Education,* 5, no. 1 (2006): 68–81; and Alan Wolfe, *Moral Freedom: The Search for Virtue in a World of* Choice (New York: W. W. Norton, 2002).

[40] Kim S. Cameron, "Good or Not Bad: Standards and Ethics in Managing Change," *Academy of Management Learning and Education,* 5, no. 3 (2006): 317–323; also Kim S. Cameron, Jane E. Dutton, and Robert E. Quinn, eds., *Positive Organizational Scholarship: Foundations of a New Discipline* (San Francisco: Berrett-Koehler, 2003).

[41] Robert H. Moorman, Gerald Blakely, and Brian Niehoff, "Does Perceived Organizational Support Mediate the Relationship Between Procedural Justice and Organizational Citizenship Behavior?" *Academy of Management Journal,* 41, no. 3 (1998): 351–357; also Linn Van Dyne, Jill Graham, and Richard Dienesch, "Organizational Citizenship Behavior: Construct Redefinition, Measurement, and Validation," *Academy of Management Journal,* 37 (1994): 765–802.

Altruism: Unselfish concern for the welfare of others.

Character: A stable organized personality with a composite of good and bad moral habits within a person.

Ethics: The principles of conduct governing an individual or a group, and the methods for applying them.

Habit: An acquired behavior pattern followed until it becomes almost automatic.

Moral: Dealing with or capable of distinguishing right from wrong.

Moral habit: A morally good or bad behavior pattern.

Value: A lasting belief that a certain goal or mode of conduct is better than the opposite goal or conduct.

Vice: A bad moral habit.

Virtue: A good moral habit that has been acquired by choosing the good.

FIGURE 4 Moral Habits Terms

Trust and a healthy community life is a foundation for prosperity. Francis Fukuyama maintains that some cultures have low trust (China, Italy, and France), while others possess high trust (Germany, the United States, and Japan). And some nonrational factors, such as religion, tradition, honor, and loyalty, are essential in building trust. But he warns that the predominant American value of individualism is a threat to trust.[42]

Character and virtue (for definitions, see Figure 4) are essential for a good manager. But high intelligence does not bring character. The example of intelligent people who supported Hitler (Martin Heidegger, Carl Jung, Ezra Pound), or the straight "A" student who sexually exploits others, demonstrates that intelligence and a good education do not result in good character.[43] Moreover, we often speak of honesty, trust, and integrity as if people are born with those virtues. This is not the case. Virtue is achieved by effort. For centuries, the philosopher **Aristotle** (384–322 BC) has helped us understand virtue. Aristotle shows how the virtuous person avoids extremes, and "what we call selfishness is guaranteed to be self-destructive as well."[44]

A **morally mature** person will develop good moral habits or virtues; "the ultimate aim of the Aristotelian approach to business is to cultivate whole human beings, not jungle fighters, efficiency automatons, or 'good soldiers.'" Certain virtues are important for business: honesty, fairness, trust, and toughness; friendliness, honor, loyalty, caring (developed from using ethical norm of caring), compassion, and justice (developed from using ethical norm). Each of these virtues is strengthened by repeated

---

[42] Francis Fukuyama, *Trust: The Social Virtues and the Creation of Prosperity* (New York: Free Press, 1995).
[43] Robert Coles, "The Disparity Between Intellect and Character," *Chronicle of Higher Education,* September 22, 1995, p. A68.
[44] Robert C. Solomon, "Victims of Circumstances: A Defense of Virtue Ethics in Business," *Business Ethics Quarterly,* 13, no. 1 (2003): 46–62.

actions. Envy and resentment are vices for the businessperson; they poison the firm. Vices are bad habits that develop through repeated acts.

A person is able to develop a good habit by consciously and repeatedly performing that act.[45] As Aristotle put it, "We are what we repeatedly do." Developing a good habit takes effort, but once a habit is established, later similar actions come easily and naturally. Thus a person who intentionally develops good habits through good acts makes additional similar good acts easier to perform. The development of good moral habits is also a test of the basic spiritual values of the individual person.[46] Moreover, people who possess virtue will be more reliable colleagues and will build a more effective firm in the long term.

Ethical decisions are the foundation of moral acts, and these good acts then provide the building blocks for good habits. Once a person has developed a good moral habit, say courage or prudence, that person is able to act with courage or prudence more easily in each new instance. This ability we identify as *virtue*. Before we proceed further, let us provide two examples of good and bad moral habits:

> A demented person placed cyanide in Tylenol capsules, and seven people in Chicago died. Consultants and the FBI advised against a recall of Tylenol, since they thought it would encourage other unstable people to do the same thing. Moreover, a recall of all existing capsules would cost manufacturer Johnson & Johnson hundreds of millions of dollars. However, James Burke, CEO at J&J, quickly decided on a recall rather than endanger additional lives. By Burke's account, this was because he and other managers based their decision on the mission and basic values of J&J and the good moral habits that thus developed among J&J people over the years.[47]

> The New York Stock Exchange (NYSE) is a non-profit, self-regulatory body that oversees the exchange of equity stock in the largest U.S. firms. NYSE's chairman, Richard Grasso, was voted $188 million in pay in 2003. The CEO's of some of the Wall Street firms that he regulated, Goldman Sachs, Lehman Brothers, and Bear Stearns, were on the compensation committee of NYSE that awarded the pay. These and other executives are criticized by shareholders for their own excessive pay. Grasso was fired as head of the NYSE after his pay was revealed.[48]

---

[45] Rushworth M. Kidder makes this same point with examples in his chapter "Ethical Fitness" in *How Good People Make Tough Choices* (New York: William Morrow, 1995); see also George P. Klubertanz, S.J., *Habits and Virtues*, "How is Virtue Acquired," (New York: Appleton-Century-Crofts, 1965), pp. 171–177; For references, see Klubertanz and Alasdair MacIntyre, *After Virtue* (Notre Dame: University of Notre Dame Press, 1981).

[46] Gerald F. Cavanagh and Mark R. Bandsuch, "Virtue as a Benchmark for Spirituality in Business," *Journal of Business Ethics*, 38 (June 2002): 109–117.

[47] See Laura L. Nash, "Johnson & Johnson's Credo," in *Corporate Ethics: A Prime Business Asset* (New York: The Business Roundtable, 1988), pp. 80–82.

[48] Michael Useem, "Behind Closed Doors," *The Wall Street Journal*, September 23, 2003, p. B2; Landon Thomas, "Big Board Said to Want Legal Action in Grasso Pay Case," *The New York Times*, January 8, 2004, pp. 1, 11.

Why did the above two men act so differently? Why did Burke of J&J almost instinctively look to the welfare of customers, while Grasso of NYSE ignored his conflict of interest and seemed to be more concerned with his own compensation? Grasso and executives at Bausch and Lomb sought primarily their own self-interest at the expense of those for whom they have responsibilities, the firm's stakeholders. We will show that moral habits, virtue or vice, account for most of the difference. Virtue inclines a person (Burke) toward doing the right thing, while vice disposes one toward selfishness (Grasso). Moreover, the presence or absence of such moral habits is an accurate predictor of good or bad future behavior. Let us examine moral habits in greater detail.

Courage, Self-Discipline, and Prudence

A virtue is a development of character, and it shows personal excellence in that area of human activity. Virtue is a stable, good moral habit that moves one toward the middle ground or between extremes in acting. Four basic moral virtues were identified by Aristotle and examined in detail by **Thomas Aquinas**. These four virtues are often called the **principal or chief virtues**: self-discipline (temperance), courage (fortitude), justice (fairness), and prudence.[49]

Self-discipline is the developed habit of not pursuing a good excessively. In our appetites (e.g., eating, drinking, sex) or in wanting to possess or control things, we often experience a temptation to have or consume too much of these goods. A temperate person is not greedy. Our senses in themselves are not disciplined, yet we understand that there is a need to stop at a suitable, harmonious mean before we destroy ourselves from gluttony, sclerosis of the liver, or sexually transmitted diseases. Richard Grasso appears to have lacked the virtue of self-discipline when he arranged for his $188 million compensation. Rather he displayed greed. The vice of greed is common today. Many businesspeople rationalize their greed by explaining that the market system encourages them to make as much money as possible. Providing the necessary capital for business is important and generally demands virtue to achieve it. However, Aristotle maintains that to own significantly more than is required for one's family or more than is ultimately a benefit to others is a vice. This assessment on the role of wealth runs counter to the view that the amount of a person's money shows the value of that person.

Courage enables one to overcome obstacles to do what is necessary to achieve a good goal. An entrepreneur must have courage to risk time and resources to begin a new business. Courage enables one to overcome temptations to both cowardliness and rashness, but it also requires the virtues of patience and perseverance. For example, James Burke of J&J had courage to order the $100 million recall of Tylenol. On the other hand, given its nonprofit status of NYSE and the conflict of interest, the members of its board of directors lacked courage when they agreed to the large compensation for

---

[49] Thomas Aquinas, *Summa Theologia*, I-II, Questions 49–67; Aristotle, *Ethics, op. cit.* See Edwin M. Hartman's discussion of virtue, "The Good Life and the Good Community" in his *Organizational Ethics and the Good Life* (New York: Oxford University Press, 1996), pp. 182–185.

Grasso. In our everyday work, it is easy to dodge difficult issues; we need courage to deal with troublesome problems.[50]

The virtue of *Justice* is the regular and constant habit to give another person her or his due. The virtue of justice is related to the ethical norm of justice, which we discussed earlier. The norm enables one to make an ethical judgment. The virtue disposes one to behave justly *because it is just*. The virtue of justice would dispose a manager to pay an equitable wage and to avoid race and gender discrimination—even before having to make a particular ethical judgment. When Bausch and Lomb CEO Daniel Gill forced unrealistic sales goals on his division executives and distributors, he violated the virtue of justice. Rather than foster a corporate culture that promoted justice, Gill's policies pressed subordinates into vicious behavior.

Prudence is the concrete judgment that a person makes to determine the means or strategy to be used to obtain a good goal. The other virtues require prudent judgment in order to be exercised. While the virtues can be assessed independently, they are nevertheless intertwined in each person. For example, without self-discipline greed will lead us to unjust actions. In classes business students often learn the techniques of marketing *any* product, or financing *any* endeavor, and some might call this prudence. However, developing strategies to obtain goals that are not good is not prudence. For example, to develop strategies to sell a product that kills, such as tobacco, or to take over a firm, loot its retirement plan, and fire its employees, is an act of shrewdness, but not the virtue of prudence.[51]

A manager cannot develop virtue in people by forcing them do things. It is harder to develop virtue in a control environment: in China, Saudi Arabia, Iran, or a jail. The motivation must come from within; a person must *intend* the good act. So developing virtue requires a good intention and perseverance, and this is often difficult because of our instinctive self-interest. As one expert puts it, "If people cared as much about the rights of others as they care about their own rights no virtue of justice would be needed . . . and rules about such things as contracts and promises would only need to be made public, like the rules of a game that everyone was eager to play."[52]

Good moral behavior is nurtured by mentoring, modeling, executive vision, and the corporate culture that this creates. Just as individuals choose to be virtuous and repeatedly act to bring that about, so, too, managers must choose a specific style of managing if they seek to encourage a moral corporate culture. However, the contrary is also true. Managers who engage in morally selfish acts thus foster bad behavior and vicious habits in their colleagues and subordinates.[53]

---

[50] See Gerald F. Cavanagh and Dennis J. Moberg, "The Virtue of Courage Within the Organization," in *Research in Ethical Issues in Organizations,* vol. 1 (Stamford, CT: JAI Press, 1999): 1–25.

[51] George P. Klubertanz, *Habits and Virtues.* See also, Charles M. Horvath, "Excellence v. Effectiveness: MacIntyre's Critique of Business," *Business Ethics Quarterly,* 5 (July 1995): 499–532.

[52] Philippa Foot, *Virtues and Vices and Other Essays in Moral Philosophy* (Berkeley: University of California Press, 1978), p. 9. The virtue of loyalty was featured in several articles in a special issue of *Business Ethics Quarterly,* 11, no. 1 (2001). See, for example, Daniel R. Gilbert, Jr., "An extraordinary Concept in the Ordinary Service of Management."

[53] See Rushworth M. Kidder, *Moral Courage* (New York: William Morrow, 2005); and Valerie Folkes and Ykun-Oh Whang, "Account-Giving For a Corporate Transgression Influences Moral Judgment: When Those Who 'Spin' Condone Harm-Doing," *Journal of Applied Psychology,* 88, no. 1 (2003): 79–86.

Leaders of organizations want their organizations to be successful over the long term. To accomplish long-term results requires good moral habits of honesty, fairness, and courage. Good moral habits, like moral principles, enable one to achieve moral goals. There is evidence that a manager's religious belief in God as a person makes a manager more likely to be ethical and socially responsible.[54] Most managers also would like to foster ethical behavior and good moral habits in their colleagues and subordinates. Traits such as honesty, trust, respect for other people, and an ability to cooperate and work with others help make an organization effective.

A good moral habit grows when one repeats morally good actions. Hence, when a person regularly makes ethical decisions and performs ethical acts, it will develop that person's good moral habits or virtues. Good moral acts performed by the members of the work group will also encourage good moral habits in other members of the work group.[55]

The Virtuous Organization

To develop a habit of a particular good moral act requires that the individual **choose** that moral act. Virtue will grow to the extent that the person performs the act because she chooses the behavior for its own sake. However, good moral acts that are motivated largely by fear, peer pressure, a control-oriented supervisor, or extrinsic rewards like compensation will not develop virtue. Nevertheless, motives are seldom pure.

Virtue in organizations is of concern to both managers and scholars.[56] Leaders attempt to select people appropriate for the job and the firm, and to communicate the values of the organization to these new hires and to those who are already colleagues; they socialize them so that they will work better within that organization. Nevertheless here we mention the importance of leaders performing acts of, for example, trust, honesty, justice, and courage, because they are morally *good* acts. When the modeling behavior of leaders support virtue, it can be effective in developing good moral habits, which then change behavior and form a person's character.

A leader must have a vision of how she wishes to operate and must be proactive, if she wishes to affect the behavior of members.[57] Stories of managers who are models of the values of the firm's mission statement support that vision. The compensation system of the organization must also support the kind of behavior that is to be encouraged. A reward system that relies on narrowly defined and easily measurable financial returns may encourage vice rather than virtue. Bausch and Lomb managers inflated profits, coerced distributors, and engaged in other vicious activities. We often build reward systems around measurable standards of performance, but trust, honesty, and courage are not easily measured. A "colleague-of-the-week"

---

[54] Johan Graafland, Muel Kaptein, and Corrie Mazereeuw, "Conceptions of God, Normative Convictions, and Socially Responsible Business Conduct," *Business and Society*, 46, no. 3 (September 2007): 331–369.

[55] Helen J. Alford, O.P. and Michael J. Naughton, *Managing as if Faith Mattered* (Notre Dame: University of Notre Dame Press, 2002), pp. 70–96; and Alasdair MacIntyre, *After Virtue*.

[56] See Dennis J. Moberg, "Practical Wisdom and Business Ethics," *Business Ethics Quarterly*, 71, no. 1 (2007): 535–561; and Cameron, Dutton, and Quinn, *op. cit.*; H. M. Trice and J. M. Beyer, *The Cultures of Work Organizations* (Englewood Cliffs, NJ: Prentice Hall, 1993).

[57] Linda Klebe Trevino and Michael E. Brown, "Managing to Be Ethical: Debunking Five Business Ethics Myths," *Academy of Management Executive*, 18 (May 2004): 69–80; Bruno Dyck and Rob Kleysen, "Aristotle's Virtues and Management Thought," *Business Ethics Quarterly*, 11, no. 4 (2002): 561–74.

program, bonuses, and other rewards can identify people who have generously done something of benefit for others and for the firm.

The development of good moral habits is diagramed in Figure 5. Each person has his or her own unique package of good moral habits. Practice in making ethical decisions and performing good acts develop those moral habits. Examining the diagram, Jessica possesses better developed moral habits or virtue, so for her the ethical issues that require judgment and action are easier to identify and decide. So each new act of that virtue will come more easily. That is, each individual act strengthens the virtue, so that the act is easier to perform the next time. Lauren has lesser developed good habits, so it will be harder for her to identify the issues, and more difficult (i.e., a greater stretch) to make an ethical judgment. But notice that for both women, the level of virtue is increased after each individual good moral act.

A person's **character** is formed by the aggregate of that person's moral habits. Every group or organization of which a person is a part influences that person's attitudes, builds good and bad habits, and ultimately forms a person's character. Moreover, an organization made up of people with mostly good habits, and hence good character, will possess a better climate and thus a better corporate culture.

The *goal* of a business, as with any organization, is to increase the well-being of women and men; this includes the development of virtue in colleagues in the working group. Virtue will not develop if a business focuses exclusively on its goals of profit and growth. Profit, return on investment, and increasing market share are important measurable *means* to achieve the *ultimate goals* of the firm.

In the process of becoming a manager, a good manager generally develops many good habits, many virtues. For example, a manager who regularly trusts subordinates develops the virtue of trust and eventually trusts almost instinctively, and encourages the trust of others. A manager who does not trust will spread distrust throughout his unit. That manager finds that it takes far more time and energy for him to be a good manager—if indeed he ever becomes a good manager.

One method of developing virtue is to help the disadvantaged. Ford Motor Company, even in the midst of its financial difficulties, encourages its people to help in

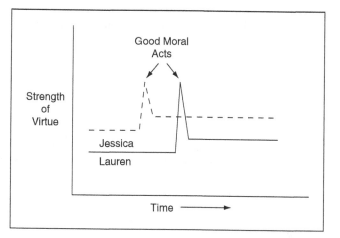

FIGURE 5   **Development of Good Moral Habits**

soup kitchens and homeless shelters, tutor inner-city youth, and engage in other projects for those in need. Ford will provide time off from work for up to 20 hours a year for these service projects. Other firms encourage their people to volunteer to help the poor overseas. Service projects are also common in colleges and universities; a person's horizons are generally broadened by personal contact with disadvantaged people: "If not for the good luck of birth, that homeless man might be me." The virtue and good character that is thus shaped also builds trust, cooperation, and honesty—the social capital of the firm. Moreover, research by health care professionals shows that helping other people is good for one's heart, immune system, and longevity.[58]

For those interested in character education, the organization *Character Education Partnership* provides a Web site that offers resources, conferences, and news.[59] Unfortunately, building character is not a priority in most U.S. colleges and universities. Arthur Schwartz, director of character education programs at the John Templeton Foundation, says,

> Only relatively few institutions—usually small liberal arts colleges or those that are religiously affiliated or faith-inspired—have a comprehensive commitment to character development in all dimensions of college life.[60]

This leads us into the next subject: how ethics and character education are taught in business schools.

ETHICS IN BUSINESS EDUCATION

After the financial and ethical bankruptcies of Enron and Arthur Andersen, the ethical debacles at NASDAQ, Solomon Brothers, Merrill Lynch, and Bear Stearns, and the subprime loan failures, many claim that business education is at the root of the problem. A veteran faculty member of Columbia University Graduate School of business places the responsibility squarely on business schools when he says, "Many business programs still don't even require any course work on ethics or social responsibility"; he then points out how business school faculty have little incentive to expose unethical practices, because their status and extra income come from being paid well as consultants or lecturers in corporate executive development programs.[61]

A study of business school students' attitudes found that at the beginning of their MBA program most felt that the purpose of business was to produce quality

[58] S. D. Papamarcos, "The Next Wave in Service-learning: Integrative, Team-based Engagements with Structural Objectives," *Review of Business,* 23, no. 2 (2002); Bruce Speck and Sherry Hoppe, *Service-Learning: History, Theory, and Issues* (Westport, CT: Praeger, 2004); Paul S. Adler and Seok-Woo Kwon, "Social Capital: Prospects for a New Concept," *The Academy of Management Review,* 27, no. 1 (2002): 17–40; Eileen Rockefeller Growald and Allan Luks, "Beyond Self: The Immunity of Samaritans," *American Health,* March 1988, pp. 51–53.

[59] See: www.character.org, accessed July 26, 2007.

[60] Arthur J. Schwartz, "It's Not Too Late to Teach College Students about Values," *Chronicle of Higher Education,* 46 (June 9, 2000).

[61] Leonard R. Sayles and Cynthia J. Smith, *The Rise of the Rogue Executive: How Good Companies Go Bad and How to Stop the Destruction* (Upper Saddle River: Pearson, 2006).

goods and services. But by the end of their MBA education, only one-third continued to see producing goods and services as the purpose, and more than two-thirds said that the purpose of business was to increase shareholder value. Often finance and economics professors give excessive respect for anything that is a result of the free market. In that model a person is expected to be selfish, and not to consider others except as competing economic agents. So it is not surprising that business students become more self-centered during their studies and that business graduate students cheat more than non-business graduate students.[62]

Another empirical study of ethics teaching in business schools found that ethics was not taken seriously at the majority of business schools, and this was especially true at large state universities. As an illustration, the author related how students tried for many decades unsuccessfully to have a required business ethics course in the undergraduate and MBA curriculum. He found that ethics at his own "big 10" university is treated by his peers somewhere between "ambivalence and disdain". Surprisingly, in the last few years and even since the public scandals, many business schools have dropped or downgraded their business ethics courses.[63]

Most agree that the ethical debacles at Tyco, ImClone, Qwest, and Computer Associates were the result of an "overemphasis American corporations have been forced to give in recent years to maximizing shareholder value without regard for the effects of their actions on other stakeholders." Yet most business school faculty teach "running the numbers" and take little account of the effect that these decisions have on employees, customers, or the local community. Ethics and corporate responsibility courses "are considered 'soft' subjects . . . and are given short shrift in favor of applied analytical tools and techniques, conceptual models, and measures of profitability."[64] A quality business education requires a consideration of the ethical consequences of any major decision and policy. Supporting this effort are 85 percent of firm recruiters who say that personal ethics and integrity is "very important" in any person that they seek to hire for their firm.[65]

Recognizing that ethics is as important as finance and marketing, hundreds of business faculty asked the business school accrediting association (AACSB) to require an ethics course in the business curriculum. The accrediting body refused

---

[62] Donald McCabe, Kenneth Butterfield, and Linda Klebe Trevino, "Academic Dishonesty in Graduate Business Programs: Prevalence, Causes, and Proposed Action," *Academy of Management Learning and Education*, 5, no. 3 (2006): 294–305; also Robert J. Shiller, "How Wall Street Learns to Look the Other Way," *The New York Times,* February 8, 2005, p. 15.

[63] LaRue T. Hosmer, "Somebody Out There Doesn't Like Us," *Journal of Business Ethics,* 22 (November, 1999): 91–106; and Marjorie Kelly, "It's a Heckuva Time to Be Dropping Business Ethics Courses: MBA Programs are Downsizing Ethics Requirements at Precisely the Wrong Time," *Business Ethics,* Fall 2002, pp. 17–18.

[64] Sandra Waddock, "Hollow Men at the Helm: Until Business Schools Teach Future Managers How Deep the Connections are Between Business, Society, Nature, and the World, Corporations Will Continue to be Run by Hollow Leaders with No Sense of Ethics or Responsibility," *BusEd,* July/August 2004, pp. 24–29. *BusEd* is published by AACSB, the international business school accrediting Agency.

[65] Ronald Alsop, "Business Schools Recruiters' Top Picks," *The Wall Street Journal,* September 22, 2004, p. R8.

to require ethics, but urged that ethics be an integral part of any graduate or undergraduate program and has provided materials for teaching ethics.[66] Will integrity, ethics, social responsibility, and character be learned at most business schools? Probably not.

The concern for ethics in business education is not new. Executives and citizens have agreed for many years that there was a need for ethics in business and in schools. In a survey two decades ago of corporate CEOs, business school deans, and members of Congress, 94 percent said that the business community is troubled by ethical problems. Further, 63 percent of these leaders believe that a business firm strengthens its competitive position by maintaining high ethical standards. These leaders also said that there was an observable difference in the quality of ethics in various parts of the United States. Areas of the country they ranked from most ethical to least are as follows: Midwest, Northwest, New England, South, Southwest, West, and East.[67]

Difficulties in arriving at an ethical judgment often stem from our lack of knowledge of ethical norms. Most managers are not immoral, but rather amoral. They simply fail to adequately consider the morality of their actions.[68] They are hampered by the fact that ethics and good character generally are not learned in American schools, from grade schools to universities. Competitive and individualistic methods of learning and grading hinder the development of a sense of community and obligations to others. In this way, schools often impede the development of moral maturity and ethics. Managers are constrained by their own lack of moral imagination; that is, their options are narrowed because they often fail to consider the more ethical act.[69]

Ethics was not always so unknown. Ethics, or **moral philosophy**, was the center of the curriculum of American colleges and universities throughout the nineteenth century. An ethics course was required of all seniors and, because of its importance, it was often taught by the college president.[70] This course was designed as an integration of all that students had learned, and prepared them for the working world. It sharpened their ethical sensitivity and enabled them to better address the ethical problems they were about to face.

Educators during this period judged that no nation could prosper without common social and moral values. For a society such as the United States, which is fragmented because of differences in ethnic backgrounds, allegiances, and interests, it was even more important to provide a structure whereby students could unify their

---

[66] *Ethics Education in Business Schools,* Report of the Ethics Education Task Force to AACSB International's Board of Governors (St. Louis: AACSB International, 2004); also available at http://www.aacsb.edu/metf.

[67] *Ethics in American Business: An Opinion Survey of Key Business Leaders on Ethical Standards and Behavior* (New York: Touche Ross, 1988), pp. 1, 10; see also "Why Ethics is Also B-School Business", *BusinessWeek,* January 27, 2003, p. 105.

[68] Archie B. Carroll, "In Search of the Moral Manager," *Business Horizons,* March–April 1987, pp. 7–15.

[69] Patricia C. Werhane, *Moral Imagination and Management Decision Making* (New York: Oxford University Press, 1999).

[70] Douglas Sloan, "The Teaching of Ethics in American Undergraduate Curriculum, 1876–1976," in *Ethics Teaching in Higher Education,* ed. Daniel Callahan and Sissela Bok (New York: Plenum Press, 1980), p. 2.

learning: "The entire college experience was meant above all to be an experience in character development and the moral life, as epitomized, secured, and brought to focus in the moral philosophy course."[71] Is this need still present today?

Business education has long been criticized for being too narrow, analytic, and technical by businesspeople and also by a committee set up by the business school accrediting association (AACSB).[72] This authoritative report concluded that MBA curricula lacked vision and integration. Among other omissions, there was insufficient attention given to ethics and the social and political environment of business.

There are practical reasons for including ethics in the business program. Making ethical judgments before one is exposed to real business pressures to act unethically can result in behavior that is more ethical. In an experiment, college students were given a case involving an ethical dilemma and asked to judge a course of action. The experimenters then presented the actual situation to these same students two weeks later. The students acted more ethically than did a control group that had not earlier discussed the case. On the job, the pressures of time and potential short-term cost savings push one to compromise.[73]

When considering a dilemma away from the pressures of the actual situation, one is more inclined to consider the ethical issues in an objective and balanced way. Moral reasoning ability is also improved when ethics is taught in courses.[74] The conclusion is that an informed discussion of ethical cases and making ethical judgments will have a positive effect on ethical behavior, and it can provide the foundation for developing good moral habits.

Executives and firms have policies and training to help workers understand ethical issues. A survey of firms showed that ethics policies and codes are distributed to almost all workers. Moreover, more than 85 percent of firms require that people verify in writing that they have received the ethics policy and are in compliance with it. In addition, 55 percent of workers say that their employers provide ethics training; this number goes to 68 percent if restricted to firms of 500 or more workers. Ethics training programs are more effective when they are integrated into other training at the firm. The goals of ethics programs are, on the one hand, to provide information and policies on what is and what is not acceptable, and on the other hand, to lessen penalties on the firm if an errant worker is charged with a crime. General Electric, IBM, Johnson & Johnson, Boeing, Merck, and many other firms all provide ethics training and have done so for many decades.[75]

---

[71] *Ibid.*, p. 7.

[72] Lyman Porter and Lawrence McKibbin, *Management Education and Development: Drift or Thrust into the 21st Century?* (New York: McGraw-Hill, 1988).

[73] Steven J. Sherman, "On the Self-Erasing Nature of Errors of Prediction," *Journal of Personality and Social Psychology,* 39 (March 1980): 211–219.

[74] Elinar Marnburg, "Educational Impacts on Academic Business Practitioner's Moral Reasoning and Behavior: Effects of Short Courses in Ethics or Philosophy," *Business Ethics: A European Review,* 12 (October 2003): 403–413.

[75] Linda Klebe Trevino and Gary Weaver, *Managing Ethics in Business Organizations* (Stanford: Stanford University Press, 2003), pp. 79–80; also Susan J. Harrington, "What Corporate America is Teaching About Ethics," *Academy of Management Executive,* 5 (February 1991): 21–30.

Summary and Conclusions

We examined moral development in the last chapter and found that selfish (Kohlberg's Level I) behavior is more typical of adolescents and the immature than of mature women and men. Most businesspeople want to be ethical; they have many good moral habits. Nevertheless, fraud, bribery, overstating revenues, hiding expenses and important information from customers, and stealing trade secrets remain major ethical problems for business. In many cases, managers say that they could not distinguish the right action from the wrong action. Generations now growing up have fewer moral skills. Many people have not learned how to recognize ethical problems and how to make ethical judgments. Furthermore, the media and advertising tell us that ethics is relative.

The ethical principles, models, and cases in this chapter are intended to aid the development of ethical skills and character. The decision norms and models are not perfect; they will not solve all ethical problems easily. But these ethical norms and models can be learned and used, and thus be an aid to businesspeople. Making ethical judgments in the classroom brings about more ethical behavior in business. Moreover, ethical acts affect behavior, enabling people to be more honest, trustworthy, and ultimately possess greater integrity and virtue.

Business leaders lament the lack of ethical skills among new workers and the lack of formal ethics in college curricula. In earlier centuries, ethics had a central place in the education of college students. It is a paradox that businesspeople learn precise decision rules for inventory, finance, and brand marketing, but have few models for moral decisions and actions. If businesspeople are not moral, business will become a wasteful, inefficient jungle that is hostile to people.

The intentional repetition of good moral acts develops good habits or virtues. Superior moral habits among colleagues can make a working environment more productive and humane. Few business schools are thorough in presenting ethics and ethical tools for future businesspeople. Yet graduates who have learned ethics and developed character are more trusted and mature, will not cost their firm its reputation, and will more likely achieve executive responsibilities.

Discussion Questions

1. What is the principal difference between rights and duties and utilitarian norms? Do an individual's intentions have any role in utilitarianism? Do intentions have a role in the theory of rights? Explain.
2. What does John Rawls add to the traditional theory of justice? Compare Rawls' theory and the traditional theory of justice with utilitarianism.
3. Upon what is the norm of caring built? How does it compare with rights and duties, justice, and utilitarianism?
4. Indicate the strengths and weaknesses of using the norms of (a) utility, (b) justice, (c) rights, and (d) caring.
5. Is anything always morally right or always morally wrong (e.g., murder)? Is lying or stealing always or generally wrong, or is it relative, a matter of social expectations, and the law?

6. Outline the criteria for whistle-blowing. If you knew of payments by a manager in your firm to a manager in a competing firm for insider information, should you blow the whistle? Apply the criteria in deciding this question.

7. How can the four principle virtues—self-discipline, courage, justice, and prudence—help an individual succeed?

8. Do many college students take a course in ethics? What is the advantage of such a course? What is the disadvantage of ethics not being learned? Have you had such a course?

9. Is the purpose of studying ethics to develop ethical decision-making skills or to influence good behavior? Does the former affect the latter? How?

10. Describe how a person can develop good habits. What is the relation of virtue and character?

11. Give an example of when you have exercised a virtue. What virtues do you see in others?

12. As a manager would you prefer that the members of your work group have good character? As a peer in a firm, would you prefer colleagues have good character? Why?

13. What is the purpose of business, according to graduate business students at the beginning of their program? How does that attitude shift by the end of their program?

14. In a fragmented, pluralistic society of the nineteenth and twentieth centuries, colleges and universities saw the need for integration of education with a capstone ethics course for all students. Is this need still present today?

15. Do business schools have a responsibility to help student learn ethics and develop good character? Why or why not? Do most business schools offer a required ethics course?

Selected Additional Readings

Daniel Callahan and Sissela Bok, eds., *Ethics Teaching in Higher Education* (New York: Plenum Press, 1980).

David Callahan, *The Cheating Culture: Why More Americans are Doing Wrong to Get Ahead* (New York: Harcourt, 2004).

Richard T. De George, *Business Ethics,* 6th ed. (Upper Saddle River: Prentice Hall, 2006).

Thomas Donaldson and Thomas W. Dunfee, *Ties That Bind: A Social Contracts Approach to Business Ethics* (Boston: Harvard Business School Press, 1999).

Rushworth M. Kidder, *Moral Courage* (New York: William Morrow, 2005).

Stephan Rothlin, *Eighteen Rules of International Business Ethics* (Beijing, 2004).

Manuel Velasquez, *Business Ethics: Concepts and Cases,* 6th ed. (Upper Saddle River, NJ: Prentice Hall, 2006).

CASES

Case 1   Encyclopedia of Ethical Failure

Government workers found misbehaving are generally fined, suspended, fired, and/or prosecuted. In addition, Stephen Epstein, director of the Pentagon Standards of Conduct Office, enters them and their actions on an Internet list with others who have been caught; he calls it the *Encyclopedia of Ethical Failure*. While names are not listed, it is not difficult to find out to who the culprit is. With huge amounts of money in the defense budget, the temptation is great to cheat; in five years Epstein has listed more than 250 people. It is a community punishment for wrongdoing, and thus is a deterrent; Epstein says, "It is like public executions."

1. Is this a wise procedure? Would such a list be a deterrent to people?
2. Is it acceptable to publicly list the names of people who have misbehaved or broken the law?
3. What ethical norm is most helpful in this case?

■ ■ ■

Case 2   PepsiCo and Bottled Water

PepsiCo uses a mountain top design on the label of its popular Aquafina brand of bottled water, but it has agreed to notify consumers that Aquafina actually comes from ordinary tap water. Meanwhile, environmentalists argue that producing plastic bottles needlessly uses energy, and the used bottles pollute the environment. Others point out that if a consumer drank eight glasses of water a day from plastic bottles, it would cost them up to $1,400 a year.

1. What are the ethical issues in this case?
2. Is it deceptive to sell bottled water that is no more pure than tap water? Should water bottlers notify consumers of the source of their bottled water?
3. Is there any ethical problem in producing the plastic bottles?
4. What ethical norms help in deciding this case?

■ ■ ■

Case 3   Double Expense Account

Frank Waldron is a second-year MBA student at Eastern State University. Although he has had many job offers, he continues to have the university placement office arrange interviews. He reasons that the interview experience is good for him and he may receive a better job offer. Frank has also discovered a way to make money from job interviews.

Two firms invited Waldron to Los Angeles for visits to their home offices. He scheduled both visits on the same day and billed each for his full travel expenses. In this way he was able to pocket $1,000. When a friend objected that this was dishonest, Frank replied that each firm had told him to submit his expenses and that therefore he was not taking something to which he had no right. One firm had not asked for receipts, so he determined it was making him a gift of the money.

1. What are the ethical issues in this case? Is what Frank doing unethical?
2. Which norms help most in deciding the question?
3. What advice would you give Frank?

■ ■ ■

Case 4   PETA vs. Pfizer

People for the Ethical Treatment of Animals (PETA) want all drug companies to stop or do less testing on animals. PETA filed a shareholder resolution with Pfizer, asking the firm to reduce the amount of animal testing that it does. The occasion of the resolution was that Pfizer lost a dog which was left in a cage that was sent through scalding water to be cleaned. The U.S. Department of Agriculture's investigation labeled the death as an accident. Nevertheless, PETA pressed its case against Pfizer with a shareholder resolution. Pfizer's Board voted unanimously against the resolution. In Britain animal rights activists have slashed researcher's tires and have placed pipe bombs at laboratories. Additional security costs British pharmaceutical firms $128 million per year, and some estimate that Britain with more stringent regulations on animal testing than the United States is losing $2 billion a year in new investment.[76]

1. What are the ethical issues involved in Pfizer's use of animals when testing pharmaceuticals?
2. Should Pfizer curtail or stop its use of animals in its testing?
3. What are the ethics of the protesters tactics?
4. What ethical norm (s) are most helpful here?

■ ■ ■

Case 5   Tax Assessment Kickback

You own a large building in a major city. The real estate assessor offers, for a fee, to underestimate the value of your property and save you a substantial amount in real estate taxes. Assume that this is a common practice in the city.

1. What are the ethical issues in this case?
2. Do you pay the fee?
3. Which ethical norm is most helpful here?

Exercises

Exercise 1: Memo to the Chief Executive

You are a manager in a firm in a very competitive industry. A competitor has made an important scientific discovery that could give it an advantage that would substantially reduce, but not eliminate, the profits of your company for about a year. A scientist who knows the details of the discovery applies for a job at your firm. There are no legal barriers to hiring the scientist.

The CEO knows that you studied ethics in your MBA program and so asks you to give her your advice. In a single-page memo to the CEO, indicate the major issues and ethical norms to be used, and make a recommendation.

---

[76] "Animal-Rights Activism Turns Rabid: Attacks on Drug Companies and University Labs are Chilling Research," *BusinessWeek,* August 30, 2004, p. 54.

Exercise[77] 2: What are Your Values?

In class answer each of the following questions as either T = True or F = False

1. _____ Ethics and religion are the same thing.

2. _____ Males, more than females, will "dump" friends when opportunities for career advancement come.

3. _____ Insurance companies are justified in charging higher auto insurance premiums for young males because their accident rate is higher.

4. _____ When a manager's personal value system conflicts with the organization's value system, the organization is the first priority.

5. _____ It is just to deny the vote to people on welfare because they are not contributing to society.

6. _____ Few people reach the stage of moral development at which they are willing to challenge either authority or generally agreed belief systems.

7. _____ There is a widening gap in the United States between the values held by the wealthy and powerful and those values held by common people.

8. _____ When a conflict develops between liberty and justice, liberty should come first.

9. _____ Given globalization, the best guide to ethical behavior when in other cultures is to follow the rule "When in Rome, do as the Romans do."

10. _____ People who possess great power in an organization and who violate the law showed be punished more severely than people with little power who commit the same illegal act.

11. _____ The American belief that "big is better" is the best organizational philosophy, because not to grow is to shrink.

12. _____ Capitalism rests on the value of self-interest—a value that, by its very nature, should worry church leaders who stress sacrifice.

Exercise 3: Ethical Climate of a Firm Compared to Caux Round Table

Principles for Business

This exercise will show how the Caux Round Table's (CRT) *Principles for Business* might be used as a benchmark for evaluating a firm's code. Compare one firm's (if possible, the one for which you work) *Mission, Vision,* and *Code of Conduct* with the CRT's *Principles for Business* (see http://www.cauxroundtable.org/principles.html).

Specifically, the assignment is to:

1. Obtain a copy of the firm's Mission, Vision, and Code of Ethics.
2. Compare the (a) firm's statements with (b) CRT's *Principles for Business*. In your comparison, note the major issues that are covered by both documents. Compare the content of both codes and evaluate the adequacy and comprehensiveness of your firm's code.
3. Write a paper to summarize your comparison of the firm's *Mission, Vision,* and *Code of Conduct* with the CRT's *Principles for Business*.

The following questions may help you to examine and compare:

General Principles

Does your firm's *Code, Mission, or Vision* have any statements like Caux's "General Principles?"

Briefly describe them. Does the firm's code cover the material of the seven *Principles*? Answer for each. If so, briefly describe how it is covered.

---

[77] Thanks to the late Clarence C. Walton for these questions.

Stakeholder Principles

Does your firm's Code have a section on responsibilities to customers?

If so, briefly compare the two codes.

Does it have a section on responsibilities to employees? If so, briefly compare the two codes.

Does it . . . on responsibilities to owners/investors? If so, briefly compare the two codes.

Does it . . . on responsibilities to suppliers? If so, briefly compare the two codes.

Does it . . . on responsibilities to competitors? If so, briefly compare the two codes.

Does it . . . on responsibilities to the community? If so, briefly compare the two codes.

Finally and most importantly, is your firm's Code designed to protect only the company? Or is it designed to protect customers, employees, and outside stakeholders, also? Does it give proportionate coverage to both the firm and the various stakeholders?

Summarize your comparison of the firm's *Mission, Vision,* and *Code of Conduct* with the CRT's *Principles for Business*. The paper should be no more than 10 double-spaced pages. Use any format that is useful for your comparison. Include a copy of the relevant *Mission, Values,* and *Code of Conduct* of the firm you use in an Appendix. Organization, spelling, punctuation, and grammar will be included in the evaluation.

Business Ethics and Social Responsibility

From Chapter 2 of *Business Essentials*, 7/e. Ronald J. Ebert. Ricky W. Griffin. Copyright © 2009 Pearson Prentice Hall.

Business Ethics and Social Responsibility

After reading this chapter, you should be able to:

1 Explain how individuals develop their personal codes of ethics and why ethics are important in the workplace.

2 Distinguish social responsibility from ethics, identify organizational stakeholders, and characterize social consciousness today.

3 Show how the concept of social responsibility applies both to environmental issues and to a firm's relationships with customers, employees, and investors.

4 Identify four general approaches to social responsibility, and describe the four steps that a firm must take to implement a social responsibility program.

5 Explain how issues of social responsibility and ethics affect small business.

Shutterstock

Under the Guise of Green

Oil companies aren't usually known for their environmentally responsible reputations. Global energy giant BP, however, has made an effort to market an environmentally friendly image. For the most part, this strategy has worked—leading many to overlook the facts suggesting that BP is not entirely the environmentally responsible exception it claims to be.

For the past several years, BP has committed environmental offenses almost annually. In 2000, the company was convicted of an environmental felony for failing to report that its subcontractor was dumping hazardous waste in Alaska. In 2005, BP allegedly ignored knowledge that its Texas City refinery was unsafe in a cost-cutting effort that led to an explosion, 15 deaths, and even more injuries. The following year, BP's negligence at its Prudhoe Bay oil field caused a 200,000-gallon oil spill and misdemeanor violation of the Clean Water Act. Then, in 2007, BP lobbied Indiana regulators for an exemption allowing it to increase its daily release of ammonia and sludge into Lake Michigan.

Despite these misdeeds, BP maintains its image as a "green" company. The Natural Resource Defense Council has even praised it for being a leader in the industry's move toward renewable energy. Indeed, true to the tag line, "Beyond Petroleum," that accompanies its green logo, BP's 2007 Sustainability Report projects spending $8 billion over the next ten years on renewable energy products. Its Web site even offers a carbon footprint calculator that lets visitors see how their own choices affect the environment.

BP risks compromising its green image by engaging in what Greenpeace calls the "greatest climate crime" in history—extracting oil from the tar sands of Alberta, Canada. The project is energy- and water-intensive, produces excessive amounts of greenhouse gases, destroys acres of forest, and harms indigenous communities, but it comes at a time when oil prices are high and western consumers are dependent on Middle Eastern oil. It remains to be seen whether BP's seemingly socially responsible ends can justify their environmentally damaging means.[1]

What's in It for Me?

To make an informed judgment about a company's social responsibility, it's important to understand how individual codes of ethics develop and play a role in the workplace, to distinguish between ethics and social responsibility, and to understand social consciousness. In addition to these elements, this chapter will explore the ethical and social responsibility issues that businesses face in terms of their customers, employees, investors, and immediate and global communities. In addition, it will look at general approaches to social responsibility, the steps businesses must take to implement social responsibility programs, and issues of social responsibility and ethics in small businesses.

Ethics in the Workplace

ETHICS beliefs about what is right or wrong and good or bad in actions that affect others

ETHICAL BEHAVIOR behavior conforming to generally accepted social norms concerning beneficial and harmful actions

UNETHICAL BEHAVIOR behavior that does not conform to generally accepted social norms concerning beneficial and harmful actions

BUSINESS ETHICS ethical or unethical behaviors by employees in the context of their jobs

MANAGERIAL ETHICS standards of behavior that guide individual managers in their work

Ethics are beliefs about what's right or wrong and good or bad based on an individual's values and morals, plus a behavior's social context. In other words, **ethical behavior** conforms to individual beliefs and social norms about what's right and good. **Unethical behavior** conforms to individual beliefs and social norms about what's wrong or bad. **Business ethics** refers to ethical or unethical behaviors by employees in the context of their jobs.

Individual Ethics

Because ethics are based on both individual beliefs and social concepts, they vary among individuals, situations, and cultures. People may develop personal

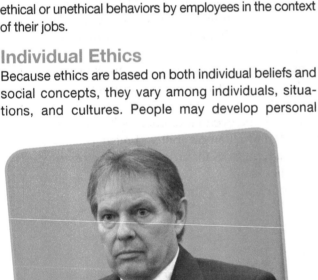

© NIGEL TREBLIN/Getty Images

Former Volkswagen personnel director Klaus Volkert was given a two-year jail sentence for his involvement in the bribery scandal that financed prostitutes and exotic holidays for union officials in exchange for their support of management plans.[4]

Tax Revenues Disappear into Bermuda Triangle

The epidemic of scandals that dominated business news over the past decade shows how willing people can be to take advantage of potentially ambiguous situations—indeed, to create them. For example, in 1997, Tyco sold itself to the smaller ADT Ltd. Because its new parent company was based in the tax haven of Bermuda, Tyco no longer had to pay U.S. taxes on its non-U.S. income. In 2000 and 2001, Tyco's subsidiaries in such tax-friendly nations doubled, and the company slashed its 2001 U.S. tax bill by $600 million. "Tyco," complained a U.S. congressman, "has raised tax avoidance to an art," but one tax expert replies that Tyco's schemes "are very consistent with the [U.S.] tax code."[2] Even in the face of blistering criticism and the indictment of its former CEO, Tyco retains its offshore ownership structure.[3]

codes of ethics reflecting a wide range of attitudes and beliefs without violating general standards. Thus, some ethical and unethical behaviors are widely agreed upon, while others fall into gray areas.

Ambiguity, the Law, and the Real World

Societies generally adopt formal laws that reflect prevailing ethical standards or social norms. We try to make unambiguous laws, but interpreting and applying them can still lead to ethical ambiguities. It isn't always easy to apply statutory standards to real-life behavior. For instance, during the aftermath of Hurricane Katrina in 2005, desperate survivors in New Orleans looted grocery stores for food and other essentials. While few people criticized this behavior, such actions were technically illegal.

Individual Values and Codes The ethics of business start with the ethics of individuals—managers, employees, and other legal representatives. Each person's personal code of ethics is determined by a combination of factors that are formed and refined throughout our lives.

Business and Managerial Ethics

Managerial ethics are the standards of behavior that guide individual managers in their work.[5] Although managerial ethics can affect business in any number of ways, it's helpful to classify them into three broad categories.

Behavior Toward Employees This category covers such matters as hiring and firing, wages and working conditions, and privacy and respect. Ethical and legal guidelines suggest that hiring and firing decisions should be based solely on the ability to perform a job.

Wages and working conditions, while regulated by law, are also controversial. Consider a manager who pays a worker less than he deserves because the manager knows that the employee can't afford to quit or

Say What You Mean

The Ethical Soft-Shoe

To bribe or not to bribe? That is the question. Although the textbook answer is a nonnegotiable "no" regardless of the business environment, culture, or country you're in, the real-world answer is much less clear. To varying degrees, complicated business dealings that ignore the strict letter of the law—offering or accepting incentives to get things done, extracting a personal favor or two, using the power and influence of people we know—happen all the time.

In fact, in some cultures ethically ambiguous practices are hallmarks of business culture. Brazilians, for example, apply the philosophy of *jeitinho*—"to find a way"—in which there's always another way to get something done—using personal connections, bending the rules, making a "contribution," or simply approaching the problem from a different angle. If you need an official document, for instance, you might set out determined to take all the proper bureaucratic steps to get it. However, when you find yourself in a maze of rules and regulations, you're likely to resort to *jeitinho*. *Jeitinho* almost never involves butting heads with authority, but is rather a complex dance that enables individuals to go around problems instead of having to go through them.

Even if you're operating in a country like Brazil, in which sidestepping the rules is business as usual, you don't *have* to do an ethical soft-shoe. Many global companies have strict ethical guidelines for doing business: International

U.S. business practices, for example, are regulated by the Foreign Corrupt Practices Act. The key to dancing with a foreign partner is understanding the culture—observing the way business is conducted and preparing yourself for any challenges—before you get out on the dance floor.

© AFP photo/Vanderlie/ALMEDIA/Newscom

In Brazil, someone pressed for time might invoke the philosophy of *jeitinho* when facing a long wait in line. The philosophy allows for rule-bending like cutting in line if fairness and practicality are overriding factors.

risk his job by complaining. While some see the behavior as unethical, others see it as a smart business move.

Behavior Toward the Organization Employee behavior toward employers involves ethical issues in such areas as conflict of interest, confidentiality, and honesty. A *conflict of interest* occurs when an activity may benefit the individual to the detriment of his or her employer. To avoid even the appearance of bribery or favoritism, most companies have policies that forbid buyers from accepting gifts from suppliers. Businesses in highly competitive industries—software and fashion apparel, for example—have safeguards, such as nondisclosure agreements, against designers selling company secrets to competitors. Relatively common problems in the general area of honesty include stealing supplies and padding expense accounts.

Behavior Toward Other Economic Agents Advertising, bargaining and negotiation, financial disclosure, ordering and purchasing—ethical ambiguity is possible in just about every activity businesses conduct with *primary agents of interest*—mainly customers, competitors, stockholders, suppliers, dealers, and unions.

Global variations can complicate ethical business practices. For example, while U.S. law forbids bribes, many countries incorporate them into normal business

practices. A U.S. power-generating company recently lost a $320 million contract in the Middle East because it refused to pay bribes that a Japanese firm was willing to pay to get the job.

"From a purely business viewpoint, taking what doesn't belong to you is usually the cheapest way to go."

The Cartoon Bank

Assessing Ethical Behavior

The following steps set a simplified course for applying ethical judgments to ethically subjective and ambiguous business situations:

1. Gather the relevant factual information.

2. Analyze the facts to determine the most appropriate moral values.

3. Make an ethical judgment based on the rightness or wrongness of the proposed activity or policy.

The process may not work this smoothly, though; facts may not be clear-cut, and moral values may not be agreed upon. Nevertheless, a judgment and a decision must be made in order to maintain trust, an indispensable element in any business transaction.

Consider a complex dilemma faced by managers with expense accounts to cover work-related expenses when they're traveling for business or entertaining clients for business purposes. If a manager takes a client to a $150 dinner, submitting a $150 reimbursement receipt for that dinner is accurate and appropriate. But suppose that this manager has a $150 dinner the next night with a friend for purely social purposes. Submitting that receipt for reimbursement would be unethical. But some employees would disagree, rationalizing that they're underpaid, so submitting this receipt as well is just a means of "recovering" income due to them.

Consider the following ethical *norms*, which Figure 1 incorporates into a model of ethical judgment making that can be applied in cases like this:[6]

1. *Utility*. Does a particular act optimize the benefits to those who are affected by it? (That is, do all relevant parties receive equally useful benefits?)

2. *Rights*. Does it respect the rights of all individuals involved?

3. *Justice*. Is it fair?

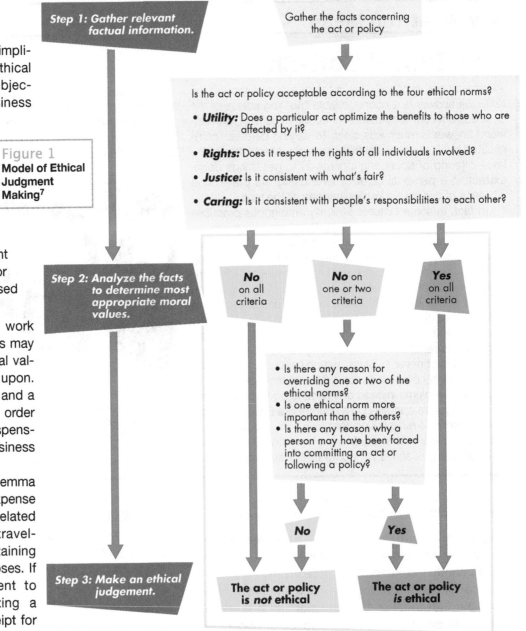

Figure 1
Model of Ethical Judgment Making[7]

4. *Caring*. Is it consistent with people's responsibilities to one another?

While the utility norm acknowledges that the manager benefits from a padded account, others, such as coworkers and owners, don't. Most would also agree that the act doesn't respect the rights of others (such as investors, who have to foot the bill). Moreover, it's clearly unfair and compromises the manager's responsibilities to others. This particular act, then, appears to be clearly unethical.

Figure 1, however, also provides mechanisms for dealing with unique circumstances that make ethical issues more or less clear-cut. Suppose, for example, that our manager loses the receipt for the legitimate dinner but retains the receipt for the social dinner. Some will now argue that it's okay to submit the illegitimate receipt because the manager is only doing so to get proper reimbursement. Others, however, will reply that submitting the alternative receipt is wrong under any circumstances.

Company Practices and Business Ethics

To discourage unethical and illegal activities, companies have taken formal steps, such as setting up codes of conduct, developing clear ethical positions, and perhaps most effectively, demonstrating upper-management support of ethical standards. These policies contribute to a corporate culture that values ethical standards and announce that the firm is equally concerned with good citizenship and profits.

Two of the most common approaches to formalizing top management commitment to ethical business practices are *adopting written codes* and *instituting ethics programs*.

Adopting Written Codes Many companies have written codes that formally announce intent to do business ethically. The number of such companies has risen dramatically in the last three decades, and today almost all major corporations have written codes of ethics. Even Enron had a code of ethics, but managers must follow the code if it's going to work. On one occasion, Enron's board of directors voted to set aside the code in order to complete a deal that would violate it; after the deal was completed, they then voted to reinstate the code!

Instituting Ethics Programs Many examples suggest that ethical responses can be learned through experience. In the classic 1982 case of a corporate saboteur who poisoned Tylenol capsules and caused the deaths of several consumers, employees at Johnson & Johnson, the maker of Tylenol, didn't wait for instructions or a company directive before informing retailers and pulling the product from shelves. In retrospect, they reported simply knowing that this was what the company would want them to do. Business schools are important players in ethics education, but most analysts agree that companies must take the chief responsibility for educating employees.

More and more firms, like ExxonMobil and Boeing, require managers to go through periodic ethics training

Do No Evil

Although strategies, practices, and objectives can change, an organization's core principles and values should remain steadfast. For example, Google must be flexible enough to adapt its strategies and practices to meet the challenges posed by the rapidly evolving technology industry. Google's core principle is simple: "Don't be evil." Google's code of conduct is built around this idea—ethical responsibility is central to Google's identity, which is especially important for a company that has access to vast amounts of private and sensitive information.

to remind them of the importance of ethical decision making and to update them on current laws and regulations. Others, such as Texas Instruments, have ethics hotlines that employees may call to discuss the ethics of a particular problem or situation or to report unethical behavior or activities by others.

SOCIAL RESPONSIBILITY the attempt of a business to balance its commitments to groups and individuals in its environment, including customers, other businesses, employees, investors, and local communities

ORGANIZATIONAL STAKEHOLDERS those groups, individuals, and organizations that are directly affected by the practices of an organization and who therefore have a stake in its performance

Social Responsibility

While ethics affect individual behavior in the workplace, **social responsibility** refers to the overall way in which a business attempts to balance its commitments to relevant groups and individuals in its social environment. These groups and individuals who are directly affected by the practices of an organization and have a stake in its performance are **organizational stakeholders**.[8]

The Stakeholder Model of Responsibility

Most companies that strive to be responsible to their stakeholders concentrate first and foremost on *customers, employees, investors, suppliers,* and *local communities*. They may then select other stakeholders who are particularly relevant or important to the organization and try to address their needs and expectations as well.

© Showcasepix/Newscom

Apple has maintained a strong customer service reputation with features like the Apple Store's "Genius Bar," where Mac specialists answer questions for Mac users.

Entrepreneurship and New Ventures

The Electronic Equivalent of Paper Shredding

In virtually every major corporate scandal of the last few years, the best-laid plans of managerial miscreants have come unraveled, at least in part, when e-mail surfaced as key evidence. For example, Citigroup analyst Jack Grubman changed stock recommendations in exchange for favors from CEO Sandy Weill and confirmed the arrangement via e-mail. Investigators found that David Duncan, Arthur Andersen's head Enron auditor, had deleted incriminating e-mails shortly after the start of the Justice Department's investigation. After Tim Newington, an analyst for Credit Suisse First Boston, refused to give in to pressure to change a client's credit rating, an e-mail circulated on the problem of Newington's troublesome integrity: "Bigger issue," warned an upper manager, "is what to do about Newington in general. I'm not sure he's salvageable at this point."

Many corporations are nervous about the potential liability that employee e-mails may incur. Software developer Omniva Policy Systems saw this concern as an opportunity. Their e-mail software allows users to send encrypted messages, specify an expiration date after which they can no longer be decrypted, and prevent resending or printing. In the event of a lawsuit or investigation, administrators can hit a "red button" that prevents any e-mail from being deleted.

"Our goal," says Omniva CEO Kumar Sreekanti, "is to keep the honest people honest . . . We help organizations comply with regulations automatically so they don't have to rely on people to do it."

E-mails like Jack Grubman's often provide investigators with a smoking gun.

© zumaphotos/Newscom

Customers Businesses that are responsible to their customers treat them fairly and honestly, charge fair prices, honor warranties, meet delivery commitments, and stand behind product quality. Apple, Wegmans Food Markets, UPS, and Lexus are among those companies with excellent reputations in this area.[9]

Employees Businesses that are socially responsible in their dealings with employees treat workers fairly, make them part of the team, and respect their dignity and basic human needs. Many of these firms are also committed to hiring and promoting qualified minorities.

Investors A socially responsible stance toward investors means following proper accounting procedures, providing appropriate information about financial performance, and protecting shareholder rights and investments. Accurate and candid assessments of future growth and profitability are also important, as is avoiding even the appearance of impropriety in such sensitive areas as insider trading, stock-price manipulation, and the withholding of financial data.

Suppliers Relations with suppliers should also be managed with care, and firms should recognize the importance of mutually beneficial partnerships.

A large corporation might easily take advantage of suppliers by imposing unrealistic delivery schedules and pushing for lower prices. Instead, it should keep suppliers informed about future plans, negotiate mutually agreeable delivery schedules and prices, and so forth.

Local and International Communities Most businesses try to be socially responsible to local communities by contributing to local programs, getting involved in charities, and minimizing negative impact on communities. Target stores, for example, give over $2 million each week to local neighborhoods, programs, and schools.[10]

Starbucks helps local farmers gain access to credit, works to develop and maintain sustainability of the coffee crop, and is building farmer support centers in Costa Rica, Ethiopia, and Rwanda to provide local farmers with agricultural and technical education and support.[11]

© Tony Karumba/Getty Images

An organization should also recognize international stakeholders. The actions of international businesses affect their suppliers, employees, and customers in multiple countries. International businesses must also address their responsibilities in areas such as wages, working conditions, and environmental protection across different countries with varying regulatory laws and norms.

Contemporary Social Consciousness

Social consciousness and views toward social responsibility have been evolving since entrepreneurs such as John D. Rockefeller, J.P. Morgan, and Cornelius Vanderbilt raised concerns about abuses of power and led to the nation's first laws regulating basic business practices. In the 1930s, many blamed the Great Depression on a climate of business greed and lack of restraint. Out of this economic turmoil emerged new laws that dictated an expanded role for business in protecting and enhancing the general welfare of society, formalizing the concept of accountability.

In the 1960s and 1970s, business was again characterized negatively. Some charged that defense contractors had helped promote the Vietnam War to spur their own profits. Eventually, increased social activism prompted increased government regulation that led to changes such as health warnings on cigarette packaging and stricter environmental protection laws.

The general economic prosperity of the 1980s and 1990s led to another period of laissez-faire attitudes toward business. For the most part, business was viewed as a positive force. Many businesses continue to operate in enlightened and socially responsible ways: Wal-Mart and Target have policies against selling weapons, GameStop refuses to sell Mature-rated games to minors, and Anheuser-Busch promotes the concept of responsible drinking in its advertising.

Unfortunately, the recent spate of corporate scandals may revive negative attitudes toward business and result in increased control and constraint of business practices by the government.[12] As just a single illustration, widespread moral outrage erupted when some of former Tyco CEO Dennis Kozlowski's extravagant perquisites were made public. In addition to the almost $300 million he made between 1998 and 2001 in salary, bonuses, and stock proceeds, his perks included a $50 million Florida mansion, an $18 million New York apartment, $11 million for antiques and furnishings, and a $2.1 million birthday party in Italy for his wife. In 2005, Kozlowski was sentenced to 25 years in prison for misappropriating Tyco funds.[13]

Areas of Social Responsibility

When defining its sense of social responsibility, a firm typically confronts four areas of concern: responsibilities toward the *environment*, *customers*, *employees*, and *investors*.

Responsibility Toward the Environment

The devastating effects of increasing carbon dioxide (Figure 2) and other greenhouse gas emissions have begun to reveal themselves in the shrinking Arctic ice cap and the increase in severe weather incidents. With

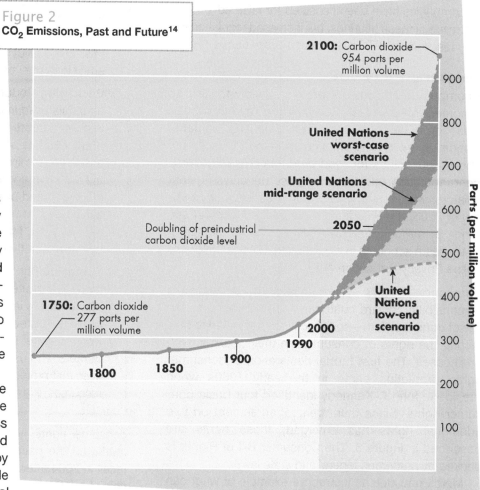

Figure 2
CO_2 Emissions, Past and Future[14]

2100: Carbon dioxide 954 parts per million volume

United Nations worst-case scenario

United Nations mid-range scenario

Doubling of preindustrial carbon dioxide level

2050

United Nations low-end scenario

1750: Carbon dioxide 277 parts per million volume

1800   **1850**   **1900**   **1990**   **2000**

Parts (per million volume)

900
800
700
600
500
400
300
200
100

GREENWASHING using advertising to project a green image without adopting substantive environmentally friendly changes

CONSUMERISM form of social activism dedicated to protecting the rights of consumers in their dealings with businesses

increased attention to global climate change comes pressure on business, both from governments and consumers, to control negative environmental impact.

Many socially responsible companies go beyond what government regulations require. For example, in addition to developing hydrogen fuel technologies, Honda reduced its own CO_2 emissions by five percent between 2000 and 2005 and has pledged to reduce them another five percent by 2010.[15] Although cost concerns have created reluctance to "go green," the opportunity to make money by marketing green products to environmentally conscious consumers is becoming increasingly apparent.

Not all businesses make a sincere effort to adopt green policies and procedures. Some are guilty of **greenwashing**—using advertising to project a green image without adopting substantive environmentally friendly changes. In January 2008, the U.S. Federal Trade Commission (FTC) began a series of hearings to determine the veracity of many green marketing claims. No companies have been censured for false advertising as a result of these hearings, but increased regulation will likely result as the FTC catches up to new trends.[16]

Responsibility Toward Customers

A company that does not act responsibly toward its customers will ultimately lose their trust and their business. To encourage responsibility, the FTC regulates advertising and pricing practices, and the FDA enforces labeling guidelines for food products. These government regulating bodies can impose penalties against violators, who may also face civil litigation. For example, in 2006, the FTC fined the social networking site Xanga $1 million for allowing children under the age of 13 to create accounts in clear violation of the Children's Online Privacy Protection Act.[17]

Consumer Rights Current interest in business responsibility toward customers can be traced to the rise of **consumerism**—social activism dedicated to protecting the rights of consumers in their dealings with businesses. The first formal declaration of consumer rights protection came in the early 1960s when President John F. Kennedy identified four basic consumer rights. Since then, general agreement on two additional rights has emerged; these rights are described in Figure 3. The Consumer Bill of Rights is backed by numerous federal and state laws.

Merck provides an instructive example of what can happen to a firm that violates one or more of these

Green marketing (also environmental or ecological marketing)—the marketing of environmentally friendly goods—encompasses a wide variety of business strategies and practices.

- **Production Processes** Businesses, like Ford Motors and General Electric, modify their production processes to limit the consumption of valuable resources like fossil fuels by increasing energy efficiency and reduce their output of waste and pollution by cutting greenhouse gas emissions.

- **Product Modification** Products can be modified to use more environmentally friendly materials, a practice S.C. Johnson encourages with its Greenlist of raw materials classified according to their impact on health and the environment. Committed to only using the safest materials on this list, S.C. Johnson eliminated 1.8 million pounds of volatile organic compounds from its glass cleaner Windex.[18]

- **Carbon Offsets** Many companies are committed to offsetting the CO_2 produced by their products and manufacturing processes. In 2007, Volkswagen began a program of planting trees (which consume CO_2 during photosynthesis) in the so-called VW Forest in the lower Mississippi alluvial valley to offset the CO_2 emissions of every car they sell.[19]

- **Packaging Reduction** Reducing and reusing materials used in packaging products is another important strategy of green marketing, which Starbucks has pioneered. In 2004 the U.S. Food and Drug Administration gave the coffee retailer the first-ever approval to use recycled materials in its food and beverage packaging. Starbucks estimates that using cups composed of 10 percent recycled fibers reduces its packaging waste by more than five million pounds per year.[20]

- **Sustainability** Using renewable resources and managing limited resources responsibly and efficiently are important goals for any business pursuing a green policy. For example, Whole Foods Market is committed to buying food from farmers who use sustainable agriculture practices that protect the environment and agricultural resources, like land and water.

consumer rights. For several years the firm aggressively marketed the painkiller Vioxx, which it was forced to recall in 2004 after clinical trials linked it to an increased risk of heart attacks and strokes. After the recall was announced, it was revealed that Merck had known about

The U.S.-based environmental group Nature Conservancy has recently teamed up with Indonesian logging company Sumalindo Lestari Jaya to help local villagers log a forest in a remote area of Indonesia. Why? The group believes that by working together with the company, it can better enforce sustainable practices.

Korean Air Lines were heavily fined, but in exchange for turning them in, Virgin and Lufthansa were not penalized.[22]

Firms can also come under attack for *price gouging*—responding to increased demand with overly steep (and often unwarranted) price increases. For example, during threats of severe weather, people often stock up on bottled water and batteries. Unfortunately, some retailers take advantage of this pattern by marking up prices. Reports were widespread of gasoline retailers doubling or even tripling prices immediately after the events of September 11, 2001, and following the U.S. invasion of Iraq in 2003. Similar problems arose after hurricanes Katrina and Rita damaged oil refineries along the Gulf Coast in late 2005.

COLLUSION illegal agreement between two or more companies to commit a wrongful act

GREEN MARKETING the marketing of environmentally friendly goods

these risks as early as 2000 and downplayed them so that they could continue selling it. In 2007, Merck agreed to pay $4.85 billion to individuals or families of those who were injured or died as a result of taking the drug.[21]

Unfair Pricing   Interfering with competition can take the form of illegal pricing practices. **Collusion** occurs when two or more firms collaborate on such wrongful acts as price fixing. In 2007, the European airlines Virgin and Lufthansa admitted to colluding with rivals to raise the prices of fuel surcharges on passenger flights as much as 12 times the regular price between August 2004 and January 2006. British Airways and

Ethics in Advertising   In recent years, increased attention has been given to ethics in advertising and product information. Controversy arose when *Newsweek* magazine reported that Sony had literally created a movie critic who happened to be particularly fond of movies released by Sony's Columbia Pictures. When advertising its newest theatrical releases, the studio had been routinely using glowing quotes from a fictitious critic. After the story broke, Sony hastily stopped the practice and apologized.

Another issue concerns advertising that some consumers consider morally objectionable—for products such as underwear, condoms, alcohol, tobacco products, and firearms. Laws regulate some of this advertising (for instance, tobacco can no longer be promoted in television commercials, but can be featured in print ads in magazines), and many advertisers use common sense and discretion in their promotions. But some companies, such as Calvin Klein and Victoria's Secret, have come under fire for being overly explicit in their advertising.

Figure 3
Consumer Bill of Rights

Consumer Bill of Rights

1   Consumers have a right to safe products.

2   Consumers have a right to be informed about all relevant aspects of a product.

3   Consumers have a right to be heard.

4   Consumers have a right to choose what they buy.

5   Consumers have a right to be educated about purchases.

6   Consumers have a right to courteous service.

Responsibility Toward Employees

Recruiting, hiring, training, promoting, and compensating are essential human resource

WHISTLE-BLOWER
employee who detects and tries to put an end to a company's unethical, illegal, or socially irresponsible actions by publicizing them

Because of controversies surrounding the potential misinterpretation of words and phrases, such as *light, reduced calorie, diet*, and *low fat*, food producers are now required to use a standardized format for listing ingredients on product packages.

© Ross Halley/Fort Worth Star-Telegram/MCT/Newscom

management activities that provide the basis for social responsibility toward employees.

Legal and Social Commitments By law, businesses cannot discriminate against people in any facet of the employment relationship. For example, a company cannot refuse to hire someone because of ethnicity or pay someone a lower salary than someone else on the basis of gender. A company that provides its employees with equal opportunities without regard to race, sex, or other irrelevant factors is meeting both its legal and its social responsibilities. Firms that ignore these responsibilities risk losing good employees and leave themselves open to lawsuits.

Most would also agree that an organization should strive to ensure that the workplace is physically and socially safe. Companies with a heightened awareness of social responsibility also recognize an obligation to provide opportunities to balance work and life pressures and preferences, help employees maintain job skills, and, when terminations or layoffs are necessary, treat them with respect and compassion.

Ethical Commitments: The Special Case of Whistle-Blowers Respecting employees as people also means respecting their behavior as ethical individuals. Ideally, an employee who discovers that a business has been engaging in illegal, unethical, or socially irresponsible practices should be able to report the problem to higher-level management and feel confident that managers will stop the questionable practices. However, if no one in the organization will take action, the employee might elect to drop the matter, or he or she may inform a regulatory agency or the media and become what is known as a **whistle-blower**—an employee who discovers and tries to put an end to a company's unethical, illegal, or socially irresponsible actions by publicizing them.[23]

PERSONS OF THE YEAR

TIME

The Whistleblowers

CYNTHIA COOPER OF WORLDCOM • COLEEN ROWLEY OF THE FBI • SHERRON WATKINS OF ENRON

© Gregory Heisler/Getty Images/Time Life Pictures

Enron's Sherron Watkins (right) reported concerns about the company's accounting practices well before the company's problems were made public, warning top management that Enron would "implode in a wave of accounting scandals." CEO Kenneth Lay commissioned a legal review of the firm's finances, but told his investigators not to "second-guess" decisions by Enron's auditor, accounting firm Arthur Andersen.[24]

Unfortunately, whistle-blowers may be demoted, fired, or, if they remain in their jobs, treated with mistrust, resentment, or hostility by coworkers. One recent study suggests that about half of all whistle-blowers eventually get fired, and about half of those who get fired subsequently lose their homes and/or families.[25] The law offers some recourse to employees who take action. The current whistle-blower law stems from the False Claims Act of 1863, which was designed to prevent contractors from selling defective supplies to the Union Army during the Civil War. With 1986 revisions to the law, the government can recover triple damages from fraudulent contractors. If the Justice Department does not intervene, a whistle-blower can proceed with a civil suit. In that case, the whistle-blower receives 25 to 30 percent of any money recovered.[26] Unfortunately, however, the prospect of large cash awards has generated a spate of false or questionable accusations.[27]

Responsibility Toward Investors

Managers can abuse their responsibilities to investors in several ways. As a rule, irresponsible behavior toward shareholders means abuse of a firm's financial resources so that shareholder-owners do not receive their due earnings or dividends. Companies can also act irresponsibly toward shareholder-owners by misrepresenting company resources.

Improper Financial Management Blatant financial mismanagement—such as paying excessive salaries to senior managers, sending them on extravagant "retreats" to exotic resorts, and providing frivolous perks—are unethical, but not necessarily illegal. In such situations, creditors and stockholders have few options for recourse. Forcing a management changeover is a difficult process that can drive down stock prices—a penalty that shareholders are usually unwilling to impose on themselves.

Insider Trading   **Insider trading** is using confidential information to gain from the purchase or sale of stocks. Suppose, for example, that a small firm's stock is currently trading at $50 a share. If a larger firm is going to buy the smaller one, it might have to pay as much as $75 a share for a controlling interest. Individuals aware of the impending acquisition before it is publicly announced, such as managers of the two firms or the financial institution making the arrangements, could gain by buying the stock at $50 in anticipation of selling it for $75 after the proposed acquisition is announced.

Informed executives can also avoid financial loss by selling stock that's about to drop in value. Legally, stock can only be sold on the basis of public information available to all investors. Potential violations of this regulation were at the heart of the Martha Stewart scandal. Sam Waksal, president of ImClone, learned that the company's stock was going to drop in value and hastily tried to sell his own stock in 2001. He allegedly tipped off close friend Martha Stewart, who subsequently sold her stock as well. Stewart, who argued that she never received Waksal's call and sold her stock only because she wanted to use the funds elsewhere, eventually pled guilty to other charges (lying to investigators) and served time in prison. Waksal, meanwhile, received a much stiffer sentence because his own attempts to dump his stock were well documented.

Misrepresentation of Finances   In maintaining and reporting its financial status, every corporation must conform to generally accepted accounting principles (GAAP). Unethical managers might project profits in excess of what they actually expect to earn, hide losses and/or expenses in order to boost paper profits, or slant financial reports to make the firm seem stronger than is really the case. In 2002, the U.S. Congress passed the *Sarbanes-Oxley Act*, which requires an organization's chief financial officer to personally guarantee the accuracy of all financial reporting.

Implementing Social Responsibility Programs

Opinions differ dramatically concerning social responsibility as a business goal. While some oppose any business activity that threatens profits, others argue that social responsibility must take precedence. Some skeptics fear that businesses will gain too much control over the ways social projects are addressed by society as a whole, or that they lack the expertise needed to address social issues. Still, many believe that corporations should help improve the lives of citizens because they are citizens themselves, often control vast resources, and may contribute to the very problems that social programs address.

> **INSIDER TRADING** illegal practice of using special knowledge about a firm for profit or gain
>
> **OBSTRUCTIONIST STANCE** approach to social responsibility that involves doing as little as possible and may involve attempts to deny or cover up violations
>
> **DEFENSIVE STANCE** approach to social responsibility by which a company meets only minimum legal requirements in its commitments to groups and individuals in its social environment

Approaches to Social Responsibility

Given these differences of opinion, it is little wonder that corporations have adopted a variety of approaches to social responsibility. As Figure 4 illustrates, the four stances that an organization can take concerning its obligations to society fall along a continuum ranging from the lowest to the highest degree of socially responsible practices.

Obstructionist Stance   The few organizations that take an **obstructionist stance** to social responsibility usually do as little as possible to solve social or environmental problems, have little regard for ethical conduct, and will go to great lengths to deny or cover up wrongdoing. For example, IBP, a leading meat-processing firm, has a long record of breaking environmental protection, labor, and food processing laws and then trying to cover up its offenses.

Defensive Stance   Organizations who take a **defensive stance** will do everything that is legally required, including admitting to mistakes and taking corrective actions, but nothing more. Defensive stance managers insist that their job is to generate profits and might, for example, install pollution-control equipment dictated by law but not higher-quality equipment to further limit pollution.

Tobacco companies generally take this position in their marketing efforts. In the United States, they are legally required to include product warnings and to limit advertising to prescribed media. Domestically, they follow these rules to the letter of the law, but in many Asian and African countries, which don't have these rules, cigarettes are heavily promoted, contain higher levels of tar and nicotine, and carry few or no health warning labels.

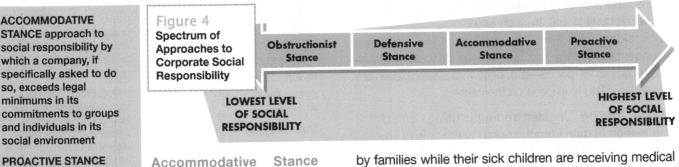

Figure 4
Spectrum of Approaches to Corporate Social Responsibility

ACCOMMODATIVE STANCE approach to social responsibility by which a company, if specifically asked to do so, exceeds legal minimums in its commitments to groups and individuals in its social environment

PROACTIVE STANCE approach to social responsibility by which a company actively seeks opportunities to contribute to the well-being of groups and individuals in its social environment

SOCIAL AUDIT systematic analysis of a firm's success in using funds earmarked for meeting its social responsibility goals

Accommodative Stance

A firm that adopts an **accommodative stance** meets and, in certain cases exceeds, its legal and ethical requirements. Such firms will agree to participate in social programs if solicitors convince them that given programs are worthy of their support. Both Shell and IBM, for example, will match contributions made by their employees to selected charitable causes.

Proactive Stance Firms with the highest degree of social responsibility exhibit the **proactive stance**; they take to heart the arguments in favor of social responsibility, view themselves as citizens in a society, indicate sincere commitment to improve the general social welfare, and surpass the accommodative stance by proactively seeking opportunities to contribute. The most common—and direct—way to implement this stance is to set up a foundation for providing direct financial support for various social programs. An excellent example of a proactive stance is the McDonald's Corporation's Ronald McDonald House program. These houses, located close to major medical centers, can be used for minimal cost by families while their sick children are receiving medical treatment nearby.

However, these categories are not sharply distinct: Organizations do not always fit neatly into one category or another. The Ronald McDonald House program has been widely applauded, but McDonald's has also been accused of misleading consumers about the nutritional value of its food products.

Managing Social Responsibility Programs

A full commitment to social responsibility requires a carefully organized and managed program and managers who take steps to foster a companywide sense of social responsibility:[29]

1. *Social responsibility must start at the top and be considered a factor in strategic planning.* No program can succeed without the support of top management, who must embrace a strong stand on social responsibility and develop a policy statement outlining that commitment.

2. *A committee of top managers must develop a plan detailing the level of management support.* Companies may set aside percentages of profits for social programs or set specific priorities, such as supporting the arts.

Table 1 **Top 10 Corporate Foundations[28]**

Foundation	State	Total Giving (In U.S. Dollars)	Fiscal Date
1 Aventis Pharmaceuticals Health Care Foundation	NJ	217,845,821	12/31/05
2 Wal-Mart Foundation	AR	155,073,614	1/31/06
3 The Bank of America Charitable Foundation, Inc.	NC	123,287,819	12/31/05
4 The JPMorgan Chase Foundation	MI	85,458,083	12/31/05
5 Citigroup Foundation	CA	80,764,000	12/31/05
6 Ford Motor Company Fund	TX	79,881,090	12/31/05
7 GE Foundation	NY	70,635,496	12/31/05
8 The Wells Fargo Foundation	NJ	65,007,124	12/31/05
9 ExxonMobil Foundation	NY	63,660,965	12/31/05
10 Verizon Foundation	CT	61,834,820	12/31/05

3 *One executive must be put in charge of the firm's agenda.* Whether a separate job or part of an existing one, the selected individual must monitor the program and ensure implementation consistent with the firm's policy statement and strategic plan.

4 *The organization must conduct occasional* **social audits**—*systematic analyses of its success in using funds earmarked for its social responsibility goals.* Consider the case of a company whose strategic plan calls for spending $200,000 to train 300 unemployed people and to place 275 of them in jobs. If, at the end of a year, the firm has spent $198,000, trained 305 people, and filled 270 jobs, a social audit will confirm the program's success. But if the program has cost $350,000, trained only 190 people, and placed only 40 of them, the audit will reveal the program's failure. Such failure should prompt a rethinking of the program's implementation and its priorities.

Social Responsibility and the Small Business

Small-businesses owners are faced with similar ethical questions, although they may largely be a question of individual ethics. As the owner of a garden supply store, how would you respond to a building inspector's suggestion that a cash payment will speed your building permit application? As a liquor store manager, would you sell alcohol to a customer whose identification card looks forged? As the owner of a small laboratory, would you verify the license of your medical waste disposal company? Who will really be harmed if you pad your small firm's income statement to get a much-needed bank loan?

What about questions of social responsibility? Can your small business afford a social agenda? Should you sponsor Little League teams and donate to the United Way? Do joining the chamber of commerce and supporting the Better Business Bureau cost too much? Clearly, all managers in all organizations have to make decisions about ethics and social responsibility. One key to business success is to decide in advance how to respond to the issues that underlie all questions of ethical and social responsibility.

For additional topics related to this material and end-of-chapter exercises and practices, please visit www.mybizlab.com.

Questions for Review

1 What basic factors should be considered in any ethical decision?

2 Who are an organization's stakeholders? Who are the major stakeholders with which most businesses must be concerned?

3 What are the major areas of social responsibility with which businesses should be concerned?

4 What are the four basic approaches to social responsibility?

5 In what ways do you think your personal code of ethics might clash with the operations of some companies? How might you try to resolve these differences?

Questions for Analysis

6 What kind of wrongdoing would most likely prompt you to be a whistle-blower? What kind of wrongdoing would least likely cause you to blow the whistle? Why?

7 In your opinion, which area of social responsibility is most important? Why? Are there areas other than those noted in the chapter that you consider important?

8 Identify some specific ethical or social responsibility issues that might be faced by small-business managers and employees in each of the following areas: environment, customers, employees, and investors.

Application Exercises

9 Develop a list of the major stakeholders of your college or university. How do you think the school prioritizes these stakeholders? Do you agree or disagree with this prioritization?

10 Using newspapers, magazines, and other business references, identify and describe at least three companies that take a defensive stance to social responsibility, three that take an accommodative stance, and three that take a proactive stance.

Reference Notes
• •

1 "Oil company BP pleads guilty to environmental crime," *International Herald Tribune* (November 29, 2007), at http://www.iht.com/articles/ap/2007/11/30/business/ NA-FIN-US-BP-Settlement-Alaska.php?page=1; Michael Hawthorne, "BP gets break on dumping in lake," *Chicago Tribune* (July 15, 2007), at http://www. chicagotribune.com/news/nationworld/chi-pollute_15jul15,1,386727; Terry Macalister "Greenpeace calls BP's oil sands plan an environmental crime," *guardian.co.uk* (December 7, 2007), at http://www. guardian.co.uk/business/2007/dec/07/bp; Sharon Epperson, "BP's Fundamental But Obscured Energy Contradiction," cnbc.com (May 21, 2008), at http://www. cnbc.com/id/24758394; Brad Hem, "10 plaintiffs in BP case will seek $950 million," *Houston Chronicle* (May 23, 2008), at http://www.chron.com/disp/story.mpl/ headline/biz/5797579.html.

2 William G. Symonds, Geri Smith, "The Tax Games Tyco Played," *Business Week* (July 1, 2002), 40–41.

3 "Tyco Votes to Stay Offshore," *BBC News* (March 6, 2003), at http://news.bbc.co.uk/2/hi/business/ 2827683.stm.

4 Seib, Christine. "Volkswagen union boss Klaus Volkert jailed for two years," *Times Online* (February 22, 2008), at http://business.timesonline.co.uk/tol/ business/industry_sectors/engineering/ article3417994.ece.

5 This section follows the logic of Gerald F. Cavanaugh, *American Business Values: A Global Perspective*, 5th ed. (Upper Saddle River, NJ: Prentice Hall, 2006), Chapter 3.

6 Manuel G. Velasquez, Business Ethics: Concepts and Cases, 6th ed. (Upper Saddle River, NJ: Prentice Hall, 2006), Chapter 2. See also John R. Boatright, *Ethics and the Conduct of Business*, 4th ed. (Upper Saddle River, NJ: Prentice Hall, 2003), 34–35, 57–59.

7 Based on Gerald S. Cavanaugh, *American Business Values: With International Perspectives*, 4th ed. (Upper Saddle River, NJ: Prentice Hall, 1998) 71, 84.

8 Jeffrey S. Harrison, R. Edward Freeman, "Stakeholders, Social Responsibility, and Performance: Empirical Evidence and Theoretical Perspectives," *Academy of Management Journal*, 1999, vol. 42, no. 5, 479–485. See also David P. Baron, *Business and Its Environment*, 5th ed. (Upper Saddle River, NJ: Prentice Hall, 2006), Chapter 18.

9 http://bwnt.businessweek.com/ interactive_reports/customer_satisfaction/index. asp, Accessed May 30, 2008.

10 http://target.com/target_group/ community_giving/index.jhtml, Accessed January 15, 2006.

11 Starbucks About Us, at http://www.starbucks. com/aboutus/origins.asp, Accessed May 30, 2008; "Starbucks to Open Regional Farmer Support Center in Rwanda," (December 1, 2007), at http://www. csrwire.com/News/10275.html.

12 Gerald Seib, "What Could Bring 1930s-Style Reform of U.S. Business?" *Wall Street Journal* (July 24, 2002), A1, A8.

13 William G. Symonds, Geri Smith, "The Tax Games Tyco Played," *Business Week*, July 1, 2002, 40–41; "Tyco Titan Charged with Tax Violations," *CBSNews.com* (June 4, 2002), at www.cbsnew.com/stories/2002/06/ 04/national/main511051.shtm; Nicholas Varchaver, "CEOs Under Fire," *Fortune.com* (December 6, 2002), at www.fortune.com/fortune/ceo/articles/ 0,15114,442883,00.html; "Kozlowski Gets up to 25 Years," *money.cnn.com* (September 19, 2005).

14 Based on Andrew C. Revkin, "Who Cares About a Few Degrees?" *New York Times*, December 12, 1997, F1.

15 http://money.cnn.com/galleries/2007/fortune/ 0703/gallery.green_giants.fortune/index.html, Accessed May 30, 2008.

16 Louise Story, "F.T.C. Asks if Carbon-Offset Money Is Well Spent," *New York Times* (January 8, 2008), at http://www.nytimes.com/2008/01/09/business/09of fsets.html?_r=2&ei=5088&en=05dc8be5247f9737&e x=1357707600&oref=slogin&partner=rssnyt&emc=r ss&pagewanted=print.

17 Bob Sullivan, "FTC fines Xanga for violating kids' privacy," (September 7, 2006), at http://www.msnbc. msn.com/id/14718350.

18 http://money.cnn.com/galleries/2007/fortune/ 0703/gallery.green_giants.fortune/7.html, Accessed May 30, 2008; http://www.scjohnson.com/ environment/growing_1.asp, Accessed May 30, 2008.

19 http://www.nytimes.com/2008/01/09/business/09of fsets.html?_r=1&ex=1357707600&en=05dc8be5247f9 737&ei=5088&partner=rssnyt&emc=rss&oref= slogic, Accessed May 30, 2008.

20 http://www.starbucks.com/csrnewsletter/ winter06/csrEnvironment.asp, Accessed May 30, 2008.

21 Alex Berenson, "Merck Agrees to Pay $4.85 Billion in Vioxx Claims," *New York Times,* (November 9, 2007), at http://www.nytimes.com/2007/11/09/business/ 09cnd-merck.html?ref=business; Rita Rubin, "How did Vioxx debacle happen?" *USA Today*, (October 12, 2004), at http://www.usatoday.com/news/health/ 2004-10-12-vioxx-cover_x.htm.

[22] "British Airways and Korean Air Lines Fined in Fuel Collusion," *New York Times* (August 2, 2007), at http://www.nytimes.com/2007/08/02/business/worldbusiness/02air.html?scp=2&sq=british+airways+price+fixing&st=nyt.

[23] Jerald Greenberg and Robert A. Baron, *Behavior in Organizations: Understanding and Managing the Human Side of Work*, 8th ed. (Upper Saddle River, NJ: Prentice Hall, 2003), 410–413.

[24] Greg Farrell, "Enron Law Firm Called Accounting Practices Creative," *USA Today*, January 2002, 1B.

[25] Cora Daniels, "It's a Living Hell," *Fortune* (April 15, 2002), 367–368.

[26] Henry R. Cheeseman, *Business Law: Legal, E Commerce, Ethical, and International Environments*, 5th ed. (Upper Saddle River, NJ: Prentice Hall, 2004), 128–129.

[27] http://www.usdoj.gov/usao/iln/pr/chicago/2008/pr0318_01.pdf, Accessed May 30, 2008; Jacob Goldstein, "CVS to Pay $37.5 Million to Settle Pill Switching Case," Wall Street Journal (March 18, 2008), at http://blogs.wsj.com/health/2008/03/18/cvs-to-pay-375-million-to-settle-pill-switching-case.

[28] http://foundationcenter.org/gainknowledge/research/pdf/keyfacts_corp_2007.pdf, Accessed May 30, 2008.

[29] Michael E. Porter and Mark R. Kramer, "Philanthropy's New Agenda: Doing Well by Doing Good," *Sloan Management Review* (Winter 2000), 75–85.

Sources

Figure 1: Based on Gerald S. Cavanaugh, *American Business Values: With International Perspectives*, 4th ed. (Upper Saddle River, NJ: Prentice Hall, 1998) 71, 84. **Figure 2:** Based on Andrew C. Revkin, "Who Cares About a Few Degrees?" *New York Times*, December 12, 1997, F1.

Ethics, Social Responsibility, and the Business Manager

- ◼ DEFINITION OF BUSINESS ETHICS AND SOCIAL RESPONSIBILITY

- ◼ THEORIES OF ETHICAL THOUGHT

- ◼ CODES OF ETHICS

- ◼ SCHOOLS OF SOCIAL RESPONSIBILITY

- ◼ GLOBAL DIMENSIONS OF ETHICS AND SOCIAL RESPONSIBILITY

On December 2, 1984, in Bhopal, India, lethal methylisocyanate (MIC) gas leaked from a chemical plant owned by Union Carbide India Ltd., killing approximately 2,000 people and injuring thousands more, many of whom are still receiving treatment. Union Carbide's chairman, Warren Anderson, a lawyer, flew to India with a pledge of interim assistance totaling $7 million and medical support. He was arrested and deported from the country. Lawsuits on behalf of the deceased and injured were brought by U.S. law firms as well as by the government of India.

The price of Union Carbide stock dropped from $48 to $33. In August 1984, GAF Corporation attempted to take over Union Carbide. Union Carbide successfully fought off the takeover attempt in 1985. On May 13, 1986, a federal court judge dismissed the personal injury and wrongful death actions, stating that the complaints should be more properly heard in a court in India. The judge attached certain conditions to the dismissal, one of which was that Union Carbide would have to agree to pay any damages rendered by an Indian court. The trail began in August 1988 in a New Delhi court amidst rumors that a former disgruntled employee had sabotaged Union Carbide's Bhopal plant, causing the gas leakage. In January 1988, Union Carbide shares traded on the New York Stock Exchange for $49, and the much leaner company was one of the 30 companies making up the composite Dow Jones Industrial Average.

In an unrelated, but similarly disturbing situation, the death toll for accidents involving Ford Explorers equipped with Firestone tires rose to at least 174 by

From Chapter 8 of *The Legal Environment of Business: A Critical Thinking Approach*, 5/e. Nancy K. Kubasek. Bartley A. Brennan. M. Neil Browne. Copyright © 2009 by Pearson Prentice Hall. All rights reserved.

June 2001, and the number of reported injuries topped 700. Ford recalled most of the Firestone tires on Explorers, and eventually it switched to other brands. Meanwhile, the tire manufacturer maintained that the problem was not the tires but the design of the Explorer. As the two companies continued to try to place responsibility primarily on each other, consumers continued to purchase Ford Explorers, although not quite at the same rate as before all the negative publicity.

The Bhopal incident in 1984, along with a stream of insider trading cases beginning in 1986 and continuing into the 1990s, as well as a number of white-collar crime cases in the 2000s have brought a heightened awareness of the need for debate as to whether the business community has a responsibility solely to shareholders or to other stakeholders as well.

Such cases force us to ask ourselves, What should be the legal rules that businesses must obey in their daily operations? Additionally, there are ethical questions that force us to consider how we should behave if we are to live in a better world. Business ethics is the study of the moral practices of the firms that play such an important role in shaping that better world.

Whenever you wonder whether a business decision requires us to think about ethics, simply ask yourself, Will this decision affect the quality of life of other people? If the answer is yes, the decision involves ethics. We think you will agree that business ethics is an extremely important aspect of our environment because almost all business decisions influence the quality of our lives.

This chapter presents material on business ethics in a neutral way. Readers are left to make their own choices about what part ethics should play in business decision making and about whether the business community, the trade groups that represent it, and individual managers should act in a "socially responsible" manner. This chapter includes (1) a broad definition of ethics and social responsibility; (2) some recognized theories of ethical thought and their application to business problems; (3) a discussion of individual, corporate, trade association, and professional ethical codes; and (4) schools of social responsibility as applied to business problems. The chapter ends with a brief discussion of some current trends in the area of ethics and social responsibility as well as some proposals now being debated, which, if implemented, would change the structure of corporate governance.

CRITICAL THINKING ABOUT THE LAW

Business ethics is perhaps one of the most personal and emotional areas in business decision making. Business ethics can be confusing and complex because a right or wrong answer often does not exist. Because this area is so emotional and controversial, it is extremely important to use your critical thinking skills when thinking about business ethics. It would be very easy to make arguments based on your gut reaction to cases such as the Bhopal gas incident. You should, however, carefully use your critical thinking skills to draw an informed conclusion. The following questions can help you begin to understand the complexity surrounding business ethics.

1. As critical thinkers, you have learned that ambiguous words—words that have multiple possible meanings—can cause confusion in the legal environment. Perhaps the best example of ambiguity in the legal environment is the phrase *social responsibility*. What definitions of responsibility can you generate?

   Clue: Consider the Bhopal incident. Do you think Union Carbide would have the same definition of social responsibility as the families of the victims of the accident in India?

2. It is common for individuals, businesses, judges, and juries to each have different meanings of the phrase *social responsibility*. Preferences for certain ethical norms might account for these different meanings. If executives of

a company thought that security was extremely important, how might their definition of social responsibility be affected?

Clue: If Union Carbide valued security, how might the company treat the victims of the Bhopal incident?

3. Your friend discovers that you are taking a legal environment of business class. He says, "I'm extremely angry at the cigarette companies. They knew that cigarettes cause cancer. Don't those companies have a responsibility to protect us?" Because you are trained in critical thinking, you know that his question does not have a simple answer. Keeping your critical thinking skills in mind, how would you intelligently respond to his question?

Clue: Consider the critical thinking questions about ambiguity, ethical norms, and missing information.

Definition of Business Ethics and Social Responsibility

BUSINESS ETHICS

Ethics is the study of good and bad behavior. **Business ethics** is a subset of the study of ethics and is defined as the study of what makes up good and bad business conduct. This conduct occurs when the firm acts as an organization, as well as when individual managers make decisions inside the organization. For example, there may be differences between the way Warren Anderson personally looked at the Bhopal tragedy (a failure of the plant to implement company operating standards) and the way the corporation's board of directors and the chemical industry did (the Indian government allowed people to live too close to the plant). It is important to look at "business" ethics not as a single monolithic system but from the perspective of individual managers, corporations, and industry-wide ethical concerns. Each may judge a particular happening in a different way.

How these groups think depends on their ethical norms and on their philosophy or theory of ethics. To help you understand their thinking, we include a discussion of three schools of ethical thought. Individual managers, corporations, or industries may belong to any one of the schools, as each school has its advocates and refinements. In addition, each school attempts to explain why an action is right or wrong and how one knows it to be right or wrong.

ethics The study of what makes up good and bad conduct inclusive of related actions and values.

business ethics The study of what makes up good and bad conduct as related to business activities and values.

THE SOCIAL RESPONSIBILITY OF BUSINESS

The **social responsibility** of business is defined as a concern by business about both its profit-seeking and its non-profit-seeking activities and their intended and unintended impact on groups and individuals other than management or the owners of a corporation (e.g., consumers, environmentalists, and political groups). Since the late 1960s, an outcry has arisen for business to be more socially responsible. This outcry of public concern has resulted in part from three factors:

social responsibility Concern of business entities about profit and nonprofit activities and their unintended impact on others directly or indirectly involved.

1. *The complexity and interdependence of a postindustrial society.* No individual or business is an island unto itself. If a company builds a chemical plant in Bhopal, India, and its primary purpose is to make profits for its shareholders, can it be held responsible to the public that lives around the plant when there is a gas leak? The public is dependent on the firm's good conduct, and

the firm is dependent on the public and its political representatives to supply labor, an adequate water supply, tax forgiveness, roads, and so on.

2. *Political influence that has translated public outcry for socially responsible conduct into government regulation.* Whether a malfunction occurs at a nuclear plant at Three Mile Island or a human disaster is caused by a gas leak in Bhopal, India, the political arm of government at all levels sees the solution in the form of more regulation. This attitude pleases the government's constituents and makes its official more electable.

3. *Philosophical differences about what should be the obligations of business.* Neoclassical economic theory would argue that the sole purpose of business is to make a profit for its investing shareholders, who, in turn, reinvest, creating expanded or new businesses that employ more people, thus creating a higher standard of living.

Others hold different theories of social responsibility. Some would argue for a managerial or coping approach; that is, "throw money" at the problem when it occurs, such as the Bhopal disaster, and it will go away. Others would argue a more encompassing theory of social responsibility that purports that business, like any other institution in our society (e.g., unions, churches), has a social responsibility not only to shareholders (or members or congregations) but also to diverse groups, such as consumers and political, ethnic, racial group, and gender-oriented organizations. These and other schools of social responsibility are discussed later in this chapter.

The case below offers serveral possible theories of social responsibility as applied to a controversial factual situation.

CASE **1**

In re Exxon Valdez
U.S. District Court District of Alaska
296 F. Supp 2d 107 (2004)

On Good Friday, March 24, 1989, the oil tanker *Exxon Valdez* was run aground on Bligh Reef in Prince William Sound, Alaska. On March 24, 1989, Joseph Hazelwood was in command of the *Exxon Valdez*. Defendant Exxon Shipping [Company] owned the *Exxon Valdez*. Exxon employed Captain Hazelwood, and kept him employed knowing that he had an alcohol problem. The captain had supposedly been rehabilitated, but Exxon knew better before March 24, 1989. Hazelwood had sought treatment for alcohol abuse in 1985 but had "fallen off the wagon" by the spring of 1986. Yet, Exxon continued to allow Hazelwood to command a supertanker carrying a hazardous cargo. Because Exxon did nothing despite its knowledge that Hazelwood was once again drinking, Captain Hazelwood was the person in charge of a vessel as long as three football fields and carrying 53 million gallons of crude oil. The best available estimate of the crude oil lost from the *Exxon Valdez* into Prince William Sound is about 11 million gallons. Commercial fisheries throughout this area were totally disrupted, with entire fisheries being closed for the 1989 season. Subsistence fishing by residents of Prince William Sound and Lower Cook Inlet villages was also disrupted. Shore-based businesses dependent upon the fishing industry were also disrupted as were the resources of cities such as Cordova. Exxon undertook a massive cleanup effort. Approximately $2.1 billion was ultimately spent in efforts to remove the spilled crude oil from the waters and beaches of Prince William Sound, Lower Cook Inlet, and Kodiak Island. Also, Exxon undertook a voluntary claims program, ultimately paying out $303 million, principally to fishermen whose livelihood was disrupted. [Lawsuits] (involving thousands of plaintiffs) were ultimately consolidated into this case.

The jury awarded a breathtaking $5 billion in punitive damages against Exxon. Exxon appealed the amount of punitive damages [to the U.S. Court of Appeals for the

178

Ninth Circuit]. [T]he Ninth Circuit Court of Appeals in this case reiterated the guideposts for use in determining whether punitive damages are grossly excessive [include] the reprehensibility of the defendant's conduct. The court of appeals remanded the case [and] unequivocally told this court that "[t]he $5 billion punitive damages award is too high" and "[i]t must be reduced."

Justice Holland

[T]he reprehensibility of the defendant's conduct is the most important indicium [indication] of the reasonableness of a punitive damages award. In determining whether a defendant's conduct is reprehensible, the court considers whether "The harm caused was physical as opposed to economic; the tortious conduct evinced an indifference to or a reckless disregard of the health or safety of others; the target of the conduct had financial vulnerability; the conduct involved repeated actions or was an isolated incident; and the harm was the result of intentional malice, trickery, or deceit, or mere accident."

The reprehensibility of a party's conduct, like truth and beauty, is subjective. One's view of the quality of an actor's conduct is the result of complex value judgments. The evaluation of a victim will vary considerably from that of a person not affected by an incident. Courts employ disinterested, unaffected lay jurors in the first instance to appraise the reprehensibility of a defendant's conduct. Here, the jury heard about what Exxon knew, and what its officers did and what they failed to do. Knowing what Exxon knew and did through its officers, the jury concluded that Exxon's conduct was highly reprehensible.

Punitive damages should reflect the enormity of the defendant's offense. Exxon's conduct did not simply cause economic harm to the plaintiffs. Exxon's decision to leave Captain Hazelwood in command of the *Exxon Valdez* demonstrated reckless disregard for a broad range of legitimate Alaska concerns: the livelihood, health, and safety of the residents of Prince William Sound, the crew of the *Exxon Valdez*, and others. Exxon's conduct targeted some financially vulnerable individuals, namely subsistence fishermen. Plaintiffs' harm was not the result of an isolated incident but was the result of Exxon's repeated decisions, over a period of approximately three years, to allow Captain Hazelwood to remain in command despite Exxon's knowledge that he was drinking and driving again. Exxon's bad conduct as to Captain Hazelwood and his operating of the *Exxon Valdez* was intentionally malicious. [Emphasis added.]

Exxon's conduct was many degrees of magnitude more egregious [flagrant] [than defendant's conduct in other cases]. For approximately three years, Exxon management, with knowledge that Captain Hazelwood had fallen off the wagon, willfully permitted him to operate a fully loaded crude oil tanker in and out of Prince William Sound—a body of water which Exxon knew to be highly valuable for its fisheries resources. Exxon's argument that its conduct in permitting a relapsed alcoholic to operate an oil tanker should be characterized as less reprehensible than [in other cases] suggests that Exxon, even today, has not come to grips with the opprobrium [disgracefulness] which society rightly attaches to drunk driving. Based on the foregoing, the court finds Exxon's conduct highly reprehensible.

[T]he court reduces the punitive damages award to $4.5 billion as the means of resolving the conflict between its conclusion and the directions of the court of appeals.

[T]here is no just reason to delay entry of a final judgment in this case. The Court's judgment as to the $4.5 billion punitive damages award is deemed final.

COMMENT: In February 2008, the U.S. Supreme Court heard the oral argument on appeals from the U.S. Court of Appeals (D.C. Circuit), which affirmed the U.S. District Court.

Theories of Ethical Thought

CONSEQUENTIAL THEORIES

Ethicists, businesspeople, and workers who adhere to a consequential theory of ethics judge acts as ethically good or bad based on whether the acts have achieved their desired results. The actions of a business or any other societal unit are looked at as right or wrong only in terms of whether the results can be rationalized (Table 1).

This theory is best exemplified by the utilitarian school of thought, which is divided into two subschools: act utilitarianism and rule utilitarianism. In general, adherents of this school judge all conduct of individuals or businesses on whether it brings net happiness or pleasure to a society. They judge an act ethically correct after adding up the risks (unhappiness) and the benefits (happiness) to society

---

LINKING LAW AND BUSINESS

Business Ethics

Managers often attempt to encourage ethical practices in the workplace. A significant reason for managers' concern with ethics is to portray their organizations in a favorable light to consumers, investors, and employees. As a means of creating an ethical workplace, there are several methods that managers should implement that you may recall from your management class: (1) Create a code of ethics, which is a formal statement that acts as a guide for making decisions and actions within an organization. Distribution and continual improvement of the code of ethics are also important steps. (2) Establish a workplace or office for the sole purpose of overseeing organizational practices to determine if actions are ethical. (3) Conduct training programs to encourage ethical practices in the organization. (4) Minimize situations in which unethical behavior is common and create conditions in which people are likely to behave ethically. Two practices that often result in unethical behavior are to give unusually high rewards for good performance and uncommonly harsh punishments for poor performance. By eliminating these two causal factors of unethical behavior, managers are more likely to create conditions in which employees choose to behave ethically within the organization. Therefore, a manager's hope to represent the organization in a respectable manner may be achieved through the execution of these methods.

Source: S. Certo, *Modern Management* (Upper Saddle River, NJ: Prentice Hall, 2000), 66-69.

---

and obtaining a net outcome. For example, if it is necessary for a company to pay a bribe to a foreign official in order to get several billion dollars in airplane contracts, utilitarians would argue, in general, that the payment is ethically correct because it will provide net happiness to society; that is, it will bring jobs and spending to the community where the airplane company is located. If the bribe is not paid, the contracts, jobs, and spending will go to a company somewhere else.

Act utilitarians determine if an action is right or wrong on the basis of whether that individual act (the payment of a bribe) alone brings net happiness to the society as opposed to whether other alternatives (e.g., not paying the bribe or allowing others to pay the bribe) would bring more or less net happiness. Rule utilitarians argue that an act (the payment of the bribe) is ethically right if the performance of similar acts by all similar agents (other contractors) would produce the best results in society or has done so in the past. Rule utilitarians hold the position that whatever applicable rule has been established by political representatives must be followed and should serve as a standard in the evaluation of similar acts. If payment of bribes has been determined by the society to bring net happiness,

TABLE 1

THEORIES OF ETHICAL THOUGHT

Consequential Theories	Acts are judged good or bad based on whether the acts have achieved their desired results. Acts of the business community or any other social unit (e.g., government, school, fraternity, and sorority). Act and rule utilitarianisms are two subschools.
Deontological Theories	Actions can be judged good or bad based on rules and principles that are applied universally.
Humanist Theories	Actions are evaluated as good or bad depending on whether they contribute to improving inherent human capacities such as intelligence, wisdom, and self-restraint.

and a rule allowing bribes exists, then rule utilitarians would allow the bribe. On the other hand, the Foreign Corrupt Practices Act of 1977, as amended in 1988, which forbids paying bribes to foreign government officials to get business that would not have been obtained without such a payment, is an example of a standard that rule utilitarians would argue must be followed but that would lead to a different result. So the act utilitarians might get the airplane plant, but the rule utilitarians, if they were following the Foreign Corrupt Practices Act, would not.

We must note that both act and rule utilitarians focus on the consequences of an act and not on the question of verifying whether an act is ethically good or bad.[1] Either one of these theories can be used by individuals or businesses to justify their actions.[2] Act utilitarians use the principle of utility (adding up the costs and benefits of an act to arrive at net happiness) to focus on an individual action at one point in time. Rule utilitarians believe that one should not consider the consequences of a single act in determining net happiness but, instead, should focus on a general rule that exemplifies net happiness for the whole society. Case 1 illustrates a rule-utilitarian view of jurisprudence.

DEONTOLOGICAL THEORIES

Deontology is derived from a Greek word meaning "duty." For advocates of deontology, rules and principles determine whether actions are ethically good or bad. The consequences of individual actions are not considered. The golden rule, "do unto others as you would have them do unto you," is the hallmark of the theory.

Absolute deontology claims that actions can be judged ethically good or bad on the basis of absolute moral principles arrived at by human reason regardless of the consequences of an action, that is, regardless of whether there is net happiness.[3] Immanuel Kant (1724–1804) provided an example of an absolute moral principle in his widely studied "categorical imperative." He stated that a person ought to engage only in acts that he or she could see becoming a universal standard. For example, if a U.S. company bribes a foreign official to obtain a contract to build airplanes, then U.S. society and business should be willing to accept the principle that foreign multinationals will be morally free to bribe U.S. government officials to obtain defense contracts. Of course, the reverse will be true if nonbribery statutes are adopted worldwide. Kant, as part of his statement of the categorical imperative, assumed that everyone is a rational being having free will, and he warned that one ought to "treat others as having intrinsic values in themselves, and not merely as a means to achieve one's end."[4] For deontologists such as Kant, ethical reasoning means adopting universal principles that are applied to all equally. Segregation of one ethnic or racial group is unethical because it denies the intrinsic value of each human being and, thus, violates a general universal principle. See Case 2 in which the court appears to leave the decision making to a trial jury.

---

[1] W. Lacroix, *Principles for Ethics in Business,* rev. ed., 6 (Washington, DC: University Press, 1979).

[2] B. Brennan, "Amending the Foreign Corrupt Practices Act of 1977: Clarifying or Gutting a Law," *Journal of Legislation 2* (1984), for an examination of the rule and act utilitarian schools of thought within the context of the proposed amending process of the 1977 Foreign Corrupt Practices Act.

[3] Lacroix, supra note 1, at 13.

[4] R. Wolff, ed., *Foundations of the Metaphysics of Moral Thought and Critical Essays 44* (Bobbs-Merrill, 1964).

HUMANIST THEORIES

A third school of thought, the humanist school, evaluates actions as ethically good or bad depending on what they contribute to improving inherent human capacities such as intelligence, wisdom, and self-restraint. Many natural law theorists believe that humans would arrive by reason alone at standards of conduct that ultimately derive from a divine being or another ultimate source such as nature. For example, if a U.S. business participates in bribing a foreign official, it is not doing an act that improves inherent human capacities such as intelligence and wisdom; thus, the act is not ethical. In a situation that demanded choice, as well as the use of the intelligence and restraint that would prevent a violation of law (the Foreign Corrupt Practices Act of 1977), the particular business would have failed ethically as well as legally.

Case 2 illustrates a consequential theory of ethics, but if read carefully, the other two schools of thought outlined here could be argued as well.

CASE 2

Pavlik v. Lane
U.S. Court of Appeals 3d Cir.
135 F.3d 876 (1998)

Pavlik (plaintiff) filed a suit, on behalf of his son, against Lane (defendant) and others. Butane, a fuel used in lighters, had a warning on each distributed can "DO NOT BREATHE SPRAY." Zeus was the brand name under which butane was distributed in small aerosol cans. Pavlik's son died after intentionally inhaling the contents of one of the cans. The plaintiff argued that the warning on the can did not warn users adequately of the hazards of butane. The defendants argued for a summary judgment claiming the warning was adequate and a 20-year-old young man must have been aware of the dangers of butane. The federal district court granted a summary judgment. The plaintiff appealed.

Justice Backer

[A]n otherwise properly designed product may still be unreasonably dangerous (and therefore "defective") for strict liability purposes if the product is distributed without sufficient warnings to apprise the ultimate user of the latent dangers in the product.

[W]e have serious doubts that the Zeus warning (on the can) sufficiently warns users of the potentially fatal consequences of butane inhalation, and we are not convinced of its adequacy. More specifically, the "DO NOT BREATHE SPRAY" warning appears to give the user no notice of the serious nature of the danger posed by inhalation, intentional or otherwise, and no other language on the Zeus can does so. Yet, we similarly cannot find that such a directive is inadequate as a matter of law, and so we must leave the question for the jury.

Reversed for Plaintiff, and *remanded* to the trial court for new trial.

Codes of Ethics

INDIVIDUAL CODES OF ETHICS

When examining business ethics, one must recognize that the corporations, partnerships, and other entities that make up the business community are a composite of individuals. If the readers of this book are asked where they obtained their ethical values, they might respond their values come from parents, church, peers, teachers, brothers and sisters, or the environment. In any event, corporations and the culture of a corporation are greatly influenced by what ethical values individuals bring to them. Often, business managers are faced with a conflict between their individual ethical values and those of the corporation. For example, a father of three young children, who is divorced and their sole support, is asked by his supervisor to "slightly change" figures that will make the tests on rats of a new drug look more favorable when reported to the Food and Drug Administration. His supervisor hints that if he fails to do so, he may be looking for another job. The individual is faced with a conflict in ethical values: individual values of honesty and humaneness toward potential users of the drug versus business values of profits, efficiency, loyalty to the corporation, and the need for a job. Which values should he adopt?

Individual Ethical Codes Versus Groupthink

On January 28, 1986, just 74 seconds into its space shuttle launch, *Challenger* exploded, killing the first schoolteacher in space, Christa McAuliffe, and six other astronauts on board. A presidential commission was set up and found that faulty O-rings in the booster rockets were to blame. Two engineers testified before the commission that they opposed the launch but were overruled by their immediate supervisor and other officials of the Thikol Corporation that manufactured the booster rockets. Warnings by the two engineers of problems with the O-rings continued to take place until the day before the launch. After the launch, one engineer was assigned to "special projects" for the firm. Another took leave and founded a consulting firm. The second schoolteacher in space was a backup to McAuliffe. Her name was Babara Morgan. She returned to teaching for 22 years after the *Challenger* incident until August 8, 2007, when she and six other astronauts were sent (successfully) to the International Space Station on the shuttle *Endeavor*.[a]

On September 11, 2001, two planes flew into (the Twin Towers) of the World Trade Center in New York City; one plane flew into the Pentagon in Washington, D.C., and another flew into a field near Pittsburgh, Pennsylvania. Approximately 3,000 people were killed by terrorists flying the planes. Again, a presidential commission was set up. In 2004, the commission reported that the failure of intermediate-level employees to be heard within intelligence agencies, as well as the inability of agencies such as the Central Intelligence Agency (CIA), Defense Intelligence Agency (DIA), and National Security Agencies (NSA) to bring early warning information forward to the decision makers (in the White House), was in part responsible for the events that took place. The CIA director resigned and other officials at some agencies retired. A new structure was set up for intelligence gathering in 2004, which allows a single individual to be responsible for intelligence provided to the president of the United States.

These factual situations are very different, but when reading the presidential commissions' testimonies, it appears, in both cases, there were conflicts between individual ethical values and groupthink. Groupthink here will be defined as a form of thinking that people engage in when they are involved in a cohesive in-group, striving for unanimity, which overrules a realistic appraisal of alternative courses of action. Groupthink refers "to a deterioration of mental efficiency, reality testing, and moral efficiency that results from in-group pressures."[b] For the engineers in the Challenger case and the middle-level managers of intelligence agencies, the question always will remain—were they part of a groupthink process that altered the outcome? Are there important factual differences in these cases: private sector employment (Thikol) as opposed to public sector intelligence agencies?

Groupthink, on the other hand, may be necessary in our society. Without it, how would we organize our corporations, the military, and government agencies? If we allowed everyone to think independently, would anyone follow orders in the military or build rocket boosters in industry? Also, people often do not think like whistle-blowers (see discussion of the Sarbanes-Oxley Act later in this chapter for fear of losing their status and their jobs, which are often necessary to support egos and families.

[a]W. Leary, "Teacher Astronaut to Fly Decade After Challenger," *New York Times,* 11 (August 7, 2007).
[b]Irving L., Janis, *Victims of Groupthink* (Boston: Houghton-Mifflin, 1972).

CORPORATE CODES OF ETHICS

The total of individual employees' ethical values influences corporate conduct, especially in a corporation's early years. The activities during these years, in turn, form the basis of what constitutes a corporate culture or an environment for doing business. In a free-market society, values of productivity, efficiency, and profits become part of the culture of all companies. Some companies seek to generate productivity by cooperation between workers and management; others motivate through intense production goals that may bring about high labor turnover. Some companies have marketed their product through emphasis on quality and service; others emphasize beating the competition through lower prices.[5] Over time, these production and marketing emphases have evolved into what is called a corporate culture, often set forth in corporate codes.

Approximately 90 percent of all major corporations have adopted codes of conduct since the mid-1960s. In general, the codes apply to upper- and middle-level managers. They are usually implemented by a chief executive officer or a designated agent. They tend to provide sanctions ranging from personal reprimands that are placed in the employee's file to dismissal. Some formal codes allow for due process hearings within the corporation, in which an employee accused of a violation is given a chance to defend himself or herself. With many employees bringing wrongful dismissal actions in courts of law, more formal internal procedures are developing to implement due process requirements. A study of corporate codes reveals that the actions most typically forbidden are[6]

- paying bribes to foreign government officials;
- fixing prices;
- giving gifts to customers or accepting gifts from suppliers;
- using insider information; and
- revealing trade secrets.

[5] C. Power and D. Vogel, *Ethics in the Education of Business Managers* 6 (Hastings Center, 1980).
[6] K. Chatov, "What Corporate Ethics Statements Say," *California Management Review* 22: 206 (1980).

Corporate Ethics

Internal Housecleaning

Following several financial scandals involving companies such as Enron, Martha Stewart Living, Inc., ImClone Systems, WorldCom, Inc. (now MCI), and Tyco International, Congress passed the Sarbanes-Oxley Act in 2002. This act required publicly traded companies to set up confidential internal systems by April 2003 so that employees and others could have a method of reporting possible illegal or unethical auditing and accounting practices as well as other areas including sexual harassment.

Web reporting systems such as Ethicspoint allow employees of companies to click on an icon on their computers and anonymously be linked to the reporting services. Employees may report alleged unethical or illegal activity. The reporting system then alerts a management person or the audit committee of the board of directors to any possible problem. Other systems include a special phone number (800 or 900). None are perfect but the key factor is that Sarbanes-Oxley has given impetus to "cleaning house" internally.

Whistle-blowing protection under Section 806 of Sarbanes-Oxley[a] prohibits any publicly traded company from "discharging, demoting, suspending, threatening or otherwise discriminating against an employee who provides information to the government or assists in a government investigation regarding conduct that an employee believes may be a violation of the securities laws."

[a] H.R. 3782 signed into law by President George W. Bush on July 30, 2002, effective on August 29, 2002. P.L. 109–204; 15 U.S.C. Section 78d (I)–(3) codified in Exchange Act, Section 4.

INDUSTRY CODES OF ETHICS

In addition to corporate ethical codes, industry codes exist, such as those of the National Association of Broadcasters or the National Association of Used Car Dealers. In most cases, these codes are rather general and contain either affirmative inspirational guidelines or a list of "shall-nots." A "hybrid model" including "dos and don'ts" generally addresses itself to subjects such as[7]

- honest and fair dealings with customers;
- acceptable levels of safety, efficacy, and cleanliness;
- nondeceptive advertising; and
- maintenance of experienced and trained personnel, competent performance of services, and furnishing of quality products.

Most trade associations were formed for the purpose of lobbying Congress, the executive branch, and the regulatory agencies, in addition to influencing elections through their political action committees (PACs). They have not generally been effective in monitoring violations of their own ethical codes. In light of the

[7] See R. Jacobs, "Vehicles for Self-Regulation Codes of Conduct, Credentialing and Standards," in *Self Regulation, Conference Proceedings* (Washington, DC: Ethics Resource).

reasons for their existence and the fact that membership dues support their work, it is not likely that they will be very effective disciplinarians.

Some effective self-regulating mechanisms, however, do exist in industries. Self-regulating organizations (SROs) such as the National Association of Securities Dealers and the New York Stock Exchange have carried out authority delegated to them by the Securities and Exchange Commission (SEC) in an extremely efficient manner. In addition, the Council of Better Business Bureaus, through its National Advertising Division (NAD), has provided empirical evidence that self-regulation can be effective. The NAD seeks to monitor and expose false advertising through its local bureaus and has done an effective job, receiving commendations from a leading consumer advocate, Ralph Nader.[8]

PROFESSIONAL CODES OF ETHICS

Within a corporation, managers often interact with individual employees who have "professional" codes of conduct that may supersede corporate or industry-wide codes in terms of what activities they can participate in and still remain licensed professionals. For example, under the Model Code of Professional Responsibility, a lawyer must reveal the intention of his or her client to commit a crime and the information necessary to prevent the crime.[9] When a lawyer, a member of the law department of Airplane Corporation X, learns that his company deliberately intends to bribe a high-level foreign official in order to obtain an airplane contract, he may be forced, under the model code, to disclose this intention because the planned bribe is a violation of the Foreign Corrupt Practices Act of 1977, as amended, an act that has criminal penalties. Failure to disclose could lead to suspension or disbarment by the lawyer's state bar. Management must be sensitive to this and to the several professional codes that are to be discussed.

Professionals is an often-overused term, referring to everything from masons to hair stylists to engineers, lawyers, and doctors. When discussing professions or professionals here, we mean a group that has the following characteristics:

- Prelicensing mandatory university educational training, as well as continuing education requirements
- Licensing-examination requirements
- A set of written ethical standards that is recognized and continually enforced by the group
- A formal association or group that meets regularly
- An independent commitment to the public interest
- Formal recognition by the public as a professional group

Management must often interact with the professions outlined in the following paragraphs. Each of them has a separate code of conduct. An awareness of this factor may lead to a greater understanding of why each group acts as it does.

---

[8] See R. Tankersley, "Advertising: Regulation, Deregulation and Self-Regulation," in *Self-Regulation, Conference Proceedings,* supra note 7, at 45.

[9] See Model Code of Professional Responsibility DR 4-401(C) and Formal Op. 314 (1965).

Accounting. The American Institute of Certified Public Accountants (AICPA) has promulgated a code of professional ethics and interpretive rules. The Institute of Internal Auditors has set out a code of ethics, as well as a Statement of Responsibilities of Internal Auditors. In addition, the Association of Government Accountants has promulgated a Code of Ethics.

Disciplinary procedures are set forth for individuals as well as for firms in the Code of Professional Ethics for Certified Public Accountants (CPAs). Membership in the AICPA is suspended without a hearing if a judgment of conviction is filed with the secretary of the institute as related to the following:[10]

- A felony as defined under any state law
- The willful failure to file an income tax return, which the CPA as an individual is required to file
- The filing of a fraudulent return on the part of the CPA for his or her own return or that of a client
- The aiding in the preparation of a fraudulent income tax return of a client

The AICPA Division for CPA Firms is responsible for disciplining firms as opposed to individuals. Through its SEC practice and its private company sections, this division requires member firms to (1) adhere to quality-control standards, (2) submit to peer review of their accounting and audit practices every 3 years, (3) ensure that all professionals participate in continuing education programs, and (4) maintain minimum amounts of liability insurance.

Accountants' ethical responsibility is reinforced by the Sarbanes-Oxley Act of 2002, which was passed by Congress following a series of financial scandals.[11] A Public Company Accounting Oversight Board was created and provisions that require auditor independence were included in this statute. Under Section 802 of the act, accountants are required to maintain working papers on file relating to an audit or review for 5 years. A willful violation will be subject to a fine or imprisonment for up to 10 years or both.

Other statutory provisions affecting accountants include Sections 11 and 12 (2) of the 1933 Securities Act, as well as Section 10(b) and (18) of the 1934 Securities Exchange Act. The 1933 act deals with accountant liability for false statements or omission of a material fact in auditing financial statements required for registration of securities. A defense is due diligence and a reasonable belief that the work is complete.

Under the 1934 act Section 10(b), accountants are liable for false and misleading reports required by the act. Willful violations bring criminal penalties. Additionally, provisions of the Internal Revenue Code provide criminal penalties (felony) for tax preparers who willfully prepare or assist in preparing a false return.[12] Additionally, tax preparers who negligently or willfully understate tax liability are subject to criminal penalties. Failure to provide a taxpayer with a copy of his or her return may subject a tax preparer to criminal penalties.[13]

---

[10] See AICPA Professional Standards, vol. 2, Disciplinary Suspensions and Termination of Membership Hearings, GL 730.01.

[11] H.R. 3762 signed into law by President George W. Bush on July 30, 2002, effective August 30, 2002.

[12] 26 U.S.C. Section 7208 (2).

[13] 26 U.S.C. Section 7101 (a) (36).

Insurance and Finance. The American Society of Chartered Life Underwriters (ASCLU) had adopted a Code of Ethics consisting of eight guides to professional conduct and six rules of professional conduct. The guides are broad in nature, whereas the rules are specific. Enforcement of the Code of Ethics is left primarily to local chapters. Discipline includes reprimand, censure, and dismissal. A local chapter can additionally recommend suspension or revocation to a national board. Very few disciplinary actions have been forthcoming.[14]

In addition, the Society of Chartered Property and Casualty Underwriters (CPCU) has a code of ethics consisting of seven Specified Unethical Practices, as well as three Unspecified Unethical Practices of a more general nature. On receipt of a written and signed complaint, the president of the society appoints a three-member conference panel to hear the case. If a panel finds a member guilty of an "unspecified unethical practice," the president directs the member to cease such action. If a member is found guilty of a "specified unethical practice," the society's board of directors may reprimand or censure the violator or suspend or expel her or him from membership in the society.

Law. The American Bar Association's Model Rules of Professional Responsibility were submitted to the highest state courts and the District of Columbia for adoption, after the association's House of Delegates approved them in August 1983 (before then, the states had adopted the Model Code of Professional Responsibility). There are nine canons of professional responsibility. From these are derived Ethical Considerations and Disciplinary Rules. The Model Rules set out a minimal level of conduct that is expected of an attorney. Violation of any of these rules may lead to warnings, reprimands, public censure, suspension, or disbarment by the enforcement agency of the highest state court in which the attorney is admitted to practice. Most state bar disciplinary actions are published in state bar journals and local newspapers, so lawyers and the public in general are aware of attorneys who have been subject to disciplinary action.

The case excerpted here illustrates some legal problems surrounding professional ethical codes when they result in price-fixing.

CASE 3

Bates v. State Bar of Arizona
United States Supreme Court 433
U.S. 350 (1977)

Plaintiff-appellants Bates and O'Steen, licensed to practice law in the state of Arizona, opened a "legal clinic" in 1974. The clinic provided legal services to people with modest incomes for approximately 2 years, after which the clinic placed an advertisement in the *Arizona Republic*, a daily newspaper circulated in the Phoenix area, stating prices charged for legal services. The plaintiffs conceded that this advertisement was a violation of Disciplinary Rule

2-101(B) incorporated in Rule 29(a) of the Arizona Supreme Court rules, which stated in part:

A lawyer shall not publicize himself or his partner or associate, or any other lawyer affiliated with him or his firm, as a lawyer through newspapers, or magazine advertisements, radio, television announcements, display advertisements in the city telephone directories or other means of commercial publicity, nor shall he authorize others to do so in his behalf.

[14] See R. Horn, *On Professions, Professionals, and Professional Ethics* (Malvern, Penn.: American Institute for Property and Liability Underwriters, 1978), p. 74.

A complaint was initiated by the president of the State Bar of Arizona, and a hearing was held before a three-member special local administrative committee. The com-mittee recommended to the Arizona Supreme Court that each of the plaintiffs be suspended from practice for not less than 6 months. The court agreed and ordered the plaintiffs suspended. The plaintiffs appealed to the U.S. Supreme Court.

Justice Blackmun

The heart of the dispute before us today is whether lawyers may constitutionally advertise the prices at which certain routine services will be performed. Numerous justifications are proffered for the restriction of such price advertising. We consider each in turn:

1. The Adverse Effect on Professionalism. Appellee places particular emphasis on the adverse effects that it feels price advertising will have on the legal profession. The key to professionalism, it is argued, is the sense of pride that involvement in the discipline generates. It is claimed that price advertising will bring about commercialization, which will undermine the attorney's sense of dignity and self-worth. The hustle of the marketplace will adversely affect the profession's service orientation, and irreparably damage the delicate balance between the lawyer's need to earn and his obligation selflessly to serve. Advertising is also said to erode the client's trust in his attorney. Once the client perceives that the lawyer is motivated by profit, his confidence that the attorney is acting out of a commitment to the client's welfare is jeopardized. And advertising is said to tarnish the digni-fied public image of the profession.

We recognize, of course, and commend the spirit of public service with which the profession of law is practiced and to which it is dedicated. The present Members of this Court, licensed attorneys all, could not feel otherwise. And we would have reason to pause if we felt that our decision today would under-cut that spirit. But we find the postulated connection between advertising and the erosion of true profes-sionalism to be severely strained. At its core, the argu-ment presumes that attorneys must conceal from themselves and from their clients the real-life fact that lawyers earn their livelihood at the bar. We suspect that few attorneys engage in such self-deception. And rare is the client, moreover, even one of modest means, who enlists the aid of an attorney with the expecta-tion that his services will be rendered free of charge.

Moreover, the assertion that advertising will dimin-ish the attorney's reputation in the community is open to question. Bankers and engineers advertise, and yet these professionals are not regarded as undignified. In fact, it has been suggested that the failure of lawyers to advertise creates public disillusionment with the profession. The absence of advertising may be seen to reflect the profession's failure to reach out and serve the community. Studies reveal that many persons do not obtain counsel even when they perceive a need because of the feared price of services or because of an inability to locate a competent attorney. Indeed, cynicism with regard to the profession may be created by the fact that it long has publicly eschewed advertis-ing, while condoning the actions of the attorney who structures his social or civic associations so as to provide contacts with potential clients.

2. Inherently Misleading Nature of Attorney Advertising. It is argued that advertising of legal services inevitably will be misleading. The argument that legal services are so unique that fixed rates cannot meaningfully be established is refuted by the record in this case. The appellee State Bar itself sponsors a Legal Services Program in which the participating attorneys agree to perform services like those advertised by the appellants at standardized rates.

3. The Adverse Effect on the Administration of Justice. Advertising is said to have the undesirable effect of stirring up litigation. But advertising by attorneys is not an unmitigated source of harm to the administra-tion of justice. It may offer great benefits. Although advertising might increase the use of the judicial machinery, we cannot accept the notion that it is always better for a person to suffer a wrong silently than to redress it by legal action.

4. The Undesirable Economic Effects of Advertising. It is claimed that advertising will increase the overhead costs of the profession, and that these costs then will be passed along to consumers in the form of increased fees. Moreover, it is claimed that the additional cost of practice will create a substantial entry barrier, deter-ring or preventing young attorneys from penetrating the market and entrenching the position of the bar's established members.

These two arguments seem dubious at best. Neither distinguishes lawyers from others and neither appears relevant to the First Amendment. The ban on advertising serves to increase the difficulty of discovering the lowest cost seller of acceptable ability. As a result, to this extent attorneys are isolated from competition, and the incen-tive to price competitively is reduced. Although it is true that the effect of advertising on the price of services has not been demonstrated, there is revealing evidence with regard to products: where consumers have the benefit of price advertising, retail prices often are dramatically lower than they would be without advertising. It is entirely possible that advertising will serve to reduce, not advance, the cost of legal services to the consumer.

The entry-barrier argument is equally unpersua-sive. In the absence of advertising, an attorney must rely on his contacts with the community to generate a flow of business. In view of the time necessary to develop such contacts, the ban in fact serves to perpetuate the market position of established attorneys. Consideration of entry-barrier problems would urge that advertising be allowed so as to aid the new competitor in penetrating the market.

5. The Adverse Effect of Advertising on the Quality of Service. It is argued that the attorney may advertise a given "package" of service at a set price, and will be inclined to provide, by indiscriminate use, the standard package regardless of whether it fits the client's needs . . . Even if advertising leads to the creation of "legal clinics" like that of appellants—clients that emphasize standardized procedures for routine problems—it is possible that such clinics will improve service by reducing the likelihood of error.

6. The Difficulties of Enforcement. Finally, it is argued that the wholesale restriction is justified by the problems of enforcement if any other course is taken. Because the public lacks sophistication in legal matters, it may be particularly susceptible to misleading or deceptive advertising by lawyers.

It is at least somewhat incongruous for the opponents of advertising to extol the virtues and altruism of the legal profession at one point, and, at another, to assert that its members will seize the opportunity to mislead and distort. We suspect that, with advertising, most lawyers will behave as they always have: They will abide by their solemn oaths to uphold the integrity and honor of their profession and of the legal system.

In sum, we are not persuaded that any of the proffered justifications rise to the level of an acceptable reason for the suppression of all advertising by attorneys. As with other varieties of speech, it follows as well that there may be reasonable restrictions on the time, place, and manner of advertising.

The constitutional issue in this case is only whether the State may prevent the publication in a newspaper of appellants' truthful advertisement concerning the availability and terms of routine legal services. We rule simply that the flow of such information may not be restrained, and we therefore hold the present application of the disciplinary rule against appellants to be violative of the First Amendment.

Reversed in favor of Plaintiff, Bates

CRITICAL THINKING ABOUT THE LAW

As you know, a judge's reasoning is not always clear. In the course of writing an opinion, a judge may discuss an assortment of topics. Your task, as a reader, is to organize those topics into a meaningful pattern and then locate the reasoning in the decision. Only then are you ready to think critically about the case. The following questions should help you better understand the reasoning in Case 2.

1. The Court clearly listed the reasons the State Bar of Arizona offered for restricting price advertising. Justice Blackmun evaluated those reasons. As critical thinkers, you realize that identifying the link between the conclusion and reasons is imperative. What reasons did the Court offer for allowing attorneys to advertise their prices?

   Clue: Remember that the Court concluded that, under the First Amendment, the state may not suppress advertising by attorneys. What reasons did Justice Blackmun use to reach this conclusion?

2. What primary ethical norm dominated the Court's consideration of the advertisement of prices for attorney services?

   Clue: Go back to the Court's examination of the reasons offered by the State Bar of Arizona. Look closely at Justice Blackmun's response to reason 3. Furthermore, consider the last two paragraphs of the opinion.

3. Suppose the State Bar of Arizona had introduced evidence that advertising causes the price of attorney's services to increase. Do you think Justice Blackmun would have come to a different conclusion? Why or why not?

   Clue: Look at the discussion of undesirable economic effects on advertising. Consider the primary ethical norm you identified in question 2. Do you think Justice Blackmun would consider this piece of evidence to be extremely persuasive?

Schools of Social Responsibility

Early in this chapter, the social responsibility of business was defined as concern by business about both its profit and its nonprofit activities and their intended and unintended impact on others. As you will see, theories of ethics and schools of social responsibility are not necessarily mutually exclusive. For example, the primary purpose of a steel company is to make a profit for its individual and institutional shareholders. The unintended effects of this company's actions might be that the surrounding community has polluted waters and homes are affected by ash that falls from the company's smokestack. Similarly, in the Union Carbide incident set out at the beginning of this chapter, the purpose of Union Carbide India Ltd. was to make a profit for its shareholders. By doing so, it was able to employ people. The unintended effect of this activity was a gas leak that killed approximately 2,000 people and injured many more. The question in both of these cases is, What responsibility, if any, do firms have for the unintended effects of their profit-seeking activity? This section of the chapter discusses five views of social responsibility that seek to answer that question: profit oriented, managerial, institutional, professional obligation, and regulation (Table 2). Each of these schools reflects, or is an implementation of, the ethical values or culture of a corporation. The reader should analyze each, realizing, as in the case of ethical theories, that each has its strong advocates but that the "answer" may not lie in any one.

PROFIT-ORIENTED SCHOOL

The profit-oriented school of social responsibility begins with a market-oriented concept of the firm that most readers were exposed to in their first or second course in economics. Holders of this theory argue that business entities are distinct organizations in our society and their sole purpose is to increase profits for shareholders. Businesses are to be judged solely on criteria of economic efficiency and how well they contribute to growth in productivity and technology. Corporate social responsibility is shown by managers who maximize profits for their shareholders, who, in turn, are able to reinvest such profits, providing

TABLE 2 SCHOOLS OF SOCIAL RESPONSIBILITY

Profit-Oriented School	Business entities are distinct organizations in our society whose sole purpose is to increase profits for shareholders.
Managerial School	Advocates of this theory argue that business entities (particularly large ones) have a number of groups that they must deal with. They include not only stockholders but also employees, customers, activist groups, and government regulators, all of whom may make claims on the entities' resources.
Institutional School	Business entities have a responsibility to act in a manner that benefits all society.
Professional Obligation School	Business managers and members of boards of directors must be certified as "professionals" before they assume managerial responsibilities. They must have a responsibility to the public interest beyond making profits. The Sarbanes-Oxley Act may be leading in that direction.
Regulation School	All business units are accountable to elected officials. See the Sarbanes-Oxley Act, as to dealing with independent financial audits.

for increased productivity, new employment opportunities, and increased consumption of goods. Classical economists, who advocate this position, recognize that there will be unintended effects of such profit-seeking activities (externalities) that affect society and cannot be incorporated into or passed on in the price of output. They would argue that this is the "social cost" of doing business. Such social costs are a collective responsibility of the government. Individual businesses should not be expected to voluntarily incorporate in their product's price the cost of cleaning up water or air, because this incorporation will distort the market mechanism and the efficient use of resources. Profit-seeking advocates argue that, when government needs to act in a collective manner, it should act in a way that involves the least interference with the efficiency of the market system, preferably through direct taxation.

In summary, efforts at pollution control, upgrading minority workers, and bringing equality of payment to the workforce are all tasks of the government and not of the private sector, which is incapable of making such choices and is not elected in a democratic society to do so. Its sole responsibility is to seek profits for its shareholders. The following box represents an important set of issues.

"Old Joe Camel" was adopted by R. J. Reynolds (RJR) in 1913 as the symbol for the brand Camel. In late 1990, RJR revived Old Joe with a new look in the form of a cartoon that appealed to young smokers.

In December 1991, the *Journal of the American Medical Association* (*JAMA*) published three surveys that found the cartoon character Joe Camel reached children very effectively.[15] Of children between ages 3 and 6 who were surveyed, 51.1 percent of them recognized Old Joe Camel as being associated with Camel cigarettes. The 6-year-olds were as familiar with Joe Camel as they were with the Mickey Mouse logo for the Disney Channel.

An RJR spokeswoman claimed that "just because children can identify our logo doesn't mean they will use our product." Since the introduction of Joe Camel, however, Camel's share of the under-18 market has climbed to 33 percent from 5 percent. Among 18- to 24-year-olds, Camel's market share has climbed to 7.9 percent from 4.4 percent.

The Centers for Disease Control reported in March 1992 that smokers between ages 12 and 18 preferred Marlboro, Newport, or Camel cigarettes, the three brands with the most extensive advertising.[16]

Teenagers throughout the country were wearing Joe Camel T-shirts. Brown & Williamson, the producer of Kool cigarettes, began testing a cartoon character for its advertisements, a penguin wearing sunglasses and Day-Glo sneakers. Company spokesman Joseph Helewicz stated that the advertisements were geared to smokers between 21 and 35 years old. Helewicz added that cartoon advertisements for adults were not new and cited the Pillsbury Doughboy and the Pink Panther as effective advertising images.

In mid-1992, then–Surgeon General Novella, along with the American Medical Association, began a campaign called "Dump the Hump" to pressure the tobacco industry to stop advertisement campaigns that teach kids to smoke. In 1993, the FTC staff recommended a ban on the Joe Camel advertisements. In 1994, then–Surgeon General Joycelyn Elders blamed the tobacco industry's $4 billion in advertisements for

---

[15] K. Deveny, "Joe Camel Ads Reach Children," *Wall Street Journal,* December 11, 1991, p. B-1.
[16] *Id.*

increased smoking rates among teens. RJR's tobacco division chief, James W. Johnston, responded, "I'll be damned if I'll pull the ads." RJR put together a team of lawyers and others it referred to as in-house censors to control Joe's influence. A campaign to have Joe wear a bandana was nixed, as was one for a punker Joe with pink hair.

In 1994, RJR's CEO James Johnston testified before a congressional panel on the Joe Camel controversy and stated, "We do not market to children and will not," and added, "We do not survey anyone under the age of 18."

Internal documents about targeting young people were damaging. A 1981 RJR internal memorandum on marketing surveys cautioned research personnel to tally underage smokers as "age 18." A 1981 Philip Morris internal document indicated that information about smoking habits in children as young as 15 was important, because "today's teenager is tomorrow's potential regular customer." Other Philip Morris documents from the 1980s expressed concerns that Marlboro sales would soon decline because teenage smoking rates were falling.

A 1987 marketing survey in France and Canada by RJR before it launched the Joe Camel campaign showed that the cartoon image with its fun and humor attracted attention. One 1987 internal document used the phrase *young adult smokers* and noted a campaign targeted at the competition's "male Marlboro smokers ages 13–24."

A 1997 survey of 534 teens by *USA Today* revealed the following:

Advertisement	Have Seen Advertisement	Liked Advertisement
Joe Camel	95%	65%
Marlboro Man	94%	44%
Budweiser Frogs	99%	92%

Marlboro was the brand smoked by most teens in the survey. The survey found 28 percent of teens between ages 13 and 18 smoked—an increase of 4 percent since 1991. In 1987, Camels were the cigarette of choice for 3 percent of teenagers when Joe Camel debuted. By 1993, the figure had climbed to 16 percent.

In early 1990, the Federal Trade Commission (FTC) began an investigation of RJR and its Joe Camel advertisements to determine whether underage smokers were illegally targeted by the 10-year Joe Camel Campaign. The FTC had dismissed a complaint in 1994 but did not have the benefits of the newly discovered internal memorandums.

In late 1997, RJR began phasing out Joe Camel. New Camel advertisements featured healthy-looking men and women in their twenties, in clubs and swimming pools, with just a dromedary logo somewhere in the advertisement. RJR also vowed not to feature the Joe Camel character on nontobacco items such as T-shirts. The cost of the abandonment was estimated at $250 million.

Philip Morris proposed its own plan to halt youth smoking in 1996, which included no vending machine advertisements, no billboard advertisements, no tobacco advertisements in magazines with 25 percent or more youth subscribers, and limits on sponsorships to events (rodeos, motor sports) where 75 percent or more of attendees were adults.

In 1998, combined pressure from Congress, the state attorneys general, and ongoing class action suits produced what came to be known as "the tobacco settlement." In addition to payment of $206 billion, the tobacco settlement in all of its various forms bars outdoor advertising, the use of human images (Marlboro man) and cartoon characters (Joe Camel), and vending-machine sales. This portion of the settlement was advocated by those who were concerned about teenagers and their attraction to cigarettes via these advertisements and their availability in machines.

MANAGERIAL SCHOOL

Advocates of the managerial school of social responsibility argue that businesses, particularly large institutions, have a number of interest groups or constituents both internally and externally that they must deal with regularly, not just stockholders and a board of directors. A business has employees, customers, suppliers, consumers, activist groups, government regulators, and others that influence decision making and the ability of the entity to make profits. In effect, modern managers must balance conflicting claims on their time and the company's resources. Employees want better wages, working conditions, and pensions; suppliers want prompt payment for their goods; and consumers want higher-quality goods at lower prices. These often conflicting demands lead advocates of a managerial theory of social responsibility to argue that the firm must have the trust of all groups, both internal and external. Thus, it must have clear ethical standards and a sense of social responsibility for its unintended acts in order to maximize profits and to survive in the short and long run. A firm that seeks to maximize short-run profits and ignores the claims of groups, whether they be unions, consumer activists, or government regulators, will not be able to survive in the complex environment that business operates in.

If one reviews the Union Carbide India Ltd. incident described earlier, it is clear that the explosion in Bhopal, India, had at least three consequences: (1) It precipitated an attempt by GAF to take over the company. (2) Union Carbide made a successful but costly attempt to fight off this takeover. (3) The value of the stock decreased and, thus, the investors suffered large losses. Advocates of managerial theory would point to the investors' trust in management's ability to deal with this disaster as being important to how the market evaluated Union Carbide's stock. They also would argue that the management of Johnson & Johnson took decisive action in dealing with the poison in its Tylenol product and was, thus, perceived by investors and customers as being trustworthy.[17] As a result its stock value recovered relatively quickly.

In this case, see the conflicting claims of stakeholders.

CASE 4

Cooper Industries v. Leatherman Tool Group, Inc.
United States Supreme Court
121 S.Ct. 1678 (2001)

Leatherman (plaintiff) sued Cooper (defendant) in federal district court for unfair competition. Leatherman Tool Group, Inc., manufactured and sold a multifunctional tool called the PST that improved on the classic Swiss army knife. Leatherman dominated the market for multifunctional pocket tools. In 1995, Cooper Industries, Inc., decided to design and sell a competing multifunctional tool under the name "ToolZall." Cooper introduced the ToolZall in August 1996 at the National Hardware Show in Chicago. At that show, Cooper used photographs in its posters, packaging, and advertising materials that purported to be a ToolZall but were actually of a modified PST. When those materials were prepared, the first of the ToolZalls had not yet been manufactured. A Cooper employee created a ToolZall "mock-up" by grinding the Leatherman trademark from a PST and substituting the unique fastenings that were to be used on the

---

[17] See M. Krikorian, "Ethical Conduct: An Aid to Management," Address at Albion College, Albion, Mich., April 16, 1985.

ToolZall. At least one of the photographs was retouched to remove a curved indention, where the Leatherman trademark had been. The photographs were used, not only at the trade show but also in marketing materials and catalogs used by Cooper's sales force throughout the United States.

The lower court found for Leatherman in the amount of $50,000 in compensatory damages and $4.5 million in punitive damages.

Cooper appealed to the court of appeals, which affirmed the lower court seeing no "abuse of discretion" by the lower court as to punitive damages. Cooper appealed to the U.S. Supreme Court petitioning for a de novo review of the facts as to the size of the punitive damages.

Justice Stevens

Although compensatory damages and punitive damages are typically awarded at the same time by the same decision maker, they serve distinct purposes. The former are intended to redress the concrete loss that the plaintiff has suffered by reason of the defendant's wrongful conduct. The latter, which have been described as "quasi-criminal," operate as private fines intended to punish the defendant and to deter future wrongdoing. A jury's assessment of the extent of a plaintiff's injury is essentially a factual determination, whereas its imposition of punitive damages is an expression of its moral condemnation. The question whether a fine is constitutionally excessive calls for the application of a constitutional standard to the facts of a particular case, and in this context de novo review of that question is appropriate.

Reversed and *remanded* based on a de novo standard in favor of Cooper, to determining whether the punitive damage award is excessive.

INSTITUTIONAL SCHOOL

Advocates of an institutional school of social responsibility for business argue that business entities have a responsibility to act in a manner that benefits all of society just as churches, unions, courts, universities, and governments have. Whether a single proprietorship, a partnership, or a corporation, a business is a legal entity in our society that must be held responsible for its activities. Proponents of this theory argue that the same civil and criminal sanctions should be applied to business activities that injure the social fabric of a society (e.g., the pollution of water and air) as are applied to acts of individuals and of other institutions. When managers fail to deal adequately with "externalities," they should be held accountable not only to their board of directors but also to government enforcement authorities and individual citizens as well.

PROFESSIONAL OBLIGATION SCHOOL

Advocates of a professional obligation school of social responsibility state that business managers and members of boards of directors should be certified as "professionals" before they can assume managerial responsibility. In our discussion of professional ethical codes, we defined professionals as persons having (1) educational entrance requirements and continuing-education standards, (2) licensing-examination requirements, (3) codes of conduct that are enforced, (4) a formal association that meets regularly, and (5) an independent commitment to the public interest. Advocates of a professional obligation theory argue that business directors and managers, like doctors and lawyers, have a responsibility to the public beyond merely making profits and that the public must be able to be sure that they are qualified to hold their positions. They should be licensed by meeting university requirements and passing a state or a national test. They should be subject to a disciplinary code that could involve revocation or suspension of their license to "practice the management of a business" if they are found by state or national boards to have failed to meet their codified responsibilities. Such responsibilities would include accountability for the unintended effects of their profit-making activities (externalities).

REGULATION SCHOOL

A regulation school of social responsibility sees all business units as accountable to elected public officials. Proponents of this theory argue that, because business managers are responsible only to a board of directors that represents shareholders, the corporation cannot be trusted to act in a socially responsible manner. If society is to be protected from the unintended effects of profit-making business activities (e.g., pollution, sex discrimination in the workplace, and injuries to workers), it is necessary for government to be involved. The degree of government involvement is much debated by advocates of this theory. Some would argue in the extreme for a socialist state. Others argue for government representatives on boards of directors, and still others argue that government should set up standards of socially responsible conduct for each industry. The last group advocates an annual process of reporting conduct, both socially responsible and otherwise, similar to the independent financial audits required now by the SEC of all publicly registered firms. The growth of ethics offices within corporations has played a role in dealing with ethical and legal problems. Sometimes these offices are mandated by courts when sentencing takes place in white-collar criminal cases. Often, corporations set up such offices as preventive measures.

Global Dimensions of Ethics and Social Responsibility

Code of Conduct for Transnational Corporations. A United Nations effort to prevent misconduct by transnational corporations has been promulgated. Four objectives include

1. *Respect for national sovereignty in countries where such companies operate.* Often transnational companies operate in developing nations where governments are less stable and more corrupt, making this goal very difficult to carry out.
2. *Adherence to sociocultural values.* The code seeks to prevent transnational companies from imposing value systems that are detrimental to those of the host country.
3. *Respect for human rights.* Companies should not discriminate on the basis of race, color, sex, religion, language, or political or other opinion. In developing nations this sometimes is very difficult when the host country does discriminate on the basis of some of these factors.
4. *Abstention from corrupt practices.* Transnational corporations shall refrain from the offering, promising, or giving of any payment, gift, or other advantage to a public official or refrain from performing a duty in accordance with a business transaction.

Corruption is endemic to many developing countries and a way of doing business. The United States has set forth one approach and the Organization for Economic and Cultural Development another.

SUMMARY

We have sought to define ethics and social responsibility within the context of business associations. We examined consequential theories of ethics based on the consequences of the company's actions. In contrast, deontology schools of ethics are based on duties. Humanist theories of ethics evaluate actions as good or bad based on how the actions improved inherent human capacities. Codes of ethics emanating from businesses and professions were also examined. Five schools of social responsibility based on the unintended effects of corporate and human conduct were examined. Finally, global dimensions of ethical and socially responsible conduct are highlighted with an examination of the United Nations' Code of Conduct for Transnational Corporations.

REVIEW QUESTIONS

1 Define the humanist theory of ethics. On the basis of this theory and a reading of the Union Carbide case synopsis, do you think that Union Carbide acted ethically after the Bhopal, India, incident? Explain.

2 List the differing views on whether corporations should act in a socially responsible manner. Explain each one.

3 How are professional codes of ethics different from individual codes? Explain.

4 What actions are typically forbidden by corporate codes? Explain.

5 Why are industry ethical codes not generally effective? Explain.

REVIEW PROBLEMS

6 A, a middle-level manager of Drug Company X, has been told by her boss, B, to change some figures on the percentage of rats that died as a result of injections of a new drug that will need Food and Drug Administration approval. The percentage of animals that died in the testing will need to be reported as lower, she is told. A is the single mother of two children and makes $65,000 a year. Choose one ethical theory outlined in the chapter and, on the basis of that theory, advise A what to do.

7 B knows that 200 percent cost overruns exist because of the negligence of the management of Company Y in carrying out a federal government contract to build an airplane. He works in the comptroller's office and has been told by his boss to "keep his mouth shut" when the auditors from the General Accounting Office (a government agency) come. He is told that there will be "severe consequences" if he does not keep quiet. He earns $65,000 annually and

is the father of three children attending private colleges. His wife works at home but is not compensated. Select a single ethical theory and advise B what he should do.

8 C, a student at University Z, learns a method of bypassing the telephone system to make free telephone calls. C tells his roommate, D. How would you advise D to act on the basis of one of the ethical theories discussed in this chapter?

9 You are hiring a new manager for your department. You have several good applicants. Assume that the one who is best suited for the job in training and experience has also been found to have done one of the things listed on the next page. How would knowing what the person has done affect your decision? Would your answer be the same regardless of which theory of ethical thought you applied? Examine each factual situation on the next page and explain how your answer is affected.

1. The individual listed on his résumé that he had an MBA from Rutgers. He does not have an MBA.

2. The individual listed that his prior salary was $40,000. The prior salary was actually $43,000.

10 You are a purchasing manager for Alphs Corporation. You are responsible for buying two $1 million generators. Your company has a written policy prohibiting any company buyer from receiving a gratuity in excess of $50 and requiring that all gratuities be reported. The company has no policy regarding whistle-blowing. A salesperson for a generator manufacturer offers to arrange it so that you can buy a $20,000 car for $7,000. The car would be bought from a third party. You decline the offer. Do you now report it to your superior? To the salesperson's superior? How would the various schools of social responsibility influence your decision? Pick one school to justify your decision. Explain.

11 You are a laboratory technician for the Standard Ethical Drug Company. You run tests on animals and prepare a summary that is then doctored by your superior to make a drug appear safe when in fact it is not. Your supervisor determines your salary and has significant influence on whether you retain the job. You are the sole source of support for your two children, have no close relative to help you, and are just making it financially. Jobs equivalent to yours are difficult to find. You are convinced that if the company markets the drug, the risk of cancer to the drug users will increase significantly. The drug provides significant relief for hemorrhoids. What will you do? Which school of social responsibility would be the basis for your decision. Explain.

CASE PROBLEMS

12 Samara Brothers, Inc., (Samara) is a designer and manufacturer of children's clothing. The core of Samara's business is its annual new line of spring and summer children's garments. Samara sold its clothing to retailers, who in turn sold the clothes to consumers. Wal-Mart Stores, Inc., (Wal-Mart) operates a large chain of budget warehouse stores that sell thousands of items at very low prices. In 1995, Wal-Mart contacted one of its suppliers, Judy-Philippine, Inc., (JPI) about the possibility of making a line of children's clothes just like Samara's successful line. Wal-Mart sent photographs of Samara's children's clothes to JPI (the name "Samara" was readily discernible on the labels of the garments) and directed JPI to produce children's clothes exactly like those in the photographs. JPI produced a line of children's clothes for Wal-Mart that copied the designs, colors, and patterns of Samara's clothing. Wal-Mart then sold this line of children's clothing in its stores, making a gross profit of over $1.15 million on these clothes sales during the 1996 selling season.

Samara discovered that Wal-Mart was selling the knock-off clothes at a price that was lower than Samara's retailers were paying Samara for its clothes. After sending unsuccessful cease-and-desist letters to Wal-Mart, Samara sued Wal-Mart, alleging that Wal-Mart copied Samara's trade dress (i.e., look and feel) in

violation of Section (43a) of the Lanham Act. Although not finding that Samara's clothes had acquired a secondary meaning in the minds of the public, the district court held in favor of Samara and awarded damages. The court of appeals affirmed. Wal-Mart appealed to the U.S. Supreme Court. Was it ethical conduct for Wal-Mart to sell the alleged knock-off clothes at a lower price. *Wal-Mart v. Samara Brothers*, 529 U.S. 205 (2000).

13 McDonald's Corporation operates the largest fast-food restaurant chain in the United States and the world. It produces such famous foods as the "Big Mac" hamburger, chicken "McNuggests," the egg "McMuffin," French fries, shakes, and other foods. A McDonald's survey showed that 22 percent of its customers are "Super Heavy Users," meaning that they eat at McDonald's at least 10 times or more a month. Super Heavy Users make up approximately 75 percent of McDonald's sales. The survey also found that 72 percent of McDonald's customers were "Heavy Users," meaning they ate at McDonald's at least once a week.

Jazlym Bradley consumed McDonald's foods her entire life during school lunch breaks and before and after school, approximately five times per week, ordering two meals per day. When Bradley was 19 years old she sued McDonald's Corporation for causing her obesity and health problems associated with obesity.

Plaintiff Bradley sued McDonald's in U.S. district court for violating the New York Consumer Protection Act, which prohibits deceptive and unfair acts. She alleged that McDonald's misled her, through its advertising campaigns and other publicity, that its food products were nutritious, of a beneficial nutritional nature, and easily part of a healthy lifestyle if consumed on a daily basis. The plaintiff sued on behalf of herself and a class of minors residing in New York State who purchased and consumed McDonald's products. McDonald's filed a motion with the district court to dismiss the plaintiff's complaint. Which ethical school of thought does McDonald's belong to? *Bradley v. McDonald's* 2003 U.S. Dist. Lexis 15202 (2003).

14 The Johns-Manville Corporation made a variety of building and other products. It was a major producer of asbestos, which was used for insulation in buildings. It has been medically proven that excessive exposure to asbestos causes asbestosis, a fatal lung disease. Thousands of employees of the company and consumers who were exposed to asbestos and had contracted this fatal disease sued the company for damages.

As a response, the company filed for reorganization bankruptcy. It argued that if it did not, an otherwise viable company that provided thousands of jobs and served a useful purpose in this country would be destroyed, and that without the declaration of bankruptcy a few of the plaintiffs who first filed their lawsuits would win awards of millions of dollars, leaving nothing for the remainder of the plaintiffs. Under the bankruptcy court's protection, the company was restructured to survive. As part of the release from bankruptcy, the company contributed money to a fund to pay current and future claimants. The fund was not large enough to pay all injured persons the full amount of their claims.

Was it ethical for Johns-Manville to declare bankruptcy? Select a school of social responsibility that the board of directors may use to rationalize its conduct in declaring bankruptcy. Explain. *In re Johns-Manville Corporation*, 36 B.R. 727 (B.C.S.D.N.Y. 1984)

15 Richard Fraser was an "exclusive career insurance agent" under a contract with Nationwide Mutual Insurance Co. Fraser leased computer hardware and software from Nationwide for his business. During a dispute between Nationwide and the Nationwide Insurance Independent Contractors Association, an organization representing Fraser and other exclusive career agents, Fraser prepared a letter to Nationwide competitors asking whether they were interested in acquiring the represented agents' policyholders. Nationwide obtained a copy of the letter and searched its electronic file server for e-mail indicating that the letter had been sent. It found a stored e-mail that Fraser had sent to a coworker indicating that the letter had been sent to at least one competitor. The e-mail was retrieved from the coworker's file of already received and discarded messages stored on the receiver. When Nationwide canceled its contract with Fraser, he filed a suit in a federal district court against the firm, alleging, among other things, violations of various federal laws that prohibit the interception of electronic communications during transmission. Had Nationwide acted ethically in retrieving the e-mail? Which school of socially responsible conduct did Richard Fraser represent in his conduct? Explain. Which school did Nationwide represent? Explain. *Fraser v. Nationwide Mutual Insurance Co.,* 135 F.Supp.3d 623 (E.D.Pa 2001).

16 Charles Zandford was a securities broker for Prudential Securities, Inc., in Annapolis, Maryland. In 1987, he persuaded William Wood, an elderly man in poor health, to open a joint investment account for himself and his mentally retarded daughter. The stated investment objectives for the account were "safety of principal and income." The Woods gave Zandford discretion to manage their account and to engage in transactions for their benefit without prior approval. Relying on Zandford's promise to "conservatively invest" their money, the Woods entrusted him with $419,255. Zandford immediately began writing checks to himself on the account. Paying the checks required selling securities in the account. Before William's death in 1991, all of the money was gone. Zandford was convicted of wire fraud and sentenced to more than 4 years in prison. The SEC filed a suit in a federal district court against Zandford, alleging in part misappropriation of $343,000 of the Woods' securities and seeking disgorgement of that amount. Which theory of ethics did Zanford represent? Explain. Which theory of ethics did the SEC represent? Explain. *SEC v. Zandford,* 535 U.S. 813 (2002).

199

THINKING CRITICALLY ABOUT RELEVANT LEGAL ISSUES

Disbarment of Lawyers

Egil Krogh, Jr., was admitted [to practice] law in the state of Washington on September 20, 1968. On February 4, 1974, he was suspended as a result of his having been convicted of a felony. [Krogh now appeals the disciplinary board's decision to disbar him.]

The information referred to in the complaint charged that while the respondent was an officer and employee of the United States Government . . . and acting in his official capacity, in conjunction with others who were officials and employees of the United States Government, the defendant unlawfully, willfully and knowingly did combine, conspire, confederate and agree with his co-conspirators to injure, oppress, threaten and intimidate Dr. Lewis J. Fielding . . . in the free exercise and enjoyment of a right and privilege secured to him by the Constitution and laws of the United States, and to conceal such activities. It further charged that the co-conspirators did, without legal process, probable cause, search warrant or other lawful authority, enter the offices of Dr. Fielding in Los Angeles County, California, with the intent to search for, examine and photograph documents and records containing confidential information concerning Daniel Ellsberg, and thereby injure, oppress, threaten and intimidate Dr. Fielding in the free exercise and enjoyment of the right and privilege secured to him by the fourth amendment to the Constitution of the United States, to be secure in his person, house, papers and effects against unreasonable searches and seizures. . . . To all of these allegations, the respondent had pleaded guilty.

Both the hearing panel and the disciplinary board found that moral turpitude was an element of the crime of which respondent was convicted. The panel found that he has a spotless record except for the incident involved in these proceedings; that he is outstanding in character and ability; that his reputation is beyond reproach; that he acted, although mistakenly, out of a misguided loyalty to [President Nixon]; that the event was an isolated one, and that in all probability there would be no repetition of any such error on his part. The panel further found that the respondent had accepted responsibility and had made amends to the best of his ability; that he testified fully and candidly and that his attitude in the proceeding was excellent. The panel concluded that in this case which it found to

be distinguishable from all other cases, the respondent apparently followed the order of a "somewhat distraught President of the United States" under the guise of national security to stop by all means further security leaks.

Th[e] rule [that attorneys are disbarred automatically when they are found guilty of a felony] still governs the disposition of such disciplinary proceedings in a number of jurisdictions. However, under our disciplinary rules, some flexibility is permitted, and the court retains its discretionary power to determine whether, on the facts of the particular case, the attorney should be disbarred.

We cannot accept the assumption that attorneys . . . can ordinarily be expected to abandon the principles which they have sworn to uphold, when asked to do so by a person who holds a constitutional office. Rather than being overawed by the authority of one who holds such an office . . . the attorney who is employed by such an officer should be the most keenly aware of the Constitution and all of its provisions, the most alert to discourage the abuse of power. In such a position those powers of discernment and reason, which he holds himself out as possessing, perform their most important function. If, when given a position of power himself, he forgets his oath to uphold the Constitution and laws of the land and instead flaunts the constitutional rights of other citizens and holds himself above the law, can we say to the public that a person so weak in his dedication to constitutional principles is qualified to practice law?

That the reputation and honor of the bar have suffered severe damage as a result is now a matter of common knowledge. We find it difficult to believe that the respondent was not aware, when he authorized the burglary of Dr. Fielding's office, that if his conduct became known, it would reflect discredit upon his profession.

For the reasons set forth herein, we must conclude that the respondent, in spite of his many commendable qualities and achievements, has shown himself to be unfit to practice law.

The recommendation of the disciplinary board is *approved*, and the respondent's name shall be stricken from the roll of attorneys in this state.

1. What ethical norm is central to the court's decision in this case?

2. What fact seems especially powerful in shaping the court's reasoning?

3. What reasons does the court provide for upholding the respondent's disbarment?

4. Outline the reasons that Egil Krogh, Jr., believed he should not be disbarred by the disciplinary board of the State of California.

ASSIGNMENT ON THE INTERNET

This chapter introduces you to three theories of ethical thought and five schools of social responsibility. Explore how the three theories of ethical thought are put into practice. Using the Internet, find the code of ethics for a business or corporation that does business in your city or town. This site provides links to codes of ethics for hundreds of corporations: **www.business-ethics.com.**

Applying your critical thinking skills, determine if the code of ethics chosen relies more heavily on one theory of ethical thought than the others. Are there aspects of that business's code of ethics that you would like to see changed? Why?

ON THE INTERNET

www.business-ethics.com This site provides codes of ethics from hundreds of corporations and articles detailing current trends or methods of bringing ethics into the business environment.

ethics.acusd.edu/index.html Ethics Updates is designed primarily to be used by ethics instructors and their students. It is intended to provide updates on current literature.

www.legalethics.com This comprehensive ethics page provides numerous hot links to other valuable Web sites.

www.ethicsweb.ca/resources/business/institutions.html This site contains links to numerous business ethics centers and institutions, as well as business ethics consultants.

www.mapnp.org/library/ethics/ethics.htm#anchor1419177 This site provides information on managing ethics in the workplace. A number of links also address the social responsibility of a business.

www.globalethics.org The Web site for the Global Ethics Institute provides information about business ethics from countries around the world.

FOR FUTURE READING

Besmer, Veronica. "Student Note: The Legal Character of Private Codes of Conduct: More Than Just a Pseudo-Formal Gloss on Corporate Social Responsibility." *Hastings Business Law Journal* 2 (2006): 279.

Epstein, Edwin. "Commentary: The Good Company: Rhetoric or Reality? Corporate Social Responsibility and Business Ethics Redux." *American Business Law Journal* 44 (2007): 207.

Jackall, Robert. *Moral Mazes: The World of Corporate Managers.* New York: Oxford University Press, 1998.

Lee, Ian B. "Is There a Cure for Corporate 'Psychopathy'?," *American Business Law Journal* 42 (2005): 65.

Ostas, Daniel T. "Deconstructing Corporate Social Responsibility: Insights from Legal and Economic Theory." *American Business Law Journal* 38 (2004): 261.

Social Responsibility and Managerial Ethics

From Chapter 5 of *Management*, 10/e. Stephen P. Robbins. Mary Coulter. Copyright © 2009 by Pearson Prentice Hall.
All rights reserved.

Let's Get Real:
Meet the Manager

Sally Yagan
Editorial Director
Pearson Education
Upper Saddle River, New Jersey

MY JOB: Editorial Director, Pearson Business School publishing.

BEST PART OF MY JOB: Transforming lives through education. We receive amazing feedback from people whose lives changed after using our products!

WORST PART OF MY JOB: Sometimes, no matter how hard we try, we can't solve every situation.

BEST MANAGEMENT ADVICE EVER RECEIVED: Surround yourself by the very best team possible and then seek (and truly listen) to their input.

You'll be hearing more from this real manager throughout the chapter.

Social Responsibility and Managerial Ethics

How important is it for organizations and managers to be socially responsible and ethical? In this chapter, we're going to look at what it means to be socially responsible and ethical and what role managers play in both. Focus on the following learning outcomes as you read and study this chapter.

LEARNING OUTCOMES

▷ 1 Discuss what it means to be socially responsible and what factors influence that decision.

2 Explain green management and how organizations can go green.

3 Discuss the factors that lead to ethical and unethical behavior.

4 Describe management's role in encouraging ethical behavior.

5 Discuss current social responsibility and ethics issues.

A Manager's Dilemma

Matt Hagen/Matt Hagen Photography

Most people would expect REI (Recreational Equipment, Inc.), a retailer of outdoor gear and clothing, to care passionately about the natural environment.[1] The company has long been committed to working with communities to keep parks and trails clean. Sally Jewell, president and CEO of REI, says, "What we are doing is important to the long-term health of the planet and therefore the long-term health of our business." In 2007, the company published its first stewardship report, which "tells its stakeholders what it's been doing to address environmental and social issues and the steps it's taking to do better." And the company has set some challenging environmental sustainability goals for itself. Living up to those commitments is hard. It means that employees may have to change some of their work habits, and change isn't easy in any organization. It also entails coordinating sustainability efforts across numerous business units of a large company. Instead of being discouraged, however, REI is focusing on the things it can do to make a difference. Put yourself in Sally's position. How does she balance being socially responsible and being focused on profits?

Courtesy REI / Matt Hagen Photography

What would you do?

Deciding how socially responsible an organization needs to be is just one example of the complicated types of ethical and social responsibility issues that managers, such as Sally Jewell, may have to cope with as they plan, organize, lead, and control. As managers manage, these issues can and do influence their actions.

LEARNING OUTCOME 1 ▷ WHAT IS SOCIAL RESPONSIBILITY?

By using digital technology and file sharing Web sites, music and video users all over the world obtain and share many of their favorite recordings for free. Large global corporations lower their costs by outsourcing to countries where human rights are not a high priority and justify it by saying they're bringing in jobs and helping strengthen the local economies. Businesses facing a drastically changed industry environment offer employees early retirement and buyout packages. Are these companies being socially responsible? Managers regularly face decisions that have a dimension of social responsibility, such as those involving employee relations, philanthropy, pricing, resource conservation, product quality and safety, and doing business in countries that devalue human rights. What does it mean to be socially responsible?

FROM OBLIGATIONS TO RESPONSIVENESS TO RESPONSIBILITY

The concept of *social responsibility* has been described in different ways. For instance, it has been called "profit making only," "going beyond profit making," "any discretionary corporate activity intended to further social welfare," and "improving social or environmental conditions."[2] We can understand it better if we first compare it to two similar concepts: social obligation and social responsiveness.[3] **Social obligation** is a firm's engaging in social actions because of its obligation to meet certain economic

206

and legal responsibilities. The organization does what it's obligated to do and nothing more. This idea reflects the **classical view** of social responsibility, which says that management's only social responsibility is to maximize profits. The most outspoken advocate of this approach is economist and Nobel laureate Milton Friedman. He argued that managers' primary responsibility is to operate the business in the best interests of the stockholders, whose primary concerns are financial.[4] He also argued that when managers decide to spend the organization's resources for "social good," they add to the costs of doing business, which have to be passed on to consumers through higher prices or absorbed by stockholders through smaller dividends. You need to understand that Friedman doesn't say that organizations shouldn't be socially responsible. But his interpretation of social responsibility is to maximize profits for stockholders.

The other two concepts—social responsiveness and social responsibility—reflect the **socioeconomic view**, which says that managers' social responsibilities go beyond making profits to include protecting and improving society's welfare. This view is based on the belief that corporations are *not* independent entities responsible only to stockholders but have an obligation to the larger society. Organizations around the world have embraced this view, as shown by a recent survey of global executives in which 84 percent said that companies must balance obligations to shareholders with obligations to the public good.[5] But how do these two concepts differ?

Social responsiveness means that a company engages in social actions in response to some popular social need. Managers in these companies are guided by social norms and values and make practical, market-oriented decisions about their actions.[6] For instance, managers at American Express Company identified three themes—community service, cultural heritage, and leaders for tomorrow—to guide it in deciding which worldwide projects and organizations to support. By making these choices, managers "responded" to what they felt were important social needs.[7]

A socially *responsible* organization views things differently. It goes beyond what it's obligated to do or chooses to do because of some popular social need and does what it can to help improve society because it's the right thing to do. We define **social responsibility** as a business's intention, beyond its legal and economic obligations, to do the right things and act in ways that are good for society.[8] Our definition assumes that a business obeys the law and cares for its stockholders, and it adds an ethical imperative to do those things that make society better and not to do those that make it worse. As Exhibit 1 shows, a socially responsible organization does what is right because it feels it has an ethical responsibility to do so. For example, Abt Electronics in Glenview, Illinois, would be described as socially responsible according to our definition. As one of the largest single-store electronics retailers in the United States, it

thinking critically about Ethics

In an effort to be (or at least appear to be) socially responsible, many organizations donate money to philanthropic and charitable causes. In addition, many organizations ask their employees to make individual donations to these causes. Suppose you're the manager of a work team, and you know that several of your employees can't afford to pledge money right now because of personal or financial problems. You've also been told by your supervisor that the CEO has been known to check the list of individual contributors to see who is and is not "supporting these very important causes." What would you do? What ethical guidelines might you suggest for individual and organizational contributions in such a situation?

social obligation
A firm's engaging in social actions because of its obligation to meet certain economic and legal responsibilities.

classical view
The view that management's only social responsibility is to maximize profits.

socioeconomic view
The view that management's social responsibility goes beyond making profits and includes protecting and improving society's welfare.

social responsiveness
A firm's engaging in social actions in response to some popular social need.

social responsibility
A business's intention, beyond its legal and economic obligations, to do the right things and act in ways that are good for society.

Exhibit 1

Social Responsibility Versus
Social Responsiveness

	Social Responsibility	Social Responsiveness
Major consideration	Ethical	Pragmatic
Focus	Ends	Means
Emphasis	Obligation	Responses
Decision framework	Long term	Medium and short term

Source: Adapted from S. L. Wartick and P. L. Cochran, "The Evolution of the Corporate Social Performance Model," *Academy of Management Review*, October 1985, p. 766.

Let's Get Real:
F2F

BEING SOCIALLY RESPONSIBLE
MEANS:

For us - it's improving lives through education, whether it's developing products that support successful student outcomes or investing in projects to improve lives around the globe.

responded to soaring energy costs and environmental concerns by shutting off lights more frequently and reducing air conditioning and heating. However, an Abt family member said, "These actions weren't just about costs, but about doing the right thing. We don't do everything just because of money."[9]

So, how should we view an organization's social actions? A U.S. business that meets federal pollution control standards or that doesn't discriminate against employees over age 40 in job promotion decisions is meeting its social obligation because laws mandate these actions. However, when it provides on-site child-care facilities for employees or packages products using recycled paper, it's being socially responsive. Why? Working parents and environmentalists have voiced these social concerns and demanded such actions.

For many businesses, their social actions are better viewed as being socially responsive than socially responsible (at least according to our definition). However, such actions are still good for society. For example, Wal-Mart Stores sponsored a program to address a serious social problem—hunger. Customers donated money to America's Second Harvest by purchasing puzzle pieces, and Wal-Mart matched the first $5 million raised. As part of this program, the company ran advertisements in major newspapers showing the word H_NGER and the tag line, "The problem can't be solved without You."[10]

SHOULD ORGANIZATIONS BE SOCIALLY INVOLVED?

Other than meeting their social obligations (which they *must* do), should organizations be socially involved? One way to look at this is by examining arguments for and against social involvement. Several points are outlined in Exhibit 2.[11]

Another way to look at this is whether social involvement affects a company's economic performance, which numerous studies have done.[12] Although most have found a small positive relationship, no generalizable conclusions can be made because the studies haven't use standardized measures of social responsibility and economic performance.[13] Another concern in these studies has been causation: If a study showed that social involvement and economic performance were positively related, this didn't necessarily mean that social involvement *caused* higher economic performance. It could simply mean that high profits afforded companies the "luxury" of being socially involved.[14] Such methodological concerns can't be taken lightly. In fact, one study found that if the flawed empirical analyses in these studies were "corrected," social responsibility had a neutral impact on a company's financial performance.[15] Another found that participating in social issues not related to the organization's primary stakeholders was negatively associated with shareholder value.[16] A recent re-analysis of several studies concluded that managers can afford to be (and should be) socially responsible.[17]

Another way to view social involvement and economic performance is by looking at socially responsible investing (SRI) funds, which provide a way for individual investors to support socially responsible companies. (You can find a list of SRI funds at www.socialfunds.com.) Typically, these funds use some type of **social screening**; that is, they apply social and environmental criteria to investment decisions. For instance, SRI funds usually do not invest in companies that are involved in liquor, gambling, tobacco, nuclear power, weapons, price fixing, or fraud or in companies that have poor product safety, employee relations, or environmental track records. Assets in these funds have grown to more than $2.7 trillion—about 11 percent of total assets in managed funds in the United States.[18] (See Exhibit 3 for SRI trends.) But, more

Exhibit 2

Arguments For and Against
Social Responsibility

For	Against
Public expectations Public opinion now supports businesses pursuing economic and social goals.	**Violation of profit maximization** Business is being socially responsible only when it pursues its economic interests.
Long-run profits Socially responsible companies tend to have more secure long-run profits.	**Dilution of purpose** Pursuing social goals dilutes business's primary purpose—economic productivity.
Ethical obligation Businesses should be socially responsible because responsible actions are the right thing to do.	**Costs** Many socially responsible actions do not cover their costs and someone must pay those costs.
Public image Businesses can create a favorable public image by pursuing social goals.	**Too much power** Businesses have a lot of power already and if they pursue social goals they will have even more.
Better environment Business involvement can help solve difficult social problems.	**Lack of skills** Business leaders lack the necessary skills to address social issues.
Discouragement of further governmental regulation By becoming socially responsible, businesses can expect less government regulation.	**Lack of accountability** There are no direct lines of accountability for social actions.
Balance of responsibility and power Businesses have a lot of power and an equally large amount of responsibility is needed to balance against that power.	
Stockholder interests Social responsibility will improve a business's stock price in the long run.	
Possession of resources Businesses have the resources to support public and charitable projects that need assistance.	
Superiority of prevention over cures Businesses should address social problems before they become serious and costly to correct.	

Exhibit 3

Trends in SRI

Socially Responsible Investing in the US • 1995–2007							
(In billions)	1995	1997	1999	2001	2003	2005	2007
Social Screening	$162	$529	$1,497	$2,010	$2,143	$1,685	$2,098
Shareholder Advocacy	$473	$736	$922	$897	$448	$703	$739
Screening and Shareholder	N/A	($84)	($265)	($592)	($441)	($117)	($151)
Community Investing	$4	$4	$5	$8	$14	$20	$26
Total	$639	$1,185	$2,159	$2,323	$2,164	$2,290	$2,711

Source: Social Investment Forum Foundation.

Notes: Social Screening includes socially and environmentally screened funds and separate account assets. Overlapping assets involved in Screening and Shareholder Advocacy are subtracted to avoid potential double-counting. Tracking Screening and Shareholder Advocacy together only began in 1997, so there is no datum for 1995. There are also potentially overlapping assets in the relatively small screened funds categories of Alternative Investments and Other Pooled Products; therefore these categories are also excluded from the SRI universe aggregated in this Report. See Chapter II for details.

social screening
Applying social criteria (screens) to investment decisions.

important than the total amount invested in these funds is that the Social Investment Forum reports that the performance of SRI funds is comparable to the performance of non-SRI funds.[19]

So, what can we conclude about social involvement and economic performance? It appears that a company's social actions *don't hurt* its economic performance. Given political and societal pressures to be socially involved, managers probably need to take into consideration social issues and goals as they plan, organize, lead, and control.

LEARNING OUTCOME 1

- Differentiate between social obligation, social responsiveness, and social responsibility.
- Discuss whether organizations should be socially involved.

- Describe what conclusion can be reached regarding social involvement and economic performance.

—Go to Learning Outcomes Summary to see how well you know this material.

LEARNING

OUTCOME 2 ▷ GREEN MANAGEMENT

The plastic shopping bag. An ugly symbol of American consumerism. Some 110 billion (that's not a typo!) are used each year, and only an estimated 2 percent of those bags are recycled. Plastic shopping bags can last 1,000 years in landfills. These bags are made from oil, and our "bag habit" costs 1.6 billion gallons each year.[20] But the good news is that things are changing. Being green is in! For instance, IKEA encourages customers to use fewer bags by charging a nickel (which it donates to American Forests) for each bag used. It also cut the price of its large reusable totes from 99 cents to 59 cents. Whole Foods Market is using wind energy for all its electricity needs, making it the largest corporate user of renewable energy in the United States. At UK-based Scottish Power, the importance of energy and environmental goals is obvious, as each division has a senior manager who's accountable for complying with those goals. Tokyo-based Ricoh hires workers to sort through company trash to analyze what might be reused or recycled. And company employees have two cans—one for recycling and one for trash. If a recyclable item is found in a trash bin, it's placed back on the offender's desk for proper removal. At Marriott International's employee cafeteria, plastic and paper containers have been replaced with real plates and compostable, potato-based containers called SpudWare.[21]

Until the late 1960s, few people (and organizations) paid attention to the environmental consequences of their decisions and actions. Although some groups were concerned with conserving natural resources, about the only reference to saving the environment was the ubiquitous printed request "Please Don't Litter." However, a number of environmental disasters brought a new spirit of environmentalism to individuals, groups, and organizations. Increasingly, managers have begun to consider the impact of their organizations on the natural environment, which we call **green management**. What do managers need to know about going green?

HOW ORGANIZATIONS GO GREEN

Managers and organizations can do many things to protect and preserve the natural environment.[22] Some do no more than what is required by law—that is, they fulfill their social obligation. However, others have radically changed their products and production processes. For instance, Fiji Water is using renewable energy sources, preserving forests, and conserving water. Carpet-maker Shaw Industries transforms its carpet and wood manufacturing waste into energy. Google and Intel initiated an effort to get computer makers and customers to adopt technologies that reduce energy consumption. Paris-based TOTAL, SA, one of the world's largest integrated oil companies, is going green by implementing tough new rules on oil tanker safety and working

Exhibit 4

Green Approaches

Source: Based on R. E. Freeman, J. Pierce, and R. Dodd, *Shades of Green: Business Ethics and the Environment* (New York: Oxford University Press, 1995).

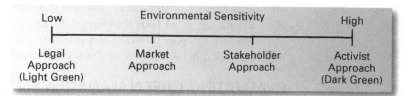

with groups such as Global Witness and Greenpeace. UPS, the world's largest package delivery company, has done several things—from retrofitting its aircraft with advanced technology and fuel-efficient engines to developing a computer network that efficiently dispatches its fleet of brown trucks to using alternative fuel to run those trucks. Although interesting, these examples don't tell us much about how organizations go green. One model uses the terms *shades of green* to describe the different environmental approaches that organizations may take (see Exhibit 4).[23]

The first approach, the *legal* (or *light green*) *approach*, is simply doing what is required legally. In this approach, which illustrates social obligation, organizations exhibit little environmental sensitivity. They obey laws, rules, and regulations without legal challenge, and that's the extent of their being green.

As an organization becomes more sensitive to environmental issues, it may adopt the *market approach* and respond to environmental preferences of customers. Whatever customers demand in terms of environmentally friendly products will be what the organization provides. For example, DuPont developed a new type of herbicide that helped farmers around the world reduce their annual use of chemicals by more than 45 million pounds. By developing this product, the company was responding to the demands of its customers (farmers) who wanted to minimize the use of chemicals on their crops. This is a good example of social responsiveness, as is the next approach.

In the *stakeholder approach*, an organization works to meet the environmental demands of multiple stakeholders, such as employees, suppliers, or community. For instance, Hewlett-Packard has several corporate environmental programs in place for its supply-chain (suppliers), product design and product recycling (customers and society), and work operations (employees and community).

Finally, if an organization pursues an *activist* (or *dark green*) *approach*, it looks for ways to protect the earth's natural resources. The activist approach reflects the highest degree of environmental sensitivity and illustrates social responsibility. For example, the Belgian company Ecover produces ecological cleaning products in a near-zero-

Subway is helping to lead the way among retail food stores when it comes to "going green." The sandwich chain is testing ways to reduce its use of paper by serving its famous subs with less wrapping and using baskets made partly of recycled material to hold food instead. It has also switched to 100% recycled paper napkins, which the store estimates is saving 147,000 trees each year.

Clive Sawyer/Alamy Images

green management
A form of management in which managers consider the impact of their organization on the natural environment.

emissions factory. This factory (the world's first ecological one) is an engineering marvel, with a huge grass roof that keeps things cool in summer and warm in winter and a water treatment system that runs on wind and solar energy. The company chose to build this facility because of its deep commitment to the environment.

EVALUATING GREEN MANAGEMENT ACTIONS

As businesses become "greener," they often release detailed reports on their environmental performance. Some 1,500 companies around the globe are voluntarily reporting their efforts in promoting environmental sustainability, using the guidelines developed by the Global Reporting Initiative (GRI). These reports, which can be found on the GRI Web site (www.globalreporting.org), describe the numerous green actions of these organizations.

Another way that organizations show their commitment to being green is through pursuing standards developed by the nongovernmental International Organization for Standardization (ISO). Although the ISO has developed more than 17,000 international standards, it's probably best known for its ISO 9000 (quality management) and ISO 14000 (environmental management) standards. An organization that wants to become ISO 14000 compliant must develop a total management system for meeting environmental challenges. This means it must minimize the effects of its activities on the environment and continually improve its environmental performance. If an organization can meet these standards, it can state that it's ISO 14000 compliant, which organizations in 138 countries have achieved. In addition to its environmental management standards, ISO is developing standards for social responsibility and for energy management. The one for social responsibility (known as ISO 26000) will be published in 2010 and will be voluntary, which means that organizations won't be able to obtain any type of certification for meeting the standards. And no date has been announced for the energy management standards because the committee developing those standards was only recently created.[24]

The final way to evaluate a company's green actions is to use the Global 100 list of the most sustainable corporations in the world (www.global100.org).[25] To be named to this list, which is announced each year at the renowned World Economic Forum in Davos, Switzerland, a company must have displayed a superior ability to effectively manage environmental and social factors. In 2008, the United Kingdom led the list with 23 Global 100 companies. The United States followed with 19 and Japan with 13. Some companies on the 2008 list included BASF (Germany), Diageo PLC (United Kingdom), Mitsubishi (Japan), and Nike (United States).

QUICK LEARNING REVIEW:
LEARNING OUTCOME 2

- Define green management.
- Describe how organizations can go green.

- Explain how green management actions can be evaluated.

Go to Learning Outcomes Summary to see how well you know this material.

LEARNING
OUTCOME 3 ▷ MANAGERS AND ETHICAL BEHAVIOR

Two weeks after firing seven top managers for failing to meet company standards, Wal-Mart issued an extensive ethics policy for employees. Takafumi Horie, founder of the Tokyo-based Internet company Livedoor, was sentenced to 2.5 years in jail for securities violations. Former WorldCom CEO Bernie Ebbers is serving a 25-year prison sentence for financial fraud, conspiracy, and false filings. The Gemological Institute of America, which grades diamonds for independent dealers and large retailers, fired four employees and made changes to top management after an internal investigation showed that lab workers took bribes to inflate the quality of diamonds in grading reports.[26] When you hear about such behaviors—especially after the high-profile financial misconduct at Enron, WorldCom, and other companies—you might conclude that businesses aren't ethical. Although that's not the case, managers—at all levels, in all areas, in all sizes, and in all kinds of organizations—do face ethical issues and dilemmas. For instance, is it ethical for a sales representative to bribe a purchasing agent as an inducement to buy? Would it make a difference if the bribe came out of the sales rep's commission? Is it ethical for someone to use a company car for private use? How about using company e-mail for personal correspondence or using a company phone to make personal phone calls? What if you managed an employee who worked all weekend on an emergency situation, and you told him to take off two days sometime later and mark it down as "sick days" because your company had a clear policy that overtime would not be compensated for any reason?[27] Would that be okay? How will you handle such situations? As managers plan, organize, lead, and control, they must consider ethical dimensions.

What do we mean by **ethics**? We define it as the principles, values, and beliefs that define right and wrong decisions and behavior.[28] Many decisions that managers make require them to consider both the process and who's affected by the result.[29] To better understand the ethical issues involved in such decisions, let's look at the factors that determine whether a person acts ethically or unethically.

FACTORS THAT DETERMINE ETHICAL AND UNETHICAL BEHAVIOR

Whether someone behaves ethically or unethically when faced with an ethical dilemma is influenced by several things: his or her stage of moral development and other moderating variables, including individual characteristics, the organization's structural design, the organization's culture, and the intensity of the ethical issue (see Exhibit 5). People who lack a strong moral sense are much less likely to do the wrong things if they're constrained by rules, policies, job descriptions, or strong cultural norms that disapprove of such behaviors. Conversely, intensely moral individuals can be corrupted by an organizational structure and culture that permits or encourages unethical practices. Let's look more closely at these factors.

Stage of Moral Development. Research confirms there are three levels of moral development, each having two stages.[30] At each successive stage, an individual's moral judgment becomes less dependent on outside influences and more internalized.

At the first level, the *preconventional* level, a person's choice between right and wrong is based on personal consequences from outside sources, such as physical punishment, reward, or exchange of favors. At the second level, the *conventional* level, ethical decisions rely on maintaining expected standards and living up to the expectations of others. At the *principled* level, individuals define moral values apart from the authority of the groups to which they belong or society in general. The three levels and six stages are described in Exhibit 6.

Exhibit 5

Factors that Determine Ethical and Unethical Behavior

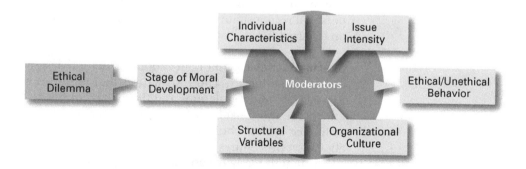

ethics
Principles, values, and beliefs that define what is right
and what is wrong behavior.

Exhibit 6

Stages of Moral Development

Source: Based on L. Kohlberg, "Moral Stages and Moralization: The Cognitive-Development Approach," in T. Lickona (ed.), *Moral Development and Behavior: Theory, Research, and Social Issues* (New York: Holt, Rinehart & Winston, 1976), pp. 34–35.

Level	Description of Stage
Principled	6. Following self-chosen ethical principles even if they violate the law
	5. Valuing rights of others and upholding absolute values and rights regardless of the majority's opinion
Conventional	4. Maintaining conventional order by fulfilling obligations to which you have agreed
	3. Living up to what is expected by people close to you
Preconventional	2. Following rules only when doing so is in your immediate interest
	1. Sticking to rules to avoid physical punishment

What can we conclude about moral development?[31] First, people proceed through the six stages sequentially. Second, there is no guarantee of continued moral development. Third, the majority of adults are at stage 4: They're limited to obeying the rules and will be inclined to behave ethically, although for different reasons. A manager at stage 3 is likely to make decisions based on peer approval; a manager at stage 4 will try to be a "good corporate citizen" by making decisions that respect the organization's rules and procedures; and a stage 5 manager is likely to challenge organizational practices that he or she believes to be wrong.

Individual Characteristics. Two individual characteristics—values and personality—play a role in determining whether a person behaves ethically. Each person comes to an organization with a relatively entrenched set of personal **values**, which represent basic convictions about what is right and wrong. Our values develop from a young age, based on what we see and hear from parents, teachers, friends, and others. Thus, employees in the same organization often possess very different values.[32] Although *values* and *stage of moral development* may seem similar, they're not. Values are broad and cover a wide range of issues; the stage of moral development is a measure of independence from outside influences.

Two personality variables have been found to influence an individual's actions according to his or her beliefs about what is right or wrong: ego strength and locus of control. **Ego strength** measures the strength of a person's convictions. People with high ego strength are likely to resist impulses to act unethically and instead follow their convictions. That is, individuals high in ego strength are more likely to do what they think is right and be more consistent in their moral judgments and actions than those with low ego strength.

Locus of control is the degree to which people believe they control their own fate. People with an *internal* locus of control believe they control their own destinies. They're more likely to take responsibility for consequences and rely on their own internal standards of right and wrong to guide their behavior. They're also more likely to be consistent in their moral judgments and actions. People with an *external* locus believe that what happens to them is due to luck or chance. They're less likely to take personal responsibility for the consequences of their behavior and more likely to rely on external forces.[33]

Structural Variables. An organization's structural design can influence whether employees behave ethically. Those structures that minimize ambiguity and uncertainty with formal rules and regulations and those that continuously remind employees of what is ethical are more likely to encourage ethical behavior. Other structural variables that influence ethical choices include goals, performance appraisal systems, and reward allocation procedures.

Although many organizations use goals to guide and motivate employees, those goals can create some unexpected problems. One study found that people who don't reach set goals are more likely to engage in unethical behavior, regardless of whether there are economic incentives to do so. The researchers concluded that "goal setting can lead to unethical behavior."[34] Examples of such behaviors abound—from companies shipping unfinished products just to reach sales goals or "managing earnings" to

meet financial analysts' expectations, to schools excluding certain groups of students when reporting standardized test scores to make their "pass" rate look better.[35]

An organization's performance appraisal system can also influence ethical behavior. Some systems focus exclusively on outcomes, while others evaluate means as well as ends. When employees are evaluated only on outcomes, they may be pressured to do whatever is necessary to look good on the outcomes and not be concerned with how they got those results. Research suggests that "success may serve to excuse unethical behaviors."[36] The danger of such thinking is that if managers are more lenient in correcting unethical behaviors of successful employees, other employees will model their behavior on what they see.

Closely related to the organization's appraisal system is how rewards are allocated. The more that rewards or punishment depend on specific goal outcomes, the more employees are pressured to do whatever they must to reach those goals, perhaps to the point of compromising their ethical standards.

Organization's Culture. As Exhibit 5 shows, the content and strength of an organization's culture influence ethical behavior.[37] An organization's culture consists of the shared organizational values. These values reflect what the organization stands for and what it believes in, and they create an environment that influences employee behavior ethically or unethically. When it comes to ethical behavior, a culture most likely to encourage high ethical standards is one that's high in risk tolerance, control, and conflict tolerance. Employees in such a culture are encouraged to be aggressive and innovative, are aware that unethical practices will be discovered, and feel free to openly challenge expectations they consider to be unrealistic or personally undesirable.

Because shared values can be powerful influences, many organizations are using **values-based management**, in which the organization's values guide employees in the way they do their jobs. For instance, Timberland is an example of a company that uses values-based management. Based on the simple statement "Make It Better," employees at Timberland know what's expected and valued: They know they need to find ways to "make it better"—whether it's creating quality products for customers, performing community service activities, designing employee training programs, or figuring out ways to make the company's packaging more environmentally friendly. As CEO Jeffrey Swartz says on the company's Web site, "Everything we do at Timberland grows out of our relentless pursuit to find a way to make it better." And Timberland isn't alone in its use of values-based management. A survey of global companies found that a large number—more than 89 percent—said they had written corporate values statements.[38] This survey also found that most of the companies believed that their values influenced relationships and reputation, the top-performing companies consciously connected values with the way employees did their work, and top managers were important to reinforcing the importance of the values throughout the organization.

Thus, an organization's managers do play an important role in ethics. They're responsible for creating an environment that encourages employees to embrace the culture and the desired values as they do their jobs. In fact, research shows that the behavior of managers is the single most important influence on an individual's decision to act ethically or unethically.[39] People look to see what those in authority are doing and use that as a benchmark for acceptable practices and expectations.

Finally, a strong culture exerts more influence on employees than a weak one. A culture that is strong and supports high ethical standards has a very powerful and positive influence on the decision to act ethically or unethically. For example, IBM has a strong culture that has long stressed ethical dealings with customers,

---

values
Basic convictions about what is right and what is wrong.

ego strength
A personality measure of the strength of a person's convictions.

locus of control
A personality attribute that measures the degree to which people believe they control their own fate.

values-based management
A form of management in which an organization's values guide employees in the way they do their jobs.

employees, business partners, and communities.[40] To reinforce the importance of ethical behaviors, the company developed an explicitly detailed set of guidelines for business conduct and ethics. And the penalty for violating the guidelines: disciplinary actions, including dismissal. IBM's managers continually reinforce the importance of ethical behavior and reinforce the fact that a person's actions and decisions are important to the way the organization is viewed.

Issue Intensity. A student who would never consider breaking into an instructor's office to steal an accounting exam may not think twice about asking a friend who took the same course from the same instructor last semester what questions were on an exam. Similarly, a manager might think nothing about taking home a few office supplies yet be highly concerned about the possible embezzlement of company funds. These examples illustrate the final factor that influences ethical behavior: the intensity of the ethical issue itself.[41]

As Exhibit 7 shows, six characteristics determine issue intensity or how important an ethical issue is to an individual: greatness of harm, consensus of wrong, probability of harm, immediacy of consequences, proximity to victim(s), and concentration of effect. These factors suggest that the greater the number of people harmed, the more agreement that the action is wrong; the greater the likelihood that the action will cause harm, the more immediately that the consequences of the action will be felt; and the closer the person feels to the victim(s) and the more concentrated the effect of the action on the victim(s), the greater the issue intensity or importance. When an ethical issue is important, employees are more likely to behave ethically.

ETHICS IN AN INTERNATIONAL CONTEXT

Are ethical standards universal? Although some common moral beliefs exist, social and cultural differences between countries are important factors that determine ethical and unethical behavior.[42] For example, say that a manager in a Mexican firm bribes several high-ranking government officials in Mexico City to secure a profitable government contract. Although this business practice is unethical (and illegal) in the United States, it's acceptable in Mexico.

Should Coca-Cola employees in Saudi Arabia adhere to U.S. ethical standards, or should they follow local standards of acceptable behavior? If Airbus (a European company) pays a "broker's fee" to a middleman to get a major contract with a Middle Eastern airline, should Boeing be restricted from doing the same because such practices are considered improper in the United States? (Note that in the United Kingdom, the Law Commission, a governmental advisory body, has said that bribing

Exhibit 7

Issue Intensity

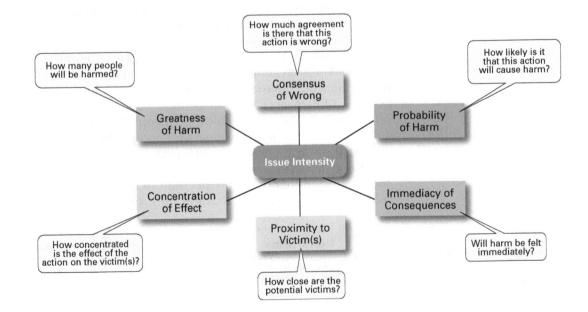

officials in foreign countries should be a criminal offense. It said that claims of "it's local custom" should not be a reason for allowing it.)[43]

In the case of payments to influence foreign officials or politicians, U.S. mangers are guided by the Foreign Corrupt Practices Act (FCPA), which makes it illegal to knowingly corrupt a foreign official. However, even this law doesn't always reduce ethical dilemmas to black and white. In some countries, government bureaucrat salaries are low because custom dictates that they receive small payments from those they serve. Payoffs to these bureaucrats "grease the machinery" and ensure that things get done. The FCPA does not expressly prohibit small payoffs to foreign government employees whose duties are primarily administrative or clerical *when* such payoffs are an accepted part of doing business in that country. Any action other than this is illegal. In 2007, the U.S. Department of Justice brought 16 FCPA enforcement actions against corporations and 8 against individuals.[44]

It's important for individual managers working in foreign cultures to recognize the social, cultural, and political/legal influences on what is appropriate and acceptable behavior.[45] And international businesses must clarify their ethical guidelines so that employees know what's expected of them while working in a foreign location, which adds another dimension to making ethical judgments.

Another guide to being ethical in international business is the Global Compact, which is a document created by the United Nations that outlines principles for doing business globally in the areas of human rights, labor, and the environment and anti-corruption (see Exhibit 8). "More than 3,000 CEOs have signed the Compact, making it the world's largest voluntary corporate citizenship initiative."[46] The goal of the Compact is a more sustainable and inclusive global economy. Organizations making this commitment do so because they believe that the world business community plays a significant role in improving economic and social conditions. In addition, the Organisation for Economic Co-operation and Development (OECD) has made fighting bribery and corruption in international business a high priority. The centerpiece of its efforts is the Anti-Bribery Convention (or set of rules and guidelines), which was the first global instrument to combat corruption in cross-border business deals. To date, significant gains have been made in fighting corruption in the 37 countries that have ratified it.[47]

Exhibit 8

Ten Principles of the UN

Human Rights	
Principle 1:	Support and respect the protection of international human rights within their sphere of influence.
Principle 2:	Make sure business corporations are not complicit in human rights abuses.
Labor Standards	
Principle 3:	Freedom of association and the effective recognition of the right to collective bargaining.
Principle 4:	The elimination of all forms of forced and compulsory labor.
Principle 5:	The effective abolition of child labor.
Principle 6:	The elimination of discrimination in respect of employment and occupation.
Environment	
Principle 7:	Support a precautionary approach to environmental challenges.
Principle 8:	Undertake initiatives to promote greater environmental responsibility.
Principle 9:	Encourage the development and diffusion of environmentally friendly technologies.
Principle 10:	Businesses should work against corruption in all its forms, including extortion and bribery.

Source: Courtesy of UN Global Compact.

QUICK LEARNING REVIEW:
LEARNING OUTCOME 3

- Define ethics.
- Discuss the factors that influence whether a person behaves ethically or unethically.

- Describe what managers need to know about international ethics.

Go to Learning Outcomes Summary and see how well you know this material.

LEARNING
OUTCOME 4 ▷ ENCOURAGING ETHICAL BEHAVIOR

Managers can do a number of things if they're serious about encouraging ethical behaviors—hire employees with high ethical standards, establish codes of ethics, lead by example, and so forth. By themselves, such actions won't have much of an impact. But having a comprehensive ethics program in place can potentially improve an organization's ethical climate. The key variable, however, is *potentially*. There are no guarantees that a well-designed ethics program will lead to the desired outcome. Sometimes corporate ethics programs are little more than public relations gestures that do little to influence managers and employees. For instance, Sears had a long history of encouraging ethical business practices through its corporate Office of Ethics and Business Practices. However, its ethics programs didn't stop managers from illegally trying to collect payments from bankrupt charge account holders or from routinely deceiving automotive service center customers into thinking they needed unnecessary repairs. Even Enron, often referred to as the "poster child" of corporate wrongdoing, outlined values in its 2000 Annual Report that most would consider ethical—communication, respect, integrity, and excellence. Yet the way top managers behaved didn't reflect those values at all.[48] Let's look at some specific ways that managers can encourage ethical behavior and create a comprehensive ethics program.

EMPLOYEE SELECTION

The selection process (interviews, tests, background checks, and so forth) should be viewed as an opportunity to learn about an individual's level of moral development, personal values, ego strength, and locus of control.[49] But even a carefully designed selection process isn't foolproof! Even under the best circumstances, individuals with questionable standards of right and wrong may be hired. However, this shouldn't be a problem if other ethics controls are in place.

CODES OF ETHICS AND DECISION RULES

George David, former CEO and chairman of Hartford, Connecticut-based United Technologies Corporation (UTC), believes in the power of a code of ethics. That's why UTC has one that's quite explicit and detailed. Employees know the behavioral expectations, especially when it comes to ethics.[50] However, that's not the way it is in all organizations.

Uncertainty about what is and is not ethical can be a problem for employees. A **code of ethics**, a formal statement of an organization's values and the ethical rules it expects employees to follow, is a popular choice for reducing that ambiguity. Research shows that 97 percent of organizations with more than 10,000 employees have written codes of ethics. Even in smaller organizations, nearly 93 percent have them.[51] And codes of ethics are becoming more popular globally. Research by the Institute for Global Ethics says that shared values such as honesty, fairness, respect, responsibility, and caring are pretty much universally embraced worldwide.[52] In addition, a survey of businesses in 22 countries found that 78 percent have formally stated ethics standards and codes of ethics.[53]

What should a code of ethics look like? It should be specific enough to show employees the spirit in which they're supposed to do things yet loose enough to allow for freedom of judgment. A survey of companies' codes of ethics found that their content tended to fall into three categories, as shown in Exhibit 9.[54]

Unfortunately, codes of ethics don't appear to work very well. A survey of employees in U.S. businesses found that 56 percent of those surveyed had observed ethical or

Exhibit 9

Codes of Ethics

Cluster 1. Be a Dependable Organizational Citizen

1. Comply with safety, health, and security regulations.
2. Demonstrate courtesy, respect, honesty, and fairness.
3. Illegal drugs and alcohol at work are prohibited.
4. Manage personal finances well.
5. Exhibit good attendance and punctuality.
6. Follow directives of supervisors.
7. Do not use abusive language.
8. Dress in business attire.
9. Firearms at work are prohibited.

Cluster 2. Do Not Do Anything Unlawful or Improper That Will Harm the Organization

1. Conduct business in compliance with all laws.
2. Payments for unlawful purposes are prohibited.
3. Bribes are prohibited.
4. Avoid outside activities that impair duties.
5. Maintain confidentiality of records.
6. Comply with all antitrust and trade regulations.
7. Comply with all accounting rules and controls.
8. Do not use company property for personal benefit.
9. Employees are personally accountable for company funds.
10. Do not propagate false or misleading information.
11. Make decisions without regard for personal gain.

Cluster 3. Be Good to Customers

1. Convey true claims in product advertisements.
2. Perform assigned duties to the best of your ability.
3. Provide products and services of the highest quality.

Source: F. R. David, "An Empirical Study of Codes of Business Ethics: A Strategic Perspective," paper presented at the 48th Annual Academy of Management Conference, Anaheim, California, August 1988.

---

legal violations in the previous 12 months, including such things as conflicts of interest, abusive or intimidating behavior, and lying to employees. And 42 percent of those employees don't report observed misconduct. Even in companies with comprehensive ethics and compliance programs, 29 percent failed to report misconduct.[55] Does this mean that codes of ethics shouldn't be developed? No. However, in doing so, managers should use these suggestions:[56]

1. Organizational leaders should model appropriate behavior and reward those who act ethically.
2. All managers should continually reaffirm the importance of the ethics code and consistently discipline those who break it.
3. The organization's stakeholders (employees, customers, and so forth) should be considered as an ethics code is developed or improved.

code of ethics
A formal statement of an organization's primary values and the ethical rules it expects its employees to follow.

4. Managers should communicate and reinforce the ethics code regularly.

5. Managers should use the 12 questions approach (see Exhibit 10) to guide employees when faced with ethical dilemmas.[57]

TOP MANAGEMENT'S LEADERSHIP

Doing business ethically requires a commitment from top managers. Why? Because they're the ones who uphold the shared values and set the cultural tone. They're role models in terms of both words and actions, though what they *do* is far more important than what they *say*. If top managers, for example, take company resources for their personal use, inflate their expense accounts, or give favored treatment to friends, they imply that such behavior is acceptable for all employees.

Top managers also set the tone with their reward and punishment practices. The choices of whom and what are rewarded with pay increases and promotions send a strong signal to employees. As we said earlier, when an employee is rewarded for achieving impressive results in an ethically questionable manner, it indicates to others that those ways are acceptable. When an employee does something unethical, managers must punish the offender and publicize the fact by making the outcome visible to everyone in the organization. This practice sends a message that doing wrong has a price, and it's not in employees' best interests to act unethically.

JOB GOALS AND PERFORMANCE APPRAISAL

Employees in three Internal Revenue Service offices were found in the bathrooms flushing tax returns and other related documents down the toilets. When questioned, they openly admitted doing it but offered an interesting explanation for their behavior. The employees' supervisors had been pressuring them to complete more work in less time. If the piles of tax returns weren't processed and moved off their desks more quickly, they were told their performance reviews and salary raises would be adversely affected. Frustrated because they had few resources and an overworked computer system, the employees decided to "flush away" the paperwork on their desks, even though they knew what they were doing was wrong. This story illustrates how powerful unrealistic goals and performance appraisals can be.[58] Under the stress of unrealistic goals, otherwise ethical employees may feel that they have no choice but to do whatever is necessary to meet those goals. Also, goal achievement is usually a key issue in performance appraisal. If performance appraisals focus only on economic goals, ends

---

Exhibit 10

12 Questions Approach

1. Have you defined the problem accurately?

2. How would you define the problem if you stood on the other side of the fence?

3. How did this situation occur in the first place?

4. To whom and to what do you give your loyalty as a person and as a member of the corporation?

5. What is your intention in making this decision?

6. How does this intention compare with the probable results?

7. Whom could your decision or action injure?

8. Can you discuss the problem with the affected parties before you make the decision?

9. Are you confident that your position will be as valid over a long period of time as it seems now?

10. Could you disclose without qualm your decision or action to your boss, your chief executive officer, the board of directors, your family, society as a whole?

11. What is the symbolic potential of your action if understood? If misunderstood?

12. Under what conditions would you allow exceptions to your stand?

Source: Reprinted by permission of *Harvard Business Review.* An exhibit from "Ethics Without the Sermon," by L. L. Nash. November–December 1981, p. 81. Copyright © 1981 by the President and Fellows of Harvard College. All rights reserved.

will begin to justify means. To encourage ethical behavior, both ends and means should be evaluated. For example, a manager's annual review of employees might include a point-by-point evaluation of how their decisions measured up against the company's code of ethics as well as how well goals were met.

ETHICS TRAINING

Organizations are increasingly setting up seminars, workshops, and similar ethics training programs to encourage ethical behavior. Such training programs aren't without controversy; the primary concern is whether ethics can be taught. Critics stress that the effort is pointless because people establish their individual value systems when they're young. Proponents note, however, that several studies have shown that values can be learned after early childhood. In addition, they cite evidence which shows that teaching ethical problem solving can make a difference in ethical behaviors;[59] that training has increased individuals' level of moral development;[60] and that, if nothing else, ethics training increases awareness of ethical issues in business.[61]

How can ethics be taught? Let's look at an example involving global defense contractor Lockheed Martin, one of the pioneers in the case-based approach to ethics training.[62] Lockheed Martin's employees take annual ethics training courses delivered by their managers. The main focus of these short courses is Lockheed Martin–specific case situations "chosen for their relevance to department or job-specific issues." In each department, employee teams review and discuss the cases and then apply an "Ethics Meter" to "rate whether the real-life decisions were ethical, unethical, or somewhere in between." For example, one of the possible ratings on the Ethics Meter, "On Thin Ice," is explained as "bordering on unethical and should raise a red flag." After the teams have applied their ratings, managers lead discussions about the ratings and examine "which of Lockheed Martin's core ethics principles were applied or ignored in the cases." In addition to its ethics training, Lockheed Martin has a widely used written code of ethics, an ethics helpline that employees can call for guidance on ethical issues, and ethics officers based in the company's various business units.

INDEPENDENT SOCIAL AUDITS

The fear of being caught can be an important deterrent to unethical behavior. Independent social audits, which evaluate decisions and management practices in terms of the organization's code of ethics, increase that likelihood. Such audits can

Green Mountain Coffee Roasters prides itself on conducting ethical business operations. Ethics, sustainability, personal excellence, appreciating differences, and being "a force for good in the world" are among the principles by which Green Mountain employees make business decisions every day. For instance, the company recently joined the Jane Goodall Institute to support small-scale coffee farms in Tanzania, near the imperiled Gombe National Park where Dr. Goodall conducted her legendary studies of primates. The partners hope to give farmers there an incentive to restore the forests that constitute one of the last remaining habitats of chimpanzees.

Toby Talbot/AP Wide World Photos

be regular evaluations, or they can occur randomly, with no prior announcement. An effective ethics program probably needs both. To maintain integrity, auditors should be responsible to the company's board of directors and present their findings directly to the board. This arrangement gives the auditors clout and reduces the opportunity for retaliation from those being audited. Because the Sarbanes-Oxley Act holds businesses to more rigorous standards of financial disclosure and corporate governance, more organizations are finding the idea of independent social audits appealing. As the publisher of *Business Ethics* magazine stated, "The debate has shifted from *whether* to be ethical to *how* to be ethical."[63]

PROTECTIVE MECHANISMS

Employees who face ethical dilemmas need protective mechanisms so they can do what's right without fear of reprimand. An organization might designate ethical counselors for employees facing an ethics dilemma. These advisors also might advocate the ethically "right" alternatives. Other organizations have appointed ethics officers who design, direct, and modify the organization's ethics programs as needed.[64] The Ethics and Compliance Officer Association reports its total membership at over 1,300 (including more than half of the *Fortune* 100 companies) and covering several countries, including the United States, Germany, India, Japan, and Canada.[65]

QUICK LEARNING REVIEW:

LEARNING OUTCOME 4

- Describe managers' important role in encouraging ethical behavior.

- Discuss specific ways managers can encourage ethical behavior.

Go to Learning Outcomes Summary and see how well you know this material.

LEARNING

OUTCOME 5 ▷ SOCIAL RESPONSIBILITY AND ETHICS ISSUES IN TODAY'S WORLD

Today's managers continue to face challenges in being socially responsible and ethical. Next we examine three current issues: managing ethical lapses and social irresponsibility, encouraging social entrepreneurship, and promoting positive social change.

MANAGING ETHICAL LAPSES AND SOCIAL IRRESPONSIBILITY

Even after public outrage over the Enron-era misdeeds, irresponsible and unethical practices by managers in all kinds of organizations haven't gone away. What's more alarming is what's going on "in the trenches" in offices, warehouses, and stores. One survey reported that of more than 5,000 employees, 45 percent admitted having fallen asleep at work; 22 percent said they had spread a rumor about a coworker; 18 percent said they had snooped after hours; and 2 percent said that they had taken credit for someone else's work.[66]

Unfortunately, it's not just at work that we see such behaviors. They're prevalent throughout society. Studies conducted by the Center for Academic Integrity showed that 26 percent of college and university business majors admitted to "serious cheating" on exams, and 54 percent admitted to cheating on written assignments. But business students weren't the worst cheaters; that distinction belonged to journalism majors, of whom 27 percent said they had cheated.[67] And a survey by Students in Free Enterprise (SIFE) found that only 19 percent of students would report a classmate who cheated.[68] But even more frightening is what today's teenagers say is "acceptable." In a survey, 23 percent said they thought violence toward another person is acceptable on some level.[69] What do such statistics say about what managers may have to deal with in the future? It's not too far-fetched to say that organizations may have

AN ETHICAL LEADER IS:
I hold myself to high standards to set an example. People tend to live up to expectations, and I do my best to set them high.

difficulty upholding high ethical standards when their future employees so readily accept unethical behavior.

What can managers do? Two actions seem to be particularly important: ethical leadership and protection of those who report wrongdoing.

Ethical Leadership. Not long after Herb Baum took over as CEO of Dial Corporation, he got a call from Reuben Mark, the CEO of competitor Colgate-Palmolive, who told him he had a copy of Dial's strategic marketing plan that had come from a former Dial salesperson who had recently joined Colgate-Palmolive. Mark told Baum that he had not looked at it, didn't intend to look at it, and was returning it. In addition, he himself was going to deal appropriately with the new salesperson.[70] As this example illustrates, managers must provide ethical leadership. As we said earlier, what managers *do* has a strong influence on employees' decisions to behave ethically or not. When managers cheat, lie, steal, manipulate, take advantage of situations or people, or treat others unfairly, what kind of signal are they sending to employees (or other stakeholders)? Probably not the one they want to send. Exhibit 11 gives some suggestions on how managers can provide ethical leadership.

Protection of Employees Who Raise Ethical Issues. What would you do if you saw other employees doing something illegal, immoral, or unethical? Would you step forward? Many of us wouldn't because of the perceived risks. That's why it's important for managers to assure employees who raise ethical concerns or issues that they will face no personal or career risks. These individuals, often called **whistle-blowers**, can be a key part of any company's ethics program. One well-known whistle-blower in recent memory is Sherron Watkins, a vice president at Enron who clearly outlined her concerns about the company's accounting practices in a letter to chairman Ken Lay. Her statement "I am incredibly nervous that we will implode in a wave of accounting scandals" couldn't have been more prophetic.[71] However, surveys show that most observers of wrongdoing don't report it, and that's the attitude managers have to address.[72] How can they protect employees so they're willing to step up if they see unethical or illegal things occurring?

One way is to set up toll-free ethics hotlines. For instance, Dell has an ethics hotline that employees can call anonymously to report infractions that the company will then investigate.[73] In addition, managers need to create a culture where bad news can be heard and acted on before it's too late. Michael Josephson, founder of the Josephson Institute of ethics (www.josephsoninstitute.org), said, "It is absolutely and unequivocally important to establish a culture where it is possible for employees to complain and protest and to get heard."[74] Even if some whistle-blowers have a personal agenda they're pursuing, it's important to take them seriously. Finally, the Sarbanes-Oxley Act offers some legal protection. Any manager who retaliates against an employee for reporting violations faces a stiff penalty: a 10-year jail sentence.[75] Unfortunately, despite this protection, hundreds of employees who have stepped forward and revealed wrongdoings at their companies have been fired or let go from their jobs.[76] So at the present time, it's not a perfect solution, but it is a step in the right direction.

Exhibit 11

Being an Ethical Leader

- Be a good role model by being ethical and honest.
  - Tell the truth always.
  - Don't hide or manipulate information
  - Be willing to admit your failures.
- Share your personal values by regularly communicating them to employees.
- Stress the organization's or team's important shared values.
- Use the reward system to hold everyone accountable to the values.

whistle-blower
An individual who raises ethical concerns or issues to others.

ENCOURAGING SOCIAL ENTREPRENEURSHIP

The world's social problems are many, and viable solutions are few. But numerous people and organizations are trying to do something. For instance, Teresa Fritschi, James Potemkin, and Raquel Marchenese share a common bond even though they don't know each other. Each sells unique handmade items made by artisans from different parts of the globe—Scotland, Mexico, Guatemala, Pakistan, Peru. But they also share a passionate belief in fair trade and act on this belief by paying their supplier artisans more than the going rate for their works. Fair trade proponents seek to "give businesses or solo artists in poor or marginalized parts of the world a higher price for what they create and a more direct route into lucrative markets in America, Europe, and Asia."[77] Each of these individuals is also an example of a **social entrepreneur**, an individual or organization who seeks out opportunities to improve society by using practical, innovative, and sustainable approaches.[78] "What business entrepreneurs are to the economy, social entrepreneurs are to social change."[79] Social entrepreneurs want to make the world a better place and have a driving passion to make that happen. For example, the nonprofit International Senior Lawyers Project matches experienced U.S. attorneys with needs in developing countries. The group has taught black attorneys in South Africa how to practice business law and has provided assistance to public defenders in Bulgaria.[80] Also, social entrepreneurs use creativity and ingenuity to solve problems. For instance, the Seattle-based Program for Appropriate Technology in Health (PATH) is an international nonprofit organization that uses low-cost technology to provide needed health care solutions for poor, developing countries. By collaborating with public groups and for-profit businesses, PATH has developed simple life-saving solutions, such as clean birthing kits, credit card–sized lab test kits, and disposable vaccination syringes that can't be reused. Because of PATH's innovative approaches to solving global medical problems, it was named to the 2008 Social Capitalists Award list.[81]

What can we learn from social entrepreneurs? Although many organizations have committed to doing business ethically and responsibly, perhaps there is more they can do, as social entrepreneurs show. Maybe, as in the case of PATH, it's simply a matter of business organizations collaborating with public groups or nonprofit organizations to address a social issue. Or maybe, as in the case of the Senior Lawyers Project, it's providing expertise where needed. Or, it may involve nurturing individuals who passionately and unwaveringly believe they have an idea that could make the world a better place and simply need the organizational support to pursue it.

BUSINESSES PROMOTING POSITIVE SOCIAL CHANGE

Since 1946, Target has contributed 5 percent of its annual income to support community needs, an amount that adds up to over $3 million per week. And it's not alone in those efforts. "Over the past two decades, a growing number of corporations, both within and beyond the United States, have been engaging in activities that promote positive social change."[82] Businesses can do this in a couple ways: through corporate philanthropy and through employee volunteering.

Corporate Philanthropy. Corporate philanthropy can be an effective way for companies to address societal problems.[83] For instance, the breast cancer "pink" campaign and the global AIDS Red campaign (started by Bono) are ways that companies support social causes.[84] Many organizations also donate money to various causes that employees and customers care about. In 2006 (latest numbers available), the 15 largest cash donors—which included Wal-Mart, Bank of America, Target, and others—donated a total of $1.9 billion.[85] Others have funded their own foundations through which to support various social issues. For example, Google's foundation—called DotOrg by its employees—has about $2 billion in assets that it will use to support five areas: developing systems to help predict and prevent disease pandemics, empowering the poor with information about public services, creating jobs by investing in small and midsize businesses in the developing world, accelerating the commercialization of plug-in cars, and making renewable energy cheaper than coal.[86]

Employee Volunteering Efforts. Employee volunteering is a popular way for businesses to be involved in promoting social change. For instance, the 11-member Molson-Coors executive team spent a full day at their annual team-building retreat building a house in Las Vegas with Habitat for Humanity. PricewaterhouseCoopers employees renovated an abandoned school in Newark, New Jersey. Every Wachovia employee is given six paid days off from work each year to volunteer in his or her community. Other businesses are encouraging their employees to volunteer in various ways. The Committee Encouraging Corporate Philanthropy says that more than 90 percent of its members had volunteer programs and almost half encouraged volunteerism by providing paid time off or by creating volunteer events.[87] Many businesses have found that such efforts not only benefit communities but enhance employees' work efforts and motivation.

QUICK LEARNING REVIEW:
LEARNING OUTCOME 5

- Describe how managers can manage ethical lapses and social irresponsibility.
- Explain the role of social entrepreneurs.

- Discuss how businesses can promote positive social change.

Go to Learning Outcomes Summary and see how well you know this material.

social entrepreneur
An individual or organization who seeks out opportunities to improve society by using practical, innovative, and sustainable approaches.

Let's Get Real:
My Turn

Sally Yagan

Editorial Director
Pearson Education
Upper Saddle River, New Jersey

Social responsibility defines everything we do as individuals, and as a company.

Much of our business involves keeping faith with the public: we're an educational technology company with a responsibility to serve the purpose of learning. We do this through the products and services we offer and our support of charitable projects in the communities in which we do business. For example, we've raised or donated millions to support literacy programs for at-risk children; collaborated with faculty to create online learning tools that have cast a lifeline to struggling college students; and increased our efforts to be sensitive to the environment and limit the impact our products and colleagues have on the environment.

My colleagues and I feel grateful to work for a company like Pearson that proactively looks for ways to help others.

LEARNING OUTCOMES
SUMMARY

1 ▷ WHAT IS SOCIAL RESPONSIBILITY?

- Differentiate between social obligation, social responsiveness, and social responsibility.
- Discuss whether organizations should be socially involved.
- Describe what conclusion can be reached regarding social involvement and economic performance.

Social obligation, which reflects the classical view of social responsibility, involves a firm engaging in social actions because of its obligation to meet certain economic and legal responsibilities. Social responsiveness involves a firm engaging in social actions in response to some popular social need. Social responsibility is a business's intention, beyond its economic and legal obligations, to pursue long-term goals that are good for society. Both of these reflect the socioeconomic view of social responsibility. Determining whether organizations should be socially involved can be done by looking at arguments for and against it. Other ways are to assess the impact of social involvement on a company's economic performance and evaluate the performance of SRI funds versus non-SRI funds. Based on such information, we can conclude that a company's being socially responsible doesn't appear to hurt its economic performance.

2 ▷ GREEN MANAGEMENT

- Define *green management*.
- Describe how organizations can go green.
- Explain how green management actions can be evaluated.

With green management, managers consider the impact of their organization on the natural environment. Organizations can "go green" in different ways. The light green approach involves doing what is required legally, which is social obligation. Using the market approach, organizations respond to the environmental preferences of their customers. Using the stakeholder approach, organizations respond to the environmental demands of multiple stakeholders. Both the market and stakeholder approaches can be viewed as social responsiveness. The activist, or dark green, approach involves an organization looking for ways to respect and preserve the earth and its natural resources, which can be viewed as social responsibility.

Green actions can be evaluated by examining reports that companies compile about their environmental performance, by looking for compliance with global standards for environmental management (ISO 14000), and by using the Global 100 list of the most sustainable corporations in the world.

3 ▷ MANAGERS AND ETHICAL BEHAVIOR

- Define *ethics*.
- Discuss the factors that influence whether a person behaves ethically or unethically.
- Describe what managers need to know about international ethics.

Ethics refers to the principles, values, and beliefs that define right and wrong decisions and behavior. The factors that affect ethical and unethical behavior include an individual's level of moral development (preconventional, conventional, or principled); individual characteristics (values and personality variables—ego strength and locus of control); structural variables (structural design, use of goals, performance appraisal systems, and reward allocation procedures); organizational culture (shared values and cultural strength); and issue intensity (greatness of harm, consensus of wrong, probability of harm, immediacy of consequences, proximity to victims, and concentration of effect).

Because ethical standards aren't universal, managers should know what they can and cannot do legally, according to the Foreign Corrupt Practices Act. It's also important to recognize any cultural differences and to clarify ethical guidelines for employees working in different global locations. Finally, managers should know about the principles of the Global Compact and the Anti-Bribery Convention.

4 ▷ ENCOURAGING ETHICAL BEHAVIOR

- Describe managers' important role in encouraging ethical behavior.
- Discuss specific ways managers can encourage ethical behavior.

The behavior of managers is the single most important influence on an individual's decision to act ethically or unethically. Some specific ways managers can encourage ethical behavior include paying attention to employee selection, having and using a code of ethics, recognizing the important ethical leadership role they play and how what they do is far more important than what they say, making sure that goals and the performance appraisal process don't reward goal achievement without taking into account how goals were achieved, using ethics training and independent social audits, and establishing protective mechanisms.

5 ▷ SOCIAL RESPONSIBILITY AND ETHICS ISSUES IN TODAY'S WORLD

- Describe how managers can manage ethical lapses and social irresponsibility.
- Explain the role of social entrepreneurs.
- Discuss how businesses can promote positive social change.

Managers can manage ethical lapses and social irresponsibility by being strong ethical leaders and by protecting employees who raise ethical issues. The example set by managers has a strong influence on whether employees behave ethically. Ethical leaders also are honest, share their values, stress important shared values, and use the reward system appropriately. Managers can protect whistle-blowers (employees who raise ethical issues or concerns) by encouraging them to come forward, by setting up toll-free ethics hotlines, and by establishing a culture where employees can complain and get heard without fear of reprisal. Social entrepreneurs play an important role in solving social problems by seeking out opportunities to improve society by using practical, innovative, and sustainable approaches. Social entrepreneurs want to make the world a better place and have a driving passion to make that happen. Businesses can promote positive social change through corporate philanthropy and employee volunteering efforts.

THINKING ABOUT MANAGEMENT ISSUES

1. What does social responsibility mean to you personally? Do *you* think business organizations should be socially responsible? Explain.
2. Do you think values-based management is just a "do-gooder" ploy? Explain your answer.
3. Internet file sharing programs are popular among college students. These programs work by allowing non-organizational users to access any local network where desired files are located. These types of file sharing programs tend to clog bandwidth and reduce local users' ability to access and use a local network. What ethical and social responsibilities does a university have in such a situation? To whom does it have a responsibility? What guidelines might you suggest for university decision makers?
4. What are some problems that could be associated with employee whistle-blowing for (a) the whistle-blower and (b) the organization?
5. Describe the characteristics and behaviors of someone you consider to be an ethical person. How could the types of decisions and actions this person engages in be encouraged in a workplace?
6. This question was posed in an article in the October 10, 2006, issue of *USA Today*: "Is capitalism going to be the salvation of the world or the cause of its demise?" Discuss.

YOUR TURN *to be a* Manager

- **Find five different examples of organizational codes of ethics. Using Exhibit 9, describe what each contains. Compare and contrast the examples.**

- **Using the examples of codes of ethics you found, create what you feel would be an appropriate and effective organizational code of ethics. In addition, create your own *personal code of ethics* that you can use as a guide to ethical dilemmas.**

- Start a portfolio that contains each of the "Thinking Critically About Ethics" dilemmas found in each chapter. Write a response to each of the dilemmas and include these responses in your portfolio.

- Take advantage of volunteer opportunities and be sure to include them on your résumé. If possible, try to do things in volunteer positions that will improve your managerial skills in planning, organizing, leading, or controlling.

- Go to the Global Reporting Initiative Web site, www.globalreporting.org, and choose three businesses from the list of organizations that have filed reports. Look at those reports and describe/evaluate what's in them. In addition, identify the stakeholders that might be affected and how they might be affected by the company's actions.

- Find out what green management activities your school or employer is doing and write up a list of them. Do some research on being green. Are there additional things your school or employer could be doing? Write a report to your school or employer, describing any suggestions. (Also look for ways that you can be green in your personal life.)

- Over the course of two weeks, see what ethical "dilemmas" you observe. These could be ones that you personally face, or they could be ones that others (friends, colleagues, other students talking in the hallway or before class starts, and so forth) face. List these dilemmas and think about what you might do if faced with each one.

- Interview two different managers about how they encourage their employees to be ethical. Write down their comments and discuss how these ideas might help you be a better manager.

- Steve's and Mary's suggested readings: Bethany McLean and Peter Elkind, *The Smartest Guys in the Room: The Amazing Rise and Scandalous Fall of Enron* (Portfolio, 2003); Barbara Ley Toffler, *Final Accounting: Ambition, Greed, and the Fall of Arthur Andersen* (Broadway Books, 2003); Joseph L. Badaracco, Jr., *Leading Quietly: An Unorthodox Guide to Doing the Right Thing* (Harvard Business School Press, 2002); and Kenneth Blanchard and Norman Vincent Peale, *The Power of Ethical Management* (Morrow, 1988).

- If you have the opportunity, take a class on ethics (business or management) or on social responsibility—often called business and society—or both. Not only will this look good on your résumé, it could help you personally grapple with some of the tough issues managers face in being ethical and responsible.

- In your own words, write down three things you learned in this chapter about being a good manager.

- Self-knowledge can be a powerful learning tool. Go to mymanagementlab and complete these self-assessment exercises: What Do I Value? How Do My Ethics Rate? Do I Trust Others? and Do Others See Me as Trusting? Using the results of your assessments, identify personal strengths and weaknesses. What will you do to reinforce your strengths and improve your weaknesses?

PEARSON
mymanagementlab   For more resources, please visit www.mymanagementlab.com

CASE APPLICATION

Not Just Another Outdoor Company

We opened the chapter with a story about an outdoor company, and we end it with a story about another outdoor company. The company we're discussing this time, based in Portland, Oregon, was the brainchild of a small group of executives who left big-time jobs at Patagonia, Nike, and Adidas. These individuals shared a belief that "in addition to generating a profit, companies have an equal responsibility to create positive social and environmental change." Putting their beliefs into action, the group formed Nau (which is Maori for "Welcome! Come in"). And Nau is not just another outdoor company!

When deciding what Nau was going to be like and how it was going to do business, the founders knew they didn't want to do things the way they'd always been done by traditional businesses. CEO Chris Van Dyke said, "We

Smith Rock State Park, Oregon.

started with a clean whiteboard. We believed every single operational element in our business was an opportunity to turn traditional business notions inside out, integrating environmental, social, and economic factors." From design to sales to finances, Nau is driven by these factors. Everything in Nau's operation has been approached with a sustainability and social justice "filter."

In the design area, the company, in partnership with its suppliers, developed 24 of its 32 fabrics to be more sustainable and to combine performance and visual appeal. Each supplier, manufacturer, and even Nau itself is bound by a code of conduct. To ensure that all parties are living up to the standards, their actions are overseen by an independent, nonprofit auditing and research firm. In the sales area, the way the company retails its product is also unique. Using a concept it calls a "Web-front," Nau has combined the efficiency of the Web with the intimacy of a gallery-like boutique. In the "store," customers can try on clothes, but they use self-serve kiosks to purchase from the Web. Because in-store inventory is

greatly reduced, the stores are small (2,400 square feet compared to the standard 4,000-plus-square-foot outdoor retail store). This approach saves operating expenses because less energy and fewer materials are used. Good for the planet...good for the business. Finally, Nau has a unique financial approach it calls "aggressive altruism." The company has pledged 5 percent of sales to charitable organizations dedicated to solving crucial environmental and humanitarian problems. The "philanthropic gold standard" is 1 percent of sales, and the average among all corporations is .047 percent. But although the amount it gives is unusual, what happens with Nau's dollars is really exceptional: Nau puts the giving decision in the hands of its customers. They're asked to indicate which "Partners for Change" they'd like their 5 percent to go to. Using this "conscious choice" process, Nau is "calling its customers out, daring them to connect the dots."

Discussion Questions

1. What do you think of Nau's approach to doing business? Is it being ethical and responsible? Discuss.

2. Will Nau's approach have a limited appeal, or do you think it has staying power? What drawbacks might there be to what Nau is doing?

3. Is it a business's responsibility to get customers to "connect the dots" and make choices about social issues?

4. Are there lessons here for other businesses? Discuss.

Sources: Nau Web site, www.nau.com; and P. LaBarre, "Leap of Faith," *Fast Company*, June 2007, pp. 96–103.

NOTES

1. B. Wingfield, "Q&A: REI's Sally Jewell on Green Business," *Forbes.com*, www.forbes.com, November 29, 2007; A. Schultz, "The REI-ight Stuff," *CRO*, May/June 2007, pp. 28–33; and D. Buss, "REI—Working Out," *BusinessWeek* online, www.businessweek.com, November 15, 2005.

2. M. L. Barnett, "Stakeholder Influence Capacity and the Variability of Financial Returns to Corporate Social Responsibility," *Academy of Management Review*, July 2007, pp. 794–816; A. Mackey, T. B. Mackey, and J. B. Barney, "Corporate Social Responsibility and Firm Performance: Investor Preferences and Corporate Strategies," *Academy of Management Review*, July 2007, pp. 817–835; and A. B. Carroll, "A Three-Dimensional Conceptual Model of Corporate Performance," *Academy of Management Review*, October 1979, p. 499.

3. See K. Basu and G. Palazzo, "Corporate Social Performance: A Process Model of Sensemaking," *Academy of Management Review*, January 2008, pp. 122–136; and S. P. Sethi, "A Conceptual Framework for Environmental Analysis of Social Issues and Evaluation of Business Response Patterns," *Academy of Management Review*, January 1979, pp. 68–74.

4. M. Friedman, *Capitalism and Freedom* (Chicago: University of Chicago Press, 1962); and M. Friedman, "The Social Responsibility of Business Is to Increase Profits," *New York Times Magazine*, September 13, 1970, p. 33.

5. S. Liebs, "Do Companies Do Good Well?" *CFO*, July 2007, p. 16.

6. See, for example, D. J. Wood, "Corporate Social Performance Revisited," *Academy of Management Review*, October 1991, pp. 703–708; and S. L. Wartick and P. L. Cochran, "The Evolution of the Corporate Social Performance Model," *Academy of Management Review*, October 1985, p. 763.

7. Information from "Giving Back," found on American Express Web site, www.americanexpress.com, March 28, 2008.

8. See, for example, R. A. Buccholz, *Essentials of Public Policy for Management*, 2d ed. (Upper Saddle River, NJ: Prentice Hall, 1990).

9. I. Brat, "The Extra Step," *Wall Street Journal*, March 24, 2008, p. R12.

10. Information from Wal-Mart Web site, www.walmartstores.com, March 16, 2006; and an advertisement from *USA Today*, March 6, 2006, p. 5A.

11. This section is based on J. D. Margolis and J. P. Walsh, "Misery Loves Companies: Rethinking Social Initiatives by Business," *Administrative Science Quarterly*, vol. 48 (2), 2003, pp. 268–305; K. Davis and W. C. Frederick, *Business and Society: Management, Public Policy, Ethics*, 5th ed. (New York: McGraw-Hill, 1984), pp. 28–41; and R. J. Monsen, Jr., "The Social Attitudes of Management," in J. M. McGuire (ed.), *Contemporary Management: Issues and Views* (Upper Saddle River, NJ: Prentice Hall, 1974), p. 616.

12. See, for instance, R. Trudel and J. Cotte, " Does Being Ethical Pay?" *Wall Street Journal,* May 12, 2008, p. R8; J. D. Margolis and H. Anger Elfenbein, "Do Well by Doing Good? Don't Count on It," *Harvard Business Review*, January 2008, pp. 19–20; M. L. Barnett, "Stakeholder Influence Capacity and the Variability of Financial Returns to Corporate Social Responsibility," 2007; D. O. Neubaum and S. A. Zahra, "Institutional Ownership and Corporate Social Performance: The Moderating Effects of Investment Horizon, Activism, and Coordination," *Journal of Management*, February 2006, pp. 108–131; B. A. Waddock and S. B. Graves, "The Corporate Social Performance–Financial Performance Link," *Strategic Management Journal*, April 1997, pp. 303–319; J. B. McGuire, A. Sundgren, and T. Schneeweis, "Corporate Social Responsibility and Firm Financial Performance," *Academy of Management Journal*, December 1988, pp. 854–872; K. Aupperle, A. B. Carroll, and J. D. Hatfield, "An Empirical Examination of the Relationship Between Corporate Social Responsibility and Profitability," *Academy of Management Journal*, June 1985, pp. 446–463; and P. Cochran and R. A. Wood, "Corporate Social Responsibility and Financial Performance," *Academy of Management Journal*, March 1984, pp. 42–56.

13. See J. Surroca and J. A. Tribo, "The Corporate Social and Financial Performance Relationship: What's the Ultimate Determinant?" *Academy of Management Proceedings* Best Conference Paper, 2005; D. J. Wood and R. E. Jones, "Stakeholder Mismatching: A Theoretical Problem in Empirical Research on Corporate Social Performance," *International Journal of Organizational Analysis*, July 1995, pp. 229–267; R. Wolfe and K. Aupperle, "Introduction to Corporate Social Performance: Methods for Evaluating an Elusive Construct," pp. 265–268, in J. E. Post (ed.), *Research in*

Corporate Social Performance and Policy, vol. 12, 1991; and A. A. Ullmann, "Data in Search of a Theory: A Critical Examination of the Relationships among Social Performance, Social Disclosure, and Economic Performance of U.S. Firms," *Academy of Management Review*, July 1985, pp. 540–557.

14. B. Seifert, S. A. Morris, and B. R. Bartkus, "Having, Giving, and Getting: Slack Resources, Corporate Philanthropy, and Firm Financial Performance," *Business & Society*, June 2004, pp. 135–161; and McGuire, Sundgren, and Schneeweis, "Corporate Social Responsibility and Firm Financial Performance."

15. A. McWilliams and D. Siegel, "Corporate Social Responsibility and Financial Performance: Correlation or Misspecification?" *Strategic Management Journal*, June 2000, pp. 603–609.

16. A. J. Hillman and G. D. Keim, "Shareholder Value, Stakeholder Management, and Social Issues: What's the Bottom Line?" *Strategic Management Journal*, vol. 22, 2001, pp. 125–139.

17. M. Orlitzky, F. L. Schmidt, and S. L. Rynes, "Corporate Social and Financial Performance," *Organization Studies*, vol. 24 (3), 2003, pp. 403–441.

18. Social Investment Forum, *2007 Report on Socially Responsible Investing Trends in the United States: 12-Year Review*, www.socialinvest.org.

19. Social Investment Forum, *Socially Responsible Mutual Fund Charts: Financial Performance*, February 29, 2008, www.socialinvest.org.

20. T. Delis, "Bag Revolution," *Fortune,* May 12, 2008, pp. 18–19; and E. Royte, "Moneybags," *Fast Company*, October 2007, p. 64.

21. M. Conlin, "Sorry, I Composted Your Memorandum," *BusinessWeek*, February 18, 2008, p. 60; CBS News Online, "Whole Foods Switching to Wind Power," www.cbsnews.com, January 12, 2006; A. Aston and B. Helm, "Green Culture, Clean Strategies," *BusinessWeek*, December 12, 2005, p. 64; and J. Esty "Never Say Never," *Fast Company*, July 2004, p. 34.

22. A. White, "The Greening of the Balance Sheet," *Harvard Business Review*, March 2006, pp. 27–28; N. Guenster, J. Derwall, R. Bauer, and K. Koedijk, "The Economic Value of Eco-Efficiency," *Academy of Management Conference*, Honolulu, Hawaii, August 2005; F. Bowen and S. Sharma, "Resourcing Corporate Environmental Strategy: Behavioral and Resource-Based Perspectives," *Academy of Management Conference*, August 2005; M. P. Sharfman, T. M. Shaft, and L. Tihanyi, "A Model of the Global and Institutional Antecedents of High-Level Corporate Environmental Performance," *Business & Society*, March 2004, pp. 6–36; S. L. Hart and M. B. Milstein, "Creating Sustainable Value," *Academy of Management Executive*, May 2003, pp. 56–67; K. Buysse and A. Verbeke, "Proactive Environmental Strategies: A

Stakeholder Management Perspective," *Strategic Management Journal,* May 2003, pp. 453–470; C. Marsden, "The New Corporate Citizenship of Big Business: Part of the Solution to Sustainability?" *Business & Society Review,* Spring 2000, pp. 9–25; R. D. Klassen and D. C. Whybark, "The Impact of Environmental Technologies on Manufacturing Performance," *Academy of Management Journal,* December 1999, pp. 599–615; H. Bradbury and J. A. Clair, "Promoting Sustainable Organizations With Sweden's Natural Step," *Academy of Management Executive,* October 1999, pp. 63–73; F. L. Reinhardt, "Bringing the Environment Down to Earth," *Harvard Business Review,* July–August 1999, pp. 149–157; I. Henriques and P. Sadorsky, "The Relationship Between Environmental Commitment and Managerial Perceptions of Stakeholder Importance," *Academy of Management Journal,* February 1999, pp. 87–99; and M. A. Berry and D. A. Rondinelli, "Proactive Corporate Environmental Management: A New Industrial Revolution," *Academy of Management Executive,* May 1998, pp. 38–50.

23. The concept of shades of green can be found in R. E. Freeman, J. Pierce, and R. Dodd, *Shades of Green: Business Ethics and the Environment* (New York: Oxford University Press, 1995).

24. Information from ISO Web site, www.iso.org.

25. The Global 100 list is a collaborative effort of Corporate Knights Inc. and Innovest Strategic Value Advisors. Information from Global 100 Web site, www.global100.org.

26. C. Chandler, "Livedoor Slammed," *Fortune,* February 20, 2006, p. 25; "$64B Diamond Industry Rocked by Fraud," *CNNMoney,* cnnmoney.com, December 20, 2005; D. Searcey, S. Young, and K. Scannell, "Ebbers Is Sentenced to 25 Years for $11 Billion WorldCom Fraud," *Wall Street Journal,* July 14, 2005, p. A1+; and E. B. Smith, "Wal-Mart Sets New Policy on Ethics," *USA Today,* January 28, 2005, p. 1B.

27. This last example is based on J. F. Viega, T. D. Golden, and K. Dechant, "Why Managers Bend Company Rules," *Academy of Management Executive,* May 2004, pp. 84–90.

28. Davis and Frederick, *Business and Society,* p. 76.

29. F. D. Sturdivant, *Business and Society: A Managerial Approach,* 3d ed. (Homewood, IL: Richard D. Irwin, 1985), p. 128.

30. L. K. Treviño, G. R. Weaver, and S. J. Reynolds, "Behavioral Ethics in Organizations: A Review," *Journal of Management,* December 2006, pp. 951–990; T. Kelley, "To Do Right or Just to Be Legal," *New York Times,* February 8, 1998, p. BU12; J. W. Graham, "Leadership, Moral Development, and Citizenship Behavior," *Business Ethics Quarterly,* January 1995, pp. 43–54; L. Kohlberg, *Essays in Moral Development: The Psychology of Moral Development,* vol. 2 (New York: Harper & Row, 1984); and L. Kohlberg, *Essays in Moral Development: The Philosophy of Moral Development,* vol. 1 (New York: Harper & Row, 1981).

31. See, for example, J. Weber, "Managers' Moral Reasoning: Assessing Their Responses to Three Moral Dilemmas," *Human Relations,* July 1990, pp. 687–702.

32. W. C. Frederick and J. Weber, "The Value of Corporate Managers and Their Critics: An Empirical Description and Normative Implications," in W. C. Frederick and L. E. Preston (eds.), *Business Ethics: Research Issues and Empirical Studies* (Greenwich, CT: JAI Press, 1990), pp. 123–144; and J. H. Barnett and M. J. Karson, "Personal Values and Business Decisions: An Exploratory Investigation," *Journal of Business Ethics,* July 1987, pp. 371–382.

33. M. E. Baehr, J. W. Jones, and A. J. Nerad, "Psychological Correlates of Business Ethics Orientation in Executives," *Journal of Business and Psychology,* Spring 1993, pp. 291–308; and L. K. Treviño and S. A. Youngblood, "Bad Apples in Bad Barrels: A Causal Analysis of Ethical Decision-Making Behavior," *Journal of Applied Psychology,* August 1990, pp. 378–385.

34. M. E. Schweitzer, L. Ordonez, and B. Douma, "Goal Setting as a Motivator of Unethical Behavior," *Academy of Management Journal,* June 2004, pp. 422–432.

35. M. C. Jensen, "Corporate Budgeting Is Broken—Let's Fix It," *Harvard Business Review,* June 2001, pp. 94–101.

36. R. L. Cardy and T. T. Selvarajan, "Assessing Ethical Behavior Revisited: The Impact of Outcomes on Judgment Bias," paper presented at the Annual Meeting of the Academy of Management, Toronto, 2000.

37. G. Weaver, "Ethics and Employees: Making the Connection," *Academy of Management Executive,* May 2004, pp. 121–125; V. Anand, B. E. Ashforth, and M. Joshi, "Business as Usual: The Acceptance and Perpetuation of Corruption in Organizations," *Academy of Management Executive,* May 2004, pp. 39–53; J. Weber, L. B. Kurke, and D. W. Pentico, "Why Do Employees Steal?" *Business & Society,* September 2003, pp. 359–380; V. Arnold and J. C. Lampe, "Understanding the Factors Underlying Ethical Organizations: Enabling Continuous Ethical Improvement," *Journal of Applied Business Research,* Summer 1999, pp. 1–19; R. R. Sims, "The Challenge of Ethical Behavior in Organizations," *Journal of Business Ethics,* July 1992, pp. 505–513; and J. B. Cullen, B. Victor, and C. Stephens, "An Ethical Weather Report: Assessing the Organization's Ethical Climate," *Organizational Dynamics,* Autumn 1989, pp. 50–62; and B. Victor and J. B. Cullen, "The Organizational Bases of Ethical Work Climates," *Adminis-trative Science Quarterly,* March 1988, pp. 101–125.

38. P. Van Lee, L. Fabish, and N. McCaw, "The Value of Corporate Values," *Strategy & Business*, Summer 2005, pp. 52–65.

39. G. Weaver, "Ethics and Employees: Making the Connection," May 2004; G. R. Weaver, L. K. Treviño, and P. L. Cochran, "Integrated and Decoupled Corporate Social Performance: Management Commitments, External Pressures, and Corporate Ethics Practices," *Academy of Management Journal*, October 1999, pp. 539–552; G. R. Weaver, L. K. Treviño, and P. L. Cochran, "Corporate Ethics Programs as Control Systems: Influences of Executive Commitment and Environmental Factors," *Academy of Management Journal*, February 1999, pp. 41–57; R. B. Morgan, "Self- and Co-Worker Perceptions of Ethics and Their Relationships to Leadership and Salary," *Academy of Management Journal*, February 1993, pp. 200–214; and B. Z. Posner and W. H. Schmidt, "Values and the American Manager: An Update," *California Management Review*, Spring 1984, pp. 202–216.

40. IBM Corporate Responsibility Report, 2007, www.ibm.com; and A. Schultz, "Integrating IBM," *CRO Newsletter*, March/April 2007, pp. 16–21.

41. T. Barnett, "Dimensions of Moral Intensity and Ethical Decision Making: An Empirical Study," *Journal of Applied Social Psychology*, May 2001, pp. 1038–1057; and T. M. Jones, "Ethical Decision Making by Individuals in Organizations: An Issue-Contingent Model," *Academy of Management Review*, April 1991, pp. 366–395.

42. W. Bailey and A. Spicer, "When Does National Identity Matter? Convergence and Divergence in International Business Ethics," *Academy of Management Journal*, December 2007, pp. 1462–1480; and R. L. Sims, "Comparing Ethical Attitudes Across Cultures," *Cross Cultural Management: An International Journal*, vol. 13 (2), 2006, pp. 101–113.

43. "Legal Review of Overseas Bribery," *BBC News* online, http://news.bbc.co.uk, November 29, 2007.

44. U.S. Department of Justice, *Fact Sheet*, March 27, 2008.

45. L. Paine, R. Deshpande, J. D. Margolis, and K. E. Bettcher, "Up to Code: Does Your Company's Conduct Meet World-Class Standards?" *Harvard Business Review*, December 2005, pp. 122–133; G. R. Simpson, "Global Heavyweights Vow 'Zero Tolerance' for Bribes," *Wall Street Journal*, January 27, 2005, pp. A2+; A. Spicer, T. W. Dunfee, and W. J. Bailey, "Does National Context Matter in Ethical Decision Making? An Empirical Test of Integrative Social Contracts Theory," *Academy of Management Journal*, August 2004, pp. 610–620; J. White and S. Taft, "Frameworks for Teaching and Learning Business Ethics Within the Global Context: Background of Ethical Theories," *Journal of Management Education*, August 2004, pp. 463–477; J. Guyon, "CEOs on Managing Globally," *Fortune*, July 26, 2004, p. 169; A. B. Carroll, "Managing Ethically with Global Stakeholders: A Present and Future Challenge," *Academy of Management Executive*, May 2004, pp. 114–120; and C. J. Robertson and W. F. Crittenden, "Mapping Moral Philosophies: Strategic Implications for Multinational Firms," *Strategic Management Journal*, April 2003, pp. 385–392.

46. "The New Social Steward," *Fortune*, Special Advertising Section, November 12, 2007, pp. 57–63; and A. Savitz and M. Choi, "The Future of the Global Compact," *CRO Newsletter*, January/February 2007, pp. 47–48.

47. Organization for Economic Cooperation and Development, "About Bribery in International Business," www.oecd.org, March 28, 2008.

48. Enron example taken from P. M. Lencioni, "Make Your Values Mean Something," *Harvard Business Review*, July 2002, p. 113; and Sears example taken from series of posters called "Sears Ethics and Business Practices: A Century of Tradition," *Business Ethics*, May/June 1999, pp. 12–13; and B. J. Feder, "The Harder Side of Sears," *New York Times*, July 20, 1997, pp. BU1+.

49. Treviño and Youngblood, "Bad Apples in Bad Barrels," p. 384.

50. J. L. Lunsford, "Transformer in Transition," *Wall Street Journal*, May 17, 2007, pp. B1+; and J. S. McClenahen, "UTC's Master of Principle," *IndustryWeek*, January 2003, pp. 30–36.

51. M. Weinstein, "Survey Says: Ethics Training Works," *Training*, November 2005, p. 15.

52. J. E. Fleming, "Codes of Ethics for Global Corporations," *Academy of Management News*, June 2005, p. 4.

53. "Global Ethics Codes Gain Importance as a Tool to Avoid Litigation and Fines," *Wall Street Journal*, August 19, 1999, p. A1; and J. Alexander, "On the Right Side," *World Business*, January/February 1997, pp. 38–41.

54. F. R. David, "An Empirical Study of Codes of Business Ethics: A Strategic Perspective," paper presented at the 48th Annual Academy of Management Conference, Anaheim, California, August 1988.

55. *National Business Ethics Survey* (Arlington, VA: Ethics Resource Center, 2007).

56. Codes of conduct information from the Center for Ethical Business Cultures Web site, www.cebcglobal.org, February 15, 2006; Paine, et al., "Up to Code: Does Your Company's Conduct Meet World-Class Standards"; and A. K. Reichert and M. S. Webb, "Corporate Support for Ethical and Environmental Policies: A Financial Management Perspective," *Journal of Business Ethics*, May 2000, pp. 53–64.

57. L. Nash, "Ethics Without the Sermon," *Harvard Business Review*, November–December 1981, p. 81.

58. V. Wessler, "Integrity and Clogged Plumbing," *Straight to the Point*, Fall 2002, pp. 1–2.

59. T. A. Gavin, "Ethics Education," *Internal Auditor*, April 1989, pp. 54–57.

60. L. Myyry and K. Helkama, "The Role of Value Priorities and Professional Ethics Training in Moral Sensitivity," *Journal of Moral Education*, vol. 31 (1), 2002, pp. 35–50; and W. Penn and B. D. Collier, "Current Research in Moral Development as a Decision Support System," *Journal of Business Ethics*, January 1985, pp. 131–136.

61. J. A. Byrne, "After Enron: The Ideal Corporation," *BusinessWeek*, August 19, 2002, pp. 68–71; D. Rice and C. Dreilinger, "Rights and Wrongs of Ethics Training," *Training & Development Journal*, May 1990, pp. 103–109; and J. Weber, "Measuring the Impact of Teaching Ethics to Future Managers: A Review, Assessment, and Recommendations," *Journal of Business Ethics*, April 1990, pp. 182–190.

62. E. White, "What Would You Do? Ethics Courses Get Context," *Wall Street Journal*, June 12, 2006, p. B3; and D. Zielinski, "The Right Direction: Can Ethics Training Save Your Company," *Training*, June 2005, pp. 27–32.

63. G. Farrell and J. O'Donnell, "Ethics Training As Taught by Ex-Cons: Crime Doesn't Pay," *USA Today*, November 16, 2005, p. 1B+.

64. J. Weber, "The New Ethics Enforcers," *BusinessWeek*, February 13, 2006, pp. 76–77.

65. The Ethics and Compliance Officer Association Web site, www.theecoa.org; and K. Maher, "Global Companies Face Reality of Instituting Ethics Programs," *Wall Street Journal*, November 9, 2004, p. B8.

66. Ethics Newsline, "Survey Reveals How Many Workers Commit Office Taboos," www.globalethics .org, September 18, 2007.

67. H. Oh, "Biz Majors Get an F for Honesty," *BusinessWeek*, February 6, 2006, p. 14.

68. "Students Aren't Squealers," *USA Today*, March 27, 2003, p. 1D; and J. Merritt, "You Mean Cheating Is Wrong?" *BusinessWeek*, December 9, 2002, p. 8.

69. J. Hyatt, "Unethical Behavior: Largely Unreported in Offices and Justified by Teens," *CRO Newsletter* online, www.thecro.com/enewsletter, February 13, 2008.

70. D. Lidsky, "Transparency: It's Not Just for Shrink Wrap Anymore," *Fast Company*, January 2005, p. 87.

71. W. Zellner, et al., "A Hero—And a Smoking-Gun Letter," *BusinessWeek*, January 28, 2002, pp. 34–35.

72. *National Business Ethics Survey* (Arlington, VA: Ethics Resource Center, 2007).

73. S. Armour, "More Companies Urge Workers to Blow the Whistle," *USA Today*, December 16, 2002, p. 1B.

74. J. Wiscombe, "Don't Fear Whistleblowers," *Workforce*, July 2002, pp. 26–27.

75. T. Reason, "Whistle Blowers: The Untouchables," *CFO*, March 2003, p. 18; and C. Lachnit, "Muting the Whistle-Blower?" *Workforce*, September 2002, p. 18.

76. J. Hyatt, "Corporate Whistleblowers Might Need a Monetary Nudge, Researchers Suggest," *CRO Newsletter* online, www.thecro.com/enewsletter, April 11, 2007; J. O'Donnell, "Blowing the Whistle Can Lead to Harsh Aftermath, Despite Law," *USA Today*, August 1, 2005, p. 2B; and D. Solomon, "For Financial Whistle-Blowers, New Shield Is an Imperfect One," *Wall Street Journal*, October 4, 2004, pp. A1+.

77. B. Dobbin, "Dealers Market Global Trade with Social Conscience," The Associated Press, *Springfield Missouri) News-Leader*, February 16, 2005, p. 5B.

78. This definition based on P. Tracey and N. Phillips, "The Distinctive Challenge of Educating Social Entrepreneurs: A Postscript and Rejoinder to the Special Issue on Entrepreneurship Education," *Academy of Management Learning & Education*, June 2007, pp. 264–271; Schwab Foundation for Social Entrepreneurship, www.schwabfound.org, February 20, 2006; and J. G. Dees, J. Emerson, and P. Economy, *Strategic Tools for Social Entrepreneurs* (New York: John Wiley & Sons, Inc., 2002).

79. D. Bornstein, *How to Change the World: Social Entrepreneurs and the Power of New Ideas* (New York: Oxford University Press, 2004), inside cover jacket.

80. K. Greene, "Tapping Talent, Experience of Those Age 60-Plus," *Wall Street Journal*, November 29, 2005, p. B12.

81. K. H. Hammonds, "Now the Good News," *Fast Company*, December 2007/ January 2008, pp. 110–121; C. Dahle, "Filling the Void," *Fast Company*, January/February 2006, pp. 54–57; and PATH Web site, www.path.org.

82. R. J. Bies, J. M. Bartunek, T. L. Fort, and M. N Zald, "Corporations as Social Change Agents: Individual, Interpersonal, Institutional, and Environmental Dynamics," *Academy of Management Review*, July 2007, pp. 788–793.

83. "The State of Corporate Philanthropy: A McKinsey Global Survey," *The McKinsey Quarterly* online, www.mckinseyquarterly.com, February 2008.

84. R. Nixon, The Associated Press, "Bottom Line for (Red)," *New York Times* online, www.nytimes.com, February 6, 2008; and G. Mulvihill, "Despite Cause, Not Everyone Tickled Pink by Campaign,"

Springfield Missouri News-Leader, October 15, 2007, p. 2E.

85. C. Wilson, "How Companies Dig Deep," *Business-Week*, November 26, 2007, pp. 52–54.

86. K. J. Delaney, "Google: From 'Don't Be Evil' to How to Do Good," *Wall Street Journal*, January 18, 2008, pp. B1+; H. Rubin, "Google Offers a Map for Its Philanthropy," *New York Times* online, www. nytimes.com, January 18, 2008; and K. Hafner, "Philanthropy Google's Way: Not the Usual," *New York Times* online, www.nytimes.com, September 14, 2006.

87. Committee Encouraging Corporate Philanthropy, www.corporatephilanthropy.org, April 7, 2008; "Investing in Society," *Leaders*, July–September 2007, pp. 12+; M. C. White, "Doing Good on Company Time," *New York Times* online, www.nytimes.com, May 8, 2007; and M. Lowery, "How Volunteerism is Changing the Face of Philanthropy," *DiversityInc*, December 2006, pp. 45–47.

Ethics of Managers and Social Responsibility of Business

Ethics of Managers and Social Responsibility of Business

> ❝*Ethical considerations can no more be excluded from the administration of justice, which is the end and purpose of all civil laws, than one can exclude the vital air from his room and live.* ❞
>
> —JOHN F. DILLON
> Laws and Jurisprudence of England and America Lecture I (1894)

CHAPTER OBJECTIVES

After studying this chapter, you should be able to:

1. Describe how law and ethics intertwine.
2. Describe the moral theories of business ethics.
3. Describe the theories of the social responsibility of business.
4. Describe corporate social audits.
5. Examine how international ethical standards differ from country to country.

CHAPTER CONTENTS

- Introduction to Ethics of Managers and Social Responsibility of Business
- Ethics and the Law
- Business Ethics
- Social Responsibility of Business
- Chapter Summary
- Test Review Terms and Concepts
- Case Problems
- Ethics Issues

Introduction to Ethics of Managers and Social Responsibility of Business

Businesses organized in the United States are subject to its laws. They are also subject to the laws of other countries in which they operate. In addition, businesspersons owe a duty to act ethically in the conduct of their affairs, and businesses owe a social responsibility not to harm society.

Although much of the law is based on ethical standards, not all ethical standards have been enacted as law. The law establishes a minimum degree of conduct expected by persons and businesses in society. Ethics demands more. This chapter discusses business ethics and the social responsibility of business.

Myanmar

Some companies refuse to do business with Myanmar because of allegations that its military-led government engages in humanitarian violations.

Ethics and the Law

Sometimes the rule of law and the golden rule of **ethics** demand the same response by a person confronted with a problem. For example, federal and state laws make bribery unlawful. A person violates the law if he or she bribes a judge for a favorable decision in a case. Ethics would also prohibit this conduct. However, the law may permit something that would be ethically wrong.

Example Occupational safety laws set standards for emissions of dust from toxic chemicals in the workplace. Suppose a company can reduce the emission below the legal standard by spending additional money. The only benefit from the expenditure would be better employee health. Ethics would require the extra expenditure; the law would not.

Another alternative occurs where the law demands certain conduct but a person's ethical standards are contrary.

Example Federal law prohibits employees from hiring certain illegal alien workers. Suppose an employer advertises the availability of a job and receives no response except from a person who cannot prove he or she is a citizen of this country or does not posses a required visa. The worker and his or her family are destitute. Should the employer hire him or her? The law says no, but ethics says yes (see Exhibit 1).

Ethics precede laws as man precedes society.

Jason Alexander
Philosophy for Investors (1979)

Law   Ethics

EXHIBIT 1

Law and Ethics

239

He who seeks equality must do equity.

Joseph Story
Equity Jurisprudence (1836)

Business Ethics

How can ethics be measured? The answer is very personal: What is considered ethical by one person may be considered unethical by another. However, there do seem to be some universal rules about what conduct is ethical and what conduct is not. The following discussion highlights five major theories of ethics.

ETHICS SPOTLIGHT

Wal-Mart Pays Big for Meal Break Violations

> **"** *At Wal-Mart, not only is there no such thing as a free lunch for employees but, in this sad case, there is no lunch at all.* **"**
>
> —Wal-Mart Watch

In recent years, the retail giant Wal-Mart has been the target of hundreds of lawsuits by employees in dozens of states, claiming the company violated wage-and-hour laws. In Colorado, Wal-Mart settled with a group of employees for $50 million because of denied meal break violations. In Oregon, workers were rewarded with nearly $2,000 each for similar violations.

A group of California Wal-Mart employees became the first in a series of class-action lawsuits involving the denied meal breaks. In *Wal-Mart Stores v. S.C. (Savaglio),* **Web** 2004 Cal. Lexis 3284 (Supreme Court of California, 2004), both current and former employees argued that Wal-Mart had violated California's meal period law. Wal-Mart fought back, saying that it didn't break any law.

The Oakland, California, jury watched four months of testimony and deliberated for three days before coming back with its verdict: 116,000 current and former Wal-Mart employees were to receive $172 million in general and punitive damages. Wal-Mart employees and community activists felt vindicated and insisted that the company fix the broken system. Wal-Mart Watch, a union-backed group that keeps a very close eye on everything the company does, commented, "At Wal-Mart, not only is there no such thing as a free lunch for employees but, in this sad case, there is no lunch at all."

Less than a year after the meal break case, Wal-Mart was in court in Pennsylvania. This time the jury hit the company with over $78 million in damages for forcing employees to work "off the clock" and during rest breaks.

Law & Ethics Questions

1. **ETHICS** Did Wal-Mart act ethically in this case?
2. **ETHICS** Why does Wal-Mart engage in such practices?

Web Exercises

1. WEB Visit the website of Wal-Mart, at *www.walmart.com.*
2. WEB Use *www.google.com* to find a recent case in which Wal-Mart has been found to engage in an illegal activity.
3. WEB Use *www.google.com* to find Wal-Mart's code of ethics.
4. WEB Visit the website of the Wal-Mart watchdog group, at *www.walmartwatch.com.* What is one of the current issues discussed?

Ethical Fundamentalism

Under **ethical fundamentalism**, a person looks to an *outside source* for ethical rules or commands. This may be a book (e.g., the Bible, the Koran) or a person (e.g., Karl Marx). Critics argue that ethical fundamentalism does not permit people to determine right and wrong for themselves. Taken to an extreme, the result could be considered unethical under most other moral theories. For example, a literal interpretation of the maxim "an eye for an eye" would permit retaliation.

ETHICS SPOTLIGHT

Qui Tam Lawsuit

The Bayer Corporation (Bayer) is a U.S. subsidiary corporation of giant German-based Bayer A.G. Bayer is a large pharmaceutical company that produces prescription drugs, including its patented antibiotic Cipro. Bayer sold Cipro to private health providers and hospitals, including Kaiser Permanente Medical Care Program, the largest health maintenance organization in the United States. Bayer also sold Cipro to the federal government's Medicaid program, which provides medical insurance to the poor. Federal law contains a "best price" rule that prohibits a company that sells a drug to Medicaid to charge Medicaid a price higher than the lowest price for which it sells the drug to private purchasers.

Kaiser told Bayer that it would not purchase Cipro from Bayer—and would switch to a competitor's antibiotics—unless Bayer reduced the price of Cipro. Bayer's executives came up with a plan whereby Bayer would put a private label on its Cipro and not call it Cipro and sell the antibiotic to Kaiser at a 40 percent discount. Thus, Bayer continued to charge Medicaid the full price for Cipro while giving Kaiser a 40 percent discount through the private labeling program. One of Bayer's executives who negotiated this deal with Kaiser was corporate account manager George Couto.

Everything went well for Bayer until Couto attended a mandatory ethics training class at Bayer at which a video of Heige Wehmeier, then company chief executive, was shown. When the video stated that Bayer employees were to obey not only "the letter of the law but the spirit of the law as well," some of the Bayer executives laughed. Later that day, Couto attended a staff meeting at which it was disclosed that Bayer kept $97 million from Medicaid by using the discounted private labeling program for Kaiser and other health care companies. Two days later, Couto wrote a memorandum to his boss, questioning the legality of the private labeling program in light of Medicaid's "best price" law.

When he received no response to his memo, Couto contacted a lawyer. Couto filed a ***qui tam*** lawsuit under the federal **False Claims Act**—also known as the **Whistleblower Statute**—which permits private parties to sue companies for fraud on behalf of the government. The riches: The whistleblower can be awarded up to 25 percent of the amount recovered on behalf of the federal government, even if the informer has been a co-conspirator in perpetrating the fraud.

Once the case was filed, the U.S. Department of Justice took over the case, as allowed by law, and filed criminal as well as civil charges against Bayer. After discovery was taken, Bayer pleaded guilty to one criminal felony and agreed to pay federal and state governments $257 million to settle the civil and criminal cases. Couto, age 39, died of pancreatic cancer three months prior to the settlement. Couto was awarded $34 million, which will go to his three children. *United States v. Bayer Corporation*.

Law & Ethics Questions

1. **ETHICS** Was it very difficult for the Bayer executives to devise the private labeling plan to cheat the federal government?

2. **ETHICS** Did Couto act ethically in this case? Should a fraudulent co-conspirator be allowed to recover an award under the Whistleblower Statute? Explain.

Web Exercises

1. **WEB** Visit the website of the Bayer Corporation, at *www.bayer.com*. Can you find the corporation's code of ethics?

2. **WEB** Use *www.google.com* to find an article that discusses a recent application of the Whistleblower Statute.

Utilitarianism

Utilitarianism is a moral theory with origins in the works of Jeremy Bentham (1748–1832) and John Stuart (1806–1873). This moral theory dictates that people must choose the actions or follow the rule that provides the *greatest good to society*. This does not mean the greatest good for the greatest number of people. For instance, if an action would increase the good of 25 people 1 unit each and an alternative action would increase the good of 1 person 26 units, the latter action should be taken.

Utilitarianism has been criticized because it is difficult to estimate the "good" that will result from different actions, it is hard to apply in an imperfect world, and it treats morality as if it were an impersonal mathematical calculation.

Example A company is trying to determine whether it should close an unprofitable plant located in a small community. Utilitarianism would require that the benefits to shareholders from closing the plant be compared to the benefits to employees, their families, and others in the community in keeping it open.

The following case examined the ethics of a fast-food restaurant chain.

Bradley v. McDonald's Corporation

Web 2003 U.S. Dist. Lexis 15202 (2003)
United States District Court for the Southern District of New York

> "Advertising campaigns run by McDonald's claimed that it sold "Good basic nutritious food. Food that's been the foundation of well-balanced diets for generations. And will be for generations to come.""

—Judge Sweet

Facts

McDonald's Corporation operates the largest fast-food restaurant chain in the United States and the world. It produces such famous foods as the "Big Mac" hamburger, chicken McNuggets, the egg McMuffin, French fries, shakes, and other foods. A McDonald's survey showed that 22% of its customers are "Super Heavy Users," meaning that they eat at McDonald's 10 times or more a month. Super Heavy Users make up approximately 75% of McDonald's sales. The survey also found that 72% of McDonald's customers were "Heavy Users," meaning they ate at McDonald's at least once a week.

Jazlyn Bradley consumed McDonald's foods her entire life during school lunch breaks and before and after school, approximately five times per week, ordering two meals per day. When Bradley was 19 years old, she sued McDonald's Corporation for causing her obesity and health problems associated with obesity.

Plaintiff Bradley sued McDonald's in U.S. District Court for violating the New York Consumer Protection Act, which prohibits deceptive and unfair acts and practices. She alleged that McDonald's misled her, through its advertising campaigns and other publicity, that its food products were nutritious, of a beneficial nutritional nature, and easily part of a healthy lifestyle if consumed on a daily basis. The plaintiff sued on behalf of herself and a class of minors residing in New York State who purchased and consumed McDonald's products. McDonald's filed a motion with the U.S. District Court to dismiss the plaintiff's complaint.

Issue

Did the plaintiff state a valid case against McDonald's for deceptive and unfair acts and practices in violation of the New York Consumer Protection Act?

Language of the Court

It is well-known that fast food in general, and McDonald's products in particular, contain high levels of cholesterol, fat, salt and sugar, and that such attributes are bad for one. The plaintiff therefore either knew or should have known enough of the critical facts of her injury that her claims accrued upon being injured. The complaint does specify how often the plaintiff ate at McDonald's. Jazlyn Bradley is alleged to have "consumed McDonald's foods her entire life during school lunch breaks and before and after school, approximately five times per week, ordering two meals per day."

What the plaintiff has not done, however, is to address the role that a number of other factors other than diet may come to play in obesity and the health problems of which the plaintiff complains. In order to allege that McDonald's products were a significant factor in the plaintiff's obesity and health problems, the complaint must address these other variables and, if possible, eliminate them or show that a McDiet is a substantial factor despite these other variables. Similarly, with regards to plaintiff's health problems that she claims resulted from her obesity, it would be necessary to allege that such diseases were not merely hereditary or caused by environmental or other factors. Without this additional information, McDonald's does not have sufficient information to determine if its foods are the cause of the plaintiff's obesity, or if instead McDonald's foods are only a contributing factor.

Decision

The U.S. District Court granted the motion of defendant McDonald's to dismiss the plaintiff's complaint. *Note:* Because of this case and other threatened obesity-related litigation, fast-food franchisors introduced salads, low-fat fare, and low-carb offerings to their menus.

Law & Ethics Questions

1. What is the purpose of consumer protection laws?

2. **ETHICS** Do you think McDonald's has a duty to warn consumers of the dangers of eating its fast food? Do parents owe a duty to their children not to let them eat fast food too often?

3. What would have been the effect on McDonald's and other fast-food companies if the plaintiff had won her lawsuit against McDonald's? Explain.

Web Exercises

1. WEB For the complete opinion of this case, go to *www.prenhall.com/cheesemancases*.

2. WEB Visit the website of the United States District Court for the Southern District of New York, at *www.nysd.uscourts.gov*.

3. WEB Visit the website of McDonald's Corporation, at *www.mcdonalds.com*. Can you find the corporation's code of ethics?

4. WEB Use *www.google.com* to find the nutrition facts about BigMacs, French fries, and chocolate shakes.

ETHICS SPOTLIGHT
New York City Bans Trans Fats

Amid the controversy around how to handle the country's increasing weight problem, New York City's Board of Health voted unanimously to ban nearly all the artificial trans fats from the city's 24,000 restaurants. This is believed to be the first law of its kind in the nation and could possibly lead to other cities creating similar laws.

Trans fats are the artery-clogging cooking oils that are used in foods such as French fries, donuts, pies, chips, cookies, and even bread. Trans fats are known to dramatically increase the risk of heart disease and stroke, even more than the better-known saturated fats. They do so by raising bad cholesterol while simultaneously lowering good cholesterol. Restaurants were given 18 months to phase out the oils and find safer alternatives.

While health officials and consumers around the country praised the new law, not everyone was happy. Restaurant owners argued that getting rid of trans fats should be on a voluntary basis only and that the government should not force the issue. The National Restaurant Association threatened to sue the city because it feared the law would quickly spread across the nation, putting some restaurants out of business due to the high cost. But New York City's health commissioner, Thomas Frieden, called the matter a public health issue and applauded the Board of Health decision, saying that the new law could, "save between 200 and 500 lives per year."

Law & Ethics Questions

1. **ETHICS** Do food manufacturers, restaurants, and other food-service businesses owe a duty of social responsibility to warn consumers of dangerous propensities of the food they sell and serve?

2. **ETHICS** Why do food companies use trans fats in their products? Should food companies voluntarily remove all trans fats from their products?

3. **ETHICS** Should New York City have enacted this law? Why or why not?

Web Exercises

1. **WEB USE** *www.google.com* to find an article that discusses the health risks of trans fats.

2. **WEB** To read more about New York City's new law, visit *www.nyc.gov/html/doh/html/cardio/cardio-transfat.shtml.*

Kantian Ethics

Immanuel Kant (1724–1804) is the best-known proponent of **duty ethics**, also called **Kantian ethics**. Kant believed that people owe moral duties that are based on *universal* rules. For example, keeping a promise to abide by a contract is a moral duty even if that contract turns out to be detrimental to the obligated party. Kant's philosophy is based on the premise that people can use reasoning to reach ethical decisions. His ethical theory would have people behave according to the *categorical imperative* "Do unto others as you would have them do unto you."

The universal rules of Kantian ethics are based on two important principles: (1) consistency—that is, all cases are treated alike, with no exceptions—and (2) reversibility—that is, the actor must abide by the rule he or she uses to judge the morality of someone else's conduct. Thus, if you are going to make an exception for yourself, that exception becomes a universal rule that applies to all others. For example, if you rationalize that it is all right for you to engage in deceptive practices, it is all right for competitors to do so also. A criticism of Kantian ethics is that it is hard to reach a consensus as to what the universal rules should be.

In the following case, a company alleged that a competitor had engaged in false advertising.

CASE 2
Ethics

Pizza Hut, Inc. v. Papa John's International, Inc.

227 F.3d 489, **Web** 2000 U.S. App. Lexis 23444 (2000)
United States Court of Appeals for the Fifth Circuit

> ❝This simple statement, "Better Pizza.," epitomizes the exaggerated advertising, blustering and boasting by a manufacturer upon which no consumer would reasonably rely. ❞
>
> —Judge Jolly

Facts

Papa John's International, Inc., is the third-largest pizza chain in the United States, with more than 2,050 locations. Papa John's adopted a new slogan—"Better Ingredients. Better Pizza."—and applied for and received a federal trademark for this slogan. Papa John's spent over $300 million building customer recognition and goodwill for this slogan. This slogan has appeared on millions of signs, shirts, menus, pizza boxes, napkins, and other items, and it has regularly appeared as the tag line at the end of Papa John's radio and television advertisements.

Pizza Hut, Inc., is the largest pizza chain in the United States, with more than 7,000 restaurants. Two years after Papa John's advertisements began, Pizza Hut launched a new advertising campaign in which it declared "war" on poor-quality pizza. The advertisements touted the "better taste" of Pizza Hut's pizza and "dared" anyone to find a better pizza.

A few weeks later, Papa John's countered with a comparative advertising campaign that touted the superiority of Papa John's pizza over Pizza Hut's pizza. Papa John's claimed it had superior sauce and dough to Pizza Hut. Many of these advertisements were accompanied by the Papa John's slogan "Better Ingredients. Better Pizza."

Pizza Hut filed a civil action in U.S. District Court, charging Papa John's with false advertising in violation of Section 43(a) of the federal Lanham Act. The U.S. District Court found that the Papa John's slogan "Better Ingredients. Better Pizza." standing alone was mere puffery and did not constitute false advertising. The District Court found, however, that Papa John's claims of superior sauce and dough were misleading and that Papa John's slogan "Better Ingredients. Better Pizza." became tainted because it was associated with these misleading statements. The U.S. District Court enjoined Papa John's from using the slogan "Better Ingredients. Better Pizza." Papa John's appealed.

Issue

Is the Papa John's slogan "Better Ingredients. Better Pizza." false advertising?

Language of the Court

Essential to any claim under Section 43(a) of the Lanham Act is a determination whether the challenged statement is one of fact—actionable under Section 43(a)—or one of general opinion—not actionable under Section 43(a). One form of non-actionable statements of general opinion under Section 43(a) of the Lanham Act has been referred to as "puffery." We think that non-actionable "puffery" comes in at least two possible forms: (1) an exaggerated, blustering, and boasting statement upon which no reasonable buyer would be justified in relying; or (2) a general claim of superiority over comparable products that is so vague that it can be understood as nothing more than a mere expression of opinion. Prosser and Keeton on the Law of Torts (5th edition) define "puffing" as "a seller's privilege to lie his head off, so long as he says nothing specific, on the theory that no reasonable man would believe him, or that no reasonable man would be influenced by such talk."

We turn now to consider the case before us. Reduced to its essence, the question is whether the evidence established that Papa John's slogan "Better Ingredients. Better Pizza." is misleading and violative of Section 43(a) of the Lanham Act. Bisecting the slogan "Better Ingredients. Better Pizza.," it is clear that the assertion by Papa John's that it makes a "Better Pizza." is a general statement of opinion regarding the superiority of its product over all others. This simple statement, "Better Pizza.," epitomizes the exaggerated advertising, blustering and boasting by a manufacturer upon which no consumer would reasonably rely. Consequently, it appears indisputable that Papa John's assertion "Better Pizza." is non-actionable puffery.

Moving next to consider the phrase "Better Ingredients," the same conclusion holds true. Like "Better Pizza." it is typical puffery. The word "better," when used in this context, is unquantifiable. What makes one food ingredient "better" than another comparable ingredient, without further description, is wholly a matter of individual taste or preference not subject to scientific quantification. Indeed, it is difficult to think of any product, or any component of any product, to which the term "better," without more quantifiable measurements. Thus, it is equally clear that Papa John's assertion that it uses "Better Ingredients." is one of opinion not actionable under the Lanham Act.

Consequently, the slogan as a whole is a statement of non-actionable opinion. Thus, there is no legally sufficient basis to support the jury's finding that the slogan is a "false or misleading" statement of fact.

Decision

The U.S. Court of Appeals held that the Papa John's trademarked slogan "Better Ingredients. Better Pizza." was mere puffery and a statement of opinion that was not false advertising and did not violate Section 43(a) of the Lanham Act. The U.S. Court of Appeals reversed the judgment of the U.S. District Court and remanded the case to the District Court for entry of judgment for Papa John's.

Law & Ethics Questions

1. What is false advertising? What is puffery? How do they differ from one another?

2. **ETHICS** Do businesses sometimes make exaggerated claims about their products? Are consumers smart enough to see through companies' puffery?

3. If the Court of Appeals had found in favor of Pizza Hut, what would have been the effect on advertising in this country? Explain.

Web Exercises

1. WEB For the complete opinion of this case, go to *www.prenhall.com/cheesemancases*.

2. WEB Visit the website of the United States Court of Appeals for the Fifth Circuit, at *www.ca5.uscourts.gov*.

3. WEB Visit the website of Papa John's International, Inc., at *www.papajohns.com*. Can you find the corporation's code of ethics?

4. WEB Visit the website of Pizza Hut, Inc., at *www.pizzahut.com*. Can you find the corporation's code of ethics?

5. WEB Use *www.google.com* to find a comparative advertising campaign. How exaggerated are the company's claims in this campaign?

ETHICS SPOTLIGHT

Procter & Gamble Wins "Satanism" Lawsuit

> ❝*The ram's horn will form the number 666, which is known as Satan's number.*❞
>
> —Amway distributor flier

A U.S. District Court jury found that the Devil is not in cahoots with Procter & Gamble (P&G), the world's largest consumer products company, and rewarded the company $19.25 million in unfair competition and false advertising damages. The verdict concluded a 12-year lawsuit in which P&G had accused four distributors of its rival, Amway Corporation, of propagating rumors that P&G was involved in Satanism and that the president of P&G had gone on national television to announce that a large portion of P&G profits would go to support the Church of Satan.

Procter & Gamble, the maker of such household names as Tide and Pampers, claimed in court documents that four Amway distributors had told customers that P&G's logo—which featured a bearded man looking over a field of 13 stars—was a symbol of Satan. P&G lawyers also produced a transcript of a voice mail message in which an Amway distributor could be heard alleging that the P&G president had avowed his personal allegiance to Satan on the *Phil Donahue* show, a nationally televised talk show. Other damaging evidence in trial was a written flier that spread like wildfire through mail, fax, and later e-mail that listed all of P&G's products and gave supposed details on the company's undying love for the Prince of Darkness. According to an Amway distributor flier:

> If you are not sure about the product, look for Procter & Gamble written on the products, or the symbol of a ram's horn, which will appear on each product beginning in April. The ram's horn will form the number 666, which is known as Satan's number.

The case was originally dismissed by a three-judge panel of the U.S. Circuit Court of Appeals, who proclaimed that the rumors were not defamatory and that P&G had not made a case for specific damages. However, P&G successfully got the case reinstated through further appeals. "This is about protecting our reputation," said Jim Johnson, P&G's chief legal officer. Amway, which focuses on direct selling through independent business owners, claimed that it acted quickly and thoroughly to stop the rumors, and the company was subsequently dismissed from the case, leaving only the four ex-distributors. "We are stunned. All of us," replied one of the distributors after the trial.

Law & Ethics Questions

1. **ETHICS** What is false advertising?
2. **ETHICS** Why did the Amway distributors make the claims about P&G that they did?

Web Exercises

1. **WEB** Visit the website of Proctor & Gamble, at *www.pg.com*. Locate P&G's logo.
2. **WEB** Visit the website of Amway Corporation, at *www.amway.com*. Can you find this corporation's code of ethics?
3. **WEB** Use *www.google.com* to find a recent article or website that criticizes P&G for Satanism.

Rawls's Social Justice Theory

John Locke (1632–1704) and Jean-Jacques Rousseau (1712–1778) proposed a **social contract** theory of morality. Under this theory, each person is presumed to have entered into a social contract with all others in society to obey moral rules that are necessary for people to live in peace and harmony. This implied contract states, "I will keep the rules if everyone else does." These moral rules are then used to solve conflicting interests in society.

The leading proponent of the modern justice theory is John Rawls, a contemporary philosopher at Harvard University. Under **Rawls's social justice theory**, fairness is considered the essence of justice. The principles of justice should be chosen by persons who do not yet know their station in society—thus, their "veil of ignorance" would permit the fairest possible principles to be selected. For example, the principle of equal opportunity would be promulgated by people who would not yet know if they were in a favored class. As a caveat, Rawls also propose that the least advantaged in society must receive special assistance to allow them to realize their potential.

Rawls's theory of social justice is criticized for two reasons. First, establishing the blind "original position" for choosing moral principles is impossible in the real world.

> The notion that a business is clothed with a public interest and has been devoted to the public use is little more than a fiction intended to beautify what is disagreeable to the sufferers.
>
> Justice Holmes
> *Tyson & Bro-United Theatre Ticket Officers v. Banton (1927)*

Second, many persons in society would choose not to maximize the benefit to the least advantaged persons in society.

In the following case, the U.S. Supreme Court examined the legality of giving gifts to politicians.

CASE 3

Ethics

U.S. SUPREME COURT

United States v. Sun-Diamond Growers of California

526 U.S. 398, 119 S.Ct. 1402, 143 L.Ed.2d 576,
Web 1999 U.S. Lexis 3001
Supreme Court of the United States

> 66 *The Solicitor General of the United States contends that the statute requires only a showing that a gift was motivated, at least in part, by the recipient's capacity to exercise governmental power or influence in the donor's favor without necessarily showing that it was connected to a particular official act.* 99

—Justice Scalia

Facts

The Sun-Diamond Growers of California is a trade association that engages in marketing and lobbying activities on behalf of its 5,000 member-growers of raisins, figs, walnuts, prunes, and hazelnuts. Sun-Diamond gave Michael Epsy, U.S. secretary of agriculture, tickets to sporting events (worth $2,295), luggage ($2,427), meals ($665), and a crystal bowl ($524) while several matters in which Sun-Diamond members had an interest in were pending before the secretary. The two matters were decided in Sun-Diamond's favor. The United States sued Sun-Diamond for making illegal gifts to a public official in violation of the federal antibribery and gratuity statute [18 U.S.C. Sections 201(b) and 201(c)]. The jury convicted Sun-Diamond, and the U.S. District Court ordered it to pay a fine of $400,000. The U.S. Court of Appeals reversed, finding that Sun-Diamond had not violated the federal antibribery and gratuity statute. The United States appealed to the U.S. Supreme Court.

Issue

Does a conviction under the federal antibribery and gratuity statute require a showing of a direct nexus between the value conferred on the public official and the official act performed by the public official in favor of the giver?

Language of the U.S. Supreme Court

The Solicitor General of the United States contends that the statute requires only a showing that a gift was motivated, at least in part, by the recipient's capacity to exercise governmental power or influence in the donor's favor without necessarily showing that it was connected to a particular official act. We are inclined to believe this meaning incorrect because

of the peculiar results that the government's reading would produce. It would criminalize, for example, token gifts to the President based on his official position and not linked to any identifiable act—such as the replica jerseys given by championship sports teams each year during ceremonial White House visits. Similarly, it would criminalize a high school principal's gift of a school baseball cap to the secretary of education, by reason of his office, on the occasion of the latter's visit to the school.

Decision

The U.S. Supreme Court held that there must be proof of a direct nexus between the gratuity given and the public official's act before the federal antibribery and gratuity statute is violated. Because no such direct nexus was proven in this case, there is no violation of the federal antibribery and gratuity statute. The U.S. Supreme Court affirmed the judgment of the U.S. Court of Appeals that found that Sun-Diamond had not violated the federal antibribery and gratuity statute.

Law & Ethics Questions

1. What does the federal antibribery and gratuity statute prohibit? Explain.
2. Do you think the Supreme Court should have read the statute so narrowly? Why or why not?
3. **ETHICS** Is it ethical for a government official to accept gifts and gratuities from parties who have actions or matters pending before the official? Do you think such gifts and gratuities are given with any return favor in mind?
4. **ETHICS** What is lobbying? Are there any winners and losers of successful lobbying? Explain.

Ethical Relativism

Ethical relativism holds that individuals must decide what is ethical based on their own feelings as to what is right or wrong. Under this moral theory, if a person meets his or her own moral standard in making a decision, no one can criticize him or her for it. Thus, there are no universal ethical rules to guide a person's conduct. This theory has been criticized because action that is usually thought to be unethical (e.g., committing fraud) would not be unethical if the perpetrator thought it was in fact ethical. Few philosophers advocate ethical relativism as an acceptable moral theory.

ETHICS SPOTLIGHT

Disney Loses "Pooh Bear" Lawsuit

For years, the Walt Disney Company had battled a Beverly Hills family over millions of dollars in Winnie the Pooh royalties. In early 2007, a federal judge dismissed Disney's lawsuit, essentially clearing the way for the family to seek its own lawsuit for lost profits and damages. The ruling was a major turning point in the legal copyright drama that has spanned decades.

In 1930, Stephen Slesinger, a cartoon character marketer, had acquired the rights to "Winnie the Pooh" merchandise from the author A.A. Milne. When Slesinger died in 1953, Shirley Slesinger, his widow, continued to market Pooh by herself. In 1961, the Slesingers dealt the Pooh rights to Disney in exchange for continuous royalty payments. Disney used its marketing might to turn the bear into its most profitable cartoon character, pulling in over $1 billion a year. In 1983, Mrs. Slesinger renegotiated the deal with Disney, agreeing that Disney would keep 98% of gross worldwide royalties and that the Slesingers would get the other 2%. Today, Disney makes over $6 billion annually from Winnie the Pooh sales and licensing.

One decade after granting Disney the Pooh rights, the Slesingers slapped Disney with a fraud and breach-of-contract lawsuit, alleging that the media giant had been cheating them out of hundreds of millions in profits from Pooh products. Specifically, the family accused Disney of failing to report Winnie the Pooh computer software and video sales of $3 billion, which would have brought the family tens of millions in royalties. The court appointed a task force of so-called forensic accountants to examine Disney's books, but before the court could rule, Disney produced evidence that the Slesingers had stolen confidential documents from the company's trash, lied about it, and altered court filings to cover it up. The judge dismissed the lawsuit with prejudice.

Disney wasn't finished, however. In 2002, the families of Pooh author A.A. Milne and illustrator E.H. Shepard filed a copyright lawsuit against the Slesingers which was funded by Walt Disney Co. The lawsuit sought to get all of the Pooh rights removed from the Slesingers and given to the other families, which in turn would revert them to Disney permanently. Disney hoped this would stop all royalty payments to the Slesingers and end the family's pending appeal for lost profits and damages. Unfortunately for Disney, that didn't happen.

In February 2007, U.S. District Court Judge Florence-Marie Cooper dismissed the Disney-sponsored lawsuit against the Slesingers. The Slesinger family immediately launched a $2 billion lawsuit against the company for damages, trademark and copyright infringement, breach of contract, and fraudulent underpayment of royalties. The long legal battle over Pooh is not yet over.

Law & Ethics Questions

1. What are royalty payments?
2. **ETHICS** How could the Slesinger family determine if Disney had been cheating them out of royalties over the years?

Web Exercises

1. WEB Visit the website of the Walt Disney Company, at *www.disney.com.*
2. WEB Find out all about Winnie the Pooh at *http://disney.go.com/characters/pooh/index.html.*

CONCEPT SUMMARY

Theories of Ethics

THEORY	DESCRIPTION
Ethical fundamentalism	Persons look to an outside source (e.g., the Bible, the Koran) or a central figure for ethical guidelines.
Utilitarianism	Persons choose the alternative that would provide the greatest good to society.
Kantian ethics	A set of universal rules establishes ethical duties. The rules are based on reasoning and require (1) consistency in application and (2) reversibility.
Rawls's social justice theory	Moral duties are based on an implied social contract. Fairness is justice. The rules are established from an original position of a "veil of ignorance."
Ethical relativism	Individuals decide what is ethical based on their own feelings as to what is right or wrong.

Vietnam

Many U.S. multinational corporations "outsource" the manufacture of goods to workers in foreign countries. The goods are then imported into the United States and sold to consumers. Are there any ethical problems with this practice?

Social Responsibility of Business

Businesses do not operate in a vacuum. Decisions made by businesses have far-reaching effects on society. In the past, many business decisions were based solely on a cost–benefit analysis and how they affected the "bottom line." Such decisions, however, may cause negative externalities for others. For example, the dumping of hazardous wastes from a manufacturing plant into a river affects the homeowners, farmers, and others who use the river's waters. Thus, corporations are considered to owe some degree of **social responsibility** for their actions. Four theories of the social responsibility of business are discussed in the following paragraphs.

The ultimate justification of the law is to be found, and can only be found, in moral considerations.

Lord Macmillan
Law and Other Things (1937)

Maximizing Profits

The traditional view of the social responsibility of business is that business should **maximize profits** for shareholders. This view, which dominated business and the law during the nineteenth century, holds that the interests of other constituencies (e.g., employees, suppliers, residents of the communities in which businesses are located) are not important in and of themselves.

In the famous case *Dodge v. Ford Motor Company*,[1] a shareholder sued the car company when Henry Ford introduced a plan to reduce the prices of cars so that more people would be put to work and more people could own cars. The shareholders alleged that such a plan would not increase dividends. Mr. Ford testified, "My ambition is to employ still more men, to spread the benefits of this industrial system to the greatest number, to help them build up their lives and their homes." The court sided with the shareholders and stated that:

> [Mr. Ford's] testimony creates the impression that he thinks the Ford Motor company has made too much money, has had too large profits and that, although large profits might still be earned, a sharing of them with the public, by reducing the price of the output of the company, ought to be undertaken.

> There should be no confusion of the duties which Mr. Ford conceives that he and the stockholders owe to the general public and the duties which in law he and his codirectors owe to protesting, minority stockholders. A business corporation is organized and carried on primarily for the profit of the stockholders. The powers of the directors are to be employed for that end. The discretion of directors is to be exercised in the choice of means to attain that end and does not extend to a change in the end itself, to the reduction of profits, or to the nondistribution of profits among stockholders in order to devote them to other purposes.

Milton Friedman, who won the Nobel Prize in economics when he taught at the University of Chicago, advocated this theory. Friedman asserted that in a free society, "there is one and only one social responsibility of business—to use its resources and engage in activities designed to increase its profits as long as it stays within the rules of the game, which is to say, engages in open and free competition without deception and fraud."[2]

In the following case, one company was accused of knocking off another company's product design.

> Public policy: That principle of the law which holds that no subject can lawfully do that which has a tendency to be injurious to the public or against the public good.
>
> Lord Truro
> *Egerton v. Brownlow (1853)*

CASE 4
Business Ethics

U.S. SUPREME COURT

Wal-Mart Stores, Inc. v. Samara Brothers, Inc.

529 U.S. 205, 120 S.Ct. 1339, 146 L.Ed.2d 182,
Web 2000 U.S. Lexis 2197 (2000)
Supreme Court of the United States

> " *Their suspicions aroused, however, Samara officials launched an investigation, which disclosed that Wal-Mart [was] selling the knockoffs of Samara's outfits.* "
>
> —Justice Scalia

Facts

Samara Brothers, Inc. (Samara), is a designer and manufacturer of children's clothing. The core of Samara's business is its annual new line of spring and summer children's garments. Samara sold its clothing to retailers, who in turn sold the clothes to consumers. Wal-Mart Stores, Inc. (Wal-Mart), operates a large chain of budget warehouse stores that sell thousands of items at very low prices. Wal-Mart contacted one of its suppliers, Judy-Philippine, Inc. (JPI), about the possibility of making a line of children's clothes just like Samara's successful line. Wal-Mart sent photographs of Samara's children's clothes to JPI (the name "Samara" was readily discernible on the labels of the garments) and directed JPI to produce children's clothes exactly like those in the photographs. JPI produced a line of children's clothes for Wal-Mart that copied the designs,

colors, and patterns of Samara's clothing. Wal-Mart then sold this line of children's clothing in its stores, making a gross profit of over $1.15 million on these clothes sales during the 1996 selling season.

Samara discovered that Wal-Mart was selling the knockoff clothes at a price that was lower than Samara's retailers were paying Samara for its clothes. After sending unsuccessful cease-and-desist letters to Wal-Mart, Samara sued Wal-Mart, alleging that Wal-Mart stole Samara's trade dress (i.e., look and feel) in violation of Section 43(a) of the Lanham Act. Although not finding that Samara's clothes had acquired a *secondary meaning* in the minds of the public, the U.S. District Court held in favor of Samara and awarded damages. The U.S. Court of Appeals affirmed the award to Samara. Wal-Mart appealed to the U.S. Supreme Court.

Issue

Must a product's design have acquired a secondary meaning before it is protected as trade dress?

Language of the U.S. Supreme Court

The Lanham Act, in Section 43(a), gives a producer a cause of action for the use by any person of "any word, term, name, symbol, or device, or any combination thereof which is likely to cause confusion as to the origin, sponsorship, or approval of his or her goods." The text of Section 43(a) provides little guidance as to the circumstances under which unregistered trade dress may be protected. It does require that a producer show that the allegedly infringing feature is likely to cause confusion with the product for which protection is sought. In an action for infringement of unregistered trade dress a product's design is protectable only upon a showing of secondary meaning.

Decision

The U.S. Supreme Court held that a product's design has to have acquired a secondary meaning in the public's eye before it is protected as

trade dress under Section 43(a) of the Lanham Act. The Supreme Court reversed the decision of the U.S. Court of Appeals and remanded the case for further proceedings consistent with its opinion.

Law & Ethics Questions

1. What is trade dress? Should it have been protected in this case?
2. **ETHICS** Even though Wal-Mart's conduct was ruled legal, was it ethical?
3. Before reading this case, had you heard or read about Samara's children's clothing?

Web Exercises

1. WEB For the complete opinion of this case, go to *www.prenhall.com/cheesemancases*.
2. WEB Visit the website of the Supreme Court of the United States, at *www.supremecourtus.gov*, and try to find documents that relate to this case.
3. WEB Visit the website of Wal-Mart, at *www.walmart.com*. Can you find the corporation's code of ethics?
4. WEB Use *www.google.com* to find a recent article about another legal dispute that Wal-Mart is currently engaged in.

ETHICS SPOTLIGHT

Student Loan Scandal Comes to Light

> **❝** *Loan decisions should be made in the best interest of the students and not the best interest of the school.* **❞**
>
> —Andrew Cuomo, New York Attorney General

Sallie Mae, the largest U.S. student-loan provider, has agreed to pay $2 million and alter its business practices after being caught up in an ever-widening scandal. New York Attorney General Andrew Cuomo, who is spearheading the investigation into the $85 billion student loan industry, said he has found numerous deceptive practices that benefit lenders and colleges at the expense of students.

Some of the arrangements Cuomo's office have investigated include revenue sharing between school employees and lenders, kickbacks to school officials who steer students toward certain lenders, and paid trips to exotic locations for school financial aid officers who direct students to "preferred lenders." Some college officials were fired after Cuomo's office accused them of receiving stock or consulting fees from student loan lenders.

Sallie Mae has also agreed to stop offering perks to college employees and to adopt a code of conduct created by Cuomo. The new code is aimed at making the loan process more transparent. It prohibits revenue sharing between schools and lenders, sets restrictions on how lenders are chosen to be preferred lenders, insists on full disclosure of the relationship between lenders and schools, and bans gifts and trips from lenders to college employees.

"The $2 million," Cuomo said, "will be paid into a fund to help educate college-bound students and their parents on financial aid issues."

Sallie Mae is not alone. So far, six colleges in the New York area, including New York University and Syracuse University, have agreed to reimburse students millions of dollars' worth of inflated loan prices, due to the revenue-sharing agreements with lenders. The probe is just beginning, as Sallie Mae alone has relationships with more than 5,600 colleges throughout the nation and serves nearly 10 million borrowers.

Law & Ethics Questions

1. **ETHICS** Did Sallie Mae act ethically in giving bribes to college loan officers for steering student loan business its way? Why do you think Sallie Mae did this?
2. **ETHICS** Did the college administrators act ethically in accepting "perks" from student lenders? Should these college administrators be fired?
3. Do you have a student loan? Are you concerned that you may not have gotten the best loan terms you could have?

Web Exercises

1. WEB Visit the website of Sallie Mae, at *www.salliemae.com*.
2. WEB Visit the website of the New York Attorney General's Office, at *www.oag.state.ny.us*.

Moral Minimum

Some proponents of corporate social responsibility argue that a corporation's duty is to *make a profit while avoiding causing harm to others*. This theory of social responsibility is called the **moral minimum**. Under this theory, as long as business avoids or corrects the social injury it causes, it has met its duty of social responsibility.

Example A corporation that pollutes the waters and then compensates those whom it injures has met its moral minimum duty of social responsibility.

The legislative and judicial branches of government have established laws that enforce the moral minimum of social responsibility on corporations. For example, occupational safety laws establish minimum safety standards for protecting employees from injuries in the workplace. Consumer protection laws establish safety requirements for products and make manufacturers and sellers liable for injuries caused by defective products. Other laws establish similar minimum standards for conduct for business in other areas.

ETHICS SPOTLIGHT

Media Giant Pays for Bomb Scare

❝ *It's all about corporate greed.* ❞

—Thomas Menino, Mayor of Boston, Massachusetts

On January 31, 2006, Boston, Massachusetts went in panic mode as multiple 911 calls were made, reporting suspicious blinking bomb-like structures attached to a subway station, a hospital, Fenway Park baseball stadium, and other high-profile spots. Local, state, and federal authorities shut down a university, bridges, and highways. The Department of Homeland Security and the U.S. Northern Command began monitoring the situation.

What authorities found was 38 blinking electronic signs with duct-tape wrapped around a package and black wires protruding from the back, but these weren't bombs. Instead, they were box-like cartoon characters giving an obscene gesture, paid for by one of the country's biggest media giants—Time Warner.

The entire debacle was part of a marketing campaign by Time Warner subsidiaries Turner Broadcasting Systems (TBS), the Cartoon Network, and Adult Swim. The campaign was part of a nationwide guerrilla marketing effort to promote the network's cartoon "Aqua Teen Hunger Force."

Not long after the devices were found, authorities arrested two men for installing the boxes and charged them with the placing of a hoax device and disorderly conduct. The men were traced back to Interference, Inc., a New York City marketing firm that Time Warner had hired to conduct the campaign. Boston's proximity to the terrorist attacks of 9/11 made it particularly sensitive to perceived threats.

After learning that the devices were part of a publicity stunt, local politicians blasted those involved. Massachusetts Attorney General Martha Coakley, Mayor Thomas Menino, and others threatened criminal charges and a civil suit. Menino told reporters, "I just think this is outrageous, what they've done. It's all about corporate greed."

Within days, all corporate parties issued public apologies, with TBS and Interference agreeing to pay $2 million in compensation for the emergency response. Officials said $1 million will be used to reimburse the agencies that dealt with the incident and the other half will go toward homeland security. The agreement also resolved any potential civil or criminal claims against the companies.

Law & Ethics Questions

1. Was this a very smart advertising campaign?

2. **ETHICS** Should TBS have been punished more harshly for its actions?

Web Exercises

1. **WEB** Visit the website of Time Warner, at *www.timewarner.com*.

2. **WEB** Visit *www.interferenceinc.com*, the website of the marketing firm that developed this hoax.

3. **WEB** Go to *www.adultswim.com/shows/athf* to view the "Aqua Teen Hunger Force" characters.

Stakeholder Interest

Businesses have relationships with all sorts of people besides their stockholders, including employees, suppliers, customers, creditors, and the local community. Under the **stakeholder interest** theory of social responsibility, a corporation must consider the effects its actions have on these *other stakeholders*. For example, a corporation would violate the stakeholder interest theory if it viewed employees solely as a means of maximizing stockholder wealth.

The stakeholder interest theory is criticized because it is difficult to harmonize the conflicting interests of stakeholders. For example, in closing a plant, certain stakeholders may benefit (e.g., stockholders and creditors) while other stakeholders may not (e.g., current employees and the local community).

BUSINESS ETHICS
State Farm: Not Such a Good Neighbor

> **❝** *The punitive award of $ 145 million, therefore, was neither reasonable nor proportionate to the wrong committed, and it was an irrational and arbitrary deprivation of the property of the defendant.* **❞**
>
> —Justice Kennedy

Curtis Campbell was driving with his wife in Utah when he decided to pass six vans traveling ahead of him on a two-lane highway. Todd Ospital, who was driving on the opposite side of the road toward Campbell, swerved to avoid a collision with Campbell and collided with an automobile driven by Robert Slusher. Ospital was killed; Slusher was rendered permanently disabled; the Campbells escaped unscathed. Early investigations determined that Campbell made an unsafe pass and had caused the crash. Ospital's heirs and Slusher sued Campbell for wrongful death and injuries, respectively. Campbell's insurance company, State Farm Mutual Automobile Insurance Company (State Farm) declined offers by Ospital's estate and Slusher to settle their claims for the insurance policy limit of $50,000 and took the case to trial. The jury determined that Campbell was 100 percent at fault and returned a judgment for $185,000.

Campbell reached a settlement with Ospital's and Slusher's attorneys whereby Campbell agreed to pursue a bad faith tort action against State Farm, and Ospital's estate and Slusher would receive 90 percent of any verdict against State Farm. One and one-half years after the initial judgment, State Farm paid all of the $185,000 judgment against Campbell, even though it exceeded the $50,000 policy limit.

State Farm has consistently used the advertising slogan "Like a good neighbor, State Farm is there." The plaintiffs did not think so, and their bad faith tort case went to trial against State Farm in a Utah trial court. At trial, evidence was introduced that State Farm had a policy to take many cases to trial even though they could be settled within the insurance policy limits. The jury held against State Farm and awarded Campbell $2.6 million in compensatory damages and $145 million in punitive damages. The trial court judge reduced the compensatory damages to $1 million and punitive damages to $25 million. The Utah supreme court reinstated the $145 million punitive damages award. State Farm appealed to the U.S. Supreme Court.

The issue on appeal was whether an award of $145 million in punitive damages, where compensatory damages were $1 million, was excessive and a violation of the Due Process Clause of the Fourteenth Amendment to the Constitution of the United States.

The U.S. Supreme Court noted that while states possess discretion over the imposition of punitive damages, it is well established that there are procedural and substantive constitutional limitations on these awards. The Due Process Clause of the Fourteenth Amendment prohibits the imposition of grossly excessive or arbitrary punishments on a tortfeasor. The U.S. Supreme Court held that this case was neither close nor difficult: It was an error to reinstate the jury's $145 million punitive damages award.

The U.S. Supreme Court stated that this case was used as a platform to expose and punish the perceived deficiencies of State Farm's operations throughout the country. The Utah supreme court's opinion makes explicit that State Farm was being condemned for its nationwide policies rather than for the conduct directed toward the Campbells. The Utah court awarded punitive damages to punish and deter conduct that bore no relation to the Campbells' harm. The U.S. Supreme Court held that a defendant's dissimilar acts, independent from the acts on which liability was premised, may not serve as the basis for punitive damages. A defendant should be punished for the conduct that harmed the plaintiff, not for being an unsavory individual or business. The Court concluded that due process does not permit courts, in the calculation of punitive damages, to adjudicate the merits of other parties' hypothetical claims against a defendant, under the guise of the reprehensibility analysis.

The U.S. Supreme Court stated that few awards exceeding a single-digit ratio between punitive and compensatory damages, to a significant degree, will satisfy due process. The Supreme Court noted that single-digit multiples are more likely to comport with due process, while still achieving the state's goals of deterrence and retribution, than awards with ratios in the range of 500 to 1, or, in this case, 145 to 1. The Supreme Court concluded that there may be a few cases in which particularly egregious conduct could justify a larger ratio of punitive damages to economic damage.

The U.S. Supreme Court held that an award of $145 million in punitive damages where compensatory damages were $1 million was excessive and violated the Due Process Clause of the Fourteenth Amendment to the U.S. Constitution. The Supreme Court stated, "The punitive award of $145 million, therefore, was neither reasonable nor proportionate to the wrong committed, and it was an irrational and arbitrary deprivation of the property of the defendant." The U.S.

Supreme Court reversed the decision of the Utah supreme court and remanded the case for proceedings consistent with the U.S. Supreme Court's opinion. *State Farm Mutual Automobile Insurance Company v. Campbell*, 538 U.S. 408, 123 S.Ct. 1513, 155 L.Ed.2d 585, **Web** 2003 U.S. Lexis 2714 (Supreme Court of the United States, 2003)

Law & Ethics Questions

1. **ETHICS** What is the purpose of punitive damages? Why are they awarded?

2. What is the protection afforded by the Due Process Clause? Explain.

3. **ETHICS** Did Campbell act ethically in this case?

4. **ETHICS** Did State Farm act ethically in this case?

Web Exercises

1. **WEB** For the complete opinion of this case, go to *www.prenhall.com/cheesemancases*.

2. **WEB** Visit the website of the Supreme Court of the United States, at *www.supremecourtus.gov*, and try to find documents that relate to this case.

3. **WEB** Visit the website of State Farm Insurance, at *www.statefarm.com*. Can you find the corporation's code of ethics?

Corporate Citizenship

The **corporate citizenship** theory of social responsibility argues that business has a responsibility to do well. That is, business is responsible for helping to solve social problems that it did little, if anything, to cause. For example, under this theory, corporations owe a duty to subsidize schools and help educate children.

This theory contends that corporations owe a duty to promote the same social goals as do individual members of society. Proponents of this "do good" theory argue that corporations owe a debt to society to make it a better place and that this duty arises because of the social power bestowed on them. That is, this social power is a gift from society and should be used to good ends.

A major criticism of this theory is that the duty of a corporation to do good cannot be expanded beyond certain limits. There is always some social problem that needs to be addressed, and corporate funds are limited. Further, if this theory were taken to its maximum limit, potential shareholders might be reluctant to invest in corporations.

CONCEPT SUMMARY

Theories of Social Responsibility

THEORY	SOCIAL RESPONSIBILITY
Maximizing profits	To maximize profits for stockholders.
Moral minimum	To avoid causing harm and to compensate for harm caused.
Stakeholder interest	To consider the interests of all stakeholders, including stockholders, employees, customers, suppliers, creditors, and the local community.
Corporate citizenship	To do well and solve social problems.

ETHICS SPOTLIGHT

Sarbanes-Oxley Act Prompts Public Companies to Adopt Codes of Ethics

In the late 1990s and early 2000s, many large corporations in the United States were found to have engaged in massive financial frauds. Many of these frauds were perpetrated by the chief executive officers and other senior officers of the companies. Financial officers, such as chief financial officers and controllers, were also found to have been instrumental in committing these frauds. In response, Congress enacted the **Sarbanes-Oxley Act** of 2002, which makes certain conduct illegal and establishes criminal penalties for violations. In addition, the Sarbanes-Oxley Act prompts companies to encourage senior officers of public companies to act ethically in their dealings with shareholders, employees, and other constituents.

Section 406 of the Sarbanes-Oxley Act requires a public company to disclose whether it has adopted a **code of ethics** for senior financial officers, including its principal financial officer and principal accounting officer. In response, public companies have adopted codes of ethics for their senior financial officers. Many public companies have included all officers and employees in the coverage of their codes of ethics.

A typical code of ethics is illustrated in Exhibit 2.

Law & Ethics Questions

1. Do you think the Sarbanes-Oxley Act will be effective in promoting ethical conduct by officers and directors? Explain.

2. **ETHICS** Can ethics be mandated? In other words, will crooks still be crooks?

EXHIBIT 2

Code of Ethics

Big Cheese Corporation
Code of Ethics

Big Cheese Corporation's mission includes the promotion of professional conduct in the practice of general management worldwide. Big Cheese's Chief Executive Officer (CEO), Chief Financial Officer (CFO), corporate Controller, and other employees of the finance organization and other employees of the corporation hold an important and elevated role in the corporate governance of the corporation. They are empowered and uniquely capable to ensure that all constituents' interests are appropriately balanced, protected, and preserved.

This Code of Ethics embodies principles to which we are expected to adhere and advocate. The CEO, CFO, finance organization employees, and other employees of the corporation are expected to abide by this Code of Ethics and all business conduct standards of the corporation relating to areas covered by this Code of Ethics. Any violation of the Code of Ethics may result in disciplinary action, up to and including termination of employment. All employees will:

- Act with honesty and integrity, avoiding actual or apparent conflicts of interest in their personal and professional relations.
- Provide stakeholders with information that is accurate, fair, complete, timely, objective, relevant, and understandable, including in our filings with and other submissions to the U.S. Securities and Exchange Commission.
- Comply with rules and regulations of federal, state, provincial, and local governments and other appropriate private and public regulatory agencies.
- Act in good faith, responsibly, with due care, competence, and diligence, without misrepresenting materials facts or allowing one's independent judgment to be subordinated.
- Respect the confidentiality of information acquired in the course of one's work, except when authorized or otherwise legally obligated to disclose. Confidential information acquired in the course of one's work will not be used for personal advantage.
- Share knowledge and maintain professional skills important and relevant to stakeholders' needs.
- Proactively promote and be an example of ethical behavior as a responsible partner among peers, in the work environment and the community.
- Achieve responsible use, control, and stewardship over all Big Cheese's assets and resources that are employed or entrusted to us.
- Not unduly or fraudulently influence, coerce, manipulate, or mislead any authorized audit or interfere with any auditor engaged in the performance of an internal or independent audit of Big Cheese's financial statements or accounting books and records.

If you are aware of any suspected or known violations of this Code of Ethics or other Big Cheese policies or guidelines, you have a duty to promptly report such concerns either to your manager, another responsible member of management, a Human Resources representative, or the Director of Compliance or the 24-hour Business Conduct Line.

If you have a concern about a questionable accounting or auditing matter and wish to submit the concern confidentially or anonymously, you may do so by sending an e-mail to (bc.codeofethics@bigcheese.cc) or calling the Business Conduct Line 24-hour number at 1-888-666-BIGC (2442).

Big Cheese will handle all inquiries discretely and make every effort to maintain, within the limits allowed by law, the confidentiality of anyone requesting guidance or reporting questionable behavior and/or a compliance concern.

It is Big Cheese's intention that this Code of Ethics to be its written code of ethics under Section 406 of the Sarbanes-Oxley Act of 2002 complying with the standards set forth in Securities and Exchange Commission Regulation S-K Item 406.

ETHICS SPOTLIGHT
The Corporate Social Audit

It has been suggested that corporate audits should be extended to include not only audits of the financial health of a corporation but also of its moral health. It is expected that corporations that conduct **corporate social audits** would be more apt to prevent unethical and illegal conduct by managers, employees, and agents. The audit would examine how well employees have adhered to the company's code of ethics and how well the corporation has met its duty of social responsibility.

Such audits would focus on the corporation's efforts to promote employment opportunities for members of protected classes, worker safety, environmental protection, consumer protection, and the like. Social audits are not easy. First, it may be difficult to conceptualize just what is being audited. Second, it may be difficult to measure results. Despite these factors, a growing number of companies are expected to undertake social audits.

Companies should institute the following procedures when conducting a social audit:

- An independent outside firm should be hired to conduct the audit. This ensures autonomy and objectivity in conducting the audit.

- The company's personnel should cooperate fully with the auditing firm while the audit is being conducted.

- The auditing firm should report its findings directly to the company's board of directors.

- The results of the audit should be reviewed by the board of directors.

- The board of directors should determine how the company can better meet its duty of social responsibility and can use the audit to implement a program to correct any deficiencies it finds.

Law & Ethics Questions

1. What is a corporate social audit? What purpose would such an audit serve?

2. **ETHICS** Would a corporate social audit encourage more ethical behavior by corporate officers and employees?

Web Exercises

1. **WEB** Go to *www.thecoca-colacompany.com/citizenship/index.html*. Pick out several categories that interest you and read how the Coca-Cola Company is helping in that area.

2. **WEB** Pick out a company that interests you. Use *www.google.com* to find the code of ethics of that company.

The actions of transnational corporations impact everything from local and global economies to human rights and labor laws. In the 1970s the United Nations recognized this important and increasing role of transnational corporations in the world and as a result began a committee to draft the **United Nations Code of Conduct for Transnational Corporations**.

INTERNATIONAL LAW
United Nations Code of Conduct for Transnational Corporations

Respect for National Sovereignty

Transnational corporations shall respect the national sovereignty of the countries in which they operate and the right of each state to exercise its permanent sovereignty over its natural wealth and resources.

Transnational corporations should carry out their activities in conformity with the development policies, objectives, and priorities set out by the governments of the countries in which they operate and work seriously toward making a positive contribution to the achievement of such goals at the national and, as appropriate, the regional level, with the framework of regional integration programs. Transnational corporations should cooperate with the governments of the countries in which they operate, with a view to contributing to the development process and should be responsible to requests for consultation in this respect, thereby establishing mutually beneficial relations with these countries.

Adherence to Sociocultural Objectives and Values

Transnational corporations should respect the social and cultural objectives, values, and traditions of the countries in which they operate. While economic and technological development is normally accompanied by social change, transnational corporations should avoid practices, products, or services that cause detrimental effects on cultural patterns and sociocultural objectives, as determined by governments. For this purpose, transnational corporations should respond positively to requests for consultations from governments concerned.

Respect for Human Rights and Fundamental Freedoms

Transnational corporations shall respect human rights and fundamental freedoms in the countries in which they operate. In their social and industrial relations, transnational corporations shall not discriminate on the basis of race, color, sex, religion, language, social, national and ethnic origin, or political or other opinion. Transnational corporations shall conform to government policies designed to extend quality of opportunity and treatment.

Abstention from Corrupt Practices

Transnational corporations shall refrain, in their transactions, from the offering, promising, or giving of any payment, gift, or other advantage to or for the benefit of a public official as consideration for performing or refraining from the performance of his duties in connection with those transactions.

Law & Ethics Questions

1. Do the rules of ethics vary from country to country? Explain.
2. **ETHICS** Should a multinational corporation refuse to engage in bribery or other corrupt practices even if such behavior is common in its industry or the country in which it is operating?

Louang-Phrabang, Laos

The local customs of a country should be honored when conducting business in that country.

Chapter Summary

Ethics and the Law
Ethics is a set of moral principles on values that governs the conduct of an individual or a group.

Business Ethics
A number of moral theories have been applied to business ethics.

Ethical Fundamentalism
Under the moral theory of ethical fundamentalism, persons look to an outside source (e.g., Bible, Koran) or a central figure to set ethical guidelines.

Utilitarianism
Under the moral theory of utilitarianism, persons choose the alternative that would provide the greatest good to society.

Kantian Ethics
Under the moral theory of Kantian ethics, also called duty ethics, a set of universal rules establishes ethical duties. The rules are based on reasoning and require (1) consistency in application and (2) reversibility.

Rawls's Social Justice Theory
Under Rawls's social justice theory, moral duties are based on an implied social contract. Fairness is justice, and the rules are established from an original position of a "veil of ignorance."

Ethical Relativism

Under the moral theory of ethical relativism, individuals decide what is ethical based on their own feelings of what is right or wrong.

Social Responsibility of Business

A number of theories of social responsibility have been posited.

Maximizing Profits

The goal of the maximizing profits theory is to maximize profits for shareholders.

Moral Minimum

The goal of the moral minimum theory is to make a profit and avoid harm and to compensate for harm caused.

Stakeholder Interest

The goal of the stakeholder interest theory is to consider the interests of stakeholders other than shareholders, such as employees, suppliers, customers, creditors, and the local community.

Corporate Citizenship

The goal of the corporate citizenship theory is to do good and help solve social problems.

Corporate Social Audit

A social audit is an audit of a corporation by independent auditors that examines how well employees have adhered to the company's code of ethics and how well the company has met its duty of social responsibility.

Test Review Terms and Concepts

Business ethics	False Claims Act	Social contract
Code of ethics	Kantian ethics (duty ethics)	Social responsibility of business
Corporate citizenship	Maximizing profits	Stakeholder interest
Corporate social audit	Moral minimum	United Nations Code of Conduct for
Ethical fundamentalism	*Qui tam* lawsuit	Transnational Corporations
Ethical relativism	Rawls's social justice theory	Utilitarianism
Ethics	Sarbanes-Oxley Act	Whistleblower Statute

Case Problems

1 Fraud: The Warner-Lambert Company has manufactured and distributed Listerine antiseptic mouthwash since 1879. Its formula has never changed. Ever since Listerine's introduction, the company has represented the product as being beneficial in preventing and curing colds and sore throats. Direct advertising of these claims to consumers began in 1921. Warner-Lambert spent millions of dollars annually advertising these claims in print media and in television commercials.

After 100 years of Warner-Lambert's making such claims, the Federal Trade Commission (FTC) filed a complaint against the company, alleging that it had engaged in false advertising in violation of federal law. Four months of hearings were held before an administrative law judge that produced an evidentiary record of more than 4,000 pages of documents from 46 witnesses. After examining the evidence, the FTC issued an opinion which held that the company's representations that Listerine prevented and cured colds and sore throats were false. The U.S. Court of Appeals affirmed.

Is Warner-Lambert guilty of fraud? If so, what remedies should the court impose on the company? Did Warner-Lambert act ethically in making its claims for Listerine? *Warner-Lambert Company v. Federal Trade Commission,* 183 U.S. App. D.C. 230, 562 F.2d 749, **Web** 1977 U.S. App. Lexis 11599 (United States Court of Appeals for the District of Columbia Circuit)

2 Liability: The Johns-Manville Corporation was a profitable company that made a variety of building and other products. It was a major producer of asbestos, which was used for insulation in buildings and for a variety of other uses. It has been medically proven that excessive exposure to asbestos causes asbestosis, a fatal lung disease. Thousands of employees of the company and consumers who were exposed to asbestos and contracted this fatal disease sued the company for damages. Eventually, the lawsuits were being filed at a rate of more than 400 per week.

In response to the claims, Johns-Manville Corporation filed for reorganization bankruptcy. It argued that if it did not, an otherwise viable company that provided thousands of jobs and served a useful purpose in this country would be destroyed and that without the declaration of bankruptcy, a few of the plaintiffs who first filed their lawsuits would win awards of hundreds of million of dollars, leaving nothing for

the remainder of the plaintiffs. Under the bankruptcy court's protection, the company was restructured to survive. As part of the release from bankruptcy, the company contributed money to a fund to pay current and future claimants. The fund is not large enough to pay all injured persons the full amounts of their claims.

Was Johns-Manville liable for negligence? Was it ethical for Johns-Manville to declare bankruptcy? Did it meet its duty of social responsibility in this case? *In re Johns-Manville Corporation*, 36 B.R. 727, **Web** 1984 Bankr. Lexis 6384 (United States Bankruptcy Court for the Southern District of New York)

Ethics Issues

3 Ethics: The Reverend Leon H. Sullivan, a Baptist minister from Philadelphia who was also a member of the board of directors of General Motors Corporation, proposed a set of rules to guide American-owned companies doing business in the Republic of South Africa. The *Sullivan Principles*, as they became known, call for the nonsegregation of races in South Africa. They call for employers to (a) provide equal and fair employment practices for all employees and (b) improve the quality of employees' lives outside the work environment in such areas as housing, schooling, transportation, recreation, and health facilities. The principles also require signatory companies to report regularly and to be graded on their conduct in South Africa.

Eventually, the Sullivan Principles were subscribed to by several hundred U.S. corporations with affiliates doing business in South Africa. Which of the following theories of social responsibility are the companies that subscribed to the Sullivan Principles following?

1. Maximizing profits
2. Moral minimum
3. Stakeholder interest
4. Corporate citizenship

To put additional pressure on the government of the Republic of South Africa to end apartheid, Reverend Sullivan called for the complete withdrawal of all U.S. companies from doing business in or with South Africa. Very few companies agreed to do so. Do companies owe a social duty to withdraw from South Africa? Should universities divest themselves of investments in companies that do not withdraw from South Africa?

4 Ethics: Kaiser Aluminum & Chemical Corporation entered into a collective bargaining agreement with the United Steelworkers of America, a union that represented employees at Kaiser's plants. The agreement contained an affirmative-action program to increase the representation of minorities in craft jobs. To enable plants to meet these goals, on-the-job training programs were established to teach unskilled production workers the skills necessary to become

craft workers. Assignment to the training program was based on seniority, except that the plan reserved 50 percent of the openings for black employees.

Thirteen craft trainees were selected from Kaiser's Gramercy plant for the training program. Of these, 7 were black and 6 white. The most senior black selected had less seniority than several white production workers who had applied for the positions but were rejected. Brian Weber, one of the white rejected employees, instituted a class action lawsuit alleging that the affirmative action plan violated Title VII of the Civil Rights Act of 1964, which made it "unlawful to discriminate because of race" in hiring and selecting apprentices for training programs. The U.S. Supreme Court upheld the affirmative-action plan in this case. The decision stated:

> We therefore hold that Title VII's prohibition against racial discrimination does not condemn all private, voluntary, race-conscious affirmative action plans. At the same time, the plant does not unnecessarily trammel the interests of the white employees. Moreover, the plan is a temporary measure; it is not intended to maintain racial balance, but simply to eliminate a manifest racial imbalance.

Do companies owe a duty of social responsibility to provide affirmative-action programs? *Steelworkers v. Weber*, 443 U.S. 193, 99 S.Ct. 2721, 61 L.Ed.2d 480, **Web** 1979 U.S. Lexis 40 (Supreme Court of the United States)

5 Ethics: Iroquois Brands, Ltd., a Delaware corporation, had $78 million in assets, $141 million in sales, and $6 million in profits. As part of its business, Iroquois imported pâté de foie gras (goose pâté) from France and sold it in the United States. Iroquois derived only $79,000 in revenues from sales of such pâté. The French product force-fed the geese from which the pâté was made. Peter C. Lovenheim, who owned 200 shares of Iroquois common stock, proposed to include a shareholder proposal in Iroquois's annual proxy materials to be sent to shareholders. His proposal criticized the company because the force-feeding caused "undue stress, pain and suffering" to the geese and requested that shareholders vote to have Iroquois discontinue importing and selling pâté produced by this method.

Iroquois refused to allow the information to be included in its proxy materials. Iroquois asserted that its refusal was based on the fact that Lovenheim's proposal was "not economically significant" and had only "ethical and social" significance. The company reasoned that because corporations are economic entities, only an economic test applied to its activities, and it was not subject to an ethical or a social responsibility test. Is the company correct? That is, should only an economic test be applied in judging the activities of a corporation? Or should a corporation also be subject to an ethical or a social responsibility test? *Lovenheim v. Iroquois Brands, Ltd.*, 618 F.Supp. 554, **Web** 1985 U.S. Dist. Lexis 21259 (United States District Court for the District of Columbia)

Endnotes

1. 204 Mich. 459, 170 N.W. 668, **Web** 1919 Mich. Lexis 720 (Supreme Court of Michigan).
2. Milton Friedman, "The Social Responsibility of Business Is to Increase Its Profits," *New York Times Magazine*, September 13, 1970.

Ethical, Social, and Political Issues in E-commerce

From Chapter 8 of *E-Commerce: Business, Technology, Society 2008*, 4/e. Kenneth C. Laudon. Carol Guercio Traver.

Ethical, Social, and Political Issues in E-commerce

Second Life Gets a Life:
Discovering Law and Ethics in Virtual Worlds

Second Life is a massively multiplayer online role playing game (MMORPG) experience where upwards of 600,000 active users (and over five million unique subscribers) engage in online virtual activities that can range from innocent social chit chat to hustling, buying, selling and even stealing. With liquidity provided by Linden dollars that can be purchased with real dollars ($1=270 Linden dollars), avatars that you create can buy and sell virtual assets, goods and services, from handbags and cars, to real estate, avatar design, clothing and accessories service businesses. Some popular services include simulated prostitution, strip clubs, and, not surprisingly, gambling. Second Life commerce generates somewhere between $250,000 and $1 million in U.S. dollar revenues each day.

screenshot of Secondlife.com home page, © Linden Lab, 2007

For the most part, players come not to compete with one another, but to entertain themselves, escape their real worlds, and have some fun. Others come in an attempt to make a profit, and a small number come to create mischief. Mischief, so much a part of the real world where law and custom aim to hold it in check, poses an interesting challenge for virtual worlds where there are no laws, and yet where actions taken online can injure people and corporations offline. It's like the Old West, where law and order were not quite established and people sought solutions, looking at times for a strong High Noon sheriff to bring order. Every now and then, the Sheriff sets down the law in Second Life, when its owners declare certain activities illegal and attempt to set up a system of self-regulation (if not quite law).

For instance, many of the assets, goods, and services sold on Second Life do not "belong" to the people who are selling them. You can buy virtual Gucci bags, Ferrari cars (L$ 1995—what a deal!), Rolex watches, Rayban sunglasses, Prada and Oakley clothes for your avatars, Nike shoes, and Apple iPods. In a small study conducted by several lawyers, of ten randomly selected virtual stores on Second Life, seven sold knock-off goods that exhibited obvious trademark infringements. Some stores sold nothing but brand-name goods. But because this is all virtual, none of the trademark owners above have thus far brought a lawsuit against residents. As lawyers point out, unless companies actively enforce their trademarks in the face of infringement, they can lose the trademark altogether. From a practical point of view, at some point nearly all firms will have a virtual presence, and when they seek to develop their trademarks on virtual sites, they will not want to compete with hundreds or thousands of residents selling knockoffs.

In a further sign of emerging legal and ethical issues, six major content creators on Second Life filed a real-world copyright and trademark infringement lawsuit against Thomas Simon, a Queens, New York, resident. Simon allegedly found a flaw in the Second Life program, and used a third-party copy program, which enabled him to make thousands of copies of the creators' products. Included in the alleged theft are avatar clothing, skins and shapes, scripted objects, furniture, and other objects. The plaintiffs did not want to file a lawsuit. Initially they sent letters to Simon after having identified him as the owner of the Rase Kenzo avatar. He replied to the plaintiffs in several "drop dead" e-mail messages. The plaintiffs tried to alert Linden Labs by filing copyright notices, filling out support tickets and abuse reports. To complicate matters, the plaintiffs "broke into" Rase Kenzo's skybox to find the evidence of infringement. In the real world, the evidence obtained by unlawful means would be disallowed.

Linden Labs is struggling with issues of governance and ethics on Second Life. It has banned six behaviors: intolerance (including slurs against groups), harassment, assault (including use of software tools to attack people's avatars), disclosure of information about other people's real-world lives, indecency (sexual behavior outside areas rated as mature), and disturbing the peace. Violations prompt warnings, suspension or banishment, enforced by Linden managers. There is no appeal process or due process.

The large scale trademark and copyright infringement raise concerns about virtual life and real life law and statutes. Stealing in virtual life would seem to parallel stealing in real life. Gambling is another matter. Linden Lab's terms of service ban any illegal activity, but the company itself is not sure whether in-world gambling or prostitution crosses the line. The FBI and federal prosecutors were invited to visit Second Life gambling operations in April 2007, but issued no opinion on the legality of the operation. According to Ginsu Yoon, Vice President of Business Affairs, "It's not always clear to us whether a 3-D simulation of a casino is the same thing as a casino, legally speaking—and it's not clear to the law enforcement authorities we have asked." Even if the law were clear, he said the company would have no way to monitor or prevent in-world gambling, much as law enforcement cannot police every neighborhood poker game or office basketball pool. "There are millions of registered accounts and tens of millions of different objects in Second Life; there is simply no way for us to monitor content prospectively even if we wanted to," Yoon said. "That would be a harder task than pre-monitoring all e-mail sent through Yahoo Mail or Gmail, and no one expects those services to prevent all possible use of e-mail for illegal activity." This sounds like no one is in control, and real-world laws just don't apply, an argument that used to be made by peer-to-peer music sites. Ultimately, the Supreme Court in the real world shut down those music sites because they intentionally established a mechanism to violate copyright laws. In July 2007, Linden Labs decided to outlaw all forms of gambling.

Linden Labs and Second Life have a strong libertarian history. Its founders envisaged Second Life as a self-regulating community where good people could amuse themselves in a fantasy world. Dealing with "griefers," and their growing numbers as evidenced by rapidly expanding abuse complaints at Second Life, suggest that Linden's executives should start thinking about what they have created and how they will police it. If not, real world prosecutors and courts will do it for them. Second Life will have to grow up someday.

SOURCES: "Rapid Trademark Infringement in Second Life Costs Millions, Undermines Future Enforcement," by Benjamin Duranske, Virtuallyblind.com, October 30, 2007; "Second Life Players Bring Virtual Reality to Court," by Emil Steiner, Washingtonpost.com, October 29, 2007; "Second Life Virtual Gamblers Told to Fold," by Mike Musgrove, *Washington Post*, August 1, 2007; "Fantasy Life, Real Law," by Stephanie Ward, *ABA Journal*, March, 2007; "Virtual Vandalism," by Don Clark, *Wall Street Journal*, November 27, 2006.

etermining how to regulate virtual behavior that may have a real world impact is just one of many ethical, social, and political issues raised by the rapid evolution of the Internet and e-commerce. These questions are not just ethical questions that we as individuals have to answer; they also involve social institutions such as family, schools, and business firms. And these questions have obvious political dimensions because they involve collective choices about how we should live and what laws we would like to live under.

In this chapter, we discuss the ethical, social, and political issues raised in e-commerce, provide a framework for organizing the issues, and make recommendations for managers who are given the responsibility of operating e-commerce companies within commonly accepted standards of appropriateness.

1 UNDERSTANDING ETHICAL, SOCIAL, AND POLITICAL ISSUES IN E-COMMERCE

The Internet and its use in e-commerce have raised pervasive ethical, social, and political issues on a scale unprecedented for computer technology. Entire sections of daily newspapers and weekly magazines are devoted to the social impact of the Internet. But why is this so? Why is the Internet at the root of so many contemporary controversies? Part of the answer lies in the underlying features of Internet technology itself, and the ways in which it has been exploited by business firms. Internet technology and its use in e-commerce disrupt existing social and business relationships and understandings.

Recall the list of the unique features of Internet technology. Instead of considering the business consequences of each unique feature, **Table 1** examines the actual or potential ethical, social, and/or political consequences of the technology.

We live in an "information society," where power and wealth increasingly depend on information and knowledge as central assets. Controversies over information are often in fact disagreements over power, wealth, influence, and other things thought to be valuable. Like other technologies such as steam, electricity, telephones, and television, the Internet and e-commerce can be used to achieve social progress, and for the most part, this has occurred. However, the same technologies can be used to commit crimes, despoil the environment, and threaten cherished social values. Before automobiles, there was very little interstate crime and very little federal jurisdiction over crime. Likewise with the Internet: Before the Internet, there was very little "cybercrime."

Many business firms and individuals are benefiting from the commercial development of the Internet, but this development also exacts a price from individuals, organizations, and societies. These costs and benefits must be carefully considered by those seeking to make ethical and socially responsible decisions in this new environment. The question is: How can you as a manager make reasoned judgments about what your firm should do in a number of e-commerce areas—from

TABLE 1	UNIQUE FEATURES OF E-COMMERCE TECHNOLOGY AND THEIR POTENTIAL ETHICAL, SOCIAL, AND/OR POLITICAL IMPLICATIONS
E-COMMERCE TECHNOLOGY DIMENSION	**POTENTIAL ETHICAL, SOCIAL, AND POLITICAL SIGNIFICANCE**
Ubiquity—Internet/Web technology is available everywhere: at work, at home, and elsewhere via mobile devices, anytime.	Work and shopping can invade family life; shopping can distract workers at work, lowering productivity; use of mobile devices can lead to automobile and industrial accidents. Presents confusing issues of "nexus" to taxation authorities.
Global reach—The technology reaches across national boundaries, around the earth.	Reduces cultural diversity in products; weakens local small firms while strengthening large global firms; moves manufacturing production to low-wage areas of the world; weakens the ability of all nations—large and small—to control their information destiny.
Universal standards—There is one set of technology standards, namely Internet standards.	Increases vulnerability to viruses and hacking attacks worldwide affecting millions of people at once. Increases the likelihood of "information" crime, crimes against systems, and deception.
Richness—Video, audio, and text messages are possible.	A "screen technology" that reduces use of text and potentially the ability to read by focusing instead on video and audio messages. Potentially very persuasive messages possible that may reduce reliance on multiple independent sources of information.
Interactivity—The technology works through interaction with the user.	The nature of interactivity at commercial sites can be shallow and meaningless. Customer e-mails are frequently not read by human beings. Customers do not really "co-produce" the product as much as they "co-produce" the sale. The amount of "customization" of products that occurs is minimal, occurring within predefined platforms and plug-in options.
Information density—The technology reduces information costs, raises quality.	While the total amount of information available to all parties increases, so does the possibility of false and misleading information, unwanted information, and invasion of solitude. Trust, authenticity, accuracy, completeness, and other quality features of information can be degraded. The ability of individuals and organizations to make sense of out of this plethora of information is limited.
Personalization/Customization—The technology allows personalized messages to be delivered to individuals as well as groups.	Opens up the possibility of intensive invasion of privacy for commercial and governmental purposes that is unprecedented.
Social technology—User content generation and social networking	Creates opportunities for cyberbullying, abusive language, and predation; challenges concepts of privacy, fair use, and consent to use posted information; creates new opportunities for surveillance by authorities and corporations into private lives.

securing the privacy of your customer's clickstream to ensuring the integrity of your company's domain name?

A MODEL FOR ORGANIZING THE ISSUES

E-commerce—and the Internet—have raised so many ethical, social, and political issues that it is difficult to classify them all, and hence complicated to see their relationship to one another. Clearly, ethical, social, and political issues are interrelated. One way to organize the ethical, social, and political dimensions surrounding e-commerce is shown in **Figure 1**. At the individual level, what appears as an ethical issue—"What should I do?"—is reflected at the social and political levels—"What should we as a society and government do?" The ethical dilemmas you face as a manager of a business using the Web reverberate and are reflected in social and political debates. The major ethical, social, and political issues that have developed around e-commerce over the past nine to ten years can be loosely categorized into four major dimensions: information rights, property rights, governance, and public safety and welfare.

Some of the ethical, social, and political issues raised in each of these areas include the following:

- **Information rights:** What rights to their own personal information do individuals have in a public marketplace, or in their private homes, when Internet technologies make information collection so pervasive and efficient? What rights do individuals have to access information about business firms and other organizations?

- **Property rights:** How can traditional intellectual property rights be enforced in an Internet world where perfect copies of protected works can be made and easily distributed worldwide in seconds?

- **Governance:** Should the Internet and e-commerce be subject to public laws? And if so, what law-making bodies have jurisdiction—state, federal, and/or international?

FIGURE 1	THE MORAL DIMENSIONS OF AN INTERNET SOCIETY

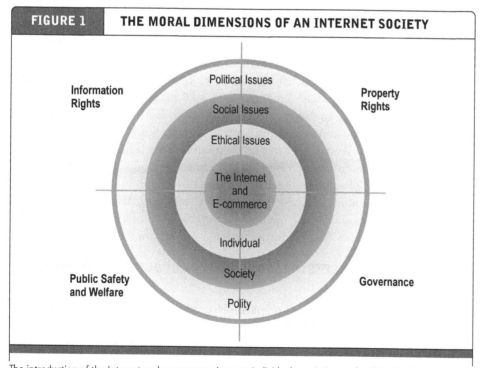

The introduction of the Internet and e-commerce impacts individuals, societies, and political institutions. These impacts can be classified into four moral dimensions: property rights, information rights, governance, and public safety and welfare.

- **Public safety and welfare:** What efforts should be undertaken to ensure equitable access to the Internet and e-commerce channels? Should governments be responsible for ensuring that schools and colleges have access to the Internet? Are certain online content and activities—such as pornography and gambling—a threat to public safety and welfare? Should mobile commerce be allowed from moving vehicles?

To illustrate, imagine that at any given moment, society and individuals are more or less in an ethical equilibrium brought about by a delicate balancing of individuals, social organizations, and political institutions. Individuals know what is expected of them, social organizations such as business firms know their limits, capabilities, and roles, and political institutions provide a supportive framework of market regulation, banking, and commercial law that provides sanctions against violators.

Now, imagine we drop into the middle of this calm setting a powerful new technology such as the Internet and e-commerce. Suddenly, individuals, business firms, and political institutions are confronted by new possibilities of behavior. For instance, individuals discover that they can download perfect digital copies of music tracks from Web sites without paying anyone, something that, under the old technology of CDs, would have been impossible. This can be done, despite the fact that these music tracks still "belong" as a legal matter to the owners of the copyright—musicians and record label companies. Then, business firms discover that they can make a business out of aggregating these digital musical tracks—or creating a mechanism for sharing musical tracks—even though they do not "own" them in the traditional sense. This, of course, is the story of Grokster, Kazaa and Napster described in Chapter 1. The record companies, courts, and Congress were not prepared at first to cope with the onslaught of online digital copying. Courts and legislative bodies will have to make new laws and reach new judgments about who owns digital copies of copyrighted works and under what conditions such works can be "shared." It may take years to develop new understandings, laws, and acceptable behavior in just this one area of social impact. In the meantime, as an individual and a manager, you will have to decide what you and your firm should do in legal "gray" areas, where there is conflict between ethical principles but no clear-cut legal or cultural guidelines. How can you make good decisions in this type of situation?

Before examining the four moral dimensions of e-commerce in greater depth, we will briefly review some basic concepts of ethical reasoning that you can use as a guide to ethical decision making, and provide general reasoning principles about the social and political issues of the Internet that you will face in the future.

BASIC ETHICAL CONCEPTS: RESPONSIBILITY, ACCOUNTABILITY, AND LIABILITY

ethics

the study of principles that individuals and organizations can use to determine right and wrong courses of action

Ethics is at the heart of social and political debates about the Internet. **Ethics** is the study of principles that individuals and organizations can use to determine right and wrong courses of action. It is assumed in ethics that individuals are free moral agents who are in a position to make choices. When faced with alternative courses of action, what is the correct moral choice? Extending ethics from individuals to business firms and even entire societies can be difficult, but it is not impossible. As long as there is a decision-making body or individual (such as a Board of Directors or CEO in a business firm, or a governmental body in a society), their decisions can be judged against a variety of ethical principles.

If you understand some basic ethical principles, your ability to reason about larger social and political debates will be improved. In western culture, there are three basic principles that all ethical schools of thought share: **responsibility**, accountability, and liability. Responsibility means that as free moral agents, individuals, organizations, and societies are responsible for the actions they take. **Accountability** means that individuals, organizations, and societies should be held accountable to others for the consequences of their actions. The third principle— **liability**—extends the concepts of responsibility and accountability to the area of law. Liability is a feature of political systems in which a body of law is in place that permits individuals to recover the damages done to them by other actors, systems, or organizations. **Due process** is a feature of law-governed societies and refers to a process in which laws are known and understood and there is an ability to appeal to higher authorities to ensure that the laws have been applied correctly.

You can use these concepts immediately to understand some contemporary Internet debates. For instance, consider the *Metro-Goldwyn-Mayer v. Grokster* lawsuit. MGM and other studios that joined it in the case argued that because the primary and intended use of Internet P2P file-sharing services such as Grokster, StreamCast and Kazaa was the swapping of copyright-protected music and video files, the file sharing services should be held accountable, and shut down. Although Grokster and the other networks acknowledged that the most common use of the software was for illegal digital music file swapping, they argued that there were substantial, nontrivial uses of the same networks for legally sharing files. They also argued they should not be held accountable for what individuals do with their software, any more than Sony could be held accountable for how people use VCRs, or Xerox for how people use copying machines. In June 2005, the case finally reached the Supreme Court, which ruled that Grokster and other P2P networks could be held accountable for the illegal actions of their users if it could be shown that they intended their software to be used for illegal downloading and sharing, and had marketed the software for that purpose. The court relied on copyright laws to arrive at its decisions, but these laws reflect some basic underlying ethical principles of responsibility, accountability, and liability.

Underlying the *Grokster* Supreme Court decision is a fundamental rejection of the notion that the Internet is an ungoverned "Wild West" environment that cannot be controlled. Under certain defined circumstances, the courts will intervene into the uses of the Internet. No organized civilized society has ever accepted the proposition that technology can flaunt basic underlying social and cultural values. Through all of the industrial and technological developments that have taken place, societies have intervened by means of legal and political decisions to ensure that the technology serves socially acceptable ends without stifling the positive consequences of innovation and wealth creation. The Internet in this sense is no different, and we can expect societies around the world to exercise more regulatory control over the Internet and e-commerce in an effort to arrive at a new balance between innovation and wealth creation, on the one hand, and other socially desirable objectives on the

responsibility

as free moral agents, individuals, organizations, and societies are responsible for the actions they take

accountability

individuals, organizations, and societies should be held accountable to others for the consequences of their actions

liability

a feature of political systems in which a body of law is in place that permits individuals to recover the damages done to them by other actors, systems, or organizations

due process

a process in which laws are known and understood and there is an ability to appeal to higher authorities to ensure that the laws have been applied correctly other. This is a difficult balancing act, and reasonable people will arrive at different conclusions.

ANALYZING ETHICAL DILEMMAS

dilemma

a situation in which there are at least two diametrically opposed actions, each of which supports a desirable outcome

Ethical, social, and political controversies usually present themselves as dilemmas. A **dilemma** is a situation in which there are at least two diametrically opposed actions, each of which supports a desirable outcome. When confronted with a situation that seems to present an ethical dilemma, how can you analyze and reason about the situation? The following is a five-step process that should help:

1. **Identify and clearly describe the facts.** Find out who did what to whom, and where, when, and how. In many instances, you will be surprised at the errors in the initially reported facts, and often you will find that simply getting the facts straight helps define the solution. It also helps to get the opposing parties involved in an ethical dilemma to agree on the facts.

2. **Define the conflict or dilemma and identify the higher-order values involved.** Ethical, social, and political issues always reference higher values. Otherwise, there would be no debate. The parties to a dispute all claim to be pursuing higher values (e.g., freedom, privacy, protection of property, and the free enterprise system). For example, supporters of the use of advertising networks such as DoubleClick argue that the tracking of consumer movements on the Web increases market efficiency and the wealth of the entire society. Opponents argue this claimed efficiency comes at the expense of individual privacy, and advertising networks should cease their activities or offer Web users the option of not participating in such tracking.

3. **Identify the stakeholders.** Every ethical, social, and political issue has stakeholders: players in the game who have an interest in the outcome, who have invested in the situation, and usually who have vocal opinions. Find out the identity of these groups and what they want. This will be useful later when designing a solution.

4. **Identify the options that you can reasonably take.** You may find that none of the options satisfies all the interests involved, but that some options do a better job than others. Sometimes, arriving at a "good" or ethical solution may not always be a balancing of consequences to stakeholders.

5. **Identify the potential consequences of your options.** Some options may be ethically correct, but disastrous from other points of view. Other options may work in this one instance, but not in other similar instances. Always ask yourself, "What if I choose this option consistently over time?"

Once your analysis is complete, you can refer to the following well-established ethical principles to help decide the matter.

CANDIDATE ETHICAL PRINCIPLES

Although you are the only one who can decide which ethical principles you will follow and how you will prioritize them, it is helpful to consider some ethical principles with deep roots in many cultures that have survived throughout recorded history:

- **The Golden Rule:** Do unto others as you would have them do unto you. Putting yourself into the place of others and thinking of yourself as the object of the decision can help you think about fairness in decision making.

- **Universalism:** If an action is not right for all situations, then it is not right for any specific situation (Immanuel Kant's categorical imperative). Ask yourself, "If we adopted this rule in every case, could the organization, or society, survive?"

- **Slippery Slope:** If an action cannot be taken repeatedly, then it is not right to take at all (Descartes' rule of change). An action may appear to work in one instance to solve a problem, but if repeated, would result in a negative outcome. In plain English, this rule might be stated as "once started down a slippery path, you may not be able to stop."

- **Collective Utilitarian Principle:** Take the action that achieves the greater value for all of society. This rule assumes you can prioritize values in a rank order and understand the consequences of various courses of action.

- **Risk Aversion:** Take the action that produces the least harm, or the least potential cost. Some actions have extremely high failure costs of very low probability (e.g., building a nuclear generating facility in an urban area) or extremely high failure costs of moderate probability (speeding and automobile accidents). Avoid the high-failure cost actions and choose those actions whose consequences would not be catastrophic, even if there were a failure.

- **No Free Lunch:** Assume that virtually all tangible and intangible objects are owned by someone else unless there is a specific declaration otherwise. (This is the ethical "no free lunch" rule.) If something someone else has created is useful to you, it has value and you should assume the creator wants compensation for this work.

- **The *New York Times* Test (Perfect Information Rule):** Assume that the results of your decision on a matter will be the subject of the lead article in the *New York Times* the next day. Will the reaction of readers be positive or negative? Would your parents, friends, and children be proud of your decision? Most criminals and unethical actors assume imperfect information, and therefore they assume their decisions and actions will never be revealed. When making decisions involving ethical dilemmas, it is wise to assume perfect information markets.

- **The Social Contract Rule:** Would you like to live in a society where the principle you are supporting would become an organizing principle of the entire society?

For instance, you might think it is wonderful to download illegal copies of music tracks, but you might not want to live in a society that did not respect property rights, such as your property rights to the car in your driveway, or your rights to a term paper or original art.

None of these rules is an absolute guide, and there are exceptions and logical difficulties with all of them. Nevertheless, actions that do not easily pass these guidelines deserve some very close attention and a great deal of caution because the appearance of unethical behavior may do as much harm to you and your company as the actual behavior.

Now that you have an understanding of some basic ethical reasoning concepts, let's take a closer look at each of the major types of ethical, social, and political debates that have arisen in e-commerce.

2 PRIVACY AND INFORMATION RIGHTS

privacy

the moral right of individuals to be left alone, free from surveillance or interference from other individuals or organizations, including the state

information privacy

includes both the claim that certain information should not be collected at all by governments or business firms, and the claim of individuals to control the use of whatever information that is collected about them

Privacy is the moral right of individuals to be left alone, free from surveillance or interference from other individuals or organizations, including the state. Privacy is a girder supporting freedom: Without the privacy required to think, write, plan, and associate independently and without fear, social and political freedom is weakened, and perhaps destroyed. **Information privacy** is a subset of privacy. The right to information privacy includes both the claim that certain information should not be collected at all by governments or business firms, and the claim of individuals to control the use of whatever information that is collected about them. Individual control over personal information is at the core of the privacy concept.

Due process also plays an important role in defining privacy. The best statement of due process in record keeping is given by the Fair Information Practices doctrine developed in the early 1970s and extended to the online privacy debate in the late 1990s (described later in this section).

There are two kinds of threats to individual privacy posed by the Internet. One threat originates in the private sector and concerns how much personal information is collected by commercial Web sites and how it will be used. A second threat originates in the public sector and concerns how much personal information federal, state, and local government authorities collect, and how they use it.

Privacy claims—and thinking about privacy—mushroomed in the United States at the end of the nineteenth century as the technology of photography and tabloid journalism enabled the invasion of the heretofore private lives of wealthy industrialists. For most of the twentieth century, however, privacy thinking and legislation focused on restraining the government from collecting and using personal information. With the explosion in the collection of private personal information by Web-based marketing firms since 1995, privacy concerns are increasingly directed toward restraining the activities of private firms in the collection and use of information on the Web. Claims to privacy are also involved at the workplace. Millions of employees are subject to various forms of electronic surveillance that in many cases is enhanced by firm intranets and Web technologies. For instance, the majority of U.S. companies monitor which Web sites their workers visit, as well as employee e-mail and instant messages. Employee posts on message boards and blogs are also coming under scrutiny (Vaughan, 2007).

In general, the Internet and the Web provide an ideal environment for both business and government to invade the personal privacy of millions of users on a scale unprecedented in history. Perhaps no other recent issue has raised as much widespread social and political concern as protecting the privacy of over 175–200 million Web users in the United States alone. The major ethical issues related to e-commerce and privacy include the following: Under what conditions should we invade the privacy of others? What legitimates intruding into others' lives through unobtrusive surveillance, market research, or other means? The major social issues related to e-commerce and privacy concern the development of "expectations of privacy" or privacy norms, as well as public attitudes. In what areas of life should we as a society encourage people to think they are in "private territory" as opposed to public view? The major political issues related to e-commerce and privacy concern the development of statutes that govern the relations between record keepers and individuals. How should both public and private organizations—which may be reluctant to remit the advantages that come from the unfettered flow of information on individuals—be restrained, if at all? In the following section, we look first at the various practices of e-commerce companies that pose a threat to privacy.

INFORMATION COLLECTED AT E-COMMERCE SITES

As you have learned in previous chapters, e-commerce sites routinely collect a variety of information from or about consumers who visit their site and/or make purchases. Some of this data constitutes **personally identifiable information (PII)**, which is defined as any data that can be used to identify, locate, or contact an individual (Federal Trade Commission, 2000a). Other data is **anonymous information**, composed of demographic and behavioral information, such as age, occupation, income, zip code, ethnicity, and other data that characterizes your life without identifying who you are. **Table 2** lists some of the personal identifiers routinely collected by online e-commerce sites. This is not an exhaustive list.

Advertising networks and search engines also track the behavior of consumers across thousands of popular sites, not just at one site, via cookies, spyware, and other techniques

Table 3 illustrates some of the major ways online firms gather information about consumers.

personally identifiable information (PII)
any data that can be used to identify, locate, or contact an individual

anonymous information
demographic and behavioral information that does not include any personal identifiers

PROFILING AND BEHAVIORAL TARGETING

On an average day, around 120 million Americans go online (Pew Internet & American Life Project, 2007). Marketers would like to know who these people are, what they are interested in, and what they buy. The more precise the information,

TABLE 2	PERSONAL INFORMATION COLLECTED BY E-COMMERCE SITES	
Name	Bank accounts	Education
Address	Credit card accounts	Preference data
Phone number	Gender	Transaction data
E-mail address	Age	Clickstream data
Social security number	Occupation	Browser type

TABLE 3	THE INTERNET'S MAJOR INFORMATION GATHERING TOOLS AND THEIR IMPACT ON PRIVACY
INTERNET CAPABILITY	**IMPACT ON PRIVACY**
Cookies	Used to track individuals at a single site.
Third-party Cookies	Cookies placed by outside third-party advertising networks. Used to monitor and track online behavior, searches, and sites visited across thousands of sites that belong to the advertising network for the purpose of displaying "relevant" advertising.
Spyware	Can be used to record all the keyboard activity of a user, including Web sites visited and security codes used; also used to display advertisements to users based on their searches or other behavior.
Search engine behavioral targeting (Google, and other search engines)	Uses prior search history, demographic, expressed interests, geographic, or other user-entered data to target advertising.
Shopping carts	Can be used to collect detailed payment and purchase information.
Forms	Online forms that users voluntarily fill out in return for a promised benefit or reward that are linked with clickstream or other behavioral data to create a personal profile.
Site transaction logs	Can be used to collect and analyze detailed information on page content viewed by users.
Search engines	Can be used to trace user statements and views on newsgroups, chat groups, and other public forums on the Web, and profile users' social and political views. Google returns name, address, and links to a map with directions to the address when a phone number is entered.
Digital Wallets (single sign-on services)	Client-side wallets and software that reveal personal information to Web sites verifying the identity of the consumer
Digital Rights Management (DRM)	Software (Windows Media Player) that requires users of online media to identify themselves before viewing copyrighted content
Trusted Computing Environments	Hardware and software that controls the viewing of copyrighted content and requires users identification

profiling

the creation of digital images that characterize online individual and group behavior

anonymous profiles

identify people as belonging to highly specific and targeted groups

the more complete the information, the more valuable it is as a predictive and marketing tool. Armed with this information, marketers can make their ad campaigns more efficient by targeting specific ads at specific groups or individuals, and they can even adjust the ads for specific groups.

Many Web sites allow third parties—including online advertising networks such as aQuantive, DoubleClick, and others—to place "third-party" cookies on a visitor's hard drive in order to engage in profiling the user's behavior across thousands of Web sites. A third-party cookie is used to track users across hundreds or thousands of other Web sites who are members of the advertising network. **Profiling** is the creation of digital images that characterize online individual and group behavior. **Anonymous profiles** identify people as belonging to highly specific and targeted groups, for example, 20-to 30-year-old males, with college degrees and incomes greater than $30,000 a year, and interested in high-fashion clothing (based on recent search engine use). **Personal profiles** add a personal e-mail address, postal address, and/or phone number to behavioral data. Increasingly, online firms are attempting to link their online profiles to offline consumer data collected by established retail and catalog firms. In the past, individual stores collected data on customer movement through a single store in order to understand consumer behavior and alter the design of stores accordingly. Also, purchase and expenditure data was gathered on consumers purchasing from multiple stores-usually long after the purchases were made—and the data was used to target direct mail and in-store campaigns, in addition to mass-media advertising.

personal profiles
add a personal e-mail address, postal address, and/or phone number to behavioral data

The online advertising networks such as DoubleClick and 24/7 Media have added several new dimensions to established offline marketing techniques. First, they have the ability to precisely track not just consumer purchases, but all browsing behavior on the Web at thousands of the most popular member sites, including browsing book lists, filling out preference forms, and viewing content pages. Second, they can dynamically adjust what the shopper sees on screen—including prices. Third, they can build and continually refresh high-resolution data images or behavioral profiles of consumers (Laudon, 1996). Other advertising firms have created spyware software that, when placed on a consumer's computer, can report back to the advertiser's server on all consumer Internet use, and is also used to display advertising on the consumer's computer.

A different kind of profiling and a more recent form of behavioral targeting is Google's results-based personalization of advertising. In October 2005, Google applied for a patent on a program that allows advertisers using Google's AdWord program to target ads to users based on their prior search histories and profiles which Google constructs based on user searches, along with any other information the user submits to Google or Google can obtain, such as age, demographics, region, and other Web activities (such as blogging). Google also applied for a second patent on a program that allows Google to help advertisers select keywords and design ads for various market segments based on search histories, such as helping a clothing Web site create and test ads targeted at teenage females. In August 2007, Google began to put some of those ideas into practice, using behavioral targeting to help it display more relevant ads based on keywords. According to Google, the new feature is aimed at capturing a more robust understanding of user intent, and thereby delivering a better ad (Tehrani, 2007) Google's Gmail, a free e-mail service, offers a powerful interface and as of November 2007, 4.7 gigabytes of free storage. In return, Google computers read all incoming and outgoing e-mail and place "relevant" advertising in the margins of the mail. Profiles are developed on individual users based on the content in their e-mail (Story, 2007).

What is different about these efforts at online profiling and behavioral targeting (when compared to offline methods used in the past) is the scope and intensity of the data dragnet, and the ability to manipulate the shopping environment to the advantage of the merchant. Most of this activity occurs in the background without the knowledge of the shopper, and it takes place dynamically online in less than a second.

Arguably, no other Web-based technique comes so close to being a real-world implementation of George Orwell's novel *1984* and its lead character, Big Brother. Here's an illustration of online profiling from "Online Profiling: A Report to Congress," an FTC report:

Online consumer Joe Smith goes to a Web site that sells sporting goods. He clicks on the pages for golf bags. While there, he sees a banner ad, which he ignores as it does not interest him. The ad was placed by USAad Network. He then goes to a travel site and enters a search on "Hawaii." The USAad Network also serves ads on this site, and Joe sees an ad for rental cars there. Joe then visits an online bookstore and browses through books about the world's best golf courses. USAad Network serves ads there as well. A week later, Joe visits his favorite online news site, and notices an ad for golf vacation packages in Hawaii. Delighted, he clicks on the ad, which was served by USAad Network. Later, Joe begins to wonder whether it was a coincidence that this particular ad appeared and, if not, how it happened (Federal Trade Commission, 2000b).

The sample online profile illustrates several features of such profiles. First, the profile created for Joe Smith was completely anonymous and did not require any personal information such as a name, e-mail address, or Social Security number. Obviously, this profile would be more valuable if the system did have personal information because then Joe could be sent e-mail marketing. Second, ad networks do not know who is operating the browser. If other members of Joe's family used the same computer to shop the Web, they would be exposed to golf vacation ads, and Joe could be exposed to ads more appropriate to his wife or children. Third, profiles are usually very imprecise, the result of "best guesses" and just plain guesses. Profiles are built using a product/service scoring system that is not very detailed, and as a result, the profiles tend to be very crude.

In the preceding example, Joe is obviously interested in golf and travel because he intentionally expressed these interests. However, he may have wanted to scuba dive in Hawaii, or visit old friends, not play golf. The profiling system in the example took a leap of faith that a golf vacation in Hawaii is what Joe really wants. Sometimes these guesses work, but there is considerable evidence to suggest that simply knowing Joe made an inquiry about Hawaii would be sufficient to sell him a trip to Hawaii for any of several activities and the USAad Network provided little additional value.

Network advertising firms argue that Web profiling benefits both consumers and businesses. Profiling permits targeting of ads, ensuring that consumers see advertisements mostly for products and services in which they are actually interested. Businesses benefit by not paying for wasted advertising sent to consumers who have no interest in their product or service. The industry argues that by increasing the effectiveness of advertising, more advertising revenues go to the Internet, which in turn subsidizes free content on the Internet. Last, product designers and entrepreneurs benefit by sensing demand for new products and services by examining user searches and profiles.

Critics argue that profiling undermines the expectation of anonymity and privacy that most people have when using the Internet, and change what should be a private experience into one where an individual's every move is recorded. As people become aware that their every move is being watched, they will be far less likely to explore sensitive topics, browse pages, or read about controversial issues. In most cases, the profiling is invisible to users, and even hidden. Consumers are not notified that profiling is occurring. Profiling permits data aggregation on hundreds or even thousands of unrelated sites on the Web. The cookies placed by ad networks are persistent, and they can be set to last days, months, years, or even forever. Their tracking occurs over an extended period of time and resumes each time the individual logs on to the Internet. This clickstream data is used to create profiles that can include hundreds of distinct data fields for each consumer. Associating so-called anonymous profiles with personal information is fairly easy, and companies can change policies quickly without informing the consumer. Some critics believe profiling permits **weblining**—charging some customers more money for products and services based on their profiles. Although the information gathered by network advertisers is often anonymous (non-PII data), in many cases, the profiles derived from tracking consumers' activities on the Web are linked or merged with personally identifiable information. DoubleClick and other advertising network firms have attempted to purchase offline marketing firms that collect offline consumer data for the purpose of matching offline and online behavioral data at the individual level. However, public reaction was so negative that no network advertising firm publicly admits to matching offline PII with online profile data. Nevertheless, client Web sites encourage visitors to register for prizes, benefits, or content access in order to capture personal information such as e-mail addresses and physical addresses. Anonymous behavioral data is far more valuable if it can be linked with offline consumer behavior, e-mail addresses, and postal addresses.

This consumer data can also be combined with data on the consumers' offline purchases, or information collected directly from consumers through surveys and registration forms. As the technology of connection to the Internet for consumers moves away from telephone modems where IP addresses are assigned dynamically, and toward static assigned IP addresses used by DSL and cable modems, then connecting anonymous profiles to personal names and e-mail addresses will become easier and more prevalent.

From a privacy protection perspective, the advertising network raises issues about who will see and use the information held by private companies, whether the user profiles will be linked to actual personally identifying information (such as name, Social Security number, and bank and credit accounts), the absence of consumer control over the use of the information, the lack of consumer choice, the absence of consumer notice, and the lack of review and amendment procedures.

The pervasive and largely unregulated collection of personal information online has raised significant fears and opposition among consumers. According to a 2007 survey, over 80% of Internet users surveyed said that the privacy of their personal information was either important or very important to them (Ponemon Institute, 2007). Another study found that over six in 10 U.S. Web searchers do not trust search engines with their information (eMarketer, Inc. 2007a). One result of the lack of trust toward online firms and specific fears of privacy invasion is a reduction in online purchases. For instance, one survey found that over 70% of respondents had decided against registering or making a purchase online because those actions required them to provide information that they did not want to divulge. A Gartner survey found that nearly half of online U.S. adults said that concerns about theft of information, data breaches, or Internet-based attacks affected their purchasing,

weblining
charging some customers more money for products and services based on their profiles

payment, online transaction or e-mail behavior (TRUSTe, 2006; eMarketer, Inc., 2007b). The actual amount of lost sales is unknown, but if 25% of consumers stopped purchasing online, that would add up to a hefty $56 billion in lost sales. If even just 10% of this number turned out to be accurate, that would still be a $22.5 billion loss in sales.

The Internet and e-commerce—as we have seen in previous chapters—strengthen the ability of private firms to collect, store, and analyze personal information at a level never envisioned by privacy thinkers and legislators. With Web technologies, the invasion of individual privacy is low-cost, profitable, and effective.

The Internet and Government Invasions of Privacy: E-commerce Surveillance

Today, the e-commerce behavior, profiles, and transactions of consumers are routinely available to a wide range of government agencies and law enforcement authorities, contributing to rising fears among online consumers, and in many cases, their withdrawal from the online marketplace. While the Internet used to be thought of as impossible for governments to control or monitor, nothing could be actually further from the truth. Law enforcement authorities have long claimed the right under numerous statutes to monitor any form of electronic communication pursuant to a court order and judicial review and based on the reasonable belief that a crime is being committed. This includes the surveillance of consumers engaged in e-commerce. In the case of the Internet, this is accomplished by placing sniffer software and servers at the ISP being used by the target suspect, in a manner similar to pen registers and trap-and-trace devices used for telephone surveillance. The Communications Assistance for Law Enforcement Act (CALEA), the USA PATRIOT Act, the Cyber Security Enhancement Act, and the Homeland Security Act all strengthen the ability of law enforcement agencies to monitor Internet users without their knowledge and, under certain circumstances when life is purportedly at stake, without judicial oversight. In addition, government agencies are among the largest users of private sector commercial data brokers, such as ChoicePoint, Acxiom, Experian, and TransUnion Corporation, that collect a vast amount of information about consumers from various offline and online public sources, such as public records and the telephone directory, and non-public sources, such as "credit header" information from credit bureaus (which typically contains name, aliases, birth date, Social Security number, current and prior addresses, and phone numbers). Information contained in individual reference services' databases ranges from purely identifying information (e.g., name and phone number) to much more extensive data (e.g., driving records, criminal and civil court records, property records, and licensing records). This information can be linked to online behavior information collected from other commercial sources to compile an extensive profile of individual's online and offline behavior (Frackman, Ray, and Martin, 2002; Federal Trade Commission, 1997).

In June 2006, the Justice Department appointed a task force to investigate a proposal that Internet companies retain records that would allow the government to identify which individuals visited certain Web sites and conducted searches using certain terms, and also records about whom users exchange e-mail with, for as long two years. The European Parliament passed similar legislation in December 2005. In 2007, the four major search engines (Google, Yahoo, MSN, and Ask.com) all announced new policies on how long they would retain search information, ranging from 18 months (Google and MSN) to 13 months (Yahoo), while Ask.com announced a new tool that would allow users to block any retention of specific search terms and the user's IP address (Hansell and Lichtblau, 2006; Zeller, 2006; Leidtke, 2007).

Congress, aware of the dangers of unregulated government intrusion into Internet communications, and its threat to e-commerce privacy, created a Privacy and Civil Liberties Oversight Board in the Office of the President in 2004 to ensure anti-terrorism laws do not decimate other privacy protection laws. The Board began meeting in 2006, and issued its first annual report to Congress in April 2007 (Privacy and Civilities Oversight Board, 2007).

LEGAL PROTECTIONS

In the United States, Canada, and Germany, rights to privacy are explicitly granted in, or can be derived from, founding documents such as constitutions, as well as in specific statutes. In England and the United States, there is also protection of privacy in the common law, a body of court decisions involving torts or personal injuries. For instance, in the United States, four privacy-related torts have been defined in court decisions involving claims of injury to individuals caused by other private parties: intrusion on solitude, public disclosure of private facts, publicity placing a person in a false light, and appropriation of a person's name or likeness (mostly concerning celebrities) for a commercial purpose (Laudon, 1996). In the United States, the claim to privacy against government intrusion is protected primarily by the First Amendment guarantees of freedom of speech and association, the Fourth Amendment protections against unreasonable search and seizure of one's personal documents or home, and the Fourteenth Amendment's guarantee of due process.

In addition to common law and the Constitution, there are both federal laws and state laws that protect individuals against government intrusion and in some cases define privacy rights vis-à-vis private organizations such as financial, educational, and media institutions (cable television and video rentals) (see **Table 4**).

Informed Consent

The concept of **informed consent** (defined as consent given with knowledge of all material facts needed to make a rational decision) also plays an important role in protecting privacy. In the United States, business firms (and government agencies) can gather transaction information generated in the marketplace and then use that information for other marketing purposes, without obtaining the informed consent of the individual. For instance, in the United States, if a Web shopper purchases books about baseball at a site that belongs to an advertising network such as DoubleClick, a cookie can be placed on the consumer's hard drive and used by other member sites

informed consent
consent given with knowledge of all material facts needed to make a rational decision

279

TABLE 4	FEDERAL AND STATE PRIVACY LAWS
NAME	DESCRIPTION

GENERAL FEDERAL PRIVACY LAWS

Name	Description
Freedom of Information Act of 1966	Gives people the right to inspect information about themselves held in government files; also allows other individuals and organizations the right to request disclosure of government records based on the public's right to know.
Privacy Act of 1974, as amended	Regulates the federal government's collection, use, and disclosure of data collected by federal agencies. Gives individuals a right to inspect and correct records.
Electronic Communications Privacy Act of 1986	Makes conduct that would infringe on the security of electronic communications illegal.
Computer Matching and Privacy Protection Act of 1988	Regulates computerized matching of files held by different government agencies.
Computer Security Act of 1987	Makes conduct that would infringe on the security of computer-based files illegal.
Driver's Privacy Protection Act of 1994	Limits access to personal information maintained by state motor vehicle departments to those with legitimate business purposes. Also gives drivers the option to prevent disclosure of driver's license information to marketers and the general public.
E-Government Act of 2002	Regulates the collection and use of personal information by federal agencies.

FEDERAL PRIVACY LAWS AFFECTING PRIVATE INSTITUTIONS

Name	Description
Fair Credit Reporting Act of 1970	Regulates the credit investigating and reporting industry. Gives people the right to inspect credit records if they have been denied credit and provides procedures for correcting information.
Family Educational Rights and Privacy Act of 1974	Requires schools and colleges to give students and their parents access to student records and to allow them to challenge and correct information; limits disclosure of such records to third parties.
Right to Financial Privacy Act of 1978	Regulates the financial industry's use of personal financial records; establishes procedures that federal agencies must follow to gain access to such records.
Privacy Protection Act of 1980	Prohibits government agents from conducting unannounced searches of press offices and files if no one in the office is suspected of committing a crime.
Cable Communications Policy Act of 1984	Regulates the cable industry's collection and disclosure of information concerning subscribers
Video Privacy Protection Act of 1988	Prevents disclosure of a person's video rental records without court order or consent.
Child Online Privacy Protection Act (1998)	Prohibits deceptive practices in connection with collection, use and/or disclosure of personal information from and about children on the Internet.
Financial Modernization Act (Graham-Leech-Bliley Act) (1999)	Requires financial institutions to inform consumers of their privacy policies and permits consumers some control over their records.
The Health Insurance Portability and Accountability Act of 1996 (HIPAA)	Requires health care providers and insurers and other third parties to promulgate privacy policies to consumers and establishes due process procedures.

TABLE 4	FEDERAL AND STATE PRIVACY LAWS (CONT'D)
NAME	**DESCRIPTION**
SELECTED STATE PRIVACY LAWS	
Online Privacy Policies	The California Online Privacy Protection Act of 2003 was the first state law in the United States requiring owners of commercial Web sites or online services to post a privacy policy. The policy must, among other things, identify the categories of PII collected about site visitors and categories of third parties with whom the information may be shared. Failure to comply can result in a civil suit for unfair business practices. Nebraska and Pennsylvania prohibit false and misleading statements in online privacy policies. At least 16 states require government Web sites to establish privacy policies or procedures or incorporate machine-readable privacy policies into their Web sites.
Spyware Legislation	A number of states, including California, Utah, Arizona, Arkansas, and Virginia, among others, have passed laws that make the installation of spyware on a user's computer without consent, illegal.
Disclosure of Security Breaches	In 2002, California enacted legislation that requires state agencies or businesses that own or license computer data with personal information to notify state residents if they experience a security breach involving that information; over 22 other states have enacted similar legislation
Privacy of Personal Information	Two states, Nevada and Minnesota, require ISPs to keep their customers' PII private unless the customer consents to disclose the information. Minnesota also requires ISPs to get permission from subscribers before disclosing information about subscribers' online surfing habits
Data Encryption	In October 2007, Nevada passed the first law that requires encryption for the transmission of customer personal information. The law takes effect October 1, 2008.

to sell the shopper sports clothing without the explicit permission or even knowledge of the user. This online preference information may also be linked with personally identifying information. In Europe, this would be illegal. A business in Europe cannot use marketplace transaction information for any purpose other than supporting the current transaction, unless of course it obtains the individual's consent in writing or by filling out an on-screen form.

There are traditionally two models for informed consent: opt-in and opt-out. The **opt-in** model requires an affirmative action by the consumer to allow collection and use of information. For instance, using opt-in, consumers would first be asked if they approved of the collection and use of information, and then directed to check a selection box if they agreed. Otherwise, the default is not to approve the collection of data. In the **opt-out** model, the default is to collect information unless the consumer takes an affirmative action to prevent the collection of data by checking a box, or by filling out a form.

opt-in
requires an affirmative action by the consumer to allow collection and use of consumer information

opt-out
the default is to collect information unless the consumer takes an affirmative action to prevent the collection of data

Until recently, many U.S e-commerce companies rejected the concept of informed consent and instead simply published their information use policy on their site. U.S. businesses argue that informing consumers about how the information will be used is sufficient to obtain the users' informed consent. Most U.S. sites that offer informed consent make opting in the default option, and require users to go to special pages to request to opt-out of promotional campaigns. Some sites have an opt-out selection box at the very bottom of their information policy statements where the consumer is unlikely to see it. Privacy advocates argue that many information/privacy policy statements on U.S. Web sites are obscure, difficult to read, and legitimate just about any use of personal information. For instance, Yahoo's privacy policy begins with the statement that "Yahoo! takes your privacy seriously." It then states that it "does not rent, sell, or share personal information about you with other people or non-affiliated companies." However, there are a number of exceptions that significantly weaken this statement. For instance, Yahoo may share the information with "trusted partners," which could be anyone that Yahoo does business with, although perhaps not a company that the user might choose to do business with.

The FTC's Fair Information Practices Principles

In the United States, the FTC has taken the lead in conducting research on online privacy and recommending legislation to Congress. The FTC is a cabinet-level agency charged with promoting the efficient functioning of the marketplace by protecting consumers from unfair or deceptive practices and increasing consumer choice by promoting competition. In addition to reports and recommendations, the FTC enforces existing legislation by suing corporations it believes are in violation of federal fair trade laws.

In 1995, the FTC began a series of investigations of online privacy based on its belief that online invasion of privacy potentially involved deceit and unfair behavior. In 1998, the FTC issued its Fair Information Practice (FIP) principles, on which it has based its assessments and recommendations for online privacy. **Table 5** describes these principles. Two of the five are designated as basic, "core" principles that must be present to protect privacy, whereas the other practices are less central. The FTC's FIP principles restate and strengthen in a form suitable to deal with online privacy the Fair Information Practices doctrine developed in 1973 by a government study group (U.S. Department of Health, Education and Welfare, 1973).

The FTC's FIP principles set the ground rules for what constitutes due process privacy protection procedures at e-commerce and all other Web sites—including government and nonprofit Web sites—in the United States.

At this point, the FTC's FIP principles are guidelines, not laws. They have stimulated private firms and industry associations to develop their own private guidelines (discussed next). However, the FTC's FIP guidelines are being used as the basis of new legislation. The most important online privacy legislation to date that was directly influenced by the FTC's FIP principles is the Children's Online Privacy Protection Act (COPPA) (1998), which requires Web sites to obtain

TABLE 5	FEDERAL TRADE COMMISSION'S FAIR INFORMATION PRACTICE PRINCIPLES
Notice/Awareness (Core principle)	Sites must disclose their information practices before collecting data. Includes identification of collector, uses of data, other recipients of data, nature of collection (active/inactive), voluntary or required, consequences of refusal, and steps taken to protect confidentiality, integrity, and quality of the data
Choice/Consent (Core principle)	There must be a choice regime in place allowing consumers to choose how their information will be used for secondary purposes other than supporting the transaction, including internal use and transfer to third parties. Opt-in/Opt-out must be available.
Access/Participation	Consumers should be able to review and contest the accuracy and completeness of data collected about them in a timely, inexpensive process.
Security	Data collectors must take reasonable steps to assure that consumer information is accurate and secure from unauthorized use.
Enforcement	There must be in place a mechanism to enforce FIP principles. This can involve self-regulation, legislation giving consumers legal remedies for violations, or federal statutes and regulation.

SOURCE: Based on data from Federal Trade Commission, 1998; 2000a.

parental permission before collecting information on children under 13 years of age.

In July 2000, the FTC recommended legislation to Congress to protect online consumer privacy from the threat posed by advertising networks. **Table 6** summarizes the Commission's recommendations. The FTC profiling recommendations significantly strengthen the FIP principles of notification and choice, while also including restrictions on information that may be collected.[1] Although the FTC supports industry efforts at self-regulation, it nevertheless recommended legislation to ensure that all Web sites using network advertising and all network advertisers comply. To date, however, Congress has not passed such legislation.

In November 2007, the FTC held a two-day workshop on online advertising, behavioral targeting and online privacy. Consumer privacy groups have asked for the institution of a "Do Not Track" list similar to the FTC's "Do Not Call" telemarketing list, that would permit people to more easily opt out of behavioral tracking programs, as well as disclosure notices that tracking is occurring, and the ability for consumers to view

[1]Much general privacy legislation affecting government, e.g., the Privacy Act of 1974, precludes the government from collecting information on political and social behavior of citizens. The FTC restrictions are significant because they are the FTC's first effort at limiting the collection of certain information.

TABLE 6	FTC RECOMMENDATIONS REGARDING ONLINE PROFILING
PRINCIPLE	DESCRIPTION OF RECOMMENDATION
Notice	Complete transparency to user by providing disclosure and choice options on the host Web site. "Robust" notice for PII (time/place of collection; before collection begins). Clear and conspicuous notice for non-PII.
Choice	Opt-in for PII, opt-out for non-PII. No conversion of non-PII to PII without consent. Opt-out from any or all network advertisers from a single page provided by the host Web site.
Access	Reasonable provisions to allow inspection and correction.
Security	Reasonable efforts to secure information from loss, misuse, or improper access.
Enforcement	Done by independent third parties, such as seal programs and accounting firms.
Restricted collection	Advertising networks will not collect information about sensitive financial or medical topics, sexual behavior or sexual orientation, or use social security numbers for profiling.

and edit any profiles about themselves that ad networks build. The online advertising industry, not surprisingly, believes that FTC regulation would stifle innovation in the industry. Although at least one FTC member suggested at the conference that rules about privacy policies might need to be established, and that the FTC needed to increase its scrutiny of the online targeting, whether any new FTC regulations will result from these efforts in the near future is unknown (Story, 2007b).

The European Directive on Data Protection

In Europe, privacy protection is much stronger than it is in the United States. In the United States, private organizations and businesses are permitted to use PII gathered in commercial transactions for other business purposes without the prior consent of the consumer (so-called secondary uses of PII). In the United States, there is no federal agency charged with enforcing privacy law. Instead, privacy law is enforced largely through self-regulation by businesses, and by individuals who must sue agencies or companies in court to recover damages. This is expensive and rarely done. The European approach to privacy protection is more comprehensive and regulatory in nature. European countries do not allow business firms to use PII without the prior consent of consumers. They enforce their privacy laws by creating data protection agencies to pursue complaints brought by citizens and to actively enforce privacy laws.

On October 25, 1998, the European Commission's Directive on Data Protection went into effect, standardizing and broadening privacy protection in the European Union (EU) nations. The Directive is based on the Fair Information Practices doctrine, but extends the control individuals can exercise over their personal information. The Directive requires companies to inform people when they collect information about them and to disclose how it will be stored and used. Customers must provide their informed consent before any company can legally use data about them, and they have the right to access that information, correct it, and request that no further data be collected. Further, the Directive prohibits the transfer of PII to organizations or countries that do not have similarly strong privacy protection policies. This means that data collected in Europe by American business firms cannot be transferred or processed in the United States (which has weaker privacy protection laws). This would potentially interfere with a $350 billion annual trade flow between the United States and Europe.

The Department of Commerce, working with the European Commission, developed a safe harbor framework for U.S. firms. A **safe harbor** is a private self-regulating policy and enforcement mechanism that meets the objectives of government regulators and legislation, but does not involve government regulation or enforcement. The government plays a role in certifying safe harbors, however. Organizations that decide to participate in the safe harbor program must develop policies that meet European standards, and they must publicly sign on to a Web-based register maintained by the Department of Commerce. Enforcement occurs in the United States and relies to a large extent on self-policing and regulation, backed up by government enforcement of fair trade statutes. For more information on the safe harbor procedures and the EU Data Directive, see www.export.gov/safeharbor.

PRIVATE INDUSTRY SELF-REGULATION

The online industry in the United States has historically opposed privacy legislation, arguing that industry can do a better job of protecting privacy than government. The online industry formed the Online Privacy Alliance (OPA) in 1998 to encourage self-regulation in part as a reaction to growing public concerns and the threat of legislation being proposed by FTC and privacy advocacy groups.

Private industry in the United States has created the idea of safe harbors from government regulation. For instance, COPPA includes a provision enabling industry groups or others to submit for the FTC's approval self-regulatory guidelines that implement the protections of the FIP principles and FTC rules. In May 2001, the FTC approved the TRUSTe Internet privacy protection program under the terms of COPPA as a safe harbor.[2]

OPA has developed a set of privacy guidelines that members are required to implement. The primary focus of industry efforts has been the development of online "seals" that attest to the privacy policies on a site. The Better Business Bureau (BBB), TRUSTe, WebTrust, and major accounting firms—among them PricewaterhouseCoopers' BetterWeb—have established seals for Web sites. To display a seal, Web site operators must conform to certain privacy principles, a complaint resolution process, and monitoring by the seal originator. Around 2,500

safe harbor

a private self-regulating policy and enforcement mechanism that meets the objectives of government regulators and legislation but does not involve government regulation or enforcement

---

[2]Another longstanding industry group with a safe harbor program for children online is CARU (Children's Advertising Review Unit), founded in 1974 as the advertising industry's self-regulation program for the protection of children.

sites now display the TRUSTe seal, and almost 40,000 display the BBB's Reliability seal. Nevertheless, online privacy seal programs have had a limited impact on Web privacy practices. Critics argue that the seal programs are not particularly effective in safeguarding privacy. For these reasons, the FTC has not deemed the seal programs as "safe harbors" yet (with the exception of TRUSTe's children's privacy seal under COPPA), and the agency continues to push for legislation to enforce privacy protection principles.

The advertising network industry has also formed an industry association, the Network Advertising Initiative (NAI), to develop privacy policies. NAI member companies include Advertising.com, Atlas (part of aQuantive), DoubleClick, Revenue Science, Tacoda, and 24/7 Real Media. The NAI has developed a set of privacy principles in conjunction with the FTC. The NAI policies have two objectives: to offer consumers a chance to opt-out of advertising network programs (including e-mail campaigns), and to provide consumers redress from abuses. In order to opt-out, the NAI has created a Web site—Networkadvertising.org—where consumers can use a global opt-out feature to prevent network advertising agencies from placing their cookies on a user's computer. If a consumer has a complaint, the NAI has a link to the Truste.org Web site where the complaints can be filed (Network Advertising Initiative, 2007).

In general, industry efforts at self-regulation in online privacy have not succeeded in reducing American fears of privacy invasion during online transactions, or in reducing the level of privacy invasion. At best, self-regulation has offered consumers notice about whether a privacy policy exists, but usually says little about the actual use of the information, does not offer consumers a chance to see and correct the information or control its use in any significant way, offers no promises for the security of that information, and offers no enforcement mechanism (Hoofnagle, 2005). At the same time, the FTC and Congress point to efforts at self-regulation as a reason for not legislating in this area.

Read *Insight on Business: Chief Privacy Officers* to see a different approach to industry self-regulation.

PRIVACY ADVOCACY GROUPS

There are a number of privacy advocacy groups on the Web that monitor developments in privacy. Some of these sites are industry-supported, while others rely on private foundations and contributions. Some of the better-known sites are listed in **Table 7**.

TECHNOLOGICAL SOLUTIONS

There are a number of privacy-enhancing technologies for protecting user privacy during interactions with Web sites that have been developed (Vijayan, 2000; Goldschlag, Reed, and Syverson, 1999; Gabber et al., 1999). Most of these tools emphasize security—the ability of individuals to protect their communications and files from illegitimate snoopers. This is just one element of privacy. The other is the development of private and public policies that enable consumers to control the collection and use of information that is gathered in the course of market transactions. **Table 8** describes some ways in which technology can be used to protect privacy.

TABLE 7	PRIVACY ADVOCACY GROUPS
ADVOCACY GROUP	**FOCUS**
Epic.org (Electronic Privacy Information Center)	Washington-based watch-dog group
Privacyinternational.org	Tracks international privacy developments
Cdt.org (Center for Democracy and Technology)	Foundation—and business-supported group with a legislative focus
Privacy.org	Clearinghouse sponsored by EPIC and Privacy International
Privacyrights.org	Educational clearinghouse
Privacyalliance.org	Industry-supported clearinghouse

TABLE 8	TECHNOLOGICAL PROTECTIONS FOR ONLINE PRIVACY	
TECHNOLOGY	**PRODUCTS**	**PROTECTION**
Spyware blockers	Spyware Doctor, ZoneAlarm, Ad-Aware and Spybot—Search and Destroy (Spybot-S&D) (freeware)	Detects and removes spyware and adware, keyloggers and other malware
Pop-up blockers	Browsers: Firefox, Internet Explorer 6.0 SP2 and 7.0, Safari, Opera Toolbars: Google, Yahoo, MSN Add-on programs: STOPzilla, Adblock, NoAds	Prevents calls to ad servers that push pop-up, pop-under and leave behind ads; restricts downloading of images at user request
Secure e-mail	ZL Technologies; SafeMessage.com; Hushmail.com; Pretty Good Privacy (PGP)	E-mail and document encryption
Anonymous remailers	W3-Anonymous Remailer; Jack B Nymble; Java Anonymous Proxy	Send e-mail without trace
Anonymous surfing	Freedom Websecure; Anonymizer.com; Tor; GhostSurf	Surf without a trace
Cookie managers	CookieCrusher, and most browsers	Prevents client computer from accepting cookies
Disk/file erasing programs	Mutilate File Wiper; Eraser; DiskVac 2.0	Completely erases hard drive and floppy files
Policy generators	OECD Privacy Policy Generator	Automates the development of an OECD privacy compliance policy
Privacy Policy Reader	P3P	Software for automating the communication of privacy policies to users
Public Key Encryption	PGP Desktop 9.0	Program that encrypts your mail and documents

INSIGHT ON BUSINESS

CHIEF PRIVACY OFFICERS

How can you tell if your own corporate practices actually conform to the privacy policy stated on your Web site? How can your business keep track of all the new privacy legislation and changes in European policies? The answer for many corporations is to create an executive position—Chief Privacy Officer (CPO). The position is a relatively new one that firms first started to create about 10 years ago, but today is one of fastest growing in corporate management. Many firms, such as IBM, AT&T, Eastman Kodak, DoubleClick, New York Life, ChoicePoint, Marriott International and many others, have added this position to senior management ranks, and it is becoming more and more common in the health care, financial services, technology, and consumer goods industries, in part due to growing regulatory requirements with respect to data privacy.

What does a CPO do? The job has several aspects. Often, a CPO's first job is to plan and then implement a privacy plan for the firm to follow. Once a plan is in place, it needs to be enforced, and monitored, and the company's business units and employees may need to be educated about the plan and the importance of privacy. For instance, at Marriott International, Chris Zoladz, vice president of information protection and privacy, notes that "Good privacy is good business." When Marriott marketing executives proposed personalizing the information that appears on the hotel chain's Web site so that it was customized based on personal information collected from guests as part of the reservation process, Zoladz got involved to make sure the information was used properly.

Another job is helping the company avoid privacy "landmines," which are mistakes in policy or technology that, had any one thought about it, would obviously be embarrassing to the company because of the potential for a storm of protest from privacy protection groups. For instance, IBM's CPO proactively led the fight within the company to ban the use of genetic data in the employment recruiting and promotion process. AOL proactively changed its privacy policy for the first time since 1998 by stopping the practice of selling mailing lists to retailers, and stopped using information from advertising networks and non-AOL sites to customize ads. In other cases, in the absence of a CPO, disaster is possible. U.S. Bancorp decided to sell personal financial data to a direct-marketing company in violation of its own stated policies. This cost Bancorp $3 million in a legal settlement in Minnesota. Real Networks had to apologize to users and change its data collection policies after a disclosure that the company's RealJukebox Internet music software captured data about users' preferences. A string of data losses, criminal intrusions, and accidents at data brokerage firms such as ChoicePoint and Reed Elsevier's LexisNexis unit resulted in the diversion and theft of hundreds of thousands of complete personal profiles. This in turn has led to Congressional investigations, fines, and the threat of restrictive legislation for the entire data brokerage industry.

The new corporate emphasis on privacy has also created a new business for the big accounting firm PricewaterhouseCoopers as one part of its Global Risk Management Solutions. PWC has

(continued)

conducted hundreds of privacy audits. Companies are taking this issue very seriously because data theft or loss and invasions of privacy directly threaten the brand names of firms. Privacy audits identify the risks that firms face and prescribe corrective actions with a view to avoiding class action suits, Internet-based protests, and shareholder enmity. And what do the auditors find? About 80% of the companies audited by PWC do not follow their own stated privacy policies. Most of the time this is the result of poor training and human error.

After Expedia completed a privacy audit led by PWC, it changed its information collection policy from opt-out to opt-in. Now Expedia's customers have to actively click a button and ask to be informed of new offers from the travel site. The result is that far fewer customers ask to unsubscribe from mailing solicitations. Expedia executives believe trust and privacy are major concerns of their customers, and anything they can do to enhance trust is good for their business.

What do CPOs worry about? They often have a hard time with their own employees taking privacy seriously and changing policies to cope with the risks. In the case of ChoicePoint's loss of 145,000 personal dossiers to criminals posing as real companies, Choice Point has hired a CPO who reports directly to the Board of Directors and the CEO, and has changed its procedures for verifying the authenticity of people claiming to be legitimate businesses. Prior to this breach of its database, ChoicePoint did not verify the authenticity or legitimacy of people claiming a business need to access their databases.

Perhaps the biggest challenge facing CPOs is federal legislation that requires companies to inform consumers of their privacy policies, and the trend away from a pro-active, pro-consumer privacy officer and towards a narrow legalistic emphasis on compliance. The Graham-Leach Bliley Act of 1999 requires all financial service firms to inform consumers of their privacy policies. This results in tens of millions of pamphlets being sent to consumers, often written in confusing legal jargon that few can understand. HIPAA, designed to make the transfer of records among health care agencies more efficient as well as to safeguard the privacy of those records, has also unleashed a flood of privacy pamphlets that few can understand. HIPAA requires that all health care providers and insurers have a privacy officer, even in small medical practices with seven doctors. Professional associations such as the International Association of Privacy Professionals openly worry that legalistic compliance with federal laws fails to take into account the real interests of consumers and the strategic implications for the firm.

SOURCES: "Gartner for IT Leaders Overview: The Chief Privacy Officer," by Arabella Hallawell and Paul E. Proctor, October 1, 2007; "Why Your Company Needs a Chief Privacy Officer," by Cara Garretson, *Network World*, May 22, 2007; "Shocking Number of Organizations without Chief Privacy Officer," Hr.com, January 26, 2007; "IBM Policy Bars Use of Gene Data in Employment," by Charles Forelle, *Wall Street Journal*, October 11, 2005; "AOL Recasts Privacy Policy," by Colin C. Haley, Internetnews.com, October 7, 2005; "Internal Privacy Audits Can Provide Companies With Excellent Value," by Jacqueline Kloske and John Kellenberger, *The Legal Inteligencer*, July 6, 2005; "What the Creation of a Chief Privacy Officer Means for CIOs," *IT BusinessEdge*, February 16, 2005.

The growth in consumer use of spyware blockers, cookie blockers, and pop-up controls on browsers threatens the online advertising industry that relies on cookies, placed mostly by advertising networks, although thus far, it has not appreciably reduced reliance on these techniques by advertisers.

P3P (Platform for Privacy Preferences)

a standard designed to communicate to Internet users a Web site's privacy policy, and to compare that policy to the user's own preferences, or to other standards such as the FTC's FIP guidelines or the EU Data Protection Directive

Perhaps the most comprehensive technological privacy protection effort is **P3P**, the **Platform for Privacy Preferences** sponsored by W3C (the World Wide Web Consortium—an international, nonprofit, industry-supported Web standards group). P3P is a standard designed to communicate a Web site's privacy policy to Internet users, and to compare that policy to the user's own preferences, or to other standards such as the FTC's FIP principles or the EU Data Protection Directive. P3P does not establish privacy standards and relies on government and industry to develop them.

P3P works through a user's Web browser. On the server side, P3P enables sites to translate their privacy policies into a standardized machine-readable XML format that can be read either by the browser or by installed software plug-ins. On the user client side, the browser automatically fetches a Web site's privacy policy and informs the user. **Figure 2(A)** illustrates how this could work.

P3P is now built into browsers such as Firefox and Internet Explorer 6.0/7.0. By using a slider, users can set the privacy policy they desire, and their browser

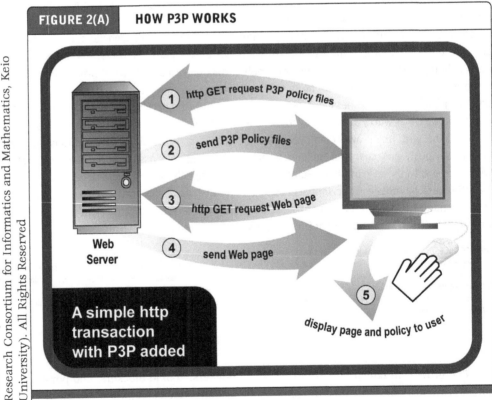

FIGURE 2(A)   HOW P3P WORKS

1. http GET request P3P policy files
2. send P3P Policy files
3. http GET request Web page
4. send Web page
5. display page and policy to user

Web Server

A simple http transaction with P3P added

The Platform for Privacy Preferences enables the automatic communication of privacy policies between e-commerce sites and consumers.

SOURCE: W3C Platform for Privacy Preferences Initiative, 2003.

will automatically read the privacy policy of sites they visit, and warn them when a site does not match their preferences (see **Figure 2 (B)**). According to a Carnegie Mellon study, about 10% of Web sites overall, and more than 20% of e-commerce sites now feature P3P, as well as about a third of the top 100 Web sites (eMarketer, Inc., 2007c).

While P3P is one step in the direction of increasing consumer awareness and understanding of Web site privacy, it fails to achieve other goals of fair information policies such as limits on what information is collected, the use of personal information, user control of over personal information, security, and enforcement of privacy rights. In this sense, it has failed to increase the consumer's sense of trust when shop-ping online. Most users simply leave the default settings for P3P at "medium," not knowing exactly what this means (Van Kirk, 2005).

Insight on Technology: The Privacy Tug of War: Advertisers vs. Consumers describes some other new technologies being used to both invade and protect privacy.

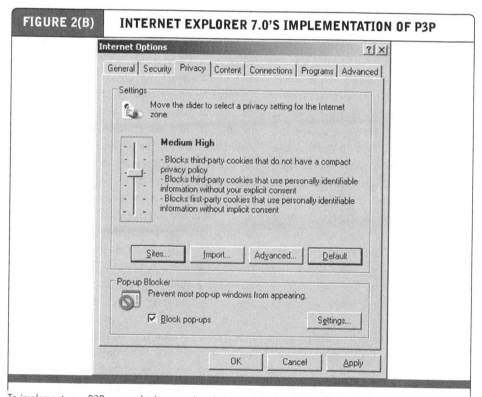

FIGURE 2(B)	INTERNET EXPLORER 7.0'S IMPLEMENTATION OF P3P

To implement your P3P personal privacy settings in Internet Explorer 7.0, click the Tools command, then Internet Options. Then click the Privacy tab in the Internet Options dialog box.

INSIGHT ON TECHNOLOGY

THE PRIVACY TUG OF WAR: ADVERTISERS VS. CONSUMERS

We are in a technological tug of war between technologies that make invading customer privacy very easy versus other technologies that make protecting privacy easier. On the privacy invasion side, Experian links Web sites to its database and provides the names and addresses of visitors to the sites in real time. Other companies such as Acxiom combine offline and online purchasing and behavioral data into one central database. In October 2007, Acxiom launched a new service, Relevance-X, that draws on that database to determine which online ads to show. MySpace has developed its HyperTargeting ad program, which scours user profiles for interests and then delivers related ads; Facebook has introduced a system that will attach names and photos of users who have indicated they like the product being advertised to the ads shown to their friends. Network advertisers place tracking cookies on your computer whenever you visit a member site and these cookies report your subsequent movements and are used to select ads you will be shown. Meanwhile, you have to be very careful not to open e-mail attachments or click on a promise of "instant rewards" on a Web site lest you accidentally download and install a spyware or adware program that will either be used to track your every keystroke or, more benignly, to swamp your screen with ads you never wanted to see in the first place.

How do the advertisers justify their intrusions into our private use of the Internet? The answer is profoundly interesting. Here's the idea, according to senior executives at advertising networks such as DoubleClick: the implicit bargain underlying the "free" Internet is that consumers get content because they are looking at ads. Never mind that you paid around $1,000 for your computer system, and $20–$50 monthly for Internet service. Take away the ads, and some other way will have to be found to pay for what you get on the Internet. The other main rationale behind all these intrusive behaviors is marketing efficiency and effectiveness: the more advertisers know about you, the more they can customize and personalize the advertising to exactly what you are looking for at right time, and, of course, the more they can charge their customers, the firms that pay for the advertising. Online advertisers believe consumers are saying, "Take my privacy, but please send the content."

The problem is that most consumers don't really accept this deal. It's possible that the advertisers don't know the consumer very well. An industry-backed survey of over 1,000 Web users found that only 14% said they liked giving information to Web sites in order to receive customized content, and 71% said they disliked it but did so only if necessary to obtain content or information. Another survey found that 41% said that, in the past six months, they had provided inaccurate information to Web sites that required personal information which respondents did not want to share. Consumers seem to be saying, "Send the content, but let me keep my privacy!" While some studies suggest that many teenagers and young adults do not care as much about privacy as older adults, privacy experts believe that this is because they do not understand how much information is being gathered about them.

On the privacy protection side, there are a great many more tools available to consumers than just a few years ago. Admittedly, P3P, an industry-sponsored effort to provide users some choice in privacy by making them aware of Web

(continued)

site privacy policies, has not been too successful. But ISPs and independent software companies now provide a host of tools that work wonders and are easy to use. AOL recently announced that it would offer a "Do Not Track" service that will link consumers directly to opt-out lists offered by the large advertising networks. The open source browser Firefox and Internet Explorer 6.0/7.0 have effective pop-up and image blockers. Google, Yahoo, MSN, and AOL also offer toolbars that provide similar help. Adoption rates of cookie blockers and anti-spyware software are increasing as software makers such as Symantec make them available as a part of their software suites that install automatically. For instance, a recent survey found that anti-virus, anti-spyware and firewall software are used by over 80% of U.S. adult Internet users, and that over two-thirds had configured their browser or operating system to block pop-ups, reject cookies or block specific Web sites. Even if these estimates are off by 50%, a significant number of ads are not actually being shown to consumers.

All these consumer self-help activities have traditional Web advertisers worried. What if consumers rejected the idea of pop-up ads, tracking their behavior, and storing all this information about them? What if consumers did not buy into the "free Internet with ads" deal? What if 50% of Internet users adopted ISP-provided privacy protection or bought their equivalents on the market? While Internet advertisers have pretty much blocked effective legislation in Washington that would preserve privacy, and while their industry associations have quite clearly failed to bring about meaningful self-regulation, the market has responded by providing consumers with some powerful tools for protecting their own privacy.

SOURCES: "Are Facebooks Social Ads Illegal?", by Saul Hansell, *New York Times*, November 8, 2007; Tracking of Web Use by Marketers Gains Favor," by Louise Story, *New York Times*, November 5, 2007; "The Higher Value of Eyeballs," by Louise Story, *New York Times*, November 5, 2007; "AOL's "Do Not Track" Effect, " by Ben Macklin, eMarketer, Inc., November 3, 2007; Privacy Groups Seek "Do Not Track" Web List," Reuters, November 1, 2007; "F.T.C. to Review Online Ads and Privacy," by Louise Story, *New York Times*, November 1, 2007; "Online Privacy? For Young People, That's Old-School," by Janet Kornbum, *USA Today*, October 22, 2007; "Firm Mines Offline Data to Target Online Ads," by Kevin J. Delaney and Emily Steel, *Wall Street Journal*, October 17, 2007; "Consumers Have False Sense of Security About Online Privacy - Actions Inconsistent with Attitudes," TRUSTe.org, December 6, 2006.

3   INTELLECTUAL PROPERTY RIGHTS

Congress shall have the power to "promote the progress of science and useful arts, by securing for limited times to authors and inventors the exclusive right to their respective writings and discoveries."

—Article I, Section 8, Constitution of the United States, 1788.

Next to privacy, the most controversial ethical, social, and political issue related to e-commerce is the fate of intellectual property rights. Intellectual property encompasses all the tangible and intangible products of the human mind. As a general rule, in the United States, the creator of intellectual property owns it. For instance, if you personally create an e-commerce site, it belongs entirely to you, and you have exclusive rights to use this "property" in any lawful way you see fit. But the Internet potentially changes things. Once intellectual works become digital, it becomes difficult to control access, use, distribution, and copying. These are precisely the areas that intellectual property seeks to control.

Digital media differ from books, periodicals, and other media in terms of ease of replication, transmission, and alteration; difficulty in classifying a software work as a program, book, or even music; compactness—making theft easy; and difficulty in establishing uniqueness. Before widespread use of the Internet, copies of software, books, magazine articles, or films had to be stored on physical media, such as paper, computer disks, or videotape, creating some hurdles to distribution.

The Internet technically permits millions of people to make perfect digital copies of various works—from music to plays, poems, and journal articles—and then to distribute them nearly cost-free to hundreds of millions of Web users. The proliferation of innovation has occurred so rapidly that few entrepreneurs have stopped to consider who owns the patent on a business technique or method their site is using. The spirit of the Web has been so free-wheeling that many entrepreneurs ignored trademark law and register domain names that can easily be confused with another company's registered trademarks. In short, the Internet has demonstrated the potential for destroying traditional conceptions and implementations of intellectual property law developed over the last two centuries.

The major ethical issue related to e-commerce and intellectual property concerns how we (both as individuals and as business professionals) should treat property that belongs to others. From a social point of view, the main questions are: Is there continued value in protecting intellectual property in the Internet age? In what ways is society better off, or worse off, for having the concept of property apply to intangible ideas? Should society make certain technology illegal just because it has an adverse impact on some intellectual property owners? From a political perspective, we need to ask how the Internet and e-commerce can be regulated or governed to protect the institution of intellectual property while at the same time encouraging the growth of e-commerce and the Internet.

TYPES OF INTELLECTUAL PROPERTY PROTECTION

There are three main types of intellectual property protection: copyright, patent, and trademark law. In the United States, the development of intellectual property law begins in the U.S. Constitution in 1788, which mandated Congress to devise a system of laws to promote "the progress of science and the useful arts." Congress passed the first copyright law in 1790 to protect original written works for a period of 14 years, with a 14-year renewal if the author was still alive. Since then, the idea of copyright has been extended to include music, films, translations, photographs, and most recently (1998), the designs of vessels under 200 feet (Fisher, 1999). The copyright law has been amended (mostly extended) 11 times in the last 40 years.

The goal of intellectual property law is to balance two competing interests—the public and the private. The public interest is served by the creation and distribution of inventions, works of art, music, literature, and other forms of intellectual expression. The private interest is served by rewarding people for creating these works through the creation of a time-limited monopoly granting exclusive use to the creator.

Maintaining this balance of interests is always challenged by the invention of new technologies. In general, the information technologies of the last century—from radio and television to CD-ROMs, DVDs, and the Internet—have at first tended to weaken the protections afforded by intellectual property law. Owners of intellectual property have often but not always been successful in pressuring Congress and the courts to strengthen the intellectual property laws to compensate for any technological threat, and even to extend protection for longer periods of time and to entirely new areas of expression. In the case of the Internet and e-commerce technologies, once again, intellectual property rights are severely challenged. In the next few sections, we discuss the significant developments in each area: copyright, patent, and trademark.

COPYRIGHT: THE PROBLEM OF PERFECT COPIES AND ENCRYPTION

In the United States, **copyright law** protects original forms of expression such as writings (books, periodicals, lecture notes), art, drawings, photographs, music, motion pictures, performances, and computer programs from being copied by others for a period of time. Up until 1998, the copyright law protected works of individuals for their lifetime plus 50 years beyond their life, and for works created for hire and owned by corporations such as Mickey Mouse of the Disney Corporation, 75 years after initial creation. Copyright does not protect ideas—just their expression in a tangible medium such as paper, cassette tape, or handwritten notes.

copyright law
protects original forms of expression such as writings, art, drawings, photographs, music, motion pictures, performances, and computer programs from being copied by others for a minimum of 70 years

In 1998, Congress extended the period of copyright protection for an additional 20 years, for a total of 95 years for corporate-owned works, and life plus 70 years of protection for works created by individuals (the Copyright Term Extension Act, also known as CETA). In *Eldred v. Ashcroft*, the Supreme Court ruled on January 16, 2003, that CETA was constitutional, over the objections of groups arguing that Congress had given copyright holders a permanent monopoly over the expression of ideas, which ultimately would work to inhibit the flow of ideas and creation of new works by making existing works too expensive (Greenhouse, 2003a). Librarians, academics, and others who depend on inexpensive access to copyrighted material opposed the legislation.

Since the first federal Copyright Act of 1790, the congressional intent behind copyright laws has been to encourage creativity and authorship by ensuring that creative people receive the financial and other benefits of their work. Most industrial nations have their own copyright laws, and there are several international conventions and bilateral agreements through which nations coordinate and enforce their laws.

In the mid-1960s, the Copyright Office began registering software programs, and in 1980, Congress passed the Computer Software Copyright Act, which clearly provides protection for source and object code and for copies of the original sold in commerce, and sets forth the rights of the purchaser to use the software while the creator retains legal title. For instance, the HTML code for a Web page—even though easily available to every browser—cannot be lawfully copied and used for a commercial purpose, say, to create a new Web site that looks identical.

Copyright protection is clear-cut: it protects against copying of entire programs or their parts. Damages and relief are readily obtained for infringement. The drawback to copyright protection is that the underlying ideas behind a work are not protected, only their expression in a work. A competitor can view the source code on your Web site to see how various effects were created and then reuse those techniques to create a different Web site without infringing on your copyright.

Look and Feel

"Look and feel" copyright infringement lawsuits are precisely about the distinction between an idea and its expression. For instance, in 1988, Apple Computer sued Microsoft Corporation and Hewlett-Packard Inc. for infringing Apple's copyright on the Macintosh interface. Among other claims, Apple claimed that the defendants copied the expression of overlapping windows. Apple failed to patent the idea of overlapping windows when it invented this method of presenting information on a computer screen in the late 1960s. The defendants counterclaimed that the idea of overlapping windows could only be expressed in a single way and, therefore, was not protectable under the "merger" doctrine of copyright law. When ideas and their expression merge (i.e., if there is only one way to express an idea), the expression cannot be copyrighted, although the method of producing the expression might be patentable (*Apple v. Microsoft*, 1989). In general, courts appear to be following the reasoning of a 1992 case—*Brown Bag Software vs. Symantec Corp.*—in which the court dissected the elements of software alleged to be infringing. There, the Federal Circuit Court of Appeals found that neither similar concept, function, general functional features (e.g., drop-down menus), nor colors were protectable by copyright law (*Brown Bag vs. Symantec Corp.*, 1992).

Fair Use Doctrine

Copyrights, like all rights, are not absolute. There are situations where strict copyright observance could be harmful to society, potentially inhibiting other rights such as the right to freedom of expression and thought. As a result, the doctrine of fair use has been created. The **doctrine of fair use** permits teachers and writers to use copyrighted materials without permission under certain circumstances. **Table 9** describes the five factors that courts consider when assessing what constitutes fair use.

doctrine of fair use
under certain circumstances, permits use of copyrighted material without permission

The fair use doctrine draws upon the First Amendment's protection of freedom of speech (and writing). Journalists, writers, and academics must be able to refer to, and cite from, copyrighted works in order to criticize or even discuss copyrighted works. Professors are allowed to clip a contemporary article just before class, copy it, and hand it out to students as an example of a topic under discussion. However, they are not permitted to add this article to the class syllabus for the next semester without compensating the copyright holder.

What constitutes fair use has been at issue in a number of recent cases, including the Google Book Search Project described in the case study at the end of the chapter, and in several recent lawsuits. In *Kelly v. ArribaSoft* (2003) and *Perfect 10, Inc. v. Amazon.com, Inc.* (2007), the federal Circuit Court of Appeals for the 10th circuit held that the display of thumbnail images in response to search requests constituted fair use. A similar result was reached by the district court for the District of Nevada with

TABLE 9	FAIR USE CONSIDERATIONS TO COPYRIGHT PROTECTIONS
FAIR USE FACTOR	**INTERPRETATION**
Character of use	Nonprofit or educational use versus for-profit use.
Nature of the work	Creative works such as plays or novels receive greater protection than factual accounts, e.g., newspaper accounts
Amount of work used	A stanza from a poem or a single page from a book would be allowed, but not the entire poem or a book chapter.
Market effect of use	Will the use harm the marketability of the original product? Has it already harmed the product in the marketplace?
Context of use	A last-minute, unplanned use in a classroom versus a planned infringement.

respect to Google's storage and display of Web sites from cache memory, in *Field v. Google, Inc.* (2006). In all of these cases, the courts accepted the argument that caching the material and displaying it in response to a search request was not only a public benefit, but also a form of marketing of the material on behalf of its copyright owner, thereby enhancing the material's commercial value. Fair use is also at issue in the lawsuit filed by Viacom against Google and YouTube in March 2007, described further in the next section.

The Digital Millennium Copyright Act of 1998

The Digital Millennium Copyright Act (DMCA) of 1998 is the first major effort to adjust the copyright laws to the Internet age. This legislation was the result of a confrontation between the major copyright holders in the United States (publishing, sheet music, record label, and commercial film industries), ISPs, and users of copyrighted materials such as libraries, universities, and consumers. While social and political institutions are sometimes thought of as "slow" and the Internet as "fast," in this instance, powerful groups of copyright owners anticipated Web music services such as Napster by several years. Napster was formed in 1999, but work by the World Intellectual Property Organization—a worldwide body formed by the major copyright-holding nations of North America, Europe, and Japan—began in 1995. **Table 10** summarizes the major provisions of the DMCA.

> **Digital Millennium Copyright Act (DMCA)**
>
> the first major effort to adjust the copyright laws to the Internet age

The penalties for willfully violating the DMCA include restitution to the injured parties of any losses due to infringement. Criminal remedies are available to federal prosecutors that include fines up to $500,000 or five years imprisonment for a first offense, and up to $1 million in fines and ten years in prison for repeat offenders. These are serious remedies.

The DMCA attempts to answer two vexing questions in the Internet age. First, how can society protect copyrights online when any practical encryption scheme imaginable can be broken by hackers and the results distributed worldwide? Second, how can society control the behavior of thousands of ISPs, who often host infringing

TABLE 10	THE DIGITAL MILLENNIUM COPYRIGHT ACT
SECTION	**IMPORTANCE**
Title I, WIPO Copyright and Performances and Phonograms Treaties Implementation	Makes it illegal to circumvent technological measures to protect works for either access or copying or to circumvent any electronic rights management information.
Title II, Online Copyright Infringement Liability Limitation	Requires ISPs to "take down" sites they host if they are infringing copyrights, and requires search engines to block access to infringing sites. Limits liability of ISPs and search engines.
Title III, Computer Maintenance Competition Assurance	Permits users to make a copy of a computer program for maintenance or repair of the computer.
Title IV, Miscellaneous Provisions	Requires the copyright office to report to Congress on the use of copyright materials for distance education; allows libraries to make digital copies of works for internal use only; extends musical copyrights to include "webcasting."

SOURCE: Based on data from United States Copyright Office, 1998.

Web sites, or who provide Internet service to individuals who are routine infringers? ISPs claim to be like telephone utilities—just carrying messages—and they do not want to put their users under surveillance or invade the privacy of users. The DMCA recognizes that ISPs have some control over how their customers use their facilities.

The DMCA implements a World Intellectual Property Organization (WIPO) treaty of 1996, which declares it illegal to make, distribute, or use devices that circumvent technology-based protections of copyrighted materials, and attaches stiff fines and prison sentences for violations. WIPO is an organization within the United Nations. Recognizing that these provisions alone cannot stop hackers from devising circumventions, the DMCA makes it difficult for such inventors to reap the fruits of their labors by making the ISPs (including universities) responsible and accountable for hosting Web sites or providing services to infringers once the ISP has been notified. ISPs are not required to intrude on their users. However, when copyright holders inform the ISP that a hosted site or individual users are infringing, they must "take down" the site immediately to avoid liability and potential fines. ISPs must also inform their subscribers of their copyright management policies. Copyright owners can subpoena the personal identities of any infringers using an ISP. There are important limitations on these ISP prohibitions that are mostly concerned with the transitory caching of materials for short periods without the knowledge of the ISP. However, should the ISP be deriving revenues from the infringement, it is as liable as the infringer, and is subject to the same penalties.

Title I of the DMCA provides a partial answer to the dilemma of hacking. It is probably true that skilled hackers can easily break any usable encryption scheme, and the means to do so on a large scale through distribution of the decryption programs already exists. The WIPO provisions accept this possibility and simply make it illegal to do so, or to disseminate, or to enable such dissemination or even storage and transmission of decrypted products or tools. These provisions put large ISPs on legal notice.

There are a number of exceptions to the strong prohibitions against defeating a copyright protection scheme outlined above. There are exceptions for libraries to examine works for adoption, for reverse engineering to achieve interoperability with other software, for encryption research, for privacy protection purposes, and for security testing. Many companies, such as YouTube, Google, and MySpace have latched on the provision of the DMCA that relates to removing infringing material upon request of the copyright owner as a "safe harbor" that precludes them from being held responsible for copyright infringement. This position is currently being tested in a $1 billion lawsuit brought by Viacom against Google and YouTube for willful copyright infringement, and by Vivendi's Universal Music Group against the News Corp.'s MySpace. These lawsuits are interesting because unlike efforts against individuals accused of file-sharing, or offshore renegade outfits such as Kazaa, they pit large established corporate institutions against one another.

In the Viacom case, Viacom alleges that YouTube and Google engaged in massive copyright infringement by deliberately building up a library of infringing works to draw traffic to the YouTube site and enhance its commercial value. In response, Google and YouTube claim that they are protected by the DMCA's safe harbor and fair use, and that it is often impossible to know whether a video is infringing or not. YouTube also does not display ads on pages where consumers can view videos unless it has an agreement with the content owner. In October 2007, Google announced a filtering system aimed at addressing the problem. It requires content owners to give Google a copy of their content so Google can load it into an auto-identification system. The copyright owner can specify whether it will allow others to post the material. Then after a video is uploaded to YouTube, the system attempts to match it with its database of copyrighted material, and removes any unauthorized material. Whether content owners will be satisfied with this system is unknown, particularly since guidelines issued by a coalition of major media and Internet companies with respect to the handling of copyrighted videos on user-generated Web sites calls for the use of filtering technology that can block infringing material before it is posted online (Helft and Fabrikant, 2007; Gentile, 2007; Swartz, 2007).

PATENTS: BUSINESS METHODS AND PROCESSES

> "Whoever invents or discovers any new and useful process, machine, manufacture, or composition of matter, or any new and useful improvement thereof, may obtain a patent therefore, subject to the conditions and requirements of this title."
>
> —Section 101, U.S. Patent Act

A **patent** grants the owner a 20-year exclusive monopoly on the ideas behind an invention. The congressional intent behind patent law was to ensure that inventors of

patent
grants the owner an exclusive monopoly on the ideas behind an invention for 20 years

new machines, devices, or industrial methods would receive the full financial and other rewards of their labor and yet still make widespread use of the invention possible by providing detailed diagrams for those wishing to use the idea under license from the patent's owner. Patents are obtained from the United States Patent and Trademark Office (USPTO), created in 1812. Obtaining a patent is much more difficult and time-consuming than obtaining copyright protection (which is automatic with the creation of the work). Patents must be formally applied for, and the granting of a patent is determined by Patent Office examiners who follow a set of rigorous rules. Ultimately, federal courts decide when patents are valid and when infringement occurs.

Patents are very different from copyrights because patents protect the ideas themselves and not merely the expression of ideas. There are four types of inventions for which patents are granted under patent law: machines, man-made products, compositions of matter, and processing methods. The Supreme Court has determined that patents extend to "anything under the sun that is made by man" (*Diamond v. Chakrabarty*, 1980) as long as the other requirements of the Patent Act are met. There are three things that cannot be patented: laws of nature, natural phenomena, and abstract ideas. For instance, a mathematical algorithm cannot be patented unless it is realized in a tangible machine or process that has a "useful" result (the mathematical algorithm exception).

In order to be granted a patent, the applicant must show that the invention is new, original, novel, nonobvious, and not evident in prior arts and practice. As with copyrights, the granting of patents has moved far beyond the original intent of Congress's first patent statute that sought to protect industrial designs and machines. Patent protection has been extended to articles of manufacture (1842), plants (1930), surgical and medical procedures (1950), and software (1981). The Patent Office did not accept applications for software patents until a 1981 Supreme Court decision that held that computer programs could be a part of a patentable process. Since that time, thousands of software patents have been granted. Virtually any software program can be patented as long as it is novel and not obvious.

Essentially, as technology and industrial arts progress, patents have been extended to both encourage entrepreneurs to invent useful devices and promote widespread dissemination of the new techniques through licensing and artful imitation of the published patents (the creation of devices that provide the same functionality as the invention but use different methods) (Winston, 1998). Patents encourage inventors to come up with unique ways of achieving the same functionality as existing patents. For instance, Amazon's patent on one-click purchasing caused Barnesandnoble.com to invent a simplified two-click method of purchasing.

The danger of patents is that they stifle competition by raising barriers to entry into an industry. Patents force new entrants to pay licensing fees to incumbents, and thus slow down the development of technical applications of new ideas by creating lengthy licensing applications and delays.

E-commerce Patents

Much of the Internet's infrastructure and software was developed under the auspices of publicly funded scientific and military programs in the United States and Europe. Unlike

Samuel F. B. Morse, who patented the idea of Morse code and made the telegraph useful, most of the inventions that make the Internet and e-commerce possible were not patented by their inventors. The early Internet was characterized by a spirit of world-wide community development and sharing of ideas without consideration of personal wealth (Winston, 1998). This early Internet spirit changed in the mid-1990s with the commercial development of the World Wide Web.

In 1998, a landmark legal decision, *State Street Bank & Trust v. Signature Financial Group, Inc.*, paved the way for business firms to begin applying for "business methods" patents. In this case, a Federal Circuit Court of Appeals upheld the claims of Signature Financial to a valid patent for a business method that allows managers to monitor and record financial information flows generated by a partner fund. Previously, it was thought business methods could not be patented. However, the court ruled there was no reason to disallow business methods from patent protection, or any "step by step process, be it electronic or chemical or mechanical, [that] involves an algorithm in the broad sense of the term" (*State Street Bank & Trust Co. v. Signature Financial Group*, 1998). The State Street decision led to an explosion in applications for e-commerce "business methods" patents, with over 10,000 in 2006 (see **Figure 3**). Note that the overall number of patents filed has also increased dramatically, from about 237,000 in 1995 to almost 444,000 in 2006.

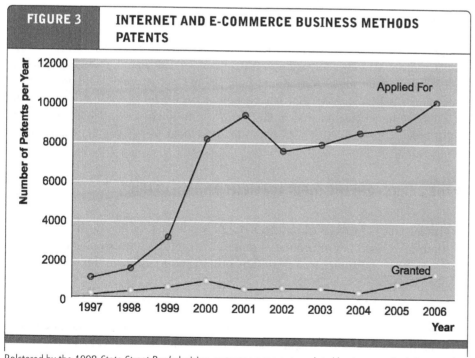

| FIGURE 3 | INTERNET AND E-COMMERCE BUSINESS METHODS PATENTS |

Bolstered by the 1998 *State Street Bank* decision, patents on computer-related business methods increased exponentially from 1998 when 1,337 applications were filed, to 2001, when 9,288 applications were submitted. During the period 2002–2005, applications dropped off somewhat and remained relatively steady at around 7,500–8,500 per year, but in 2006, they increased significantly again, to over 10,000 applications.
SOURCE: Based on data from United States Patent and Trademark Office, 2007.

Table 11 lists some of the better-known, controversial e-commerce patents. Reviewing these, you can understand the concerns of commentators and corporations. Some of the patent claims are very broad (for example, "name your price" sales methods), have historical precedents in the pre-Internet era (shopping carts), and seem "obvious" (one-click purchasing). Critics of online business methods patents argue that the Patent Office has been too lenient in granting such patents and that in most instances, the supposed inventions merely copy pre-Internet business methods and thus do not constitute "inventions" (Harmon, 2003; Thurm, 2000; Chiappetta, 2001). The Patent Office argues, on the contrary, that its Internet inventions staff is composed of engineers, lawyers, and specialists with many years of experience with Internet and network technologies, and that it consults with outside technology experts before granting patents. To complicate matters, the European Patent Convention and the patent laws of most European countries do not recognize business methods per se unless the method is implemented through some technology (Takenaka, 2001).

Patent Reform

Issues related to business method patents, patent "trolls" (companies such as Acacia Technologies that buy up broadly-worded patents on a speculative basis and then use them to threaten companies that are purportedly violating the patent) and confusing legal decisions have led to increasing calls for patent reform over the last few years, particularly by companies in the technology sector. In September 2007, the House of Representatives passed its version of a patent reform bill that includes provisions that change the patent system from a "first to invent" system to a "first to file" system, change the way damages for patent infringement are calculated, provide a new way to challenge patents out of court, limit where patent suits can be filed (to prevent suits from being filed in districts that have a reputation for being more favorable), and impose heightened standards for a finding of willful infringement. Whether the bill will ultimately be enacted into law, and if so, its final form, is unknown as of this writing (Broache, 2007)

TRADEMARKS: ONLINE INFRINGEMENT AND DILUTION

> Trademark is "any word, name, symbol, or device, or any combination thereof ... used in commerce ... to identify and distinguish ... goods . . . from those manufactured or sold by others and to indicate the source of the goods."
>
> —The Trademark Act, 1946

trademark
a mark used to identify and distinguish goods and indicate their source

Trademark law is a form of intellectual property protection for **trademarks**—a mark used to identify and distinguish goods and indicate their source. Trademark protections exist at both the federal and state levels in the United States. The purpose of trademark law is twofold. First, the trademark law protects the public in the marketplace by ensuring that it gets what it pays for and wants to receive. Second, trademark law protects the owner—who has spent time, money, and energy bringing

TABLE 11	SELECTED E-COMMERCE PATENTS	
COMPANY	SUBJECT	UPDATE
Leon Stambler	Secure communications	Private inventor with seven patents (1992–1998) covering creation of an authentication code to be used in electronic communications. In 2003, a Delaware jury found that RSA Security and VeriSign did not infringe on the patents. Stambler's appeal to the U.S. Court of Appeals for the Federal Circuit was rejected in February 2005.
Amazon.com	One-click purchasing	Amazon.com attempted to use patent originally granted to it in 1999 to force changes to Barnes & Noble's Web site, but a federal court overturned a previously issued injunction. Eventually settled out of court. In September 2007, a USPTO panel rejected most of the patent because of evidence another patent predated it, sending it back to the patent examiner for reconsideration.
Eolas Technologies	Embedding interactive content in a Web site	Eolas Technologies, a spin-off of the University of California, obtained patent in 1998. Eolas filed suit against Microsoft in 1999 for infringing the patent in Internet Explorer and was award a $520 million judgment in 2003. Decision was partially reversed in 2005, and sent back to district court for a new trial. The patent was reaffirmed in September 2005 by the USPTO. In August 2007, Eolas and Microsoft finally settled the suit on undisclosed terms.
Priceline.com	Buyer-driven "name your price" sales	Originally invented by Walker Digital, an intellectual property laboratory, and then assigned to Priceline. Granted by the USPTO in 1999. Shortly thereafter, Priceline sued Microsoft and Expedia for copying its patented business method. Expedia settled and agreed to pay a royalty in 2001.
Sightsound.com	Music downloads	Sightsound won a settlement in 2004 against Bertelsmann subsidiaries CDNow and N2K music sites for infringing its patent.
Akamai	Internet content delivery Global Hosting System	A broad patent granted in 2000 covering techniques for expediting the flow of information over the Internet. Akamai sued Digital Island (subsequently acquired Cable & Wireless) for violating the patent and in 2001 a jury found in its favor. In 2004, Akamai accepted a damages payment to finally settle the suit.
DoubleClick	Dynamic delivery of online advertising	The patent underlying DoubleClick's business of online banner ad delivery, originally granted in 2000. DoubleClick sued competitors 24/7 Media and L90 for violating the patent and ultimately reached a settlement with them.
Overture	Pay for performance search	System and method for influencing position on search result list generated by computer search engine, granted in 2001. Competitor FindWhat.com sued Overture, charging that patent was obtained illegally; Overture countered by suing both FindWhat and Google for violating patent. Google agreed to pay a license fee to Overture in 2004 to settle the suit, and the lawsuit with FindWhat resulted in a hung jury in 2005, with both sides claiming victory.
Acacia Technologies	Streaming video media transmission	Patents for the receipt and transmission of streaming digital audio and or video content originally granted to founders of Greenwich Information Technologies in 1990s. Patents were purchased by Acacia, a firm founded solely to enforce the patents, in 2001. Acacia has subsequently secured dozens of licenses.
Soverain Software	Purchase technology	The so-called "shopping cart" patent for network-based systems. Originally owned by Open Markets, then Divine Inc., and now Soverain. Soverain filed suit against Amazon for patent infringement in 2004; Amazon settled for $40 million in August 2005.
MercExchange (Thomas Woolston)	Auction technology	Patents on person-to-person auctions and database search, originally granted in 1995. eBay ordered to pay $25 million in 2003 for infringing on patent. In July 2007, the U.S. district court denied a motion for permanent patent injunction against eBay using the "Buy It Now" feature, and moved to the final stages of allowing the damages award to be paid. Issues related to a second patent were deferred pending a USPTO office reexamination.
Google	Search technology	Google PageRank patent was filed in 1998 and granted in 2001.

the product to the marketplace—against piracy and misappropriation. Trademarks have been extended from single words to pictures, shapes, packaging, and colors. Some things may not be trademarked: common words that are merely descriptive ("clock"), flags of states and nations, immoral or deceptive marks, or marks belonging to others. Federal trademarks are obtained, first, by use in interstate commerce, and second, by registration with the USPTO. Trademarks are granted for a period of ten years, and can be renewed indefinitely.

Disputes over federal trademarks involve establishing infringement. The test for infringement is twofold: market confusion and bad faith. Use of a trademark that creates confusion with existing trademarks causes consumers to make market mistakes, or misrepresents the origins of goods is an infringement. In addition, the intentional misuse of words and symbols in the marketplace to extort revenue from legitimate trademark owners ("bad faith") is proscribed.

In 1995, Congress passed the Federal Trademark Dilution Act, which created a federal cause of action for dilution of famous marks. This legislation dispenses with the test of market confusion (although that is still required to claim infringement), and extends protection to owners of famous trademarks against **dilution**, which is defined as any behavior that would weaken the connection between the trademark and the product. Dilution occurs through blurring (weakening the connection between the trademark and the goods) and tarnishment (using the trademark in a way that makes the underlying products appear unsavory or unwholesome).

dilution

any behavior that would weaken the connection between the trademark and the product

Trademarks and the Internet

The rapid growth and commercialization of the Internet have provided unusual opportunities for existing firms with distinctive and famous trademarks to extend their brands to the Internet. These same developments have provided malicious individuals and firms the opportunity to squat on Internet domain names built upon famous marks, as well as attempt to confuse consumers and dilute famous or distinctive marks (including your personal name or a movie star's name). The conflict between legitimate trademark owners and malicious firms was allowed to fester and grow because Network Solutions Inc. (NSI), originally the Internet's sole agency for domain name registration for many years, had a policy of "first come, first served." This meant anyone could register any domain name that had not already been registered, regardless of the trademark status of the domain name. NSI was not authorized to decide trademark issues (Nash, 1997).

In response to a growing number of complaints from owners of famous trademarks who found their trademark names being appropriated by Web entrepreneurs, Congress passed the **Anticybersquatting Consumer Protection Act (ACPA)** in November 1999. The ACPA creates civil liabilities for anyone who attempts in bad faith to profit from an existing famous or distinctive trademark by registering an Internet domain name that is identical, confusingly similar, or "dilutive" of that trademark. The Act does not establish criminal sanctions. The Act proscribes using "bad faith" domain names to extort money from the owners of the existing trademark (**cybersquatting**), or using the bad faith domain to divert Web

Anticybersquatting Consumer Protection Act (ACPA)

creates civil liabilities for anyone who attempts in bad faith to profit from an existing famous or distinctive trademark by registering an Internet domain name that is identical, or confusingly similar, or "dilutive" of that trademark

cybersquatting

involves the registration of an infringing domain name, or other Internet use of an existing trademark, for the purpose of extorting payments from the legitimate owners traffic to the bad faith domain that could harm the good will represented by the trademark, create market confusion, tarnish, or disparage the mark (**cyberpiracy**). The Act also proscribes the use of a domain name that consists of the name of a living person, or a name confusingly similar to an existing personal name, without that person's consent, if the registrant is registering the name with the intent to profit by selling the domain dame to that person.

Trademark abuse can take many forms on the Web. **Table 12** lists the major behaviors on the Internet that have run afoul of trademark law, and the some of the court cases that resulted.

cyberpiracy

involves the same behavior as cybersquatting, but with the intent of diverting traffic from the legitimate site to an infringing site

Cybersquatting

In one of the first cases involving the ACPA, E. & J. Gallo Winery, owner of the registered mark "Ernest and Julio Gallo" for alcoholic beverages, sued Spider Webs Ltd. for using the domain name Ernestandjuliogallo.com. Spider Webs Ltd. was a

TABLE 12	INTERNET AND TRADEMARK LAW EXAMPLES	
ACTIVITY	DESCRIPTION	EXAMPLE CASE
Cybersquatting	Registering domain names similar or identical to trademarks of others to extort profits from legitimate holders.	*E. & J. Gallo Winery v. Spider Webs Ltd.*, 129 F. Supp. 2d 1033 (S.D. Tex., 2001) aff'd 286 F. 3d 270 (5th Cir.,2002)
Cyberpiracy	Registering domain names similar or identical to trademarks of others to divert Web traffic to their own sites.	*Ford Motor Co. v. Lapertosa*, 2001 U.S. Dist. LEXIS 253 (E.D. Mich., 2001); *PaineWebber Inc. v. Fortuny*, Civ. A. No. 99-0456-A (E.D. Va., 1999); *Playboy Enterprises, Inc. v. Global Site Designs, Inc.*, 1999 WL 311707 (S.D. Fla., 1999);
		Audi AG and Volkswagen of America Inc. v. Bob D'Amato (No. 05-2359; 6th Cir., November 27, 2006).
Metatagging	Using trademark words in a site's metatags.	*Bernina of America, Inc. v. Fashion Fabrics Int'l, Inc.*, 2001 U.S. Dist. LEXIS 1211 (N.D. Ill., 2001); *Nissan Motor Co., Ltd. v. Nissan Computer Corp.*, 289 F. Supp. 2d 1154 (C.D. Cal., 2000), aff'd, 246 F. 3rd 675 (9th Cir., 2000).
Keywords	Placing trademarked keywords on Web pages, either visible or invisible.	*Playboy Enterprises, Inc. v. Netscape Communications, Inc.*, 354 F. 3rd 1020 (9th Cir., 2004); *Nettis Environment Ltd. v. IWI, Inc.*, 46 F. Supp. 2d 722 (N.D. Ohio, 1999); *Government Employees Insurance Company v. Google, Inc.*, Civ. Action No. 1:04cv507 (E.D. VA, 2004); *Google, Inc. v. American Blind & Wallpaper Factory, Inc.*, Case No. 03-5340 JF (RS) (N.D. Cal., April 18, 2007)
Linking	Linking to content pages on other sites, bypassing the home page.	*Ticketmaster Corp. v. Tickets.com*, 2000 U.S. Dist. Lexis 4553 (C.D. Cal., 2000).
Framing	Placing the content of other sites in a frame on the infringer's site.	*The Washington Post, et al. v. TotalNews, Inc., et al.*, (S.D.N.Y., Civil Action Number 97-1190).

domain name speculator that owned numerous domain names consisting of famous company names. The Ernestandjuliogallo.com Web site contained information on the risks of alcohol use, anti-corporate articles about E. & J. Gallo Winery, and was poorly constructed. The court concluded that Spider Webs Ltd. was in violation of the ACPA and that its actions constituted dilution by blurring because the Ernestandjuliogallo.com domain name appeared on every page printed off the Web site accessed by that name, and that Spider Webs Ltd. was not free to use this particular mark as a domain name (*E. & J. Gallo Winery v. Spider Webs Ltd.*, 2001).

Cyberpiracy

Cyberpiracy involves the same behavior as cybersquatting, but with the intent of diverting traffic from the legitimate site to an infringing site. In *Ford Motor Co. v. Lapertosa*, Lapertosa had registered and used a Web site called Fordrecalls.com as an adult entertainment Web site. The court ruled that Fordrecalls.com was in violation of the ACPA in that it was a bad faith attempt to divert traffic to the Lapertosa site and diluted Ford's wholesome trademark (*Ford Motor Co. v. Lapertosa*, 2001).

The Ford decision reflects two other famous cases of cyberpiracy. In the *Paine Webber Inc. v. Fortuny* case, the court enjoined Fortuny from using the domain name Wwwpainewebber.com—a site that specialized in pornographic materials—because it diluted and tarnished Paine Webber's trademark and diverted Web traffic from Paine Webber's legitimate site—Painewebber.com (*Paine Webber Inc. v. Fortuny*, 1999). In the *Playboy Enterprises, Inc. v. Global Site Designs, Inc.* case, the court enjoined the defendants from using the Playboy and Playmate marks in their domain names Playboyonline.net and Playmatesearch.net and from including the Playboy trademark in their metatags. In these cases, the defendants' intention was diversion for financial gain (*Playboy Enterprises, Inc. v. Global Site Designs, Inc.*, 1999).

In a more recent case, *Audi AG and Volkswagen of America Inc. v. Bob D'Amato*, the Federal Circuit Court of Appeals for the Sixth Circuit affirmed the District Court's ruling that the defendant Bob D'Amato infringed and diluted the plaintiffs' Audi, Quatro and Audi Four Rings logo marks, and violated the ACPA by operating the Audisport.com Web site (*Audi AG and Volkswagen of America Inc. v. Bob D'Amato*, 2006).

Typosquatting is a form of cyberpiracy in which a domain name contains a common misspelling of another site's name. Often the user ends up at a site very different from one they intended to visit. For instance, John Zuccarini is an infamous typosquatter who was jailed in 2002 for setting up pornographic Web sites with URLs based on misspellings of popular children's brands, such as Bob the Builder and Teletubbies. The FTC fined him again in October 2007 for engaging in similar practices (McMillan, 2007).

Metatagging

The legal status of using famous or distinctive marks as metatags is more complex and subtle. The use of trademarks in metatags is permitted if the use does not mislead or confuse consumers. Usually this depends on the content of the site. A car dealer would be permitted to use a famous automobile trademark in its metatags if the dealer sold this brand of automobiles, but a pornography site could not use the same trademark, nor a dealer for a rival manufacturer. A Ford dealer would most likely be infringing if it used "Honda" in its metatags, but would not be infringing if it used "Ford" in its metatags. (Ford Motor Company would be unlikely to seek an injunction against one of its dealers.)

In the *Bernina of America, Inc. v. Fashion Fabrics Int'l, Inc.* case, the court enjoined Fashion Fabrics, an independent dealer of sewing machines, from using the trademarks "Bernina" and "Bernette," which belonged to the manufacturer Bernina, as metatags. The court found the defendant's site contained misleading claims about Fashion Fabrics' knowledge of Bernina products that were likely to confuse customers. The use of the Bernina trademarks as metatags per se was not a violation of ACPA, according to the court, but in combination with the misleading claims on the site would cause confusion and hence infringement (*Bernina of America, Inc. v. Fashion Fabrics Int'l, Inc.*, 2001).

In the *Nissan Motor Co. Ltd. v. Nissan Computer Corp.* case, Uzi Nissan had used his surname "Nissan" as a trade name for various businesses since 1980, including Nissan Computer Corp. He registered Nissan.com in 1994 and Nissan.net in 1996. Nissan.com had no relationship with Nissan Motor, but over the years began selling auto parts that competed with Nissan Motor. Nissan Motor Company objected to the use of the domain name Nissan.com and the use of "Nissan" in the metatags for both sites on grounds it would confuse customers and infringe on Nissan Motor's trademarks. Uzi Nissan offered to sell his sites to Nissan Motor for several million dollars. Nissan Motor refused. The court ruled that Nissan Computer's behavior did indeed infringe on Nissan Motor's trademarks, but it refused to shut the site down. Instead, the court ruled Nissan Computer could continue to use the Nissan name, and metatags, but must post notices on its site that it was not affiliated with Nissan Motor (*Nissan Motor Co. Ltd. v. Nissan Computer Corp.*, 2000). In November 2002, a U.S. District Court issued a permanent injunction, allowing Mr. Nissan to keep the domains, but restricting the commercial, advertising, and anti-Nissan Motor content that could be placed on the Web sites. Mr. Nissan appealed, and in August 2004, the Ninth Circuit Court of Appeals found that while Nissan Computer in fact capitalized on Nissan Motors' good-will in the Nissan trademark to the extent that use of the mark for automobiles captured the attention of customers interested in Nissan cars, Nissan Motor could not gain protection against any resultant dilution of the trademark because Nissan Computer had made its first commercial use of the mark over five years before Nissan Motor's mark became famous in the United States. In addition, requiring that the Web site not contain links to anti-Nissan Web sites was inconsistent with free speech rights. The Court of Appeals therefore reversed the previous ruling, ordering Mr. Nissan to refrain only from showing car-related ads, and remanded the case back to the District Court for consideration as to whether the injunction should be broadened to include the transfer of the domains. In April 2005, the Supreme Court turned down an appeal made by Nissan Motor.

Keywording

The permissibility of using trademarks as keywords on search engines is also subtle and depends on the extent to which such use is considered to be a "use in commerce", causes "initial customer confusion" and on the content of the search results.

In *Playboy Enterprises, Inc. v. Netscape Communications, Inc.*, Playboy objected to the practice of Netscape's and Excite's search engines displaying banner ads unrelated to Playboy Magazine when users entered search arguments such as "playboy," "playmate," and "playgirl." The Ninth Circuit Court of Appeals denied the defendant's motion for a summary judgment and held that when an advertiser's banner ad is not labeled so as to identify its source, the practice could result in trademark infringement due to consumer confusion (*Playboy Enterprises, Inc. v. Netscape Communications, Inc.*, 2004).

In the *Nettis Environment Ltd. v. IWI, Inc.* case, Nettis and IWI Inc. were competitors in the ventilation business. IWI had registered the trademarks "nettis" and "nettis environmental" on over 400 search engines, and in addition, used these marks as metatags on its site. The court required IWI to remove the metatags and de-register the keywords with all search engines because consumers would be con fused—searching for Nettis products would lead them to an IWI Web site (*Nettis Environment Ltd. v. IWI, Inc.*, 1999).

Google has also faced lawsuits alleging that its advertising network illegally exploits others' trademarks. For instance, insurance company GEICO challenged Google's practice of allowing competitors' ads to appear when a searcher types "Geico" as the search query. In December 2004, a U.S. District Court ruled that this practice did not violate federal trademark laws so long as the word "Geico" was not used in the ads' text (*Government Employees Insurance Company v. Google, Inc.*, 2004). Google quickly discontinued allowing the latter, and settled the case (Associated Press, 2005). Google settled another similar lawsuit, *Google Inc. v American Blind & Wallpaper Factory, Inc.*, in August 2007, following a court ruling in April that Google's display of competitor's ads as part of Google's AdWords program was a use of those marks in commerce, and allowing American Blind to proceed with trademark infringement claims arising from the use of those marks, finding that American Blind had presented sufficient evidence of consumer confusion to survive Google's motion for summary judgment on the matter. However, these settlements have not prevented other companies from also suing Google. For instance, in August 2007, American Airlines filed suit against Google over sponsored ads that appear when a user enters a keyword search using American Airlines trademarks. Thus far, although Google has lost some trademark cases in Europe, no definitive ruling against it has been issued in the United States.

The state of Utah has attempted to pre-empt the issue and passed a controversial Trademark Protection Act in March 2007 that bans advertisers from using the trademarked terms of their competitors to target ads to Utah users. The statute also establishes an "electronic registration mark" protecting trademark owners that file marks with a registry the state intends to create. Not surprisingly, the statute has been severely criticized by search providers such as Google, AOL, Yahoo and Microsoft, and will likely face constitutional challenges (Seidenberg, 2007).

Linking

Linking refers to building hypertext links from one site to another site. This is obviously a major design feature and benefit of the Web. **Deep linking** involves bypassing the target site's home page and going directly to a content page. In *Ticketmaster Corp. v. Tickets.com*, Tickets.com—owned by Microsoft—competed directly against Ticketmaster in the events ticket market. When Tickets.com did not have tickets for an event, it would direct users to Ticketmaster's internal pages, bypassing the Ticketmaster home page. Even though its logo was displayed on the internal pages, Ticketmaster objected on the grounds that such "deep linking" violated the terms and conditions of use for its site (stated on a separate page altogether and construed by Ticketmaster as equivalent to a shrink-wrap license), and constituted false advertising, as well as the violation of copyright. The court found, however, that deep linking per se is not illegal, no violation of copyright occurred because no copies were made, the terms and conditions of use were not obvious to users, and users were not required to read the page on which the terms and conditions of use appeared in any event. The court refused to rule in favor of Ticketmaster, but left open further argument on the licensing issue. In an out-of-court settlement, Tickets.com nevertheless agreed to stop the practice of deep linking (*Ticketmaster v. Tickets. com*, 2000).

linking
building hypertext links from one site to another site

deep linking
involves bypassing the target site's home page, and going directly to a content page

Framing

Framing involves displaying the content of another Web site inside your own Web site within a frame or window. The user never leaves the framer's site and can be exposed to advertising while the target site's advertising is distorted or eliminated. Framers may or may not acknowledge the source of the content. In *The Washington Post, et al. v. TotalNews, Inc. case, The Washington Post*, CNN, Reuters, and several other news organizations filed suit against TotalNews Inc., claiming that TotalNews's use of frames on its Web site, TotalNews.com, infringed upon the respective plaintiffs' copyrights and trademarks, diluted the content of their individual Web sites, and the content of those Web sites. The plaintiffs claimed additionally that TotalNews's framing practice effectively deprived the plaintiffs' Web sites of advertising revenue.

framing
involves displaying the content of another Web site inside your own Web site within a frame or window

TotalNews's Web site employed four frames. The TotalNews logo appeared in the lower left frame, the various links were located on a vertical frame on the left side of the screen, TotalNews's advertising was framed across the screen bottom, and the "news frame," the largest frame, appeared in the center and right. Clicking on a specific news organization's link allowed the reader to view the content of that particular organization's Web site, including any related advertising, within the context of the "news frame." In some instances, the framing distorted or modified the appearance of the linked Web site, including the advertisements, while the appearance of TotalNews's advertisements, in a separate frame, remained unchanged. In addition, the URL remained fixed on the TotalNews address, even though the content in the largest frame on the Web site was from the linked Web site. The "news frame" did not, however, eliminate the linked Web site's identifying features.

The case was settled out of court. The news organizations allowed TotalNews to link to their Web sites, but prohibited framing and any attempt to imply affiliation with the news organizations (*The Washington Post, et al. v. TotalNews, Inc.*, 1997).

CHALLENGE: BALANCING THE PROTECTION OF PROPERTY WITH OTHER VALUES

In the areas of copyright, patent law, and trademark law, societies have moved quickly to protect intellectual property from challenges posed by the Internet. In each of these areas, traditional concepts of intellectual property have not only been upheld, but often strengthened. The DMCA seems to restrict journalists and academics from even accessing copyrighted materials if they are encrypted, a protection not true of traditional documents (which are rarely encrypted anyway). Patents have been extended to Internet business methods, and trademarks are more strongly protected than ever because of fears of cybersquatting. In the early years of e-commerce, many commentators believed that Internet technology would sweep away the powers of corporations to protect their property (Dueker, 1996). The case of Napster and digital music files was a powerful example of how a new technology could disrupt an entrenched business model and an entire industry. In the case of Napster, though, the industry won in court suits and forced Napster's demise. Score one for the industry. Napster was quickly replaced by a newer technology (true peer-to-peer networks). Score one for file swappers. However, the U.S. Supreme Court and courts in Australia have found Grokster and other P2P networks liable for the infringement they enable. Australian courts ordered Sharman Network's P2P network software to track over 3,000 words (author and song names) and remove them from their network. In November 2005, Grokster shut down entirely as part of a legal settlement with the record industry, and paid $50 million in damages (McBride, 2005). Advantage: industry.

It is apparent that corporations have some very powerful legal tools for protecting their digital properties. By 2007, the record industry had filed over 25,000 lawsuits for sharing files (Associated Press, 2007). In addition, there are five arbitration panels established to hear trademark disputes: WIPO, ICANN, the National Arbitration Forum (Minneapolis), eResolutions Consortium (Amherst, Massachusetts), and C.P.R. Institute for Dispute Resolutions in New York. The difficulty now may be in going too far to protect the property interests of the powerful and the rich, preventing parody sites or parody content from receiving wide distribution and recognition, and in this sense interfering with the exercise of First Amendment guarantees of freedom of expression.

4 | GOVERNANCE

governance

has to do with social control: Who will control e-commerce, what elements will be controlled, and how the controls will be implemented

Governance has to do with social control: Who will control the Internet? Who will control the processes of e-commerce, the content, and the activities? What elements will be controlled, and how will the controls be implemented? A natural question arises and needs to be answered: "Why do we as a society need to 'control' e-commerce?" Because e-commerce and the Internet are so closely intertwined (though not identical), controlling e-commerce also involves regulating the Internet.

WHO GOVERNS E-COMMERCE AND THE INTERNET?

Governance of both the Internet and e-commerce has gone through four stages. **Table 13** summarizes these stages in the evolution of e-commerce governance.

TABLE 13	THE EVOLUTION OF GOVERNANCE OF E-COMMERCE
INTERNET GOVERNANCE PERIOD	**DESCRIPTION**
Government Control Period 1970–1994	DARPA and the National Science Foundation control the Internet as a fully government-funded program.
Privatization 1995–1998	Network Solutions Inc. is given a monopoly to assign and track high-level Internet domains. Backbone is sold to private telecommunications companies. Policy issues are not decided.
Self-Regulation 1995–present	President Clinton and the Department of Commerce encourage the creation of a semiprivate body, the Internet Corporation for Assigning Numbers and Names (ICANN), to deal with emerging conflicts and establish policies. ICANN currently holds a contract with the Department of Congress to govern some aspects of the Internet.
Governmental Regulation 1998–present	Executive, legislative, and judicial bodies worldwide begin to implement direct controls over the Internet and e-commerce.

Prior to 1995, the Internet was a government program. Beginning in 1995, private corporations were given control of the technical infrastructure as well as the process of granting IP addresses and domain names. However, the NSI monopoly created in this period did not represent international users of the Internet, and was unable to cope with emerging public policy issues such as trademark and intellectual property protection, fair policies for allocating domains, and growing concerns that a small group of firms were benefiting from growth in the Internet.

In 1995, President Clinton, using funds from the Department of Commerce, encouraged the establishment of an international body called the Internet Corporation for Assigned Names and Numbers (ICANN) that hopefully could better represent a wider range of countries and a broad range of interests, and begin to address emerging public policy issues. ICANN was intended to be an Internet/e-commerce industry self-governing body, not another government agency.

The explosive growth of the Web and e-commerce created a number of issues over which ICANN had no authority. Content issues such as pornography, gambling, and offensive written expressions and graphics, along with commercial issue of intellectual property protection, ushered in the current era of growing governmental regulation of the Internet and e-commerce throughout the world. Currently, we are in a mixed-mode policy environment where self-regulation through a variety of Internet policy and technical bodies co-exists with limited government regulation.

Today, ICANN remains in charge of the domain name system that translates domain names (such as www.company.com) into IP addresses. It has subcontracted the work of maintaining the databases of the domain registries to several private corporations. The U.S. government controls the "A-root" server. However, these arrangements are increasingly challenged by other countries, including China, Russia, Saudi Arabia, and most of the European Union, all of whom want the United States to give up control over the Internet to an international body such as the International Telecommunication Union (ITU) (a UN agency). In November 2005, an Internet Summit sponsored by the ITU agreed to leave control over the Internet domain servers with the United States and instead called for an international forum to meet in future years to discuss Internet policy issues (Miller and Rhoads, 2005). For its part, the United States is currently loathe to give up control over the Internet as originally envisaged by earlier presidents.

Can the Internet Be Controlled?

Early Internet advocates argued that the Internet was different from all previous technologies. They contended that the Internet could not be controlled, given its inherent decentralized design, its ability to cross borders, and its underlying packet switching technology that made monitoring and controlling message content impossible. Many still believe this to be true today. The slogans are "Information wants to be free," and "the Net is everywhere" (but not in any central location). The implication of these slogans is that the content and behavior of e-commerce sites—indeed Internet sites of any kind—cannot be "controlled" in the same way as traditional media such as radio and television. However, attitudes have changed as many governments and corporations extend their control over the Internet and the World Wide Web (Markoff, 2005).

In fact, the Internet is technically very easily controlled, monitored, and regulated from central locations (such as network access points, as well as servers and routers throughout the network). For instance, in China, Saudi Arabia, North Korea, Thailand, Singapore, and many other countries, access to the Web is controlled from government-owned centralized routers that direct traffic across their borders and within the country, such as China's "Great Firewall of China," which permits the government to block access to certain U.S. or European Web sites, or via tightly regulated ISPs operating within the countries. In China, for instance, all ISPs need a license from the Ministry of Information Industry (MII), and are prohibited from disseminating any information that may harm the state or permit pornography, gambling, or the advocacy of cults. In addition, ISPs and search engines such as Google, Yahoo, and MSN typically self-censor their Asian content by using only government-approved news sources. MySpace also self-censors content it believes might upset the Chinese government. Despite this, in October 2007, it was reported that China was redirecting traffic from search engines operated by Google, Microsoft and Yahoo to Chinese-operated Baidu.com (Ho, 2007; Elgin and Einhorn, 2006).

In some instances, the firms have also cooperated with the Chinese government's pursuit of bloggers and journalists as a condition of its continuing business in China. For instance, Yahoo has been roundly denounced for helping the Chinese government convict and sentence a man to ten years in jail for posting information to a U.S. Web site.

In the United States, as we have seen in our discussion of intellectual property, e-commerce sites can be put out of business for violating existing laws, and ISPs can be forced to "take down" offending content, or stolen content. Government security agencies such as the FBI can obtain court orders to monitor ISP traffic and engage in widespread monitoring of millions of e-mail messages. Under the USA PATRIOT Act, passed after the World Trade Center attack on September 11, 2001, American intelligence authorities are permitted to tap into whatever Internet traffic they believe is relevant to the campaign against terrorism, in some circumstances without judicial review. And many American corporations are developing restrictions on their employees' at-work use of the Web to prevent gambling, shopping, and other activities not related to a business purpose.

In the United States, efforts to control media content on the Web have run up against equally powerful social and political values that protect freedom of expression, including several rulings by the Supreme Court which have struck down laws attempting to limit Web content in the United States. The U.S. Constitution's First Amendment says "Congress shall make no law ... abridging the freedom of speech, or of the press." As it turns out, the 200-year-old Bill of Rights has been a powerful brake on efforts to control 21st-century e-commerce content.

PUBLIC GOVERNMENT AND LAW

The reason we have governments is ostensibly to regulate and control activities within the borders of the nation. What happens in other nations, for the most part, we generally ignore, although clearly environmental and international trade issues require multinational cooperation. E-commerce and the Internet pose some unique problems to public government that center on the ability of the nation-state to govern activities within its borders. Nations have considerable powers to shape the Internet.

TAXATION

Few questions illustrate the complexity of governance and jurisdiction more potently than taxation of e-commerce sales. In both Europe and the United States, governments rely on sales taxes based on the type and value of goods sold. In Europe, these taxes are collected along the entire value chain, including the final sale to the consumer, and are called "value-added taxes" (VAT), whereas in the United States, taxes are collected on final sales to consumers and are called consumption taxes. In the United States, there are 50 states, 3,000 counties, and 12,000 municipalities, each with unique tax rates and policies. Cheese may be taxable in one state as a "snack food" but not taxable in another state (such as Wisconsin), where it is considered a basic food. Consumption taxes are generally recognized to be regressive because they disproportionately tax poorer people, for whom consumption is a larger part of total income.

Sales taxes were first implemented in the United States in the late 1930s as a Depression era method of raising money for localities. Ostensibly, the money was to be used to build infrastructure such as roads, schools, and utilities to support business development, but over the years the funds have been used for general government purposes of the states and localities. In most states, there is a state-based sales tax, and a smaller local sales tax. The total sales tax ranges from zero in some states (North Dakota) to as much as 13% in New York City.

The development of "remote sales" such as mail order/telephone order (MOTO) retail in the United States in the 1970s broke the relationship between physical presence and commerce, complicating the plans of state and local tax authorities to tax all retail commerce. States sought to force MOTO retailers to collect sales taxes for them based on the address of the recipient, but Supreme Court decisions in 1967 and 1992 established that states had no authority to force MOTO retailers to collect state taxes unless the businesses had a "nexus" of operations (physical presence) in the state. Congress could, however, create legislation giving states this authority. But every congressional effort to tax catalog merchants has been beaten back by a torrent of opposition from catalog merchants and consumers, leaving intact an effective tax subsidy for MOTO merchants (Swisher, 2001).

The explosive growth of e-commerce, the latest type of "remote sales," has once again raised the issue of how—and if—to tax remote sales. Since its inception, e-commerce has benefited from a tax subsidy of up to 13% for goods shipped to high sales tax areas. Local retail merchants have complained bitterly about the e-commerce tax subsidy. E-commerce merchants have argued that this new form of commerce needs to be nurtured and encouraged in its early years, and that in any event, the crazy quilt of sales and use tax regimes would be difficult to administer for Internet merchants. State and local governments meanwhile see a potential source of new revenue slipping from their reach.

In 1998, Congress passed the Internet Tax Freedom Act, which placed a moratorium on "multiple or discriminatory taxes on electronic commerce" as well as on taxes on Internet access, for three years until October 2001, and in November 2001, extended the moratorium to November 2003. In November 2002, delegates from 32 states approved model legislation designed to create a system to tax Web sales. Spearheaded by the National Governor's Association (NGA), the Streamlined Sales Tax Project (SSTP) requires participating states to have only one tax rate for personal property or services effective by the end of 2005. By 2007, 15 states had agreed to support the SSTP. The governors are trying to get Congress to override judicial opinions and force online merchants to start collecting taxes. Nevertheless, in December 2004, Congress enacted the Internet Tax Nondiscrimination Act (Public Law 108–435), which extended the moratorium on states and local governments imposing taxes on Internet access and taxes on electronic commerce through November 1, 2007. In October 2007, Congress extended the moratorium once again, this time for an additional 7 years. (Gross, 2007).

The merger of online e-commerce with offline commerce further complicates the taxation question. Currently, almost all of the top 100 online retailers collect taxes when orders ship to states where these firms have a physical presence. But others, like eBay, still refuse to collect and pay local taxes, arguing that the so-called tax simplification project ended up with taxes for each of 49,000 zip codes, hardly a simplification (Broache, 2005). The taxation situation is also very complex in services. For instance, none of the major online travel sites collect the full amount of state and local hotel occupancy taxes, or state and local airline taxes. Instead of remitting sales tax on the full amount of the consumer's purchase, these sites instead collect taxes on the basis of the wholesale price they pay for the hotel rooms or tickets (Hansell, 2002).

The taxation situation in Europe, and trade between Europe and the United States, is similarly complex. The Organization for Economic Cooperation and Development (OECD), the economic policy coordinating body of European, American, and Japanese governments, is currently investigating different schemes for applying consumption and business profit taxes for e-commerce digitally downloaded goods. The EU began collecting a VAT on digital goods such as music and software delivered to consumers by foreign companies in 2003. Previously, European Union companies were required to collect the VAT on sales to EU customers, but U.S. companies were not. This gave American companies a huge tax edge.

Thus, there is no integrated rational approach to taxation of domestic or international e-commerce (Varian, 2001). In the United States, the national and international character of Internet sales is wreaking havoc on taxation schemes that were built in the 1930s and based on local commerce and local jurisdictions. Although there appears to be acquiescence among large Internet retailers such as Amazon to the idea of some kind of sales tax on e-commerce sales, their insistence on uniformity will probably delay taxation for many years, and any proposal to tax e-commerce will likely incur the wrath of almost 120 million U.S. e-commerce consumers. Congress is not likely to ignore their voices.

NET NEUTRALITY

In the United States, another Internet governance issue that has recently attracted attention has been the issue of "Net neutrality". Currently, all Internet traffic is treated equally (or "neutrally") by Internet backbone owners. However, telephone and cable companies that provide the Internet backbone would like to be able to charge differentiated prices based on the amount of bandwidth consumed by content being delivered over the Internet. The content of companies that pay an additional fee would be given preferential treatment in terms of delivery speed. The content of companies that refused to pay would be delivered at a slower rate. Those who oppose this prospect have been lobbying Congress to create a new layer of Internet regulation that would require network providers to manage their networks in a nondiscriminatory manner. So far, Congress has not yet passed any legislation, although the issue is likely to be revisited as certain types of content, such as online videos and other types of file-sharing, consume more and more bandwidth.

5   PUBLIC SAFETY AND WELFARE

Governments everywhere claim to pursue public safety, health, and welfare. This effort produces laws governing everything from weights and measures to national highways, to the content of radio and television programs. Electronic media of all kinds (telegraph, telephone, radio, and television) have historically been regulated by governments seeking to develop a rational commercial telecommunications environment and to control the content of the media—which may be critical of government or offensive to powerful groups in a society. Historically, in the United States, newspapers and print media have been beyond government controls because of constitutional guarantees of freedom of speech. Electronic media such as radio and television have, on the other hand, always been subject to content regulation because they use the publicly owned frequency spectrum. Telephones have also been regulated as public utilities and "common carriers," with special social burdens to provide service and access, but with no limitations on content.

In the United States, critical issues in e-commerce center around the protection of children, strong sentiments against pornography in any public media, efforts to control gambling, and the protection of public health through restricting sales of drugs and cigarettes.

PROTECTING CHILDREN

Pornography is an immensely successful Internet business. According to various statistics, online pornography in 2007 generated somewhere between $2-$3 billion in revenue. According to comScore Media Metrix, more than a third of U.S. Internet users visit adult Web sites each month, and 4% of all Web traffic and 2% of all time spent Web surfing involved an adult site (eMarketer, Inc., 2007d; Moore, 2007).

To control the Web as a distribution medium for pornography, in 1996, Congress passed the Communications Decency Act (CDA). This act made it a felony criminal offense to use any telecommunications device to transmit "any comment, request, suggestion, proposal, image or other communications which is obscene, lewd, lascivious, filthy, or indecent" to anyone, and in particular, to persons under the age of 18 years of age (Section 502, Communications Decency Act of 1996). In 1997, the Supreme Court struck down the CDA as an unconstitutional abridgement of freedom of speech protected by the First Amendment. While the government argued the CDA was like a zoning ordinance designed to allow "adult" Web sites for people over 18 years of age, the Court found the CDA was a blanket proscription on content and rejected the "cyberzoning" argument as impossible to administer. Another 1996 law, the Child Pornography Prevention Act, which made it a crime to create, distribute, or posses "virtual" child pornography that uses computer-generated images or young adults rather than real children, was also struck down as overly broad by the Supreme Court in 2002, in the *Ashcroft v. Free Speech Coalition* case.

In 1998, Congress passed the Children's Online Protection Act (COPA). This act made it a felony criminal offense to communicate for "commercial purposes" "any material harmful to minors." Harmful material was defined as prurient, depicting sexual acts, and lacking value for minors. The act differed from the CDA by focusing on "commercial speech" and minors exclusively. In February 1999, however, a Federal District Court in Pennsylvania struck down COPA as an unconstitutional restriction on Web content that was protected under the First Amendment. The court nevertheless recognized the interest of Congress and society to protect children on the Internet and in e-commerce. In May 2002, the U.S. Supreme Court returned the case to the Court of Appeals for a decision, leaving in place an injunction barring enforcement of the law. In March 2003, the Third Circuit Court of Appeals ruled for the second time that COPA was unconstitutional, finding that the law violated the First Amendment because it improperly restricts access to a substantial amount of online speech that is lawful for adults. In 2004, the Supreme Court blocked enforcement of the law again, saying that it likely violated the First Amendment, but remanded it to the District Court for a further trial examining Internet filtering technologies that might be used to achieve the law's goals. In January 2006, it was revealed that in preparation for this trial, the Department of Justice had issued subpoenas to Google, AOL, Yahoo, and MSN seeking a week's worth of search queries and a random sampling of 1 million Web addresses in the effort to understand the prevalence of material that could be deemed harmful to minors and the effectiveness of filtering technology, raising a storm of additional controversy. AOL, MSN, and Yahoo all agreed to supply the requested data, but Google refused on a variety of grounds, including protection of its trade secrets, privacy, and public relations (Hafner and Richtel, 2006). In response, the court limited the subpoena to just a sample of URLs in Google's database. In March 2007, the district court struck down COPA, ruling once again that the law violated the 1st and 5th Amendments, and issued an order permanently enjoining the government from enforcing COPA. The government has once again appealed, and as of this writing, the case is before the Third Circuit (Urbina, 2007).

As of this writing, a 2003 law, called the Protect Act, is also before the Supreme Court. The Protect Act is an omnibus bill intended to prevent child abuse that includes prohibitions against computer-generated child pornography." Part of that statute was previously held to be unconstitutional as well by the 11th Circuit Court of Appeals.

Although Congress has had a difficult time framing constitutionally acceptable legislation to protect children and other consumers from pornography, in the Children's Online Privacy Protection Act (COPPA) (1998) (described in Section 2), it appears to have been successful in preventing e-commerce sites from collecting information on minors without parental consent. Pornographers who collect information on children without parental consent are potential felons. Because COPPA does not regulate e-commerce content per se, to date it has not been challenged in the courts.

In 2001, Congress passed the Children's Internet Protection Act (CIPA), which required schools and libraries in the United States to install "technology protection measures" (filtering software), in an effort to shield children from pornography. In June 2003, the Supreme Court upheld CIPA, overturning a Federal District Court that found the law interfered with the First Amendment guarantee of freedom of expression. The Supreme Court, in a 6-3 opinion, held that the law's limitations on access to the Internet posed no more a threat to freedom of expression than limitations on access to books that librarians choose for whatever reason not to acquire. The dissenting justices found this analogy inappropriate and instead argued the proper analogy was if librarians were to purchase encyclopedias and then rip out pages they thought were or might be offensive to patrons. All the justices agreed that existing blocking software was overly blunt, unable to distinguish child pornography from sexually explicit material (which is protected by the First Amendment), and generally unreliable (Greenhouse, 2003b). Other legislation such as the 2002 Domain

Names Act seeks to prevent unscrupulous Web site operators from luring children to pornography using misleading domain names or characters known to children, while the 2002 Dot Kids Act authorizes the creation of a second-level domain on the Internet where all Web sites would have to declare they contain no material harmful to children. An alternative plan, to create an .xxx domain for adult web site content, was rejected by ICANN for the third time in March 2007 (Moore, 2007).

In addition to government regulation, private pressure from organized groups has also been successful in forcing some Web sites to eliminate the display of pornographic materials.

CIGARETTES, GAMBLING, AND DRUGS: IS THE WEB REALLY BORDERLESS?

In the United States, both the states and the federal government have adopted legislation to control certain activities and products in order to protect public health and welfare. Cigarettes, gambling, medical drugs, and of course addictive recreational drugs, are either banned or tightly regulated by federal and state laws (see *Insight on Society: The Internet Drug Bazaar*). Yet these products and services are ideal for distribution over the Internet through e-commerce sites. Because the sites can be located offshore, they can operate beyond the jurisdiction of state and federal prosecutors. Or so it seemed until recently. In the case of cigarettes, state and federal authorities have been quite successful in shutting down tax-free cigarette Web sites within the United States and pressuring credit card firms to drop cigarette merchants from their systems. The major shipping companies—UPS, FedEx and DHL, have been pressured into refusing shipment of untaxed cigarettes, and a bill has been introduced to Congress to prohibit the shipping of cigarettes and other tobacco products via the U.S. Postal Service. Phillip Morris has also agreed to no longer ship cigarettes to any resellers that have been found to be engaging in illegal Internet and mail order sales. However, East European sites and Web sites located on American Indian reservations continue to operate using checks and money orders as payments and the postal system as logistics partner, but their level of business has plummeted as consumers fear state tax authorities will present them with huge tax bills if they are discovered using these sites. As a result of these pressures and the threat of ultimately collecting taxes from consumers who purchase at these sites, online tax-free cigarette sales have dropped precipitously.

Gambling also provides an interesting example of the clash between traditional jurisdictional boundaries and claims to a borderless, uncontrollable Web. The online gambling market, based almost entirely offshore—primarily in United Kingdom and various Caribbean Islands—grew by leaps and bounds between 2000 and 2006, generating as much as $50 billion to $60 billion a year, and with much of the action (some estimate up to 50%) coming from U.S.-based customers. Although the federal government contended online gambling was illegal under U.S. federal law, they were initially unable to stop it, with various federal courts offering mixed opinions. However, in the summer of 2006, federal officials turned up the heat and arrested two executive officers of offshore gambling operations as they passed through the United States, leading their companies to cease U.S. operations. Then in October 2006, Congress passed the Unlawful Internet Gambling Enforcement Act, which makes it a

INSIGHT ON SOCIETY

THE INTERNET DRUG BAZAAR

In July 2007, the FBI announced the indictment of Kathleen Giacobbe, the owner and operator of Youronlinedoctor.com, as well as four other defendants, including a doctor and the owner of two pharmacies located in North Carolina, on drug distribution and money laundering charges in connection with an alleged unlawful prescription drug operation. According to the indictment, from August 2002 to May 2006, the defendants conspired to distribute millions of dosage units of powerful and addictive painkillers and anxiety medications to thousands of customers nationwide based on unlawful and illegitimate prescriptions. The purported prescriptions were in fact merely drug "orders" taken by the Web site and then filled by the North Carolina pharmacies, which by pre-arrangement had agreed not to challenge the legitimacy of the orders. The Web site employed a doctor to give it the façade of legitimacy, and used a photocopy of his signature when it submitted the orders. In August 2007, in a similar case, three U.S. physicians and two pharmacists, along with eight affiliated Web site operators, were indicted for the illegal online sale of prescription drugs. According to the Department of Justice, the operation handled more than 1 million online orders and took in over $125 million during a two-year period.

According to a study done by the Treatment Research Institute at the University of Pennsylvania, addictive and potentially lethal medications are available without prescription from more than 2 million Web sites around the world, with many sites based in countries that impose little if any regulation on pharmaceuticals. The National Center on Addiction and Substance Abuse (CASA) at Columbia University found in 2006 that a majority of Web sites selling controlled prescription drugs did not require a prescription. MarkMonitor, a company specializing in online brand protection, studied 3,160 online pharmacies in the summer of 2007. It found that questionable business practices were more the norm than the exception. A Google search on "drugs" "no prescription" returns over 2 million results.

The sale of drugs without a prescription is not the only danger posed by the Internet drug bazaar. Rogue online pharmacy sites may be selling counterfeit drugs, or unapproved drugs. For example, in February 2007, the FDA issued a warning that a number of consumers who had purchased Ambien, Xanax, and Lexapro online from several different Web sites had instead received a product containing haloperial, a powerful anti-psychotic drug. In May 2007, the FDA issued another warning that 24 apparently related Web sites were involved in the distribution of counterfeit versions of Xenical, a prescription weight loss drug.

But despite these dangers, online pharmacies remain alluring and are one of the fastest-growing business models, with, oddly, senior citizens—usually some of the most law-abiding citizens—leading the charge for cheaper drugs. The top 1,000 Internet pharmacies are estimated to generate about $4 billion in revenue. The main attraction of online drug sites is price. Typically, they are located in countries where prescription drugs are price-controlled, or where the price structure is much lower, such as in Mexico. U.S. citizens can often save 50%–75% by purchasing from online pharmacies located in other countries.

Currently a patchwork regulatory structure governs the sale of drugs online. At the federal

(continued)

level, the 1938 Food, Drug, and Cosmetic Act (FDCA) requires that certain drugs may only be purchased with a valid doctor's prescription and must be dispensed by a state-licensed pharmacy. To get around this requirement, some online pharmacies use questionnaires to diagnose disease and have these questionnaires reviewed by doctors that write the prescription. Whether this constitutes a "valid" prescription differs from state to state, which regulate both pharmacies and the practice of medicine within their borders. Congress has considered legislation to establish a federal definition of what constitutes a valid prescription, but to date such legislation has not passed.

Complicating matters is the fact that many online pharmacies operate offshore, making it difficult for federal and state authorities to exercise jurisdiction over them.

In the meantime, the Food and Drug Administration recommends that consumers look for the National Association of Boards of Pharmacy (NABP) Verified Internet Pharmacy Practices Sites (VIPPS) Seal, which verifies that the site is legitimate. So far, 14 major Internet pharmacies have signed on, including Drugstore.com, Caremark.com, CVS.com, Walgreens.com, among others. However, that leaves thousands of sites that consumers should approach with a "Buyer Beware" attitude.

SOURCES: "MarkMonitor Brandjacking Index Exposes Online Scams that Threaten Top Pharmaceutical Brands and Hurt Consumers," MarkMonitor, August 20, 2007; "Online Pill Pushers Busted," by Roy Mark, Internetnews.com, August 3, 2007; "Five Defendants Indicted in Unlawful Prescription Drug Operation," Department of Justice, July 20, 2007; "Legal Issues Related to Prescription Drug Sales on the Internet," by Vanessa Burrows, CRS Report for Congress, July 12, 2007; "The Possible Dangers of Buying Medicine Online," U.S. Food and Drug Administration, July 2, 2007; "FDA Warns Consumers about Counterfeit Drugs from Multiple Internet Sellers," U.S. Food and Drug Administration, May 1, 2007; "Vantage Point: Internet Sales of Dangerous Drugs without a Prescription," by Keith Humphreys, *Stanford Report*, May 30, 2007; "FDA Alerts Consumers to Unsafe, Misrepresented Drugs Purchased Over the Internet," U.S. Food and Drug Administration, February 16, 2007; "Internet Prescriptions as Public Health Threat," by Edmund Scanlan, Chicago Accident Law Blog, February 13, 2007.

crime to use credit cards or online payment systems for Internet betting. This effectively bars online gambling companies from operating legally in the United States, and shortly thereafter a number of the leading, publicly traded companies suspended their business in the United States. However, the bill has not eliminated all online gambling in the United States, with some smaller companies still offering offshore gambling. An association of online gambling groups is also challenging the law as unconstitutional, claiming that Internet gambling is protected by First Amendment privacy rights and that filtering technology exists to make sure that children and compulsive gamblers cannot access offshore betting sites. Several countries are also seeking compensation from the United States on the basis of a World Trade Organization ruling that American Internet gambling restrictions are illegal (Parry, 2007; Rivlan, 2007; Pfanner, 2006).

6 CASE STUDY

Print the Library [Online]:
Is Google Playing Fair, or Just Out to Make a Buck?

Google is on a tear to put everything digital on its servers and then, as the founders promise in ceaseless self-congratulatory announcements, provide access to "all the world's information" through its efforts. And make a buck, as it turns out, by selling ads aimed at you that are "relevant" to your searches. A problem arises, however, when what Google wants to put on their servers does not belong to them. We're all familiar with the copyrighted music and video situation, where firms often operating offshore, beyond the law (or so they think) enable, induce, and encourage Internet users to illegally download copyrighted material without paying a dime for it, while in the meantime raking in millions of advertising dollars from companies willing to advertise on their networks.

But Google is no criminal organization. For a firm who's motto is "Don't be evil," it seems out of character for it to initiate a program of scanning millions of copyrighted books it does not own and then, without permission, providing its search

screenshot of Opencontentalliance.org home page © 2007 Open Content Alliance. Used with permission

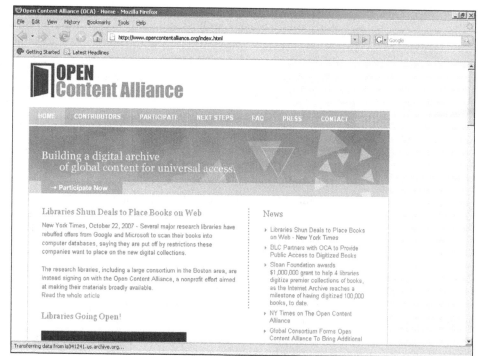

engine users with access to those books without charge, while selling ad space and pocketing millions for its own account without sharing that revenue with publishers or authors. One major difference between Google and most file-sharing firms is that Google has very deep pockets filled with cash, and they are based in the United States, making it an excellent legal target.

It's a complicated story with exaggerations on all sides. In 2004, Google announced a program it now calls the Google Book Search Project (previously called Google Print). There are two parts to the project. Under the Partner Program (previously called the Publisher Program), publishers give permission to Google to scan their books, or make scans available, and then make parts of the work, or simply bibliographic information (title, author, and publisher), available on Google's search engine. No problem there: publishers and authors get a chance to find a wider market, and Google sells more ads.

It's the second part of the project that is controversial. Under the Library Project (previously called Google Print Library), Google proposes to scan millions of books in university and public libraries and then allow users to search for key phrases, and display "relevant" portions of the text (what it calls "snippets"), all without contacting the publisher or seeking permission or paying a royalty fee. Google said it would "never show a full page without the right from the copyright holder," just the "relevant" portion. Google gave the publishing industry until November 2005 to opt-out by proving Google with a list of books they did not want to be included.

Google has the backing of a number of prestigious libraries, such as the University of Michigan, Harvard University, Stanford University, the New York Public Library, and Oxford University. But not all librarians agree. Some believe this is a marvelous extension of public access to library collections, while other librarians fear it is harmful to book authors and publishers. A number of well-known libraries, such as the Smithsonian Institution, and the Boston Public Library, as well as a consortium of 19 research and academic libraries in the Northeast, have refused to participate, in part because of restrictions that Google wants to place on the collection. Libraries that work with Google must agree to make the material unavailable to other commercial search services.

Google claims it is performing a public service by making an index of books, and relevant portions, available to millions on the Internet, and perhaps even helping publishers sell new copies of books that currently sit on dusty library shelves. The publishing industry disagrees with Google and two lawsuits were quickly filed in federal court in New York, one a class action suit by the Authors Guild, and the second by five major publishing companies (McGraw Hill, Pearson Education, Penguin Group, Simon & Schuster, and John Wiley & Sons), claiming copyright infringement. The American Association of Publishers alleges that Google is claiming the right to "unilaterally change copyright law and copy anything unless somebody tells [them] "No" [making it] impossible for people in the intellectual property community to operate. They [Google] keep talking about doing this because it is good for the world. That has never been a principle in law. They 'do no evil' except they are stealing people's property." Or, as one wag put it, it's like having a thief break into your house and clean the kitchen—it's still breaking and entering.

Google, on the other hand, claims this use is "fair" under the "fair use" doctrine that has emerged from a number of court decisions issued over the years, and which is codified in the Copyright Act in 1976 (refer to Table 11). The copying and lending of books by libraries has been considered a fair use since the late 1930s under a "gentleman's agreement" between libraries and publishers, and a library exemption was codified as Section 108 of the Copyright Act of 1976. Libraries loan books to patrons for a limited period, and they must purchase at least one copy. Many people read books borrowed from libraries and recommend them to friends, who often buy the books rather than take the time and effort to go to a library. Libraries are also considered by many in the publishing industry as helping to market a book to a larger public, and libraries are believed to be performing a public service by increasing literacy and education.

There are two lines of cases that suggest potentially different outcomes for the Google litigation. In New York, in the *UMG Recording v. MP3* case, the federal district court for the Southern District of New York ruled that a defendant that copied copyrighted works onto a server and allowed access to third-party subscribers was not protected by fair use. But in California, two Ninth Circuit cases, *Kelly v. Arriba Soft*, and *Perfect 10, Inc. v. Amazon.com Inc.*, held that the storage and display of "thumbnail" images of copyrighted works in order to make them accessible via a search engine was fair use. Motions for summary judgment in both Google lawsuits were filed in July 2007, and trial is expected in 2008.

Meanwhile, the Open Content Alliance (OCA) has begun its own mammoth book-scanning project to produce an open database of book contents that will be accessible from any search engine, including Google's. For the most part, the OCA will focus on books in the public domain, often of historical interest. But for books still under copyright protection, they will obtain permission from the publishers before scanning. In contrast, Google wants to own and control its database of books. Microsoft initially joined the OCA when it first started, as did Yahoo, but both have since launched their own book search projects. Proponents of the OCA approach worry that allowing one company, such as Google, to dominate the digital conversion of books is a dangerous proposition that gives too much control to a private entity that has profit as its primary goal.

The book industry isn't the only industry likely to have to worry about Google. Just about any digital content is in the cross-hairs of Google's plans to dominate the Internet search industry. The more digital content Google can index, from maps, to music, TV programs, books, newspapers, and reports, the larger its audience, and the more money it can make from selling space to advertisers.

SOURCES: "Libraries Shun Deals to Place Books on Web," by Katie Hafner, New York Times, October 22, 2007; "The Google Book Search Project Litigation," by Lawrence Jordan, Michigan Bar Journal, September 2007; "Scan This Book!", by Andrew Richard Albanese, Library Journal, August 15, 2007; "Search Me?, " by Bob Thompson, Washington Post, August 13, 2006.

Case Study Questions

1. Who is harmed by Google's Library Project? Make a list of harmed groups, and for each group, try to devise a solution that would eliminate or lessen the harm.

2. If you were a librarian, would you support Google's Library Project? Why or why not?

3. Do you believe Google's claim that scanning entire books fits within the concept of "fair use?" Why or why not?

4. What are some of the important differences between Google's Library Project program and the Open Content Alliance program?

5. Why is Google pursuing the Library Project program? What's in it for Google? Make a list of benefits to Google.

7   REVIEW

KEY CONCEPTS

■ Understand why e-commerce raises ethical, social, and political issues.

Internet technology and its use in e-commerce disrupts existing social and business relationships and understandings. Suddenly, individuals, business firms, and political institutions are confronted by new possibilities of behavior for which understandings, laws, and rules of acceptable behavior have not yet been developed. Many business firms and individuals are benefiting from the commercial development of the Internet, but this development also has costs for individuals, organizations, and societies. These costs and benefits must be carefully considered by those seeking to make ethical and socially responsible decisions in this new environment, particularly where there are as yet no clear-cut legal or cultural guidelines.

■ Recognize the main ethical, social, and political issues raised by e-commerce.

The major issues raised by e-commerce can be loosely categorized into four major dimensions:
- *Information rights*—What rights do individuals have to control their own personal information when Internet technologies make information collection so pervasive and efficient?
- *Property rights*—How can traditional intellectual property rights be enforced when perfect copies of protected works can be made and easily distributed worldwide via the Internet?
- *Governance*—Should the Internet and e-commerce be subject to public laws? If so, what law-making bodies have jurisdiction-state, federal, and/or international?

- *Public safety and welfare*—What efforts should be undertaken to ensure equitable access to the Internet and e-commerce channels? Do certain online content and activities pose a threat to public safety and welfare?

■ Identify a process for analyzing ethical dilemmas.

Ethical, social, and political controversies usually present themselves as dilemmas. Ethical dilemmas can be analyzed via the following process:
- Identify and clearly describe the facts.
- Define the conflict or dilemma and identify the higher-order values involved.
- Identify the stakeholders.
- Identify the options that you can reasonably take.
- Identify the potential consequences of your options.
- Refer to well-established ethical principles, such as the Golden Rule, Universalism, Descartes' Rule of Change, the Collective Utilitarian Principle, Risk Aversion, the No Free Lunch Rule, the *New York Times* Test, and the Social Contract Rule to help you decide the matter.

■ Understand basic concepts related to privacy.

To understand the issues concerning online privacy, you must first understand some basic concepts:
- *Privacy* is the moral right of individuals to be left alone, free from surveillance or interference from others.
- *Information privacy* includes both the claim that certain information should not be collected at all by governments or business firms, and the claim of individuals to control the use of information about themselves.
- *Due process* as embodied by the Fair Information Practices doctrine, informed consent, and opt-in/opt-out policies also play an important role in privacy.

■ Identify the practices of e-commerce companies that threaten privacy.

Almost all e-commerce companies collect some personally identifiable information in addition to anonymous information and use cookies to track clickstream behavior of visitors. Advertising networks and search engines also track the behavior of consumers across thousands of popular sites, not just at one site, via cookies, spyware, search engine behavioral targeting, and other techniques

■ Describe the different methods used to protect online privacy.

There are a number of different methods used to protect online privacy. They include:
- Legal protections deriving from constitutions, common law, federal law, state laws, and government regulations. In the United States, rights to online privacy may be derived the U.S. Constitution, tort law, federal laws such as the Children's Online Privacy Protection Act, the Federal Trade Commission's Fair Information Practice principles, and a variety of state laws. In Europe, the European Commission's Directive on Data Protection has standardized and broadened privacy protection in the European Union nations.
- Industry self-regulation via industry alliances, such as the Online Privacy Alliance and the Network Advertising Initiative, that seek to gain voluntary adherence to industry privacy guidelines and safe harbors. Some firms also hire Chief Privacy Officers.

- Privacy-enhancing technological solutions include secure e-mail, anonymous remailers, anonymous surfing, cookie managers, disk file-erasing programs, policy generators, and privacy policy readers.

■ **Understand the various forms of intellectual property and the challenge of protecting it.**

There are three main types of intellectual property protection: copyright, patent, and trademark law.

- *Copyright law* protects original forms of expression such as writings, drawings, and computer programs from being copied by others for a minimum of 70 years. It does not protect ideas—just their expression in a tangible medium. "Look and feel" copyright infringement lawsuits are precisely about the distinction between an idea and its expression. If there is only one way to express an idea, then the expression cannot be copyrighted. Copyrights, like all rights, are not absolute. The doctrine of fair use permits certain parties under certain circumstances to use copyrighted material without permission. The Digital Millennium Copyright Act (DMCA) is the first major effort to adjust the copyright laws to the Internet Age. The DMCA implements a World Intellectual Property Organization treaty, which declares it illegal to make, distribute, or use devices that circumvent technology-based protections of copyrighted materials, and attaches stiff fines and prison sentences for violations.

- *Patent law* grants the owner of a patent an exclusive monopoly to the ideas behind an invention for 20 years. Patents are very different from copyrights in that they protect the ideas themselves and not merely the expression of ideas. There are four types of inventions for which patents are granted under patent law: machines, man-made products, compositions of matter, and processing methods. In order to be granted a patent, the applicant must show that the invention is new, original, novel, non-obvious, and not evident in prior arts and practice. Most of the inventions that make the Internet and e-commerce possible were not patented by their inventors. This changed in the mid-1990s with the commercial development of the World Wide Web. Business firms began applying for "business methods" and software patents.

- *Trademark protections* exist at both the federal and state levels in the United States. The purpose of trademark law is twofold. First, trademark law protects the public in the marketplace by ensuring that it gets what it pays for and wants to receive. Second, trademark law protects the owner who has spent time, money, and energy bringing the product to market against piracy and misappropriation. Federal trademarks are obtained, first, by use in interstate commerce, and second, by registration with the U.S. Patent and Trademark Office (USPTO). Trademarks are granted for a period of ten years and can be renewed indefinitely. Use of a trademark that creates confusion with existing trademarks, causes consumers to make market mistakes, or misrepresents the origins of goods is an infringement. In addition, the intentional misuse of words and symbols in the marketplace to extort revenue from legitimate trademark owners ("bad faith") is proscribed. The Anticybersquatting Consumer Protection Act (ACPA) creates civil liabilities for anyone who attempts in bad faith to profit from an existing famous or distinctive trademark by registering an Internet domain name that is identical, confusingly similar, or "dilutive" of that trademark. Trademark abuse can take many forms on the Web. The major behaviors on the Internet that have run afoul of trademark law include cybersquatting, cyberpiracy, metatagging, keywording, linking, and framing.

■ **Understand how governance of the Internet has evolved over time.**

Governance has to do with social control: who will control e-commerce, what elements will be controlled, and how the controls will be implemented. Governance of both the Internet and e-commerce has gone through four stages:

- *Government control (1970–1994).* During this period, DARPA and the National Science Foundation controlled the Internet as a fully government funded program.
- *Privatization (1995–1998).* Network Solutions was given a monopoly to assign and track high-level Internet domain names. The backbone was sold to private telecommunications companies and policy issues remained undecided.
- *Self-regulation (1995–present).* President Clinton and the Department of Commerce encouraged creation of ICANN, a semi-private body, to deal with emerging conflicts and to establish policies.
- *Governmental regulation (1998–present).* Executive, legislative, and judicial bodies worldwide began to implement direct controls over the Internet and e-commerce.

We are currently in a mixed-mode policy environment where self-regulation, through a variety of Internet policy and technical bodies, co-exists with limited government regulation.

■ **Explain why taxation of e-commerce raises governance and jurisdiction issues.**

E-commerce raises the issue of how—and if—to tax remote sales. The national and international character of Internet sales is wreaking havoc on taxation schemes in the United States that were built in the 1930s and based on local commerce and local jurisdictions. E-commerce has benefited from a tax subsidy since its inception. E-commerce merchants have argued that this new form of commerce needs to be nurtured and encouraged, and that in any event, the crazy quilt of sales and use tax regimes would be difficult to administer for Internet merchants. In 1998, Congress passed the Internet Tax Freedom Act, which placed a moratorium on multiple or discriminatory taxes on electronic commerce, and any taxation of Internet access, and since that time has extended the moratorium three times, most recently until November 2014. In November 2002, delegates from 32 states approved model legislation designed to create a system to tax Web sales, and by 2007, 15 states had agreed to support the program. Although there appears to be acquiescence among large Internet retailers to the idea of some kind of sales tax on e-commerce sales, insistence on uniformity will delay taxation for many years, and any proposal to tax e-commerce will likely incur the wrath of U.S. e-commerce consumers.

■ **Identify major public safety and welfare issues raised by e-commerce.**

Critical public safety and welfare issues in e-commerce include:

- The protection of children and strong sentiments against pornography. The Children's Online Protection Act (COPA) of 1998 made it a felony criminal offense to communicate for commercial purposes any material harmful to minors. This law has thus far been struck down as an unconstitutional restriction on Web content that is protected under the First Amendment. The Children's Internet Protection Act (CIPA), which requires schools and libraries in the United States to install "technology protection measures" (filtering soft-ware) in an effort to shield children from pornography, has however, been upheld by the Supreme Court. In addition to government regulation, private pressure from organized groups has also been successful in forcing some Web sites to eliminate the display of pornographic materials.

- Efforts to control gambling and restrict sales of cigarettes and drugs. In the United States, cigarettes, gambling, medical drugs, and addictive recreational drugs are either banned or tightly regulated by federal and state laws. Yet these products and services are often distributed via offshore e-commerce sites operating beyond the jurisdiction of federal and state prosecutors. At this point, it is not clear that the Web will remain borderless or that e-commerce can continue to flaunt national, state, and local laws with impunity.

QUESTIONS

1. What basic assumption does the study of ethics make about individuals?
2. What are the three basic principles of ethics? How does due process factor in?
3. Explain Google's position that YouTube does not violate the intellectual property rights of copyright owners.
4. Define universalism, slippery slope, the *New York Times* test, and the social contract rule as they apply to ethics.
5. Explain why someone with a serious medical condition might be concerned about researching his or her condition online, through medical search engines or pharmaceutical sites, for example. What is one technology that could prevent one's identity from being revealed?
6. Name some of the personal information collected by Web sites about their visitors.
7. How does information collected through online forms differ from site transaction logs? Which potentially provides a more complete consumer profile?
8. How is the opt-in model of informed consent different from opt-out? In which type of model does the consumer retain more control?
9. What are the two core principles of the FTC's Fair Information Practice principles?
10. How do safe harbors work? What is the government's role in them?
11. Name three ways online advertising networks have improved on, or added to, traditional offline marketing techniques.
12. Explain how Web profiling is supposed to benefit both consumers and businesses.
13. What are some of the challenges that Chief Privacy Officers face in their jobs?
14. How could the Internet potentially change protection given to intellectual property? What capabilities make it more difficult to enforce intellectual property law?
15. What does the Digital Millennium Copyright Act attempt to do? Why was it enacted? What types of violations does it try to prevent?
16. Define cybersquatting. How is it different from cyberpiracy? What type of intellectual property violation does cybersquatting entail?
17. What is deep linking and why is it a trademark issue? Compare it to framing—how is it similar and different?
18. What are some of the tactics illegal businesses, such as betting parlors and casinos, successfully use to operate outside the law on the Internet?

PROJECTS

1. Go to Google's Preferences page and examine its SafeSearch filtering options. Surf the Web in search of content that could be considered objectionable for children using each of the options. What are the pros and cons of such restrictions? Are there terms that could be considered inappropriate to the filtering software but be approved by parents? Name five questionable terms. Prepare a brief PowerPoint or other form of presentation to report on your experiences and to explain the positive and negative aspects of such filtering software.

2. Develop a list a privacy protection features that should be present if a Web site is serious about protecting privacy. Then, visit at least four well-known Web sites and examine their privacy policies. Write a report that rates each of the Web sites on the criteria you have developed.

3. Review the provisions of the Digital Millennium Copyright Act of 1998. Examine each of the major sections of the legislation and make a list of the protections afforded property owners and users of copyrighted materials. Do you believe this legislation balances the interests of owners and users appropriately? Do you have suggestions for strengthening "fair use" provisions in this legislation?

4. Visit at least four Web sites that take a position on e-commerce taxation, beginning with The National Conference of State Legislatures (Ncsl.org) and The National Governor's Association (Nga.org). You might also include national associations of local businesses or citizen groups opposed to e-commerce taxation. Develop a reasoned argument for, or against, taxation of e-commerce.

5. Consider the issue of the Department of Justice's subpoena of search query records discussed above. Prepare a list of reasons why the firms subpoenaed should or should not comply with this request. What moral dilemmas present themselves? What higher-order values, and what kind of value conflicts, are revealed in this list. How do you propose that we as a society resolve these dilemmas. You might conclude by applying each of the Candidate Ethical Principles described in Section 1.

WEB SITE RESOURCES www.prenhall.com/laudon

- News: News stories relevant to the material in this chapter
- Research: Important e-commerce research abstracts and links to articles
- Additional projects, exercises, and tutorials
- Careers: Explore career opportunities in e-commerce
- Raising capital and business plans

REFERENCES

Apple Col ⌐ ater, Inc. v. Microsoft Corp. 709 F. Supp. 925, 926 (N. D. Cal. 1989); 799 F. Supp. 1006, 1017 (N. D. Cal., 1992); 35 F. 3d 1435 (9th Cir.); cert. denied, 63 U. S. L. W. 3518 (U.S., Feb. 21, 1995) (No. 94-1121).

Associated Press. "Google Settles Final Piece of Geico Case." BizReport.com (September 8, 2005).

Associated Press. "Woman Must Pay Record Labels for Sharing Copyrighted Music." USA Today (October 4, 2007).

Audi AG and Volkswagen of America, Inc. v. Bob D'Amato No. 05-2359, 6th Circuit (November 27, 2006).

Bernina of America, Inc. v. Fashion Fabrics Int'l., Inc. 2001 U. S. Dist. LEXIS 1211 (N. D. Ill., Feb. 8, 2001).

Broache, Anne. "Renewing the Push to Collect Net Taxes." CNetnews.com (September 9, 2005).

Broache, Anne. "House OKs Revamp of Patent System." C/net News.com (September 7, 2007).

Brown Bag vs. Symantec Corp., 960 F. 2d 1465 (9th Cir. 1992).

Chiappetta, Vincent. "Defining the Proper Scope of Internet Patents: If We Don't Know Where We Want to Go, We're Unlikely to Get There." Michigan Telecommunications Technology Law Review (May 2001).

Diamond v. Chakrabarty, 447 US 303 (1980).

Dueker, Kenneth Sutherlin. "Trademark Law Lost in Cyberspace: Trademark Protection for Internet Addresses." *Harvard Journal of Law and Technology* (Summer 1996).

E. & J. Gallo Winery v. Spider Webs Ltd. 129 F. Supp. 2d 1033 (S.D. Tex., 2001) aff'd 286 F. 3d 270 (5th Cir., 2002).

Elgin, Ben and Bruce Einhorn. "The Great Firewall of China." *BusinessWeek* (January 12, 2006).

eMarketer, Inc. "Some Users Distrust Search Engines." (July 23, 2007a)

eMarketer, Inc. "When Bad Ads Harm Good E-commerce." (July 3, 2007b)

eMarketer, Inc. "Online Buyers Will Pay Extra for Privacy." (June 14, 2007c)

eMarketer, Inc. "Adult Content Revenues in the US, by Segment, 2006 & 2006." (January 4, 2007d).

Federal Trade Commission. "Individual Reference Services: A Report to Congress." (December 1997).

Federal Trade Commission. "Privacy Online: Fair Information Practices in the Electronic Marketplace." (May 2000a).

Federal Trade Commission. "Online Profiling: A Report to Congress." (June 2000b).

Federal Trade Commission. "Privacy Online: A Report to Congress." (June 1998).

Field v. Google, Inc. 412 F.Supp. 2nd 1106 (D. Nev., 2006).

Fisher, William W. III. "The Growth of Intellectual Property: A History of the Ownership of Ideas in the United States." Law.harvard.edu/Academic_Affairs/coursepages/tfisher/iphistory.html (1999).

Ford Motor Co. v. Lapertosa 2001 U. S. Dist. LEXIS 253 (E. D. Mich. Jan. 3, 2001).

Frackman, Andrews; Claudia Ray, and Rebecca C. Martin. Internet and Online Privacy: A Legal and Business Guide ALM Publishing (2002).

Gabber, Eran; Phillip B. Gibbons; David M. Kristol; Yossi Matias; and Alain Mayer. "Consistent, Yet Anonymous, Web Access with LPWA." *Communications of the ACM* (February 1999).

Gentile, Gary. "Companies Set Guidelines on Copyrighted Video." *USA Today* (October 18, 2007).

Goldschlag, David M.; Michael G. Reed; and Paul F. Syverson. "Onion Routing for Anonymous and Private Internet Connections." *Communications of the ACM* (February 1999).

Google, Inc. v. American Blind & Wallpaper Factory, Inc. Case No. 03-5340 JF (RS) (N.D. Cal., April 18, 2007).

Government Employees Insurance Company v. Google, Inc. Civ. Action No. 1:04cv507 (E.D. VA, December 15, 2004).

Greenhouse, Linda. "Justices Back Law to Make Libraries Use Internet Filters." *New York Times* (June 24, 2003).

Gross, Grant. "House Panel Votes to Extend Net Tax Ban." *InfoWorld* (October 11, 2007).

Hafner, Katie and Matt Richtel. "Google Resists U.S. Subpoena of Search Data." *New York Times* (January 20, 2006).

Hansell, Saul. "Experts Contend Travel Sites May Skimp on Hotel Taxes." *New York Times* (December 23, 2002).

Hansell, Saul and Eric Lichtblau. "U.S. Wants Internet Companies to Keep Web-Surfing Records." *New York Times* (June 2006).

Harmon, Amy. "Pondering Value of Copyright vs. Innovation." *New York Times* (March 3, 2003).

Helft, Miguel and Geraldine Fabrikant. "Viacom Sues Google Over Video Clips on Its Sharing Web Site." *New York Times* (March 14, 2007).

Ho, Victoria. "China Accused of Rerouting Search Traffic to Baidu." CNETNews.com (October 22, 2007).

Hoofnagle, Chris Jay. "Privacy Self-Regulation: A Decade of Disappointment." Electronic Privacy Information Center (Epic.org) (March 4, 2005).

Kelly v. ArribaSoft. 336 F3rd 811 (CA 9th, 2003).

Laudon, Kenneth. "Markets and Privacy." *Communications of the ACM* (September 1996).

Liedtke, Michael. "Microsoft, Yahoo Tweak Privacy Policies." *USA Today* (July 23, 2007).

Markoff, John. "Control the Internet? A Futile Pursuit, Some Say." *New York Times* (Nvember 14, 2005)

McBride, Sarah. "For Groskter, It's the Day the Music Died." *Wall Street Journal* (November 8, 2005).

McMillan, Robert. "Porn Typosquatter Fined Again by FTC." *InfoWorld* (October 16, 2007).

Miller, John W. and Christopher Rhoads, "U.S. Fights to Keep Control Of Global Internet Oversight." *Wall Street Journal* (November 16, 2005).

Moore, Matt. "ICANN Rejects Creation of ".XXX" Domain." *USA Today* (March 30, 2007).

Nash, David B. "Orderly Expansion of the International Top-Level Domains: Concurrent Trademark Users Need a Way Out of the Internet Trademark Quagmire." *The John Marshall Journal of Computer and Information Law* Vol. 15, No. 3 (1997).

Nettis Environment Ltd. v. IWI, Inc. 46 F. Supp. 2d 722 (N. D. Ohio 1999).

Network Advertising Initiative. "Participating Networks." (November 2007).

Nissan Motor Co., Ltd. v. Nissan Computer Corp. 289 F. Supp. 2d 1154 (C. D. Cal.), aff'd, 2000 U. S. App. LEXIS 33937 (9th Cir. Dec. 26, 2000).

PaineWebber Inc. v. Fortuny, Civ. A. No. 99-0456-A (E. D. Va. Apr. 9, 1999).

Parry, Wayne. "N.J. Judge Hears Challenge to Online Gambling Restrictions," *Associated Press* (September 26, 2007).

Perfect 10, Inc. v. Amazon.com, Inc. 487 F3rd 701 (CA 9th, 2007).

Pew Internet & American Life Project. "Daily Internet Activities." (June 11, 2007).

Pfanner, Eric. "Online Gambling Shares Plunge on Passage of U.S. Crackdown Law." *New York Times* (October 3, 2006).

Playboy Enterprises, Inc. v. Global Site Designs, Inc. 1999 WL 311707 (S. D. Fla. May 15, 1999).

Playboy Enterprises, Inc. v. Netscape Communications, Inc. 354 F. 3rd 1020 (9th Cir., 2004).

Ponemon Institute. "2007 Most Trusted Companies for Privacy Study." (March 28, 2007).

Privacy and Civil Liberties Oversight Board. "About the Board." Privacyboard.gov (2007).

Rivlin, Garry. "Gambling Dispute with a Tiny Country Puts U.S. in a Bind." *New York Times* (August 23, 2007).

Seidenberg, Steve. "Keyword Protection." *Insidecounsel* (August 2007)

State Street Bank & Trust Co. v. Signature Financial Group, 149 F. 3d 1368 (1998).

Story, Louise. "F.T.C. to Review Online Ads and Privacy." *New York Times* (November 1, 2007a).

Story, Louise. "F.T.C. Member Vows Tighter Controls of Online Ads." *New York Times* (November 2, 2007b).

Swartz, Jon. "YouTube Gets Media Providers' Help Foiling Piracy." *USA Today* (October 15, 2007).

Swisher, Kara. "E-tailers Faced Death; Now Can They Handle Taxes?" *New York Times* (April 9, 2001).

Takenaka, Toshiko. "International and Comparative Law Perspective on Internet Patents." *Michigan Telecommunications Technology Law Review* (May 15, 2001).

Tehrani, Rich. "Behavioral Targeting at Google." VoIP Blog-Tehrani.com (August 1, 2007).

Thurm, Scott. "The Ultimate Weapon: It's the Patent." *Wall Street Journal* (April 17, 2000a).

Ticketmaster v. Tickets.com. 2000 U.S. Dist. Lexis 4553 (C.D. Cal., August 2000).

TRUSTe. "Consumers Have False Sense of Security About Online Privacy - Actions Inconsistent With Attitudes." Truste.org (December 6, 2006).

United States Copyright Office. "Digital Millennium Copyright Act of 1998: U.S. Copyright Office Summary." (December 1998).

United States Department of Health, Education and Welfare (US-DHEW). Records, Computers and Rights of Citizens. Cambridge, MA: MIT Press (1973).

United States Patent and Trademark Office. "Class 705 Application Filing and Patents Issued Data." (November 2007).

Urbina, Ian. "Court Rejects Law Limiting Online Pornography." *New York Times* (March 23, 2007).

Van Kirk, Andrew. "Platform for Privacy Preferences (P3P): Privacy Without Teeth." (March 10, 2005).

Varian, Hal, "Forget Taxing Internet Sales. In Fact, Just Forget Sales Taxes Altogether." *New York Times* (March 8, 2001).

Vaughan, Sandra. "Evolution of Employee Monitoring Stretches Far Beyond Email." Scmagazineus.com (February 21, 2007).

Vijayan, Jaikumar, "Caught in the Middle." *Computerworld* (July 24, 2000).

The Washington Post, et al. v. TotalNews, Inc., et al. S.D.N.Y, Civil Action Number 97-1190. (February 1997).

Winston, Brian. Media Technology and Society: A History From the Telegraph to the Internet. Routledge (1998).

W3C Platform for Privacy Preferences Initiative." P3P 1. 0: A New Standard in Online Privacy." Platform for Privacy Preferences Initiative. (June 16, 2003).

Zeller, Tom, Jr. "Your Life As An Open Book." *New York Times* (August 12, 2006).

The Foundation of Ethical Thought

> "The biggest corporation, like the humblest citizen, must be held to strict compliance with the will of the people."
>
> *Theodore Roosevelt*
>
> "We demand that big business give people a square deal; in return we must insist when anyone engaged in big business honestly endeavors to do right, he shall himself be given a square deal."
>
> *Theodore Roosevelt*

Chapter Outline

- Introduction
- The Foundation of Ethical Theory
- Teleological Frameworks
- Deontological Frameworks
- Mixed Frameworks
- Global Business Standards Codex

UTILITARIAN ETHICS: ONE PLAYGROUND AT A TIME[1]

The challenge to find drinking water in rural villages in the Republic of South Africa has been a long and painful one. An estimated five million people do not have easy access to clean drinking water. In the beginning of the 1800s, European explorers came to South Africa with the idea of being able to reproduce that high level of *vegetation that was found in Western Europe. As a result, when they settled in South Africa, they planted trees and plants from their native countries to try to colonize new growth in the region. The net result was that a number of nonnative species of plants survived, which meant that this foreign vegetation was consuming billions of gallons of water that had been flowing from mountain streams into lower-level rivers and lakes. Enter Trevor Field to the rescue! Field was a wealthy, retired marketing executive who wanted to give back to the community. Field watched as women from the rural villages in the eastern part of South Africa carried water every day from a watering hole back to their villages. The water was contaminated, the buckets capturing the water were leaking, and the buckets could weigh up to forty pounds. Field realized that that was a very inefficient way to get water and the time spent by the women gathering water could focus on other, more relevant activities than walking back and forth from the watering hole. Field's solution was to design a water pump that could be used by children when they play at a playground. At a cost of seven thousand dollars, the pump is designed to pull water from deeper points in the ground where the water would not be contaminated and would also be cooler. The pump would work like a merry-go-round in which the children would spin and ride on the grips at the top of the pump and the movement of the circular cylinder would result in water being pumped to the ground's surface. The water would then move through pipes and be captured in a water tower. The pump takes only a few hours to install and can be placed in any part of the rural countryside. To help generate money to pay for the pumps, Field sells advertising on the water towers to local businesses. In 2006 Field and his organization, PlayPumps International, received a check for $16.4 million from the U.S. government, the Case Foundation, and the MCJ Foundation to help support the expansion of his program. Field wants to raise $45 million by 2010 so he can help ten million African citizens get access to clean drinking water.*

INTRODUCTION

As human beings, we are accountable for our actions. Our day-to-day interactions with every activity we do have an impact on both the human and the nonhuman elements of our world. As a result, as employees of a business organization, we take on the additional burden of also being responsible for the actions of the business organization. An underlying component in guiding our behavior both within and outside a business setting is the role of ethics.

Ethics can be defined as the values an individual uses to interpret whether any particular action or behavior is considered acceptable and appropriate. Some questions that could be asked to help identify the values needed to interpret the particular action or behavior could be the following:

1. Is the behavior or action consistent with the overall basic duties of the individual in question?
2. Does the behavior or action acknowledge and respect the underlying rights of all the individuals who will be impacted by the action?

3. Would the behavior or action be considered the best practice in that specific set of circumstances?

4. Does the behavior or action match the overall entrenched beliefs of the individual?[2]

Business ethics can be defined as the collective values of a business organization that can be used to evaluate whether the behavior of the collective members of the organization are considered acceptable and appropriate.

THE FOUNDATION OF ETHICAL THEORY

Types of Ethical Examinations

The study of ethical behavior can initially be classified based on what perspective is considered by the reader. Ethics can be presented in a descriptive manner. *Descriptive ethics* is defined as the presentation of facts related to the specific ethical actions of an individual or organization. Descriptive ethics is used when an observer wants to understand the course of events that generated the ethical issue. Within the descriptive ethics context, there is no interpretation of the facts or assumptions concerning why that course of action took place.

The second way in which ethics can be examined is through an analytical lens. *Analytical ethics* can be described as understanding the reasons a course of action that may have an ethical impact took place. Analytical ethics, or metaethics, moves from the how and when inquiry, which is the basis of the descriptive ethics viewpoint, to asking why. It is from analytical ethics that hypotheses can be developed to help understand the relationships among different variables impacting ethical behavior. From a legal standpoint, analytical ethics would address the "motive" behind the actions instead of just being satisfied with a description of the actions.

The third approach to view ethics is from a normative perspective. *Normative ethics* can be defined as a prescribed course of action that attempts to ensure that ethical behavior will be followed in the future. Normative ethics moves the evaluation of the ethical behavior from the past to future tense. Normative ethics presents information on what should be done in the future rather than what was done in the past, which are both part of descriptive and analytical ethics. This prescriptive approach allows employees and managers to address potential ethical issues before they occur. As a result, the use of ethical tools such as a code of ethics helps direct the normative ethical behavior by presenting what are acceptable and unacceptable types of behavior tolerated within the firm.[3]

TELEOLOGICAL FRAMEWORKS

Teleological frameworks focus on the results of the conduct of the individual. Derived from the Greek word for fulfillment, *telos*, these frameworks focus on the ramifications, positive and negative, resulting from the actions and conduct of individuals. The three teleological frameworks are ethical egoism, utilitarianism, and Sidgwick's dualism.[4]

Ethical Egoism

Although Thomas Hobbes has been credited with the development of ethical egoism, it can be said that Plato may have actually been the father of the ideas that have evolved into it. Contemporary writers such as Ayn Rand have embraced the concept of focusing on each individual's self-interest. Ethical egoism is based on the belief that every individual should act in a way to promote him- or herself if the net result will generate, on balance, positive rather than negative results. Derived from the Latin word *ego,* which is defined as one's self, ethical egoism allows for self-interests to play a role in the actions of the individual as long as there are also positive benefits for others. Of course, individuals who abide by the philosophy of ethical egoism may have different interpretations of what would be considered on balance an action that is good for others as well as themselves. Some ethical egoists may argue that based on their own perceptions, all of their actions on balance generate more positive than negative benefits. This level of rationalization may evolve into the justification that pursuing a person's self-interest is necessary to generate a positive outcome for others. The supporters of ethical egoism argue that this framework is the only ethical model that captures the essence of motivation within individuals. Without self-interest, ethical egoists would argue, why would someone do any action? As a result, ethical egoists will argue that their philosophy supports a "win-win" proposition. An individual will reward his or her self-interest while also yielding benefits for the rest of society.

Those who argue against ethical egoism state that part of the connection of the actions that motivate an individual also require certain obligations of an individual. Moreover, human motivation is primarily based on purely selfish factors, meaning that there should also be nonselfish factors that motivate individuals and make them unique human beings.[5]

Utilitarianism

The utilitarianism movement started in England in the eighteenth century. Originally developed by Jeremy Bentham in his *Introduction to the Principles of Morals and Legislation* in 1789 and John Stuart Mill's *Utilitarianism* in 1863, utilitarianism holds the belief that any action of an individual will be based on providing the greatest good for the greatest number of people. Derived from the word *utility,* utilitarianism is based on the principle of utility where each person's actions add to the overall utility of the community impacted by those actions. As a result, utilitarians will focus on the net result of their actions instead of the means or motives that generated the reason for their actions. Utilitarianism can be based on single acts of individuals (act utilitarianism) or on guiding behavior indirectly through an evaluation of ethical conduct via rules procedures (rule utilitarianism).[6] Those who support utilitarianism state that this theory is the only one that captures the essence of benevolent behavior. Without utilitarianism as a framework, supporters would argue that people would not do actions that help others if the action doesn't benefit the self-interests of the individuals.

Those who oppose the utilitarian viewpoint state that it would be difficult to ever properly evaluate the effectiveness of utilitarianism because it is practically impossible to determine what would be the greatest good for the greatest number. They also argue that there will be some inherent contradictions with this theory. By stating that the actions support the greatest good for the greatest number, it begs the question whether the minority that does not receive the greatest good would be treated unfairly.[7] For example, the scenario at the beginning of the chapter demonstrates utilitarianism ethics at its best. Trevor Field was committed to helping the community as a whole.

Sidgwick's Dualism

First published in 1874, *The Methods of Ethics* by Henry Sidgwick attempted to bridge the gap between the two competing ethical frameworks of ethical egoism and utilitarianism. Sidgwick argued that a common ground could be found between the two theories. Hence, Sidgwick's dualism was born. At the core of the argument is that both previous theories had elements of using cost-benefit analysis to help analyze the actions of individuals. Sedgwick's dualism attempted to resolve the fundamental difference of whether the actions for one's self-benefit impact just the individual or others. Sidgwick argued that utilitarianism is a foundation component of any ethical framework, which he called *rational benevolence*. However, he also argued that the self-interest of ethical egoism must be included in the ethical framework he called *prudence*. He argued that rational benevolence is necessary in an individual's actions, but he also stated that prudence is necessary because the happiness of the individual is the common goal of the action and it would not be logical for an individual to sacrifice his or her own happiness to help others. Therefore, he argued that a harmony can exist among rational benevolence and prudence viewpoints to have a rational ethical model. He concluded by stating that there had to be some reconciliation between the two theories to explain how individuals act in their own self-interest as well as in those interests of others.[8]

As a result, these frameworks can be used to present different arguments from a business perspective. Those supporters of the ethical egoism theory would argue that businesses should focus solely on their own self-interests and maximize their level of profitability by developing a strong competitive advantage. Those who support the utilitarianism theory would accept government intervention as a way to protect the interests of the majority against the decisions of the minority within any given business. In his book, *An Inquiry into the Nature and Causes of the Wealth of Nations*, Adam Smith presented an argument that could support Sidgwick's dualism. Smith argues that the greatest good for the greatest number is achieved by individuals pursuing their self-interests in the marketplace.[9]

DEONTOLOGICAL FRAMEWORKS

As opposed to teleological frameworks, which focus on whether the results are favorable or not, deontological frameworks focus on the duty or obligation in determining whether the actions are right or wrong. Deontological is derived from the Greek word *deon*, which means *duty*. There are three deontological frameworks: existentialism, contractarianism, and Kant's ethics.[10]

Existentialism

Existentialism is based on the underlying belief that the only person who can determine right and wrong is based on the free will of the person making the decisions. As a result, each individual determines his or her own actions and is ultimately responsible for the consequences of those actions. Philosophers such as Søren Kierkegaard, Friedrich Nietzsche, and Jean-Paul Sartre have all embraced existentialism as the most viable way to connect duty with actions. It is through authenticity of their actions that individuals are able to develop their own sense of personal virtue. As a result, existentialism would not utilize universal principles because each individual determines that acceptance of his or her own actions.[11] As Polonius advises his son, Laertes, in William Shakespeare's *Hamlet* "This above all: to thine own self be true, and it must follow, as the night the day, Thou canst not be false to any man."[12]

Contractarianism

Contractarianism, or social contract theory, is based on the belief that all individuals agree to social contacts to be members within a society. This theory is based on the work of John Locke's 1689 book, *Two Treatises on Government*; Jean-Jacques Rousseau's *The Social Contract, or Principles of Political Right*, published in 1762; and more recently Garrett Hardin's 1968 book, *The Tragedy of the Commons*, and John Rawls's 1971 book, *A Theory of Justice*.

Contractarianism holds the view that membership in society comes with certain duties and responsibilities. As a result, individuals agree to the norms of society by establishing a social contract with the other members of the society. The underlying principle of contractarianism is to have guided principles that are fair to everyone. As a result, if the principles are fair, everyone in the society should agree to abide by the principles. John Rawls proposed that individuals in a society contract freely to have economic and political components help guide our day-to-day living. As a result, Rawls argues that everyone should have equal rights and duties. Furthermore, he stated that if there are social and economic inequalities, it would be acceptable to the society only if these inequalities were able to generate benefits for everyone in society. Therefore, Rawls challenged the utilitarian philosophy by stating that it would not be acceptable to focus on actions for the greater good if the minorities do not also benefit from the decision.[13]

Kant's Ethics

In his book *Foundations of the Metaphysics of Morals* (1785), Immanuel Kant discussed ethical decisions based on the free will of the individual. Kant argued that the free will to make decisions that were considered rational needed to be converted into a universal will. Kant's ethical view is considered a dualism because it attempted to bridge the gap between the existentialist and contractarian points of view. The linkage Kant made was to consider his principle pertaining to free will based on the philosophy that an individual should act in a way in which one would expect everyone to act if it were a universal will and to treat other individuals as the end, not the means to an end. As a result, Kant would reject the view of using heuristics of "gut feelings" as a justification for a decision because these findings are not always predictable nor are they acceptable. In addition, the rationale for not committing an illegal act such as dumping dangerous chemicals into a water source should not be based on the legal requirements or the potential negative image that would be created for the company. Kant would argue that the manager should consider only whether his free will action to dump the toxic waste would be acceptable as a universal will in which any company or individual could dump any chemical they want into any water supply. Kant argued that this should be the only way in which managers should consider their decisions.[14]

MIXED FRAMEWORKS

Intuitionism and Love

In his book *The Right and the Good* (1930), W. D. Ross argued that there are certain principles that individuals should follow that are considered part of the prima facie obligation an individual has to society. Ross identified in his book that there could be a possible conflict between the duties and obligations of a specific circumstance and that the actions may override an individual's actual duty. For example, Ross explained that telling a lie or breaking a promise to an individual may be acceptable in certain circumstances. The circumstances help develop the distinction between a prima facie duty based on that specific situation and an actual or absolute duty.

Ross presented seven basic principles to support his ethical philosophy. It is through these principles that individuals develop a level of intuition that becomes incorporated in their decision-making processes.

The seven guiding principles are as follows:

1. **Fidelity:** an individual needs to keep explicit and implicit promises
2. **Reparation:** an individual must act on repairing the consequences for previous wrongful acts
3. **Gratitude:** an individual must be able to show gratitude for the kindnesses that others have given him or her
4. **Justice:** an individual should try to see that any goods are fairly distributed
5. **Beneficence:** an individual should focus on trying to improve the lives of others
6. **Self-improvement:** an individual should improve oneself by focusing on virtue and intelligence
7. **Noninjury:** an individual should not cause any harm to others

Ross draws on the work from previous theories. Ethical egoism is represented in self-improvement, and utilitarianism is represented in beneficence and noninjury. Furthermore, existentialism is represented in fidelity and self-improvement, and contractarianism is represented in fidelity and justice.[15]

GLOBAL BUSINESS STANDARDS CODEX

In their study to develop a framework to evaluate the conduct of companies around the world, Paine, Deshpande, Margolis, and Bettcher established the Global Business Standards Codex.[16] This codex captures eight major underlying principles in which ethical behavior can be interpreted and evaluated. The eight ethical principles are fiduciary, property, reliability, transparency, dignity, fairness, citizenship, and responsiveness.

Fiduciary Principle

As part of the legal structure of a business organization, each officer and director of a company has a legal fiduciary duty to act in the best interests of the stakeholders and other employees within the firm. Furthermore, there is also an implied fiduciary duty for every employee within the organization to also act in a way that generates positive benefits for the firm. The traditional components of fiduciary duty include ensuring that there are no actual or potential conflicts of interests given the actions of the employee. It also is implied that each employee will not put his or her self-interests above the overall interests of the firm. Additionally, it is assumed that employees will give good-faith efforts for carrying out each of their responsibilities, they are prudent with the company's resources, and they exercise due diligence regarding the quality of their work. Specifically, due diligence would include ensuring that the employee actively promotes the interests of the company in a diligent and professional manner. The employee would also be expected to develop a sense of loyalty to the firm. From a loyalty perspective, the employee is expected to use his or her job title and the company resources available to him or her for company purposes only. A loyal employee is also expected to report any ethical violations and conflicts between the employee's own interests and the company's interests. It is also expected that a loyal employee would refuse any type of gift that could be considered excessive within a business relationship context.[17]

Property Principle

The property principle is based on the belief that every employee should respect property as well as the rights of the owners of the property. Traditional examples of violations of this principle include theft, misappropriation of funds, and wasting resources. This principle has been expanded to intangible property and now also includes the misappropriation of intellectual property or other types of information. It is expected that an employee would protect the tangible and intangible assets of the firm. It is expected that the employee should be a good steward to the resources the employee has access to. As a result, it is the duty of the employee not to damage or steal any assets or allow a third party to take any of the company's tangible or intangible assets or steal the assets of another firm. Therefore, it is the employee's responsibility to prohibit any misappropriation of company funds and to disallow the firm's proprietary information to become available to a competitor nor should the employee obtain access to a competitor's proprietary information.[18]

Reliability Principle

The reliability principle is based on the belief that it is the employee's responsibility to honor the commitments he or she has made to the firm. It is expected that the employees will follow through with the promises and commitments that have been made between the employees and the firm. Traditional violations of the reliability principle would include breaching a promise or contract or not fulfilling a promised action. It is expected that the employee will do his or her best to make a good-faith effort to fulfill all the commitments that the employee has promised. The reliability principle would also include ensuring that suppliers and other business partners are paid in a timely manner.[19]

Transparency Principle

The transparency principle is based on the belief that every employee should conduct business in a truthful and open manner. It is expected that the employees will not make decisions based on a personal agenda. As a result, employees are expected not to act in a deceptive manner and to keep accurate and current records of all the business obligations that are currently the responsibility of the employee. Employees should allow any other interested party to understand how the pattern of behavior was justified based on his or her actions. Traditional violations of this principle include fraudulent and deceptive actions of the employee. Transparency also incorporates how information is dealt with by the employee. Transparent actions would include accurate and up-to-date records of the information related to the actions and the decision-making process. It would also guarantee that the financial information presented to investors is truthful and accurate and that the information is developed within the guidelines of auditing and financial reporting standards. Furthermore, transparency guides the employees in ensuring that the relationships between the company and its suppliers and partners are handled in an honest manner. Transparency would also ensure that the firm's marketing focus would not mislead or misinform its current and potential customers. Transparency ensures that firms would present accurate and truthful customer warnings for any health and safety issues that could impact the customer's use of a product.

Transparency makes it clear to the employees that the acquisition of proprietary information from competitors is not acceptable. The benefits of following the transparency principle include the ability to make better-informed decisions, the ability to ensure that the truth is always presented to others in the organization, and allowance for improved cooperation within the firm through the development of trust among the employees.[20]

Dignity Principle

The dignity principle is based on the belief that each employee needs to respect the dignity of all individuals. Protecting the dignity of people in society includes ensuring the human rights of health, safety, and privacy. Furthermore, the dignity principle

341

encourages the enhancement of human development not only within the company and the marketplace, but also in the society at large. Therefore, any type of humiliation, coercion, or other type of human offenses is in direct violation of the dignity principle. The dignity principle involves making affirmative efforts for those individuals who need help in their personal pursuits, and it also helps protect those individuals who are vulnerable to unethical actions. Those vulnerable could be employees who potentially face harassment or other factors that could make for a hostile work environment. Under the dignity principle, it is the responsibility of the company to also ensure that employees do not face unnecessary physical risks as they perform their work responsibilities. Furthermore, the company is responsible for respecting employees' and customers' privacy and for protecting their confidential information. It is also expected that the company would not accept any labor opportunities in which child labor would be directly or indirectly involved in the manufacturing of the firm's products. The firm would allow the employees to form a union and permit collective bargaining to take place pertaining to labor issues. Moreover, the dignity principle highlights the sensitivity employees should have as they interact with people from other cultures and other countries.[21]

Fairness Principle

The fairness principle is based on the belief that stakeholders who have a vested interest in the firm should be treated fairly. There are four types of fairness: reciprocal fairness, distributive fairness, fair competition, and procedural fairness. Reciprocal fairness addresses the issues of treating another party fairly and having the other party treat the firm fairly. Distributive fairness is based on the assumption that the allocation of finite resources within the firm will be distributed fairly based on maximizing the benefits of those allocations. Fair competition focuses on the fair treatment given by the firm as it interacts with its existing and potential competitors. This would include ensuring that collusion does not occur between the firm and its competitors pertaining to factors such as price, number of products produced in geographical locations, and market share. It also includes ensuring that bribes or any other illegal financial incentives are not given to interested parties in exchange for a favorable relationship with those parties. Procedural fairness deals with ensuring that parties that interact with the firm are treated fairly from a due process perspective. This would also include ensuring that employees would not experience retaliation if they notify government officials of any legal violations.[22]

Citizenship Principle

The citizenship principle is based on the belief that every employee should act as a responsible citizen in the community. It is also expected that employees respect the laws of the community. This includes not only criminal laws, but also competition, environmental, and corporate social responsibility laws. Furthermore, it is expected that employees protect and preserve public goods or commons available to the community. This includes sustainability and other environmental issues, public space issues, and legitimate government. It is also expected that employees should be cooperative with community officials. This includes notifying the proper authorities if there are health and safety issues that relate to the goods and services provided by the firm. Employees should not become involved in unacceptable involvement in political or government issues, including illegal financial involvement or other illegal use of resources to support a political official. The employees contribute to the general well-being of the community by volunteering to help the community through charitable organizations or other community-based programs.[23]

Responsiveness Principle

The responsiveness principle is based on the belief that employees have a responsibility to respond to requests for information about the operations from the various stakeholders. As a result, employees must not only reply to stakeholders' requests for information, but also be responsive to ideas presented by the stakeholders to help improve the operations of the firm. From a customer perspective, a responsive firm would be one in which the goods and services offered would at least meet, if not exceed, the expectations of the customers. A timely response to any complaints from the customers concerning the firm's products should also occur. That level of responsiveness is also expected with the firm's interaction with its employees. A responsive firm is expected to react in a timely manner to resolve any outstanding issues that have been raised by the employees, interest groups, suppliers, the local community, and any other stakeholder that has a vested interest in the company.[24]

Questions for Thought

1. Choose an event in your life where you believe you acted ethically. Discuss the event in terms of the teleological frameworks discussed in the text.

2. Using the same event you chose in question 1 above, discuss the event in terms of the deontological frameworks discussed in the text.

3. Choose any Fortune 500 company. Locate the company's code of ethics published on the company's Web page. Evaluate the code of ethics in terms of the Global Business Standards Codex.

4. Using the principles set forth in the Global Business Standards Codex, find an example of a company that does or did not follow one of the principles. Discuss the implications of the company's actions.

Endnotes

1. www.pbs.org/frontlineworld/rough/2005/10/south_africa_th.html.

2. Lynn Sharp Paine, *Ethics: A Basic Framework* (Boston: Harvard Business School, 2006), 2.

3. Kenneth E. Goodpaster, *Ethical Frameworks for Management* (Boston: Harvard Business School, 1983), 2.

4. Ibid., 5.

5. Ibid.

6. www.britannica.com.

7. Kenneth E. Goodpaster, *Ethical Frameworks for Management* (Boston: Harvard Business School, 1983), 6.

8. Ibid.

9. Ibid., 7.

10. Ibid., 8.

11. Ibid.

12. William Shakespeare, *Hamlet*, Act I Scene iii.

13. Kenneth E. Goodpaster, *Ethical Frameworks for Management* (Boston: Harvard Business School, 1983), 9.

14. Ibid., 9–10.

15. Ibid., 11–12.

16. Lynn Paine, Rohit Deshpande, Joshua D. Margolis, and Kim Eric Bettcher, "Up to Code: Does Your Company's Conduct Meet World-Class Standards?" *Harvard Business Review* 83, no. 12 (2005): 122–33.

17. Ibid.

18. Ibid.

19. Ibid.

20. Ibid.

21. Ibid.

22. Ibid.

23. Ibid.

24. Ibid.

Establishing a Code of Ethics and Ethical Guidelines

"I have found that the greatest help in meeting any problem with decency and self-respect and whatever courage is demanded, is to know where you yourself stand. That is, to have in words what you believe and are acting from."

William Faulkner

Chapter Outline

- Role of a Code of Ethics
- Code of Ethics and Stakeholders
- Benefits of a Code of Ethics
- Content of a Code of Ethics
- The Role of Total Responsibility Management and a Code of Ethics
- Steps for an Effective Code of Ethics
- Value of a Code of Ethics
- How to Make a Code of Ethics More Effective
- Examples of Codes of Ethics
- Role of Government Regulations
- Global Code of Ethics

From Chapter 10 of *Understanding Business Ethics*. Peter A. Stanwick. Sarah D. Stanwick. Copyright © 2008 by Pearson Prentice Hall. All rights reserved.

How We're Fixing Up Tyco[1]

The new senior vice president of corporate governance at Tyco, Eric Pillmore, had a big problem. How was he going to try to repair the tarnished image of the diversified conglomerate Tyco? A major difference between the Tyco scandal and the WorldCom and Enron scandals was that Tyco had strong financial performance from its divisions. While the other scandals falsified financial statements to give the appearance of financial strength, Tyco was still profitable during the scandal.

Realizing that to re-create its image, Tyco needed to start with a clean slate, it changed all the board members who were part of the Kozlowski era to try to separate the company from $6,000 shower curtains. It went through a two-stage process in which the board evaluated all the activities of the former top executives as well as reviewed all the financial statements for each business unit within the company. The board established Pillmore's job of vice president of corporate governance, which reported directly to the board of directors.

Tyco also realized that it would have to start from scratch to develop a new code of ethics. In order to reestablish credibility with its stakeholders, Tyco had to incorporate its new value system in a formal document. Tyco examined the code of ethics and corporate governance practices at General Electric, Johnson & Johnson, and Coca-Cola as a starting point to rewrite its code of ethics. From that foundation, Tyco established the Guide to Ethical Conduct, which was applicable to all employees at Tyco. The guide covered such ethical areas as sexual harassment, potential conflicts of interest, compliance rules, and what is considered to be fraudulent behavior of the employees. As a complement to the guide, Tyco also developed ethical vignette videos to highlight potentially unethical behavior in different situations. In the summer of 2003, the guide and access to the vignettes were given to every employee at Tyco.

ROLE OF A CODE OF ETHICS

A code of ethics can be defined as a written document that explicitly states what acceptable and unacceptable behaviors are for all of the employees in the organization. The code of ethics of a firm represents the identification and interpretation of what the firm considers acceptable behavior. Singh proposes that a number of components impact the development of the ethical standards of the firm.[2] Those factors are social value, institutional factors, personal factors, and organizational factors that result in the establishment of ethical standards. A model presenting the relationships proposed by Singh is shown in Figure 1.

The value of society drives the development of a code of ethics by impacting the relationship among institutional, personal, and organizational factors. Institutional factors would be voluntary industry guidelines and government regulations. Personal factors would be the values and ethical morals of the decision makers creating the code of ethics. Organizational factors would be the development of a code of ethics within the firm. The net result would be the establishment of a strong positive ethical climate within the firm.

FIGURE 1   The Role of a Code of Ethics in the Development of Ethical Standards

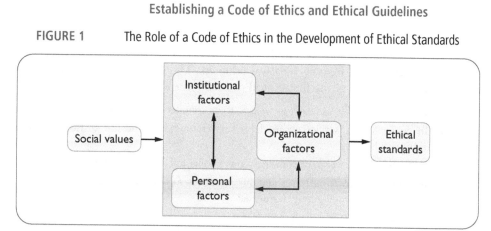

Source: Jang B. Singh, "A Comparison of the Contents of the Code of Ethics of Canada's Largest Corporations in 1992 and 2003," Journal of Business Ethics *64 (2006): 18.*

There are four types of statements that a corporation may adopt to communicate the corporation's view of the subject of ethics:[3]

- Values Statements: a succinct document that is intended to set out the guiding principles of a company
- Corporate Credos: a statement that sets forth the company's beliefs and responsibilities to stakeholders
- Codes of Ethics: a detailed statement of a firm's ethical policies
- Internet Privacy Policies: a statement discussing the company's privacy policy for Internet transactions, usually written in very legal terms

No matter what term is used, they all really represent the same thing—the company's commitment to doing the right thing. They represent a statement of values to give employees and management guidelines about what to do in those gray areas that they may be faced with when working for the company to help guide them away from ethical misconduct. What is covered in each company's code may differ, being tailored to the specific industry or to the specific instances that the employees may face working for a particular company.

CODE OF ETHICS AND STAKEHOLDERS

The code of ethics gives a firm an opportunity to declare to all of its stakeholders its ethical vision. It is from information provided in the code of ethics that firms can address the ethical needs of various stakeholders. Raiborn and Payne suggest that firms consider four ethical values when developing and/or modifying a code of ethics.[4] Those four values are integrity, justice, competence, and utility. Raiborn and Payne define *integrity* as presenting ideals in the code of ethics that highlight the attributes of honesty, sincerity, and transparency. They define *justice* as presenting the firm's commitment to unbiased and good-faith interactions with its stakeholders. *Competence* is identified as the duties and capabilities of the firm to execute its ethical vision. *Utility* is incorporating within the code of ethics values and actions that will do the greatest good to the greatest number.

One of the first corporate codes of ethics was developed by JCPenney, whose stores were originally called the Golden Rule Stores. In 1913, when the JCPenney stores were formed, the Penney Idea was adopted. The company introduced seven ideas, which formed one of the first ethical codes for corporations:

1. To serve the public, as nearly as we can, to its complete satisfaction
2. To expect for the service we render a fair remuneration and not all the profit the traffic will bear
3. To do all in our power to pack the customer's dollar full of value, quality, and satisfaction
4. To continue to train ourselves and our associates so that the service we give will be more and more intelligently performed
5. To improve constantly the human factor in our business
6. To reward men and women in our organization through participation in what the business produces
7. To test our every policy, method, and act in this wise: "Does it square with what is right and just?"[5]

It is important to put a code of ethics into writing regardless of the size of the business because it helps stakeholders know which behaviors are acceptable and which are not. Many codes of ethics leave out sanctions sections. It is important for employees and management to understand the implications if they violate the code. By having a sanctions section, it shows the employees that this is a living document. However, if the sanctions section is overlooked or used on only select employees, then the code of ethics is nothing more than a piece of paper.

The Enron code of ethics began with a letter from the chairman and chief executive officer. Ken Lay stated, "We want to be proud of Enron and to know that it enjoys a reputation for fairness and honesty and that it is respected. Gaining such respect is one aim of our advertising and public relations activities, but no matter how effective they may be, Enron's reputation finally depends on its people, on you and me. Let's keep that reputation high."[6] The sixty-five-page code of ethics at Enron highlighted the conditional value of a code of ethics. A code of ethics is valuable to a firm only if the employees believe in the code and the code has a direct impact on their actions within the firm.

Sometimes companies require their employees to sign a statement that they have read the code of ethics and accept it. This signature may be used as part of the performance evaluation and/or as part of the requirement to advance in the organization.

BENEFITS OF A CODE OF ETHICS

Ethical issues are faced by business professionals on a daily basis. By having a code of ethics in place and enforcing that code, the following happens:

- Employee loyalty increases.
- Questionable behavior decreases.
- Competitive positions improve.
- Managers get more confident.

- Employee relations improve.
- Customer relationships get more solid.[7]

W. Edwards Deming is best known for his fourteen points, which define quality from a business perspective. When examining these points, which deal with employee skill, empowerment, and the absence of fear, approximately half of them can be related to ethical concepts. These include the following:

- Adopt a philosophy that encourages high-quality and effective training and ensures effective supervision.
- Institute training.
- Institute leadership.
- Drive out fear.
- Break down barriers among staff.
- Eliminate quotas.
- Remove barriers to pride of workmanship.[8]

CONTENT OF A CODE OF ETHICS

Stimson believes that these ideas came from a Deming-inspired code of ethics, providing benefits to performers and consumers, which ultimately provide benefits to the marketplace. Beginning with a statement that says that profit is the company's goal and integrity is the means by which they will achieve that goal, these benefits are as follows:

- Meeting customer expectations
- Honesty
- Nondelegable quality
- Traceability, which reduces occasions for waste and fraud
- Respect for privacy and avoidance of conflicts of interest
- Antidiscrimination, which is required by law but inserted to complete the code
- Empowerment through organizational freedom, responsibility, and authority
- True reports
- Integrity (encouragement of whistle-blowing reduces animosity and punitive action)[9]

For example, General Electric published its 2007 Citizenship Report, called "Investing in a Sustainable Future." In this 116-page document, the company sets forth its policy on several different areas and discusses each in detail. Areas include governance, compliance, public policy, environment, health and safety, globalization, community, customers, products and services, suppliers, investors, and employees.[10]

Code of ethics content areas could include the following:

- Fiduciary responsibilities
- Compliance
- Accounting
- Governance

- Member communications and confidentiality
- Commitment to learning and skill enhancement
- Absence of prejudice and harassment
- Conflict of interest
- Human resources
- Cooperation with other credit unions
- Social responsibility

THE ROLE OF TOTAL RESPONSIBILITY MANAGEMENT AND A CODE OF ETHICS

An extension to Deming's Total Quality Management (TQM) approach to firms is Waddock and Bodwell's Total Responsibility Management (TRM).[11] TRM starts with the premise that the vision of the firm drives the development of the code of ethics. It is argued that the vision of the creators of the code of ethics must include the responsibilities that the firm has to its stakeholders and to the natural environment. It is from the identification of the firm's responsibilities to its stakeholders that the firm can explicitly state what it considers acceptable conduct to support the needs and demands of the stakeholders. The firm's vision also establishes the benchmark goals in which the firm is now accountable to its stakeholders. It is the firm's ethical vision that was highlighted in the Tyco example at the beginning of the chapter. As Tyco tried to start its ethical commitment from scratch, it needed to start its ethical vision from scratch as well. Therefore, Tyco used a method very similar to TRM to reestablish the ethical commitment to its stakeholders. The three major stages of the TRM system are inspiration process, integration process, and innovation and improvement process.

Inspiration Process

Vision Setting and Leadership Commitment It is during the inspiration process that the firm identifies the establishment of its ethical leadership commitment as well as establishes the vision-setting process. Vision setting is based on the identification of the unique relationship each firm has with its competitive advantage, its stakeholders, and its historical development. Each of these three factors impacts what will be appropriate for the firm's overall vision as it relates to its responsibilities to its stakeholders.

Responsibility Vision and Leadership Commitments It is during this stage that the formalization of the responsibilities and commitments to the ethical vision take place. The responsibility vision and leadership commitments are needed to be consistent and repeated often over time to all stakeholders. The two questions that need to be addressed during this step are "What business are we in?" and "What do we stand for?" It is the second question that is critical in the development of a strong ethical vision because the answer to the question identifies the core ethical values of the firm.

Stakeholder Engagement Processes Furthermore, the inspiration stage also incorporates the process to engage with the firm's stakeholders. It is during the engagement step of the process that the firm interacts with the stakeholders to ensure that the ethical vision that the firm is developing coincides with the needs and expectations of all the stakeholders.

Foundation Values   It is during the inspiration stage that a firm identifies its foundation values along with the international standards that are applicable to its operations. The foundation values are the minimally acceptable standards to do any transactions with any stakeholder. Because it is the minimally acceptable standards, firms are expected to move well beyond the minimal standards when they are developing their ethical visions to drive the TRM system.

Integration: Changes in Strategies and Management Practices

The integration process involves top management integrating the ethical vision, value, and leadership into the strategic decision-making process. The integration process involves integration into the corporate- and business-level strategies of the firm as well as identifying strategic implementation responsibilities, which include human resource and management systems issues.

Strategy   From a total responsibility management perspective, the ethical vision developed in the inspiration is incorporated in all aspects of the firm's corporate- and business-level strategies. This integration process allows the firm to be proactive if a crisis that must be dealt with arises. Furthermore, integration of the ethical vision in the strategic formulation stage of the decision-making process can eliminate the potential conditions for a crisis before they can be formulated. The question to ask from a strategic integration perspective is "How do we do business here?"

Building Human Resource Capacity   The integration of the ethical vision requires that human resource issues be identified for the effective execution of the ethical vision. The ethical vision will incorporate the beliefs on the most effective ways to treat employees and the most effective ways to develop the employees' skills. Furthermore, because the employees are the individuals responsible for the execution of the ethical vision, the employees must be trained on and informed of their specific role in the execution of the ethical vision. It is also during this stage that decisions are made and implemented pertaining on the allocation of resources to execute the ethical vision. Firms are able to set the tone for their visions and acceptable codes of conduct by establishing training and rewards programs that are linked to ethical behavior. As a result, the human resource element is usually a key and comprehensive component of any firm's code of ethics. It is through the explicit explanation of what responsibilities the employees have within the firm and the expectations of how they will be treated by the firm that become the cornerstone of the tone set in the code of ethics.

Integration into Management Systems   Another component of the integration process is to establish the link between the responsibilities of executing the ethical vision and the management systems within the firm. The integration impacts the direct relationship the firm has with its external stakeholders. An example of the integration into the management systems would be for the firm to coordinate its ethical practices with its suppliers. In fact, firms can and will demand complete compliance with their ethical visions from suppliers, or they will shift to another supplier who will agree to their ethical commitments. As a result, the code of ethics will highlight the relationship that management systems play in the overall integration of the ethical vision of the firm.

Innovation: Focusing on Assessment, Improvement, and Learning Systems

Through use of the Total Responsibility Management system, firms are not only able to present their ethical vision to their stakeholders via their codes of ethics, but they also will be able to generate new ideas on how to improve their TRM systems.

The Responsibility Measurement System   Firms that use a TRM system have the ability to measure goals not only related to operating practices, but also relating to their stakeholder relationships. Therefore, by focusing on multiple stakeholders, TRM allows for the measurement of multiple bottom lines. Each stakeholder's interests can be evaluated based on how well the firm is able to execute its strategic ethical vision.

Transparency and Accountability   Firms that implement a TRM system are able to generate relevant information of interest for both internal and external stakeholders. As a result, an effective ethical vision would not only allow, but encourage the release of all relevant information that could impact the stakeholders. Therefore, firms that use TRM are transparent in their information and are accountable. The firms have nothing to hide from their stakeholders.

Innovation, Improvement, and Learning Systems   Firms that adopt a TRM system are able to learn from the implementation of the system. Similar to its cousin TQM, TRM is a continuous cycle in which the feedback from one year's execution becomes part of the input for the next year's cycle. From a code of ethics perspective, the innovative aspect of TRM allows the code of ethics to be a living document. By constantly measuring and reevaluating the ethical vision of the firm, the firm can make adjustments on how the ethical vision is presented in the code of ethics.

STEPS FOR AN EFFECTIVE CODE OF ETHICS

Many companies begin their codes of ethics with mission statements. This statement sets forth a brief explanation about what the company stands for and why it exists. The mission statement also identifies many of the stakeholders of the company and explains the interactions within the company. The code should not be written by one person or one group. A task force should be developed with representatives from every level of employees. Companies attempt to establish effective ethics programs, which include both the code of ethics and the implementation of the code, to allow their employees to actively think about ethics programs and to provide them with a way to address ethical issues on the job. By having an ethics program, employee concerns about ethical issues are validated, and they should no longer be wary of identifying and bringing these issues to light. These programs should provide a means for employees to evaluate ethical issues. Many use training programs to discuss the draft of the code. This would give employees a chance to participate in the actual writing of the code. The employees may feel empowered to see the code change based on their input.

When developing a code of ethics, there are several standard recommendations of what to include in the code. Deloitte recommends the following:

- An introductory letter from the senior leadership team or CEO that sets the tone at the top and defines the importance of ethics and compliance to each employee and the company

- The company's mission statement, vision, values, and guiding principles that reflect the company's commitment to ethics, integrity, and quality

- An ethical decision framework to assist employees in making choices. For example, a code might ask employees to answer some questions to guide them in making an ethical decision about a possible course of action. The goal is for employees to think before acting and to seek guidance when unsure. They should be encouraged to think about this type of question in the context of an ethical dilemma: "Would you be unwilling or embarrassed to tell your family, friends, or coworkers?"

- A listing of available resources for obtaining guidance and for good-faith reporting of suspected misconduct; for example, consider the following:
  - A means to report issues anonymously, such as a helpline or postal address
  - How to contact the ethics and compliance officer or office
  - A definition of the reporting chain of command (e.g., supervisor, department head, etc.)
  - A listing of any internal ethics and compliance Web sites

- A listing of any additional ethics and compliance resources and the identification of supplementary policies and procedures and their location

- Enforcement and implementation mechanisms that address the notion of accountability and discipline for unethical behavior; for example, unethical behavior will be subject to disciplinary action up to and including termination

- Generic examples of what constitutes acceptable and unacceptable behavior could be included to further explain risk areas; examples could be based on relevant company or industry experiences[12]

Some trade organizations and governmental departments are encouraging companies to develop codes of ethics by publishing guidelines for codes of ethics. For example, the Federal Deposit Insurance Corporation has developed a short guide for financial institutions, "Guidance on Implementing an Effective Ethics Program." This document encourages management of financial institutions, including the board of directors, to convey the message of integrity and ethical values to all those involved with the organization. They suggest policies be developed that discuss the following:

- Safeguarding confidential information
- Ensuring integrity of records
- Providing strong internal controls over assets
- Providing candor in dealing with auditors, examiners, and legal counsel
- Avoiding self-dealings and acceptance of gifts or favors
- Observing applicable laws
- Implementing appropriate background checks

- Involving internal auditors in monitoring the corporate code of conduct or ethics policy
- Providing a mechanism to report questionable activity
- Outlining penalties for a breach of the corporate code of conduct or ethics policy
- Providing periodic training and acknowledgment of policy
- Periodically updating policies to reflect new business activities[13]

The importance of establishing the code of ethics means that companies need to cover everyone in the organization while encouraging each employee to follow the code and question and report any ethical issues or ethical violations. All codes of ethics will be different. Murphy and Swenson suggest twenty questions companies ask when developing a code of ethics:

1. Should there be one code, two, or even more?
2. Does the code cover newly developing risks?
3. For what you already cover, have you kept up with developments in the law?
4. What do you tell employees about raising questions?
5. Do employees certify the code?
6. Does the code include examples?
7. Is the format inviting and effective?
8. What does the code say about values?
9. Is the code's organization useful?
10. Are there "finding" aids in the code?
11. Does the code lead to other information sources?
12. Did the code get the benefit of input from key constituencies?
13. Is there a communications plan for use after the code is issued?
14. Has the code entered the electronic age?
15. Does the code's message reach third parties?
16. Is the code global?
17. Is the code translated?
18. Does the code include things that no longer make sense?
19. Does the code cover all employees?
20. Is the code ethical and legal?[14]

A good ethics program can be a value-added service to a company if it consists of the right elements.[15] These elements should include the following:

- A well-designed code of ethics
- The assignment of functional responsibility
- The proper employee training
- An ethics hotline

Rather than feeling the code is something that is imposed on them, employees should feel included in the process if they are involved in the writing of the code. The code of ethics should be seen as a document that can help strengthen the ethical working environment as well as protect the company legally. Management needs to view the code as being a work in progress. It is important to stress that ownership of the code of ethics is important. The code is never actually finished. The company's code should be made public and should be readily available for public scrutiny to help increase transparency. Corporations need to be more sensitive about the public's expectations of their behaviors. Is it necessary to have the firm's legal team look over or even write the code of ethics? It is probably necessary for the legal team to look over the document to make sure that what the firm has expressed in the code is legal. However, it is probably unnecessary for management to have the firm's legal team write the code for the company. The code should realistically be written by those who use it.

VALUE OF A CODE OF ETHICS

In all cases actions will speak louder than words. Having good statements, or any statements at all, will never ensure that employees will comply with the code. If no one follows the code, the ethical code is a useless piece of information in the company. Consider, for example, Enron. Enron had a code of ethics in place at the time of its collapse, as mentioned at the beginning of this chapter. However, few actually believe that given the collapse of this organization that they ever enforced this code of ethics. In fact, when the code of ethics was distributed to Enron employees on July 1, 2000, Ken Lay stated in his letter to employees, "The Code of Ethics contains common-sense rules of conduct with which the great majority of Enron employees routinely conform. However, I ask that you read them carefully and completely and that, as you do, you reflect on your past actions to make certain that you have complied with the policies. It is absolutely essential that you fully comply with these policies in the future. If you have any questions, talk them over with your supervisor, manager, or Enron legal counsel (Interoffice Memorandum, Enron, July 1, 2000)."[16] In fact, the board of directors suspended Enron's code of ethics twice to approve the off–balance sheet transactions that were later shown to be illegal.

Bondy, Matten, and Moon offer several reasons codes of ethics might be adopted:[17]

- Part of an internal control system
- Product differentiation in the marketplace
- Signal to stakeholders about a firm's quality and when these stakeholders may subsequently reward firms for participation
- Reduced insurance premiums (due to potential for risk) and to provide evidence of due diligence
- Peer pressure within the same industry
- Government failure
- Applicability of codes of conduct across boundaries and borders beyond the borders of one nation-state
- Improvement of customer relationships
- Maintenance of standards along the supply chain

TABLE 1   Directives for Making Codes of Conduct More Effective

Good Practice	Poor Practice
Integrate the code in core ethical values	Post the code to the notice board without any action
Distribute to everyone in the company	Do not get the commitment of the board of directors
Allow a hotline or other method to report ethical breaches	Assign one unit within the company to be responsible for the effectiveness of the firm's ethical commitment
Include ethical training programs	Do not ask for employee feedback pertaining to their ethical concerns
Set up an ethics committee within the board of directors	Do not feature the code of ethics in training and management development
Include a report on the code's use in the annual report	Do not review the code of ethics for revisions
Make ethical commitment part of a contract for employment	Make exceptions to the code's application in certain circumstances
Make the code available in all the languages in which the firm does business	Fail to follow up when there is a breach of the code's standards
Distribute the code to business partners, including suppliers	Failure by top managers to set a good ethical example
Review and make adjustments to the code when necessary	View the code as a confidential and/or internal document
Make sure senior staff set the correct example by "walking the talk"	Make it difficult for staff to have continuous access to the code

Source: Adapted from www.ibe.org.uk/effective.html.

HOW TO MAKE A CODE OF ETHICS MORE EFFECTIVE

The Institute of Business Ethics offers guidance to companies desiring to develop a code of ethics. One area that they focus on is making codes of ethics effective. Table 1 presents their comparison of good and poor practices in making codes of ethics effective.

EXAMPLES OF CODES OF ETHICS

MetLife has a comprehensive Employee Code of Business Conduct and Ethics.[18] All employees are responsible for "reading, understanding, and adhering" to the code. The code covers many different areas, including these:

1. In the workplace
   a. Respect
   b. Equal employment opportunity
   c. Sexual harassment and other discriminatory harassment
2. Business conduct certification program

3. Conflicts of interest
   a. Corporate opportunities
   b. Outside opportunities
      i. Office or director of another business
      ii. Second job
   c. Vendors, suppliers, and consultants
   d. Gifts and entertainment
   e. Communication of conflicts
4. Compliance with laws, rules, and regulations
   a. Insider trading
   b. Antitrust
   c. Money laundering
   d. Foreign Corrupt Practices Act
   e. Boycotts
5. Financial management and disclosure
   a. Accounting standards
   b. Audits and outside examinations
6. Protection and proper use of company assets
   a. Confidentiality
   b. Technology
7. Administration
   a. Reporting of any illegal or unethical behavior; points of contact
   b. Responding to improper conduct

Some believe that a code of ethics should begin with a statement of the company's value statements. Two codes that do just that are the codes of ethics for two accounting firms, Ernst & Young and KPMG. While very different in their approach, each states the firm's values in a very succinct manner. Table 2 provides a comparison of the value statements of these two firms. Notice that each of these values statements reinforces the concept of integrity as being one of the core values of the firm's operations.

Enron represents a company that stated its corporate values but didn't practice them at the senior management level.[19] Consider the values stated in the Enron code of ethics:

- Respect: We treat others as we would like to be treated ourselves. We do not tolerate abusive or disrespectful treatment. Ruthlessness, callousness, and arrogance don't belong here.

- Integrity: We work with customers and prospects openly, honestly, and sincerely. When we say we will do something, we will do it; when we say we cannot or will not do something, then we won't do it.

- Communication: We have an obligation to communicate. Here, we take the time to talk with one another . . . and to listen. We believe that information is meant to move and that information moves people.

TABLE 2   Comparison of Value Statements

Ernst & Young: Our Values Statement—Who We Are and What Our Employees Stand For	KPMG—Our Core Values
■ Employees who value integrity, respect, and teamwork	■ Our employees lead by our actions.
■ Employees with energy, enthusiasm, and the drive to lead others	■ Our employees work together to achieve common goals.
■ Employees who establish relationships with others based on the belief that they should always do the right thing	■ Our employees respect the rights of others.
	■ Our employees gather information and make insightful decisions.
	■ Our employees foster an honest, two-way communication process
	■ Our employees are committed to the communities in which they live.
	■ Our employees act with integrity.

Source: Adapted from www.ey.com and www.kpmg.com.

■ Excellence: We are satisfied with nothing less than the very best in everything we do. We will continue to raise the bar for everyone. The great fun here will be for all of us to discover just how good we can really be.

ROLE OF GOVERNMENT REGULATIONS

In an effort to educate financial institutions about establishing an appropriate code of ethics, the Federal Deposit Insurance Corporation issued guidance in 2005. The publication, "Corporate Codes of Conduct: Guidance on Implementing an Effective Ethics Program," provides suggestions for the components of a code of conduct for financial institutions. These areas include (1) safeguarding confidential information; (2) ensuring the integrity of records; (3) providing strong internal controls over assets; (4) providing candor in dealing with auditors, examiners, and legal counsel; (5) avoiding self-dealings and acceptance of gifts or favors; (6) observing applicable laws; (7) implementing appropriate background checks; (8) involving internal auditors in monitoring corporate codes of conduct or ethics policies; (9) providing a mechanism to report questionable activity; (10) outlining penalties for a breach of the corporate code of conduct or ethics policy; (11) providing periodic training and acknowledgment of the policy; and (12) periodically updating policies to reflect new business activities.[20] As in practically all corporate codes of ethics, the FDIC recommends that financial institutions include specific information of applicable laws and regulations. They specifically suggest that certain regulations be addressed, when applicable. Table 3 lists these regulations.

Section 406 of the Sarbanes-Oxley Act of 2002 requires that companies that are publicly traded disclose whether or not they have a code of ethics. If they do not have a code of ethics, they must explain why. In addition, firms must report any amendments or any waivers from the code of ethics. However, based on the SOX requirement, only top-level managers are required to be held accountable to the firm's code

TABLE 3 Applicable Laws and Regulations for Financial Institutions

Regulation	Description
Section 18(k) of the Federal Deposit Insurance Act (FDI Act)	The government has the authority to regulate or ban a select number of benefits to institution-affiliated parties
Part 359 of the FDI Act	This section of the act addresses regulations pertaining to management's golden parachutes and indemnification payments
Section 39(c) of the FDI Act	This section of the act addresses regulations pertaining to company compensation standards
Section 32 of the FDI Act	This section of the act addresses regulations pertaining to agency disapproval of directors and senior executive officers of insured depository institutions or depository institution holding companies
Section 19 of the FDI Act	This section of the act addresses regulations pertaining to penalties for unauthorized participation by convicted individuals
Part 349 of the FDIC Rules and Regulations	This section of the act addresses regulations pertaining to reports and public disclosure of indebtedness of executive officers and principal shareholders to other banks
Sections 22(g) and 22(h) of the Federal Reserve Act	This section of the act addresses regulations pertaining to loans to executive officers of banks and extensions of credit to executive officers, directors, and principal shareholders of member banks
The Federal Reserve Board's Regulation O	This section of the act addresses regulations pertaining to loans to executive officers, directors, and principal shareholders of member banks
Section 337.3 of the FDIC Rules and Regulations	This section of the act pertains to regulations pertaining to limits on extensions of credit to executive officers and directors and principal shareholders of insured nonmember banks
Part 348 of the FDIC Rules and Regulations	This section of the act pertains to regulations pertaining to management official interlocks with other firms
Section 737 of the Gramm-Leach-Bliley Act	This section of the act pertains to regulations pertaining to bank officers and directors as officers and directors of public utilities
Section 8(e) of the FDI Act	This section of the act pertains to regulations pertaining to removal and prohibition authority given to the FDIC
Section 8(g) of the FDI Act	This section of the act pertains to regulations pertaining to felony charges involving dishonesty or breach of trust as cause for suspension, removal, or prohibition by the individual

Source: Adapted from www.fdic.org.

of ethics. In a survey done in August and September of 2002, which was shortly after the passage of the Sarbanes-Oxley Act, 44 percent of the 291 executive respondents stated that their companies did not have a formal code of ethics.[21] Therefore, to be in compliance with the act, a company's code of ethics must be composed of standards that are "reasonably necessary to promote

- honest and ethical conduct, including the ethical handling of actual or apparent conflicts of interest between personal and professional relationships.
- full, fair, accurate, timely, and understandable disclosure in the periodic reports required to be filed by the issuer.
- compliance with applicable governmental rules and regulations."[22]

The U.S. Sentencing Guidelines were revised in 2004.[23] These new guidelines strengthened the need for companies to have an ethics program and an associated compliance program related to ethics. By implementing an ethics program and compliance program, a company may be able to reduce the sentence if a company is convicted of a federal crime.

GLOBAL CODE OF ETHICS

A number of organizations have shown the foresight to develop a global code of ethics that both for-profit and nonprofit organizations can use as a starting point to develop and/or revise their codes of the ethics. Three of the major global codes of ethics are the Caux Round Table principles, the Organization of Economic Co-operation and Development guidelines for multinational enterprises, and the United Nations Global Compact.

Caux Round Table Principles[24]

The Caux Round Table (CRT) is an international network of business leaders who are committed to promoting the concept of moral capitalism. It is through the CRT principles that businesses will be able to be socially responsible and promote sustainability of these ideals. The principles are based on the ethical ideals of kyosei and human dignity. *Kyosei* is defined as the ability to live and work together for the common good that allows for mutual prosperity through cooperation. CRT defines *human dignity* as the sacred value of each human life, which should not be used solely for the betterment of others.

Organization of Economic Co-operation and Development Guidelines for Multinational Enterprises[25]

OECD guidelines are recommendations made by governments for multinational enterprises to adopt into their own codes of ethics. The guidelines are voluntary principles and standards that support responsible and accountable business conduct. The goal of the guidelines is to encourage multinational enterprises to make a positive contribution to the economic, environmental, and social progress of countries around the world.

United Nations Global Impact[26]

Established in January 1999, the UN Global Impact was based on a challenge by former Secretary-General of the United Nations Kofi Annan for businesses to adopt universal environmental and social principles. The principles are categorized into four major areas: human rights, labor, the natural environment, and anticorruption.

A comparison of the principles presented by these three organizations is shown in Table 4. Table 5 presents some advice for companies that want to develop and/or revise their codes of ethics to ensure that they have captured all the global issues that directly or indirectly impact the firm.

TABLE 4   A Comparison of Global Ethical Principles

CRT Principles

Principle 1: The responsibilities of business are beyond shareholders and are to all stakeholders.

Principle 2: The economic and social impact of business should be toward innovation, justice, and world community.

Principle 3: Business behavior should be beyond the letter of the law toward a spirit of trust.

Principle 4: Businesses need to respect the global rules.

Principle 5: Businesses need to support multilateral trade.

Principle 6: Businesses must respect the environment.

Principle 7: Businesses must avoid illicit operations.

Stakeholder Principles: Businesses must treat all stakeholders with respect and dignity including customers, employees, owners/investors, suppliers, competitors, and communities.

Source: www.cauxroundtable.org/documents/Principles%20for%20Business.PDF.

OECD Guidelines for Multinational Enterprises

Principle 1: Organizations must focus on sustainable development when contributing to economic, social, and environmental progress.

Principle 2: Organizations must respect human rights of all those individuals impacted by the organization.

Principle 3: Organizations must encourage local economic development through cooperation with the local community.

Principle 4: Organizations must encourage employment opportunities and employee training opportunities.

Principle 5: Organizations must not ask local or regional government for legal exemptions from legal requirements based on environmental, health/safety, labor, taxation, financial incentives, or any other legal issue.

Principle 6: Organizations must support and uphold good corporate governance principles and apply good corporate governance practices.

Principle 7: Organizations must develop and apply effective self-regulatory practices and management systems.

Principle 8: Organizations must make all of their employees aware of all compliance and company policies that impact the behavior of the employees.

Principle 9: Organizations must not be involved in any discriminatory behavior toward employees nor should they be unjust in the treatment of their employees.

Principle 10: Organizations must whenever possible do business with partners and suppliers who also agree to the OECD principles.

Principle 11: Organizations must avoid any improper conduct involving local political activities.

Source: www.oecd.org/daf/investment/guidelines.

United Nations Global Impact Principles

Human Rights

Principle 1: Businesses should support and respect global human rights.

Principle 2: Businesses should make sure they are not associated with any human rights abuses.

Labor Standards

Principle 3: Businesses should allow the freedom of association and recognize collective bargaining of their employees.

Principle 4: Businesses should eliminate all forms of forced and/or compulsory labor.

Principle 5: Businesses should abolish all child labor.

Principle 6: Businesses should eliminate all forms of discrimination in the workplace.

Environment

Principle 7: Businesses should support a precautionary approach to global environmental challenges.

Principle 8: Businesses should undertake all initiatives that promote a higher level of environmental responsibility.

Principle 9: Businesses should encourage the development and dissemination of environmentally-friendly technologies.

Anticorruption

Principle 10: Businesses should stop all forms of corruption including extortion and bribery.

Source: www.unglobalcompact.org/AboutTheGC/TheTenPrinciples/index.html.

TABLE 5 Common Mistakes that Companies Make when Developing Global Ethics Programs

Not having consensus on objectives for globalization of ethics commitment

Not incorporating international-based employees in the development of the company's ethics policies

Not focusing on the potential competitive advantages of having a strong positive ethical program

Making the ethical policy in other countries match the country's legal requirements

Not committing resources and/or employees who focus on ethics issues in other countries

Selecting only home country employees to fill any ethics-based positions

Not offering ethics training in languages other than English

Not making sure that all countries interpret the meaning of the ethics policy consistently

Failing to acknowledge the many cultural differences related to business ethics

Source: Adapted from International Business Ethics Institute.

Questions for Thought

1. Do you think codes of ethics really make a difference in an organization? Explain.

2. Comment on the topics addressed in JCPenney Code of Ethics. Do you feel the code adequately achieves its purpose? Is the Code as valid today as it was in 1913?

3. Many companies ignore or overlook differences in translating codes of ethics into other languages. Why is it important to have codes of ethics translated into the native languages of the countries in which the company may operate?

Endnotes

1. Eric Pillmore, "How We're Fixing Up Tyco," *Harvard Business Review* December (2003).

2. Jang Singh, "A Comparison of the Contents of the Code of Ethics of Canada's Largest Corporations in 1992 and 2003," *Journal of Business Ethics* 64 (2006).

3. Patrick E. Murphy, "Developing, Communicating, and Promoting Corporate Ethics Statements: A Longitudinal Analysis," *Journal of Business Ethics* 62 (2005): 183–89.

4. C. Raiborn and D. Payne, "Corporate Codes of Conduct: A Collective Conscience and Continuum," *Journal of Business Ethics* 9, no. 11 (1990): 879–89.

5. www.jcpenney.net/company/history/history/idea.htm.

6. Enron's Code of Ethics, www.thesmokinggun.com.

7. Jeff Turner, "Business Ethics: What Would You Do?" www.refresher.com/archives44.html.

8. William A. Stimson, "A Deming-Inspired Management Code of Ethics," *Quality Progress* 38 (2005): 67–75.

9. Ibid.

10. www.ge.com/company/citizenship/downloads/pdf/GE_2007_citiizen_07rep.pdf.

11. Sandra Waddock and Charles Bodwell, "From TQM to TRM: Total Responsibility Management Approaches," *Journal of Corporate Citizenship* Autumn (2002): 113–26.

12. www.deloitte.com/us/corpgov.

13. www.fdic.gov/news/news/financial/2005/fil10505a.html.

14. www.ethikosjournal.com/html/20questions.html.

15. C. Calhoun and P. Wolitzer, "Ethics as a Value-Added Service," *The CPA Journal* 71 (2001).

16. www.smokingun.com.

17. K. Bondy, D. Matten, and J. Moon, "The Adoption of Voluntary Codes of Conduct in MNCs: A Three-Country Comparative Study," *Business and Society Review* 109, no. 4 (2004): 449–77.

18. www.metlife.com.

19. www.smokingun.com.

20. www.fdic.gov.

21. Randy Myers, "Ensuring Ethical Effectiveness," *Journal of Accountancy* February (2003): 28–29.

22. Sarbanes-Oxley Act of 2002, Section 406.

23. www.ussc.gov/2004guid/862_1.htm.

24. www.cauxroundtable.org.

25. www.oecd.org/daf/investment/guidelines.

26. www.unglobalcompact.org/AboutTheGC/index.html.

Index

A

Abu Ghraib prison, 121
Acacia Technologies, 302–303
Accountability, 165, 269
Act utilitarianism, 179–180
Activist (or dark green) approach, to going green, 211–212
Act–of–state doctrine, 97
Acxiom, 278, 292
Adversarial system, 56–57
Advertising, 135, 150
   ethics, 167
Affirm, use of term, 69
Akamai Technologies, 303
Alexander, Jason, 239
A&M Records, Inc. v. Napster, Inc., 36
Amazon
   copyright issues and, 296, 323
   Internet sales tax and, 315
   One–click purchasing patent, 300, 303
Ambiguity, 15
Ambiguous word, 8
Ambrosia Coal & Construction Company v. Hector Carlos Morales, et al., 45–47
American Bar Association, 54
American Institute of Certified Public Accountants (AICPA), 187
American realist school of jurisprudence, 25
American Society of Chartered Life Underwriters (ASCLU), code of ethics, 188
Analogies, 14–15
Analytical ethics, 335
Andean Common Market (ANCOM), 103
Anderson, Warren, 177
Anheuser–Busch, 165
Annan, Kofi, 360
Anonymous information, 273
Anonymous profiles, 274
Anonymous remailers, 287
Anonymous surfing, 287
Anti–Bribery Convention, 217
Anticybersquatting Consumer Protection Act (ACPA), 304–305
AOL
   Chief Privacy Officer (CPOs) and, 288

Department of Justice subpoena and, 317
Do Not Track Service, 293
Utah Trademark Protection Act and, 308
Appellate court procedure, 69–71
Appellate judges, 54
Appellate jurisdiction, 39–40
Apple
   Apple v. Microsoft, 296
   iPod, 263
Apple Computer, 163–164
Aquinas, Thomas, 142
Aristotle, 121, 140–142, 144
Arnold Schwarzenegger v. Fred Martin Motors, 76
Arthur Andersen, 117, 146, 164, 168
Ashcroft v. Free Speech Coalition, 316
Asian–Pacific Economic Cooperation (APEC), 20, 103
Ask.com, 279
Assisi, St. Francis, 117
Association of Government Accountants, 187
Association of Southeast Asian Nations (ASEAN), 103
Attorney–client privilege, 53
Attorneys, 52–54
Audi AG and Volkswagen of America Inc. v. Bob D'Amato, 306
Avatar, 263–264

B

Bates v. State Bar of Arizona, 188–190
Batson v. Kentucky, 64, 66
Baumhart, Raymond C., 120
Bausch and Lomb, 134, 144
BBBonline, 285
Bear Stearns, 141, 146
Beattie v. Beattie, 36
Behavioral targeting, 273–279
Beneficence, 339
Bentham, Jeremy, 122, 336
Bernina of America, Inc. v. Fashion Fabrics International, 307
Better Business Bureau (BBB), 285
BetterWeb, 285
Bhopal, India, gas leak accident, 175–178, 194
Big Brother, 276

Bilateral investment treaties (BITs), 95
Black & White Taxicab & Transfer Co. v. Brown & Yellow Taxicab & Transfer Co., 46
Blogs, 272, 275
   Chinese government and, 312
Board of directors, 142
Bochan v. LaFontaine, 76–77
Boeing, 149, 163
Bourne v. Walt Disney Co., 35
BP, 160
Bradley v. McDonald's, 199
Bramble Bush, The (Llewellyn), 25
Brazil, 161
Brennan, B., 181
Bribery, 150, 161
Brierly, J., 87
British Airways, 167
Brown Bag Software v. Symantec Corp., 296
Brown v. Thaler, 76
Buffet, Warren, 117, 139
Burke, James, 141–142
Business ethics, 149, 160, 335
   company practices and, 163
Business ethics, theories of, 240–248
Business managers, 3
Business methods patents, 301–302

C

Cable Communications Policy Act, 280
Calvin Klein, 167
Capital, 126
Carbon dioxide emissions, 165
Carbon offsets, 166
Carefirst of Maryland, Inc. v. Carefirst Pregnancy Centers, Inc., 48
Caring, 124, 129–130, 134, 136, 140, 162
Case Foundation, 334
Case law, 31
Categorical imperative, 243
Caux Round Table Principles, 360
Center for Democracy and Technology (CDT), 287
Certified mail, 40
Certo, S., 73, 90, 180
Character, 118, 138–150
Character development, 139, 146, 149

Character education, 146

Character Education
     Partnership, 146

Chatov, K., 184

Cheating, 133

Chief executive officer(CEO), 117,
     134, 139, 141, 143, 148

Chief privacy officers
     (CPOs), 288–289

Child Pornography Prevention
     Act, 316

Children, lifestyle impact of Internet
     on
     pornography and, 306, 316–318
     privacy and, 280, 282–283,
         285–286

Children's Internet Protection Act
     (CIPA), 317

Children's Online Privacy Protection
     Act, 166

Children's Online Privacy Protection
     Act (COPPA), 282, 285–286, 317

Children's Online Protection Act
     (COPA), 316–317

China, 135, 140, 143

China, Internet censorship by, 312

ChoicePoint, 278, 288–289

Christ, Jesus, 126

Cigarettes, and Internet, 316, 318

Circuit court of appeals, 49

Citigroup, 164

Citizenship principle, 342

Civil law, 32

Civil Rights Act of 1964, 33

Class Action Fairness Act, 71–72

Class actions, 71–72

Classical view, 207

Climate change, 165–166

Closing arguments, 69

Coca–Cola Company, 346

Code of ethics, 218–219, 254,
     346–347

Code of ethics content, 349

Code of Professional Ethics for
     Certified Public
     Accountants, 187

Codes of conduct, 163

Collective utilitarian principle, 271

Collusion, 167

Commercial Court (London), 111

Committee Encouraging Corporate
     Philanthropy, 225

Common law, 86–87

Communications Assistance for Law
     Enforcement Act (CALEA), 278

Communications Decency Act
     (CDA), 316

Community, 140, 142

Comparative advantage, theory of, 90

Competence, 347

Complaint, 40, 59

Computer Associates, 147

Computer Matching and Privacy
     Protection Act, 280

Computer Security Act, 280

Computer Software Copyright
     Act, 295

Conclusion, 3

Concurrent federal jurisdiction, 44

Concurrent jurisdiction, 44

Conference on jury instructions, 68

Confidentiality, 161

Conflict of interest, 161

Congressional Record, 30

Consensus, 130

Consequential theories of ethical
     thought, 179–181

Constitution of the United
     States, 279, 294, 313

Construction, green, 212

Consumer Bill of Rights, 167

Consumer rights, 166–167

Consumerism, 166

Context and legal decisions, 97

Convention on Combating Bribery of
     Foreign Officials in International
     Business Transactions
     (CCBFOIBT), 83

Conventional stage of moral
     development, 213

Cookie managers, 287

Cookies, 273–274, 277, 279,
     286–287, 289, 292–293

Cooper, Cynthia, 136

Cooper Industries v. Leatherman Tool
     Group, Inc., 194–195

Copyright, 264, 268–269, 294–299,
     309–310, 321–323

Copyright Act of 1790, 295

Copyright law, 295

Copyright Term Extension Act
     (CETA), 295

Corporate attorneys, 53

Corporate citizenship, 253

Corporate codes of ethics, 184–185

Corporate credos, 347

Corporate culture, 184

Corporate foundations, 170

Corporate philanthropy, 224

Corporate scandals, 164–165

Corporate social audits, 255

Corruption Perception Index
     (CPI), 86

Cost–benefit analysis, 73

Council of Better Business
     Bureaus, 186

Counterclaim, 60–61

Credit Suisse First Boston, 164

Criminal law, 31–32

Critical legal studies school of
     jurisprudence, 26

Crosby v. National Foreign Trade
     Council, 89

Cross–examination, 68

Cultural dimensions, of international
     environment of business, 83

Culture
     ethics and, 215–216

Culture, defined, 83

Cuomo, Andrew, 250

Currency controls, 99

Currency fluctuations, 100

Customers, 164
     responsibility toward, 166–167

Cyber Security Enhancement
     Act, 278

Cyberlaw, 33

Cyberpiracy, 305–306

Cybersquatting, 304–306

D

DaimlerChrysler Corp. v. Unites
     States, 114

Daniels, J., 90

Data brokerage firms, 288

Data brokers, 278

Data protection European directive
     on, 284–285

Davids, R., 87

Deep linking, 309

Defendant, 40

Defendant's case, 68

Defensive stance, 169

Deming, W. Edwards, 349–350

Deontological framework, 337

Deontological theories of ethical
     thought, 180–181

Deontology, defined, 181

Department of Commerce, 285

Deposition, 63

Descriptive ethics, 335

Deveny, K., 192

Dharmasastra (Hindu law), 88

DHL, 318

Diamond v.Chakrabarty, 300

Diamond–grading scandal, 212
Digital media, 294
Digital Millennium Copyright Act (DMCA), 297–298
Dignity of human beings, 127
Dignity principle, 341–342
Dilemma, 270
Dillon, John F., 238
Dilution, 304
Direct examination, 68
Disbarment of lawyers, 200–201
Discovery, 62–63
Discrimination, employment, 168
Distribution of
    benefits and burdens, 121, 123, 127
Distributive fairness, 342
Distributive justice, 127
Doctrine of fair use, 296
Domain names
    cyberpiracy and, 306
    cybersquatting and, 304–306
    Domain Names act and, 317–318
    Dot Kids act and, 318
    governance over, 311–312
    trademark abuse and, 294, 304–305
DoubleClick, 270, 274–275, 277, 279, 292
    chief privacy officer, 288
    Network Advertising Initiative (NAI), 286
    patents and, 303
Drugs, online sales of, 319–320
Due process, 269, 272, 279–280, 282
Duncan, David, 164

E
E & J Gallo Winery, 305–306
eBay
    Internet taxes and, 314
    patents, 303
E–commerce (Electronic commerce)
    ethical issues, 265–272
    patents for, 300–303
E–commerce technology impact of unique features of on business environment
    potential ethical, social and/or political impact of unique features, 266
Economic dimensions, of international environment of business, 82–83
Economics, 122, 147
Education, 139, 146–150

EEOC v. Trabucco, 36
Efficiency, as ethical norm, 9, 14
Ego strength *A personality measure of the strength of a person's convictions*, 214–215
E&JGalloWinery v.SpiderWebs Ltd, 305–306
Eldred v.Ashcroft, 295
E–mail
    privacy issues, 164
Employee e–mails, 164
Employee training
    ethics, 221
Employees
    as stakeholders, 164
    behavior toward, 160–161
    performance appraisal methods for, 219
    protecting those who raise ethical issues, 223
    responsibility toward, 167–168
    selection process, ethics and, 218
    social responsibility, promoting, 223–225
Employment discrimination, 168
Energy consumption, 210–211
Enron, 118, 136, 164, 168, 346, 348, 355, 357
Entrepreneur, 124, 133
Environment
    greening of management and, 210–212
Environment, responsibility toward, 165–166
Eolas Technologies, 303
Epic.org, 287
Equal Employment Opportunity Commission (EEOC), 31, 33
Ernst & Young, 357–358
Ethical
    issue, 149
    judgment, 149
    norm, 134–135, 140, 143, 148, 150
Ethical behavior, 160
    assessing, 162–163
Ethical concepts, basic, 268–270
Ethical dilemmas, analyzing, 270
Ethical egoism, 336, 339
Ethical fundamentalism, 240
Ethical norms, 8–9, 14–15, 162
Ethical principles, 270–271
Ethical relativism, 247
Ethics, 160, 175, 213, 264, 268–272, 334

advertising, 167
business, 240–248
cheating by students on exams, 222
code of, 254
codes of, and decision rules, 218–220
company practices and, 163
corporate social audits, 255
Disney losses "Pooh Bear" lawsuit, 247
employees, and factors affecting, 218–222
in an international context, 216–217
in leadership, 220
in philanthropic and charitable donations, 207
in social entrepreneurship, 224
individual, 160
international, 161
issue intensity, 216–221
issue intensity and, 216
law and, 239
managerial, 160–161, 212–217
methods of encouraging, 218–222
misrepresentation and lying, 222
pledges to philanthropic and charitable causes, 207
Procter & Gamble, 245
Sarbanes–Oxley Act, 253–254
stages of moral development, 214
State Farm case, 252–253
student loan scandal, 250
Wal–Mart and meal break violations, 240
Ethics and Compliance Officer Association, 222
Ethics programs, 163
European Central Bank (ECB), 108
European Directive on Data Protection, 284–285, 290
European Free Trade Association (EFTA), 103
European Monetary Institute, 106
European Monetary Union (EMU), 108
European Union (EU), 20, 102–108
European Union (EU), and Internet taxation, 315
Evidence, preponderance of, 32
Exchange rates, manipulating, 100
Exclusive federal jurisdiction, 43–44
Executive orders, 31
Existentialism, 338–339

Expedia
   patent lawsuit by Priceline,   303
   privacy audit by PWC,   289
Expense account,   152
Experian,   278, 292
Exploitation,   128
Export controls,   98–99
Expropriation of private property,   95
ExxonMobil,   163

F

Facebook
   privacy and,   292
Fair competition,   342
Fair Credit Reporting Act,   280
Fair information practices (FIP)
      principles,   282–284
Fair use,   266, 296–297, 299, 323
Fairness principle,   342
False Claims Act,   168, 240
Family Educational Rights and Privacy
      Act,   280
Fashion Fabrics International,   307
Fastow, Andrew S.,   118, 133
Faulkner, William,   345
Favoritism,   161
Federal Communications Act,   33
Federal Communications Commission
      (FCC),   33
Federal court judges,   54
Federal court system,   49
Federal Deposit Insurance
      Corporation,   353, 358
Federal law,   27
Federal Register,   31
Federal Rules of Criminal
      Procedure,   7
Federal Trade Commission
      (FTC),   31–32, 166, 276,
      282–284, 286, 290, 306, 325
Federal Trademark Dilution Act,   304
Felonies,   31
Feminist school of jurisprudence,   26
Fidelity,   339
Fiduciary principle,   340
Field, Trevor,   334, 337
File–sharing,   269, 299, 315, 322
Filtering software,   299, 317, 320
Financial fraud,   212
Financial mismanagement,   168–169
Financial Modernization Act
      (Graham–Leach–Bliley Act),   280
Financial reporting,   169
Firefox (Mozilla).   120,   287, 290, 293

First Amendment,   279, 296, 310,
      313, 316–317, 320
Food and Drug Administration
      (FDA),   166, 319–320
Food, Drug, and Cosmetic Act
      (FDCA),   320
Ford, Henry,   249
Ford Motor Company,   145–146
Ford Motor Co.v.Lapertosa,   306
Ford Motors,   166
Foreign Corrupt Practices Act,   161,
      217
Foreign Corrupt Practices Act (FCPA)
      of 1977,   34, 83, 181–182, 186,
      196
Foreign direct investment,   92–95
Foreign Sovereign Immunities Act
      (FSIA),   96
Foreign subsidiary,   92
Forms, as information–gathering
      tool,   274–275
Forum non conveniens,   47–48
Foundation,   121, 139–140, 146
Fourteenth Amendment,   279
Fourth Amendment,   279
Framing,   309
Fraser v. Nationwide Mutual
      Insurance Co.,   199
Free market,   147
Freedom,   127, 139
Freedom, as ethical norm,   9, 14
Freedom of Information Act,   270
Freedom Websecure,   287
Friedman, Milton,   249
Fukuyama, Francis,   140

G

Galanter, M.,   57
Gambling and the Internet,   263–264,
      268, 311–313, 316, 318–320
GameStop,   165
Gasoline prices,   167
Gator.com, Inc. v. L.L. Bean,
      Inc.,   48
General Electric,   346, 349
General Electric (GE),   149, 166
Generally accepted accounting
      principles (GAAP),   169
Getty, J. Paul,   117
Giacobbe, Kathleen,   319
Gilligan, Carol,   129
Global 100 (100 Most Sustainable
      Corporations in the World),   212
Global business, of international
      environment of business,   90

Global Business Standards
      Codex,   340
Global code of ethics,   360
Global Compact,   217
Global environment
      problems in,   210–211
Global Ethics Institute Web site,   201
Global Reporting Initiative
      (GRI),   212
Globalization,   154
Globalization of business, pros and
      cons,   112
Goals
   ethics and,   220
God,   144
Golden Rule,   126, 271
Golden Rule Stores,   348
Goldman Sachs,   141
Good behavior,   119
Good moral behavior,   143
Good moral habit,   144
Google,   163, 275, 321
   Book Search Project,   296, 319–323
   China and,   312
   copyright issues and,   296–297,
      299, 321–323
   Department of Justice
      subpoena,   317
   patents,   303
   pop–up blocking toolbar,   287, 293
   privacy and,   274–275, 279
   trademarks in keywords, litigation
      vs.,   305, 308
Google AdWords,   275
Google Gmail,   275
*Google Inc.v.American Blind
      &Wallpaper Factory, Inc.,*   308
Governance,   310–315
   of the Internet,   267
*Government Employees Insurance
      Company v. Google,Inc.,*   308
Government regulation,   165
Governmental laws and regulations
      for clarification of financial
      information,   222–223
Graham–Leach Bliley Act of
      1999,   289
Grand juries,   56
Gratitude,   339
Green management,   211
   evaluating,   212
   global environmental problems
      associated with,   210–211
   going green, approaches

to, 210–212
shades of green and, 211–212
Green marketing, 166–167
Green policies, 166
Greenwashing, 166
Grokster, 268–269, 310
Grubman, Jack, 164
Gulf Cooperation Council
(GCC), 103

H
Hamlet, 338
Hardin, Garrett, 338
Health, 136
Health Insurance Portability and
Accountability Act (HIPPA), 280,
289
Hedging, 101
Hewlett Packard, 296
Hindu law, 86, 88
Hobbes, Thomas, 336
Holmes, Oliver Wendell, Jr., 245
Homeland Security Act of 2002, 278
Honda, 166
Honesty, 161
Horn, R., 188
Human dignity, 121–122, 126, 360
Humanistic theories of ethical
thought, 180, 182
Hurricane Katrina, 160

I
IBM, 170, 288
IBP, 169
Ignorance, 127
ImClone, 147, 169
Import controls, 99
In personam jurisdiction, 40
In re Exxon Valdez, 178–179
In Re Union Carbide Corporation Gas
Plant Disaster at Bhopal, India, in
December 1984 v. Union Carbide
Corporation, 93–94
In rem jurisdiction, 43
Incapacitating factors, 134, 136
coercion, 134, 136
lack of information, 134
Independent social audits, 221–222
Indictment, 56
Individual chooses moral acts, 144
Individual codes of ethics, 182–184
Individual ethics, 160
Individualism, 140
Individualistic, 123, 126, 148

Industry codes of ethics, 185–186
Inequality, 127
Information privacy, 272
Information rights, 267
Informed consent, 279
In–house counsel, 53
Innovation, 352
Insider trading, 169
Inspiration process, 350
Institute of Business Ethics, 356
Institute of Internal Auditors, 187
Institutional school of social
responsibility, 191, 195
Integration, 351
Integrity, 347
Intellectual property
protection of, 294–295
rights for, 293–310
Interdisciplinary nature, 22
Internal Revenue Code, 187
International Association of Privacy
Professionals, 289
International business:
practices, 161
International business activity, legal
and economic integration as a
means of encouraging, 102–109
International Business Machines
(IBM), 149
International Center for the
Settlement of Investment Disputes
(ICSID), 110
International commerce and currency
markets, 101
International franchising, 91–92
International law, 88–89
United Nations Code of Conduct
for Transnational
Corporations, 255–256
International legal environment of
business, 80
International licensing, 91
International Securities Enforcement
Cooperation Act (ISECA) of
1990, 196
International stakeholders, 165
International Telecommunications
Union (ITU), 312
International trade, 89–91
International Trade Administration
(ITA), 99
International Trade Commission
(ITC), 99
Internet, 16, 37, 118, 151
borderlessness, 318

government regulation of, 267
neutrality, 315
Internet privacy, 347
Internet Tax Freedom Act, 314
Interstate Commerce Commission
(ICC), 28
Intertwined, 143
Intuitionism and love, 339
Investors, 164, 168–169
Islamic law, 86–87
Issue intensity, 216
Issue intensity, ethics and, 216

J
Jacobs, R., 185
Janis, I. L., 184
JCPenney, 348
J.E.B v. Alabama, EX REL.
T.B., 64–66
Jeitinho, 161
Jeremy, 241
Johnson & Johnson, 163, 346
Johnson & Johnson (J&J), 141–142,
149
Joint ventures, 94–95
Jolly, Judge, 243
Judges, 54–55
Judicial activism, 55
Judicial restraint, 55
Judicial system in Germany, 73
Jurisdiction, 39
Jurisprudence, 23
Jury, 55–56
Just law, 24
Justice, 121, 126–134, 162, 339, 347
Justice, as ethical norm, 9, 14

K
Kant, Immanuel, 121, 123, 126, 181,
243, 271, 338
Kant's ethics, 338
Kantian ethics, 243–244
Karatnycky, A., 81
Kazaa, 268–269, 299
Keller v. Central Bank of Nigeria, 96
Kelly v.ArribaSoft, 296, 323
Kennedy, John F., 166
Kennedy, Justice, 252
Kenzo, Rase, 264
Keywording, 308
Kierkegaard, Soren, 338
King, Martin Luther Jr., 23–24
Kohlberg, Lawrence, 130, 150

Korean Air Lines, 167
Koyo Seiko Co. v. United States, 114
Kozlowski, Dennis, 165, 346
KPMG, 357–358
Kramer v. Caribbean Mills, 46
Kyosei, 360

L

Lacroix, W., 181
Laertes, 338
Lane, Maureen E., 67
Law and economics school of
    jurisprudence, 26–27
Law, public government and, 313
Law(s)
    ethics and, 239
Lawyers, disbarment of, 200–201
Lay, Ken, 348, 355
Lay, Kenneth, 168
Layoffs, 124
Leadership
    ethics, and top management as role
        models, 220, 223
Leary, W., 184
Legal literacy, 22
Legal protections, 279–285
Legal rights, 122
Legislative process, steps in, 28–29
Legislature, as source of statutory
    law, 27–29
LexisNexis, 288
Lexus, 164
Liability, 269
Linden Dollars, 263–264
Linden Labs, 263–264
Linking, 309
Lisbon Treaty (Reform Treaty), 208
Litigation, global dispute
    resolution, 111
Llewellyn, K., 25
Local communities, 164
Local law, 27
Locke, John, 121, 123, 245, 338
Locus of control
    *A personality attribute that
        measures the degree to which
        people believe they control their
        own fate*, 214–215
Long–arm statutes, 41
Love, 117, 126
Lufthansa, 167

M

Maastricht Summit Treaty, 103–105,
    107–108
Macmillan, Lord, 248
Management, 73
Management Accounting Quarterly, 2
Managerial ethics, 160–161
Managerial school of social
    responsibility, 191, 194–195
Marbury v. Madison, 30, 55
Market approach, 211
MarkMonitor, 319
Martindale–Hubble Law Directory
    Web site, 78
Massively multiplayer online role
    playing game (MMORPG), 263
McDonald's, 170
MCJ Foundation, 334
Media, 136–138, 150
Menino, Thomas, 251
Mercado Commun del Ser Mercosul
    (Mercosul), 103
MercExchange, 303
Merck, 149, 166–167
Merrill Lynch, 146
Meta tags, 305–308
Metaethics, 335
Metatagging, 305–307
MetLife, 356
*Metro Goldwyn Mayer Studios v.
    Grokster, et al*, 269
Microsoft, 296
    Apple v. Microsoft, 296
    book search project and, 323
    China and, 309
    Eolas Technologies, patent suit
        vs., 303
    Tickets.com, 309
    Utah Trademark Protection Act
        and, 309
Microsoft Internet
    Explorer, 290–291, 293, 303
Mill, John Stuart, 122, 241
Mills, John Stuart, 336
Ministry of Information Industry
    (MII), 312
Misdemeanors, 31–32
Missing information, 10, 15–16
Mobile commerce
    (m–commerce), 268
Mock jury, 67
Model Code of Professional
    Responsibility, 186
Modify, use of term, 69
Monopoly, 294–295, 299, 311

Moral
    development, 117, 129–130, 150,
        154
    judgment, 118, 143
    philosophy, 148–149
    reasoning, 149
Moral minimum, 251
Morally
    mature person, 140
Morgan, J.P., 165
Morse, Samuel F.B., 301
Motion for a directed verdict, 68
Motions to dismiss, 60
Motivation, 143
Moving party, 68
Myers v. The Bennett Law
    Offices, 77
MySpace
    China and, 312
    copyright issues and, 299
    Digital Millenium Copyright Act
        and, 299
    privacy and, 292
    Vivendi Universal Music Group,
        lawsuit vs., 299

N

Napster, 268, 297, 310
National Advertising Division
    (NAD), 186
National Association of Boards of
    Pharmacy (NABP), 320
National Association of Securities
    Dealers (NASD), 186
National Governor's Association
    (NGA), 314
National legal systems, 86–88
Natural law school, 23–24
Natural Resource Defense
    Council, 159
Nature Conservancy, 167
Net neutrality, 315
Netscape, 308
Nettis Environment Ltd. v. IWI,
    Inc., 308
Network Advertising Initiative
    (NAI), 286, 325
New York Stock Exchange
    (NYSE), 186
New York Times test, 271
Newington, Tim, 164
Newsweekmagazine, 167
Nietzsche, Friedrich, 338
Nissan Motor Co., 307

Nissan Motor Co.Ltd.v.Nissan Computer Corp., 307
Nissan, Uzi, 307
No free lunch, 271
Nondisclosure agreements, 161
Noninjury, 339
Normative ethics, 335
Norms, 13
North American Free Trade Agreement (NAFTA), 20, 103

O

Obstructionist stance, 169
Occupational Safety and Health Administration (OSHA), 31
Office of Management and Budget (OMB), 30
Office of Personnel Management (OPM), 30
Omniva Policy Systems, 164
100 Most Sustainable Corporations in the World (Global 100), 212
1984, 276
Online gambling, U.S. ban on, 109
Online Privacy Alliance, 325
Open Content Alliance (OCA), 323
Opening statements, 68
Opt–in, 281
Opt–out, 281
Organisation for Economic Co–operation and Development (OECD), 217
Organization
  structure and ethical behavior, 214–215
Organization for Economic and Cultural Development, 196
Organization for Economic Cooperation and Development (OECD), 83, 103, 315, 360
Organizational stakeholders, 163
Original jurisdiction, 39–40
Orwell, George, 276
Overriding factors, 134
Overseas Private Investment Corporation (OPIC), 95

P

Packaging reduction, 166
Paine Webber Inc. v. Fortuny, 306
Patents, 299–302
  reform, 302
PATH (Program for Appropriate Technology in Health), 224

Pavlik v. Lane, 182
Peer pressure, 144
Penney Idea, 348
PepsiCo, 152
Peremptory challenges, 64
Perfect10
  v. Amazon.com, Inc., 296, 323
Performance appraisal, ethics and, 220–221
Personal profiles, 275
Personal service, 40
Personally identifiable information (PII), 273
Petit juries, 56
Pharmacies, online, 319–320
Philip Morris, 318
Pillmore, Eric, 346
Plaintiff, 40
Plaintiff's case, 68
Plastic shopping bags, 210
Platform for Privacy Preferences (P3P), 290
Plato, 121, 336
Playboy Enterprises, Inc.v.Global Site Designs, Inc., 306
Playboy Enterprises, Inc.v.Netscape Communications, Inc., 308
PlayPumps International, 334
Pleadings, 59
Pocket–veto, 29
Political action committees (PACs), 185
Political dimensions, of international environment of business, 81–82
Polonius, 338
Poor, 127, 136, 146
Pornography, on Internet, 316–318
Positivist school of jurisprudence, 24
Post–trial motions, 69
Power, C., 184
Preconventional stage of moral development, 213
Preponderance of evidence, 32
Pretrial conference, 63
Pretrial motions, civil cases, 62
Pretrial stage, 57–63
Price fixing, 167
Price gouging, 167
Priceline
  patents and, 303
Pricing
  unfair, 167
Primary ethical norms, 14
Principled stage of moral development, 213

Privacy, 272–293
  advertisers vs. consumers, 292–293
  advocacy groups, 286–287
  Chief Privacy Officers, 288–289
  European Directive on Data Protection, 284–285
  federal privacy laws, 280
  FTC's Fair Information Practices principles, 282–284
  government surveillance and e–commerce, 278–279
  industry self–regulation and, 285–286
  information gathering tools, 274
  informed consent, 279, 281–282
  legal protections for, 279–285
  P3P, 290–291
  profiling and behavioral targeting, 273–278
  state privacy laws, 280–281
  technological solutions, 286–287, 289–293
Privacy and Civil Liberties Oversight Board, 279
Privacy laws, federal and state, 280
Privacy Policy Reader, 287
Private advocacy groups, 287
Private industrial networks self–regulation and, 285–286
Private international law, 88
Private law, 33
Private property, 122, 125
  rights, 122, 125
Procedural fairness, 342
Procedural law, 33
Procter & Gamble (P&G), 135
Product modification, 166
Production processes
  green, 166
Productivity, 124, 127, 135
Professional codes of ethics, 186–190
Professional obligation school of social responsibility, 191, 195
Profiling, 273–274
Profit, 145
  social responsibility and, 229–230
Profit–oriented school of social responsibility, 191–193
Profits
  maximizing, 248–249
Property principle, 340
Property rights, 267
Protect Act, 317
Prudence, 337

Public Company Accounting Oversight Board, 187
Public government, law and, 313
Public international law, 88
Public law, 32–33

Q

Qui tam lawsuits, 241
Qwest, 147

R

R & D Transport, Inc. v. A.H., 76
Radebaugh, L., 90
Rand, Ayn, 336
Rational benevolence, 337
Rawls, John, 122–123, 127, 245–247, 338
Rawls' social justice theory, 245–247
Real–world problems, 22
Reasonable likelihood, 8
Rebuttal, 69
Reciprocal fairness, 343
Recycling, 210
Redirect examination, 68
Reed Elsevier, 288
Reform Treaty, 208
Regulation school of social responsibility, 191, 196
Regulations for financial institutions, 359
Relationships, 129, 131, 139
Relevance–X, 292–293
Relevant facts, 130–131
Reliability principle, 341–342
Remand, use of term, 69
Reparation, 339
Republic of Nicaragua v. Standard Fruit Company and Steamship Company, 110–111
Republic of the Philippines v. Ferdinand E. Marcos, 97–98
Responsibility, 269
Responsiveness principle, 344
Reverse, use of term, 69
Reward, 117, 134
Reward system, 144
Right to Financial Privacy Act, 280
Rights, 162
Rights and duties, 121–126, 129–130, 132
Risk aversion, 271
R.J. Reynolds (RJR), 192–193
Rockefeller, John D., 165
Romano–Germanic civil law, 86–88

Ronald McDonald House program, 170
Ross, W. D., 339
Roth v. United States, 25
Rousseau, Jean–Jacques, 245, 338
Rule utilitarianism, 181
Rules of civil procedure, 57

S

Safe harbor, 285
Safemessage.com, 287
Sallie Mae, 250
Sarbanes–Oxley Act, 169, 222–223, 358–359
Sarbanes–Oxley Act (2002), 253–254
code of ethics, 254
Sarbanes–Oxley Act of 2002, 187
Sarbanes–Oxley Act, Section 406, 358
Sartre, Jean–Paul, 338
Satisfaction, 118
S.C. Johnson, 166
Scalia, Antonin, 246, 249
Search engines
book search, 321–323
censoring of content on, 312
copyright issues and, 298–299, 321–323
patents, 303
privacy and, 273–275, 277, 279
trademarks as keywords on, 308
SEC v. Zandford, 199
Second Life, 263–264
Securities Act of 1933, 187
Securities and Exchange Commission (SEC), 31–32, 186
Securities Exchange Act of 1934, 187
Security, as ethical norm, 9, 14
Self–centered, 147
Self–improvement, 339
Self–interest, 121, 124, 142–143
Self–regulation, private industry and, 285
Service, 40, 60
Shadow jury, 67
Shakespeare, William, 338
Shareholder, 139, 141, 147, 153
value, 147
Shell, 170
Sidgwick, 337
Sidgwick's dualism, 337
SIFE (Students in Free Enterprise), 222
Simon, Thomas, 264

Single European Act (SEA), 103–104, 107
Slippery slope, 271
Small business
social responsibility and, 171
Smith, Adam, 122, 337
Snowney v. Harrah's Entertainment, Inc., 42, 75–76
Social audit, 170–171
Social audits, corporate, 255
Social capital, 146
Social consciousness, 165
Social Contract, 130
Social contract rule, 271
Social contract theory, of morality, 245
Social entrepreneur, 224–225
Social involvement, and economic performance, 208, 210
Social irresponsibility and ethical lapses, managing, 222–223
Social justice theory, Rawls', 245–247
Social networks
technology for, 266
Social obligation, 207
Social responsibility, 159, 163, 207, 229–230
approaches to, 169–170
areas of, 165–169
arguments for and against, 208–209
economic performance and, 208, 210
investing, 209
management of, 170–171
program implementation, 169–171
progression, four–stage model of, 206–207
small business and, 171
social consciousness, 165
social entrepreurship, encouraging, 224
social responsiveness and, 208
stakeholder model of, 163–165
toward customers, 166–167
toward employees, 167–168
toward environment, 165–166
toward investors, 168–169
views of, 208
Social responsibility of business, 177–178, 248–255
corporate citizenship, 253
maximizing profits, 248–249
moral minimum, 251
stakeholder interest, 253

Social responsiveness, 207
Social screening, 209
Socialist law, 86–88
Society of Chartered Property and Casualty Underwriters (CPCU), code of ethics, 188
Socioeconomic view, 207
Sociological school of jurisprudence, 25
SONY, 167
South American Common Market, 102–103
Soverain Software, 303
Sovereign immunity doctrine, 95–96
Spybot Seach and Destroy (Spybot–S&D), 287
Spyware Doctor, 287
Sreekanti, Kumar, 164
SRI (Socially Responsible Investing), 208–210
Stakeholder interest, 251–252
Stakeholders
    customers, 164
    employees, 164
    going green, 211
    international, 165
    investors, 164
    local communities, 164
    organizational, 163
    suppliers, 164
Starbucks, 164, 166
State court judges, 54
State court system, 43
State jurisdiction, 43
State law, 27
State Street Bank &Trust v. Signature Financial Group, Inc., 301
Statutory law, 31
Stewart, Martha, 169
Stockholders, obligations to, 206–208
StopZilla, 287
Story, Joseph, 240
Streamlined Sales Tax Project (SSTP), 314
Subject matter jurisdiction, 43–47
Substantive law, 33
Sullivan, D., 90
Summons, 40
Supplier, 121
Suppliers, 164
Supremacy Clause of the U.S. Constitution (Article VI), 30
Sustainability, 166

Sustainability 100 Most Sustinable Corporations in the World (Global 100), 212
Sustainability Reporting Guidelines, 212
Sweet, Judge, 242

T

Tacoda, 286
Tankersley, R., 186
Target, 165
Targeting
    behavioral, 273–279
Taxation, 313–315
Technological protections for online privacy, 287
Teleological frameworks, 337
Templeton Foundation, John, 146
Texas Instruments, 163
Thomas Aquinas, Saint, 24
Three Mile Island, 178
Ticketmaster Corp. v. Tickets.com, 309
Tobacco companies, 169
Tonoga, Ltd. v. Ministry of Public Works and Housing of Kingdom of Saudi Arabia, 114
Top managers
    ethics, leadership in, 220, 223
Total Quality Management, 350
Total Responsibility Management, 350
Trademark Act, 302
Trademark law, list of Internet–related cases, 305
Trademarks, 294, 302–309
    arbitration panels, 310
    Second Life stores and infringements of, 263–264
    test for infringement, 304
Transnational Corporations, 255–256
Transparency principle, 342
Treaty making, 30
Trial, civil litigation, 63–69
Trial court judges, 54
Truro, Lord, 249
Trust, 140, 144, 146
TRUSTe, 278, 285–286
Trusted computing environment, as information gathering tool, 274
Truthfulness, 125
12 questions approach, 220
2002 Dot Kids Act, 318
24/7 Real Media, 275, 286
Tyco, 147, 160, 165, 346, 350
Tylenol, 163
Typosquatting, 306

U

UMG Recording v. MP3, 323
Undisclosed principal, liability of, 47
Unethical behavior, 160
Union Carbide, 175, 191
Union Carbide India Ltd, 194
United Nations
    Universal Declaration of Human Rights, 122
United Nations Code of Conduct for Transnational Corporations, 255–256
United Nations Convention on the Recognition and Enforcement of Foreign Arbitral Awards, 110
United Nations Global Impact, 360
United States
    Bill of Rights, 122
    Constitution, 122
    Federal Aviation Administration, 136
    Securities and Exchange Commission, 134
United States Code Annotated, 29
United States of America v. Martha Stewart and Peter Bacanovic, 4–5
United States v. Haggar Apparel Company, 101–102
United States v. Wallach, 7, 9
Universal rules, 243
Universalism, 271
Unjust law, 24
Unlawful Internet Gambling Enforcement Act, 318
UPS, 164
Uruguay Round Amendments Act, 102
U.S. Code Congressional News and Administrative Reports, 30
U.S. Department of Justice, 317, 319
U.S. Patent Act, 299
U.S. Patent and Trademark Office (USPTO), 300–301, 303–304
U.S. Postal Service, 318
U.S. Sentencing Guidelines, 360
U.S. Supreme Court, 24, 30, 41, 49, 51, 64, 70, 88–89
U.S. v. Kay, 84–85
USA PATRIOT Act, 278
Utah Trademark Protection Act, 308
Utilitarian principle, 271
Utilitarianism:, 122, 125–130, 241–242, 336, 340
    Consequences, 128

Good of the group,   129
Greatest net benefit,   128
Utility,   162, 347

V

Value–added tax (VAT),   313, 315
Value–based management
  corporate values, bottom line
    on,   215
Values,   214–215
Values statements,   347
Values–based management,   215
Vanderbilt, Cornelius,   165
Veil of ignorance,   127–128
Velasquez, Manuel,   130
Venue,   47–49
Verified Internet Pharmacy Practices
  Sites (VIPPS),   320
VeriSign,   303
Veterans' Court of Appeals,   49
Viacom, lawsuit v. Google and
  YouTube,   299
Vice,   140
Victoria's Secret,   167
Video, streaming 75,   303
Vioxx,   166–167
Virgin,   167
Virtue,   118, 139–145
Virtues
  intertwined in each person,   143
Virtues, chief,   142
Virtues, principal,   142
  courage,   142
  justice,   143
  prudence,   143
  self–discipline,   142
Viruses,   266
Vision,   144, 149
Vivendi Universal Music Group,   299
Vogel, D.,   184
Voir dire,   64, 67

Volkert, Klaus,   160
Volkswagon,   166
Volunteering, employee,   225

W

Waksal, Sam,   169
Wal–Mart,   165
Wal–Mart v. Samara Brothers,   198
Walt Disney Company,   247
*Washington Post, et al v. Total News,
  Inc.*,   309
Watkins, Sherron,   168
Web browsers
  P3P and,   290
Weblining,   277
Wegmans Food Markets,   164
Weill, Sandy,   164
Whistle–blower,   168, 223
Whistleblower Statute,   241
Whistle–blowing,   136–139
  common good,   137
  evidence,   138
  informed,   138
  legislation,   139
  specific act,   138
Whole Foods Market,   166
Wiedenbaum, M.,   112
Wolff, R.,   181
Women,   122, 129, 135, 137
  advertising,   135
  caring,   129
  relationships,   129
  Time magazine 'Women of the
    Year',   137
Work,   120, 122, 126–127, 129,
    133–134, 143–146
Workers,   134, 149
Work–product doctrine,   53
World Bank,   82–83
World Intellectual Property
  Organization,   297

World Trade Organization
  (WTO),   20, 103
WorldCom,   117, 136, 346
World–Wide Volkswagen Corporation
  v. Woodson District Judge of
  Cook County,   41–42
Wrongdoing within the firm,   138

X

Xanga,   166

Y

Yahoo
  book search project,   323
  China and,   311
  Department of Justice subpoena
    and,   317
  pop–up blocking toolbar,   287, 293
  privacy policy,   282
  search engine information retention
    policies,   279
  Utah Trademark Protection Act
    and,   308
Yahoo Mail,   264
Yoon, Ginsu,   264
Young people,   118
YouTube
  copyright infringement issues
    and,   299
  Viacom lawsuit against,   297

Z

Zeran v. AOL,   36
ZL Technologies,   287
Zoladz, Chris,   288
Zone Alarm,   287
Zuccarini, John,   306